Analytical Key to the Old Testament

EXODUS

JOHN JOSEPH OWENS

1817

Published in San Francisco by

HARPER & ROW, PUBLISHERS

New York, Hagerstown, San Francisco, London

 For information address Harper & Row, Publishers, Inc., 10 East 53rd Street, New York, N.Y. 10022. Published simultaneously in Canada by Fitzhenry & Whiteside Limited, Toronto.

FIRST EDITION

Library of Congress Cataloging in Publication Data

Owens, John Joseph, 1918-
EXODUS.

(His Analytical key to the Old Testament)
1. Bible. O.T. Exodus–Translating. 2. Hebrew language–Glossaries, vocabularies, etc. 3. Hebrew language–Translating into English. I. Bible. O. T. Exodus. Hebrew. Asher. 1977. II. Title. III. Series.
BS1245.5.09 1977 222'.12'044 77-14404

Preface

The *Analytical Key to the Old Testament* identifies grammatically and lexicographically each form of the Hebrew text. It has been compiled to enable you to make ready use of your lexicon for every word in context. The grammatical information and the dictionary page number for each word provide you with a basis for an interpretation of the text of the Old Testament.

Verbs are analyzed by a specific explanation of each element. This gives the basis for you to define the various shades of meaning included in the author's selection of verbs. Nouns are clearly explained as to usage and relationship. The presence of articles, prepositions, and conjunctions is noted. A key to the abbreviations used is found at the back of this volume.

Also provided for each word is the page number of the standard Hebrew-English dictionary [Francis Brown, S. R. Driver, and Charles A. Briggs, *A Hebrew and English Lexicon of the Old Testament* (Oxford: Clarendon Press, 1975)] on which it can be found. This enables you to pursue easily the word that you wish to understand. Other printed aids treat some words, but this volume treats every word. Other books give possible explanations of some forms, but this volume parses each word as used in the specific verse without omissions. Thus, you can interpret more accurately the nuances which the author expressed within the thought pattern of his time and language.

Best use can be made of the *Analytical Key to the Old Testament* by following an established method of study. Most students examine a particular verse, pericope, or chapter at a time. Each verse can be readily found in this book from the headings at the tops of the pages.

When you locate the verse or passage to be studied, you can pursue the material in accord with your facility in Hebrew. You can translate the Hebrew words by reading the left-hand side of the column. If you have not obtained or retained confidence in your Hebrew reading, you will be able to isolate any specific word or words by reading the English translation, which generally follows the Revised Standard Version, provided at the right-hand side of the column. When you find the desired word you will find the abbreviated explanations that provide the needed grammatical tools. At this point you can turn to the page of the Hebrew dictionary to find the shades of meaning which that word may convey.

The Hebrew text is the best complete Ben Asher text available [Rudolf Kittel, ed., *Biblia Hebraica*, 7th ed., by Alt, Eissfeldt, and Kahle (Stuttgart: Württembergische Bibelanstalt, 1951)]. When there is an insoluble difficulty in the text, a variant reading has been provided from the best translations or grammars.

A quite literal translation has been given for some words since the goal is to discover what the Hebrew text means. Oftentimes, the English Bible translations give such a free rendering or a loose paraphrase that one cannot be sure what the Hebrew text really said.

I want to express a special word of gratitude to my colleague, Dr. Page H. Kelley, who has assisted and encouraged me continuously. His invaluable suggestions in format and content are incorporated throughout the series. My appreciation also goes to my graduate fellow, Gerald Keown, and to my students, Kandy Queen Sutherland, Kathe Brown, and Gary Light, who have typed much of the material. Also, I want to thank Mr. Allan Farson of the Church Press, Glendale, California, who invented the process by which this material has been put into printed form.

JOHN JOSEPH OWENS

Exodus 1:1

וְאֵלֶּה conj.-demons. adj. p. (41) *these are*

שְׁמוֹת n.m.p. cstr. (1027) *the names of*

בְּנֵי n.m.p. cstr. (119) *the sons of Israel*

יִשְׂרָאֵל pr.n. (975) *Israel*

הַבָּאִים def.art.-Qal act.ptc. m.p. (בּוֹא 97) *who came*

מִצְרָיְמָה pr.n.-dir.he paus. (595) *to Egypt*

אֵת יַעֲקֹב prep. (II 85)-pr.n. (784) *with Jacob*

אִישׁ n.m.s. (35) *each*

וּבֵיתוֹ conj.-n.m.s.-3 m.s. sf. (108) *with his household*

בָּאוּ Qal pf. 3 c.p. (בּוֹא 97) *(came)*

1:2

רְאוּבֵן pr.n. (910) *Reuben*

שִׁמְעוֹן pr.n. (1035) *Simeon*

לֵוִי pr.n. (532) *Levi*

וִיהוּדָה conj.-pr.n. (397) *and Judah*

1:3

יִשָּׂשכָר pr.n. (441) *Issachar*

זְבוּלֻן pr.n. (259) *Zebulun*

וּבִנְיָמִן conj.-pr.n. (122) *and Benjamin*

1:4

דָּן pr.n. (192) *Dan*

וְנַפְתָּלִי conj.-pr.n. (836) *and Naphtali*

גָּד pr.n. (151) *Gad*

וְאָשֵׁר conj.-pr.n. (81) *and Asher*

1:5

וַיְהִי consec.-Qal impf. 3 m.s. (הָיָה 224) *were*

כָּל־נֶפֶשׁ n.m.s. cstr. (481)-n.f.s. cstr. (654) *all of*

יֹצְאֵי יֶרֶךְ־ Qal act. ptc. m.p. cstr. (יָצָא 422)-n.f.s. cstr. (437) *the offspring of (ones going out of the loin of)*

יַעֲקֹב pr.n. (784) *Jacob*

שִׁבְעִים num. p. (988) *seventy*

נָפֶשׁ n.f.s. paus. (659) *persons*

וְיוֹסֵף conj.-pr.n. (415) *Joseph already*

הָיָה Qal pf. 3 m.s. (224) *was*

בְמִצְרָיִם prep.-pr.n. paus. (595) *in Egypt*

1:6

וַיָּמָת consec.-Qal impf. 3 m.s. (מוּת 559) *then died*

יוֹסֵף pr.n. (415) *Joseph*

וְכָל־אֶחָיו conj.-n.m.s. cstr. (481) - n.m.p.-3 m.s. sf. (26) *and all his brothers*

וְכֹל conj.-n.m.s. cstr. (481) *and all (of)*

הַדּוֹר הַהוּא def.art.-n.m.s. (189)-def.art.-demons. adj. m.s. (214) *that generation*

1:7

וּבְנֵי conj.-cf.1:1 n.m.p. cstr. (119) *but the descendants of*

יִשְׂרָאֵל pr.n. (975) *Israel*

פָּרוּ Qal pf. 3 c.p. (פָּרָה 826) *were fruitful*

וַיִּשְׁרְצוּ consec.-Qal impf. 3 m.p. (1056) *and increased greatly (swarmed)*

וַיִּרְבּוּ consec.-Qal impf. 3 m.p. (רָבָה I 915) *they multiplied*

וַיַּעַצְמוּ consec. - Qal impf. 3 m.p. (עָצַם I 782) *and grew ... strong (were numerous)*

בִּמְאֹד מְאֹד prep.-adv. (547) - *exceedingly*

וַתִּמָּלֵא consec.-Ni. impf. 3 f.s. (569) *so that ... was filled*

הָאָרֶץ def.art.-n.f.s. (75) *the land*

אֹתָם prep.-3 m.p. sf. (II 85) *with them*

1:8

וַיָּקָם consec.-Qal impf. 3 m.s. (קוּם 877) *now there arose*

מֶלֶךְ־חָדָשׁ n.m.s. (I 572)-adj. m.s. (I 294) *a new king*

עַל־מִצְרָיִם prep.-pr.n. paus. (595) *over Egypt*

אֲשֶׁר rel. *who*

לֹא־יָדַע neg.-Qal pf. 3 m.s. (393) *did*

not know

אֶת־יוֹסֵף dir.obj.-pr.n. (415) *Joseph*

1:9

וַיֹּאמֶר consec.-Qal impf. 3 m.s. (55) *and he said*

אֶל־עַמּוֹ prep.-n.m.s.-3 m.s. sf. (I 766) *to his people*

הִנֵּה demons. part. (243) *behold*

עַם n.m.s. cstr. (I 766) *the people of*

בְּנֵי יִשְׂרָאֵל n.m.p. cstr. (119)-pr.n. (975) *(the sons of) Israel*

רַב adj. (I 912) *are ... many*

וְעָצוּם conj.-adj. (783) *and ... mighty*

מִמֶּנּוּ prep.-1 c.p. sf. (577; 6) *too ... for us*

1:10

הָבָה Qal impv. 2 m.s.-vol. he (יָהַב 396) *come*

נִתְחַכְּמָה Hith. impf. 1 c.p.-vol. he (חָכַם 314) *let us deal shrewdly*

לוֹ prep.-3 m.s. sf. *with them*

פֶּן־יִרְבֶּה conj. (814)-Qal impf. 3 m.s. (רָבָה I 915) *lest they multiply*

וְהָיָה conj.-Qal pf. 3 m.s. (224) *and (it is)*

כִּי־תִקְרֶאנָה conj.-Qal impf. 3 f.p. (קָרָא II 896)(rd.poss. תִּקְרָאֵנוּ Qal impf. 3 f.s.-1 c.p. sf.) *if ... befall us*

מִלְחָמָה n.f.s. (536) *war*

וְנוֹסַף conj.-Ni. pf. 3 m.s. (יָסַף 414) *join*

גַּם־הוּא adv. (168)-pers.pr. 3 m.s. (214) *they*

עַל־שֹׂנְאֵינוּ prep.-Qal act. ptc. m.p.-1 c.p. sf. (שָׂנֵא 971) *our enemies*

וְנִלְחַם־בָּנוּ conj.-Ni. pf. 3 m.s. (לָחַם 535)-prep.-1 c.p. sf. *and fight against us*

וְעָלָה conj.-Qal pf. 3 m.s. (748) *and escape (go up)*

מִן־הָאָרֶץ prep.-def.art.-n.f.s. (75) *from the land*

1:11

וַיָּשִׂימוּ consec.-Qal impf. 3 m.p. (שִׂים I 962) *therefore they set*

עָלָיו prep.-3 m.s. sf. *over them*

שָׂרֵי מִסִּים n.m.p. cstr. (978)-n.m.p. (מַס I 586) *taskmasters*

לְמַעַן prep. (775) *to*

עַנֹּתוֹ Pi. inf. cstr.-3 m.s. sf. (עָנָה III 776) *afflict them*

בְּסִבְלֹתָם prep.-n.f.p.-3 m.p. sf. (688) *with (their) heavy burdens*

וַיִּבֶן consec.-Qal impf. 3 m.s. (בָּנָה 124) *and they built*

עָרֵי מִסְכְּנוֹת n.f.p. cstr. (עִיר 746)-n.f.p. (698) *store-cities*

לְפַרְעֹה prep.-pr.n. (829) *for Pharaoh*

אֶת־פִּתֹם dir.obj.-pr.n. (837) *Pithom*

וְאֶת־רַעַמְסֵס conj.-dir.obj.-pr.n. (947) *and Raamses*

1:12

וְכַאֲשֶׁר conj.-prep.-rel. *but the more (as)*

יְעַנּוּ Pi. impf. 3 m.p. (עָנָה III 776) *they ... oppressed*

אֹתוֹ dir.obj.-3 m.s. sf. *were (them)*

כֵּן יִרְבֶּה adv. (I 485)-Qal impf. 3 m.s. (רָבָה I 915) *the more (thus) they multiplied*

וְכֵן יִפְרֹץ conj.-adv. (I 485)-Qal impf. 3 m.s. (פָּרַץ I 829) *and the more they spread abroad*

וַיָּקֻצוּ consec.-Qal impf. 3 m.p. (קוּץ I 880) *and were in dread*

מִפְּנֵי prep.-n.m.p. cstr. (815) *of (from the faces of)*

בְּנֵי יִשְׂרָאֵל cf.1:1,9 n.m.p. cstr. (119)-pr.n. (975) *the people of Israel*

1:13

וַיַּעֲבִדוּ consec. - Hi. impf. 3 m. p. (עָבַד 712) *so they made ... serve*

מִצְרַיִם pr.n. (595) *the Egyptians*

אֶת־בְּנֵי יִשְׂרָאֵל v.supra *the people of Israel*

בְּפָרֶךְ prep.-n.m.s. paus. (827) *with rigor*

1:14

וַיְמָרְרוּ consec.-Pi. impf. 3 m.p. (מָרַר I 600) *and made bitter*

אֶת־חַיֵּיהֶם dir.obj.-n.m.p.-3 m.p. sf.

(313) *their lives*

בַּעֲבֹדָה prep.-n.f.s. (715) *with ... service*

קָשָׁה adj. f.s. (904) *hard*

בְּחֹמֶר prep.-n.m.s. (I 330) *in mortar*

וּבִלְבֵנִים conj.-prep.-n.f.p. (527) *and brick*

וּבְכָל־ conj.-prep.-n.m.s. cstr. (481) *and in all kinds of*

עֲבֹדָה v.supra *work*

בַּשָּׂדֶה prep.-def.art.-n.m.s. (961) *in the field*

אֵת כָּל־ dir.obj.-n.m.s. cstr. (481) *in all*

עֲבֹדָתָם n.f.s.-3 m.p. sf. (715) *their work*

אֲשֶׁר עָבְדוּ rel.-Qal pf. 3 c.p.(עָבַד 712) *they made serve*

בָהֶם prep.-3 m.p. sf. *them*

בְּפָרֶךְ cf.1:13 prep.-n.m.s. paus. (827) *with rigor*

1:15

וַיֹּאמֶר consec.-Qal impf. 3 m.s. (55) *then said*

מֶלֶךְ n.m.s. cstr. (I 572) *the king of*

מִצְרַיִם pr.n. (595) *Egypt*

לַמְיַלְּדֹת prep.-def.art.-Pi. ptc. f.p. (יָלַד 408) *to the ... midwives*

הָעִבְרִיֹּת def.art.-adj. f.p. (I 720) *Hebrew*

אֲשֶׁר rel. *whom*

שֵׁם הָאַחַת n.m.s. cstr. (1027)-def.art.-num. f.s. (25) *name of one*

שִׁפְרָה pr.n. (II 1051) *Shiphrah*

וְשֵׁם הַשֵּׁנִית conj.-n.m.s. cstr. (1027)-def.art.-num. f.s. (1041) *and the other*

פּוּעָה pr.n. (806) *Puah*

1:16

וַיֹּאמֶר cf.1:15 Qal impf. 3 m.s. (55) *(and he said)*

בְּיַלֶּדְכֶן prep.-Pi. inf. cstr.-2 f.p. sf. (408) *when you serve as midwife*

אֶת־הָעִבְרִיּוֹת dir.obj.-def.art.-adj. f.p. (I 720) *to the Hebrew women*

וּרְאִיתֶן conj.-Qal pf. 2 f.p. (רָאָה 906) *and you see them*

עַל־הָאָבְנָיִם prep.-def.art.-n.m. du. paus. (7) *upon the birthstool*

אִם־בֵּן hypoth.part. (49)-n.m.s. (119) *if ... a son*

הוּא pers.pr. 3 m.s. (214) *it is*

וַהֲמִתֶּן conj.-Hi. pf. 2 f.p. (מוּת 559) *you shall kill*

אֹתוֹ dir.obj.-3 m.s. sf. *him*

וְאִם־בַּת conj.-hypoth.part. (49)-n.f.s. (I 123) *but if a daughter*

הִיא pers.pr. 3 f.s. (214) *it is*

וָחָיָה conj.-Qal pf. 3 f.s. (310) *she shall live*

1:17

וַתִּירֶאןָ consec.-Qal impf. 3 f.p. (יָרֵא 431) *but ... feared*

הַמְיַלְּדֹת def.art.-Pi. ptc. f.p. (יָלַד 408) *the midwives*

אֶת־הָאֱלֹהִים dir.obj.-def.art.-n.m.p. (43) *God*

וְלֹא עָשׂוּ conj.-neg.-Qal pf. 3 c.p. (עָשָׂה I 793) *and did not do*

כַּאֲשֶׁר prep.-rel. *as*

דִּבֶּר Pi. pf. 3 m.s. (180) *commanded*

אֲלֵיהֶן prep.-3 f.p. sf. *them*

מֶלֶךְ n.m.s. cstr. (I 572) *the king of*

מִצְרָיִם pr.n. paus. (595) *Egypt*

וַתְּחַיֶּיןָ consec.-Pi. impf. 3 f.p. (310) *but let live*

אֶת־הַיְלָדִים dir.obj.-def.art.-n.m.p. (409) *the male children*

1:18

וַיִּקְרָא consec.-Qal impf. 3 m.s. (894) *so ... called*

מֶלֶךְ־ cf. 1:17 *the king of*

מִצְרַיִם pr.n. (595) *Egypt*

לַמְיַלְּדֹת prep.-def. art.-Pi. ptc. f.p. (יָלַד 408) *the midwives*

וַיֹּאמֶר consec.-Qal impf. 3 m.s. (55) *and said*

לָהֶן prep.-3 f.p. sf. *to them*

מַדּוּעַ adv. (396) *why*

עֲשִׂיתֶן Qal pf. 2 f.p. (I 793) *have you done*

הַדָּבָר def. art.-n.m.s. (182) *(thing)*

הַזֶּה def. art.-demons. adj. m.s. (260) *this*

וַתְּחַיֶּיןָ consec.-Pi. impf. 2 f.p. (310) *and let live*

אֶת־הַיְלָדִים cf. 1:17 dir. obj.-def. art.-n.m.p. (409) *the male children*

1:19

וַתֹּאמַרְןָ consec.-Qal impf. 3 f.p. (55) *said*

הַמְיַלְּדֹת def. art.-Pi. ptc. f.p. (יָלַד 408) *the midwives*

אֶל־פַּרְעֹה prep.-pr.n. (829) *to Pharaoh*

כִּי לֹא conj.-neg. *because ... not*

כַּנָּשִׁים prep.-def.art.-n.f.p. (61) *like the ... women*

הַמִּצְרִיֹּת def. art.-adj. f.p. (596) *Egyptian*

הָעִבְרִיֹּת def. art.-adj. f.p. (I 720) *the Hebrew women*

כִּי־חָיוֹת conj.-adj. f.p. (313) *for are vigorous*

הֵנָּה pers. pr. 3 f.p. (241) *they*

בְּטֶרֶם prep.-adv. (382) *before*

תָּבוֹא Qal impf. 3 f.s. (בּוֹא 97) *comes*

אֲלֵהֶן prep.-3 f.p. *to them*

הַמְיַלֶּדֶת def. art.-Pi. ptc. f.s. (יָלַד 408) *the midwife*

וְיָלָדוּ conj.-Qal pf. 3 c.p. paus. (408) *they are delivered*

1:20

וַיֵּיטֶב consec.-Qal impf. 3 m.s. (יָטַב 405) *so ... dealt well*

אֱלֹהִים n.m.p. (43) *God*

לַמְיַלְּדֹת prep.-def. art.-Pi. ptc. f.p. (יָלַד 408) *with the midwives*

וַיִּרֶב consec.-Qal impf. 3 m.s. (רָבָה I 915) *and ... multiplied*

הָעָם def. art.-n.m.s. (I 766) *the people*

וַיַּעַצְמוּ consec.-Qal impf. 3 m.p. (I 782) *and grew strong*

מְאֹד adv. (547) *very*

1:21

וַיְהִי consec.-Qal impf. 3 m.s. (224) *and*

כִּי־יָרְאוּ conj.-Qal pf. 3 c.p. (יָרֵא 431) *feared*

הַמְיַלְּדֹת def.art.-Pi. ptc. f.p. (יָלַד 408) *the midwives*

אֶת־הָאֱלֹהִים dir.obj.-def.art.-n.m.p. (43) *God*

וַיַּעַשׂ consec.-Qal impf. 3 m.s. (עָשָׂה I 793) *he gave*

לָהֶם prep.-3 m.p. sf. *them*

בָּתִּים n.m.p. (108) *families*

1:22

וַיְצַו consec.-Pi. impf. 3 m.s. (צָוָה 845) *then ... commanded*

פַּרְעֹה pr.n. (829) *Pharaoh*

לְכָל־עַמּוֹ prep.-n.m.s. cstr. (481)-n.m.s.-3 m.s. sf. (I 766) *all his people*

לֵאמֹר prep.-Qal inf. cstr. (55) *(saying)*

כָּל־הַבֵּן n.m.s. cstr. (481)-def.art.-n.m.s. (119) *Every son*

הַיִּלּוֹד def.art.-adj. (409) *that is born*

הַיְאֹרָה def.art.-n.m.s.-dir.he (384) *into the Nile*

תַּשְׁלִיכֻהוּ Hi. impf. 2 m.p.-3 m.s. sf. (1020) *you shall cast (him)*

וְכָל־הַבַּת conj.-n.m.s. cstr. (481)-def.art.-n.f.s. (I 123) *but every daughter*

תְּחַיּוּן Pi. impf. 2 m.p. (חָיָה 310) *you shall let live*

2:1

וַיֵּלֶךְ consec.-Qal impf. 3 m.s. (הָלַךְ 229) *now went*

אִישׁ n.m.s. (35) *a man*

מִבֵּית לֵוִי prep.-n.m.s. cstr. (108)-pr.n. (I 532) *from the house of Levi*

וַיִּקַּח consec.-Qal impf. 3 m.s. (לָקַח 542) *and took to wife*

אֶת־בַּת־לֵוִי dir.obj.-n.f.s. cstr. (I 123)-pr.n. (I 532) *a daughter of Levi*

2:2

וַתַּהַר consec.-Qal impf. 3 f.s. (הָרָה 247) *conceived*

הָאִשָּׁה def.art.-n.f.s. (61) *the woman*

וַתֵּלֶד consec.-Qal impf. 3 f.s. (יָלַד 408) *and bore*

בֵּן n.m.s. (119) *a son*

וַתֵּרֶא consec.-Qal impf. 3 f.s. (רָאָה 906) *and when she saw*

אֹתוֹ dir.obj.-3 m.s. sf. *(him)*

כִּי־טוֹב conj.-adj. m.s. (373) *that a goodly child*

הוּא pers.pr. 3 m.s. (214) *he was*

וַתִּצְפְּנֵהוּ consec.-Qal impf. 3 f.s.-3 m.s. sf. (צָפַן 860) *she hid him*

שְׁלֹשָׁה num. f.s. (1025) *three*

יְרָחִים n.m.p. (437) *months*

2:3

וְלֹא־יָכְלָה conj.-neg.-Qal pf. 3 f.s. (יָכֹל 407) *and when she could ... no*

עוֹד adv. (728) *longer*

הַצְּפִינוֹ Hi. inf. cstr.-3 m.s. sf. (860) *hide him*

וַתִּקַּח־לוֹ consec. - Qal impf. 3 f.s. (לָקַח 542) - prep.-3 m.s. sf. *she took for him*

תֵּבַת n.f.s. cstr. (1061) *a basket of*

גֹּמֶא n.m.s. (167) *bulrushes*

וַתַּחְמְרָה consec. - Qal impf. 3 f. s. (חָמַר II 330) *and daubed it*

בַחֵמָר prep.-def.art.-n.m.s. (330) *with bitumen*

וּבַזָּפֶת conj.-prep.-def.art.-n.f.s. paus. (278) *and pitch*

וַתָּשֶׂם consec.-Qal impf. 3 f.s. (שִׂים I 962) *and she put*

בָּהּ prep.-3 f.s. sf. *in it*

אֶת־הַיֶּלֶד dir.obj.-def.art.-n.m.s. (409) *the child*

וַתָּשֶׂם v.supra *and placed it*

בַּסּוּף prep.-def.art.-n.m.s. (I 693) *among the reeds*

עַל־שְׂפַת prep.-n.f.s. cstr. (973) *at the brink of*

הַיְאֹר def.art.-n.m.s. (384) *the river*

2:4

וַתֵּתַצַּב consec. - Hith. impf. 3 f. s. (יָצַב 426) *and ... stood*

אֲחֹתוֹ n.f.s.-3 m.s. sf. (27) *his sister*

מֵרָחֹק prep.-n.m.s. (935) *at a distance*

לְדֵעָה prep.-Qal inf. cstr. (יָדַע 393) *to know*

מַה־יֵּעָשֶׂה interr. (552)-Ni. impf. 3 m.s. (עָשָׂה I 793) *what would be done*

לוֹ prep.-3 m.s. sf. *to him*

2:5

וַתֵּרֶד consec.-Qal impf. 3 f.s. (יָרַד 432) *now ... came down*

בַּת־פַּרְעֹה n.f.s. cstr. (I 123)-pr.n. (829) *the daughter of Pharaoh*

לִרְחֹץ prep.-Qal inf. cstr. (934) *to bathe*

עַל־הַיְאֹר prep.-def.art.-n.m.s. (384) *at the river*

וְנַעֲרֹתֶיהָ conj.-n.f.p.-3 f.s. sf. (655) *and her maidens*

הֹלְכֹת Qal act. ptc. f.p. (הָלַךְ 229) *walked*

עַל־יַד prep.-n.f.s. cstr. (388) *beside*

הַיְאֹר v.supra *the river*

וַתֵּרֶא consec.-Qal impf. 3 f.s. (רָאָה 906) *she saw*

אֶת־הַתֵּבָה dir.obj.-def.art.-n.f.s. (1061) *the basket*

בְּתוֹךְ הַסּוּף prep.-n.m.s. cstr. (1063)-def.art.-n.m.s. (I 693) *among the reeds*

וַתִּשְׁלַח consec.-Qal impf. 3 f.s. (1018) *and sent*

אֶת־אֲמָתָהּ dir.obj.-n.f.s.-3 f.s. sf. (51) *her maid*

וַתִּקָּחֶהָ consec.-Qal impf. 3 f.s.-3 f.s. sf. (לָקַח 542) *to fetch it*

2:6

וַתִּפְתַּח consec.-Qal impf. 3 f.s. (פָּתַח 834) *when she opened it*

וַתִּרְאֵהוּ consec.-Qal impf. 3 f.s.-3 m.s. sf. (רָאָה 906) *she saw*

אֶת־הַיֶּלֶד dir.obj.-def.art.-n.m.s. (409) *the child*

וְהִנֵּה־ conj.-demons.part. (243) *and lo*

נַעַר n.m.s. (654) *the babe*

בֹּכֶה Qal act. ptc. (בָּכָה 113) *was crying*

וַתַּחְמֹל consec.-Qal impf. 3 f.s. (חָמַל 328) *she took pity*

עָלָיו prep.-3 m.s. sf. *on him*

וַתֹּאמֶר consec.-Qal impf. 3 f.s. (55) *and said*

מִיַּלְדֵי prep.-n.m.p. cstr. (409) *of the children of*

הָעִבְרִים def.art.-adj. m.p. (720) *the Hebrews*

זֶה demons.adj. m.s. (260) *this*

2:7

וַתֹּאמֶר consec.-Qal impf. 3 f.s. (55) *then said*

אֲחֹתוֹ n.f.s.-3 m.s. sf. (27) *his sister*

אֶל־בַּת־ prep.-n.f.s. cstr. (I 123) *to daughter of*

פַּרְעֹה pr.n. (829) *Pharaoh*

הַאֵלֵךְ interr.-Qal impf. 1 c.s. (הָלַךְ 229) *shall I go?*

וְקָרָאתִי conj.-Qal pf. 1 c.s. (894) *and call?*

לָךְ prep.-2 f.s. sf. *for you*

אִשָּׁה n.f.s. (61) *a woman*

מֵינֶקֶת Hi. ptc. f.s. (יָנַק 413) *nursing*

מִן הָעִבְרִיֹּת prep.-def.art.-adj. f.p. (720) *from the Hebrew women*

וְתֵינִק conj.-Hi. impf. 3 f.s. (יָנַק 413) *to nurse*

לָךְ prep.-2 f.s. sf. *for you*

אֶת־הַיָּלֶד dir.obj.-def.art.-n.m.s. paus. (409) *the child*

2:8

וַתֹּאמֶר־ consec.-Qal impf. 3 f.s. (55) *and said*

לָהּ prep.-3 f.s. sf. *to her*

בַּת־פַּרְעֹה n.f.s. cstr. (I 123)-pr.n. (829) *Pharaoh's daughter*

לֵכִי Qal impv. 2 f.s. paus. (הָלַךְ 229) *Go*

וַתֵּלֶךְ consec.-Qal impf. 3 f.s. (הָלַךְ 229) *so ... went*

הָעַלְמָה def.art.-n.f.s. (761) *the girl*

וַתִּקְרָא consec.-Qal impf. 3 f.s. (894) *and called*

אֶת־אֵם dir.obj.-n.f.s. cstr. (51) *the mother of*

הַיָּלֶד def.art.-n.m.s. paus. (409) *the child*

2:9

וַתֹּאמֶר לָהּ cf.2:8 consec.-Qal impf. 3 f.s. (550)-prep.-3 f.s. sf. *and ... said to her*

בַּת־פַּרְעֹה cf.2:8 n.f.s. cstr. (I 123)-pr.n. (829) *Pharaoh's daughter*

הֵילִיכִי Hi. impv. 2 f.s. (הָלַךְ 229) *take away*

אֶת־הַיֶּלֶד הַזֶּה dir.obj.-def.art.-n.m.s. (409)-def.art.-demons. adj. (260) *this child*

וְהֵינִקִהוּ conj.-Hi. impv. 2 f.s.-3 m.s. sf. (יָנַק 413) *and nurse him*

לִי prep.-1 c.s. sf. *for me*

וַאֲנִי אֶתֵּן conj.-pers.pr. 1 c.s. (58)-Qal impf. 1 c.s. (נָתַן 678) *and I will give you*

אֶת־שְׂכָרֵךְ dir.obj.-n.m.s.-2 f.s. sf. (I 969) *your wages*

וַתִּקַּח consec. - Qal impf. 3 f. s. (לָקַח 542) *so ... took*

הָאִשָּׁה def.art.-n.f.s. (61) *the woman*

הַיֶּלֶד def.art.-n.m.s. (409) *the child*

וַתְּנִיקֵהוּ consec.-Hi. impf. 3 f.s.-3 m.s. sf. (יָנַק 413) *and nursed him*

2:10

וַיִּגְדַּל consec.-Qal impf. 3 m.s. (152) *and ... grew*

הַיֶּלֶד cf.2:9 def.art.-n.m.s. (409) *the child*

וַתְּבִאֵהוּ consec.-Hi. impf. 3 f.s.-3 m.s. sf. (בּוֹא 97) *and she brought him*

לְבַת־פַּרְעֹה prep.-n.f.s. cstr. (I 123)-pr.n. (829) *to Pharaoh's daughter*

וַיְהִי־לָהּ consec.-Qal impf. 3 m.s. (הָיָה 224)-prep.-3 f.s. sf. *and he became her*

לְבֵן prep.-n.m.s. (119) *son*

וַתִּקְרָא consec.-Qal impf. 3 f.s. (894)

and she (called)

שְׁמוֹ n.m.s.-3 m.s. sf. (1027) *named him*

מֹשֶׁה pr.n. (602) *Moses*

וַתֹּאמֶר consec.-Qal impf. 3 f.s. (55) *for she said*

כִּי מִן־הַמַּיִם conj.-prep.-def.art.-n.m.p. (565) *Because ... out of the water*

מְשִׁיתִהוּ Qal pf. 1 c.s.-3 m.s. sf. (מָשָׁה 602) *I drew him*

2:11

וַיְהִי consec.-Qal impf. 3 m.s. (הָיָה 224) *(and it was)*

בַּיָּמִים הָהֵם prep.-def.art.-n.m.p. (יוֹם 398)-def.art.-demons. adj. m.p. (241) *one day (in those days)*

וַיִּגְדַּל cf.2:10 consec.-Qal impf. 3 m.s. (152) *when ... had grown up*

מֹשֶׁה pr.n. (602) *Moses*

וַיֵּצֵא consec.-Qal impf. 3 m.s. (יָצָא 422) *he went out*

אֶל־אֶחָיו prep.-n.m.p.-3 m.s. sf. (26) *to his people (brothers)*

וַיַּרְא consec.-Qal impf. 3 m.s. (רָאָה 906) *and looked*

בְּסִבְלֹתָם prep.-n.f.p.-3 m.p. sf. (688) *on their burdens*

וַיַּרְא v.supra *and he saw*

אִישׁ מִצְרִי n.m.s. cstr. (35)-adj. (596) *an Egyptian*

מַכֶּה Hi. ptc. (נָכָה 645) *beating*

אִישׁ־עִבְרִי n.m.s. cstr. (35)-adj. (720) *a Hebrew*

מֵאֶחָיו prep.-n.m.p.-3 m.s. sf. (26) *one of his people*

2:12

וַיִּפֶן consec.-Qal impf. 3 m.s. (פָּנָה 815) *he looked (turned)*

כֹּה וָכֹה adv. (462)-conj.-adv. (462) *this way and that*

וַיַּרְא cf.2:11 consec.-Qal impf. 3 m.s. (רָאָה 906) *and seeing*

כִּי אֵין אִישׁ conj.-subst.cstr. (II 34)-n.m.s. (35) *no one*

וַיַּךְ consec.-Hi. impf. 3 m.s. (נָכָה 645) *and he killed*

אֶת־הַמִּצְרִי dir.obj.-def.art.-adj. (596) *the Egyptian*

וַיִּטְמְנֵהוּ consec.-Qal impf. 3 m.s.-3 m.s. sf. (טָמַן 380) *and hid him*

בַּחוֹל prep.-def.art.-n.m.s. (297) *in the sand*

2:13

וַיֵּצֵא cf.2:11 consec.-Qal impf. 3 m.s. (יָצָא 422) *when he went out*

בַּיּוֹם הַשֵּׁנִי prep.-def.art.-n.m.s. (398)-def.art.-num.adj. (1041) *the next day*

וְהִנֵּה conj.-demons.part. (243) *behold*

שְׁנֵי־ num. p. cstr. (1040) *two (of)*

אֲנָשִׁים עִבְרִים n.m.p. (35)-adj. m.p. (720) *Hebrew men*

נִצִּים Ni. ptc. m.p. (נָצָה II 663) *were struggling together*

וַיֹּאמֶר consec.-Qal impf. 3 m.s. (55) *and he said*

לָרָשָׁע prep.-def.art.-n.m.s. (957) *to the man that did the wrong*

לָמָּה interr. (552: 4,d) *why*

תַכֶּה Hi. impf. 2 m.s. (נָכָה 645) *do you strike?*

רֵעֶךָ n.m.s.-2 m.s. sf. (945) *your fellow*

2:14

וַיֹּאמֶר consec.-Qal impf. 3 m.s. (55) *he answered*

מִי שָׂמְךָ interr. (566)-Qal pf. 3 m.s.-2 m.s. sf. (שִׂים 962) *who made you*

לְאִישׁ prep.-n.m.s. (35) *(for a man)*

שַׂר n.m.s. (978) *a prince*

וְשֹׁפֵט conj.-Qal act. ptc. (שָׁפַט 1047) *and a judge*

עָלֵינוּ prep.-1 c.p. sf. *over us*

הַלְהָרְגֵנִי interr.-prep.-Qal inf. cstr.-1 c.s. sf. (הָרַג 246) *to kill me*

אַתָּה אֹמֵר pers.pr. 2 m.s. (61)-Qal act. ptc. (55) *Do you mean*

כַּאֲשֶׁר prep.-rel. *as*

הָרַגְתָּ Qal pf. 2 m.s. (הָרַג 246) *you killed*

אֶת־הַמִּצְרִי dir.obj.-def.art.-adj. (596) *the Egyptian*

וַיִּירָא consec.-Qal impf. 3 m.s. (יָרֵא 431) *then ... was afraid*

מֹשֶׁה pr.n. (602) *Moses*

וַיֹּאמַר v.supra Qal impf. 3 m.s. (55) *and thought (said)*

אָכֵן adv. (38) *Surely*

נוֹדַע Ni. pf. 3 m.s. (יָדַע 393) *is known*

הַדָּבָר def.art.-n.m.s. (182) *the thing*

2:15

וַיִּשְׁמַע consec.-Qal impf. 3 m.s. (1033) *when ... heard*

פַּרְעֹה pr.n. (829) *Pharaoh*

אֶת־הַדָּבָר הַזֶּה dir.obj.-def.art.-n.m.s. (182)-def.art.-demons.adj. (260) *of it*

וַיְבַקֵּשׁ consec.-Pi. impf. 3 m.s. (בָּקַשׁ 134) *he sought*

לַהֲרֹג prep.-Qal inf. cstr. (הָרַג 246) *to kill*

אֶת־מֹשֶׁה dir.obj.-pr.n. (602) *Moses*

וַיִּבְרַח consec.-Qal impf. 3 m.s. (בָּרַח 137) *but ... fled*

מֹשֶׁה pr.n. (602) *Moses*

מִפְּנֵי prep.-n.m.p. cstr. (815) *from (the face of)*

פַּרְעֹה pr.n. (829) *Pharaoh*

וַיֵּשֶׁב consec.-Qal impf. 3 m.s. (יָשַׁב 442) *and stayed*

בְּאֶרֶץ־ prep.-n.f.s. cstr. (75) *in the land of*

מִדְיָן pr.n. (193) *Midian*

וַיֵּשֶׁב v.supra *he sat down*

עַל־הַבְּאֵר prep.-def.art.-n.f.s. (91) *by a well*

2:16

וּלְכֹהֵן conj.-prep.-n.m.s. cstr. (463) *now the priest of*

מִדְיָן pr.n. (193) *Midian*

שֶׁבַע בָּנוֹת num. m.s. (987)-n.f.p. (בַּת I 123) *seven daughters*

וַתָּבֹאנָה consec.-Qal impf. 3 f.p. (בּוֹא 97) *and they came*

וַתִּדְלֶנָה consec.-Qal impf. 3 f.p. (דָּלָה 194) *and drew water*

וַתְּמַלֶּאנָה consec.-Pi. impf. 3 f.p. (מָלֵא 569) *and filled*

אֶת־הָרְהָטִים dir.obj.-def.art.-n.m.p. (I 923) *the troughs*

לְהַשְׁקוֹת prep.-Hi. inf. cstr. (שָׁקָה 1052) *to water*

צֹאן n.f.s. cstr. (838) *flock (of)*

אֲבִיהֶן n.m.s.-3 f.p. sf. (3) *their father*

2:17

וַיָּבֹאוּ consec.-Qal impf. 3 m.p. (בּוֹא 97) *came*

הָרֹעִים def.art.-Qal act. ptc. m.p. (רָעָה I 944) *the shepherds*

וַיְגָרְשׁוּם consec.-Pi. impf. 3 m.p.-3 m.p. sf. (גָּרַשׁ 176) *and drove them away*

וַיָּקָם consec.-Qal impf. 3 m.s. (קוּם 877) *but ... stood up*

מֹשֶׁה pr.n. (602) *Moses*

וַיּוֹשִׁעָן consec.-Hi. impf. 3 m.s.-3 f.p. sf. (יָשַׁע 446) *and helped them*

וַיַּשְׁקְ consec.-Hi. impf. 3 m.s. (שָׁקָה 1054) *and watered*

אֶת־צֹאנָם dir.obj.-n.f.s.-3 m.p. sf. (838) *their flock*

2:18

וַתָּבֹאנָה consec.-Qal impf. 3 f.p. (בּוֹא 97) *when they came*

אֶל־רְעוּאֵל prep.-pr.n. (946) *to Reuel*

אֲבִיהֶן n.m.s.-3 f.p. sf. (3) *their father*

וַיֹּאמֶר consec.-Qal impf. 3 m.s. (55) *he said*

מַדּוּעַ adv. (396) *How*

מִהַרְתֶּן Pi. pf. 2 f.p. (מָהַר I 554) *You have ... so soon (hastened)*

בֹּא Qal inf. cstr. (בּוֹא 97) *come*

הַיּוֹם def.art.-n.m.s. (398) *today*

2:19

וַתֹּאמַרְןָ consec.-Qal impf. 3 f.p. (55) *they said*

אִישׁ מִצְרִי n.m.s. cstr. (35)-adj. m.s. (596) *an Egyptian*

הִצִּילָנוּ Hi. pf. 3 m.s.-1 c.p. sf. (נָצַל 664) *delivered us*

מִיַּד prep.-n.f.s. cstr. (388) *out of the hand of*

הָרֹעִים def.art.-Qal act. ptc. m.p.

(רָעָה I 944) *the shepherds*

וְגַם־דָּלֹה conj.-adv. (168)-Qal inf. abs. (דָּלָה 194) *and even*

דָּלָה לָנוּ Qal pf. 3 m.s. (194)-prep.-1 c.p. sf. *drew water for us*

וַיַּשְׁקְ consec.-Hi. impf. 3 m.s. (שָׁקָה 1052) *and watered*

אֶת־הַצֹּאן dir.obj.-def.art.-n.f.s. (838) *the flock*

2:20

וַיֹּאמֶר consec.-Qal impf. 3 m.s. (55) *he said*

אֶל־בְּנֹתָיו prep.-n.f.p.-3 m.s. sf. (בַּת I 123) *to his daughters*

וְאַיּוֹ conj.-interr. (32)-3 m.s. sf. *and where is he?*

לָמָּה זֶּה interr. (552)-demons.adj. (260) *why*

עֲזַבְתֶּן Qal pf. 2 f.p. (עָזַב I 736) *have you left*

אֶת־הָאִישׁ dir.obj.-def.art.-n.m.s. (35) *the man*

קִרְאֶן לוֹ Qal impv. 2 f.p. (894)-prep.-3 m.s. sf. *call him*

וְיֹאכַל conj.-Qal impf. 3 m.s. (אָכַל 37) *that he may eat*

לָחֶם n.m.s. paus. (536) *bread*

2:21

וַיּוֹאֶל consec.-Hi. impf. 3 m.s. (יָאַל II 383) *and ... was content*

מֹשֶׁה pr.n. (602) *Moses*

לָשֶׁבֶת prep.-Qal inf. cstr. (יָשַׁב 442) *to dwell*

אֶת־הָאִישׁ prep. (II 85)-def.art.-n.m.s. (35) *with the man*

וַיִּתֵּן consec.-Qal impf. 3 m.s. (נָתַן 678) *and he gave*

אֶת־צִפֹּרָה dir.obj.-pr.n. (862) *Zipporah*

בִתּוֹ n.f.s.-3 m.s. sf. (I 123) *his daughter*

לְמֹשֶׁה prep.-pr.n. (602) *(to) Moses*

2:22

וַתֵּלֶד בֵּן consec.-Qal impf. 3 f.s. (יָלַד 408)-n.m.s. (119) *she bore a son*

וַיִּקְרָא consec.-Qal impf. 3 m.s. (894) *and he called*

אֶת־שְׁמוֹ dir.obj.-n.m.s.-3 m.s. sf. (1027) *his name*

גֵּרְשֹׁם pr.n. (177) *Gershom*

כִּי אָמַר conj.-Qal pf. 3 m.s. (55) *for he said*

גֵּר הָיִיתִי n.m.s. (158)-Qal pf. 1 c.s. (הָיָה 224) *I have been a sojourner*

בְּאֶרֶץ prep.-n.f.s. (75) *in a ... land*

נָכְרִיָּה adj. f.s. (648) *foreign*

2:23

וַיְהִי consec.-Qal impf. 3 m.s. (הָיָה 224) *in the course of*

בַיָּמִים הָרַבִּים prep.-def.art.-n.m.p. (יוֹם 398)-def.art.-adj.m.p. (I 912) *many days*

הָהֵם def.art.-demons.adj.m.p. (241) *those*

וַיָּמָת consec.-Qal impf. 3 m.s. (מוּת 559) *died*

מֶלֶךְ מִצְרַיִם n.m.s. cstr. (I 572)-pr.n. (595) *the king of Egypt*

וַיֵּאָנְחוּ consec.-Ni. impf. 3 m.p. (אָנַח 58) *and ... groaned*

בְנֵי־יִשְׂרָאֵל n.m.p. cstr. (119)-pr.n. (975) *the people of Israel*

מִן־הָעֲבֹדָה prep.-def.art.-n.f.s. (715) *under their bondage*

וַיִּזְעָקוּ consec.-Qal impf. 3 m.p. paus. (זָעַק 277) *and cried out for help*

וַתַּעַל consec.-Qal impf. 3 f.s. (עָלָה 748) *and ... came up*

שַׁוְעָתָם n.f.s.-3 m.p. sf. (1003) *their cry*

אֶל־הָאֱלֹהִים prep.-def.art.-n.m.p. (43) *to God*

מִן־הָעֲבֹדָה v.supra *under bondage*

2:24

וַיִּשְׁמַע consec. - Qal impf. 3 m. s. (שָׁמַע 1033) *and ... heard*

אֱלֹהִים n.m.p. (43) *God*

אֶת־נַאֲקָתָם dir.obj.-n.f.s.-3 m.p. sf. (611) *their groaning*

וַיִּזְכֹּר consec.-Qal impf. 3 m.s. (זָכַר 269) *and ... remembered*

אֱלֹהִים v.supra *God*

אֶת־בְּרִיתוֹ dir.obj.-n.f.s.-3 m.s. sf. (136) *his covenant*

אֶת־אַבְרָהָם prep. (II 85)-pr.n. (אַבְרָם 4) *with Abraham*

אֶת־יִצְחָק prep. (II 85)-pr.n. (850) *with Isaac*

וְאֶת־יַעֲקֹב conj.-prep. (II 85) - pr.n. (784) *and with Jacob*

2:25

וַיַּרְא consec.-Qal impf. 3 m.s. (רָאָה 906) *and ... saw*

אֱלֹהִים n.m.p. (43) *God*

אֶת־בְּנֵי יִשְׂרָאֵל dir.obj.-n.m.p. cstr. (119)-pr.n. (975) *the people of Israel*

וַיֵּדַע consec.-Qal impf. 3 m.s. (יָדַע 393) *and ... knew*

אֱלֹהִים v.supra *God*

3:1

וּמֹשֶׁה הָיָה conj.-pr.n. (602)-Qal pf. 3 m.s. (224) *now Moses was*

רֹעֶה Qal act. ptc. (רָעָה I 944) *keeping*

אֶת־צֹאן dir.obj.-n.f.s. cstr. (838) *the flock of*

יִתְרוֹ pr.n. (452) *Jethro*

חֹתְנוֹ verb.n.-3 m.s. sf. (368) *his father-in-law*

כֹּהֵן n.m.s. cstr. (463) *the priest of*

מִדְיָן pr.n. (193) *Midian*

וַיִּנְהַג consec.-Qal impf. 3 m.s. (נָהַג 624) *and he led*

אֶת־הַצֹּאן dir.obj.-def.art.-n.f.s. (838) *his flock*

אַחַר הַמִּדְבָּר prep. (29)-def.art.-n.m.s. (184) *to the west side of (behind) the wilderness*

וַיָּבֹא consec.-Qal impf. 3 m.s. (בּוֹא 97) *and came*

אֶל־הַר prep.-n.m.s. cstr. (249) *to the mountain of*

הָאֱלֹהִים def.art.-n.m.p. (43) *God*

חֹרֵבָה pr.n.-dir.he paus. (352) *to Horeb*

3:2

וַיֵּרָא consec.-Ni. impf. 3 m.s. (רָאָה 906) *and ... appeared*

מַלְאַךְ n.m.s. cstr. (521) *the angel of*

יהוה pr.n. (217) *Yahweh*

אֵלָיו prep.-3 m.s. sf. *to him*

בְּלַבַּת־ prep.-n.f.s. cstr. (לֶהָבָה 529) *in a flame of*

אֵשׁ n.f.s. (77) *fire*

מִתּוֹךְ prep.-n.m.s. cstr. (1063) *out of the midst of*

הַסְּנֶה def. art.-n.m.s. (702) *the bush*

וַיַּרְא consec.-Qal impf. 3 m.s. (רָאָה 906) *and he looked*

וְהִנֵּה conj.-demons. part. (243) *and lo*

הַסְּנֶה v. supra *the bush*

בֹּעֵר Qal act. ptc. (בָּעַר 128) *was burning*

בָּאֵשׁ prep.-def. art.-n.f.s. (77) *(by the fire)*

וְהַסְּנֶה conj.-v. supra *yet it (the bush)*

אֵינֶנּוּ subst.-3 m.s. sf. (II 34) *was not*

אֻכָּל Pu. ptc. (אָכַל 37) *consumed*

3:3

וַיֹּאמֶר consec.-Qal impf. 3 m.s. (55) *and ... said*

מֹשֶׁה pr.n. (602) *Moses*

אָסֻרָה־נָּא Qal impf. 1 c.s.-coh. he (סוּר 693)-part. of entreaty (609) *I will turn aside*

וְאֶרְאֶה conj.-Qal impf. 1 c.s. (רָאָה 906) *and see*

אֶת־הַמַּרְאֶה dir. obj.-def. art.-n.m.s. (909) *sight*

הַגָּדֹל הַזֶּה def. art.-adj. m.s. (152)-def. art.-demons. adj. m.s. (260) *this great*

מַדּוּעַ adv. (יָדַע 396) *why*

לֹא־יִבְעַר neg.-Qal impf. 3 m.s. (128) *is not burnt*

הַסְּנֶה def. art.-n.m.s. (702) *the bush*

3:4

וַיַּרְא consec.-Qal impf. 3 m.s. (רָאָה 906) *when ... saw*

יהוה pr.n. (217) *Yahweh*

כִּי סָר conj.-Qal pf. 3 m.s. (סוּר 693) *that he turned aside*

לִרְאוֹת prep.-Qal inf. cstr. (רָאָה 906) *to see*

וַיִּקְרָא consec.-Qal impf. 3 m.s. (קָרָא 894) *called*

אֵלָיו prep.-3 m.s. sf. *to him*

אֱלֹהִים n.m.p. (43) *God*

מִתּוֹךְ prep.-n.m.s. cstr. (1063) *out of*

הַסְּנֶה def. art.-n.m.s. (702) *the bush*

וַיֹּאמֶר consec.-Qal impf. 3 m.s. (55) *(and said)*

מֹשֶׁה מֹשֶׁה pr.n. (602)-pr.n. (602) *Moses, Moses*

וַיֹּאמֶר v. supra *and he said*

הִנֵּנִי demons. part.-1 c.s. sf. paus. (243) *Here am I*

3:5

וַיֹּאמֶר consec.-Qal impf. 3 m.s. (55) *then he said*

אַל־תִּקְרַב neg.-Qal impf. 2 m.s. (קָרַב 897) *Do not come near*

הֲלֹם adv. (240) *(hither)*

שַׁל־נְעָלֶיךָ Qal impv. 2 m.s.(נָשַׁל 675) - n.f. du.-n.m.s. sf. (653) *put off your shoes*

מֵעַל prep.-prep. *from*

רַגְלֶיךָ n.f. du.-2 m.s. sf. (919) *your feet*

כִּי הַמָּקוֹם conj.-def. art.-n.m.s. (879) *for the place*

אֲשֶׁר rel. *which*

אַתָּה עוֹמֵד pers. pr. 2 m.s. (61)-Qal act. ptc. (763) *you are standing*

עָלָיו prep.-3 m.s. sf. *upon (it)*

אַדְמַת־קֹדֶשׁ n.f.s. cstr. (9)-n.m.s. (871) *holy ground*

הוּא pers. pr. 3 m.s. (214) *(it)*

3:6

וַיֹּאמֶר consec.-Qal impf. 3 m.s. (55) *and he said*

אָנֹכִי pers. pr. 1 c.s. (59) *I am*

אֱלֹהֵי n.m.p. cstr. (43) *the God of*

אָבִיךָ n.m.s.-2 m.s. sf. (3) *your father*

אֱלֹהֵי v. supra *the God of*

אַבְרָהָם pr.n. (אַבְרָם; II אָבָה 4) *Abraham*

אֱלֹהֵי v. supra *the God of*

יִצְחָק pr.n. (850) *Isaac*

וֵאלֹהֵי conj.-v. supra *and the God of*

יַעֲקֹב pr.n. (784) *Jacob*

וַיַּסְתֵּר consec.-Hi. impf. 3 m.s. (711) *and hid*

מֹשֶׁה pr.n. (602) *Moses*

פָּנָיו n.m.p.-3 m.s. sf. (815) *his face*

כִּי יָרֵא conj.-Qal pf. 3 m.s. (יָרֵא 431) *for he was afraid*

מֵהַבִּיט prep.-Hi. inf. cstr. (נָבַט 613) *to look*

אֶל־הָאֱלֹהִים prep.-def. art.-n.m.p. (43) *at God*

3:7

וַיֹּאמֶר consec.-Qal impf. 3 m.s. (55) *then ... said*

יהוה pr.n. (217) *Yahweh*

רָאֹה רָאִיתִי Qal inf. abs. (רָאָה 906)-Qal pf. 1 c.s. (906) *I have seen*

אֶת־עֳנִי dir.obj.-n.m.s. cstr. (777) *the affliction of*

עַמִּי n.m.s.-1 c.s. sf. (I 766) *my people*

אֲשֶׁר rel. *who are*

בְּמִצְרָיִם prep.-pr.n. paus. (595) *in Egypt*

וְאֶת־צַעֲקָתָם conj.-dir. obj.-n.f.s.-3 m.p. sf. (858) *and their cry*

שָׁמַעְתִּי Qal pf. 1 c.s. (1033) *I have heard*

מִפְּנֵי prep.-n.m.p. cstr. (815) *because of*

נֹגְשָׂיו Qal act. ptc. m.p.-3 m.s. sf. (נָגַשׂ 621) *their taskmasters*

כִּי יָדַעְתִּי conj.-Qal pf. 1 c.s. (יָדַע 393) *I know*

אֶת־מַכְאֹבָיו dir. obj.-n.m.p.-3 m.s. sf. (456) *their sufferings*

3:8

וָאֵרֵד consec.-Qal impf. 1 c.s. (יָרַד 432) *and I have come down*

לְהַצִּילוֹ prep.-Hi. inf. cstr.-3 m.s. sf. (נָצַל 664) *to deliver them*

מִיַּד prep.-n.f.s. cstr. (388) *out of the hand of*

מִצְרַיִם v. supra *the Egyptians*

וּלְהַעֲלֹתוֹ conj.-prep.-Hi. inf. cstr.-3

m.s. sf. (עָלָה 748) *and to bring them up*

מִן־הָאָרֶץ prep.-def. art.-n.f.s. (75) *out of ... land*

הַהִוא def. art.-demons. adj. f.s. (214) *that*

אֶל־אֶרֶץ prep.-n.f.s. (75) *to a ... land*

טוֹבָה adj. f.s. (II 373) *good*

וּרְחָבָה conj.-adj. f.s. (I 932) *and broad*

אֶל־אֶרֶץ v. supra *(to) a land*

זָבַת חָלָב Qal act. ptc. f.s. cstr. (זוּב 264)-n.m.s. (316) *flowing with milk*

וּדְבָשׁ conj.-n.m.s. paus. (185) *and honey*

אֶל־מְקוֹם prep.-n.m.s. cstr. (879) *to the place of*

הַכְּנַעֲנִי def. art.-pr.n. gent. (489) *the Canaanites*

וְהַחִתִּי conj.-def. art.-pr.n. gent. (366) *the Hittites*

וְהָאֱמֹרִי conj.-def. art.-pr.n. gent. (57) *the Amorites*

וְהַפְּרִזִּי conj.-def.art.-pr.n. gent. (827) *the Perizzites*

וְהַחִוִּי conj.-def. art.-pr.n. gent. (295) *the Hivites*

וְהַיְבוּסִי conj.-def. art.-pr.n. gent. (בּוּס 101) *and the Jebusites*

3:9

וְעַתָּה conj.-adv. (773) *and now*

הִנֵּה demons.part. (243) *behold*

צַעֲקַת n.f.s. cstr. (858) *the cry of*

בְּנֵי־יִשְׂרָאֵל n.m.p. cstr. (119)-pr.n. (975) *the people of Israel*

בָּאָה Qal pf. 3 f.s. (בּוֹא 97) *has come*

אֵלָי prep.-1 c.s. sf. paus. *to me*

וְגַם־רָאִיתִי conj.-adv. (168)-Qal pf. 1 c.s. (רָאָה 906) *and I have seen*

אֶת־הַלַּחַץ dir.obj.-def.art.-n.m.s. (537) *the oppression*

אֲשֶׁר rel. *with which*

מִצְרַיִם pr.n. (595) *the Egyptians*

לֹחֲצִים Qal act. ptc. m.p. (לָחַץ 537) *oppress*

אֹתָם dir.obj.-3 m.p. sf. *them*

3:10

וְעַתָּה cf.3:9 *(and now)*

לְכָה Qal impv. 2 m.s.-coh.he (הָלַךְ 229) *Come*

וְאֶשְׁלָחֲךָ conj.-Qal impf. 1 c.s.-2 m.s. sf. (שָׁלַח 1018) *I will send you*

אֶל־פַּרְעֹה prep.-pr.n. (829) *to Pharaoh*

וְהוֹצֵא Hi. impv. 2 m.s. (יָצָא 422) *that you may bring forth*

אֶת־עַמִּי dir.obj.-n.m.s.-1 c.s. sf. (I 766) *my people*

בְנֵי־יִשְׂרָאֵל cf.3:9 *the sons of Israel*

מִמִּצְרָיִם prep.-pr.n. paus. (595) *out of Egypt*

3:11

וַיֹּאמֶר consec.-Qal impf. 3 m.s. (55) *but ... said*

מֹשֶׁה pr.n. (602) *Moses*

אֶל־הָאֱלֹהִים prep.-def.art.-n.m.p. (43) *to God*

מִי אָנֹכִי interr. (566)-pers.pr. 1 c.s. (59) *Who am I?*

כִּי אֵלֵךְ conj.-Qal impf. 1 c.s. (הָלַךְ 229) *that I should go*

אֶל־פַּרְעֹה prep.-pr.n. (829) *to Pharaoh*

וְכִי אוֹצִיא conj.-conj.-Hi. impf. 1 c.s. (יָצָא 422) *and bring out*

אֶת־בְּנֵי יִשְׂרָאֵל dir.obj.-v.supra *the sons of Israel*

מִמִּצְרָיִם prep.-pr.n. paus. (595) *out of Egypt*

3:12

וַיֹּאמֶר consec.-Qal impf. 3 m.s. (אָמַר 55) *he said*

כִּי־אֶהְיֶה conj.-Qal impf. 1 c.s. (הָיָה 224) *But I will be*

עִמָּךְ prep.-2 m.s. sf. paus. *with you*

וְזֶה־לְּךָ conj.-demons.adj. (260)-prep.-2 m.s. sf. *and this shall be ... for you*

הָאוֹת def.art.-n.m.s. (16) *the sign*

כִּי אָנֹכִי conj.-pers.pr. 1 c.s. (59) *that I*

שְׁלַחְתִּיךָ Qal pf. 1 c. s. - 2 m. s. sf. (שָׁלַח) (1018) *have sent you*

בְּהוֹצִיאֲךָ prep.-Hi. inf. cstr. - 2 m.s. sf. (יָצָא 422) *when you have brought forth*

אֶת־הָעָם dir.obj.-def.art.-n.m.s. (I 766) *the people*

מִמִּצְרַיִם prep.-pr.n. (595) *out of Egypt*

תַּעַבְדוּן Qal impf. 2 m.p. (עָבַד 712) *you shall serve*

אֶת־הָאֱלֹהִים dir.obj.-def.art.-n.m.p. (43) *God*

עַל הָהָר prep.-def.art.-n.m.s. (249) *upon ... mountain*

הַזֶּה def.art.-demons. adj. (260) *this*

3:13

וַיֹּאמֶר cf.3:12 *then ... said*

מֹשֶׁה pr.n. (602) *Moses*

אֶל־הָאֱלֹהִים cf.3:12 *to God*

הִנֵּה demons.part. (243) *If*

אָנֹכִי בָא pers.pr. 1 c.s. (59)-Qal act. ptc. (בּוֹא 97) *I come*

אֶל־בְּנֵי prep.-n.m.p. cstr. (119) *to the people (sons) of*

יִשְׂרָאֵל pr.n. (975) *Israel*

וְאָמַרְתִּי conj.-Qal pf. 1 c.s. (55) *and say*

לָהֶם prep.-3 m.p. sf. *to them*

אֱלֹהֵי n.m.p. cstr. (43) *The God of*

אֲבוֹתֵיכֶם n.m.p.-2 m.p. sf. (אָב 3) *your fathers*

שְׁלָחַנִי Qal pf. 3 m.s.-1 c.s. sf. (שָׁלַח 1018) *has sent me*

אֲלֵיכֶם prep.-2 m.p. sf. *to you*

וְאָמְרוּ־לִי conj.-Qal pf. 3 c.p. (55)-prep.-1 c.s. sf. *and they ask me*

מַה־שְּׁמוֹ interr. (552)-n.m.s.-3 m.s. sf. (1027) *what is his name?*

מָה אֹמַר interr. (552)-Qal impf. 1 c.s. (אָמַר 55) *what shall I say*

אֲלֵהֶם prep.-3 m.p. sf. *to them*

3:14

וַיֹּאמֶר cf.3:12,13 *said*

אֱלֹהִים n.m.p. (43) *God*

אֶל־מֹשֶׁה prep.-pr.n. (602) *to Moses*

אֶהְיֶה Qal impf. 1 c.s. (הָיָה 224) *I am*

אֲשֶׁר rel. *who*

אֶהְיֶה v.supra *I am*

וַיֹּאמֶר v.supra *and he said*

כֹּה תֹאמַר adv. (462)-Qal impf. 2 m.s. (55) *Say this (thus)*

לִבְנֵי prep.-n.m.p. cstr. (119) *to the people of*

יִשְׂרָאֵל pr.n. (975) *Israel*

אֶהְיֶה v.supra *I am ('ehyeh)*

שְׁלָחַנִי cf.3:13 Qal pf. 3 m.s.-1 c.s. sf. (1018) *has sent me*

אֲלֵיכֶם cf.3:13 prep.-2 m.p. sf. *to you*

3:15

וַיֹּאמֶר consec.-Qal impf. 3 m.s. (55) *said*

עוֹד adv. (728) *also*

אֱלֹהִים n.m.p. (43) *God*

אֶל־מֹשֶׁה prep.-pr.n. (602) *to Moses*

כֹּה־תֹאמַר v.3:14 adv. (462) - Qal impf. 2 m.s. (55) *say this (thus)*

אֶל־בְּנֵי prep.-n.m.p. cstr. (119) *to the people of*

יִשְׂרָאֵל pr.n.(975) *Israel*

יהוה pr.n.(217) *Yahweh*

אֱלֹהֵי n.m.p. cstr. (43) *the God of*

אֲבֹתֵיכֶם n.m.p. - 2 m.p. sf. (אָב 3) *your fathers*

אֱלֹהֵי v.supra *the God of*

אַבְרָהָם pr.n. (4) *Abraham*

אֱלֹהֵי v.supra *the God of*

יִצְחָק pr.n. (850) *Isaac*

וֵאלֹהֵי conj.-v.supra *and the God of*

יַעֲקֹב pr.n. (784) *Jacob*

שְׁלָחַנִי v.3:13, 14 Qal pf. 3 m.s.-1 c.s. sf. (1018) *has sent me*

אֲלֵיכֶם v. 3:13,14 prep. - 2 m.p. sf. *to you*

זֶה־שְּׁמִי demons. adj. (260)-n.m.s.-l c.s. sf. (1027) *this is my name*

לְעֹלָם prep.-n.m.s. (761) *for ever*

וְזֶה conj.-demons. adj. (260) *and thus (this)*

זִכְרִי n.m.s. - 1 c.s. sf. (271) *I am to be remembered (my memorial)*

לְדֹר דֹּר prep. - n.m.s. (189) - n.m.s. (189) *throughout all generations*

3:16

לֵךְ Qal impv. 2 m.s. (הָלַךְ 229) *go*

וְאָסַפְתָּ conj.-Qal pf.2 m.s.(אָסַף 62) *and gather*

אֶת־זִקְנֵי dir.obj.-n.m.p.cstr.(278) *the elders of*

יִשְׂרָאֵל pr.n.(975) *Israel*

וְאָמַרְתָּ conj.-Qal pf.2 m.s.(55) *and say*

אֲלֵהֶם prep.-3 m.p.sf. *to them*

יהוה pr.n.(217) *Yahweh*

אֱלֹהֵי v.3:15 n.m.p. cstr. (43) *the God of*

אֲבֹתֵיכֶם v.3:15 n.m.p. - 2 m.p. sf. (3) *your fathers*

נִרְאָה Ni.pf.3 m.s.(רָאָה 906) *has appeared*

אֵלַי prep.-1 c.s.sf. *to me*

אֱלֹהֵי v.supra *the God of*

אַבְרָהָם pr.n.(4) *Abraham*

יִצְחָק pr.n.(850) *Isaac*

וְיַעֲקֹב conj.-pr.n.(784) *and Jacob*

לֵאמֹר prep.-Qal inf. cstr. (55) *saying*

פָּקֹד פָּקַדְתִּי Qal inf.abs.(823)-Qal pf.1 c.s.(823) *I have observed (visited)*

אֶתְכֶם dir.obj.-2 m.p.sf. *you*

וְאֶת־הֶעָשׂוּי conj.-dir.obj.-def.art. - Qal pass. ptc. (עָשָׂה I 793) *and what has been done*

לָכֶם prep.-2 m.p.sf. *to you*

בְּמִצְרָיִם prep.-pr.n.paus.(595) *in Egypt*

3:17

וָאֹמַר consec.-Qal impf.1 c.s.(אָמַר 55) *and I promise*

אַעֲלֶה Hi.impf.1 c.s.(עָלָה 748) *that I will bring up*

אֶתְכֶם dir.obj.-2 m.p.sf. *you*

מֵעֳנִי prep.-v.3:7 n.m.s. cstr. (777) *out of the affliction of*

מִצְרַיִם pr.n.(595) *Egypt*

אֶל־אֶרֶץ prep.-n.f.s.cstr.(75) *to the land of*

הַכְּנַעֲנִי def.art.-pr.n.gent.(489) *the Canaanites*

וְהַחִתִּי conj.-def.art.-pr.n.gent.(366) *the Hittites*

וְהָאֱמֹרִי conj.-def.art.-pr.n.gent.(57) *the Amorites*

וְהַפְּרִזִּי conj.-def.art.-pr.n.gent.(827) *the Perizzites*

וְהַחִוִּי conj.-def.art.-pr.n.gent.(295) *the Hivites*

וְהַיְבוּסִי conj.-def.art.-pr.n.gent.(בּוּס 101) *the Jebusites*

אֶל־אֶרֶץ prep.-n.f.s.(75) *to a land*

זָבַת Qal act.ptc.f.s.cstr.(זוב 264) *flowing with*

חָלָב n.m.s.(316) *milk*

וּדְבָשׁ conj.-n.m.s.paus.(185) *and honey*

3:18

וְשָׁמְעוּ conj.-Qal pf. 3 c.p. (שָׁמַע 1033) *and they will hearken*

לְקֹלֶךָ prep.-n.m.s.-2 m.s. sf. (876) *to your voice*

וּבָאתָ conj.-Qal pf.2 m.s.(בּוֹא 97) *and shall go*

אַתָּה pers.pr.2 m.s.(61) *you*

וְזִקְנֵי conj.-n.m.p.cstr.(278) *and the elders of*

יִשְׂרָאֵל pr.n.(975) *Israel*

אֶל־מֶלֶךְ prep.-n.m.s. cstr. (I 572) *to the king of*

מִצְרַיִם pr.n.(595) *Egypt*

וַאֲמַרְתֶּם conj.-Qal pf.2 m.p.(55) *and say*

אֵלָיו prep.-3 m.s.sf. *to him*

יהוה pr.n.(217) *Yahweh*

אֱלֹהֵי n.m.p.cstr.(43) *the God of*

הָעִבְרִיִּים def.art.-pr.n.gent.m.p.(I 720) *the Hebrews*

נִקְרָה Ni.pf.3 m.s.(קָרָה 899) *has met*

עָלֵינוּ prep.-1 c.p.sf. *with us*

וְעַתָּה conj.-adv.(773) *and now*

נֵלְכָה־נָּא Qal impf. 1 c.p.-coh. he (הָלַךְ 229) - part.of entreaty (609) *we pray you let us go*

דֶּרֶךְ n.m.s. cstr. (202) *journey (of)*

שְׁלֹשֶׁת num.f.s.cstr.(1025) *three (of)*
יָמִים n.m.p.(398) *days'*
בַּמִּדְבָּר prep.-def.art.-n.m.s.(184) *into the wilderness*
וְנִזְבְּחָה conj.-Qal impf. 1 c.p.-coh. he (זָבַח 256) *that we may sacrifice*
ליהוה prep.-pr.n.(217) *to Yahweh*
אֱלֹהֵינוּ n.m.p.-1 c.p.sf.(43) *our God*

3:19

וַאֲנִי conj.-pers.pr.1 c.s.(58) *I*
יָדַעְתִּי Qal pf.1 c.s.(יָדַע 393) *know*
כִּי לֹא יִתֵּן conj.-neg.-Qal impf. 3 m.s. (נָתַן 678) *that ... will not let*
אֶתְכֶם dir.obj.-2 m.p. sf. *you*
מֶלֶךְ n.m.s. cstr. (I 572) *the king of*
מִצְרַיִם pr.n. (595) *Egypt*
לַהֲלֹךְ prep.-Qal inf. cstr. (הָלַךְ 229) *go*
וְלֹא conj.-neg. *unless compelled*
בְּיָד prep.-n.f.s.(388) *by a ... hand*
חֲזָקָה adj.f.s.(305) *mighty*

3:20

וְשָׁלַחְתִּי conj.-Qal pf.1 c.s.(שָׁלַח 1018) *so I will stretch out*
אֶת־יָדִי dir.obj.-n.f.s.-1 c.s.sf.(388) *my hand*
וְהִכֵּיתִי conj.-Hi.pf.1 c.s.(נָכָה 645) *and smite*
אֶת־מִצְרַיִם dir.obj.-pr.n.(595) *Egypt*
בְּכֹל prep.-n.m.s.cstr.(481) *with all (of)*
נִפְלְאֹתַי Ni.ptc.f.p.-1 c.s.sf (פָּלָא 810) *the (my) wonders*
אֲשֶׁר rel. *which*
אֶעֱשֶׂה Qal impf. 1 c.s. (I 793) *I will do*
בְּקִרְבּוֹ prep.-n.m.s.-3 m.s.sf.(899) *in it*
וְאַחֲרֵי־כֵן conj.-prep.(29)-adv.(I 485) *after that*
יְשַׁלַּח Pi. impf.3 m.s.(שָׁלַח 1018) *he will let go*
אֶתְכֶם dir.obj.-2 m.p.sf. *you*

3:21

וְנָתַתִּי conj.-Qal pf. 1 c.s. (נָתַן 678) *and I will give*
אֶת־חֵן dir.obj.-n.m.s. (336) *favor*
הָעָם־הַזֶּה def.art.-n.m.s. (I 766)-def.art.-demons.adj. (260) *this people*
בְּעֵינֵי prep.-n.f.p. cstr. (744) *in the sight of*
מִצְרָיִם pr.n. paus. (595) *the Egyptians*
וְהָיָה conj.-Qal pf. 3 m.s. (224) *and (it will be)*
כִּי תֵלֵכוּן conj.-Qal impf. 2 m.p. (הָלַךְ 229) *when you go*
לֹא תֵלְכוּ neg.-Qal impf. 2 m.p. (הָלַךְ 229) *you shall not go*
רֵיקָם adv. (938) *empty*

3:22

וְשָׁאֲלָה conj.-Qal pf. 3 f.s. (שָׁאַל 981) *but ... shall ask*
אִשָּׁה n.f.s. (61) *each woman*
מִשְּׁכֶנְתָּהּ prep.-adj. f.s.-3 f.s. sf. (1015) *of her neighbor*
וּמִגָּרַת conj.-prep.-Qal act. ptc. f.s. cstr. (גּוּר I 157) *and of her who sojourns in*
בֵּיתָהּ n.m.s.-3 f.s. sf. (108) *her house*
כְּלֵי־כֶסֶף n.m.p. cstr. (479)-n.m.s. (494) *jewelry of silver*
וּכְלֵי זָהָב conj.-v.supra-n.m.p. cstr. (479) - n.m.s. (262) *and of gold*
וּשְׂמָלֹת conj.-n.f.p. (971) *and clothing*
וְשַׂמְתֶּם conj.-Qal pf. 2 m.p. (שִׂים 962) *and you shall put them*
עַל־בְּנֵיכֶם prep.-n.m.p.-2 m.p. sf. (119) *on your sons*
וְעַל־בְּנֹתֵיכֶם conj.-prep.-n.f.p.-2 m.p. sf. (I 123) *and on your daughters*
וְנִצַּלְתֶּם conj.-Pi. pf. 2 m.p. (נָצַל 664) *thus you shall despoil*
אֶת־מִצְרָיִם dir.obj.-pr.n. paus. (595) *the Egyptians*

4:1

וַיַּעַן consec.-Qal impf. 3 m.s. (עָנָה I 772) *then ... answered*
מֹשֶׁה pr.n. (602) *Moses*

וַיֹּאמֶר consec.-Qal impf. 3 m.s. (אָמַר 55) *(and said)*

וְהֵן conj.-demons.part. (243) *but behold*

לֹא־יַאֲמִינוּ neg. - Hi. impf. 3 m. p. (אָמַן 52) *they will not believe*

לִי prep.-1 c.s. sf. *me*

וְלֹא יִשְׁמְעוּ conj.-neg.-Qal impf. 3 m.p. (שָׁמַע 1033) *or listen*

בְּקֹלִי prep.-n.m.s.-1 c.s. sf. (876) *to my voice*

כִּי יֹאמְרוּ conj.-Qal impf. 3 m.p. (55) *for they will say*

לֹא־נִרְאָה neg.-Ni. pf. 3 m.s. (רָאָה 906) *did not appear*

אֵלֶיךָ prep.-2 m.s. sf. *to you*

יהוה pr.n. (217) *Yahweh*

4:2

וַיֹּאמֶר consec.-Qal impf. 3 m.s. (55) *said*

אֵלָיו prep.-3 m.s. sf. *to him*

יהוה pr.n. (217) *Yahweh*

מַזֶּה interr. (552)-demons.adj. (260) *what is that*

בְיָדֶךָ prep.-n.f.s.-2 m.s. sf. (388) *in your hand*

וַיֹּאמֶר v.supra *he said*

מַטֶּה n.m.s. (641) *a rod*

4:3

וַיֹּאמֶר cf.4:2 *and he said*

הַשְׁלִיכֵהוּ Hi. impv. 2 m.s.-3 m.s. sf. (שָׁלַךְ 1020) *Cast it*

אַרְצָה n.f.s.-dir.he (75) *on the ground*

וַיַּשְׁלִיכֵהוּ consec.-Hi. impf. 3 m.s.-3 m.s. sf. (שָׁלַךְ 1020) *so he cast it*

אַרְצָה v.supra *on the ground*

וַיְהִי consec.-Qal impf. 3 m.s. (הָיָה 224) *and it became*

לְנָחָשׁ prep.-n.m.s. (638) *a serpent*

וַיָּנָס consec.-Qal impf. 3 m.s. (נוּס 630) *and ... fled*

מֹשֶׁה pr.n. (602) *Moses*

מִפָּנָיו prep.-n.m.p.-3 m.s. sf. (815) *from it*

4:4

וַיֹּאמֶר cf.4:2,3 consec.-Qal impf. 3 m.s. (55) *but ... said*

יהוה pr.n. (217) *Yahweh*

אֶל־מֹשֶׁה prep.-pr.n. (602) *to Moses*

שְׁלַח Qal impv. 2 m.s. (1018) *Put out*

יָדְךָ n.f.s.-2 m.s. sf. (388) *your hand*

וֶאֱחֹז conj.-Qal impv. 2 m.s. (אָחַז 28) *and take it*

בִּזְנָבוֹ prep.-n.m.s.-3 m.s. sf. (275) *by the tail*

וַיִּשְׁלַח consec.-Qal impf. 3 m.s. (1018) *so he put out*

יָדוֹ n.f.s.-3 m.s. sf. (388) *his hand*

וַיַּחֲזֶק consec.-Hi. impf. 3 m.s. (חָזַק 304) *and caught*

בּוֹ prep.-3 m.s. sf. *it*

וַיְהִי consec.-Qal impf. 3 m.s. (הָיָה 224) *and it became*

לְמַטֶּה prep.-n.m.s. (641) *a rod*

בְּכַפּוֹ prep.-n.f.s.-3 m.s. sf. (496) *in his hand*

4:5

לְמַעַן prep.-prep. (775) *that*

יַאֲמִינוּ Hi. impf. 3 m.p. (אָמַן 52) *they may believe*

כִּי־נִרְאָה conj.-Ni. pf. 3 m.s. (רָאָה 906) *that ... has appeared*

אֵלֶיךָ prep.-2 m.s. sf. *to you*

יהוה pr.n. (217) *Yahweh*

אֱלֹהֵי cf.3:16 n.m.p. cstr. (43) *the God of*

אֲבֹתָם n.m.p.-3 m.p. sf. (3) *their fathers*

אֱלֹהֵי v.supra *the God of*

אַבְרָהָם pr.n. (4) *Abraham*

אֱלֹהֵי v.supra *the God of*

יִצְחָק pr.n. (850) *Isaac*

וֵאלֹהֵי conj.-v.supra *and the God of*

יַעֲקֹב pr.n. (784) *Jacob*

4:6

וַיֹּאמֶר consec.-Qal impf. 3 m.s. (55) *said*

יהוה pr.n. (217) *Yahweh*

לוֹ prep.-3 m.s. sf. *to him*

עוֹד adv. (728) *again*

הָבֵא־נָא Hi. impv. 2 m.s. (בּוֹא 97)-

part.of entreaty (609) *Put*
יָדְךָ n.f.s.-2 m.s. sf. (388) *your hand*
בְּחֵיקֶךָ prep.-n.m.s.-2 m.s. sf. (300) *into your bosom*
וַיָּבֵא consec.-Hi. impf. 3 m.s. (בּוֹא 97) *and he put*
יָדוֹ n.f.s.-3 m.s. sf. (388) *his hand*
בְּחֵיקוֹ prep.-n.m.s.-3 m.s. sf. (300) *into his bosom*
וַיּוֹצִאָהּ consec.-Hi. impf. 3 m.s.-3 f.s. sf. (יָצָא 422) *and when he took it out*
וְהִנֵּה conj.-demons. part. (243) *behold*
יָדוֹ v. supra *his hand*
מְצֹרַעַת Pu. ptc. f.s. (צָרַע 863) *was leprous*
כַּשָּׁלֶג prep.-def. art.-n.m.s. paus. (1017) *as snow*

4:7

וַיֹּאמֶר consec.-Qal impf. 3 m.s. (55) *then said*
הָשֵׁב Hi. impv. 2 m.s. (שׁוּב 996) *Put back*
יָדְךָ n.f.s.-2 m.s. sf. (388) *your hand*
אֶל־חֵיקֶךָ prep.-n.m.s.-2 m.s. sf. (300) *into your bosom*
וַיָּשֶׁב consec.-Hi. impf. 3 m.s. (שׁוּב 996) *so he put back*
יָדוֹ n.f.s.-3 m.s. sf. (388) *his hand*
אֶל־חֵיקוֹ prep.-n.m.s.-3 m.s. sf. (300) *into his bosom*
וַיּוֹצִאָהּ consec.-Hi. impf. 3 m.s.-3 f.s. sf. (יָצָא 422) *and when he took it out*
מֵחֵיקוֹ prep.-n.m.s.-3 m.s. sf. (300) *(from his bosom)*
וְהִנֵּה־ conj.-demons. part. (243) *behold*
שָׁבָה Qal pf. 3 f.s. (שׁוּב 996) *it was restored*
כִּבְשָׂרוֹ prep.-n.m.s.-3 m.s. sf. (142) *like the rest of his flesh*

4:8

וְהָיָה conj.-Qal pf 3 m.s. (224) *(and it shall be)*
אִם־לֹא יַאֲמִינוּ hypoth.part. (49)-neg.-Hi. impf. 3 m.p. (אָמַן 52) *if they will not believe*
לָךְ prep.-2 m.s. sf. paus. *you*
וְלֹא יִשְׁמְעוּ conj.-neg.-Qal impf. 3 m.p. (1033) *or (hearken) heed*
לְקֹל prep.-n.m.s. cstr. (876) *(to the voice of)*
הָאֹת def. art.-n.m.s. (16) *the ... sign*
הָרִאשׁוֹן def. art.-adj. m.s. (911) *first*
וְהֶאֱמִינוּ conj.-Hi. pf. 3 c.p. (אָמַן 52) *they may believe*
לְקֹל v. supra *(the voice of)*
הָאֹת v. supra *the ... sign*
הָאַחֲרוֹן def. art.-adj. m.s. (30) *latter*

4:9

וְהָיָה v. 4:8 *(and it shall be)*
אִם־לֹא יַאֲמִינוּ v. 4:8 *if they will not believe*
גַּם adv. (168) *even*
לִשְׁנֵי prep.-num. m.p. cstr. (1040) *two (of)*
הָאֹתוֹת def art.-n.m.p. (16) *signs*
הָאֵלֶּה def. art.-demons. adj. c.p. (41) *these*
וְלֹא יִשְׁמְעוּן conj.-neg.-Qal impf. 3 m.p. (שָׁמַע 1033) *or heed*
לְקֹלֶךָ prep.-n.m.s.-2 m.s. sf. (876) *your voice*
וְלָקַחְתָּ conj.-Qal pf. 2 m.s. (לָקַח 542) *you shall take*
מִמֵּימֵי prep.-n.m.p. cstr. (565) *some water from (of)*
הַיְאֹר def. art.-n.m.s. (384) *the Nile*
וְשָׁפַכְתָּ conj.-Qal pf. 2 m.s. (שָׁפַךְ 1049) *and pour it*
הַיַּבָּשָׁה def. art.-n.f.s. (387) *upon the dry ground*
וְהָיוּ conj.-Qal pf. 3 c.p. (הָיָה 224) *and (shall be)*
הַמַּיִם def. art.-n.m.p. (565) *the water*
אֲשֶׁר rel. *which*
תִּקַּח Qal impf. 2 m.s. (לָקַח 542) *you shall take*
מִן־הַיְאֹר prep.-def. art.-n.m.s. (384) *from the Nile*
וְהָיוּ v. supra *will become*

לְדָם prep.-n.m.s. (196) *blood*

בַּיַּבָּשֶׁת prep.-def. art.-n.f.s. (387) *upon the dry ground*

4:10

וַיֹּאמֶר consec.-Qal impf. 3 m.s. (55) *but ... said*

מֹשֶׁה pr.n. (602) *Moses*

אֶל־יהוה prep.-pr.n. (217) *to Yahweh*

בִּי part. of entreaty (106) *Oh*

אֲדֹנָי n.m.p.-1 c.s. sf. (10) *my Lord*

לֹא אִישׁ neg.-n.m.s. cstr. (35) *not (a man of)*

דְּבָרִים n.m.p. (182) *(words) eloquent*

אָנֹכִי pers. pr. 1 c.s. (59) *I*

גַּם מִתְּמוֹל adv. (168)-prep.-subst. as adv. acc. (1069) *either*

גַּם מִשִּׁלְשֹׁם adv. (168)-prep.-adv. (1026) *henceforth*

גַּם מֵאָז adv. (168) - prep.-adv. (23) *or since*

דַּבֶּרְךָ Pi. inf. cstr.-2 m.s. sf. (180) *thou hast spoken*

אֶל־עַבְדֶּךָ prep.-n.m.s.-2 m.s. sf. (712) *to thy servant*

כִּי כְבַד־פֶּה conj.-adj. m.s. cstr. (458)-n.m.s. (804) *but ... slow of speech*

וּכְבַד לָשׁוֹן conj.-v. supra.-n.f.s. (546) *and (slow) of tongue*

אָנֹכִי pers. pr. 1 c.s. (59) *I*

4:11

וַיֹּאמֶר consec.-Qal impf. 3 m.s. (55) *then ... said*

יהוה pr.n. (217) *Yahweh*

אֵלָיו prep.-3 m.s. sf. *to him*

מִי שָׂם interr. (566) - Qal pf. 3 m.s. (שׂוּם 962) *who has made*

פֶּה n.m.s. (804) *mouth*

לָאָדָם prep.-n.m.s. (9) *man's*

אוֹ מִי־ conj. (14)-interr. (566) *(or) who*

יָשׂוּם Qal impf. 3 m.s. (שׂוּם 962) *makes*

אִלֵּם adj. (48) *dumb*

אוֹ חֵרֵשׁ conj. (14)-adj. (361) *or deaf*

אוֹ פִקֵּחַ conj. (14)-adj. (824) *or seeing*

אוֹ עִוֵּר conj. (14)-adj. (734) *or blind*

הֲלֹא אָנֹכִי interr. part.-neg.-pers. pr. 1 c.s. (59) *Is it not I*

יהוה pr.n. (217) *Yahweh*

4:12

וְעַתָּה conj.adv. (773) *now therefore*

לֵךְ Qal impv. 2 m.s. (הָלַךְ 229) *go*

וְאָנֹכִי conj.-pers. pr. 1 c.s. (59) *and I*

אֶהְיֶה Qal impf. 1 c.s. (הָיָה 224) *I will be*

עִם־פִּיךָ prep. (767)-n.m.s.-2 m.s. sf. (804) *with your mouth*

וְהוֹרֵיתִיךָ conj.-Hi. pf. 1 c.s.-2 m.s. sf. (יָרָה 434) *and teach you*

אֲשֶׁר rel. *what*

תְּדַבֵּר Pi. impf. 2 m.s. (180) *you shall speak*

4:13

וַיֹּאמֶר consec.-Qal impf. 3 m.s. (55) *but he said*

בִּי אֲדֹנָי v.4:10 part. of entreaty (106)-n.m.p.-1 c.s. sf. (10) *Oh, my Lord*

שְׁלַח־נָא Qal impv. 2 m.s. (1018) - part. of entreaty (609) *send, I pray*

בְּיַד־תִּשְׁלָח prep.-n.f.s. cstr. (388)-Qal impf. 2 m.s. paus. (1018) *some other person (by the hand of whom you shall send)*

4:14

וַיִּחַר־ consec.-Qal impf. 3 m.s. (חָרָה 354) *then ... was kindled*

אַף יהוה n.m.s. cstr. (I 60)-pr.n. (217) *the anger of Yahweh*

בְּמֹשֶׁה prep.-pr.n. (602) *against Moses*

וַיֹּאמֶר consec.-Qal impf. 3 m.s. (55) *and he said*

הֲלֹא אַהֲרֹן interr. part.-neg.-pr.n. (14) *Is there not Aaron*

אָחִיךָ n.m.s.-2 m.s. sf. (26) *your brother*

הַלֵּוִי def. art.-adj. gent. (II 532) *the Levite*

יָדַעְתִּי Qal pf. 1 c.s. (393) *I know*

כִּי־דַבֵּר conj.-Pi. inf. abs. (180) *that ... well*

יְדַבֵּר Pi. impf. 3 m.s. (180) *he can speak*

הוּא pers. pr. 3 m.s. (214) *he*

וְגַם conj.-adv. (168) *and*

הִנֵּה־הוּא demons. part. (243)-pers. pr. 3 m.s. (214) *behold he*

יֹצֵא Qal act. ptc. (יָצָא 422) *is coming out*

לִקְרָאתֶךָ prep.-Qal inf. cstr.-2 m.s. sf. (קָרָא 894) *to meet you*

וְרָאֲךָ conj.-Qal pf. 3 m.s.-2 m.s. sf. (רָאָה 906) *and when he sees you*

וְשָׂמַח conj.-Qal pf. 3 m.s. (970) *he will be glad*

בְּלִבּוֹ prep.-n.m.s.-3 m.s. sf. (523) *in his heart*

4:15

וְדִבַּרְתָּ conj.-Pi. pf. 2 m.s. (180) *and you shall speak*

אֵלָיו prep.-3 m.s. sf. *to him*

וְשַׂמְתָּ conj.-Qal pf. 2 m.s. (שׂוּם 962) *and put*

אֶת־הַדְּבָרִים dir.obj.-def.art.-n.m.p. (182) *the words*

בְּפִיו prep.-n.m.s.-3 m.s. sf. (804) *in his mouth*

וְאָנֹכִי conj.-pers.pr. 1 c.s. (59) *and I*

אֶהְיֶה Qal impf. 1 c.s. (הָיָה 224) *will be*

עִם־פִּיךָ prep. (767)-n.m.s.-2 m.s. sf. (804) *with your mouth*

וְעִם־פִּיהוּ conj.-prep.-n.m.s.-3 m.s. sf. (804) *and with his mouth*

וְהוֹרֵיתִי conj.-Hi. pf. 1 c.s. (יָרָה 434) *and will teach*

אֶתְכֶם dir.obj.-2 m.p. sf. *you*

אֵת אֲשֶׁר dir.obj.-rel. *what*

תַּעֲשׂוּן Qal impf. 2 m.p. (עָשָׂה I 793) *you shall do*

4:16

וְדִבֶּר־הוּא conj.-Pi. pf. 3 m.s. (180)-pers.pr 3 m.s. (214) *he shall speak*

לְךָ prep.-2 m.s. sf. *for you*

אֶל־הָעָם prep.-def.art.-n.m.s. (I 766) *to the people*

וְהָיָה הוּא conj.-Qal pf. 3 m.s. (224)-pers.pr. 3 m.s. (214) *and (it shall be) he*

יִהְיֶה־ Qal impf. 3 m.s. (224) *shall be*

לְּךָ v.supra *for you*

לְפֶה prep.-n.m.s. (804) *a mouth*

וְאַתָּה conj.-pers.pr. 2 m.s. (61) *and you*

תִּהְיֶה־לּוֹ Qal impf. 2 m.s. (224)-prep.-3 m.s. sf. *shall be to him*

לֵאלֹהִים prep.-n.m.p. (43) *as God*

4:17

וְאֶת־הַמַּטֶּה conj.-dir.obj.-def.art.-n.m.s. (641) *and ... rod*

הַזֶּה def.art.-demons.adj. (260) *this*

תִּקַּח Qal impf. 2 m.s. (לָקַח 542) *you shall take*

בְּיָדֶךָ prep.-n.f.s.-2 m.s. sf. (388) *in your hand*

אֲשֶׁר rel. *which*

תַּעֲשֶׂה־בּוֹ Qal impf. 2 m.s. (עָשָׂה I 793)-prep.-3 m.s. sf. *with ... you shall do*

אֶת־הָאֹתֹת dir.obj.-def.art.-n.m.p. (16) *the signs*

4:18

וַיֵּלֶךְ consec.-Qal impf. 3 m.s. (הָלַךְ 229) *went*

מֹשֶׁה pr.n. (602) *Moses*

וַיָּשָׁב consec.-Qal impf. 3 m.s. (שׁוּב 996) *back (and returned)*

אֶל־יֶתֶר prep.-pr.n. (III 452) *to Jethro*

חֹתְנוֹ n.m.s.-3 m.s. sf. (368) *his father-in-law*

וַיֹּאמֶר לוֹ consec.-Qal impf. 3 m.s. (55)-prep.-3 m.s. sf. *and said to him*

אֵלְכָה נָּא Qal impf. 1 c.s.-coh. he (הָלַךְ 229)-part. of entreaty (609) *let me go ... I pray thee*

וְאָשׁוּבָה conj.-Qal impf. 1 c.s.-coh. he (שׁוּב 996) *back (and let me return)*

אֶל־אַחַי prep.-n.m.p.-1 c.s. sf. (26)

to my kinsmen
אֲשֶׁר־ rel. *(who)*
בְּמִצְרַיִם prep.-pr.n. (595) *in Egypt*
וְאֶרְאֶה conj.-Qal impf. 1 c.s. (906) *and (let me) see*
הַעוֹדָם interr.-adv.-3 m.p. sf. (728) *whether they are still*
חַיִּים adj. m.p. (I 311) *alive*
וַיֹּאמֶר v. supra *and ... said*
יִתְרוֹ pr.n. (452) *Jethro*
לְמֹשֶׁה prep.-pr.n. (602) *to Moses*
לֵךְ Qal impv. 2 m.s. (הָלַךְ 229) *Go*
לְשָׁלוֹם prep.-n.m.s. (1022) *in peace*

4:19

וַיֹּאמֶר consec.-Qal impf. 3 m.s. (55) *and ... said*
יהוה pr.n. (217) *Yahweh*
אֶל־מֹשֶׁה prep.-pr.n. (602) *to Moses*
בְּמִדְיָן prep.-pr.n. (193) *in Midian*
לֵךְ Qal impv. 2 m.s. (הָלַךְ 229) *Go*
שֻׁב Qal impv. 2 m.s. (שׁוּב 996) *back (return)*
מִצְרָיִם pr.n. paus. (595) *to Egypt*
כִּי־מֵתוּ conj.-Qal pf. 3 c.p. (מוּת 559) *for ... are dead*
כָּל־הָאֲנָשִׁים n.m.s. cstr. (481) - def.art.-n.m.p. (35) *all the men*
הַמְבַקְשִׁים def.art. - Pi. ptc. m. p. (בָּקַשׁ 134) *who were seeking*
אֶת־נַפְשֶׁךָ dir. obj.-n.f.s.-2 m.s. sf. (659) *your life*

4:20

וַיִּקַּח consec.-Qal impf. 3 m.s. (לָקַח 542) *so ... took*
מֹשֶׁה pr.n. (602) *Moses*
אֶת־אִשְׁתּוֹ dir. obj.-n.f.s.-3 m.s. sf. (61) *his wife*
וְאֶת־בָּנָיו conj.-dir. obj.-n.m.p.-3 m.s. sf. (119) *and his sons*
וַיַּרְכִּבֵם consec.-Hi. impf. 3 m.s.-3 m.p. sf. (רָכַב 938) *and set them (caused them to ride)*
עַל־הַחֲמֹר prep.-def. art.-n.m.s. (331) *on an ass*
וַיָּשָׁב consec.-Qal impf. 3 m.s. (שׁוּב 996) *and went back*
אַרְצָה n.f.s.-dir. he (75) *to the land*
מִצְרָיִם pr.n. paus. (595) *Egypt*
וַיִּקַּח consec.-Qal impf. 3 m.s. (לָקַח 542) *and ... took*
מֹשֶׁה pr.n. (602) *Moses*
אֶת־מַטֵּה dir. obj.-n.m.s. cstr. (641) *the rod of*
הָאֱלֹהִים def. art.-n.m.p. (43) *God*
בְּיָדוֹ prep.-n.f.s.-3 m.s. sf. (388) *in his hand*

4:21

וַיֹּאמֶר consec.-Qal impf. 3 m.s. (55) *and ... said*
יהוה pr.n. (217) *Yahweh*
אֶל־מֹשֶׁה prep.-pr.n. (602) *to Moses*
בְּלֶכְתְּךָ prep.-Qal inf. cstr.-2 m.s. sf. (הָלַךְ 229) *when you go*
לָשׁוּב prep.-Qal inf. cstr. (996) *back (to return)*
מִצְרַיְמָה pr.n.-dir. he (595) *to Egypt*
רְאֵה Qal impv. 2 m.s. (רָאָה 906) *see*
כָּל־הַמֹּפְתִים n.m.s. cstr. (481)-def. art.-n.m.p. (68) *all the miracles*
אֲשֶׁר־שַׂמְתִּי rel.-Qal pf. 1 c.s. (שׂוּם 962) *which I have put*
בְיָדֶךָ prep.-n.f.s.-2 m.s. sf. (388) *in your power*
וַעֲשִׂיתָם conj.-Qal pf. 2 m.s.-3 m.p. sf. (עָשָׂה I 793) *that you do (them)*
לִפְנֵי prep.-n.m.p. cstr. (815) *before*
פַרְעֹה pr.n. (829) *Pharaoh*
וַאֲנִי conj.-pers.pr. 1 c.s. (58) *but I*
אֲחַזֵּק Pi. impf. 1 c.s. (חָזַק 304) *will harden*
אֶת־לִבּוֹ dir. obj.-n.m.s.-3 m.s. sf. (523) *his heart*
וְלֹא יְשַׁלַּח conj.-neg.-Pi. impf. 3 m.s. (1018) *so that he will not let go*
אֶת־הָעָם dir. obj.-def. art.-n.m.s. (I 766) *the people*

4:22

וְאָמַרְתָּ conj.-Qal pf. 2 m.s. (55) *and you shall say*
אֶל־פַּרְעֹה prep.-pr.n. (829) *to Pharaoh*
כֹּה אָמַר adv. (462)-Qal pf. 3 m.s.

(55) *thus says*

יהוה pr.n. (217) *Yahweh*

בְּנִי n.m.s.-1 c.s. sf. (119) *my son*

בְכֹרִי n.m.s.-1 c.s. sf. (114) *my first-born*

יִשְׂרָאֵל pr.n. (975) *Israel*

4:23

וָאֹמַר consec. - Qal impf. 1 c.s. (55) *and I say*

אֵלֶיךָ prep.-2 m.s. sf. *to you*

שַׁלַּח Pi. impv. 2 m.s. (1018) *let ... go*

אֶת־בְּנִי dir. obj.-n.m.s.-1 c.s. sf. (119) *my son*

וְיַעַבְדֵנִי conj.-Qal impf. 3 m.s.-1 c.s. sf. (עָבַד 712) *that he may serve me*

וַתְּמָאֵן consec.-Pi. impf. 2 m.s. (מָאֵן 549) *if you refuse*

לְשַׁלְּחוֹ prep.-Pi. inf. cstr.-3 m.s. sf. (1018) *to let him go*

הִנֵּה demons. part. (243) *behold*

אָנֹכִי הֹרֵג pers. pr. 1 c.s. (59)-Qal act. ptc. (הָרַג 246) *I will slay*

אֶת־בִּנְךָ dir. obj.-n.m.s.-2 m.s. sf. (119) *your son*

בְּכֹרֶךָ n.m.s.-2 m.s. sf. (114) *your first-born*

4:24

וַיְהִי consec.-Qal impf. 3 m.s. (הָיָה 224) *(and it shall be)*

בַדֶּרֶךְ prep.-def.art.-n.m.s. (202) *on the way*

בַּמָּלוֹן prep.-def.art.-n.m.s. (533) *at a lodging place*

וַיִּפְגְּשֵׁהוּ consec.-Qal impf. 3 m.s.-3 m.s. sf. (פָּגַשׁ 803) *met him*

יהוה pr.n. (217) *Yahweh*

וַיְבַקֵּשׁ consec.-Pi. impf. 3 m.s. (134) *and sought*

הֲמִיתוֹ Hi. inf. cstr.-3 m.s. sf. (מוּת 559) *to kill him*

4:25

וַתִּקַּח consec.-Qal impf. 3 f.s. (לָקַח 542) *then ... took*

צִפֹּרָה pr.n. (862) *Zipporah*

צֹר n.m.s. (II 866) *a flint*

וַתִּכְרֹת consec.-Qal impf. 3 f.s. (כָּרַת 503) *and cut off*

אֶת־עָרְלַת dir.obj.-n.f.s. cstr. (790) *foreskin (of)*

בְּנָהּ n.m.s.-3 f.s. sf. (119) *her son's*

וַתַּגַּע consec.-Hi. impf. 3 f.s. (נָגַע 619) *and touched*

לְרַגְלָיו prep.-n.f. du.-3 m.s. sf. (919) *Moses' (his) feet*

וַתֹּאמֶר consec.-Qal impf. 3 f.s. (55) *and said*

כִּי חֲתַן־ conj.-n.m.s. cstr. (368) *surely a bridegroom of*

דָּמִים n.m.p. (196) *blood*

אַתָּה pers.pr. 2 m.s. (61) *you*

לִי prep.-1 c.s. sf. *to me*

4:26

וַיִּרֶף consec.-Qal impf. 3 m.s. (רָפָה 951) *so he let alone (he withdrew)*

מִמֶּנּוּ prep.-3 m.s. sf. *(from) him*

אָז אָמְרָה adv. (23)-Qal pf. 3 f.s. (55) *then she said*

חֲתַן cf.4:25 n.m.s. cstr. (368) *a bridegroom of*

דָּמִים cf.4:25 n.m.p. (196) *blood*

לַמּוּלֹת prep.-def.art.-n.f.p. (558) *because of the circumcision*

4:27

וַיֹּאמֶר consec.-Qal impf. 3 m.s. (55) *said*

יהוה pr.n. (217) *Yahweh*

אֶל־אַהֲרֹן prep.-pr.n. (14) *to Aaron*

לֵךְ Qal impv. 2 m.s. (הָלַךְ 229) *Go*

לִקְרַאת prep.-Qal inf. cstr. (קָרָא 894) *to meet*

מֹשֶׁה pr.n. (602) *Moses*

הַמִּדְבָּרָה def.art.-n.m.s.-dir.he (184) *into the wilderness*

וַיֵּלֶךְ consec.-Qal impf. 3 m.s. (הָלַךְ 229) *so he went*

וַיִּפְגְּשֵׁהוּ consec.-Qal impf. 3 m.s.-3 m.s. sf. (פָּגַשׁ 803) *and met him*

בְּהַר prep.-n.m.s. cstr. (249) *at the mountain of*

הָאֱלֹהִים def.art.-n.m.p. (43) *God*

וַיִּשַּׁק־לוֹ consec.-Qal impf. 3 m.s.

(נָשַׁק I 676) - prep.-3 m.s. sf. *and kissed him*

4:28

וַיַּגֵּד consec.-Hi. impf. 3 m.s. (נָגַד 616) *and ... told*

מֹשֶׁה pr.n. (602) *Moses*

לְאַהֲרֹן prep.-pr.n. (14) *Aaron*

אֵת כָּל־ dir. obj.-n.m.s. cstr. (481) *all*

דִּבְרֵי n.m.p. cstr. (182) *the words of*

יהוה pr.n. (217) *Yahweh*

אֲשֶׁר rel. *with which*

שְׁלָחוֹ Qal pf. 3 m.s.-3 m.s. sf. (1018) *he had sent him*

וְאֵת כָּל־ conj.-dir. obj.-n.m.s. cstr. (481) *and all*

הָאֹתֹת def. art.-n.m.p. (16) *the signs*

אֲשֶׁר rel. *which*

צִוָּהוּ Pi. pf. 3 m.s.-3 m.s. sf. (צָוָה 845) *he had charged him*

4:29

וַיֵּלֶךְ consec.-Qal impf. 3 m.s. (הָלַךְ 229) *then ... went*

מֹשֶׁה pr.n. (602) *Moses*

וְאַהֲרֹן conj.-pr.n. (14) *and Aaron*

וַיַּאַסְפוּ consec. - Qal impf. 3 m. p. (אָסַף 62) *and gathered together*

אֶת־כָּל־ dir. obj.-n.m.s. cstr. (481) *all*

זִקְנֵי n.m.p. cstr. (278) *the elders of*

בְּנֵי n.m.p. cstr. (119) *the people of*

יִשְׂרָאֵל pr.n. (975) *Israel*

4:30

וַיְדַבֵּר consec.-Pi. impf. 3 m.s. (180) *and ... spoke*

אַהֲרֹן pr.n. (14) *Aaron*

אֵת כָּל־ dir. obj.-n.m.s. cstr. (481) *all*

הַדְּבָרִים def. art.-n.m.p. (182) *the words*

אֲשֶׁר־ rel. *which*

דִּבֶּר יהוה Pi. pf. 3 m.s. (180)-pr.n. (217) *Yahweh had spoken*

אֶל־מֹשֶׁה prep.-pr.n. (602) *to Moses*

וַיַּעַשׂ consec.-Qal impf. 3 m.s. (עָשָׂה 793) *and did*

הָאֹתֹת def. art.-n.m.p. (16) *the signs*

לְעֵינֵי prep.-n.f.p. cstr. (744) *in the sight of*

הָעָם def. art.-n.m.s. (I 766) *the people*

4:31

וַיַּאֲמֵן consec.-Hi. impf. 3 m.s. (אָמַן I 52) *and ... believed*

הָעָם def. art.-n.m.s. (I 766) *the people*

וַיִּשְׁמְעוּ consec.-Qal impf. 3 m.p. (1033) *and when they heard*

כִּי־פָקַד conj.-Qal pf. 3 m.s. (823) *that ... had visited*

יהוה pr.n. (217) *Yahweh*

אֶת־בְּנֵי dir. obj.-n.m.p. cstr. (119) *the people of*

יִשְׂרָאֵל pr.n. (975) *Israel*

וְכִי רָאָה conj.-conj.-Qal pf. 3 m.s. (906) *and that he had seen*

אֶת־עָנְיָם dir. obj.-n.m.s.-3 m.p. sf. (777) *their affliction*

וַיִּקְּדוּ consec.-Qal impf. 3 m.p. (קָדַד I 869) *they bowed their heads*

וַיִּשְׁתַּחֲוּוּ consec.-Hithpalel impf. 3 m.p. (שָׁחָה 1005) *and worshiped*

5:1

וְאַחַר conj.-adv. (29) *afterward*

בָּאוּ Qal pf. 3 c.p. (בּוֹא 97) *went*

מֹשֶׁה pr.n. (602) *Moses*

וְאַהֲרֹן conj.-pr.n. (14) *and Aaron*

וַיֹּאמְרוּ consec.-Qal impf. 3 m.p. (55) *and said*

אֶל־פַּרְעֹה prep.-pr.n. (829) *to Pharaoh*

כֹּה־אָמַר adv. (462)-Qal pf. 3 m.s. (55) *Thus says*

יהוה pr.n. (217) *Yahweh*

אֱלֹהֵי n.m.p. cstr. (43) *the God of*

יִשְׂרָאֵל pr.n. (975) *Israel*

שַׁלַּח Pi. impv. 2 m.s. (1018) *let go*

אֶת־עַמִּי dir. obj.-n.m.s.-1 c.s. sf. (I 766) *my people*

וְיָחֹגּוּ conj.-Qal impf. 3 m.p. (חָגַג 290) *that they may hold a feast*

לִי prep.-1 c.s. sf. *to me*

בַּמִּדְבָּר prep.-def. art.-n.m.s. (184) *in the wilderness*

5:2

וַיֹּאמֶר consec.-Qal impf. 3 m.s. (55) *but ... said*

פַּרְעֹה pr.n. (829) *Pharaoh*

מִי יהוה interr. (566)-pr.n. (217) *Who is Yahweh*

אֲשֶׁר rel. *that*

אֶשְׁמַע Qal impf. 1 c.s. (שָׁמַע 1033) *I should heed*

בְּקֹלוֹ prep.-n.m.s.-3 m.s. sf. (876) *his voice*

לְשַׁלַּח prep.-Pi. inf. cstr. (1018) *and (to) let go*

אֶת־יִשְׂרָאֵל dir. obj.-pr.n. (975) *Israel*

לֹא יָדַעְתִּי neg.-Qal pf. 1 c.s. (393) *I do not know*

אֶת־יהוה dir. obj.-pr.n. (217) *Yahweh*

וְגַם conj.-adv. (168) *and moreover*

אֶת־יִשְׂרָאֵל dir. obj.-pr.n. (975) *Israel*

לֹא אֲשַׁלֵּחַ neg.-Pi. impf. 1 c.s. (שָׁלַח 1018) *I will not let go*

5:3

וַיֹּאמְרוּ consec.-Qal impf. 3 m.p. (55) *then they said*

אֱלֹהֵי n.m.p. cstr. (43) *the God of*

הָעִבְרִים def. art.-n.m.p. gent. (I 720) *the Hebrews*

נִקְרָא Ni. pf. 3 m.s. (קָרָא 894) *has met*

עָלֵינוּ prep.-1 c.p. sf. *with us*

נֵלֲכָה נָּא Qal impf. 1 c.p.-coh. he (הָלַךְ 229)-part. of entreaty (609) *let us go, we pray*

דֶּרֶךְ n.m.s. cstr. (202) *a journey (of)*

שְׁלֹשֶׁת num. f.s. cstr. (1025) *three*

יָמִים n.m.p. (398) *days*

בַּמִּדְבָּר prep.-def. art.-n.m.s. (184) *into the wilderness*

וְנִזְבְּחָה conj.-Qal impf. 1 c.p.-coh. he (זָבַח 256) *and sacrifice*

ליהוה prep.-pr.n. (217) *to Yahweh*

אֱלֹהֵינוּ n.m.p.-1 c.p. sf. (43) *our God*

פֶּן־יִפְגָּעֵנוּ conj.-Qal impf. 3 m.s.-1 c.p. sf. (פָּגַע 803) *lest he fall upon us*

בַּדֶּבֶר prep.-def. art.-n.m.s. (184) *with pestilence*

אוֹ בֶחָרֶב conj. (14)-prep.-def. art.-n.f.s. paus. (352) *or with the sword*

5:4

וַיֹּאמֶר consec.-Qal impf. 3 m.s. (55) *but ... said*

אֲלֵהֶם prep.-3 m.p. sf. *to them*

מֶלֶךְ מִצְרַיִם n.m.s. cstr. (I 572)-pr.n. (595) *the king of Egypt*

לָמָּה prep.-interr. (552) *why*

מֹשֶׁה pr.n. (602) *Moses*

וְאַהֲרֹן conj.-pr.n. (14) *and Aaron*

תַּפְרִיעוּ Hi. impf. 2 m.p. (פָּרַע III 828) *do you take ... away (cause to refrain)*

אֶת־הָעָם dir. obj.-def. art.-n.m.s. (I 766) *the people*

מִמַּעֲשָׂיו prep.-n.m.p.-3 m.s. sf. (795) *from their work*

לְכוּ Qal impv. 2 m.p. (הָלַךְ 229) *Get*

לְסִבְלֹתֵיכֶם prep.-n.f.p.-2 m.p. sf. (688) *to your burdens*

5:5

וַיֹּאמֶר consec.-Qal impf.3 m.s.(55) *and ... said*

פַּרְעֹה pr.n.(829) *Pharaoh*

הֵן־רַבִּים demons.part.(243)-adj.m.p.(I 912) *Behold, ... are many*

עַתָּה adv.(773) *now*

עַם הָאָרֶץ n.m.s.cstr.(I 766)-def.art.-n.f.s.(75) *the people of the land*

וְהִשְׁבַּתֶּם conj.-Hi.pf.2 m.p.(שָׁבַת 991) *and you make rest*

אֹתָם dir.obj.-3 m.p.sf. *them*

מִסִּבְלֹתָם prep.-n.f.p.-3 m.p.sf.(688) *from their burdens*

5:6

וַיְצַו consec.-Pi.impf.3 m.s.(צָוָה 845) *commanded*

פַּרְעֹה pr.n.(829) *Pharaoh*

בַּיּוֹם הַהוּא prep.-def.art.-

n.m.s.(398)-def.art.-demons.adj.(214) *The same day*

אֶת־הַנֹּגְשִׂים dir.obj.-def.art.-Qal act.ptc.m.p. (נָגַשׂ 620) *the taskmasters*

בָּעָם prep.-def.art.-n.m.s.(I 766) *of the people*

וְאֶת־שֹׁטְרָיו conj.-dir.obj.-n.m.p.-3 m.s. sf. (1009) *and their foremen*

לֵאמֹר prep.-Qal inf.cstr.(55) *saying*

5:7

לֹא תֹאסִפוּן neg.-Hi. impf.2 m.p.(יָסַף 414) *you shall no longer*

לָתֵת prep.-Qal inf.cstr.(נָתַן 678) *give*

תֶּבֶן לָעָם n.m.s.(1061)-prep.-def.art.-n.m.s.(I 766) *straw (to) the people*

לִלְבֹּן prep.-Qal inf.cstr.(לָבַן 527) *to make (bricks)*

הַלְּבֵנִים def.art.-n.f.p.(527) *bricks*

כִּתְמוֹל prep.-adv.acc.(1069) *as heretofore*

שִׁלְשֹׁם adv.(1025) with previous word an idiom

הֵם יֵלְכוּ pers.pr. 3 m.p. (241) - Qal impf. 3 m.p. (הָלַךְ 229) *let them go*

וְקֹשְׁשׁוּ conj.-Po'el pf. 3 c.p. (קָשַׁשׁ 905) *and gather (stubble)*

לָהֶם prep.-3 m.p.sf. *for themselves*

תֶּבֶן v.supra *straw*

5:8

וְאֶת־מַתְכֹּנֶת conj.-dir.obj.-n.f.s. cstr. (1067) *but the number of*

הַלְּבֵנִים def.art.-n.f.p.(527) *bricks*

אֲשֶׁר rel. *which*

הֵם עֹשִׂים pers.pr.3 m.p.(241)-Qal act.ptc.m.p.(עָשָׂה 793) *they made*

תְּמוֹל שִׁלְשֹׁם adv.acc.(1069)-adv.(1026) *heretofore*

תָּשִׂימוּ Qal impf.2 m.p.(שִׂים 962) *you shall lay*

עֲלֵיהֶם prep.-3 m.p.sf. *on them*

לֹא תִגְרְעוּ neg.-Qal impf. 2 m.p. (רָגַע 175) *you shall by no means lessen*

מִמֶּנּוּ prep.-3 m.s. sf. *it*

כִּי־נִרְפִּים conj.-Ni. ptc. m.p. (רָפָה 951) *for ... idle*

הֵם pers.pr.3 m.p.(241) *they are*

עַל־כֵּן prep.-adv.(487) *therefore*

הֵם צֹעֲקִים pers.pr.3 m.p.(241)-Qal act.ptc.m.p.(צָעַק 858) *they cry*

לֵאמֹר prep.-Qal inf.cstr.(55) *(saying)*

נֵלְכָה Qal impf. 1 c.p.-coh. he (הָלַךְ 229) *let us go*

נִזְבְּחָה Qal impf.1 c.p.-coh.he (זָבַח 256) *and offer sacrifice*

לֵאלֹהֵינוּ prep.-n.m.p.-1 c.p.sf. (43) *to our God*

5:9

תִּכְבַּד Qal impf. 3 f.s. (כָּבֵד 457) *let heavier ... be laid (make heavy)*

הָעֲבֹדָה def.art.-n.f.s.(715) *work*

עַל־הָאֲנָשִׁים prep.-def.art.-n.m.p.(35) *upon the men*

וְיַעֲשׂוּ־ conj.-Qal impf.3 m.p.(עָשָׂה 793) *that they may labor*

בָהּ prep.-3 f.s.sf. *at it*

וְאַל־יִשְׁעוּ conj.-neg.-Qal impf. 3 m.p. (שָׁעָה 1043) *and pay no regard*

בְּדִבְרֵי־ prep.-n.m.p.cstr.(182) *to ... words (of)*

שָׁקֶר n.m.s.paus.(1055) *lying*

5:10

וַיֵּצְאוּ consec.-Qal impf.3 m.p.(יָצָא 422) *so ... went out*

נֹגְשֵׂי Qal act.ptc.m.p.cstr.(נָגַשׂ 620) *taskmasters of*

הָעָם def.art.-n.m.s.(I 766) *the people*

וְשֹׁטְרָיו conj.-n.m.p.-3 m.s.sf.(1009) *and (their) foremen*

וַיֹּאמְרוּ consec.-Qal impf.3 m.p.(55) *and said*

אֶל־הָעָם prep.-def.art.-n.m.s.(I 766) *to the people*

לֵאמֹר prep.-Qal inf.cstr.(55) *(saying)*

כֹּה אָמַר adv. (462)-Qal pf.3 m.s.(55) *Thus says*

פַּרְעֹה pr.n. (829) *Pharaoh*

אֵינֶנִּי subst.-1 c.s.sf.(II 34) *I will not*

נֹתֵן Qal act.ptc.(נָתַן 678) *give*

לָכֶם prep.-2 m.p.sf. *you*

תֶּבֶן n.m.s.(1061) *straw*

5:11

אַתֶּם לְכוּ pers.pr. 2 m.p. (61) - Qal impv. 2 m.p. (הָלַךְ 229) *go yourselves*

קְחוּ לָכֶם Qal impv.2 m.p.(לָקַח 542)-prep.-2 m.p.sf. *get your*

תֶּבֶן n.m.s.(1061) *straw*

מֵאֲשֶׁר prep.-rel. *wherever*

תִּמְצָאוּ Qal impf. 2 m.p. (מָצָא 592) *you can find it*

כִּי אֵין conj.-subst. (II 34) *but will not be*

נִגְרָע Ni.ptc. (גָּרַע 175) *lessened*

מֵעֲבֹדַתְכֶם prep.-n.f.s.-2 m.p.sf.(715) *(from) your work*

דָּבָר n.m.s.(182) *in the least*

5:12

וַיָּפֶץ consec.-Hi. impf. 3 m.s. (I פּוּץ 806) *so ... were scattered abroad*

הָעָם def.art.-n.m.s.(I 766) *the people*

בְּכָל־אֶרֶץ prep.-n.m.s.cstr.(481)-n.f.s.cstr.(75) *throughout all the land of*

מִצְרָיִם pr.n.paus.(595) *Egypt*

לְקֹשֵׁשׁ קַשׁ prep.-Po'el inf. cstr. (קָשַׁשׁ 905) - n.m.s. (905) *to gather stubble*

לַתֶּבֶן prep.-def.art.-n.m.s. (1061) *for straw*

5:13

וְהַנֹּגְשִׂים conj.-def.art.-Qal act.ptc.m.p.(נָגַשׂ 620) *the taskmasters*

אָצִים Qal act.ptc.m.p.(אוּץ 21) *were urgent (pressing)*

לֵאמֹר prep.-Qal inf. cstr. (55) *saying*

כַּלּוּ Pi.impv.2 m.p.(כָּלָה 477) *complete*

מַעֲשֵׂיכֶם n.m.p.-2 m.p.sf.(795) *your work*

דְּבַר־יוֹם n.m.s.cstr.(182)-n.m.s.(398) *daily task (task of a day)*

בְּיוֹמוֹ prep.-n.m.s.-3 m.s.sf.(398) *(in its day)*

כַּאֲשֶׁר prep.-rel. *as*

בִּהְיוֹת prep.-Qal inf. cstr. (הָיָה 224) *when there was*

הַתֶּבֶן def.art.-n.m.s.(1061) *straw*

5:14

וַיֻּכּוּ consec.-Ho. impf. 3 m.p. (נָכָה 645) *and ... were beaten*

שֹׁטְרֵי n.m.p.cstr. (1009) *the foremen of*

בְּנֵי n.m.p.cstr.(119) *the people of*

יִשְׂרָאֵל pr.n. (975) *Israel*

אֲשֶׁר־ rel. *whom*

שָׂמוּ Qal pf.3 c.p.(שׂוּם 962) *had set*

עֲלֵהֶם prep.-3 m.p. sf. *over them*

נֹגְשֵׂי Qal act.ptc.m.p.cstr.(נָגַשׂ 620) *the taskmasters of*

פַּרְעֹה pr.n. (829) *Pharaoh*

לֵאמֹר prep.-Qal inf.cstr.(55) *and were asked*

מַדּוּעַ adv.(396) *why*

לֹא כִלִּיתֶם neg.-Pi. pf. 2 m.p. (כָּלָה 477) *have you not done all (finished)*

חָקְכֶם n.m.s.-2 m.p.sf.(349) *your task*

לִלְבֹּן prep.-Qal inf.cstr.(לָבַן 527) *of making bricks*

כִּתְמוֹל שִׁלְשֹׁם prep.-adv.(1069)-adv.(1026) *as hitherto*

גַּם־תְּמוֹל גַּם־הַיּוֹם adv.(168)-adv.(1069)-adv.(168)-def.art.-n.m.s.(398) *today*

5:15

וַיָּבֹאוּ consec.-Qal impf.3 m.p.(בּוֹא 97) *then ... came*

שֹׁטְרֵי n.m.p.cstr.(1009) *the foremen of*

בְּנֵי n.m.p. cstr. (119) *the people of*

יִשְׂרָאֵל pr.n. (975) *Israel*

וַיִּצְעֲקוּ consec. - Qal impf. 3 m.p. (צָעַק 858) *and cried*

אֶל־פַּרְעֹה prep.-pr.n.(829) *to Pharaoh*

לֵאמֹר prep.-Qal inf.cstr.(55) *(say-*

ing)
לָמָּה adv.(552) *why*
תַעֲשֶׂה Qal impf.2 m.s.(עָשָׂה I 793) *do you deal*
כֹּה adv.(462) *thus*
לַעֲבָדֶיךָ prep.-n.m.p.-2 m.s. sf. (712) *with your servants*

5:16

תֶּבֶן n.m.s. (1061) *straw*
אֵין subst. (II 34) *No*
נִתָּן Ni. ptc. (678) *is given*
לַעֲבָדֶיךָ prep.-n.m.p.-2 m.s. sf. (712) *to your servants*
וּלְבֵנִים conj.-n.m.p. (527) *yet ... bricks*
אֹמְרִים Qal act. ptc. m.p. (55) *they say*
לָנוּ prep.-1 c.p. sf. *to us*
עֲשׂוּ Qal impv. 2 m.p. (עָשָׂה I 793) *make*
וְהִנֵּה conj.-demons. part. (243) *and behold*
עֲבָדֶיךָ n.m.p.-2 m.s. sf. (712) *your servants*
מֻכִּים Ho. ptc. m.p. (נָכָה 645) *are beaten*
וְחָטָאת conj.-Qal pf. 3 f.s. (חָטָא 306) *but the fault is in (are wrong)*
עַמֶּךָ n.f.s.-2 m.s. sf. (I 766) *your own people*

5:17

וַיֹּאמֶר consec.-Qal impf. 3 m.s. (55) *but he said*
נִרְפִּים Ni. ptc. m.p. (רָפָה 951) *are idle*
אַתֶּם pers. pr. 2 m.p. (61) *you*
נִרְפִּים v. supra *you are idle*
עַל־כֵּן prep.-adv. (485) *therefore*
אַתֶּם v. supra *you*
אֹמְרִים Qal act. ptc. m.p. (55) *say*
נֵלְכָה Qal impf. 1 c.p.-coh. he (הָלַךְ 229) *let us go*
נִזְבְּחָה Qal impf. 1 c.p.-coh. he (זָבַח 256) *and sacrifice*
ליהוה prep.-pr.n. (217) *to Yahweh*

5:18

וְעַתָּה conj.-adv. (773) *now*
לְכוּ Qal impv. 2 m.p. (הָלַךְ 229) *Go*
עִבְדוּ Qal impv. 2 m.p. (712) *work*
וְתֶבֶן conj.-n.m.s. (1061) *for ... straw*
לֹא־יִנָּתֵן neg.-Ni. impf. 3 m.s. (נָתַן 678) *will not be given*
לָכֶם prep.-2 m.p. sf. *(to) you*
וְתֹכֶן conj.-n.m.s. cstr. (I 1067) *yet the same number of*
לְבֵנִים n.f.p. (527) *bricks*
תִּתֵּנוּ Qal impf. 2 m.p. (נָתַן 678) *you shall deliver*

5:19

וַיִּרְאוּ consec.-Qal impf. 3 m.p. (רָאָה 906) *saw*
שֹׁטְרֵי n.m.p. cstr. (1009) *the foremen of*
בְנֵי־ n.m.p. cstr. (119) *the people of*
יִשְׂרָאֵל pr.n. (975) *Israel*
אֹתָם dir. obj.-3 m.p. sf. *(them) that they were*
בְּרָע prep.-n.m.s. (II 948) *in evil plight*
לֵאמֹר prep.-Qal inf. cstr. (55) *when they said*
לֹא־תִגְרְעוּ neg.-Qal impf. 2 m.p. (גָּרַע 175) *you shall by no means lessen*
מִלִּבְנֵיכֶם prep.-n.f.p.-2 m.p. sf. (527) *(from) your bricks*
דְּבַר־יוֹם n.m.s. cstr. (182)-n.m.s. (398) *daily number*
בְּיוֹמוֹ prep.-n.m.s.-3 m.s. sf. (398) *(on its day)*

5:20

וַיִּפְגְּעוּ consec.-Qal impf. 3 m.p. (פָּגַע 803) *they met*
אֶת־מֹשֶׁה dir.obj.-pr.n. (602) *Moses*
וְאֶת־אַהֲרֹן conj.-dir.obj.-pr.n. (14) *and Aaron*
נִצָּבִים Ni. ptc. m.p. (נָצַב 662) *who were waiting*
לִקְרָאתָם prep.-Qal inf. cstr.-3 m.p. sf. (קָרָא 894) *for them (to meet them)*

בְּצֵאתָם prep.-Qal inf. cstr.-3 m.p. sf. (יָצָא 422) *as they came forth*

מֵאֵת פַּרְעֹה prep.-prep. (II, 4; 85) - pr.n. (829) *from Pharaoh*

5:21

וַיֹּאמְרוּ consec.-Qal impf. 3 m.p. (55) *and they said*

אֲלֵהֶם prep.-3 m.p. sf. *to them*

יֵרֶא Qal impf. 3 m.s. apoc. juss. (רָאָה 906) *(let) ... look*

יהוה pr.n. (217) *Yahweh*

עֲלֵיכֶם prep.-2 m.p. sf. *upon you*

וְיִשְׁפֹּט conj.-Qal impf. 3 m.s. (1047) *and judge*

אֲשֶׁר rel. *because*

הִבְאַשְׁתֶּם Hi. pf. 2 m.p. (בָּאַשׁ 92) *you have made offensive*

אֶת־רֵיחֵנוּ dir.obj.-n.m.s.-1 c.p. sf. (926) *us (our odor)*

בְּעֵינֵי prep.-n.f.p. cstr. (744) *in the sight of*

פַּרְעֹה pr.n. (829) *Pharaoh*

וּבְעֵינֵי conj.-prep.-n.f.p. cstr. (744) *and (in the sight of)*

עֲבָדָיו n.m.p.-3 m.s. sf. (712) *his servants*

לָתֶת־חֶרֶב prep.-Qal inf. cstr. (נָתַן 678)-n.f.s. (352) *and have put (to put) a sword*

בְּיָדָם prep.-n.f.s.-3 m.p. sf. (388) *in their hand*

לְהָרְגֵנוּ prep.-Qal inf. cstr.-1 c.p. sf. (הָרַג 246) *to kill us*

5:22

וַיָּשָׁב consec.-Qal impf. 3 m.s. (שׁוּב 996) *then ... turned again*

מֹשֶׁה pr.n. (602) *Moses*

אֶל־יהוה prep.-pr.n. (217) *to Yahweh*

וַיֹּאמַר consec.-Qal impf. 3 m.s. (55) *and said*

אֲדֹנָי n.m.p.-1 c.s. sf. (10) *O Lord*

לָמָה prep.-interr. (552) *why*

הֲרֵעֹתָה Hi. pf. 2 m.s. (רָעַע 949) *hast thou done evil*

לָעָם הַזֶּה prep.-def. art.-n.m.s. (I 766)-def. art.-demons. adj. m.s. (260) *to this people*

לָמָּה v. supra *why*

זֶּה demons. adv. (260) *(now) ever*

שְׁלַחְתָּנִי Qal pf. 2 m.s.-1 c.s. sf. (שָׁלַח 1018) *didst thou send me*

5:23

וּמֵאָז conj.-prep.-adv. (23) *for since*

בָּאתִי Qal pf. 1 c.s. (בּוֹא 97) *I came*

אֶל־פַּרְעֹה prep.-pr.n. (829) *to Pharaoh*

לְדַבֵּר prep.-Pi. inf. cstr. (180) *to speak*

בִּשְׁמֶךָ prep.-n.m.s.-2 m.s. sf. (1027) *in thy name*

הֵרַע Hi. pf. 3 m.s. (רָעַע 949) *he has done evil*

לָעָם הַזֶּה prep.-def. art.-n.m.s. (I 766)-def. art.-demons. adj. m.s. (260) *to this people*

וְהַצֵּל conj.-Hi. inf. abs. (נָצַל 664) *and ... at all (delivering)*

לֹא־הִצַּלְתָּ neg.-Hi. pf. 2 m.s. (נָצַל 664) *thou hast not delivered*

אֶת־עַמֶּךָ dir. obj.-n.m.s.-2 m.s. sf. (I 766) *thy people*

6:1

וַיֹּאמֶר consec.-Qal impf. 3 m.s. (55) *but ... said*

יהוה pr.n. (217) *Yahweh*

אֶל־מֹשֶׁה prep.-pr.n. (602) *to Moses*

עַתָּה adv. (773) *now*

תִרְאֶה Qal impf. 2 m.s. (רָאָה 906) *you shall see*

אֲשֶׁר rel. *what*

אֶעֱשֶׂה Qal impf. 1 c.s. (עָשָׂה I 793) *I will do*

לְפַרְעֹה prep.-pr.n. (829) *to Pharaoh*

כִּי conj. *for*

בְּיָד prep.-n.f.s. (388) *with a ... hand*

חֲזָקָה adj. f.s. (305) *strong*

יְשַׁלְּחֵם Pi. impf. 3 m.s.-3 m.p. sf. (1018) *he will send them out*

וּבְיָד חֲזָקָה conj.-v. supra *yea, with a strong hand*

יְגָרְשֵׁם Pi. impf. 3 m.s.-3 m.p. sf. (גָּרַשׁ 176) *he will drive them out*

מֵאַרְצוֹ prep.-n.f.s.-3 m.s. sf. (75) *of his land*

6:2

וַיְדַבֵּר consec.-Pi. impf. 3 m.s. (180) *and ... said*

אֱלֹהִים n.m.p. (43) *God*

אֶל־מֹשֶׁה prep.-pr.n. (602) *to Moses*

וַיֹּאמֶר consec.-Qal impf. 3 m.s. (55) *(and he said)*

אֵלָיו prep.-3 m.s. sf. *(to him)*

אֲנִי יהוה pers. pr. 1 c.s. (58)-pr.n. (217) *I am Yahweh*

6:3

וָאֵרָא consec.-Ni. impf. 1 c.s. (רָאָה 906) *I appeared*

אֶל־אַבְרָהָם prep.-pr.n. (4) *to Abraham*

אֶל־יִצְחָק prep.-pr.n. (850) *to Isaac*

וְאֶל־יַעֲקֹב conj.-prep.-pr.n. (784) *and to Jacob*

בְּאֵל שַׁדָּי prep.-n.m.s. (42) - n.m. (994) *as God Almighty ('el Shaddai)*

וּשְׁמִי conj.-n.m.s.-1 c.s. sf. (1027) *but by my name*

יהוה pr.n. (217) *Yahweh*

לֹא נוֹדַעְתִּי neg.-Ni. pf. 1 c.s. (יָדַע 393) *I did not make myself known*

לָהֶם prep.-3 m.p. sf. *to them*

6:4

וְגַם הֲקִמֹתִי conj.-adv. (168)-Hi. pf. 1 c.s. (קוּם 877) *I also established*

אֶת־בְּרִיתִי dir. obj.-n.f.s.-1 c.s. sf. (136) *my covenant*

אִתָּם prep. (II 85)-3 m.p. sf. *with them*

לָתֵת לָהֶם prep.-Qal inf. cstr. (נָתַן 678)-prep.-3 m.p. sf. *to give them*

אֶת־אֶרֶץ dir. obj.-n.f.s. cstr. (75) *the land of*

כְּנָעַן pr.n. paus. (489) *Canaan*

אֵת אֶרֶץ dir. obj.-n.f.s. cstr. (75) *the land (of)*

מְגֻרֵיהֶם n.m.p.-3 m.p. sf. (158) *their sojourning*

אֲשֶׁר־ rel. *which*

גָּרוּ בָהּ Qal pf. 3 c.p. (גּוּר I 157) - prep.-3 f.s. sf. *they sojourned in it*

6:5

וְגַם אֲנִי conj.-adv. (168)-pers.pr. 1 c.s. (58) *moreover I*

שָׁמַעְתִּי Qal pf. 1 c.s. (שָׁמַע 1033) *have heard*

אֶת־נַאֲקַת dir.obj.-n.f.s. cstr. (611) *the groaning of*

בְּנֵי n.m.p. cstr. (119) *the people of*

יִשְׂרָאֵל pr.n. (975) *Israel*

אֲשֶׁר rel. *whom*

מִצְרַיִם pr.n. (595) *the Egyptians*

מַעֲבִדִים Hi. ptc. m.p. (712) *hold in bondage*

אֹתָם dir.obj.-3 m.p. sf. *(them)*

וָאֶזְכֹּר consec.-Qal impf. 1 c.s. (זָכַר 269) *and I have remembered*

אֶת־בְּרִיתִי dir.obj.-n.f.s.-1 c.s. sf. (136) *my covenant*

6:6

לָכֵן prep.-adv. (485) *therefore*

אֱמֹר Qal impv. 2 m.s. (אָמַר 55) *Say*

לִבְנֵי־ prep.-n.m.p. cstr. (119) *to the people of*

יִשְׂרָאֵל pr.n. (975) *Israel*

אֲנִי יהוה pers.pr. 1 c.s. (58)-pr.n. (217) *I am Yahweh*

וְהוֹצֵאתִי conj.-Hi. pf. 1 c.s. (יָצָא 422) *and I will bring ... out*

אֶתְכֶם dir.obj.-2 m.p. sf. *you*

מִתַּחַת prep.-prep. (1065) *from under*

סִבְלֹת n.f.p. cstr. (688) *the burdens of*

מִצְרַיִם pr.n. (595) *the Egyptians*

וְהִצַּלְתִּי conj.-Hi. pf. 1 c.s. (נָצַל 664) *and I will deliver*

אֶתְכֶם dir.obj.-2 m.p. sf. *you*

מֵעֲבֹדָתָם prep.-n.f.s.-3 m.p. sf. (715) *from their bondage*

וְגָאַלְתִּי conj.-Qal pf. 1 c.s. (גָּאַל I 145) *and I will redeem*

אֶתְכֶם dir.obj.-2 m.p. sf. *you*

בִּזְרוֹעַ prep.-n.f.s. (283) *with an ... arm*

נְטוּיָה Qal pass. ptc. f.s. (639) *outstretched*

וּבִשְׁפָטִים conj.-prep.-n.m.p. (1048) *and with ... acts of judgment*

גְּדֹלִים adj. m.p. (152) *great*

6:7

וְלָקַחְתִּי conj.-Qal pf. 1 c.s. (לָקַח 542) *and I will take*

אֶתְכֶם dir.obj.-2 m.p. sf. *you*

לִי prep.-1 c.s. sf. *(to me) my*

לְעָם prep.-n.m.s. (I 766) *for ... people*

וְהָיִיתִי conj.-Qal pf. 1 c.s. (הָיָה 224) *and I will be*

לָכֶם prep.-2 m.p. sf. (*to you*) *your*

לֵאלֹהִים prep.-n.m.p. (43) *God*

וִידַעְתֶּם conj.-Qal pf. 2 m.p. (יָדַע 393) *and you shall know*

כִּי אֲנִי conj.-pers.pr. 1 c.s. (58) *that I*

יהוה pr.n. (217) *Yahweh*

אֱלֹהֵיכֶם n.m.p.-2 m.p. sf. (43) *your God*

הַמּוֹצִיא def.art.-Hi. ptc. (יָצָא 422) *who has brought*

אֶתְכֶם dir.obj.-2 m.p. sf. *you*

מִתַּחַת prep.-prep. (1065) *from under*

סִבְלוֹת n.f.p. cstr. (688) *the burdens of*

מִצְרָיִם pr.n. paus. (595) *the Egyptians*

6:8

וְהֵבֵאתִי conj.-Hi. pf. 1 c.s. (בּוֹא 97) *and I will bring*

אֶתְכֶם dir. obj.-2 m.p. sf. *you*

אֶל־הָאָרֶץ prep.-def. art.-n.f.s. (75) *into the land*

אֲשֶׁר rel. *which*

נָשָׂאתִי Qal pf. 1 c.s. (נָשָׂא 669) *I swore (lifted up)*

אֶת־יָדִי dir. obj.-n.f.s.-1 c.s. sf. (388) *(my hand)*

לָתֵת אֹתָהּ prep.-Qal inf. cstr. (נָתַן 678)-dir. obj.-3 f.s. sf. *to give (it)*

לְאַבְרָהָם prep.-pr.n. (4) *to Abraham*

לְיִצְחָק prep.-pr.n. (850) *to Isaac*

וּלְיַעֲקֹב conj.-prep.-pr.n. (784) *and to Jacob*

וְנָתַתִּי אֹתָהּ conj. - Qal pf. 1 c.s. (נָתַן 678) - dir.obj.-3 f.s. sf. *I will give it*

לָכֶם prep.-2 m.p. sf. *to you*

מוֹרָשָׁה n.f.s. (440) *for a possession*

אֲנִי יהוה pers. pr. 1 c.s. (58)-pr.n. (217) *I am Yahweh*

6:9

וַיְדַבֵּר consec.-Pi. impf. 3 m.s. (180) *spoke*

מֹשֶׁה pr.n. (602) *Moses*

כֵּן adv. (485) *thus*

אֶל־בְּנֵי prep.-n.m.p. cstr. (119) *to the people of*

יִשְׂרָאֵל pr.n. (975) *Israel*

וְלֹא שָׁמְעוּ conj.-neg.-Qal pf. 3 c.p. (1033) *but they did not listen*

אֶל־מֹשֶׁה prep.-pr.n. (602) *to Moses*

מִקֹּצֶר prep.-n.m.s. cstr. (894) *because of shortness of*

רוּחַ n.f.s. (924) *spirit*

וּמֵעֲבֹדָה conj.-prep.-n.f.s. (715) *and ... bondage*

קָשָׁה adj. f.s. (904) *cruel*

6:10

וַיְדַבֵּר consec.-Pi. impf. 3 m.s. (180) *and ... said*

יהוה pr.n. (217) *Yahweh*

אֶל־מֹשֶׁה prep.-pr.n. (602) *to Moses*

לֵאמֹר prep.-Qal inf. cstr. (55) *(saying)*

6:11

בֹּא Qal impv. 2 m.s. (בּוֹא 97) *Go in*

דַּבֵּר Pi. impv. 2 m.s. (180) *tell*

אֶל־פַּרְעֹה prep.-pr.n. (829) *Pharaoh*

מֶלֶךְ n.m.s. cstr. (I 572) *king of*

מִצְרָיִם pr.n. paus. (595) *Egypt*

וִישַׁלַּח conj.-Pi. impf. 3 m.s. (שָׁלַח 1018) *to let go*

אֶת־בְּנֵי־ dir. obj.-n.m.p. cstr. (119) *the people of*

יִשְׂרָאֵל pr.n. (975) *Israel*

מֵאַרְצוֹ prep.-n.f.s.-3 m.s. sf. (75) *out of his land*

6:12

וַיְדַבֵּר consec.-Pi. impf. 3 m.s. (180) *but ... said*

מֹשֶׁה pr.n. (602) *Moses*

לִפְנֵי prep.-n.m.p. cstr. (815) *to (before)*

יהוה pr.n. (217) *Yahweh*

לֵאמֹר prep.-Qal inf. cstr. (55) *(saying)*

הֵן demons. part. (243) *behold*

בְּנֵי־יִשְׂרָאֵל n.m.p. cstr. (119)-pr.n. (975) *the people of Israel*

לֹא־שָׁמְעוּ neg.-Qal pf. 3 c.p. (1033) *have not listened*

אֵלַי prep.-1 c.s. sf. *to me*

וְאֵיךְ conj.-interr. (32) *how then*

יִשְׁמָעֵנִי Qal impf. 3 m.s.-1 c.s. sf. (1033) *shall ... listen to me*

פַּרְעֹה pr.n. (829) *Pharaoh*

וַאֲנִי conj.-pers. pr. 1 c.s. (58) *who am a man (for I)*

עֲרַל adj. m.s. cstr. (790) *uncircumcised of*

שְׂפָתָיִם n.f. du. paus. (973) *lips*

6:13

וַיְדַבֵּר consec.-Pi. impf. 3 m.s. (180) *but ... spoke*

יהוה pr.n. (217) *Yahweh*

אֶל־מֹשֶׁה prep.-pr.n. (602) *to Moses*

וְאֶל־אַהֲרֹן conj.-prep.-pr.n. (14) *and Aaron*

וַיְצַוֵּם consec.-Pi. impf. 3 m.s.-3 m.p. sf. (צָוָה 845) *and gave them a charge*

אֶל־בְּנֵי prep.-n.m.p. cstr. (119) *to the people of*

יִשְׂרָאֵל pr.n. (975) *Israel*

וְאֶל־פַּרְעֹה conj.-prep.-pr.n. (829) *and to Pharaoh*

מֶלֶךְ n.m.s. cstr. (I 572) *king of*

מִצְרָיִם pr.n. paus. (595) *Egypt*

לְהוֹצִיא prep.-Hi. inf. cstr. (יָצָא 422) *to bring*

אֶת־בְּנֵי־ dir. obj.-n.m.p. cstr. (119) *the people of*

יִשְׂרָאֵל pr.n. (975) *Israel*

מֵאֶרֶץ prep.-n.f.s. cstr. (75) *out of the land of*

מִצְרָיִם pr.n. paus. (595) *Egypt*

6:14

אֵלֶּה demons. adj. c.p. (41) *these are*

רָאשֵׁי n.m.p. cstr. (910) *the heads of*

בֵית־אֲבֹתָם n.m.s. cstr. (108)-n.m.p.-3 m.p. sf. (3) *their fathers' house*

בְּנֵי רְאוּבֵן n.m.p. cstr. (119)-pr.n. (910) *the sons of Reuben*

בְּכֹר יִשְׂרָאֵל n.m.s. cstr. (114)-pr.n. (975) *the first-born of Israel*

חֲנוֹךְ pr.n. (335) *Hanoch*

וּפַלּוּא conj.-pr.n. (811) *Pallu*

חֶצְרוֹן pr.n. (348) *Hezron*

וְכַרְמִי conj.-pr.n. (I 501) *and Carmi*

אֵלֶּה v. supra *these are*

מִשְׁפְּחֹת n.f.p. (1046) *the families of*

רְאוּבֵן pr.n. (910) *Reuben*

6:15

וּבְנֵי שִׁמְעוֹן conj.-n.m.p. cstr. (119)-pr.n. (1035) *The sons of Simeon*

יְמוּאֵל pr.n. (410) *Jemuel*

וְיָמִין conj.-pr.n. (II 412) *Jamin*

וְאֹהַד conj.-pr.n. (13) *Ohad*

וְיָכִין conj.-pr.n. (467) *Jachin*

וְצֹחַר conj.-pr.n. (850) *Zohar*

וְשָׁאוּל conj.-pr.n. (982) *and Shaul*

בֶּן־הַכְּנַעֲנִית n.m.s. cstr. (119)-def. art.-pr.n. gent. f. (I 489) *the son of a Canaanite woman*

אֵלֶּה v. 6:14 *these are*

מִשְׁפְּחֹת v. 6:14 *the families of*

שִׁמְעוֹן v. supra *Simeon*

6:16

וְאֵלֶּה conj.-demons. adj. c.p. (41) *these are*

שְׁמוֹת n.m.p. cstr. (1027) *the names of*

בְּנֵי־לֵוִי n.m.p. cstr. (119)-pr.n. (532) *the sons of Levi*

לְתֹלְדֹתָם prep.-n.f.p.-3 m.p. sf. (410) *according to their generations*

גֵּרְשׁוֹן pr.n. (177) *Gershon*

וּקְהָת conj.-pr.n. (875) *Kohath*

וּמְרָרִי conj.-pr.n. (I 601) *and Merari*

וּשְׁנֵי חַיֵּי conj.-n.f.p. cstr. (1040)-n.m.p. cstr. (313) *the years of the life of*

לֵוִי pr.n. (II 532) *Levi*

שֶׁבַע num. (988) *seven*

וּשְׁלֹשִׁים conj.-num. p. (1025) *and thirty*

וּמְאַת conj.-num. cstr. (547) *and a hundred of*

שָׁנָה n.f.s. (1040) *years*

6:17

בְּנֵי גֵרְשׁוֹן n.m.p. cstr. (119)-pr.n. (177) *the sons of Gershon*

לִבְנִי pr.n. (I 526) *Libni*

וְשִׁמְעִי conj.-pr.n. (I 1035) *and Shimei*

לְמִשְׁפְּחֹתָם prep.-n.f.p.-3 m.p. sf. (1046) *by their families*

6:18

וּבְנֵי קְהָת conj.-n.m.p. cstr. (119)-pr.n. (875) *the sons of Kohath*

עַמְרָם pr.n. (771) *Amram*

וְיִצְהָר conj.-pr.n. (II 844) *Izhar*

וְחֶבְרוֹן conj.-pr.n. (II 289) *Hebron*

וְעֻזִּיאֵל conj.-pr.n. (739) *and Uzziel*

וּשְׁנֵי חַיֵּי conj.-n.f.p. cstr. (1040)-n.m.p. cstr. (313) *the years of the life of*

קְהָת pr.n. (875) *Kohath*

שָׁלֹשׁ num. s. (1025) *three*

וּשְׁלֹשִׁים num. p. (1025) *and thirty*

וּמְאַת conj.-n.f.s. cstr. (547) *and a hundred of*

שָׁנָה n.f.s. (1040) *years*

6:19

וּבְנֵי מְרָרִי conj.-n.m.p. cstr. (119)-pr.n. (I 601) *the sons of Merari*

מַחְלִי pr.n. (I 563) *Mahli*

וּמוּשִׁי conj.-pr.n. (I 559) *and Mushi*

אֵלֶּה demons. c.p. (41) *these are*

מִשְׁפְּחֹת n.f.p. cstr. (1046) *the families of*

הַלֵּוִי def. art.-pr.n. (II 532) *the Levites*

לְתֹלְדֹתָם prep.-n.f.p.-3 m.p. sf. (410) *according to their generations*

6:20

וַיִּקַּח consec.-Qal impf. 3 m.s. (לָקַח 542) *took*

עַמְרָם pr.n. (771) *Amram*

אֶת־יוֹכֶבֶד dir. obj.-pr.n. (222) *Jochebed*

דֹּדָתוֹ n.f.s.-3 m.s. sf. (187) *his father's sister*

לוֹ לְאִשָּׁה prep.-3 m.s. sf.-prep.-n.f.s. (61) *(to him) to wife*

וַתֵּלֶד לוֹ consec.-Qal impf. 3 f.s. (יָלַד 408)-prep.-3 m.s. sf. *and she bore him*

אֶת־אַהֲרֹן dir. obj.-pr.n. (14) *Aaron*

וְאֶת־מֹשֶׁה conj.-dir. obj.-pr.n. (602) *and Moses*

וּשְׁנֵי חַיֵּי conj.-n.f.p. cstr. (1040)-n.m.p. cstr. (313) *the years of the life of*

עַמְרָם pr.n. (771) *Amram*

שֶׁבַע num. (988) *seven*

וּשְׁלֹשִׁים conj.-num. p. (1025) *and thirty*

וּמְאַת conj.-n.f.s. cstr. (547) *and a hundred of*

שָׁנָה n.f.s. (1040) *years*

6:21

וּבְנֵי יִצְהָר conj.-n.m.p. cstr. (119)-pr.n. (II 844) *the sons of Izhar*

קֹרַח pr.n. (901) *Korah*

וָנֶפֶג conj.-pr.n. (655) *Nepheg*

וְזִכְרִי conj.-pr.n. (271) *and Zichri*

6:22

וּבְנֵי עֻזִּיאֵל conj.-n.m.p. cstr. (119)-pr.n. (739) *and the sons of Uzziel*

מִישָׁאֵל pr.n. (567) *Mishael*

וְאֶלְצָפָן conj.-pr.n. (45) *Elzaphan*

וְסִתְרִי conj.-pr.n. (712) *and Sithri*

6:23

וַיִּקַּח consec.-Qal impf. 3 m.s. (לָקַח 542) *took*

אַהֲרֹן pr.n. (14) *Aaron*

אֶת־אֱלִישֶׁבַע dir. obj.-pr.n. (45) *Elisheba*

בַּת־עַמִּינָדָב n.f.s. cstr. (I 123)-pr.n. (770) *the daughter of Amminadab*

אֲחוֹת נַחְשׁוֹן n.f.s. cstr. (27)-pr.n. (638) *the sister of Nahshon*

לוֹ לְאִשָּׁה prep.-3 m.s. sf.-prep.-n.f.s. (61) *(to him) to wife*

וַתֵּלֶד לוֹ consec.-Qal impf. 3 f.s. (יָלַד 408)-prep.-3 m.s. sf. *and she bore him*

אֶת־נָדָב dir. obj.-pr.n. (621) *Nadab*

וְאֶת־אֲבִיהוּא conj.-dir. obj.-pr.n. (4) *Abihu*

אֶת־אֶלְעָזָר dir. obj.-pr.n. (46) *Eleazar*

וְאֶת־אִיתָמָר conj.-dir. obj.-pr.n. (16) *and Ithamar*

6:24

וּבְנֵי קֹרַח conj.-n.m.p. cstr. (119)-pr.n. (901) *the sons of Korah*

אַסִּיר pr.n. (64) *Assir*

וְאֶלְקָנָה conj.-pr.n. (46) *Elkanah*

וַאֲבִיאָסָף conj.-pr.n. (4) *and Abiasaph*

אֵלֶּה demons. adj. c.p. (41) *these are*

מִשְׁפְּחֹת n.f.p. cstr. (1046) *the families of*

הַקָּרְחִי def. art.-pr.n. (901) *the Korahites*

6:25

וְאֶלְעָזָר conj.-pr.n. (46) *Eleazar*

בֶּן־אַהֲרֹן n.m.s. cstr. (119)-pr.n. (14) *Aaron's son*

לָקַח־לוֹ Qal pf. 3 m.s. (542)-prep.-3 m.s. sf. *took (to him)*

מִבְּנוֹת prep.-n.f.p. cstr. (I 123) *(from) the daughters of*

פּוּטִיאֵל pr.n. (806) *Putiel*

לוֹ לְאִשָּׁה prep.-3 m.s. sf.-prep.-n.f.s. (61) *(to him) to wife*

וַתֵּלֶד לוֹ consec.-Qal impf. 3 f.s. (יָלַד 408)-prep.-3 m.s. sf. *and she bore him*

אֶת־פִּינְחָס dir. obj.-pr.n. (810) *Phinehas*

אֵלֶּה demons. adj. c.p. (41) *these are*

רָאשֵׁי n.m.p. cstr. (910) *the heads of*

אֲבוֹת הַלְוִיִּם n.m.p. cstr. (3)-def.art.-pr.n. gent.p. (II 532) *the fathers' houses of the Levites*

לְמִשְׁפְּחֹתָם prep.-n.f.p.-3 m.p. sf. (1046) *by their families*

6:26

הוּא demons. adj. m.s. (214) *these are*

אַהֲרֹן pr.n. (14) *the Aaron*

וּמֹשֶׁה conj.-pr.n. (602) *and Moses*

אֲשֶׁר rel. *whom*

אָמַר יהוה Qal pf. 3 m.s. (55)-pr.n. (217) *Yahweh said*

לָהֶם prep.-3 m.p. sf. *to (them)*

הוֹצִיאוּ Hi. impv. 2 m.p. (יָצָא 422) *Bring out*

אֶת־בְּנֵי dir. obj.-n.m.p. cstr. (119) *the people of*

יִשְׂרָאֵל pr.n. (975) *Israel*

מֵאֶרֶץ prep.-n.f.s. cstr. (75) *from the land of*

מִצְרַיִם pr.n. (595) *Egypt*

עַל־צִבְאֹתָם prep.-n.m.p.-3 m.p. sf. (838) *by their hosts*

6:27

הֵם pers.pr. 3 m.p. (241) *it was they*

הַמְדַבְּרִים def.art.-Pi. ptc. m.p. (180) *who spoke*

אֶל־פַּרְעֹה prep.-pr.n. (829) *to Pharaoh*

מֶלֶךְ־מִצְרַיִם n.m.s. cstr. (I 572)-pr.n. (595) *king of Egypt*

לְהוֹצִיא prep.-Hi. inf. cstr. (יָצָא 422) *about bringing out*

אֶת־בְּנֵי־ dir.obj.-n.m.p. cstr. (119) *the people of*

יִשְׂרָאֵל pr.n. (975) *Israel*

מִמִּצְרָיִם prep.-pr.n. paus. (595) *from Egypt*

הוּא v. 6:26 *this*

מֹשֶׁה pr.n. (602) *Moses*

וְאַהֲרֹן conj.-pr.n. (14) *and Aaron*

6:28

וַיְהִי consec.-Qal impf. 3 m.s. (הָיָה 224) *(and it was)*

בְּיוֹם prep.-n.m.s. cstr. (398) *on the day when*

דִּבֶּר יהוה Pi. pf. 3 m.s. (180)-pr.n. (217) *Yahweh spoke*

אֶל־מֹשֶׁה prep.-pr.n. (602) *to Moses*

בְּאֶרֶץ prep.-n.f.s. cstr. (75) *in the land of*

מִצְרָיִם pr.n. paus. (595) *Egypt*

6:29

וַיְדַבֵּר consec.-Pi. impf. 3 m.s.(180) *said*

יהוה pr.n.(217) *Yahweh*

אֶל־מֹשֶׁה prep.-pr.n. (602) *to Moses*

לֵאמֹר prep.-Qal inf.cstr.(55) *(saying)*

אֲנִי יהוה pers.pr.1 c.s.(58)-pr.n.(217) *I am Yahweh*

דַּבֵּר Pi.impv.2 m.s.(180) *tell*

אֶל־פַּרְעֹה prep.-pr.n.(829) *Pharaoh*

מֶלֶךְ n.m.s. cstr. (I 572) *king of*

מִצְרַיִם pr.n.(595) *Egypt*

אֵת כָּל־אֲשֶׁר dir.obj.-n.m.s.(481)-rel. *all that*

אֲנִי דֹּבֵר pers.pr.1 c.s.(58)-Qal act.ptc.(180) *I say*

אֵלֶיךָ prep.-2 m.s. sf. *to you*

6:30

וַיֹּאמֶר consec.-Qal impf. 3 m.s. (55) *but ... said*

מֹשֶׁה pr.n.(602) *Moses*

לִפְנֵי prep.-n.m.p.cstr.(815) *to (the face of)*

יהוה pr.n.(217) *Yahweh*

הֵן demons.part.(243) *behold*

אֲנִי pers.pr.1 c.s.(58) *I am*

עֲרַל adj.s.cstr.(790) *uncircumcised of*

שְׂפָתַיִם n.f.du.(973) *lips*

וְאֵיךְ conj.-interr. (32) *how then*

יִשְׁמַע Qal impf.3 m.s.(1033) *shall ... listen*

אֵלַי prep.-1 c.s.sf. *to me*

פַּרְעֹה pr.n.(829) *Pharaoh*

7:1

וַיֹּאמֶר consec.-Qal impf.3 m.s.(55) *and ... said*

יהוה pr.n.(217) *Yahweh*

אֶל־מֹשֶׁה prep.-pr.n.(602) *to Moses*

רְאֵה Qal impv.2 m.s.(906) *see*

נְתַתִּיךָ Qal pf. 1 c.s.-2 m.s. sf. (נָתַן 678) *I make you*

אֱלֹהִים n.m.p.(43) *God*

לְפַרְעֹה prep.-pr.n.(829) *to Pharaoh*

וְאַהֲרֹן conj.-pr.n.(14) *and Aaron*

אָחִיךָ n.m.s.-2 m.s. sf. (26) *your brother*

יִהְיֶה Qal impf. 3 m.s. (224) *shall be*

נְבִיאֶךָ n.m.s.-2 m.s. sf. (611) *your prophet*

7:2

אַתָּה pers.pr.2 m.s.(61) *you*

תְדַבֵּר Pi.impf.2 m.s.(180) *shall speak*

אֵת כָּל־אֲשֶׁר dir.obj.-n.m.s.(481)-rel. *all that*

אֲצַוֶּךָּ Pi.impf.1 c.s.-2 m.s.sf.(צָוָה 845) *I command you*

וְאַהֲרֹן conj.-pr.n. (14) *and Aaron*

אָחִיךָ v.supra *your brother*

יְדַבֵּר Pi.impf.3 m.s.(180) *shall tell*

אֶל־פַּרְעֹה prep.-pr.n.(829) *Pharaoh*

וְשִׁלַּח conj.-Pi.pf.3 m.s.(1018) *to let go (send)*

אֶת־בְּנֵי־ dir.obj.-n.m.p.cstr.(119) *the people of*

יִשְׂרָאֵל pr.n.(975) *Israel*

מֵאַרְצוֹ prep.-n.f.s.-3 m.s.sf.(75) *out of his land*

7:3

וַאֲנִי conj.-pers.pr.1 c.s.(58) *but I*

אַקְשֶׁה Hi.impf.1 c.s.(קָשָׁה 904) *will harden*

אֶת־לֵב dir.obj.-n.m.s.cstr.(523) *the heart of*

פַּרְעֹה pr.n.(829) *Pharaoh*

וְהִרְבֵּיתִי conj.-Hi.pf.1 c.s.(רָבָה I 915) *and though I multiply*

אֶת־אֹתֹתַי dir.obj.-n.m.p.-1 c.s.sf.(16) *my signs*

וְאֶת־מוֹפְתַי conj.-dir.obj.-n.m.p.-1 c.s.sf.(68) *and (my) wonders*

בְּאֶרֶץ prep.-n.f.s.cstr.(75) *in the land of*

מִצְרָיִם pr.n.paus.(595) *Egypt*

7:4

וְלֹא־יִשְׁמַע conj.-neg.-Qal impf.3 m.s.(1033) *will not listen*

אֲלֵכֶם prep.-2 m.p.sf. *to you*

פַּרְעֹה pr.n.(829) *Pharaoh*

וְנָתַתִּי conj.-Qal pf.1 c.s.(נָתַן 678) *then I will lay*

אֶת־יָדִי dir.obj.-n.f.s.-1 c.s.sf.(388) *my hand*

בְּמִצְרָיִם prep.-pr.n.paus.(595) *upon Egypt*

וְהוֹצֵאתִי conj.-Hi.pf.1 c.s.(יָצָא 422) *and bring forth*

אֶת־צִבְאֹתַי dir.obj.-n.m.p.-1 c.s. sf. (838) *my hosts*

אֶת־עַמִּי dir.obj.-n.m.s.-1 c.s.sf.(I 766) *my people*

בְנֵי־יִשְׂרָאֵל n.m.p.cstr.(119)-pr.n.(975) *the sons of Israel*

מֵאֶרֶץ prep.-n.f.s. cstr. (75) *out of the land of*

מִצְרַיִם pr.n.(595) *Egypt*

בִּשְׁפָטִים prep.-n.m.p.(1048) *by ... acts of judgment*

גְּדֹלִים adj.m.p.(152) *great*

7:5

וְיָדְעוּ conj.-Qal pf.3 c.p.(393) *and ... shall know*

מִצְרַיִם pr.n. (595) *the Egyptians*

כִּי־אֲנִי conj.-pers.pr.1 c.s.(58) *that I am*

יהוה pr.n.(217) *Yahweh*

בִּנְטֹתִי prep.-Qal inf. cstr.-1 c.s. sf. (נָטָה 639) *when I stretch forth*

אֶת־יָדִי dir.obj.-n.f.s.-1 c.s.sf.(388) *my hand*

עַל־מִצְרָיִם prep.-pr.n.paus.(595) *upon Egypt*

וְהוֹצֵאתִי conj.-Hi.pf.1 c.s.(יָצָא 422) *and bring out*

אֶת־בְּנֵי־ dir.obj.-n.m.p.cstr.(119) *the people of*

יִשְׂרָאֵל pr.n.(975) *Israel*

מִתּוֹכָם prep.-n.m.s.-3 m.p.sf.(1063) *from among them*

7:6

וַיַּעַשׂ consec. - Qal impf. 3 m. s. (עָשָׂה I 793) *and ... did*

מֹשֶׁה pr.n.(602) *Moses*

וְאַהֲרֹן conj.-pr.n.(14) *and Aaron*

כַּאֲשֶׁר prep.-rel. *as*

צִוָּה Pi.pf.3 m.s.(צָוָה 845) *commanded*

יהוה pr.n.(217) *Yahweh*

אֹתָם dir.obj.-3 m.p.sf. *them*

כֵּן עָשׂוּ adv.(485)-Qal pf.3 c.p.(עָשָׂה I 793) *so they did*

7:7

וּמֹשֶׁה conj.-pr.n.(602) *Now Moses*

בֶּן־שְׁמֹנִים n.m.s.cstr.(119)-num.p.(1033) *was eighty*

שָׁנָה n.f.s.(1040) *years old*

וְאַהֲרֹן conj.-pr.n.(14) *and Aaron*

בֶּן־שָׁלשׁ n.m.s.cstr.(119)-num.(1025) *(son of) three*

וּשְׁמֹנִים num.p.(1033) *(and) eighty*

שָׁנָה v.supra *years old*

בְּדַבְּרָם prep.-Pi.inf.cstr.-3 m.p.sf.(דָּבַר 180) *when they spoke*

אֶל־פַּרְעֹה prep.-pr.n.(829) *to Pharaoh*

7:8

וַיֹּאמֶר consec.-Qal impf.3 m.s.(55) *and ... said*

יהוה pr.n.(217) *Yahweh*

אֶל־מֹשֶׁה prep.-pr.n.(602) *to Moses*

וְאֶל־אַהֲרֹן conj.-prep.-pr.n. (14) *and Aaron*

לֵאמֹר prep.-Qal inf.cstr.(55) *(saying)*

7:9

כִּי יְדַבֵּר conj.-Pi.impf.3 m.s.(180) *when ... says*

אֲלֵכֶם prep.-2 m.p.sf. *to you*

פַּרְעֹה pr.n.(829) *Pharaoh*

לֵאמֹר prep.-Qal inf.cstr.(55) *(saying)*

תְּנוּ Qal impv.2 m.p.(נָתַן 678) *Prove (give)*

לָכֶם prep.-2 m.p.sf. *(to) yourselves*

מוֹפֵת n.m.s.(68) *a miracle*

וְאָמַרְתָּ conj.-Qal pf.2 m.s.(55) *then you shall say*

אֶל־אַהֲרֹן prep.-pr.n.(14) *to Aaron*

קַח Qal impv.2 m.s.(לָקַח 542) *Take*

אֶת־מַטְּךָ dir.obj.-n.m.s.-2 m.s. sf. (641) *your rod*

וְהַשְׁלֵךְ conj.-Hi. impv. 2 m.s. (1020) *and cast it down*

לִפְנֵי־ prep.-n.m.p.cstr.(815) *before*

פַרְעֹה pr.n.(829) *Pharaoh*

יְהִי Qal impf.3 m.s.apoc.(הָיָה 224) *that it may become*

לְתַנִּין prep.-n.m.s.(1072) *a serpent*

7:10

וַיָּבֹא consec.-Qal impf.3 m.s.(בּוֹא 97) *so ... went*

מֹשֶׁה pr.n. (602) *Moses*

וְאַהֲרֹן conj.-pr.n.(14) *and Aaron*

אֶל־פַּרְעֹה prep.-pr.n.(829) *to Pharaoh*

וַיַּעֲשׂוּ consec.-Qal impf.3 m.p.(עָשָׂה I 793) *and did*

כֵּן כַּאֲשֶׁר adv.(485)-prep.-rel. *(thus) as*

צִוָּה Pi.pf. 3 m.s.(845) *commanded*

יהוה pr.n.(217) *Yahweh*

וַיַּשְׁלֵךְ consec.-Hi.impf. 3m.s.(שָׁלַךְ 1020) *(and) cast down*

אַהֲרֹן pr.n. (14) *Aaron*

אֶת־מַטֵּהוּ dir.obj.-n.m.s.-3 m.s. sf. (641) *his rod*

לִפְנֵי prep.-n.m.p.cstr.(815) *before*

פַרְעֹה pr.n.(829) *Pharaoh*

וְלִפְנֵי conj.-v.supra *and (before)*

עֲבָדָיו n.m.p.-3 m.s. sf. (712) *his servants*

וַיְהִי consec.-Qal impf.3 m.s.(הָיָה 224) *and it became*

לְתַנִּין prep.-n.m.s.(1072) *a serpent*

7:11

וַיִּקְרָא consec.-Qal impf.3 m.s.(894) *then ... summoned*

גַּם־פַּרְעֹה adv.(168)-pr.n.(829) *Pharaoh*

לַחֲכָמִים prep.-def.art.-n.m.p.(314) *the wise men*

וְלַמְכַשְּׁפִים conj.-prep.-def.art.-Pi.ptc.m.p.(כָּשַׁף 506) *and the sorcerers*

וַיַּעֲשׂוּ consec.-Qal impf.3 m.p.(עָשָׂה I 793) *and ... did*

גַם־הֵם adv.(168)-pers.pr.3 m.p.(241) *they also*

חַרְטֻמֵּי n.m.p.cstr.(355) *the magicians of*

מִצְרַיִם pr.n.(595) *Egypt*

בְּלַהֲטֵיהֶם prep.-n.m.p.-3 m.p.sf.(לָט 532) *by their secret arts*

כֵּן adv.(485) *the same (thus)*

7:12

וַיַּשְׁלִיכוּ consec.-Hi. impf. 3 m.p. (שָׁלַךְ 1020) *for ... cast down*

אִישׁ n.m.s.(35) *every man*

מַטֵּהוּ n.m.s.-3 m.s.sf.(641) *his rod*

וַיִּהְיוּ consec.-Qal impf.3 m.p.(הָיָה 224) *and they became*

לְתַנִּינִם prep.-n.m.p.(1072) *serpents*

וַיִּבְלַע consec.-Qal impf.3 m.s.(118) *but ... swallowed up*

מַטֵּה־ n.m.s.cstr.(641) *the rod of*

אַהֲרֹן pr.n.(14) *Aaron*

אֶת־מַטֹּתָם dir.obj.-n.m.p.-3 m.p.sf.(641) *their rods*

7:13

וַיֶּחֱזַק consec.-Qal impf.3 m.s.(חָזַק 304) *still ... was hardened*

לֵב פַּרְעֹה n.m.s.cstr.(523)-pr.n.(829) *Pharaoh's heart*

וְלֹא שָׁמַע conj.-neg.-Qal pf.3 m.s.(1033) *and he would not listen*

אֲלֵהֶם prep.-3 m.p.sf. *to them*

כַּאֲשֶׁר prep.-rel. *as*

דִּבֶּר Pi.pf.3 m.s.(1080) *had said*

יהוה pr.n.(217) *Yahweh*

7:14

וַיֹּאמֶר consec.-Qal impf.3 m.s.(55) *then ... said*

יהוה pr.n.(217) *Yahweh*

אֶל־מֹשֶׁה prep.-pr.n. (602) *to Moses*

כָּבֵד Qal pf.3 m.s.(457) *is hardened*

לֵב פַּרְעֹה n.m.s.cstr.(523)-pr.n.(829) *Pharaoh's heart*

מֵאֵן Pi.pf.3 m.s.(מָאֵן 549) *he refuses*

לְשַׁלַּח prep.-Pi.inf.cstr.(1018) *t*

go

הָעָם def.art.-n.m.s.(I 766) *the people*

7:15

לֵךְ Qal impv. 2 m.s. (הָלַךְ 229) *go*

אֶל־פַּרְעֹה prep.-pr.n.(829) *to Pharaoh*

בַּבֹּקֶר prep.-def.art.-n.m.s.(133) *in the morning*

הִנֵּה demons. part. (243) *(behold) as*

יֹצֵא Qal act.ptc.(יָצָא 422) *he is going out*

הַמַּיְמָה def.art.-n.m.p.-dir.he(565) *to (toward) the water*

וְנִצַּבְתָּ conj.-Ni.pf.2 m.s.(נָצַב 662) *wait for*

לִקְרָאתוֹ prep.-Qal inf.cstr.-3 m.s.sf.(894) *(to meet) him*

עַל־שְׂפַת prep.-n.f.s.cstr.(973) *by the brink of*

הַיְאֹר def.art.-n.m.s.(384) *the river*

וְהַמַּטֶּה conj.-def.art.-n.m.s.(641) *and the rod*

אֲשֶׁר־ rel. *which*

נֶהְפַּךְ Ni. pf. 3 m.s. (הָפַךְ 245) *was turned*

לְנָחָשׁ prep.-n.m.s.(638) *into a serpent*

תִּקַּח Qal impf.2 m.s.(לָקַח 542) *take*

בְּיָדֶךָ prep.-n.f.s.-2 m.s. sf. (388) *in your hand*

7:16

וְאָמַרְתָּ conj.-Qal pf. 2 m.s. (55) *and you shall say*

אֵלָיו prep.-3 m.s. sf. *to him*

יהוה pr.n. (217) *Yahweh*

אֱלֹהֵי n.m.p. cstr. (43) *the God of*

הָעִבְרִים def.art.-pr.n. gent. p. (720) *the Hebrews*

שְׁלָחַנִי Qal pf. 3 m.s.-1 c.s. sf. (1018) *sent me*

אֵלֶיךָ prep.-2 m.s. sf. *to you*

[illegible] ep.-Qal inf. cstr. (55) *saying*

[illegible] mpv. 2 m.s. (1018) *Let go*

[illegible] ir.obj.-n.m.s.-1 c.s. sf. (I [illegible] *people*

[illegible] -Qal impf. 3 m.p.-1 c.s. sf. (712) *that they may serve me*

בַּמִּדְבָּר prep.-def. art.-n.m.s. (184) *in the wilderness*

וְהִנֵּה conj.-demons. part. (243) *and behold*

לֹא־שָׁמַעְתָּ neg.-Qal pf. 2 m.s. (1033) *you have not obeyed*

עַד־כֹּה prep.-adv. (462) *yet*

7:17

כֹּה אָמַר adv. (462)-Qal pf. 3 m.s. (55) *thus says*

יהוה pr.n. (217) *Yahweh*

בְּזֹאת prep.-demons. adj. f.s. (260) *By this*

תֵּדַע Qal impf. 2 m.s. (יָדַע 393) *you shall know*

כִּי אֲנִי conj.-pers. pr. 1 c.s. (58) *that I am*

יהוה pr.n. (217) *Yahweh*

הִנֵּה demons. part. (243) *behold*

אָנֹכִי pers. pr. 1 c.s. (59) *I*

מַכֶּה Hi. ptc. (נָכָה 645) *will strike*

בַּמַּטֶּה prep.-def. art.-n.m.s. (641) *with the rod*

אֲשֶׁר־בְּיָדִי rel.-prep.-n.f.s.-1 c.s. sf. (388) *that is in my hand*

עַל־הַמַּיִם prep.-def. art.-n.m.p. (565) *the water*

אֲשֶׁר בַּיְאֹר rel.-prep.-def. art.-n.m.s. (384) *that is in the Nile*

וְנֶהֶפְכוּ conj.-Ni. pf. 3 c.p. (הָפַךְ 245) *and it shall be turned*

לְדָם prep.-n.m.s. (196) *to blood*

7:18

וְהַדָּגָה conj.-def. art.-n.f.s. (185) *and the fish*

אֲשֶׁר־בַּיְאֹר rel.-prep.-def. art.-n.m.s. (384) *in the Nile*

תָּמוּת Qal impf. 3 f.s. (מוּת 559) *shall die*

וּבָאַשׁ conj.-Qal pf. 3 m.s. (92) *and ... shall become foul*

הַיְאֹר def. art.-n.m.s. (384) *the Nile*

וְנִלְאוּ conj.-Ni. pf. 3 c.p. (לָאָה 521) *will loathe (be weary of)*

מִצְרַיִם pr.n. (595) *the Egyptians*

לִשְׁתּוֹת prep.-Qal inf. cstr. (שָׁתָה 1059) *to drink*

מַיִם n.m.p. (565) *water*

מִן־הַיְאֹר prep.-def. art.-n.m.s. (384) *from the Nile*

7:19

וַיֹּאמֶר יהוה consec.-Qal impf. 3 m.s. (55)-pr.n. (217) *and Yahweh said*

אֶל־מֹשֶׁה prep.-pr.n. (602) *to Moses*

אֱמֹר Qal impv. 2 m.s. (55) *Say*

אֶל־אַהֲרֹן prep.-pr.n. (14) *to Aaron*

קַח Qal impv. 2 m.s. (לָקַח 542) *Take*

מַטְּךָ n.m.s.-2 m.s. sf. (641) *your rod*

וּנְטֵה־יָדְךָ conj.-Qal impv. 2 m.s. (639)-n.f.s.-2 m.s. sf. (388) *and stretch out your hand*

עַל־מֵימֵי prep.-n.m.p. cstr. (565) *over the water of*

מִצְרַיִם pr.n. (595) *Egypt*

עַל־נַהֲרֹתָם prep.-n.f.p.-3 m.p. sf. (625) *over their rivers*

עַל־יְאֹרֵיהֶם prep.-n.m.p.-3 m.p. sf. (384) *their canals*

וְעַל־אַגְמֵיהֶם conj.-prep.-n.m.p.-3 m.p. sf. (8) *and their ponds*

וְעַל כָּל־ conj.-prep.-n.m.s. cstr. (481) *and all (of)*

מִקְוֵה n.m.s. cstr. (II 876) *pools (of) (collection of)*

מֵימֵיהֶם n.m.p.-3 m.p. sf. (565) *their water*

וְיִהְיוּ־דָם conj.-Qal impf. 3 m.p. (הָיָה 224)-n.m.s. (196) *that they may become blood*

וְהָיָה דָם conj.-Qal pf. 3 m.s. (224)-n.m.s. (196) *and there shall be blood*

בְּכָל־אֶרֶץ prep.-n.m.s. ctr. (481)-n.f.s. cstr. (75) *throughout all the land of*

מִצְרַיִם pr.n. (595) *Egypt*

וּבָעֵצִים conj.-prep.-def. art.-n.m.p. (781) *both in vessels of wood*

וּבָאֲבָנִים conj.-prep.-def. art.-n.f.p. (6) *and in vessels of stone*

7:20

וַיַּעֲשׂוּ־כֵן consec.-Qal impf. 3 m.p. (עָשָׂה I 793)-adv. (485) *did (so)*

מֹשֶׁה pr.n. (602) *Moses*

וְאַהֲרֹן conj.-pr.n. (14) *and Aaron*

כַּאֲשֶׁר prep.-rel. *as*

צִוָּה יהוה Pi. pf. 3 m.s. (845)-pr.n. (217) *Yahweh commanded*

וַיָּרֶם consec.-Hi. impf. 3 m.s. (רום 926) *he lifted up*

בַּמַּטֶּה prep.-def. art.-n.m.s. (641) *the rod*

וַיַּךְ consec.-Hi. impf. 3 m.s. (נָכָה 645) *and struck*

אֶת־הַמַּיִם dir. obj.-def. art.-n.m.p. (565) *the water*

אֲשֶׁר בַּיְאֹר rel.-prep.-def. art.-n.m.s. (384) *that was in the Nile*

לְעֵינֵי prep.-n.f.p. cstr. (744) *in the sight of*

פַרְעֹה pr.n. (829) *Pharaoh*

וּלְעֵינֵי conj.-prep.-n.f.p. cstr. (744) *and in the sight of*

עֲבָדָיו n.m.p.-3 m.s. sf. (712) *his servants*

וַיֵּהָפְכוּ consec.-Ni. impf. 3 m.p. (הָפַךְ 245) *and was turned*

כָּל־הַמַּיִם n.m.s. cstr. (481)-def. art.-n.m.p. (565) *all the water*

אֲשֶׁר־בַּיְאֹר v. supra *that was in the Nile*

לְדָם prep.-n.m.s. (196) *to blood*

7:21

וְהַדָּגָה conj.-def.art.-n.f.s. (185) *and the fish*

אֲשֶׁר־בַּיְאֹר rel.-prep.-def.art.-n.m.s.(384) *in the Nile*

מֵתָה Qal pf.3 f.s.(מוּת 559) *died*

וַיִּבְאַשׁ consec.-Qal impf. 3 m. s. (בָּאַשׁ 92) *and became foul*

הַיְאֹר def.art.-n.m.s. (384) *the Nile*

וְלֹא־יָכְלוּ conj.-neg.-Qal pf. 3 m.p.(יָכֹל 407) *so that could not*

מִצְרַיִם pr.n.(595) *the Egyptians*

לִשְׁתּוֹת prep.-Qal inf.cstr.(שָׁתָה 1059) *drink*

מַיִם n.m.p.(565) *water*

מִן־הַיְאֹר prep.-def.art.-n.m.s.(384)

from the Nile

וַיְהִי הַדָּם consec.-Qal impf.3 m.p. (הָיָה 224)-def.art.-n.m.s. (196) *and there was blood*

בְּכָל־אֶרֶץ prep.-n.m.s.cstr.(481)-n.f.s.cstr.(75) *throughout all the land of*

מִצְרָיִם pr.n.paus.(595) *Egypt*

7:22

וַיַּעֲשׂוּ־כֵן v.7:20 consec.-Qal impf. 3 m.p. (עָשָׂה I 793)-adv. (485) *but ... did the same*

חַרְטֻמֵּי n.m.p.cstr.(355) *the magicians of*

מִצְרַיִם pr.n.(595) *Egypt*

בְּלָטֵיהֶם prep.-n.m.p.-3 m.p.sf.(532) *by their secret arts*

וַיֶּחֱזַק consec.-Qal impf.3 m.s.(304) *so ... remained hardened*

לֵב־פַּרְעֹה n.m.s. cstr. (523) - pr.n. (829) *Pharaoh's heart*

וְלֹא־שָׁמַע conj.-neg.-Qal pf.3 m.s.(1033) *and he would not listen*

אֲלֵהֶם prep.-3 m.p.sf. *to them*

כַּאֲשֶׁר prep.-rel. *as*

דִּבֶּר Pi.pf.3 m.s.(180) *had said*

יהוה pr.n.(217) *Yahweh*

7:23

וַיִּפֶן consec.-Qal impf. 3 m.s. (פָּנָה 815) *turned*

פַּרְעֹה pr.n.(829) *Pharaoh*

וַיָּבֹא consec.-Qal impf.3 m.s.(בּוֹא 97) *and went*

אֶל־בֵּיתוֹ prep.-n.m.s.-3 m.s.sf.(108) *into his house*

וְלֹא־שָׁת conj. - neg.-Qal pf. 3 m.s. (שִׁית 1011) *and he did not lay*

לִבּוֹ n.m.s.-3 m.s.sf.(523) *to heart*

גַּם־לָזֹאת adv.(168)-prep.-demons.adj.f.s.(260) *even this*

7:24

וַיַּחְפְּרוּ consec.-Qal impf.3 m.p.(חָפַר I 343) *and ... dug*

כָל־מִצְרַיִם n.m.s.cstr.(481)-pr.n.(595) *all the Egyptians*

סְבִיבֹת subst.f.p.cstr. as prep.(686) *round about*

הַיְאֹר def.art.-n.m.s.(384) *the Nile*

מַיִם n.m.p.(565) *for water*

לִשְׁתּוֹת prep.-Qal inf.cstr.(שָׁתָה 1059) *to drink*

כִּי לֹא יָכְלוּ conj.-neg.-Qal pf.3 m.p.(יָכֹל 407) *for they could not*

לִשְׁתֹּת prep.-Qal inf.cstr.(שָׁתָה 1059) *drink*

מִמֵּימֵי prep.-n.m.p. cstr. (565) *the water of*

הַיְאֹר def.art.-n.m.s.(384) *the Nile*

7:25

וַיִּמָּלֵא consec.-Ni.impf.3 m.s.(מָלֵא 569) *passed*

שִׁבְעַת num.f.s.cstr.(988) *seven (of)*

יָמִים n.m.p.(398) *days*

אַחֲרֵי prep.(29) *after*

הַכּוֹת־ Hi.inf.cstr.(נָכָה 645) *had struck*

יהוה pr.n.(217) *Yahweh*

אֶת־הַיְאֹר dir.obj.-def.art.-n.m.s.(384) *the Nile*

7:26

וַיֹּאמֶר consec.-Qal impf.3 m.s.(55) *then ... said*

יהוה pr.n.(217) *Yahweh*

אֶל־מֹשֶׁה prep.-pr.n.(602) *to Moses*

בֹּא Qal impv.2 m.s.(בּוֹא 97) *Go in*

אֶל־פַּרְעֹה prep.-pr.n.(829) *to Pharaoh*

וְאָמַרְתָּ conj.-Qal pf.2 m.s.(55) *and say*

אֵלָיו prep.-3 m.s.sf. *to him*

כֹּה אָמַר adv.(462)-Qal pf.3 m.s.(55) *Thus says*

יהוה pr.n.(217) *Yahweh*

שַׁלַּח Pi.impv.2 m.s.(1018) *Let go*

אֶת־עַמִּי dir.obj.-n.m.s.-1 c.s.sf.(I 766) *my people*

וְיַעַבְדֻנִי conj.-Qal impf.3 m.p.-1 c.s.sf.(712) *that they may serve me*

7:27

וְאִם־מָאֵן conj.-hypoth.part.(49)-adj.verb.m.s.(549) *but if ... refuse*

אַתָּה pers.pr.2 m.s.(61) *you*

לְשַׁלֵּחַ prep.-Pi.inf.cstr.(1018) *to let go*

הִנֵּה demons.part.(243) *behold*

אָנֹכִי pers.pr.1 c.s.(59) *I*

נֹגֵף Qal act.ptc.(נָגַף 619) *will plague*

אֶת־כָּל־ dir.obj.-n.m.s.cstr.(481) *all (of)*

גְּבוּלְךָ n.m.s.-2 m.s. sf. (147) *your country*

בַּצְפַרְדְּעִים prep.-def.art.-n.f.p.(862) *with frogs*

7:28

וְשָׁרַץ conj.-Qal pf. 3 m.s.(1056) *shall swarm with*

הַיְאֹר def.art.-n.m.s.(384) *the Nile*

צְפַרְדְּעִים n.f.p.(862) *frogs*

וְעָלוּ conj.-Qal pf.3 c.p.(עָלָה 748) *which shall come up*

וּבָאוּ conj.-Qal pf.3 c.p.(בּוֹא 97) *(and come)*

בְּבֵיתֶךָ prep.-n.m.s.-2 m.s. sf. (108) *into your house*

וּבַחֲדַר conj.-prep.-n.m.s. cstr. (293) *and into the room of*

מִשְׁכָּבְךָ n.m.s.-2 m.s. sf. (1012) *your lying down*

וְעַל־מִטָּתֶךָ conj.-prep.-n.f.s.-2 m.s. sf. (641) *and on your bed*

וּבְבֵית conj.-prep.-n.m.s. cstr. (108) *and into the house of*

עֲבָדֶיךָ n.m.p.-2 m.s. sf. (712) *your servants*

וּבְעַמֶּךָ conj.-prep.-n.m.s.-2 m.s. sf. (I 766) *and upon your people*

וּבְתַנּוּרֶיךָ conj.-prep.-n.m.p.-2 m.s. sf. (1072) *and into your ovens*

וּמִשְׁאֲרוֹתֶיךָ conj.-prep.-n.f.p.-2 m.s. sf. (602) *and your kneading bowls*

7:29

וּבְכָה conj.-prep.-2 m.s.sf. *and ... on you*

וּבְעַמְּךָ conj.-prep.-n.m.s.-2 m.s. sf. (I 766) *and on your people*

וּבְכָל־עֲבָדֶיךָ conj.-prep.-n.m.s. cstr. (481) - n.m.p.-2 m.s. sf. (712) *and on all your servants*

יַעֲלוּ Qal impf.3 m.p.(עָלָה 748) *shall come up*

הַצְפַרְדְּעִים def.art.-n.f.p.(862) *the frogs*

8:1

וַיֹּאמֶר consec.-Qal impf. 3 m.s. (55) *and ... said*

יהוה pr.n.(217) *Yahweh*

אֶל־מֹשֶׁה prep.-pr.n.(602) *to Moses*

אֱמֹר Qal impv.2 m.s.(55) *Say*

אֶל־אַהֲרֹן prep.-pr.n.(14) *to Aaron*

נְטֵה Qal impv.2 m.s.(נָטָה 639) *Stretch out*

אֶת־יָדְךָ dir.obj.-n.f.s.-2 m.s. sf. (388) *your hand*

בְּמַטֶּךָ prep.-n.m.s.-2 m.s. sf. (641) *with your rod*

עַל־הַנְּהָרֹת prep.-def.art.-n.m.p.(625) *over the rivers*

עַל־הַיְאֹרִים prep.-def.art.-n.m.p.(384) *over the canals*

וְעַל־הָאֲגַמִּים conj.-prep.-def.art.-n.m.p.(8) *and over the pools*

וְהַעַל conj.-Hi. impv. 2 m.s. apoc. (עָלָה 748) *and cause to come*

אֶת־הַצְפַרְדְּעִים def.art.-n.f.p. (862) *frogs*

עַל אֶרֶץ prep.-n.f.s. cstr. (75) *upon the land of*

מִצְרָיִם pr.n.paus.(595) *Egypt*

8:2

וַיֵּט consec.-Qal impf. 3 m.s. (נָטָה 639) *so ... stretched out*

אַהֲרֹן pr.n. (14) *Aaron*

אֶת־יָדוֹ dir.obj.-n.f.s.-3 m.s. sf. (388) *his hand*

עַל מֵימֵי prep.-n.m.p. cstr. (565) *over the waters of*

מִצְרָיִם pr.n. paus. (595) *Egypt*

וַתַּעַל consec.-Qal impf. 3 f.s. (עָלָה 748) *and ... came up*

הַצְפַרְדֵּעַ def.art.-n.f.s. (862) *the frogs*

וַתְּכַס consec.-Pi. impf. 3 f.s. (כָּסָה 491) *and covered*

אֶת־אֶרֶץ dir.obj.-n.f.s. cstr. (75) *the land of*

מִצְרָיִם pr.n. paus. (595) *Egypt*

8:3

וַיַּעֲשׂוּ־כֵן consec.-Qal impf. 3 m.p. (עָשָׂה I 793)-adv. (485) *but ... did the same*

הַחַרְטֻמִּים def.art.-n.m.p. (355) *the magicians*

בְּלָטֵיהֶם prep.-n.m.p.-3 m.p. sf. (532) *by their secret arts*

וַיַּעֲלוּ consec.-Hi. impf. 3 m.p. (עָלָה 748) *and brought*

אֶת־הַצְפַרְדְּעִים dir.obj.-def.art.-n.f.p. (862) *frogs*

עַל־אֶרֶץ prep.-n.f.s. cstr. (75) *upon the land of*

מִצְרָיִם pr.n. paus. (595) *Egypt*

8:4

וַיִּקְרָא consec.-Qal impf. 3 m.s. (894) *then ... called*

פַּרְעֹה pr.n. (829) *Pharaoh*

לְמֹשֶׁה prep.-pr.n. (602) *Moses*

וּלְאַהֲרֹן conj.-prep.-pr.n. (14) *and Aaron*

וַיֹּאמֶר consec.-Qal impf. 3 m.s. (55) *and said*

הַעְתִּירוּ Hi. impv. 2 m.p. (עָתַר I 801) *entreat*

אֶל־יהוה prep.-pr.n. (217) *Yahweh*

וְיָסֵר conj.-Hi. impf. 3 m.s. apoc. (סוּר 693) *to take away*

הַצְפַרְדְּעִים def.art.-n.f.p. (862) *the frogs*

מִמֶּנִּי prep.-1 c.s. sf. *from me*

וּמֵעַמִּי conj.-prep.-n.m.s.-1 c.s. sf. (I 766) *and from my people*

וַאֲשַׁלְּחָה conj.-Pi. impf. 1 c.s. -coh.he (שָׁלַח 1018) *and I will let go*

אֶת־הָעָם dir.obj.-def.art.-n.m.s. (I 766) *the people*

וְיִזְבְּחוּ conj.-Qal impf. 3 m.p. (זָבַח 256) *to sacrifice*

ליהוה prep.-pr.n. (217) *to Yahweh*

8:5

וַיֹּאמֶר consec.-Qal impf. 3 m.s. (55) *said*

מֹשֶׁה pr.n. (602) *Moses*

לְפַרְעֹה prep.-pr.n. (829) *to Pharaoh*

הִתְפָּאֵר Hith. impv. 2 m.s. (פָּאַר I 802) *Be pleased to command*

עָלַי prep.-1 c.s. sf. (*over*) *me*

לְמָתַי prep.-interr.adv. (607) *when*

אַעְתִּיר Hi. impf. 1 c.s. (עָתַר I 801) *I am to entreat*

לְךָ prep.-2 m.s. sf. *for you*

וְלַעֲבָדֶיךָ conj.-prep.-n.m.p.-2 m.s. sf. (712) *and for your servants*

וּלְעַמְּךָ conj.-prep.-n.m.s.-2 m.s. sf. (I 766) *and for your people*

לְהַכְרִית prep.-Hi. inf. cstr. (כָּרַת 503) *that ... be destroyed*

הַצְפַרְדְּעִים def.art.-n.f.p. (862) *the frogs*

מִמְּךָ prep.-2 m.s. sf. *from you*

וּמִבָּתֶּיךָ conj.-prep.-n.m.p.-2 m.s. sf. (108) *and (from) your houses*

רַק בַּיְאֹר adv. (956)-prep.-def.art.-n.m.s. (384) *only in the Nile*

תִּשָּׁאַרְנָה Ni. impf. 3 f.p. (שָׁאַר 983) *be left*

8:6

וַיֹּאמֶר consec.-Qal impf. 3 m.s. (55) *and he said*

לְמָחָר prep.-adv. (563) *Tomorrow*

וַיֹּאמֶר v.supra *said*

כִּדְבָרְךָ prep.-n.m.s.-2 m.s. sf. (182) *Be it as you say*

לְמַעַן prep.-prep. (775) *that*

תֵּדַע Qal impf. 2 m.s. (יָדַע 393) *you may know*

כִּי־אֵין conj.-subst. (II 34) *that there is no one*

כיהוה prep.-pr.n. (217) *like Yahweh*

אֱלֹהֵינוּ n.m.p.-1 c.p. sf. (43) *our God*

8:7

וְסָרוּ conj.-Qal pf. 3 c.p. (סוּר 693) *shall depart*

הַצְפַרְדְּעִים def.art.-n.f.p. (862) *the frogs*

מִמְּךָ prep.-2 m.s. sf. *from you*

וּמִבָּתֶּיךָ conj.-prep.-n.m.p.-2 m.s. sf. (108) *and your houses*

וּמֵעֲבָדֶיךָ conj.-prep.-n.m.p.-2 m.s.

sf. (712) *and your servants*

וּמֵעַמֶּךָ conj.-prep.-n.m.s.-2 m.s. sf. (I 766) *and your people*

רַק בַּיְאֹר adv. (956)-prep.-def.art.-n.m.s. (384) *only in the Nile*

תִּשָּׁאַרְנָה Ni. impf. 3 f.p. (שָׁאַר 983) *they shall be left*

8:8

וַיֵּצֵא consec.-Qal impf. 3 m.s. (יָצָא 422) *so ... went out*

מֹשֶׁה pr.n. (602) *Moses*

וְאַהֲרֹן conj.-pr.n. (14) *and Aaron*

מֵעִם פַּרְעֹה prep.-prep.-pr.n. (829) *from Pharaoh*

וַיִּצְעַק consec.-Qal impf. 3 m.s. (858) *and ... cried*

מֹשֶׁה pr.n. (602) *Moses*

אֶל־יהוה prep.-pr.n. (217) *to Yahweh*

עַל־דְּבַר prep.-n.m.s. cstr. (182) *concerning*

הַצְפַרְדְּעִים def.art.-n.f.p. (862) *the frogs*

אֲשֶׁר־שָׂם rel.-Qal pf. 3 m.s. (שׂוּם 962) *which he had put*

לְפַרְעֹה prep.-pr.n. (829) *on Pharaoh*

8:9

וַיַּעַשׂ consec.-Qal impf. 3 m.s. (עָשָׂה I 793) *and ... did*

יהוה pr.n. (217) *Yahweh*

כִּדְבַר prep.-n.m.s. cstr. (182) *according to the word of*

מֹשֶׁה pr.n. (602) *Moses*

וַיָּמֻתוּ consec.-Qal impf. 3 m.p. (מוּת 559) *died*

הַצְפַרְדְּעִים def.art.-n.f.p. (862) *the frogs*

מִן־הַבָּתִּים prep.-def.art.-n.m.p. (108) *out of the houses*

מִן־הַחֲצֵרֹת prep.-def.art.-n.f.p. (I 346) *and courtyards*

וּמִן־הַשָּׂדֹת conj.-prep.-def.art.-n.f.p. (961) *and out of the fields*

8:10

וַיִּצְבְּרוּ consec.-Qal impf. 3 m.p. (840) *and they gathered*

אֹתָם dir.obj.-3 m.p. sf. *them*

חֳמָרִם חֳמָרִם n.m.p. (II 330)-n.m.p. (II 330) *in heaps*

וַתִּבְאַשׁ consec.-Qal impf. 3 f.s. (בָּאַשׁ 92) *and ... stank*

הָאָרֶץ def.art.-n.f.s. (75) *the land*

8:11

וַיַּרְא consec.-Qal impf. 3 m.s. (רָאָה 906) *but when ... saw*

פַּרְעֹה pr.n. (829) *Pharaoh*

כִּי הָיְתָה conj.-Qal pf. 3 f.s. (הָיָה 224) *that there was*

הָרְוָחָה def.art.-n.f.s. (926) *a respite*

וְהַכְבֵּד conj.-Hi. inf. abs. (457) *he hardened*

אֶת־לִבּוֹ dir.obj.-n.m.s.-3 m.s. sf. (523) *his heart*

וְלֹא שָׁמַע conj.-neg.-Qal pf. 3 m.s. (1033) *and would not listen*

אֲלֵהֶם prep.-3 m.p. sf. *to them*

כַּאֲשֶׁר prep.-rel. *as*

דִּבֶּר Pi. pf. 3 m.s. (180) *had said*

יהוה pr.n. (217) *Yahweh*

8:12

וַיֹּאמֶר consec.-Qal impf. 3 m.s. (55) *then ... said*

יהוה pr.n. (217) *Yahweh*

אֶל־מֹשֶׁה prep.-pr.n. (602) *to Moses*

אֱמֹר Qal impv. 2 m.s. (55) *Say*

אֶל־אַהֲרֹן prep.-pr.n. (14) *to Aaron*

נְטֵה Qal impv. 2 m.s. (639) *Stretch out*

אֶת־מַטְּךָ dir.obj.-n.m.s.-2 m.s. sf. (641) *your rod*

וְהַךְ conj.-Hi. impv. 2 m.s. (נָכָה 645) *and strike*

אֶת־עֲפַר dir.obj.-n.m.s. cstr. (779) *the dust of*

הָאָרֶץ def.art.-n.f.s. (75) *the earth*

וְהָיָה conj.-Qal pf. 3 m.s. (224) *that it may become*

לְכִנִּם prep.-n.m.p. (IV 487) *gnats*

בְּכָל־אֶרֶץ prep.-n.m.s. cstr. (481)-n.f.s. cstr. (75) *throughout all the land of*

מִצְרָיִם pr.n. paus. (595) *Egypt*

8:13

וַיַּעֲשׂוּ־כֵן consec.-Qal impf. 3 m.p. (עָשָׂה I 793)-adv. (485) *and they did so*

וַיֵּט consec.-Qal impf.3 m.s. (נָטָה 639) *stretched out*

אַהֲרֹן pr.n. (14) *Aaron*

אֶת־יָדוֹ dir.obj.-n.f.s.-3 m.s. sf. (388) *his hand*

בְמַטֵּהוּ prep.-n.m.s.-3 m.s. sf. (641) *with his rod*

וַיַּךְ consec.-Hi. impf. 3 m.s. (נָכָה 645) *and struck*

אֶת־עֲפַר dir.obj.-n.m.s. cstr. (779) *the dust of*

הָאָרֶץ def.art.-n.f.s. (75) *the earth*

וַתְּהִי consec.-Qal impf. 3 f.s. (הָיָה 224) *and there came*

הַכִּנָּם def.art.-n.m.s. (IV 487) *gnats*

בָּאָדָם prep.-def.art.-n.m.s. (9) *on man*

וּבַבְּהֵמָה conj.-prep.-def.art.-n.f.s. (96) *and beast*

כָּל־עֲפַר n.m.s. cstr. (481)-n.m.s. cstr. (779) *all the dust of*

הָאָרֶץ def.art.-n.f.s. (75) *the earth*

הָיָה Qal pf. 3 m.s. (224) *became*

כִנִּים n.m.p. (IV 487) *gnats*

בְּכָל־אֶרֶץ prep.-n.m.s. cstr. (481)-n.f.s. cstr. (75) *throughout all the land of*

מִצְרָיִם pr.n. paus. (595) *Egypt*

8:14

וַיַּעֲשׂוּ־כֵן consec.-Qal impf. 3 m.p. (עָשָׂה I 793)-adv. (485) *tried (did so)*

הַחַרְטֻמִּים def.art.-n.m.p. (355) *the magicians*

בְּלָטֵיהֶם prep.-n.m.p.-3 m.p. sf. (532) *by their secret arts*

לְהוֹצִיא prep.-Hi. inf. cstr. (יָצָא 422) *to bring forth*

אֶת־הַכִּנִּים dir.obj.-def.art.-n.m.p. (IV 487) *gnats*

וְלֹא יָכֹלוּ conj.-neg.-Qal pf. 3 c.p. (יָכֹל 407) *but they could not*

וַתְּהִי consec.-Qal impf. 3 f.s. (הָיָה 224) *so there were*

הַכִּנָּם def.art.-n.m.s. (IV 487) *gnats*

בָּאָדָם prep.-def.art.-n.m.s. (9) *on man*

וּבַבְּהֵמָה conj.-prep.-def.art.-n.f.s. (96) *and beast*

8:15

וַיֹּאמְרוּ consec.-Qal impf. 3 m.p. (55) *and ... said*

הַחַרְטֻמִּים def.art.-n.m.p. (355) *the magicians*

אֶל־פַּרְעֹה prep.-pr.n. (829) *to Pharaoh*

אֶצְבַּע n.f.s. cstr. (840) *the finger of*

אֱלֹהִים n.m.p. (43) *God*

הִוא demons. adj. f.s. (214) *this is*

וַיֶּחֱזַק consec.-Qal impf. 3 m.s. (304) *but ... was hardened*

לֵב־פַּרְעֹה n.m.s. cstr. (523)-pr.n. (829) *the heart of Pharaoh*

לֹא־שָׁמַע conj.-neg.-Qal pf. 3 m.s. (1033) *and he would not listen*

אֲלֵהֶם prep.-3 m.p. sf. *to them*

כַּאֲשֶׁר prep.-rel. *as*

דִּבֶּר Pi. pf. 3 m.s. (180) *had said*

יהוה pr.n. (217) *Yahweh*

8:16

וַיֹּאמֶר consec.-Qal impf. 3 m.s. (55) *then ... said*

יהוה pr.n. (217) *Yahweh*

אֶל־מֹשֶׁה prep.-pr.n. (602) *to Moses*

הַשְׁכֵּם Hi. impv. 2 m.s. (שָׁכַם 1014) *Rise up early*

בַּבֹּקֶר prep.-def.art.-n.m.s. (133) *in the morning*

וְהִתְיַצֵּב conj. - Hith. impv. 2 m. s. (יָצַב 426) *and wait for (take your stand)*

לִפְנֵי prep.-n.m.p. cstr. (815) *(before)*

פַרְעֹה pr.n. (829) *Pharaoh*

הִנֵּה demons.part. (243) *as (behold)*

יוֹצֵא Qal act. ptc. (422) *he goes out*

הַמָּיְמָה def.art.-n.m.p.-dir.he (565) *to (toward) the water*

וְאָמַרְתָּ conj.-Qal pf. 2 m.s. (55) *and*

say

אֵלָיו prep.-3 m.s. sf. *to him*

כֹּה אָמַר adv. (462)-Qal pf. 3 m.s. (55) *thus says*

יהוה pr.n. (217) *Yahweh*

שַׁלַּח Pi. impv. 2 m.s. (1018) *Let go*

עַמִּי n.m.s. - 1 c.s. sf. (I 766) *my people*

וְיַעַבְדֻנִי conj.-Qal impf. 3 m.p.-1 c.s. sf. (712) *that they may serve me*

8:17

כִּי אִם־אֵינְךָ conj.-hypoth.part. (49)-subst.-2 m.s. sf. (II 34) *else if you will not*

מְשַׁלֵּחַ Pi. ptc. (1018) *let go*

אֶת־עַמִּי dir.obj.-n.m.s.-1 c.s. sf. (I 766) *my people*

הִנְנִי demons. part.-1 c.s. sf. (243) *behold I*

מַשְׁלִיחַ Hi. ptc. (1018) *will send*

בְּךָ prep.-2 m.s. sf. *on you*

וּבַעֲבָדֶיךָ conj.-prep.-n.m.p.-2 m.s. sf. (712) *and your servants*

וּבְעַמְּךָ conj.-prep.-n.m.s.-2 m.s. sf. (I 766) *and your people*

וּבְבָתֶּיךָ conj.-prep.-n.m.p.-2 m.s. sf. (108) *and into your houses*

אֶת־הֶעָרֹב dir. obj.-def. art.-n.m.s. (786) *swarms of flies*

וּמָלְאוּ conj.-Qal pf. 3 c.p. (מָלֵא 569) *and ... shall be filled*

בָּתֵּי n.m.p. cstr. (108) *the houses of*

מִצְרַיִם pr.n. (595) *Egypt*

אֶת־הֶעָרֹב dir. obj.-def. art.-n.m.s. (786) *with swarms of flies*

וְגַם conj.-adv. (168) *and also*

הָאֲדָמָה def. art.-n.f.s. (9) *the ground*

אֲשֶׁר־הֵם rel.-pers. pr. 3 m.p. (241) *which they*

עָלֶיהָ prep.-3 f.s. sf. *on it*

8:18

וְהִפְלֵיתִי conj.-Hi. pf. 1 c.s. (פָּלָה 811) *but ... I will set apart*

בַיּוֹם הַהוּא prep.-def. art.-n.m.s. (398)-def. art.-demons. adj. m.s. (214) *on that day*

אֶת־אֶרֶץ dir. obj.-n.f.s. cstr. (75) *the land of*

גֹּשֶׁן pr.n. (177) *Goshen*

אֲשֶׁר עַמִּי rel.-n.m.s.-1 c.s. sf. (I 766) *where my people*

עֹמֵד Qal act. ptc. (763) *dwell (stand)*

עָלֶיהָ prep.-3 f.s. sf. *(on it)*

לְבִלְתִּי prep.-neg. (116) *so that no ...*

הֱיוֹת־שָׁם Qal inf. cstr. (הָיָה 224)-adv. (1027) *shall be there*

עָרֹב n.m.s. (786) *swarms of flies*

לְמַעַן תֵּדַע prep.-prep. (775)-Qal impf. 2 m.s. (יָדַע 393) *that you may know*

כִּי אֲנִי conj.-pers. pr. 1 c.s. (58) *that I am*

יהוה pr.n. (217) *Yahweh*

בְּקֶרֶב prep.-n.m.s. cstr. (899) *in the midst of*

הָאָרֶץ def. art.-n.f.s. (75) *the earth*

8:19

וְשַׂמְתִּי conj.-Qal pf. 1 c.s. (שׂוּם 962) *thus I will put*

פְדֻת n.f.s. (804) *division (redemption)*

בֵּין עַמִּי prep. (107)-n.m.s.-1 c.s. sf. (I 766) *between my people*

וּבֵין עַמֶּךָ conj.-prep.-n.m.s.-2 m.s. sf. (I 766) *and (between) your people*

לְמָחָר prep.-n.m.s. (563) *by tomorrow*

יִהְיֶה Qal impf. 3 m.s. (224) *shall be*

הָאֹת הַזֶּה def. art.-n.m.s. (16)-def. art.-demons. adj. m.s. (260) *this sign*

8:20

וַיַּעַשׂ consec.-Qal impf. 3 m.s. (עָשָׂה I 793) *and ... did*

יהוה pr.n. (217) *Yahweh*

כֵּן adv. (485) *so*

וַיָּבֹא consec.-Qal impf. 3 m.s. (בּוֹא 97) *there came*

עָרֹב n.m.s. (786) *swarms of flies*

כָּבֵד adj. m.s. (458) *great*

בֵּיתָה n.m.s. cstr.-dir. he (108) *into*

the house of
פַּרְעֹה pr.n. (829) *Pharaoh*
וּבֵית conj.-n.m.s. cstr. (108) *and the house of*
עֲבָדָיו n.m.p.-3 m.s. sf. (712) *his servants*
וּבְכָל־ conj.-prep.-n.m.s. cstr. (481) *and in all*
אֶרֶץ n.f.s. cstr. (75) *the land of*
מִצְרַיִם pr.n. (595) *Egypt*
תִּשָּׁחֵת Ni. impf. 3 f.s. (שָׁחַת 1007) *was ruined*
הָאָרֶץ def. art.-n.f.s. (75) *the land*
מִפְּנֵי prep.-n.m.p. cstr. (815) *by reason of (before)*
הֶעָרֹב def. art.-n.m.s. (786) *the flies*

8:21

וַיִּקְרָא consec.-Qal impf. 3 m.s. (894) *then called*
פַּרְעֹה pr.n. (829) *Pharaoh*
אֶל־מֹשֶׁה prep.-pr.n. (602) *Moses*
וּלְאַהֲרֹן conj.-prep.-pr.n. (14) *and Aaron*
וַיֹּאמֶר consec.-Qal impf. 3 m.s. (55) *and said*
לְכוּ Qal impv. 2 m.p. (הָלַךְ 229) *Go*
זִבְחוּ Qal impv. 2 m.p. (256) *sacrifice*
לֵאלֹהֵיכֶם prep.-n.m.p.-2 m.p. sf. (43) *to your God*
בָּאָרֶץ prep.-def. art.-n.f.s. (75) *within the land*

8:22

וַיֹּאמֶר consec.-Qal impf. 3 m.s. (55) *but ... said*
מֹשֶׁה pr.n. (602) *Moses*
לֹא נָכוֹן neg.-Ni. pf. 3 m.s. (כּוּן 465) *It would not be right*
לַעֲשׂוֹת prep.-Qal inf. cstr. (עָשָׂה I 793) *to do*
כֵּן adv. (485) *so*
כִּי תּוֹעֲבַת conj.-n.f.s. cstr. (1072) *for ... offerings abominable to*
מִצְרַיִם pr.n. (595) *the Egyptians*
נִזְבַּח Qal impf. 1 c.p. (256) *we shall sacrifice*
ליהוה prep.-pr.n. (217) *to Yahweh*
אֱלֹהֵינוּ n.m.p.-1 c.p. sf. (43) *our God*
הֵן hypoth. part. (II 243) *If*
נִזְבַּח v. supra *we sacrifice*
אֶת־תּוֹעֲבַת v. supra *offerings abominable to*
מִצְרַיִם v. supra *the Egyptians*
לְעֵינֵיהֶם prep.-n.f. du.-3 m.p. sf. (744) *before their eyes*
וְלֹא conj.-neg. *will ... not*
יִסְקְלֻנוּ Qal impf. 3 m.p.-1 c.p. sf. (סָקַל 709) *they stone us*

8:23

דֶּרֶךְ n.m.s. cstr. (202) *journey (of)*
שְׁלֹשֶׁת num. f.s. cstr. (1025) *three (of)*
יָמִים n.m.p. (398) *days*
נֵלֵךְ Qal impf. 1 c.p. (הָלַךְ 229) *we must go*
בַּמִּדְבָּר prep.-def. art.-n.m.s. (184) *into the wilderness*
וְזָבַחְנוּ conj.-Qal pf. 1 c.p. (256) *and sacrifice*
ליהוה prep.-pr.n. (217) *to Yahweh*
אֱלֹהֵינוּ n.m.p.-1 c.p. sf. (43) *our God*
כַּאֲשֶׁר prep.-rel. *as*
יֹאמַר Qal impf. 3 m.s. (55) *he will command*
אֵלֵינוּ prep.-1 c.p. sf. *us*

8:24

וַיֹּאמֶר consec.-Qal impf. 3 m.s. (55) *so ... said*
פַּרְעֹה pr.n. (829) *Pharaoh*
אָנֹכִי pers. pr. 1 c.s. (59) *I*
אֲשַׁלַּח Pi. impf. 1 c.s. (1018) *will let go*
אֶתְכֶם dir. obj.-2 m.p. sf. *you*
וּזְבַחְתֶּם conj.-Qal pf. 2 m.p. (זָבַח 256) *to sacrifice*
ליהוה prep.-pr.n. (217) *to Yahweh*
אֱלֹהֵיכֶם n.m.p.-2 m.p. sf. (43) *your God*
בַּמִּדְבָּר prep.-def. art.-n.m.s. (184) *in the wilderness*
רַק adv. (956) *only*
הַרְחֵק Hi. inf. abs. (934) *very*
לֹא־תַרְחִיקוּ neg.-Hi. impf. 2 m.p.

(רָחַק 934) *you shall not ... far*
לָלֶכֶת prep.-Qal inf. cstr. (הָלַךְ 229) *go*
הַעְתִּירוּ Hi. impv. 2 m.p. (עָתַר I 801) *make entreaty*
בַּעֲדִי prep.-1 c.s. sf. (126) *for me*

8:25

וַיֹּאמֶר consec.-Qal impf. 3 m.s. (55) *then ... said*
מֹשֶׁה pr.n. (602) *Moses*
הִנֵּה demons. part. (243) *Behold*
אָנֹכִי pers. pr. 1 c.s. (59) *I*
יוֹצֵא Qal act. ptc. (יָצָא 422) *am going out*
מֵעִמָּךְ prep.-prep.-2 m.s. sf. paus. *from you*
וְהַעְתַּרְתִּי conj.-Hi. pf. 1 c.s. (עָתַר I 801) *and I will pray*
אֶל־יהוה prep.-pr.n. (217) *to Yahweh*
וְסָר conj.-Qal pf. 3 m.s. (סוּר 693) *that ... may depart*
הֶעָרֹב def. art.-n.m.s. (786) *the swarms of flies*
מִפַּרְעֹה prep.-pr.n. (829) *from Pharaoh*
מֵעֲבָדָיו prep.-n.m.p.-3 m.s. sf. (712) *from his servants*
וּמֵעַמּוֹ conj.-prep.-n.m.s.-3 m.s. sf. (I 766) *and from his people*
מָחָר adv. (563) *tomorrow*
רַק adv. (956) *only*
אַל־יֹסֵף neg.-Hi. impf. 3 m.s. apoc. (יָסַף 414) *let not ... again*
פַּרְעֹה pr.n. (829) *Pharaoh*
הָתֵל Hi. inf. cstr. (תָּלַל II 1068) *deal falsely*
לְבִלְתִּי prep.-neg. (116) *by not*
שַׁלַּח Pi. inf. cstr. (1018) *letting go*
אֶת־הָעָם dir. obj.-def. art.-n.m.s. (I 766) *the people*
לִזְבֹּחַ prep.-Qal inf. cstr. (256) *to sacrifice*
ליהוה prep.-pr.n. (217) *to Yahweh*

8:26

וַיֵּצֵא consec.-Qal impf. 3 m.s. (יָצָא 422) *so ... went out*
מֹשֶׁה pr.n. (602) *Moses*
מֵעִם prep.-prep. (767) *from*
פַּרְעֹה pr.n. (829) *Pharaoh*
וַיֶּעְתַּר consec.-Qal impf. 3 m.s. (עָתַר I 801) *and prayed*
אֶל־יהוה prep.-pr.n. (217) *to Yahweh*

8:27

וַיַּעַשׂ consec.-Qal impf. 3 m.s. (עָשָׂה I 793) *and did*
יהוה pr.n. (217) *Yahweh*
כִּדְבַר prep.-n.m.s. cstr. (182) *as ... asked (according to the word of)*
מֹשֶׁה pr.n. (602) *Moses*
וַיָּסַר consec.-Qal impf. 3 m.s. (סוּר 693) *and removed*
הֶעָרֹב def. art.-n.m.s. (786) *the swarms of flies*
מִפַּרְעֹה prep.-pr.n. (829) *from Pharaoh*
מֵעֲבָדָיו prep.-n.m.p.-3 m.s. sf. (712) *from his servants*
וּמֵעַמּוֹ conj.-prep.-n.m.s.-3 m.s. sf. (I 766) *and from his people*
לֹא נִשְׁאַר neg.-Ni. pf. 3 m.s. (983) *not ... remained*
אֶחָד num. m.s. (25) *one*

8:28

וַיַּכְבֵּד consec.-Hi. impf. 3 m.s. (457) *but ... hardened*
פַּרְעֹה pr.n. (829) *Pharaoh*
אֶת־לִבּוֹ dir. obj.-n.m.s.-3 m.s. sf. (523) *his heart*
גַּם adv. (168) *also*
בַּפַּעַם prep.-def. art.-n.f.s. (821) *time*
הַזֹּאת def. art.-demons. adj. f.s. (260) *this*
וְלֹא שִׁלַּח conj.-neg.-Pi. pf. 3 m.s. (1018) *and did not let go*
אֶת־הָעָם dir. obj.-def. art.-n.m.s. (I 766) *the people*

9:1

וַיֹּאמֶר consec.-Qal impf. 3 m.s. (55) *then ... said*

יהוה pr.n. (217) *Yahweh*
אֶל־מֹשֶׁה prep.-pr.n. (602) *to Moses*
בֹּא Qal impv. 2 m.s. (בּוֹא 97) *Go in*
אֶל־פַּרְעֹה prep.-pr.n.(829) *to Pharaoh*
וְדִבַּרְתָּ conj.Pi. pf. 2 m.s. (180) *and say*
אֵלָיו prep.-3 m.s. sf. *to him*
כֹּה־אָמַר adv. (462)-Qal pf. 3 m.s. (55) *thus says*
יהוה pr.n. (217) *Yahweh*
אֱלֹהֵי n.m.p. cstr. (43) *the God of*
הָעִבְרִים def. art.-pr.n.m.p. gent. (I 720) *the Hebrews*
שַׁלַּח Pi. impv. 2 m.s. (1018) *Let go*
אֶת־עַמִּי dir. obj.-n.m.s.-1 c.s. sf. (I 766) *my people*
וְיַעַבְדֻנִי conj.-Qal impf. 3 m.p.-1 c.s. sf. (712) *that they may serve me*

9:2

כִּי אִם־מָאֵן conj.-hypoth. part. (49)-adj. from Pi. inf. cstr. (549) *for if ... refuse*
אַתָּה pers. pr. 2 m.s. (61) *you*
לְשַׁלֵּחַ prep.-Pi. inf. cstr. (1018) *to let go*
וְעוֹדְךָ conj.-adv.-2 m.s. sf. (728) *and still (you)*
מַחֲזִיק Hi. ptc. (חָזַק 304) *hold*
בָּם prep.-3 m.p. sf. *them*

9:3

הִנֵּה demons. part. (243) *behold*
יַד־יהוה n.f.s. cstr. (388)-pr.n. (217) *the hand of Yahweh*
הוֹיָה Qal act. ptc. f.s. (הָיָה 224) *will fall*
בְּמִקְנְךָ prep.-n.m.s.-2 m.s. sf. (889) *upon your cattle*
אֲשֶׁר בַּשָּׂדֶה rel.-prep.-def.art.-n.m.s. (961) *which are in the field*
בַּסּוּסִים prep.-def. art.-n.m.p. (692) *the horses*
בַּחֲמֹרִים prep.-def. art.-n.m.p. (331) *the asses*
בַּגְּמַלִּים prep.-def.art.-n.m.p. (168) *the camels*
בַּבָּקָר prep.-def.art.-n.m.s. (133) *the herds*
וּבַצֹּאן conj.-prep.-def. art.-n.f.s. (838) *and the flocks*
דֶּבֶר n.m.s. (184) *with a plague*
כָּבֵד adj. m.s. (458) *severe*
מְאֹד adv. (547) *very*

9:4

וְהִפְלָה conj.-Hi. pf. 3 m.s. (פָּלָה 811) *but ... will make a distinction*
יהוה pr.n. (217) *Yahweh*
בֵּין מִקְנֵה prep. (107)-n.m.s. cstr. (889) *between the cattle of*
יִשְׂרָאֵל pr.n. (975) *Israel*
וּבֵין conj.-prep. (107) *and (between)*
מִקְנֵה v. supra *the cattle of*
מִצְרָיִם pr.n. paus. (595) *Egypt*
וְלֹא יָמוּת conj.-neg.-Qal impf. 3 m.s. (מוּת 559) *so that no ... shall die*
מִכָּל־ prep.-n.m.s. cstr. (481) *of all*
לִבְנֵי prep.-n.m.p. cstr. (119) *that belongs to the people of*
יִשְׂרָאֵל pr.n. (975) *Israel*
דָּבָר n.m.s. (182) *thing*

9:5

וַיָּשֶׂם consec.-Qal impf. 3 m.s. (שִׂים 962) *and ... set*
יהוה pr.n. (217) *Yahweh*
מוֹעֵד n.m.s. (417) *a time*
לֵאמֹר prep.-Qal inf. cstr. (55) *saying*
מָחָר adv. (563) *Tomorrow*
יַעֲשֶׂה יהוה Qal impf. 3 m.s. (I 793) - pr.n. (217) *Yahweh will do*
הַדָּבָר def. art.-n.m.s. (182) *thing*
הַזֶּה def. art.-demons. adj. m.s. (260) *this*
בָּאָרֶץ prep.-def.art.-n.f.s. (75) *in the land*

9:6

וַיַּעַשׂ consec.-Qal impf. 3 m.s. (I 793) *and ... did*
יהוה pr.n. (217) *Yahweh*
אֶת־הַדָּבָר dir. obj.-def. art.-n.m.s. (182) *thing*
הַזֶּה def. art.-demons. adj. m.s. (260) *this*
מִמָּחֳרָת prep.-adv. (564; n.f.s.) *on*

the morrow
וַיָּמָת consec.-Qal impf. 3 m.s. (מות 559) *(and) died*
כֹּל n.m.s. cstr. (481) *all (of)*
מִקְנֵה n.m.s. cstr. (889) *the cattle of*
מִצְרָיִם pr.n. paus. (595) *the Egyptians*
וּמִמִּקְנֵה conj.-prep.-n.m.s. cstr. (889) *but of the cattle of*
בְנֵי־יִשְׂרָאֵל n.m.p. cstr. (119) - pr.n. (975) *the people of Israel*
לֹא־מֵת neg.-Qal pf. 3 m.s. (מות 559) *not died*
אֶחָד num. s. (25) *one*

9:7

וַיִּשְׁלַח consec.-Qal impf. 3 m.s. (1018) *and ... sent*
פַּרְעֹה pr.n. (829) *Pharaoh*
וְהִנֵּה conj.-demons. part. (243) *and behold*
לֹא־מֵת neg.-Qal pf. 3 m.s. (מות 559) *not ... was dead*
מִמִּקְנֵה prep.-n.m.s. cstr. (889) *of the cattle of*
יִשְׂרָאֵל pr.n. (975) *Israel*
עַד־אֶחָד adv. (III 723)-num. s. (25) *one*
וַיִּכְבַּד consec.-Qal impf. 3 m.s. (457) *but ... was hardened*
לֵב פַּרְעֹה n.m.s. cstr. (523)-pr.n. (829) *the heart of Pharaoh*
וְלֹא שִׁלַּח conj.-neg.-Pi. pf. 3 m.s. (1018) *and he did not let go*
אֶת־הָעָם dir. obj.-def. art.-n.m.s. (I 766) *the people*

9:8

וַיֹּאמֶר consec.-Qal impf. 3 m.s. (55) *and ... said*
יהוה pr.n. (217) *Yahweh*
אֶל־מֹשֶׁה prep.-pr.n. (602) *to Moses*
וְאֶל־אַהֲרֹן conj.-prep.-pr.n. (14) *and Aaron*
קְחוּ Qal impv. 2 m.p. (לָקַח 542) *take*
לָכֶם prep.-2 m.p. sf.
מְלֹא n.m.s. cstr. (571) *fulness of*
חָפְנֵיכֶם n.m. du.-2 m.p. sf. (342) *your fists*
פִּיחַ n.m.s. cstr. (806) *ashes from*
כִּבְשָׁן n.m.s. (461) *the kiln*
וּזְרָקוֹ conj.-Qal pf. 3 m.s.-3 m.s. sf. (284) *and let ... throw them*
מֹשֶׁה pr.n. (602) *Moses*
הַשָּׁמַיְמָה def.art.-n.m.p.-dir.he (1029) *toward heaven*
לְעֵינֵי prep.-n.f. du. cstr. (744) *in the sight of*
פַרְעֹה pr.n. (829) *Pharaoh*

9:9

וְהָיָה conj.-Qal pf. 3 m.s. (224) *and it shall become*
לְאָבָק prep.-n.m.s. (7) *fine dust*
עַל כָּל־ prep.-n.m.s. cstr. (481) *over all*
אֶרֶץ n.f.s. cstr. (75) *the land of*
מִצְרָיִם pr.n. paus. (595) *Egypt*
וְהָיָה v.supra *and become*
עַל־הָאָדָם prep.-def.art.-n.m.s. (9) *on man*
וְעַל־הַבְּהֵמָה conj.-prep.-def.art.-n.f.s. (96) *and beast*
לִשְׁחִין prep.-n.m.s. (1006) *boils*
פֹּרֵחַ Qal act. ptc. (פָּרַח II 827) *breaking out*
אֲבַעְבֻּעֹת n.f.p. (101) *in sores*
בְּכָל־ prep.-n.m.s. cstr. (481) *throughout all*
אֶרֶץ n.f.s. cstr. (75) *the land of*
מִצְרָיִם pr.n. paus. (595) *Egypt*

9:10

וַיִּקְחוּ consec.-Qal impf. 3 m.p. (לָקַח 542) *so they took*
אֶת־פִּיחַ dir.obj.-n.m.s. cstr. (806) *ashes from*
הַכִּבְשָׁן def.art.-n.m.s. (461) *the kiln*
וַיַּעַמְדוּ consec.-Qal impf. 3 m.p. (763) *and stood*
לִפְנֵי prep.-n.m.p. cstr. (815) *before*
פַרְעֹה pr.n. (829) *Pharaoh*
וַיִּזְרֹק consec.-Qal impf. 3 m.s. (284) *and ... threw*
אֹתוֹ dir.obj.-3 m.s. sf. *them*
מֹשֶׁה pr.n. (602) *Moses*

הַשָּׁמָיְמָה def.art.-n.m.p.-dir. he paus. (1029) *toward heaven*

וַיְהִי consec.-Qal impf. 3 m.s. (הָיָה 224) *and it became*

שְׁחִין n.m.s. (1006) *boils*

אֲבַעְבֻּעֹת n.f.p. (101) *in sores*

פֹּרֵחַ Qal act. ptc. (II 827) *breaking out*

בָּאָדָם prep.-def.art.-n.m.s. (9) *on man*

וּבַבְּהֵמָה conj.-prep.-def.art.-n.f.s. (96) *and beast*

9:11

וְלֹא־יָכְלוּ conj.-neg.-Qal pf. 3 c.p. (יָכֹל 407) *and ... could not*

הַחַרְטֻמִּים def.art.-n.m.p. (355) *the magicians*

לַעֲמֹד prep.-Qal inf. cstr. (763) *stand*

לִפְנֵי prep.-n.m.p. cstr. (815) *before*

מֹשֶׁה pr.n. (602) *Moses*

מִפְּנֵי prep.-n.m.p. cstr. (815) *because of*

הַשְּׁחִין def.art.-n.m.s. (1006) *the boils*

כִּי־הָיָה conj.-Qal pf. 3 m.s. (224) *for were*

הַשְּׁחִין v.supra *the boils*

בַּחַרְטֻמִּם prep.-def.art.-n.m.p. (355) *upon the magicians*

וּבְכָל־ conj.-prep.-n.m.s. cstr. (481) *and upon all*

מִצְרָיִם pr.n. paus. (595) *the Egyptians*

9:12

וַיְחַזֵּק consec.-Pi. impf. 3 m.s. (304) *but ... hardened*

יהוה pr.n. (217) *Yahweh*

אֶת־לֵב dir.obj.-n.m.s. cstr. (523) *the heart of*

פַּרְעֹה pr.n. (829) *Pharaoh*

וְלֹא שָׁמַע conj.-neg.-Qal pf. 3 m.s. (1033) *and he did not listen*

אֲלֵהֶם prep.-3 m.p. sf. *to them*

כַּאֲשֶׁר prep.-rel. *as*

דִּבֶּר Pi. pf.3 m.s. (180) *had spoken*

יהוה pr.n. (217) *Yahweh*

אֶל־מֹשֶׁה prep.-pr.n. (602) *to Moses*

9:13

וַיֹּאמֶר consec.-Qal impf. 3 m.s. (55) *then ... said*

יהוה pr.n. (217) *Yahweh*

אֶל־מֹשֶׁה prep.-pr.n. (602) *to Moses*

הַשְׁכֵּם Hi. impv. 2 m.s. (1014) *rise up early*

בַּבֹּקֶר prep.-def.art.-n.m.s. (133) *in the morning*

וְהִתְיַצֵּב conj. - Hith. impv. 2 m.s. (יָצַב 426) *and stand*

לִפְנֵי prep.-n.m.p. cstr. (815) *before*

פַּרְעֹה pr.n. (829) *Pharaoh*

וְאָמַרְתָּ conj.-Qal pf. 2 m.s. (55) *and say*

אֵלָיו prep.-3 m.s. sf. *to him*

כֹּה־אָמַר adv. (462)-Qal pf. 3 m.s. (55) *Thus says*

יהוה pr.n. (217) *Yahweh*

אֱלֹהֵי n.m.p. cstr. (43) *the God of*

הָעִבְרִים def.art.-pr.n. gent. p. (720) *the Hebrews*

שַׁלַּח Pi. impv. 2 m.s. (1018) *Let go*

אֶת־עַמִּי dir.obj.-n.m.s.-1 c.s. sf. (I 766) *my people*

וְיַעַבְדֻנִי conj.-Qal impf. 3 m.p.-1 c.s. sf. (עָבַד 712) *that they may serve me*

9:14

כִּי בַּפַּעַם conj.-prep.-def.art.-n.f.s. (821) *for ... time*

הַזֹּאת def.art.-demons. adj. f.s. (260) *this*

אֲנִי pers.pr. 1 c.s. (58) *I*

שֹׁלֵחַ Qal act. ptc. (1018) *will send*

אֶת־כָּל־ dir.obj.-n.m.s. cstr. (481) *all*

מַגֵּפֹתַי n.f.p.-1 c.s. sf. (620) *my plagues*

אֶל־לִבְּךָ prep.-n.m.s.-2 m.s. sf. (523) *upon your heart*

וּבַעֲבָדֶיךָ conj.-prep.-n.m.p.-2 m.s. sf. (712) *and upon your servants*

וּבְעַמֶּךָ conj.-prep.-n.m.s.-2 m.s. sf. (I 766) *and your people*

בַּעֲבוּר prep.-prep. (II 721) *that*

תֵּדַע Qal impf. 2 m.s. (יָדַע 393) *you may know*

כִּי אֵין conj.-subst. cstr. (II 34) *that there is none*

כָּמֹנִי prep.-1 c.s. sf. *like me*

בְּכָל־ prep.-n.m.s. cstr. (481) *in all (of)*

הָאָרֶץ def.art.-n.f.s. (75) *the earth*

9:15

כִּי עַתָּה conj.-adv. (773) *for by now*

שָׁלַחְתִּי Qal pf. 1 c.s. (1018) *I could have put forth*

אֶת־יָדִי dir.obj.-n.f.s.-1 c.s. sf. (388) *my hand*

וָאַךְ consec.-Hi. impf. 1 c.s. (נָכָה 645) *and struck*

אוֹתְךָ dir.obj.-2 m.s. sf. *you*

וְאֶת־עַמְּךָ conj.-dir.obj.-n.m.s.-2 m.s. sf. (I 766) *and your people*

בַּדָּבֶר prep.-def.art.-n.m.s. paus. (184) *with pestilence*

וַתִּכָּחֵד consec.-Ni. impf. 2 m.s. (כָּחַד 470) *and you would have been cut off*

מִן־הָאָרֶץ prep.-def.art.-n.f.s. (75) *from the earth*

9:16

וְאוּלָם conj.-adv. (III 19) *but*

בַּעֲבוּר prep.-prep. (II 721) *for ... purpose*

זֹאת demons.adj. f.s. (260) *this*

הֶעֱמַדְתִּיךָ Hi. pf. 1 c.s. - 2 m. s. sf. (עָמַד 763) *have I let you live (stand)*

בַּעֲבוּר v.supra *to*

הַרְאֹתְךָ Hi. inf. cstr.-2 m.s. sf. (רָאָה 906) *show you*

אֶת־כֹּחִי dir.obj.-n.m.s.-1 c.s. sf. (470) *my power*

וּלְמַעַן conj.-prep.-prep. (775) *so that*

סַפֵּר Pi. inf. cstr. (707) *may be declared*

שְׁמִי n.m.s.-1 c.s. sf. (1027) *my name*

בְּכָל־ prep.-n.m.s. cstr. (481) *throughout all (of)*

הָאָרֶץ def.art.-n.f.s. (75) *the earth*

9:17

עוֹדְךָ adv.-2 m.s. sf. (728) *you ... still*

מִסְתּוֹלֵל Hith. ptc. (סָלַל I 699) *are exalting yourself*

בְּעַמִּי prep.-n.m.s.-1 c.s. sf. (I 766) *against my people*

לְבִלְתִּי prep.-neg. (116) *and will not*

שַׁלְּחָם Pi. inf. cstr.-3 m.p. sf. (שָׁלַח 1018) *let them go*

9:18

הִנְנִי demons. part. - 1 c.s. sf. (243) *behold I*

מַמְטִיר Hi. ptc. (מָטַר 565) *will cause to fall*

כָּעֵת prep.-def.art.-n.f.s. (773) *about this time*

מָחָר adv. (563) *tomorrow*

בָּרָד n.m.s. (135) *hail*

כָּבֵד מְאֹד adj. m.s. (458)-adv. (547) *very heavy*

אֲשֶׁר rel. *such as*

לֹא־הָיָה neg.-Qal pf. 3 m.s. (224) *has never been*

כָמֹהוּ prep.-3 m.s. sf. *(like it)*

בְּמִצְרַיִם prep.-pr.n. (595) *in Egypt*

לְמִן־הַיּוֹם prep.-prep.-def.art.-n.m.s. (398) *from the day*

הִוָּסְדָה Ni. inf. cstr. (f.s.?: dir.he?: or 3 f.s. sf.?) (יָסַד 413) *it was founded*

וְעַד־עָתָּה conj.-adv. (III 723)-adv. paus. (773) *until now*

9:19

וְעַתָּה conj.-adv. (773) *now therefore*

שְׁלַח Qal impv. 2 m.s. (1018) *send*

הָעֵז Hi. impv. 2 m.s. (עוּז 731) *get into safe shelter*

אֶת־מִקְנְךָ dir.obj.-n.m.s.-2 m.s. sf. (889) *your cattle*

וְאֵת כָּל־ conj.-dir.obj.-n.m.s. cstr. (481) *and all*

אֲשֶׁר לְךָ rel.-prep.-2 m.s. sf. *that you have*

בַּשָּׂדֶה prep.-def.art.-n.m.s. (961) *in the field*

כָּל־הָאָדָם n.m.s. cstr. (481)-def.art.-n.m.s. (9) *every man*
וְהַבְּהֵמָה conj.-def.art.-n.f.s. (96) *and beast*
אֲשֶׁר־ rel. *that*
יִמָּצֵא Ni. impf. 3 m.s. (592) *is (found)*
בַשָּׂדֶה v.supra *in the field*
וְלֹא יֵאָסֵף conj.-neg.-Ni. impf. 3 m.s. (אָסַף 62) *and is not brought*
הַבַּיְתָה def.art.-n.m.s.-dir. he (108) *home*
וְיָרַד conj.-Qal pf. 3 m.s. (432) *for shall come down*
עֲלֵהֶם prep.-3 m.p. sf. *upon them*
הַבָּרָד def.art.-n.m.s. (135) *the hail*
וָמֵתוּ conj.-Qal pf. 3 c.p. (מוּת 559) *and they shall die*

9:20

הַיָּרֵא def.art.-Qal act. ptc. (יָרֵא 431) *then he who feared*
אֶת־דְּבַר dir.obj.-n.m.s. cstr. (182) *the word of*
יהוה pr.n. (217) *Yahweh*
מֵעַבְדֵי prep.-n.m.p. cstr. (712) *among the servants of*
פַּרְעֹה pr.n. (829) *Pharaoh*
הֵנִיס Hi. pf. 3 m.s. (נוּס 630) *made ... flee*
אֶת־עֲבָדָיו dir.obj.-n.m.p.-3 m.s. sf. (712) *his slaves*
וְאֶת־מִקְנֵהוּ conj.-dir.obj.-n.m.s.-3 m.s. sf. (889) *and his cattle*
אֶל־הַבָּתִּים prep.-def.art.-n.m.p. (108) *into the houses*

9:21

וַאֲשֶׁר conj.-rel. *but he who*
לֹא־שָׂם לִבּוֹ neg.-Qal act. ptc. (שׂוּם 962)-n.m.s.-3 m.s. sf. (523) *did not regard (set his heart)*
אֶל־דְּבַר prep.-n.m.s. cstr. (182) *(upon) the word of*
יהוה pr.n. (217) *Yahweh*
וַיַּעֲזֹב consec. - Qal impf. 3 m.s. (I 736) *left*
אֶת־עֲבָדָיו dir.obj.-n.m.p.-3 m.s. sf. (712) *his slaves*
וְאֶת־מִקְנֵהוּ conj.-dir.obj.-n.m.s.-3 m.s. sf. (889) *and his cattle*
בַּשָּׂדֶה prep.-def.art.-n.m.s. (961) *in the field*

9:22

וַיֹּאמֶר consec.-Qal impf. 3 m.s. (55) *and ... said*
יהוה pr.n. (217) *Yahweh*
אֶל־מֹשֶׁה prep.-pr.n. (602) *to Moses*
נְטֵה Qal impv. 2 m.s. (639) *Stretch forth*
אֶת־יָדְךָ dir.obj.-n.f.s.-2 m.s. sf. (388) *thy hand*
עַל־הַשָּׁמַיִם prep.-def.art.-n.m.p. (1029) *toward heaven*
וִיהִי conj.-Qal impf. 3 m.s. apoc. (הָיָה 224) *that there may be*
בָרָד n.m.s. (135) *hail*
בְּכָל־אֶרֶץ prep.-n.m.s. cstr. (481)-n.f.s. cstr. (75) *in all the land of*
מִצְרָיִם pr.n. paus. (595) *Egypt*
עַל־הָאָדָם prep.-def.art.-n.m.s. (9) *upon man*
וְעַל־הַבְּהֵמָה conj.-prep.-def.art.-n.f.s. (96) *and beast*
וְעַל כָּל־ conj.-prep.-n.m.s. cstr. (481) *and every*
עֵשֶׂב n.m.s. cstr. (793) *plant of*
הַשָּׂדֶה def.art.-n.m.s. (961) *the field*
בְּאֶרֶץ prep.-n.f.s. cstr. (75) *throughout the land of*
מִצְרָיִם pr.n. paus. (595) *Egypt*

9:23

וַיֵּט consec.-Qal impf. 3 m.s. (נָטָה 639) *then ... stretched out*
מֹשֶׁה pr.n. (602) *Moses*
אֶת־מַטֵּהוּ dir.obj.-n.m.s.-3 m.s. sf. (641) *his rod*
עַל־הַשָּׁמַיִם prep.-def.art.-n.m.p. (1029) *toward heaven*
ויהוה conj.-pr.n. (217) *and Yahweh*
נָתַן Qal pf. 3 m.s. (678) *sent*
קֹלֹת n.m.p. (876) *thunder*
וּבָרָד conj.-n.m.s. (135) *and hail*
וַתִּהֲלַךְ consec.-Qal impf. 3 f.s. (הָלַךְ

229) *and ran down*

אֵשׁ n.f.s. (77) *fire*

אָרְצָה n.f.s.-dir. he (75) *to the earth*

וַיַּמְטֵר consec.-Hi. impf. 3 m.s. (מָטַר 565) *and ... rained*

יהוה pr.n. (217) *Yahweh*

בָּרָד v.supra *hail*

עַל־אֶרֶץ prep.-n.f.s. cstr. (75) *upon the land of*

מִצְרָיִם pr.n. paus. (595) *Egypt*

9:24

וַיְהִי consec.-Qal impf. 3 m.s. (הָיָה 224) *there was*

בָרָד n.m.s. (135) *hail*

וְאֵשׁ conj.-n.f.s. (77) *and fire*

מִתְלַקַּחַת Hith. ptc. f.s. cstr. (לָקַח 542) *flashing continually*

בְּתוֹךְ prep.-n.m.s. cstr. (1063) *in the midst of*

הַבָּרָד def.art.-n.m.s. (135) *the hail*

כָּבֵד מְאֹד adj. m.s. (458)-adv. (547) *very heavy*

אֲשֶׁר rel. *such as*

לֹא־הָיָה neg.-Qal pf. 3 m.s. (224) *had never been*

כָּמֹהוּ prep.-3 m.s. sf. (*as it*)

בְּכָל־אֶרֶץ prep.-n.m.s. cstr. (481) - n.f.s. cstr. (75) *in all the land of*

מִצְרַיִם pr.n. (595) *Egypt*

מֵאָז prep.-adv. (23) *since*

הָיְתָה Qal pf. 3 f.s. (הָיָה 224) *it became*

לְגוֹי prep.-n.m.s. (156) *a nation*

9:25

וַיַּךְ consec.-Hi. impf. 3 m.s. (נָכָה 645) *struck down*

הַבָּרָד def.art.-n.m.s. (135) *the hail*

בְּכָל־אֶרֶץ prep.-n.m.s. cstr. (481) - n.f.s. cstr. (75) *throughout all the land of*

מִצְרַיִם pr.n. (595) *Egypt*

אֵת כָּל־ dir.obj.-n.m.s. (481) *everything*

אֲשֶׁר rel. *that*

בַּשָּׂדֶה prep.-def.art.-n.m.s. (961) *in the field*

מֵאָדָם prep.-n.m.s. (9) *man*

וְעַד־בְּהֵמָה conj.-adv. (III 723)-n.f.s. (96) *and beast*

וְאֵת כָּל־ conj.-dir.obj. n.m.s. cstr. (481) *and every*

עֵשֶׂב n.m.s. cstr. (793) *plant of*

הַשָּׂדֶה def.art.-n.m.s. (961) *the field*

הִכָּה Hi. pf. 3 m.s. (נָכָה 645) *struck down*

הַבָּרָד def.art.-n.m.s. (135) *(the hail)*

וְאֶת־כָּל־עֵץ conj.-dir.obj.-n.m.s. cstr. (481)-n.m.s. cstr. (781) *and every tree of*

הַשָּׂדֶה v.supra *the field*

שִׁבֵּר Pi. pf. 3 m.s. (990) *shattered*

9:26

רַק adv. (956) *only*

בְּאֶרֶץ prep.-n.f.s. cstr. (75) *in the land of*

גֹּשֶׁן pr.n. (177) *Goshen*

אֲשֶׁר־שָׁם rel.-adv. (1027) *where were*

בְּנֵי יִשְׂרָאֵל n.m.p. cstr. (119)-pr.n. (975) *the people of Israel*

לֹא הָיָה neg.-Qal pf. 3 m.s. (224) *there was no*

בָּרָד n.m.s. (135) *hail*

9:27

וַיִּשְׁלַח consec.-Qal impf. 3 m.s. (1018) *then ... sent*

פַּרְעֹה pr.n. (829) *Pharaoh*

וַיִּקְרָא consec.-Qal impf. 3 m.s. (894) *and called*

לְמֹשֶׁה prep.-pr.n. (602) *Moses*

וּלְאַהֲרֹן conj.-prep.-pr.n. (14) *and Aaron*

וַיֹּאמֶר consec.-Qal impf. 3 m.s. (55) *and said*

אֲלֵהֶם prep.-3 m.p. sf. *to them*

חָטָאתִי Qal pf. 1 c.s. (חָטָא 306) *I have sinned*

הַפָּעַם def.art.-n.m.s. paus. (821) *this time*

יהוה pr.n.(217) *Yahweh*

הַצַּדִּיק def.art.-adj. m.s. (843) *is in the right*

וַאֲנִי conj.-pers.pr. 1 c.s. (58) *and I*

וְעַמִּי conj.-n.m.s.-1 c.s. sf. (I 766) *and my people*

הָרְשָׁעִים def.art.-adj. m.p. (957) *in the wrong*

9:28

הַעְתִּירוּ Hi. impv. 2 m.p. (עָתַר I 801) *entreat*

אֶל־יהוה prep.-pr.n. (217) *Yahweh*

וְרַב conj.-adj. (I 912) *enough*

מִהְיֹת prep.-Qal inf. cstr. (הָיָה 224) *there has been (of being)*

קֹלֹת אֱלֹהִים n.m.p. cstr. (876)-n.m.p. (43) *thunder*

וּבָרָד conj.-n.m.s. (135) *and hail*

וַאֲשַׁלְּחָה conj.-Pi. impf. 1 c.s.-coh. he (שָׁלַח 1018) *I will let go*

אֶתְכֶם dir.obj.-2 m.p. sf. *you*

וְלֹא תֹסִפוּן conj.-neg.-Hi. impf. 2 m.p. (יָסַף 414) *and you shall no longer*

לַעֲמֹד prep.-Qal inf. cstr. (עָמַד 763) *(stand) stay*

9:29

וַיֹּאמֶר consec.-Qal impf. 3 m.s. (55) *said*

אֵלָיו prep.-3 m.s. sf. *to him*

מֹשֶׁה pr.n. (602) *Moses*

כְּצֵאתִי prep.-Qal inf. cstr.-1 c.s. sf. (יָצָא 422) *as soon as I have gone out*

אֶת־הָעִיר dir.obj.-def.art.-n.f.s. (746) *the city*

אֶפְרֹשׂ Qal impf. 1 c.s. (פָּרַשׂ 831) *I will stretch out*

אֶת־כַּפַּי dir.obj.-n.f.p.-1 c.s. sf. (496) *my hands*

אֶל־יהוה prep.-pr.n. (217) *to Yahweh*

הַקֹּלוֹת def.art.-n.m.p. (876) *the thunder*

יֶחְדָּלוּן Qal impf. 3 m.p. (חָדַל 292) *will cease*

וְהַבָּרָד conj.-def.art.-n.m.s. (135) *and hail*

לֹא יִהְיֶה־ neg.-Qal impf. 3 m.s. (224) *there will be no*

עוֹד adv. (728) *more*

לְמַעַן prep.-prep. (775) *that*

תֵּדַע Qal impf. 2 m.s. (יָדַע 393) *you may know*

כִּי ליהוה conj.-prep.-pr.n. (217) *that ... is Yahweh's*

הָאָרֶץ def.art.-n.f.s. (75) *the earth*

9:30

וְאַתָּה conj.-pers.pr. 2 m.s. (61) *but as for you*

וַעֲבָדֶיךָ conj.-n.m.p.-2 m.s. sf. (712) *and your servants*

יָדַעְתִּי Qal pf. 1 c.s. (יָדַע 393) *I know*

כִּי טֶרֶם conj.-neg. (382) *that ... not yet*

תִּירְאוּן Qal impf. 2 m.p. (יָרֵא 431) *you fear*

מִפְּנֵי prep.-n.m.p. cstr. (815) *(before)*

יהוה pr.n. (217) *Yahweh*

אֱלֹהִים n.m.p. (43) *God*

9:31

וְהַפִּשְׁתָּה conj.-def.art.-n.f.s. (834) *the flax*

וְהַשְּׂעֹרָה conj.-def.art.-n.f.s. (972) *and the barley*

נֻכָּתָה Pu. pf. 3 f.s. (נָכָה 645) *were ruined*

כִּי conj. *for*

הַשְּׂעֹרָה v.supra *the barley*

אָבִיב n.m.s. (1) *the ear*

וְהַפִּשְׁתָּה v.supra *and the flax*

גִּבְעֹל n.m.s. (149) *in bud*

9:32

וְהַחִטָּה conj.-def.art.-n.f.s. (334) *but the wheat*

וְהַכֻּסֶּמֶת conj.-def.art.-n.f.s. (493) *and the spelt*

לֹא נֻכּוּ neg.-Pu. pf. 3 c.p. (נָכָה 645) *were not ruined*

כִּי אֲפִילֹת conj.-adj. f.p. (66) *late in coming*

הֵנָּה pers.pr. 3 f.p. (II 244) *they*

9:33

וַיֵּצֵא consec.-Qal impf. 3 m.s. (יָצָא 422) *so ... went out of*

מֹשֶׁה pr.n. (602) *Moses*

מֵעִם prep.-prep. *from*

פַּרְעֹה pr.n. (829) *Pharaoh*

אֶת־הָעִיר dir.obj.-def.art.-n.f.s. (746) *the city*

וַיִּפְרֹשׂ consec.-Qal impf. 3 m.s. (פָּרַשׂ 831) *and stretched out*

כַּפָּיו n.f.p.-3 m.s. sf. (496) *his hands*

אֶל־יהוה prep.-pr.n. (217) *to Yahweh*

וַיַּחְדְּלוּ consec.-Qal impf. 3 m.p. (חָדַל 292) *and ceased*

הַקֹּלוֹת def.art.-n.m.p. (876) *the thunder*

וְהַבָּרָד conj.-def.art.-n.m.s. (135) *and the hail*

וּמָטָר conj.-n.m.s. (564) *and rain*

לֹא־נִתַּךְ neg.-Pi. pf. 3 m.s. (נָתַךְ 677) *no longer poured*

אָרְצָה n.f.s.-dir. he (75) *upon the earth*

9:34

וַיַּרְא consec.-Qal impf. 3 m.s. (רָאָה 906) *but when ... saw*

פַּרְעֹה pr.n. (829) *Pharaoh*

כִּי־חָדַל conj.-Qal pf. 3 m.s. (292) *that ... had ceased*

הַמָּטָר def.art.-n.m.s. (564) *the rain*

וְהַבָּרָד conj.-def.art.-n.m.s. (135) *and the hail*

וְהַקֹּלֹת conj.-def.art.-n.m.p. (876) *and the thunder*

וַיֹּסֶף consec.-Hi. impf. 3 m.s. (יָסַף 414) *he ... again*

לַחֲטֹא prep. - Qal inf. cstr. (306) *sinned*

וַיַּכְבֵּד consec.-Hi. impf. 3 m.s. (457) *and hardened*

לִבּוֹ n.m.s.-3 m.s. sf. (523) *his heart*

הוּא pers.pr. 3 m.s. (214) *he*

וַעֲבָדָיו conj.-n.m.p.-3 m.s. sf. (712) *and his servants*

9:35

וַיֶּחֱזַק consec.-Qal impf. 3 m.s. (חָזַק 304) *so ... was hardened*

לֵב פַּרְעֹה n.m.s. cstr. (523)-pr.n. (829) *the heart of Pharaoh*

וְלֹא שִׁלַּח conj.-neg.-Pi. pf. 3 m.s. (1018) *and he did not let go*

אֶת־בְּנֵי dir.obj.-n.m.p. cstr. (119) *the people of*

יִשְׂרָאֵל pr.n. (975) *Israel*

כַּאֲשֶׁר prep.-rel. *as*

דִּבֶּר Pi. pf. 3 m.s. (180) *had spoken*

יהוה pr.n. (217) *Yahweh*

בְּיַד־ prep.-n.f.s. cstr. (388) *through (by the hand of)*

מֹשֶׁה pr.n. (602) *Moses*

10:1

וַיֹּאמֶר consec.-Qal impf. 3 m.s. (55) *then ... said*

יהוה pr.n. (217) *Yahweh*

אֶל־מֹשֶׁה prep.-pr.n. (602) *to Moses*

בֹּא Qal impv. 2 m.s. (בּוֹא 97) *Go in*

אֶל־פַּרְעֹה prep.-pr.n. (829) *to Pharaoh*

כִּי־אֲנִי conj.-pers.pr. 1 c.s. (58) *for I*

הִכְבַּדְתִּי Hi. pf. 1 c.s. (כָּבַד 457) *have hardened*

אֶת־לִבּוֹ dir.obj.-n.m.s.-3 m.s. sf. (523) *his heart*

וְאֶת־לֵב conj.-dir.obj.-n.m.s. cstr. (523) *and the heart of*

עֲבָדָיו n.m.p.-3 m.s. sf. (712) *his servants*

לְמַעַן prep.-prep. (775) *that*

שִׁתִי Qal pass. ptc.-1 c.s. sf. (שִׁית 1011) *I may show*

אֹתֹתַי n.f.p.-1 c.s. sf. (16) *my signs*

אֵלֶּה demons.adj. c.p. (41) *these*

בְּקִרְבּוֹ prep.-n.m.s.-3 m.s. sf. (899) *among them*

10:2

וּלְמַעַן conj.-prep.-prep. (775) *and that*

תְּסַפֵּר Pi. impf. 2 m.s. (סָפַר 707) *you may tell*

בְּאָזְנֵי prep.-n.f.p. cstr. (23) *in the hearing of*

בִנְךָ n.m.s.-2 m.s. sf. (119) *your son*

וּבֶן־בִּנְךָ conj.-n.m.s. cstr. (119)-v.supra *and of your son's son*

אֵת אֲשֶׁר dir.obj.-rel. *how*

הִתְעַלַּלְתִּי Hith. pf. 1 c.s. (עָלַל I 759) *I have made sport*

בְּמִצְרַיִם prep.-pr.n. (595) *of the Egyptians*

וְאֶת־אֹתֹתַי conj.-dir.obj.-n.f.p.-1 c.s. sf. (16) *and ... signs*

אֲשֶׁר־שַׂמְתִּי rel.-Qal pf. 1 c.s. (שׂוּם 962) *what ... I have done*

בָם prep.-3 m.p. sf. *among them*

וִידַעְתֶּם conj.-Qal pf. 2 m.p. (יָדַע 393) *that you may know*

כִּי־אֲנִי conj.-pers.pr. 1 c.s. (58) *that I am*

יהוה pr.n. (217) *Yahweh*

10:3

וַיָּבֹא consec.-Qal impf. 3 m.s. (בּוֹא 97) *so ... went in*

מֹשֶׁה pr.n. (602) *Moses*

וְאַהֲרֹן conj.-pr.n. (14) *and Aaron*

אֶל־פַּרְעֹה prep.-pr.n. (829) *to Pharaoh*

וַיֹּאמְרוּ consec.-Qal impf. 3 m.p. (55) *and said*

אֵלָיו prep.-3 m.s. sf. *to him*

כֹּה־אָמַר adv. (462)-Qal pf. 3 m.s. (55) *Thus says*

יהוה pr.n. (217) *Yahweh*

אֱלֹהֵי n.m.p. cstr. (43) *the God of*

הָעִבְרִים def.art.-pr.n. (720) *the Hebrews*

עַד־מָתַי prep. (III 723)-adv. (607) *How long*

מֵאַנְתָּ Pi. pf. 2 m.s. (מָאֵן 549) *will you refuse*

לֵעָנֹת prep.-Ni. inf. cstr. (עָנָה III 776) *to humble yourself*

מִפָּנָי prep.-n.m.p.-1 c.s. sf. paus. (815) *before me*

שַׁלַּח Pi. impv. 2 m.s. (1018) *Let go*

עַמִּי n.m.s.-1 c.s. sf. (I 766) *my people*

וְיַעַבְדֻנִי conj.-Qal impf. 3 m.p. - 1 c.s. sf. (עָבַד 712) *that they may serve me*

10:4

כִּי אִם־ conj.-hypoth. part. (49) *for if*

מָאֵן adj. verb. (549) *refuse*

אַתָּה pers.pr. 2 m.s. (61) *you*

לְשַׁלֵּחַ prep.-Pi. inf. cstr. (1018) *to let go*

אֶת־עַמִּי dir.obj.-n.m.s.-1 c.s. sf. (I 766) *my people*

הִנְנִי demons.part.-1 c.s. sf. (243) *behold I*

מֵבִיא Hi. ptc. (בּוֹא 97) *will bring*

מָחָר adv. (563) *tomorrow*

אַרְבֶּה n.m.s. (916) *locusts*

בִּגְבֻלֶךָ prep.-n.m.s.-2 m.s. sf. paus. (147) *into your country (border)*

10:5

וְכִסָּה conj.-Pi. pf. 3 m.s. (כָּסָה 491) *and they shall cover*

אֶת־עֵין dir.obj.-n.f.s. cstr. (744) *the face of*

הָאָרֶץ def.art.-n.f.s. (75) *the land*

וְלֹא יוּכַל conj.-neg.-Qal impf. 3 m.s. (יָכֹל 407) *so that no one can*

לִרְאֹת prep.-Qal inf. cstr. (רָאָה 906) *see*

אֶת־הָאָרֶץ dir.obj.-def.art.-n.f.s. (75) *the land*

וְאָכַל conj.-Qal pf. 3 m.s. (37) *and they shall eat*

אֶת־יֶתֶר dir.obj.-n.m.s. cstr. (451) *(the remainder of)*

הַפְּלֵטָה def.art.-n.f.s. (812) *(the remnant)*

הַנִּשְׁאֶרֶת def.art.-Ni. ptc. f.s. cstr. (שָׁאַר 983) *what is left*

לָכֶם prep.-2 m.p. sf. *to you*

מִן־הַבָּרָד prep.-def.art.-n.m.s. (135) *after the hail*

וְאָכַל v.supra *and they shall eat*

אֶת־כָּל־ dir.obj.-n.m.s. cstr. (481) *every*

הָעֵץ def.art.-n.m.s. (781) *tree*

הַצֹּמֵחַ def.art.-Qal act. ptc. (855) *which grows*

לָכֶם prep.-2 m.p. sf. *of yours*

מִן־הַשָּׂדֶה prep.-def.art.-n.m.s. (961) *in the field*

10:6

וּמָלְאוּ conj.-Qal pf. 3 c.p. (569) *and*

they shall fill

בָּתֶּיךָ n.m.p.-2 m.s. sf. (108) *your houses*

וּבָתֵּי conj.-n.m.p. cstr. (108) *and the houses of*

כָל־עֲבָדֶיךָ n.m.s. cstr. (481)-n.m.p.-2 m.s. sf. (712) *all your servants*

וּבָתֵּי conj.-n.m.p. cstr. (108) *and (houses of)*

כָל־מִצְרַיִם n.m.s. cstr. (481)-pr.n. (595) *all the Egyptians*

אֲשֶׁר rel. *as*

לֹא־רָאוּ neg.-Qal pf. 3 c.p. (רָאָה 906) *neither have seen*

אֲבֹתֶיךָ n.m.p.-2 m.s. sf. (3) *your fathers*

וַאֲבוֹת conj.-n.m.p. cstr. (3) *and (fathers of)*

אֲבֹתֶיךָ v.supra *your fathers*

מִיּוֹם prep.-n.m.s. cstr. (398) *from the day*

הֱיוֹתָם Qal inf. cstr.-3 m.p. sf. (הָיָה 224) *they came*

עַל־הָאֲדָמָה prep.-def.art.-n.f.s. (9) *on earth*

עַד הַיּוֹם prep. (III 723)-def.art.-n.m.s. (398) *to ... day*

הַזֶּה def.art.-demons. adj. m.s. (260) *this*

וַיִּפֶן consec.-Qal impf. 3 m.s. (פָּנָה 815) *then he turned*

וַיֵּצֵא consec.-Qal impf. 3 m.s. (יָצָא 422) *and went out*

מֵעִם prep.-prep. *from*

פַּרְעֹה pr.n. (829) *Pharaoh*

10:7

וַיֹּאמְרוּ consec.-Qal impf. 3 m.p. (55) *and said*

עַבְדֵי n.m.p. cstr. (712) *servants of*

פַרְעֹה pr.n. (829) *Pharaoh*

אֵלָיו prep.-3 m.s. sf. *to him*

עַד־מָתַי prep. (III 723)-adv. (607) *How long*

יִהְיֶה Qal impf. 3 m.s. (הָיָה 224) *shall be*

זֶה demons. adj. m.s. (260) *this man*

לָנוּ prep.-1 c.p. sf. *to us*

לְמוֹקֵשׁ prep.-n.m.s. (430) *a snare*

שַׁלַּח Pi. impv. 2 m.s. (1018) *Let go*

אֶת־הָאֲנָשִׁים dir.obj.-def.art.-n.m.p. (35) *the men*

וְיַעַבְדוּ conj.-Qal impf. 3 m.p. (עָבַד 712) *that they may serve*

אֶת־יהוה dir.obj.-pr.n. (217) *Yahweh*

אֱלֹהֵיהֶם n.m.p.-3 m.p. sf. (43) *their God*

הֲטֶרֶם interr.-neg. (382) *do ... not yet?*

תֵּדַע Qal impf. 2 m.s. (יָדַע 393) *you know*

כִּי אָבְדָה conj.-Qal pf. 3 f.s. (1) *that ... is ruined*

מִצְרָיִם pr.n. paus. (595) *Egypt*

10:8

וַיּוּשַׁב consec.-Ho. impf. 3 m.s. (שׁוּב I 962) *so ... were brought back*

אֶת־מֹשֶׁה dir.obj.-pr.n. (602) *Moses*

וְאֶת־אַהֲרֹן conj.-dir.obj.-pr.n. (14) *and Aaron*

אֶל־פַּרְעֹה prep.-pr.n. (829) *to Pharaoh*

וַיֹּאמֶר consec.-Qal impf. 3 m.s. (55) *and he said*

אֲלֵהֶם prep.-3 m.p. sf. *to them*

לְכוּ Qal impv. 2 m.p. (הָלַךְ 229) *Go*

עִבְדוּ Qal impv.2 m.p. (712) *serve*

אֶת־יהוה dir.obj.-pr.n. (217) *Yahweh*

אֱלֹהֵיכֶם n.m.p.-2 m.p. sf. *your God*

מִי וָמִי interr. (566)-conj.-interr. (566) *but who*

הַהֹלְכִים def.art.-Qal act. ptc. m.p. (הָלַךְ 229) *are to go*

10:9

וַיֹּאמֶר consec.-Qal impf. 3 m.s. (55) *and ... said*

מֹשֶׁה pr.n. (602) *Moses*

בִּנְעָרֵינוּ prep.-n.m.p.-1 c.p. sf. (654) *with our young*

וּבִזְקֵנֵינוּ conj.-prep.-n.m.p.-1 c.p. sf. (278) *and (with) our old*

נֵלֵךְ Qal impf. 1 c.p. (הָלַךְ 229) *we will go*

בְּבָנֵינוּ prep.-n.m.p.-1 c.p. sf. (119) *with our sons*

וּבִבְנוֹתֵנוּ conj.-prep.-n.f.p.-1 c .p. sf. (I 123) *and (with our) daughters*

בְּצֹאנֵנוּ prep.-n.f.s.-1 c.p. sf. (838) *with our flocks*

וּבִבְקָרֵנוּ conj.-prep.-n.m.s.-1 c.p. sf. (133) *and herds*

נֵלֵךְ v.supra *we will go*

כִּי חַג־יהוה conj.-n.m.s. cstr. (290)-pr.n. (217) *for a feast to Yahweh*

לָנוּ prep.-1 c.p. sf. *we must hold*

10:10

וַיֹּאמֶר consec.-Qal impf. 3 m.s. (55) *and he said*

אֲלֵהֶם prep.-3 m.p. sf. *to them*

יְהִי Qal impf. 3 m.s. apoc. (הָיָה 224) *Let be*

כֵן adv. (485) *(so)*

יהוה pr.n. (217) *Yahweh*

עִמָּכֶם prep.-2 m.p. sf. *with you*

כַּאֲשֶׁר prep.-rel. *if ever (as)*

אֲשַׁלַּח Pi. impf. 1 c.s. (שָׁלַח 1018) *I let go*

אֶתְכֶם dir.obj.-2 m.p. sf. *you*

וְאֶת־טַפְּכֶם conj.-dir.obj.-n.m.s.-2 m.p. sf. (381) *and your little ones*

רְאוּ Qal impv. 2 m.p. (רָאָה 906) *Look*

כִּי רָעָה conj.-n.f.s. (948) *evil purpose*

נֶגֶד פְּנֵיכֶם prep.-n.m.p.-2 m.p. sf. (815) *in mind (before your faces)*

10:11

לֹא כֵן neg.-adv. (485) *No*

לְכוּ־נָא Qal impv. 2 m.p. (הָלַךְ 229)-part. of entreaty (609) *Go (I pray)*

הַגְּבָרִים def.art.-n.m.p. (149) *the men*

וְעִבְדוּ conj.-Qal impv. 2 m.p. (עָבַד 712) *and serve*

אֶת־יהוה dir.obj.-pr.n. (217) *Yahweh*

כִּי אֹתָהּ conj.-dir.obj.-3 f.s. sf. *for that*

אַתֶּם pers.pr. 2 m.p. (61) *you*

מְבַקְשִׁים Pi. ptc. m.p. (בָּקַשׁ 134) *desire*

וַיְגָרֶשׁ consec.-Pi. impf. 3 m.s. (גָּרַשׁ 176) *and he drove out*

אֹתָם dir.obj.-3 m.p. sf. *them*

מֵאֵת prep.-prep. (II 85) *from*

פְּנֵי n.m.p. cstr. (815) *presence (of)*

פַרְעֹה pr.n. (829) *Pharaoh*

10:12

וַיֹּאמֶר consec.-Qal impf. 3 m.s. (55) *then ... said*

יהוה pr.n. (217) *Yahweh*

אֶל־מֹשֶׁה prep.-pr.n. (602) *to Moses*

נְטֵה Qal impv. 2 m.s. (נָטָה 639) *Stretch out*

יָדְךָ n.f.s.-2 m.s. sf. (388) *your hand*

עַל־אֶרֶץ prep.-n.f.s. cstr. (75) *over the land of*

מִצְרַיִם pr.n. (595) *Egypt*

בָּאַרְבֶּה prep.-def.art.-n.m.s. (916) *for the locusts*

וְיַעַל conj.-Qal impf. 3 m.s. apoc (עָלָה 748) *that they may come up*

עַל־אֶרֶץ v.supra *on the land of*

מִצְרָיִם pr.n. paus. (595) *Egypt*

וְיֹאכַל conj.-Qal impf. 3 m.s. (אָכַל 37) *and (may) eat*

אֶת־כָּל־ dir.obj.-n.m.s. cstr. (481) *every*

עֵשֶׂב n.m.s. cstr. (793) *plant in*

הָאָרֶץ def.art.-n.f.s. (75) *the land*

אֵת כָּל־ dir.obj.-n.m.s. (481) *all*

אֲשֶׁר rel. *that*

הִשְׁאִיר Hi. pf. 3 m.s. (שָׁאַר 983) *has left*

הַבָּרָד def.art.-n.m.s. (135) *the hail*

10:13

וַיֵּט consec.-Qal impf. 3 m.s. (נָטָה 639) *so ... stretched forth*

מֹשֶׁה pr.n. (602) *Moses*

אֶת־מַטֵּהוּ dir.obj.-n.m.s.-3 m.s. sf. (641) *his rod*

עַל־אֶרֶץ prep.-n.f.s. cstr. (75) *over the land of*

מִצְרַיִם pr.n. (595) *Egypt*

וַיהוה conj.-pr.n. (217) *and Yahweh*

נִהַג Pi. pf. 3 m.s. (נָהַג 624) *brought*

רוּחַ n.f.s. cstr. (924) *wind*

קָדִים n.m.s. (870) *east*

בָּאָרֶץ prep.-def.art.-n.f.s. (75) *upon the land*

כָּל־הַיּוֹם n.m.s. cstr. (481)-def.art.-n.m.s. (398) *all ... day*

הַהוּא def.art.-demons. adj. m.s. (214) *that*

וְכָל־הַלָּיְלָה conj.-n.m.s. cstr. (481)-def.art.-n.m.s. paus. (538) *and all that night*

הַבֹּקֶר def.art.-n.m.s. (133) *and when morning*

הָיָה Qal pf. 3 m.s. (224) *was*

וְרוּחַ conj.-v.supra *wind*

הַקָּדִים v.supra *east*

נָשָׂא Qal pf. 3 m.s. (669) *had brought*

אֶת־הָאַרְבֶּה dir.obj.-def.art.-n.m.s. (916) *the locusts*

10:14

וַיַּעַל consec.-Qal impf. 3 m.s. (עָלָה 748) *and ... came up*

הָאַרְבֶּה def.art.-n.m.s. (916) *the locusts*

עַל כָּל־אֶרֶץ prep.-n.m.s. cstr. (481)-n.f.s. cstr. (75) *over all the land of*

מִצְרַיִם pr.n. (595) *Egypt*

וַיָּנַח consec.-Qal impf. 3 m.s. (נוּחַ 628) *and settled*

בְּכֹל prep.-n.m.s. cstr. (481) *on the whole*

גְּבוּל n.m.s. cstr. (147) *country of*

מִצְרָיִם pr.n. paus. (595) *Egypt*

כָּבֵד adj. m.s. (458) *dense*

מְאֹד adv. (547) *very*

לְפָנָיו prep.-n.m.p.-3 m.s. sf. (815) *before him*

לֹא־הָיָה neg.-Qal pf. 3 m.s. (224) *had never been*

כֵּן adv. (485) *such*

אַרְבֶּה n.m.s. (916) *swarm of locusts*

כָּמֹהוּ prep.-3 m.s. sf. *(like it)*

וְאַחֲרָיו conj.-n.m.p.-3 m.s. sf. (29) *(after it) again*

לֹא יִהְיֶה־כֵּן neg.-Qal impf. 3 m.s. (224)-adv. (485) *nor ever shall be*

10:15

וַיְכַס consec.-Pi. impf. 3 m.s. (כָּסָה 491) *for they covered*

אֶת־עֵין dir.obj.-n.f.s. cstr. (744) *the face of*

כָּל־הָאָרֶץ n.m.s. cstr. (481)-def.art.-n.f.s. (75) *the whole land*

וַתֶּחְשַׁךְ consec. - Ho. impf. 3 f. s. (חָשַׁךְ 364) *so that ... was darkened*

הָאָרֶץ def.art.-n.f.s. (75) *the land*

וַיֹּאכַל consec.-Qal impf. 3 m.s. (אָכַל 37) *and they ate*

אֶת־כָּל־ dir.obj.-n.m.s. cstr. (481) *all*

עֵשֶׂב n.m.s. cstr. (793) *the plants in*

הָאָרֶץ def.art.-n.f.s. (75) *the land*

וְאֵת כָּל־ conj.-dir.obj.-n.m.s. cstr. (481) *and all*

פְּרִי הָעֵץ n.m.s. cstr. (826)-def.art.-n.m.s. (781) *the fruit of the trees*

אֲשֶׁר rel. *which*

הוֹתִיר Hi. pf. 3 m.s. (יָתַר 451) *had left*

הַבָּרָד def.art.-n.m.s. (135) *the hail*

וְלֹא־נוֹתַר conj.-neg.-Ni. pf. 3 m.s. (יָתַר 451) *not remained*

כָּל־יֶרֶק n.m.s. cstr. (481)-n.m.s. (438) *a green thing*

בָּעֵץ prep.-def.art.-n.m.s. (781) *neither tree*

וּבְעֵשֶׂב conj.-prep.-n.m.s. cstr. (793) *nor plant of*

הַשָּׂדֶה def.art.-n.m.s. (961) *the field*

בְּכָל־אֶרֶץ prep.-n.m.s. cstr. (481)-n.f.s. cstr. (75) *through all the land of*

מִצְרָיִם pr.n. paus. (595) *Egypt*

10:16

וַיְמַהֵר consec.-Pi. impf. 3 m.s. (I 554) *then in haste*

פַּרְעֹה pr.n. (829) *Pharaoh*

לִקְרֹא prep.-Qal inf. cstr. (894) *called*

לְמֹשֶׁה prep.-pr.n. (602) *Moses*

וּלְאַהֲרֹן conj.-prep.-pr.n. (14) *and Aaron*

וַיֹּאמֶר consec.-Qal impf. 3 m.s. (55) *and said*

חָטָאתִי Qal pf. 1 c.s. (חָטָא 306) *I have sinned*

ליהוה prep.-pr.n. (217) *against Yahweh*

אֱלֹהֵיכֶם n.m.p.-2 m.p. sf. (43) *your God*

וְלָכֶם conj.-prep.-2 m.p. sf. *and against you*

10:17

וְעַתָּה conj.-adv. (773) *now therefore*

שָׂא נָא Qal impv. 2 m.s. (נָשָׂא 669)-part. of entreaty (609) *forgive I pray you*

חַטָּאתִי n.f.s.-1 c.s. sf. (308) *my sin*

אַךְ adv. (36) *only*

הַפַּעַם def.art.-n.m.s. (821) *this once*

וְהַעְתִּירוּ conj.-Hi. impv. 2 m.p. (עָתַר I 801) *and entreat*

ליהוה prep.-pr.n. (217) *Yahweh*

אֱלֹהֵיכֶם n.m.p.-2 m.p. sf. *your God*

וְיָסֵר conj.-Hi. impf.3 m.s. apoc. (סוּר 693) *to remove*

מֵעָלַי prep.-prep.-1 c.s. sf. *from me*

רַק adv. (956) *only*

אֶת־הַמָּוֶת dir.obj.-def.art.-n.m.s. (560) *death*

הַזֶּה def.art.-demons. adj. m.s. (260) *this*

10:18

וַיֵּצֵא consec.-Qal impf. 3 m.s. (יָצָא 422) *so he went out*

מֵעִם פַּרְעֹה prep.-prep.-pr.n. (829) *from Pharaoh*

וַיֶּעְתַּר consec. - Qal impf. 3 m. s. (עָתַר I 801) *and entreated*

אֶל־יהוה prep.-pr.n. (217) *Yahweh*

10:19

וַיַּהֲפֹךְ consec.-Qal impf. 3 m.s. (הָפַךְ 245) *and ... turned*

יהוה pr.n. (217) *Yahweh*

רוּחַ־יָם n.f.s. cstr. (924)-n.m.s. (410) *west wind*

חָזָק מְאֹד adj. (305)-adv. (547) *very strong*

וַיִּשָּׂא consec.-Qal impf. 3 m.s. (נָשָׂא 669) *which lifted*

אֶת־הָאַרְבֶּה dir.obj.-def.art.-n.m.s. (916) *the locusts*

וַיִּתְקָעֵהוּ consec.-Qal impf. 3 m.s.-3 m.s. sf. (תָּקַע 1075) *and drove them*

יָמָּה n.m.s.-dir.he (410) *into the Sea*

סוּף n.m.s. (I 693) *Red*

לֹא נִשְׁאַר neg.-Ni. pf. 3 m.s. (שָׁאַר 983) *not ... was left*

אַרְבֶּה n.m.s. (916) *locust*

אֶחָד num. adj. (25) *a single*

בְּכֹל גְּבוּל prep.-n.m.s. cstr. (481)-n.m.s. cstr. (147) *in all the country of*

מִצְרָיִם pr.n. paus. (595) *Egypt*

10:20

וַיְחַזֵּק consec.-Pi. impf. 3 m.s. (304) *but ... hardened*

יהוה pr.n. (217) *Yahweh*

אֶת־לֵב dir.obj.-n.m.s. cstr. (523) *heart (of)*

פַּרְעֹה pr.n. (829) *Pharaoh*

וְלֹא שִׁלַּח conj.-neg. -Pi. pf. 3 m.s. (1018) *and he did not let go*

אֶת־בְּנֵי dir.obj.-n.m.p. cstr. (119) *the children of*

יִשְׂרָאֵל pr.n. (975) *Israel*

10:21

וַיֹּאמֶר consec.-Qal impf. 3 m.s. (55) *then ... said*

יהוה pr.n. (217) *Yahweh*

אֶל־מֹשֶׁה prep.-pr.n. (602) *to Moses*

נְטֵה Qal impv. 2 m.s. (נָטָה 639) *stretch out*

יָדְךָ n.f.s.-2 m.s. sf. (388) *your hand*

עַל־הַשָּׁמַיִם prep.-def.art.-n.m. du. (1029) *toward heaven*

וִיהִי conj.-Qal impf. 3 m.s. apoc. (הָיָה 224) *that there may be*

חֹשֶׁךְ n.m.s. (365) *darkness*

עַל־אֶרֶץ prep.-n.f.s. cstr. (75) *over the land of*

מִצְרָיִם pr.n. paus. (595) *Egypt*

וְיָמֵשׁ conj.-Hi. impf. 3 m.s. apoc. (מָשַׁשׁ 606) *to be felt*

חֹשֶׁךְ v.supra *a darkness*

10:22

וַיֵּט consec.-Qal impf. 3 m.s. (נָטָה 639) *so ... stretched out*

מֹשֶׁה pr.n. (602) *Moses*

אֶת־יָדוֹ dir.obj.-n.f.s.-3 m.s. sf. (388) *his hand*

עַל־הַשָּׁמָיִם prep.-def.art.-n.m. du. paus. (1029) *toward heaven*

וַיְהִי consec.-Qal impf. 3 m.s. (הָיָה 224) *and there was*

חֹשֶׁךְ־אֲפֵלָה n.m.s. cstr. (365)-n.f.s. (66) *thick darkness*

בְּכָל־אֶרֶץ prep.-n.m.s. cstr. (481)-n.f.s. cstr. (75) *in all the land of*

מִצְרַיִם pr.n. (595) *Egypt*

שְׁלֹשֶׁת num. f.s. cstr. (1025) *three*

יָמִים n.m.p. (398) *days*

10:23

לֹא־רָאוּ neg.-Qal pf. 3 c.p. (רָאָה 906) *they did not see*

אִישׁ n.m.s. (35) *one*

אֶת־אָחִיו dir.obj.-n.m.s.-3 m.s. sf. (26) *another (his brother)*

וְלֹא־קָמוּ conj.-neg.-Qal pf. 3 c.p. (קוּם 877) *nor did arise*

אִישׁ v.supra *any*

מִתַּחְתָּיו prep.-prep.-3 m.s. sf. (1065) *from his place*

שְׁלֹשֶׁת num. f.s. cstr. (1025) *three*

יָמִים n.m.p. (398) *days*

וּלְכָל־בְּנֵי conj.-prep.-n.m.s. cstr. (481)-n.m.p. cstr. (119) *but all the people of*

יִשְׂרָאֵל pr.n. (975) *Israel*

הָיָה Qal pf. 3 m.s. (224) *had*

אוֹר n.m.s. (21) *light*

בְּמוֹשְׁבֹתָם prep.-n.f.p.-3 m.p. sf. (444) *where they dwelt*

10:24

וַיִּקְרָא consec.-Qal impf. 3 m.s. (894) *then ... called*

פַּרְעֹה pr.n. (829) *Pharaoh*

אֶל־מֹשֶׁה prep.-pr.n. (602) *Moses*

וַיֹּאמֶר consec.-Qal impf. 3 m.s. (55) *and said*

לְכוּ Qal impv. 2 m.p. (הָלַךְ 229) *Go*

עִבְדוּ Qal impv. 2 m.p. (עָבַד 712) *serve*

אֶת־יהוה dir.obj.-pr.n. (217) *Yahweh*

רַק adv. (956) *only*

צֹאנְכֶם n.f.s.-2 m.p. sf. (838) *your flocks*

וּבְקַרְכֶם conj.-n.m.s.-2 m.p. sf. (133) *and your herds*

יֻצָּג Ho. impf. 3 m.s. paus. (יָצַג 426) *let remain behind*

גַּם־טַפְּכֶם adv. (168)-n.m.s.-2 m.p. sf. (381) *your children also*

יֵלֵךְ Qal impf. 3 m.s. (הָלַךְ 229) *may go*

עִמָּכֶם prep.-2 m.p. sf. *with you*

10:25

וַיֹּאמֶר consec.-Qal impf. 3 m.s. (55) *but ... said*

מֹשֶׁה pr.n. (602) *Moses*

גַּם־אַתָּה adv. (168)-pers.pr. 2 m.s. (61) *You also*

תִּתֵּן Qal impf. 2 m.s. (נָתַן 678) *must let*

בְּיָדֵנוּ prep.-n.f.s.-1 c.p. sf. (388) *us have (in our hands)*

זְבָחִים n.m.p. (257) *sacrifices*

וְעֹלוֹת conj.-n.f.p. (750) *and burnt offerings*

וְעָשִׂינוּ conj.-Qal pf. 1 c.p. (עָשָׂה I 793) *that we may sacrifice*

ליהוה prep.-pr.n. (217) *to Yahweh*

אֱלֹהֵינוּ n.m.p.-1 c.p. sf. (43) *our God*

10:26

וְגַם־מִקְנֵנוּ conj.-adv. (168)-n.m.s.-1 c.p. sf. (889) *our cattle also*

יֵלֵךְ Qal impf. 3 m.s. (הָלַךְ 229) *must go*

עִמָּנוּ prep.-1 c.p. sf. *with us*

לֹא תִשָּׁאֵר neg.-Ni. impf. 3 f.s. (983) *shall not be left behind*

פַּרְסָה n.f.s. (828) *a hoof*

כִּי מִמֶּנּוּ conj.-prep.-3 m.s. sf. *for of them*

נִקַּח Qal impf. 1 c.p. (לָקַח 542) *we must take*

לַעֲבֹד prep.-Qal inf. cstr. (712) *to serve*

אֶת־יהוה dir.obj.-pr.n. (217) *Yahweh*

אֱלֹהֵינוּ n.m.p.-1 c.p. sf. (43) *our God*

וַאֲנַחְנוּ conj.-pers.pr. 1 c.p. (59) *and we*

לֹא־נֵדַע neg.-Qal impf. 1 c.p. (יָדַע 393) *do not know*

מַה־נַּעֲבֹד interr. (552)-Qal impf. 1 c.p. (עָבַד 712) *with what we must serve*

אֶת־יהוה dir.obj.-pr.n. (217) *Yahweh*

עַד־בֹּאֵנוּ prep.-Qal inf. cstr.- 1 c.p. sf. (בּוֹא 97) *until we arrive*

שָׁמָּה adv.-dir. he (1027) *there*

10:27

וַיְחַזֵּק consec.-Pi. impf. 3 m.s. (חָזַק 304) *but ... hardened*

יהוה pr.n. (217) *Yahweh*

אֶת־לֵב dir.obj.-n.m.s. cstr. (523) *heart (of)*

פַּרְעֹה pr.n. (829) *Pharaoh*

וְלֹא אָבָה conj.-neg.-Qal pf. 3 m.s. (אָבָה 2) *and he would not let*

לְשַׁלְּחָם prep.-Pi. inf. cstr.-3 m.p. sf. (שָׁלַח 1018) *them go*

10:28

וַיֹּאמֶר־לוֹ consec.-Qal impf. 3 m.s. (55)-prep.-3 m.s. sf. *then ... said to him*

פַּרְעֹה pr.n. (829) *Pharaoh*

לֵךְ Qal impv. 2 m.s. (הָלַךְ 229) *Get away*

מֵעָלָי prep.-prep.-1 c.s. sf. paus. *from me*

הִשָּׁמֶר Ni. impv. 2 m.s. (1036) *Take heed*

לְךָ prep.-2 m.s. sf. *to yourself*

אַל־תֹּסֶף neg.-Hi. impf. 2 m.s. apoc. (יָסַף 414) *never again*

רְאוֹת Qal inf. cstr. (רָאָה 906) *see*

פָּנַי n.m.p.-1 c.s. sf. (815) *my face*

כִּי בְּיוֹם conj.-prep.-n.m.s. cstr. (398) *for in the day (of)*

רְאֹתְךָ Qal inf. cstr.-2 m.s. sf. (רָאָה 906) *you see*

פָּנַי v. supra *my face*

תָּמוּת Qal impf. 2 m.s. (מוּת 559) *you shall die*

10:29

וַיֹּאמֶר consec.-Qal impf. 3 m.s. (55) *said*

מֹשֶׁה pr.n. (602) *Moses*

כֵּן adv. (485) *As*

דִּבַּרְתָּ Pi. pf. 2 m.s. (180) *you say*

לֹא־אֹסִף neg.-Hi. impf. 1 c.s. (יָסַף 414) *I will not again*

עוֹד adv. (728) *again*

רְאוֹת Qal inf. cstr. (רָאָה 906) *see*

פָּנֶיךָ n.m.p.-2 m.s. sf. (815) *your face*

11:1

וַיֹּאמֶר consec.-Qal impf. 3 m.s. (55) *said*

יהוה pr.n. (217) *Yahweh*

אֶל־מֹשֶׁה prep.-pr.n. (602) *to Moses*

עוֹד adv. (728) *Yet ... more*

נֶגַע אֶחָד n.m.s. (619)-num. (25) *one plague*

אָבִיא Hi. impf. 1 c.s. (בּוֹא 97) *I will bring*

עַל־פַּרְעֹה prep.-pr.n. (829) *upon Pharaoh*

וְעַל־מִצְרַיִם conj.-prep.-pr.n. (595) *and upon Egypt*

אַחֲרֵי־כֵן prep. cstr. (29)-adv. (485) *afterwards*

יְשַׁלַּח Pi. impf. 3 m.s. (1018) *he will let go*

אֶתְכֶם dir. obj.-2 m.p. sf. *you*

מִזֶּה prep.-demons. adj. m.s. (260) *hence*

כְּשַׁלְּחוֹ prep.-Pi. inf. cstr.-3 m.s. sf. (שָׁלַח 1018) *when he lets go*

כָּלָה adv. (478) *completely*

גָּרֵשׁ יְגָרֵשׁ Pi. inf. abs. (גָּרַשׁ 176)-Pi. impf. 3 m.s. (176) *he will drive*

אֶתְכֶם dir. obj.-2 m.p. sf. *you*

מִזֶּה v. supra *(hence)*

11:2

דַּבֶּר־נָא Pi. impv. 2 m.s. (180)-part. of entreaty (609) *speak now*

בְּאָזְנֵי prep.-n.f. du. cstr. (23) *in the hearing of*

הָעָם def. art.-n.m.s. (I 766) *the people*

וְיִשְׁאֲלוּ conj.-Qal impf. 3 m.p. (שָׁאַל 981) *that they ask*

אִישׁ n.m.s. (35) *every man*

מֵאֵת רֵעֵהוּ prep.-prep. (II 85)-n.m.s.-3 m.s. sf. (945) *of his neighbor*

וְאִשָּׁה conj.-n.f.s. (61) *and every woman*

מֵאֵת רְעוּתָהּ prep.-prep. (II 85)-n.f.s.-3 f.s. sf. (945) *of her neighbor*

כְּלֵי־כֶסֶף n.m.p. cstr. (479)-n.m.s. (494) *jewelry of silver*

וּכְלֵי זָהָב conj.-v. supra-n.m.s. (262) *and (vessels) of gold*

11:3

וַיִּתֵּן consec.-Qal impf. 3 m.s. (נָתַן 678) *and ... gave*

יהוה pr.n. (217) *Yahweh*

אֶת־חֵן dir. obj.-n.m.s. cstr. (336) *favor of*

הָעָם def. art.-n.m.s. (I 766) *the people*

בְּעֵינֵי prep.-n.f.p. cstr. (744) *in the sight of*

מִצְרָיִם pr.n. paus. (595) *the Egyptians*

גַּם הָאִישׁ adv. (168)-def. art.-n.m.s. (35) *Moreover, the man*

מֹשֶׁה pr.n. (602) *Moses*

גָּדוֹל מְאֹד adj. m.s. (152)-adv. (547) *very great*

בְּאֶרֶץ prep.-n.f.s. cstr. (75) *in the land of*

מִצְרַיִם pr.n. (595) *Egypt*

בְּעֵינֵי v. supra *in the sight of*

עַבְדֵי־ n.m.p. cstr. (712) *servants (of)*

פַּרְעֹה pr.n. (829) *Pharaoh*

וּבְעֵינֵי conj.-v. supra *and in the sight of*

הָעָם v. supra *the people*

11:4

וַיֹּאמֶר consec.-Qal impf. 3 m.s. (55) *and ... said*

מֹשֶׁה pr.n. (602) *Moses*

כֹּה אָמַר adv. (462)-Qal pf. 3 m.s. (55) *Thus says*

יהוה pr.n. (217) *Yahweh*

כַּחֲצֹת prep.-n.f.p. cstr. (345) *about mid-*

הַלַּיְלָה def. art.-n.m.s. (538) *night*

אֲנִי pers. pr. 1 c.s. (58) *I*

יוֹצֵא Qal act. ptc. (יָצָא 422) *will go forth*

בְּתוֹךְ prep.-n.m.s. cstr. (1063) *in the midst of*

מִצְרָיִם pr.n. paus. (595) *Egypt*

11:5

וּמֵת conj.-Qal pf. 3 m.s. (מוּת 559) *and ... shall die*

כָּל־בְּכוֹר n.m.s. cstr. (481)-n.m.s. (114) *all the first-born*

בְּאֶרֶץ prep.-n.f.s. cstr. (75) *in the land of*

מִצְרַיִם pr.n. (595) *Egypt*

מִבְּכוֹר prep.-n.m.s. cstr. (114) *from the first-born of*

פַּרְעֹה pr.n. (829) *Pharaoh*

הַיֹּשֵׁב def. art.-Qal act. ptc. (יָשַׁב 442) *who sits*

עַל־כִּסְאוֹ prep.-n.m.s.-3 m.s. sf. (490) *on the throne (of him)*

עַד בְּכוֹר prep. (III 723)-n.m.s. cstr. (114) *even to the first-born of*

הַשִּׁפְחָה def. art.-n.f.s. (1046) *the maidservant*

אֲשֶׁר rel. *who*

אַחַר prep. (29) *behind*

הָרֵחָיִם def. art.-n.m. du. paus. (932) *the mill*

וְכֹל בְּכוֹר conj.-n.m.s. cstr. (481)-n.m.s. cstr. (114) *and all the first-born of*

בְּהֵמָה n.f.s. (96) *cattle*

11:6

וְהָיְתָה conj.-Qal pf. 3 f.s. (הָיָה 224) *and there shall be*

צְעָקָה n.f.s. (858) *a ... cry*

גְדֹלָה adj. f.s. (152) *great*

בְּכָל־אֶרֶץ prep.-n.m.s. cstr. (481)-n.f.s. cstr. (75) *throughout all the land of*

מִצְרָיִם pr.n. paus. (595) *Egypt*

אֲשֶׁר כָּמֹהוּ rel.-prep.-3 m.s. sf. *such as there*

לֹא נִהְיָתָה neg.-Ni. pf. 3 f.s. (הָיָה 224) *has never been*

וְכָמֹהוּ conj.-prep.-3 m.s. sf. *nor (as there)*

לֹא תֹסִף neg.-Hi. impf. 3 f.s. (יָסַף 414) *ever shall be again*

11:7

וּלְכֹל בְּנֵי conj.-n.m.s. cstr. (481)-n.m.p. cstr. (119) *but against any of the people of*

יִשְׂרָאֵל pr.n. (975) *Israel*

לֹא יֶחֱרַץ־ neg.-Qal impf. 3 m.s. (חָרַץ I 358) *not shall growl (sharpen)*

כֶּלֶב n.m.s. (476) *a dog*

לְשֹׁנוֹ n.f.s.-3 m.s. sf. (546) *(his tongue)*

לְמֵאִישׁ prep.-prep.-n.m.s. (35) *either man*

וְעַד־בְּהֵמָה conj.-prep. (III 723)-n.f.s. (96) *or beast*

לְמַעַן prep.-prep. (775) *that*

תֵּדְעוּן Qal impf. 2 m.p. (יָדַע 393) *you may know*

אֲשֶׁר rel. *that*

יַפְלֶה Hi. impf. 3 m.s. (פָּלָה 811) *makes a distinction*

יהוה pr.n. (217) *Yahweh*

בֵּין מִצְרַיִם prep. (107)-pr.n. (595) *between the Egyptians*

וּבֵין יִשְׂרָאֵל conj.-prep. (107)-pr.n. (975) *and Israel*

11:8

וְיָרְדוּ conj.-Qal pf. 3 c.p. (יָרַד 432) *and ... shall come down*

כָל־עֲבָדֶיךָ n.m.s. cstr. (481)-n.m.p.-2 m.s. sf. (712) *all ... your servants*

אֵלֶּה demons. c.p. (41) *these*

אֵלַי prep.1 c.s. sf. *to me*

וְהִשְׁתַּחֲווּ־ conj.-Hithpalel pf. 3 c.p. (שָׁחָה 1005) *and bow down*

לִי prep.-1 c.s. sf. *to me*

לֵאמֹר prep.-Qal inf. cstr. (55) *saying*

צֵא אַתָּה Qal impv. 2 m.s. (יָצָא 422)-pers.pr. 2 m.s. (61) *Get you out*

וְכָל־הָעָם conj.-n.m.s. cstr. (481)-def.art.-n.m.s. (I 766) *and all the people*

אֲשֶׁר־ rel. *who*

בְּרַגְלֶיךָ prep.-n.f.p.-2 m.s. sf. (919) *follow you (at your feet)*

וְאַחֲרֵי־כֵן conj.-prep.- (29)-adv. (485) *and after that*

אֵצֵא Qal impf. 1 c.s. (יָצָא 422) *I will go out*

וַיֵּצֵא consec.-Qal impf. 3 m.s. (יָצָא 422) *and he went out*

מֵעִם־פַּרְעֹה prep.-prep.-pr.n. (829) *from Pharaoh*

בָּחֳרִי־אָף prep.-n.m.s. cstr. (354)-n.m.s. paus. (I 60) *hot anger*

11:9

וַיֹּאמֶר consec.-Qal impf. 3 m.s. (55) *then ... said*

יהוה pr.n. (217) *Yahweh*

אֶל־מֹשֶׁה prep.-pr.n. (602) *to Moses*

לֹא־יִשְׁמַע neg.-Qal impf. 3 m.s. (1033) *will not listen*

אֲלֵיכֶם prep.-2 m.p. sf. *to you*

פַּרְעֹה pr.n. (829) *Pharaoh*

לְמַעַן prep.-prep. (775) *that*

רְבוֹת Qal inf. cstr. (רָבָה I 915) *may be multiplied*

מוֹפְתַי n.m.p.-1 c.s. sf. (68) *my wonders*

בְּאֶרֶץ prep.-n.f.s. cstr. (75) *in the land of*

מִצְרָיִם pr.n. paus. (595) *Egypt*

11:10

וּמֹשֶׁה conj.-pr.n. (602) *Moses*

וְאַהֲרֹן conj.-pr.n. (14) *and Aaron*

עָשׂוּ Qal pf. 3 c.p. (עָשָׂה I 793) *did*
אֶת־כָּל־ dir.obj.-n.m.s. cstr. (481) *all*
הַמֹּפְתִים def.art.-n.m.p. (68) *signs*
הָאֵלֶּה def.art.-demons. adj. c.p. (41) *these*
לִפְנֵי prep.-n.m.p. cstr. (815) *before*
פַּרְעֹה prep. (829) *Pharaoh*
וַיְחַזֵּק consec.-Pi. impf. 3 m.s. (חָזַק 304) *and ... hardened*
יהוה pr.n. (217) *Yahweh*
אֶת־לֵב dir.obj.-n.m.s. cstr. (523) *heart (of)*
פַּרְעֹה pr.n. (829) *Pharaoh*
וְלֹא־שִׁלַּח conj.-neg.-Pi. pf. 3 m.s. (1018) *and he did not let go*
אֶת־בְּנֵי־ dir.obj.-n.m.p. cstr. (119) *the people of*
יִשְׂרָאֵל pr.n. (975) *Israel*
מֵאַרְצוֹ prep.-n.f.s.-3 m.s. sf. (75) *out of his land*

12:1

וַיֹּאמֶר consec.-Qal impf. 3 m.s. (55) *said*
יהוה pr.n. (217) *Yahweh*
אֶל־מֹשֶׁה prep.-pr.n. (602) *to Moses*
וְאֶל־אַהֲרֹן conj.-prep.-pr.n. (14) *and Aaron*
בְּאֶרֶץ prep.-n.f.s. cstr. (75) *in the land of*
מִצְרַיִם pr.n. (595) *Egypt*
לֵאמֹר prep.-Qal inf. cstr. (55) *(saying)*

12:2

הַחֹדֶשׁ הַזֶּה def.art.-n.m.s. (II 294)-def.art.-demons. adj. m.s. (260) *this month*
לָכֶם prep.-2 m.p. sf. *for you*
רֹאשׁ n.m.s. cstr. (910) *the beginning of*
חֳדָשִׁים n.m.p. (II 294) *months*
רִאשׁוֹן adj. m.s. (911) *the first*
הוּא לָכֶם pers. pr. 3 m.s. (214)-prep.-2 m.p. sf. *it ... for you*
לְחָדְשֵׁי prep.-n.m.p. cstr. (II 294) *month of*
הַשָּׁנָה def. art.-n.f.s. (1040) *the year*

12:3

דַּבְּרוּ Pi. impv. 2 m.p. (180) *Tell*
אֶל־כָּל־עֲדַת prep.-n.m.s. cstr. (481)-n.f.s. cstr. (II 417) *all the congregation of*
יִשְׂרָאֵל pr.n. (975) *Israel*
לֵאמֹר prep.-Qal inf. cstr. (55) *(saying)*
בֶּעָשֹׂר prep.-def. art.-num. (7970 *on the tenth day*
לַחֹדֶשׁ הַזֶּה prep.-def. art.-n.m.s. (II 294)-def. art.-demons. adj. m.s. (260) *of this month*
וְיִקְחוּ conj.-Qal impf. 3 m.p. (לָקַח 542) *they shall take*
לָהֶם prep.-3 m.p. sf. *(to them)*
אִישׁ n.m.s. (35) *every man*
שֶׂה n.m.s. (961) *a lamb*
לְבֵית־אָבֹת prep.-n.m.s. cstr. (108)-n.m.p. (3) *to father's houses*
שֶׂה v. supra *a lamb*
לַבָּיִת prep.-def.art.-n.m.s. paus. (108) *for a household*

12:4

וְאִם־יִמְעַט conj.-hypoth. part. (49)-Qal impf. 3 m.s. (מָעַט 589) *and if ... is too small*
הַבַּיִת def. art.-n.m.s. (108) *the household*
מִהְיֹת מִשֶּׂה prep.-Qal inf. cstr. (הָיָה 224)-prep.-n.m.s. (961) *for a lamb*
וְלָקַח conj.-Qal pf. 3 m.s. (542) *then ... shall take*
הוּא וּשְׁכֵנוֹ pers. pr. 3 m.s. (214)-conj.-adj. m.s.-3 m.s. sf. (1015) *a man and his neighbor*
הַקָּרֹב def art.-adj. (898) *next (the nearest)*
אֶל־בֵּיתוֹ prep.-n.m.s.-3 m.s. sf. (108) *to his house*
בְּמִכְסַת prep.-n.f.s. cstr. (493) *according to the number of*
נְפָשֹׁת n.f.p. (659) *persons*
אִישׁ n.m.s. (35) *each*
לְפִי אָכְלוֹ prep.-n.m.s. cstr. (804)-

Qal inf. cstr.-3 m.s. sf. (37) *according to what ... can eat*

תָּכֹסּוּ Qal impf. 2 m.p. (כָּסַס 493) *you shall make your count*

עַל־הַשֶּׂה prep.-def. art.-n.m.s. (961) *for the lamb*

12:5

שֶׂה תָמִים n.m.s. (961)-adj. m.s. (1071) *lamb without blemish*

זָכָר n.m.s. (271) *a male*

בֶּן־שָׁנָה n.m.s. cstr. (119)-n.f.s. (1040) *a year old*

יִהְיֶה לָכֶם Qal impf. 3 m.s. (224)-prep.-2 m.p. sf. *your ... shall be*

מִן־הַכְּבָשִׂים prep.-def. art.-n.m.p. (461) *from the sheep*

וּמִן־הָעִזִּים conj.-prep.-def. art.-n.f.p. (777) *or from the goats*

תִּקָּחוּ Qal impf. 2 m.p. paus. (לָקַח 542) *you shall take*

12:6

וְהָיָה לָכֶם conj.-Qal pf. 3 m.s. (224)-prep.-2 m.p. sf. *and you shall*

לְמִשְׁמֶרֶת prep.-n.f.s. (1038) *keep*

עַד אַרְבָּעָה prep.(III 723) - num. f.s. (916) *until four-*

עָשָׂר יוֹם num. (797)-n.m.s. (398) *teenth day*

לַחֹדֶשׁ הַזֶּה prep.-def. art.-n.m.s. (II 294)-def. art.-demons. adj. m.s. (260) *of this month*

וְשָׁחֲטוּ conj.-Qal pf. 3 c.p. (שָׁחַט 1006) *when ... shall kill*

אֹתוֹ dir. obj.-3 m.s. sf. *their lambs (it)*

כֹּל קְהַל n.m.s. cstr. (481)-n.m.s. ctr. (874) *the whole assembly of*

עֲדַת־יִשְׂרָאֵל n.f.s. cstr. (II 417)-pr.n. (975) *the congregation of Israel*

בֵּין הָעַרְבָּיִם prep. (107)-def. art.-n.f.p. (787) *in the evening*

12:7

וְלָקְחוּ conj.-Qal pf. 3 c.p. (לָקַח 542) *then they shall take*

מִן־הַדָּם prep.-def. art.-n.m.s. (196) *some of the blood*

וְנָתְנוּ conj.-Qal pf. 3 c.p. (נָתַן 678) *and put*

עַל־שְׁתֵּי prep.-num. p. cstr. (1040) *on the two (of)*

הַמְּזוּזֹת def. art.-n.f.p. (265) *doorposts*

וְעַל־הַמַּשְׁקוֹף conj.-prep.-def. art.-n.m.s. (1054) *and the lintel*

עַל הַבָּתִּים prep.-def. art.-n.m.p. (108) *of the houses*

אֲשֶׁר־ rel. *which*

יֹאכְלוּ Qal impf. 3 m.p. (37) *they eat*

אֹתוֹ dir. obj.-3 m.s. sf. *them*

בָּהֶם prep.-3 m.p. sf. *in (them)*

12:8

וְאָכְלוּ conj.-Qal pf. 3 c.p. (37) *they shall eat*

אֶת־הַבָּשָׂר dir. obj.-def. art.-n.m.s. (142) *the flesh*

בַּלַּיְלָה הַזֶּה prep.-def. art.-n.m.s. (538)-def. art.-demon. adj. m.s. (260) *that night*

צְלִי־אֵשׁ n.m.s. cstr. (852)-n.f.s. (77) *roasted (of fire)*

וּמַצּוֹת conj.-n.f.p. (595) *with unleavened bread*

עַל־מְרֹרִים prep.-n.m.p. (601) *bitter herbs*

יֹאכְלֻהוּ Qal impf. 3 c.p.-3 m.s. sf. (37) *they shall eat it*

12:9

אַל־תֹּאכְלוּ neg.-Qal impf. 3 m.p. (37) *Do not eat*

מִמֶּנּוּ prep.-3 m.s. sf. *of it*

נָא part. of entreaty (609)

וּבָשֵׁל מְבֻשָּׁל conj.-adj. (143)-Pu. ptc. (143) *or boiled*

בַּמָּיִם prep.-def. art.-n.m.p. paus. (565) *with water*

כִּי אִם־ conj.-hypcth. part. (49) *but*

צְלִי־אֵשׁ v. 12:8 *roasted*

רֹאשׁוֹ n.m.s.-3 m.s. sf. (910) *its head*

עַל־כְּרָעָיו prep.-n.f.du.-3 m.s. sf. (502) *with its legs*

וְעַל־קִרְבּוֹ conj.-prep.-n.m.s.-3 m.s. sf. (899) *and its inner parts*

12:10

וְלֹא־תוֹתִירוּ conj.-neg.-Hi. impf. 2

m.p. (יָתַר 451) *and you shall let none remain*

מִמֶּנּוּ prep.-3 m.s. sf. *of it*

עַד־בֹּקֶר prep.-n.m.s. (133) *until the morning*

וְהַנֹּתָר conj.-def. art.-Ni. ptc. (יָתַר 451) *and anything that remains*

מִמֶּנּוּ v. supra *(of it)*

עַד־בֹּקֶר v. supra *until the morning*

בָּאֵשׁ prep.-def. art.-n.f.s. (77) *(in the fire)*

תִּשְׂרֹפוּ Qal impf. 2 m.p. paus. (שָׂרַף 976) *you shall burn*

12:11

וְכָכָה conj.-adv. (462) *in this manner*

תֹּאכְלוּ Qal impf. 2 m.p. (37) *you shall eat*

אֹתוֹ dir.obj.-3 m.s. sf. *it*

מָתְנֵיכֶם n.m.p.-2 m.p. sf. (608) *your loins*

חֲגֻרִים Qal pass. ptc. m.p. (חָגַר 291) *girded*

נַעֲלֵיכֶם n.m. du.-2 m.p. sf. (653) *your sandals*

בְּרַגְלֵיכֶם prep.-n.f. du.-2 m.p. sf. (919) *on your feet*

וּמַקֶּלְכֶם conj.-n.m.s.-2 m.p. sf. (596) *and your staff*

בְּיֶדְכֶם prep.-n.f.s.-2 m.s. sf. (388) *in your hand*

וַאֲכַלְתֶּם conj.-Qal pf. 2 m.p. (37) *and you shall eat*

אֹתוֹ dir.obj.-3 m.s. sf. *it*

בְּחִפָּזוֹן prep.-n.m.s. (342) *in haste*

פֶּסַח n.m.s. (820) *passover*

הוּא pers.pr. 3 m.s. (214) *it*

ליהוה prep.-pr.n. (217) *Yahweh's*

12:12

וְעָבַרְתִּי conj.-Qal pf. 1 c.s. (עָבַר 716) *for I will pass through*

בְאֶרֶץ־ prep.-n.f.s. cstr. (75) *the land of*

מִצְרַיִם pr.n. (595) *Egypt*

בַּלַּיְלָה הַזֶּה prep.-def.art.-n.m.s. (538)-def. art.-demons. adj. m.s. (260) *that night*

וְהִכֵּיתִי conj.-Hi. pf. 1 c.s. (נָכָה 645) *and I will smite*

כָל־בְּכוֹר n.m.s. cstr. (481)-n.m.s. (114) *all the first-born*

בְּאֶרֶץ prep.-n.f.s. cstr. (75) *in the land of*

מִצְרַיִם pr.n. (595) *Egypt*

מֵאָדָם prep.-n.m.s. (9) *man*

וְעַד־בְּהֵמָה conj.-prep. (III 723)-n.f.s. (96) *and beast*

וּבְכָל־אֱלֹהֵי conj.-prep.-n.m.s. cstr. (481)-n.m.p. cstr. (43) *and on all the gods of*

מִצְרַיִם pr.n. (595) *Egypt*

אֶעֱשֶׂה Qal impf. 1 c.s. (עָשָׂה I 793) *I will execute*

שְׁפָטִים n.m.p. (1048) *judgments*

אֲנִי יהוה pers.pr. 1 c.s. (58)-pr.n. (217) *I am Yahweh*

12:13

וְהָיָה conj.-Qal pf. 3 m.s. (224) *shall be*

הַדָּם def.art.-n.m.s. (196) *the blood*

לָכֶם prep.-2 m.p. sf. *for you*

לְאֹת prep.-n.m.s. (16) *a sign*

עַל הַבָּתִּים prep.-def.art.-n.m.p. (108) *upon the houses*

אֲשֶׁר rel. *where*

אַתֶּם שָׁם pers.pr. 2 m.s. (61)-adv. (1027) *you (there)*

וְרָאִיתִי conj.-Qal pf. 1 c.s. (רָאָה 906) *and when I see*

אֶת־הַדָּם dir.obj.-def.art.-n.m.s. (196) *the blood*

וּפָסַחְתִּי conj.-Qal pf. 1 c.s. (פָּסַח I 820) *I will pass over*

עֲלֵכֶם prep.-2 m.p. sf. *over you*

וְלֹא־יִהְיֶה conj.-neg.-Qal impf. 3 m.s. (הָיָה 224) *and no ... shall fall*

בָכֶם prep.-2 m.p. sf. *on you*

נֶגֶף n.m.s. (619) *plague*

לְמַשְׁחִית prep.-Hi. ptc. (שָׁחַת 1007) *to destroy*

בְּהַכֹּתִי prep.-Hi. inf. cstr.-1 c.s. sf. (נָכָה 645) *when I smite*

בְּאֶרֶץ prep.-n.f.s. cstr. (75) *the land of*

מִצְרָיִם pr.n. paus. (595) *Egypt*

12:14

וְהָיָה Qal pf. 3 m.s. (224) *shall be*

הַיּוֹם הַזֶּה def.art.-n.m.s. (398)-def.art.-demons. adj. (260) *this day*

לָכֶם prep.-2 m.p. sf. *for you*

לְזִכָּרוֹן prep.-n.m.s. (272) *a memorial day*

וְחַגֹּתֶם conj.-Qal pf. 2 m.p. (חָגַג 290) *and you shall keep (a feast)*

אֹתוֹ dir.obj.-3 m.s. sf. *it*

חַג ליהוה n.m.s. (290)-prep.-pr.n. (217) *a feast to Yahweh*

לְדֹרֹתֵיכֶם prep.-n.m.p.-2 m.p. sf. (189) *throughout your generations*

חֻקַּת עוֹלָם n.f.s. cstr. (349)-n.m.s. (761) *an ordinance for ever*

תְּחָגֻּהוּ Qal impf. 2 m.p.-3 m.s. sf. (חָגַג 290) *you shall observe it*

12:15

שִׁבְעַת יָמִים num. f.s. cstr. (988)-n.m.p. (398) *seven days*

מַצּוֹת n.f.p. (595) *unleavened bread*

תֹּאכֵלוּ Qal impf. 2 m.p. paus. (אָכַל 37) *you shall eat*

אַךְ adv. (36) *(indeed)*

בַּיּוֹם הָרִאשׁוֹן prep.-def.art.-n.m.s. (398) - def.art.-num. adj. (911) *on the first day*

תַּשְׁבִּיתוּ Hi. impf. 2 m.p. (שָׁבַת 991) *you shall put away*

שְׂאֹר n.m.s. (959) *leaven*

מִבָּתֵּיכֶם prep.-n.m.p.-2 m.p. sf. (108) *out of your houses*

כִּי כָּל־אֹכֵל conj.-n.m.s. cstr. (481)-Qal act. ptc. (37) *for if any one eats*

חָמֵץ n.m.s. (329) *what is leavened*

וְנִכְרְתָה conj.-Ni.pf.3 f.s.(כָּרַת 503) *shall be cut off*

הַנֶּפֶשׁ הַהִוא def.art.-n.f.s.(659)-def.art.-demons.adj.f.s.(214) *that person*

מִיִּשְׂרָאֵל prep.-pr.n.(975) *from Israel*

מִיּוֹם הָרִאשֹׁן prep.-n.m.s.cstr.(398)-def.art.-adj.(911) *from the first day*

עַד־יוֹם prep.(III 723)-n.m.s.cstr.(398) *until the ... day*

הַשְּׁבִעִי def.art.-num.(988) *seventh*

12:16

וּבַיּוֹם הָרִאשׁוֹן conj.-prep.-def.art.-n.m.s. (398) - def.art.-adj. m.s. (911) *on the first day*

מִקְרָא־קֹדֶשׁ n.m.s.(896)-adj.m.s.(872) *a holy assembly*

וּבַיּוֹם הַשְּׁבִיעִי v. supra-def.art.-num.adj.(988) *and on the seventh day*

מִקְרָא־קֹדֶשׁ v. supra-v.supra *a holy assembly*

יִהְיֶה לָכֶם Qal impf.3 m.s.(הָיָה 224)-prep.-2 m.p.sf. *you shall hold*

כָּל־מְלָאכָה n.m.s.cstr.(481)-n.f.s.(521) *(any) work*

לֹא־יֵעָשֶׂה neg.-Ni.impf.3 m.s.(I 793) *shall not be done*

בָּהֶם prep.-3 m.p.sf. *on those days*

אַךְ אֲשֶׁר adv. (36)-rel. *but what*

יֵאָכֵל Ni.impf.3 m.s.(אָכַל 37) *must eat*

לְכָל־נֶפֶשׁ prep.-n.m.s.cstr.(481)-n.f.s.(659) *every one*

הוּא לְבַדּוֹ demons.adj.m.s.(214)-prep.-n.m.s.-3 m.s.sf.(94) *that only*

יֵעָשֶׂה לָכֶם Ni.impf. 3 m.s. (עָשָׂה I 793)-prep.-2 m.p. sf. *may be prepared by you*

12:17

וּשְׁמַרְתֶּם conj.-Qal pf.2 m.p.(שָׁמַר 1036) *And you shall observe*

אֶת־הַמַּצּוֹת dir.obj.-def.art.-n.f.p. (595) *the feast of unleavened bread*

כִּי בְּעֶצֶם conj.-prep.-n.f.s.cstr. (782) *on ... very*

הַיּוֹם הַזֶּה def.art.-n.m.s. (398)-def.art.-demons.adj.m.s. (260) *this day*

הוֹצֵאתִי Hi.pf.1 c.s. (יָצָא 422) *I brought*

אֶת־צִבְאוֹתֵיכֶם dir.obj.-n.f.p.-2

m.p.sf. (838) *your hosts*

מֵאֶרֶץ prep.-n.f.s.cstr. (75) *out of the land of*

מִצְרָיִם pr.n.paus.(595) *Egypt*

וּשְׁמַרְתֶּם v.supra *therefore you shall observe*

אֶת־הַיּוֹם־הַזֶּה dir.obj.-v.supra-v.supra *this day*

לְדֹרֹתֵיכֶם prep.-n.m.p.-2 m.p.sf. (189) *throughout your generations*

חֻקַּת עוֹלָם n.f.s. cstr. (349) - n.m.s. (761) *as an ordinance for ever*

12:18

בָּרִאשֹׁן prep.-def.art.-adj. (911) *in the first*

בְּאַרְבָּעָה prep.-n.f.s. (916) *on the four-*

עָשָׂר num.m.s.(797) *teenth*

יוֹם n.m.s. (398) *day*

לַחֹדֶשׁ prep.-def.art.-n.m.s. (II 294) *of the month*

בָּעֶרֶב prep.-def.art.-n.m.s. (787) *at evening*

תֹּאכְלוּ Qal impf.2 m.p. (אָכַל 37) *you shall eat*

מַצֹּת n.f.p. (595) *unleavened bread*

עַד יוֹם prep. (III 723)-n.m.s. cstr. (398) *until the ... day (of)*

הָאֶחָד def.art.-num. (25) *first*

וְעֶשְׂרִים conj.-num.m.p. (797) *twenty-*

לַחֹדֶשׁ v.supra *of the month*

בָּעָרֶב v.supra *at evening*

12:19

שִׁבְעַת n.f.s.cstr.(988) *for seven*

יָמִים n.m.p. (398) *days*

שְׂאֹר n.m.s. (959) *leaven*

לֹא יִמָּצֵא neg.-Ni.impf.3 m.s. (מָצָא 592) *no ... shall be found*

בְּבָתֵּיכֶם prep.-n.m.p.-2 m.p.sf. (108) *in your houses*

כִּי כָּל־אֹכֵל conj.-n.m.s. cstr. (481)-Qal act.ptc. (37) *for if any one eat*

מַחְמֶצֶת n.f.s. (330) *what is leavened*

וְנִכְרְתָה conj.-Ni.pf.3 f.s. (כָּרַת 503) *shall be cut off*

הַנֶּפֶשׁ הַהִוא def.art.-n.f.s. (659)-def.art.-demons. adj. f.s. (214) *that person*

מֵעֲדַת יִשְׂרָאֵל prep.-n.f.s.cstr. (II 417)-pr.n. (975) *from the congregation of Israel*

בַּגֵּר prep.-def.art.-n.m.s. (158) *whether he is a sojourner*

וּבְאֶזְרַח conj.-prep.-n.m.s.cstr. (280) *or a native of*

הָאָרֶץ def.art.-n.f.s. (75) *the land*

12:20

כָּל־מַחְמֶצֶת n.m.s. cstr. (481)-n.f.s. (330) *thing leavened*

לֹא תֹאכֵלוּ neg.-Qal impf. 2 m.p. paus. (אָכַל 37) *no ... you shall eat*

בְּכֹל prep.-n.m.s. cstr. (481) *in all*

מוֹשְׁבֹתֵיכֶם n.f.p.-2 m.p. sf. (444) *your dwellings*

תֹּאכְלוּ Qal impf.2 m.p. (37) *you shall eat*

מַצּוֹת n.f.p. (595) *unleavened bread*

12:21

וַיִּקְרָא consec.-Qal impf.3 m.s. (894) *then ... called*

מֹשֶׁה pr.n. (602) *Moses*

לְכָל־זִקְנֵי prep.-n.m.s. cstr. (481)-n.m.p. cstr. (278) *all the elders of*

יִשְׂרָאֵל pr.n. (975) *Israel*

וַיֹּאמֶר consec.-Qal impf.3 m.s. (55) *and said*

אֲלֵהֶם prep.-3 m.p. sf. *to them*

מִשְׁכוּ Qal impv.2 m.p. (604) *Select (draw)*

וּקְחוּ לָכֶם conj.-Qal impv.2 m.p. (לָקַח 542)-prep.-2 m.p. sf. *for yourselves*

צֹאן n.f.s. (838) *lambs*

לְמִשְׁפְּחֹתֵיכֶם prep.-n.f.p.-2 m.p. sf. (1046) *according to your families*

וְשַׁחֲטוּ conj.-Qal impv.2 m.p. (שָׁחַט 1006) *and kill*

הַפָּסַח def.art.-n.m.s. paus. (820) *the passover lamb*

12:22

וּלְקַחְתֶּם conj.-Qal pf.2 m.p. (לָקַח 542) *take*

אֲגֻדַּת אֵזוֹב n.f.s. cstr. (8)-n.m.s. (23) *a bunch of hyssop*

וּטְבַלְתֶּם conj.-Qal pf.2 m.p. (טָבַל I 371) *and dip*

בַּדָּם prep.-def.art.-n.m.s. (196) *in the blood*

אֲשֶׁר־בַּסַּף rel.-prep.-def.art.-n.m.s. (I 706) *which in the basin*

וְהִגַּעְתֶּם conj.-Hi.pf.2 m.p. (נָגַע 619) *and touch*

אֶל־הַמַּשְׁקוֹף prep.-def.art.-n.m.s. (1054) *the lintel*

וְאֶל־שְׁתֵּי conj.-prep.-num.m.p. cstr. (1040) *and the two*

הַמְּזוּזֹת def.art.-n.f.p. (265) *doorposts*

מִן־הַדָּם prep.-def.art.-n.m.s. (196) *with the blood*

אֲשֶׁר בַּסָּף rel.-prep.-def.art.-n.m.s. paus. (I 706) *which in the basin*

וְאַתֶּם conj.- pers.pr.2 m.p. (61) *and ... you*

לֹא תֵצְאוּ neg.-Qal impf.2 m.p. (יָצָא 422) *not ... shall go out*

אִישׁ n.m.s. (35) *one*

מִפֶּתַח־בֵּיתוֹ prep.-n.m.s. cstr. (835)-n.m.s.-3 m.s. sf. (108) *of the door of his house*

עַד־בֹּקֶר prep.-n.m.s. (133) *until morning*

12:23

וְעָבַר conj.-Qal pf. 3 m.s. (716) *for ... will pass through*

יהוה pr.n. (217) *Yahweh*

לִנְגֹּף prep.-Qal inf.cstr. (נָגַף 619) *to slay*

אֶת־מִצְרַיִם dir.obj.-pr.n. (595) *the Egyptians*

וְרָאָה conj.-Qal pf.3 m.s. (906) *and when he sees*

אֶת־הַדָּם dir.obj.-def.art.-n.m.s. (196) *the blood*

עַל־הַמַּשְׁקוֹף prep.-def.art.-n.m.s. (1054) *on the lintel*

וְעַל שְׁתֵּי conj.-prep.-num. m.p. cstr. (1040) *and on the two*

הַמְּזוּזֹת def.art.-n.f.p. (265) *doorposts*

וּפָסַח יהוה conj.-Qal pf.3 m.s. (I 820)-pr.n. (217) *Yahweh will pass over*

עַל־הַפֶּתַח prep.-def.art.-n.m.s. (835) *the door*

וְלֹא יִתֵּן conj.-neg.-Qal impf. 3 m.s. (נָתַן 678) *and will not allow*

הַמַּשְׁחִית def.art.-Hi.ptc. (שָׁחַת 1007) *the destroyer*

לָבֹא prep.-Qal inf.cstr. (בּוֹא 97) *to enter*

אֶל־בָּתֵּיכֶם prep.-n.m.p.-2 m.p. sf. (108) *your houses*

לִנְגֹּף prep.-Qal inf. cstr. (נָגַף 619) *to slay*

12:24

וּשְׁמַרְתֶּם conj.-Qal pf.2 m.p. (שָׁמַר 1036) *you shall observe*

אֶת־הַדָּבָר־הַזֶּה dir.obj.-def.art.-n.m.s. (182)-def.art.-demons.adj.m.s. (260)*this rite*

לְחָק־לְךָ prep.-n.m.s. (349)-prep.-2 m.s. sf. *as an ordinance for you*

וּלְבָנֶיךָ conj.-prep.-n.m.p.-2 m.s. sf. (119) *and for your sons*

עַד־עוֹלָם prep. (III 723) - n.m.s. (761) *for ever*

12:25

וְהָיָה conj.-Qal pf.3 m.s. (224) *and (it shall be)*

כִּי־תָבֹאוּ conj.-Qal impf.2 m.p. (בּוֹא 97) *when you come*

אֶל־הָאָרֶץ prep.-def.art.-n.f.s. (75) *to the land*

אֲשֶׁר יִתֵּן rel.-Qal impf.3 m.s. (נָתַן 678) *which ... will give*

יהוה pr.n. (217) *Yahweh*

לָכֶם prep.-2 m.p. sf. *you*

כַּאֲשֶׁר prep.-rel. *as*

דִּבֵּר Pi.pf.3 m.s. (180) *he has promised*

וּשְׁמַרְתֶּם v.supra *you shall keep*

אֶת־הָעֲבֹדָה dir.obj.-def.art.-n.f.s. (715) *service*

הַזֹּאת def.art.-demons.adj.f.s. (260) *this*

12:26

וְהָיָה כִּי־ conj.-Qal pf. 3 m.s. (224) - conj. *and when*

יֹאמְרוּ Qal impf. 3 m.p. (55) *say*

אֲלֵיכֶם prep.-2 m.p. sf. *to you*

בְּנֵיכֶם n.m.p.-2 m.p. sf. (119) *your children*

מָה interr. (552) *what*

הָעֲבֹדָה הַזֹּאת def.art.-n.f.s. (715)-def.art.- demons. adj. f.s. (260) *this service*

לָכֶם prep.-2 m.p. sf. *(to) you*

12:27

וַאֲמַרְתֶּם conj.-Qal pf. 2 m.p. (55) *you shall say*

זֶבַח־פֶּסַח n.m.s. cstr. (257)-n.m.s. (820) *sacrifice of passover*

הוּא pers.pr. 3 m.s. (214) *it is*

ליהוה prep.-pr.n. (217) *Yahweh's*

אֲשֶׁר פָּסַח rel.-Qal pf. 3 m.s. (I 820) *for he passed*

עַל־בָּתֵּי prep.-n.m.p. cstr. (108) *over the houses of*

בְּנֵי־יִשְׂרָאֵל n.m.p. cstr. (119)-pr.n. (975) *the people of Israel*

בְּמִצְרַיִם prep.-pr.n. (595) *in Egypt*

בְּנָגְפּוֹ prep.-Qal act. ptc.-3 m.s. sf. (נָגַף 619) *when he slew*

אֶת־מִצְרַיִם dir.obj.-pr.n. (595) *the Egyptians*

וְאֶת־בָּתֵּינוּ conj.-dir.obj.-n.m.p.-1 c.p. sf. (108) *but ... our houses*

הִצִּיל Hi. pf. 3 m.s. (נָצַל 664) *spared*

וַיִּקֹּד consec.-Qal impf. 3 m.s. (קָדַד I 869) *and ... bowed*

הָעָם def.art.-n.m.s. (I 766) *the people*

וַיִּשְׁתַּחֲווּ consec.-Hithpalel impf. 3 m.p. (שָׁחָה 1005) *and worshiped*

12:28

וַיֵּלְכוּ consec.-Qal impf. 3 m.p. (הָלַךְ 229) *then ... went*

וַיַּעֲשׂוּ consec.-Qal impf. 3 m.p. (עָשָׂה I 793) *and did*

בְּנֵי יִשְׂרָאֵל n.m.p. cstr. (119)-pr.n. (975) *the people of Israel*

כַּאֲשֶׁר prep.-rel. *as*

צִוָּה יהוה Pi. pf. 3 m.s. (צָוָה 845)-pr.n. (217) *Yahweh had commanded*

אֶת־מֹשֶׁה dir.obj.-pr.n. (602) *Moses*

וְאַהֲרֹן conj.-pr.n. (14) *and Aaron*

כֵּן עָשׂוּ adv. (485)-Qal pf. 3 c.p. (עָשָׂה I 793) *so they did*

12:29

וַיְהִי consec.-Qal impf. 3 m.s. (הָיָה 224) *(and it was)*

בַּחֲצִי prep.-n.m.s. cstr. (345) *at mid-*

הַלַּיְלָה def.art.-n.m.s. (538) *night*

ויהוה conj.-pr.n. (217) *Yahweh*

הִכָּה Hi. pf. 3 m.s. (נָכָה 645) *smote*

כָל־בְּכוֹר n.m.s. cstr. (481)-n.m.s. (114) *all the first-born*

בְּאֶרֶץ prep.-n.f.s. cstr. (75) *in the land of*

מִצְרַיִם pr.n. (595) *Egypt*

מִבְּכֹר prep.-n.m.s. cstr. (114) *from the first-born of*

פַּרְעֹה pr.n. (829) *Pharaoh*

הַיֹּשֵׁב def.art.-Qal act. ptc. (יָשַׁב 442) *who sat*

עַל־כִּסְאוֹ prep.-n.m.s.-3 m.s. sf. (490) *on his throne*

עַד בְּכוֹר prep. (III 723)-n.m.s. cstr. (114) *to the first-born of*

הַשְּׁבִי def.art.-n.m.s. (985) *the captive*

אֲשֶׁר בְּבֵית rel.-prep.-n.m.s. cstr. (108) *who was in (the house of)*

הַבּוֹר def.art.-n.m.s. (92) *the kingdom*

וְכֹל בְּכוֹר conj.-n.m.s. cstr. (481)-n.m.s. cstr. (114) *and all the first-born of*

בְּהֵמָה n.f.s. (96) *cattle*

12:30

וַיָּקָם consec.-Qal impf. 3 m.s. (קוּם 877) *and ... rose up*

פַּרְעֹה pr.n. (829) *Pharaoh*

לַיְלָה n.m.s. (538) *in the night*

הוּא pers.pr. 3 m.s. (214) *he*

וְכָל־עֲבָדָיו conj.-n.m.s. cstr. (481)-

n.m.p.-3 m.s. sf. (712) *and all his servants*

וְכָל־מִצְרַיִם conj.-v.supra-pr.n. (595) *and all the Egyptians*

וַתְּהִי consec.-Qal impf. 3 f.s. (הָיָה 224) *and there was*

צְעָקָה גְדֹלָה n.f.s. (858)-adj. f.s. (152) *a great cry*

בְּמִצְרָיִם prep.-pr.n. paus. (595) *in Egypt*

כִּי־אֵין בַּיִת conj.-subst. cstr. (II 34)-n.m.s. (108) *for there was not a house*

אֲשֶׁר אֵין־שָׁם rel.-v.supra-adv. (1027) *where one was not*

מֵת Qal act. ptc. (מוּת 559) *dead*

12:31

וַיִּקְרָא consec.-Qal impf. 3 m.s. (894) *and he summoned*

לְמֹשֶׁה prep.-pr.n. (602) *Moses*

וּלְאַהֲרֹן conj.-prep.-pr.n. (14) *and Aaron*

לַיְלָה n.m.s. (538) *by night*

וַיֹּאמֶר consec.-Qal impf. 3 m.s. (55) *and said*

קוּמוּ Qal impv. 2 m.p. (קוּם 877) *rise up*

צְאוּ Qal impv. 2 m.p. (יָצָא 422) *go forth*

מִתּוֹךְ עַמִּי prep.-n.m.s. cstr. (1063)-n.m.s.-1 c.s. sf. (I 766) *from among my people*

גַּם־אַתֶּם adv. (168)-pers.pr. 2 m.s. (61) *both you*

גַּם־בְּנֵי יִשְׂרָאֵל adv.(168)-n.m.p. cstr. (119) -pr.n. (975) *and the people of Israel*

וּלְכוּ conj.-Qal impv. 2 m.p. (הָלַךְ 229) *and go*

עִבְדוּ Qal impv. 2 m.p. (712) *serve*

אֶת־יהוה dir.obj.-pr.n. (217) *Yahweh*

כְּדַבֶּרְכֶם prep.-Pi. inf. cstr.-2 m.p. sf. (180) *as you have said*

12:32

גַּם־צֹאנְכֶם adv. (168)-n.f.s.-2 m.p. sf. (838) *both your flocks*

גַּם־בְּקַרְכֶם v.supra-n.m.s.-2 m.p. sf. (133) *and your herds*

קְחוּ Qal impv. 2 m.p. (לָקַח 542) *take*

כַּאֲשֶׁר prep.-rel. *as*

דִּבַּרְתֶּם Pi. pf. 2 m.p. (180) *you have said*

וָלֵכוּ conj.-Qal impv. 2 m.p. paus. (הָלַךְ 229) *and be gone*

וּבֵרַכְתֶּם conj.-Pi. pf. 2 m.p. (בָּרַךְ 138) *and bless*

גַּם־אֹתִי adv. (168) - dir.obj.-1 c.s. sf. *me also*

12:33

וַתֶּחֱזַק consec.-Qal impf. 3 f.s. (חָזַק 304) *and ... were urgent*

מִצְרַיִם pr.n. (595) *the Egyptians*

עַל־הָעָם prep.-def.art.-n.m.s. (I 766) *with the people*

לְמַהֵר prep.-Pi. inf. cstr. as adv. (I 554) *in haste*

לְשַׁלְּחָם prep.-Pi. inf. cstr.-3 m.p. sf. (1018) *to send them*

מִן־הָאָרֶץ prep.-def.art.-n.f.s. (75) *out of the land*

כִּי אָמְרוּ conj.-Qal pf. 3 c.p. (55) *for they said*

כֻּלָּנוּ n.m.s. - 1 c.p. sf. (481) *we are all*

מֵתִים Qal act. ptc. (מוּת 559) *dead men*

12:34

וַיִּשָּׂא consec.-Qal impf. 3 m.s. (נָשָׂא 669) *so ... took*

הָעָם def.art.-n.m.s. (I 766) *the people*

אֶת־בְּצֵקוֹ dir.obj.-n.m.s.-3 m.s. sf. (130) *their dough*

טֶרֶם יֶחְמָץ neg. (382)-Qal impf. 3 m.s. (חָמֵץ 329) *before it was leavened*

מִשְׁאֲרֹתָם n.f.p.-3 m.p. sf. (602) *their kneading bowls*

צְרֻרֹת Qal pass. ptc. f.p. (צָרַר I 864) *being bound up*

בְּשִׂמְלֹתָם prep.-n.f.p.-3 m.p. sf. (971) *in their mantles*

עַל־שִׁכְמָם prep.-n.m.s.-3 m.p. sf. (I

1014) *on their shoulders*

12:35

וּבְנֵי־יִשְׂרָאֵל conj.-n.m.p. cstr. (119)-pr.n. (975) *also the people of Israel*

עָשׂוּ Qal pf. 3 c.p. (עָשָׂה I 793) *had done*

כִּדְבַר מֹשֶׁה prep.-n.m.s. cstr. (182)-pr.n. (602) *as Moses told*

וַיִּשְׁאֲלוּ consec.-Qal impf. 3 m.p. (שָׁאַל 981) *for they had asked*

מִמִּצְרַיִם prep.-pr.n. (595) *of the Egyptians*

כְּלֵי־כֶסֶף n.m.p. cstr. (479)-n.m.s. (494) *jewelry of silver*

וּכְלֵי זָהָב conj.-v. supra-n.m.s. (262) *and of gold*

וּשְׂמָלֹת conj.-n.f.p. (971) *and clothing*

12:36

ויהוה conj.-pr.n. (217) *and Yahweh*

נָתַן Qal pf. 3 m.s. (678) *had given*

אֶת־חֵן dir. obj.-n.m.s. (336) *favor*

הָעָם def. art.-n.m.s. (I 766) *the people*

בְּעֵינֵי prep.-n.f.p. cstr. (744) *in the sight of*

מִצְרַיִם pr.n. (595) *the Egyptians*

וַיַּשְׁאִלוּם consec.-Hi. impf. 3 m.p.-3 m.p. sf. (שָׁאַל 981) *so that they let them have what they asked*

וַיְנַצְּלוּ consec.-Pi.impf.3 m.p. (נָצַל 664) *thus they despoiled*

אֶת־מִצְרָיִם dir. obj.-pr.n. paus. (595) *the Egyptians*

12:37

וַיִּסְעוּ consec.-Qal impf. 3 m.p. (נָסַע 652) *and ... journeyed*

בְנֵי־יִשְׂרָאֵל n.m.p. cstr. (119)-pr.n. (975) *the people of Israel*

מֵרַעְמְסֵס prep.-pr.n. (947) *from Rameses*

סֻכֹּתָה pr.n.-dir. he (697) *to Succoth*

כְּשֵׁשׁ־מֵאוֹת prep.-num. (995)-num. f.p. (547) *about six hundred*

אֶלֶף n.m.s. (48) *thousand*

רַגְלִי adj. (920) *on foot*

הַגְּבָרִים def. art.-n.m.p. (149) *men*

לְבַד מִטָּף prep.-n.m.s. (94) as adv.-prep.-n.m.s. paus. (381) *besides children*

12:38

וְגַם־ conj.-adv. (168) *also*

עֵרֶב רַב n.m.s. (I 786)-adj. m.s. (I 912) *A mixed multitude*

עָלָה אִתָּם Qal pf. 3 m.s. (748)-prep.-3 m.p. sf. (II 85) *went out with them*

וְצֹאן conj.-n.f.s. (838) *both flocks*

וּבָקָר conj.-n.m.s. (133) *and herds*

מִקְנֶה n.m.s. (889) *cattle*

כָּבֵד מְאֹד adj. (458)-adv. (547) *very many*

12:39

וַיֹּאפוּ consec.-Qal impf. 3 m.p. (אָפָה 66) *and they baked*

אֶת־הַבָּצֵק dir. obj.-def. art.-n.m.s. (130) *the dough*

אֲשֶׁר הוֹצִיאוּ rel.-Hi. pf. 3 c.p. (יָצָא 422) *which they had brought*

מִמִּצְרַיִם prep.-pr.n. (595) *out of Egypt*

עֻגֹת מַצּוֹת n.f.p. cstr. (728) - n.f.p. (595) *unleavened cakes*

כִּי לֹא חָמֵץ conj.-neg.-Qal pf. 3 m.s. (I 329) *for it was not leavened*

כִּי־גֹרְשׁוּ conj.-Pu. pf. 3 c.p. (גָּרַשׁ 176) *because they were thrust*

מִמִּצְרַיִם prep.-v. supra *out of Egypt*

וְלֹא יָכְלוּ conj.-neg.-Qal pf. 3 c.p. (יָכֹל 407) *and could not*

לְהִתְמַהְמֵהַּ prep.-Hithpilpel inf. cstr. (מָהַהּ 554) *tarry*

וְגַם־צֵדָה conj.-adv. (168)-n.f.s. (845) *provisions*

לֹא־עָשׂוּ לָהֶם neg.-Qal pf. 3 c.p. (עָשָׂה I 793)-prep.-3 m.p. sf. *neither had they prepared for themselves*

12:40

וּמוֹשַׁב conj.-n.m.s. cstr. (444) *the time (of dwelling)*

בְּנֵי יִשְׂרָאֵל n.m.p. cstr. (119)-pr.n. (975) *the people of Israel*

יָשְׁבוּ אֲשֶׁר rel.-Qal pf. 3 c.p. (יָשַׁב 442) *that dwelt*

בְּמִצְרָיִם prep.-pr.n. paus. (595) *in Egypt*

שְׁלֹשִׁים num. p. (1026) *thirty*

שָׁנָה n.f.s. (1040) *years*

וְאַרְבַּע מֵאוֹת conj.-num. (916)-n.f.p. cstr. (547) *and four hundred (of)*

שָׁנָה v. supra *(years)*

12:41

וַיְהִי consec.-Qal impf. 3 m.s. (הָיָה 224) *and*

מִקֵּץ שְׁלֹשִׁים prep.-n.m.s. cstr. (893)-num. p. (1026) *at the end of thirty*

שָׁנָה n.f.s. (1040) *years*

וְאַרְבַּע מֵאוֹת v. 12:40 conj.-num. (916)-n.f.p. cstr. (547) *and four hundred*

שָׁנָה v. supra *(years)*

וַיְהִי v. supra *(and it was)*

בְּעֶצֶם prep.-n.m.s. cstr. (782) *on ... very*

הַיּוֹם הַזֶּה def. art.-n.m.s. (398)-def. art.-demons. adj. m.s. (260) *that ... day*

יָצְאוּ Qal pf. 3 c.p. (יָצָא 422) *went out*

כָּל־צִבְאוֹת n.m.s. cstr. (481)-n.f.p. cstr. (838) *all the hosts of*

יהוה pr.n. (217) *Yahweh*

מֵאֶרֶץ prep.-n.f.s. cstr. (75) *from the land of*

מִצְרָיִם pr.n. paus. (595) *Egypt*

12:42

לֵיל n.m.s. cstr. (538) *a night of*

שִׁמֻּרִים n.m.p. (1037) *watching*

הוּא ליהוה pers. pr. 3 m.s. (214)-prep.-pr.n. (217) *It was ... by Yahweh*

לְהוֹצִיאָם prep.-Hi. inf. cstr.-3 m.p. sf. (יָצָא 422) *to bring them*

מֵאֶרֶץ prep.-n.f.s. cstr. (75) *out of the land of*

מִצְרָיִם pr.n. paus. (595) *Egypt*

הוּא־הַלַּיְלָה v. supra-def. art.-n.m.s. (538) *so ... night*

הַזֶּה def. art.-demons. adj. m.s. (260) *this*

ליהוה prep.-pr.n. (217) *to Yahweh*

שִׁמֻּרִים v. supra *watching*

לְכָל־בְּנֵי prep.-n.m.s. cstr. (481)-n.m.p. cstr. (119) *by all the people of*

יִשְׂרָאֵל pr.n. (975) *Israel*

לְדֹרֹתָם prep.-n.m.p.-3 m.p. sf. (189) *throughout their generations*

12:43

וַיֹּאמֶר יהוה consec.-Qal impf. 3 m.s. (55)-pr.n. (217) *and Yahweh said*

אֶל־מֹשֶׁה prep.-pr.n. (602) *to Moses*

וְאַהֲרֹן conj.-pr.n. (14) *and Aaron*

זֹאת חֻקַּת demons. adj. f.s. (260)-n.f.s. cstr. (349) *This is the ordinance of*

הַפָּסַח def. art.-n.m.s. paus. (820) *the passover*

כָּל־בֶּן־נֵכָר n.m.s. cstr. (481)-n.m.s. cstr. (119)-n.m.s. (648) *foreigner*

לֹא־יֹאכַל בּוֹ neg.-Qal impf. 3 m.s. (37)-prep.-3 m.s. sf. *no ... shall eat of it*

12:44

וְכָל־עֶבֶד conj.-n.m.s. cstr. (481)-n.m.s. (712) *but every slave*

אִישׁ n.m.s. (35) *each*

מִקְנַת־כָּסֶף n.f.s. cstr. (889)-n.m.s. paus. (494) *that is bought for money*

וּמַלְתָּה אֹתוֹ conj.-Qal pf. 2 m.s. (מוּל II 557)-dir. obj.-3 m.s. sf. *after you have circumcised him*

אָז adv. (23) *(then)*

יֹאכַל בּוֹ Qal impf. 3 m.s. (37)-prep.-3 m.s. sf. *may eat of it*

12:45

תּוֹשָׁב n.m.s. (444) *sojourner*

וְשָׂכִיר conj.-n.m.s. (969) *or hired servant*

לֹא־יֹאכַל־בּוֹ neg.-Qal impf. 3 m.s. (37)-prep.-3 m.s. sf. *no ... may eat of it*

12:46

בְּבַיִת אֶחָד prep.-n.m.s. (108)-num. m.s. (25) *in one house*

יֵאָכֵל Ni. impf. 3 m.s. (אָכַל 37) *shall it be eaten*

לֹא־תוֹצִיא neg.-Hi. impf. 2 m.s. (יָצָא 422) *you shall not carry forth*

מִן־הַבַּיִת prep.-def. art.-n.m.s. (108) *(from) the house*

מִן־הַבָּשָׂר prep.-def.art.-n.m.s. (142) *any of the flesh*

חוּצָה n.m.s.-dir. he (299) *outside*

וְעֶצֶם conj.-n.f.s. (782) *and a bone*

לֹא תִשְׁבְּרוּ־בוֹ neg.-Qal impf. 2 m.p. (1036)-prep.-3 m.s. sf. *you shall not break of it*

12:47

כָּל־עֲדַת n.m.s. cstr. (481)-n.f.s. cstr. (II 417) *all the congregation of*

יִשְׂרָאֵל pr.n. (975) *Israel*

יַעֲשׂוּ אֹתוֹ Qal impf. 3 m.p. (עָשָׂה I 793) - dir.obj.-3 m.s. sf. *shall keep it*

12:48

וְכִי־יָגוּר conj.-conj.-Qal impf. 3 m.s. (גּוּר 157) *and when ... shall sojourn*

אִתְּךָ גֵּר prep.-2 m.s. sf. (II 85)-n.m.s. (158) *with you a sojourner*

וְעָשָׂה conj.-Qal pf. 3 m.s. (I 793) *and would keep*

פֶּסַח ליהוה n.m.s. (820)-prep.-pr.n. (217) *passover to Yahweh*

הִמּוֹל לוֹ Ni. impv. 2 m.s. (מוּל II 557)-prep.-3 m.s. sf. *let be circumcised ... his*

כָּל־זָכָר n.m.s. cstr. (481)-n.m.s. (271) *all ... males*

וְאָז יִקְרַב conj.-adv. (23)-Qal impf. 3 m.s. (897) *then he may come near*

לַעֲשֹׂתוֹ prep.-Qal inf. cstr.-3 m.s. sf. (עָשָׂה I 793) *and keep it*

וְהָיָה conj.-Qal pf. 3 m.s. (224) *he shall be*

כְּאֶזְרַח prep.-n.m.s. cstr. (280) *as a native of*

הָאָרֶץ def. art.-n.f.s. (75) *the land*

וְכָל־עָרֵל conj.-n.m.s. cstr. (481)-n.m.s. (790) *but ... uncircumcised person*

לֹא־יֹאכַל בּוֹ neg.-Qal impf. 3 m.s. (37)-prep.-3 m.s. sf. *no ... shall eat of it*

12:49

תּוֹרָה אַחַת n.f.s. (435) - num. adj. f.s. (25) *one law*

יִהְיֶה Qal impf. 3 m.s. (הָיָה 224) *there shall be*

לָאֶזְרָח prep.-def. art.-n.m.s. paus. (280) *for the native*

וְלַגֵּר conj.-prep.-def. art.-n.m.s. (158) *and for the stranger*

הַגָּר def. art.-Qal act. ptc. (גּוּר 157) *who sojourns*

בְּתוֹכְכֶם prep.-n.m.s. cstr. (1063)-2 m.p. sf. *among you*

12:50

וַיַּעֲשׂוּ consec.-Qal impf. 3 m.p. (עָשָׂה I 793) *thus did*

כָּל־בְּנֵי n.m.s. cstr. (481) - n.m.p. cstr. (119) *all the people of*

יִשְׂרָאֵל pr.n. (975) *Israel*

כַּאֲשֶׁר prep.-rel. *as*

צִוָּה יהוה Pi. pf. 3 m.s. (צָוָה 845)-pr.n. (217) *Yahweh commanded*

אֶת־מֹשֶׁה dir. obj.-pr.n. (602) *Moses*

וְאֶת־אַהֲרֹן conj.-dir. obj.-pr.n. (14) *and Aaron*

כֵּן עָשׂוּ adv. (485)-Qal pf. 3 c.p. (עָשָׂה I 793) *so they did*

12:51

וַיְהִי consec.-Qal impf. 3 m.s. (הָיָה 224) *and (it was)*

בְּעֶצֶם prep.-n.m.s. cstr. (782) *on ... very*

הַיּוֹם הַזֶּה def. art.-n.m.s. (398)-def. art.-demons. adj. m.s. (260) *that ... day*

הוֹצִיא יהוה Hi. pf. 3 m.s. (יָצָא 422)-pr.n. (217) *Yahweh brought*

אֶת־בְּנֵי dir.obj.-n.m.p. cstr. (119) *the people of*

יִשְׂרָאֵל pr.n. (975) *Israel*

מֵאֶרֶץ prep.-n.f.s. cstr. (75) *out of the land of*

מִצְרַיִם pr.n. (595) *Egypt*

עַל־צִבְאֹתָם prep.-n.f.p.-3 m.p. sf. (838) *by their hosts*

13:1

וַיְדַבֵּר consec.-Pi. impf. 3 m.s. (180) *said*

יהוה pr.n. (217) *Yahweh*

אֶל־מֹשֶׁה prep.-pr.n. (602) *to Moses*

לֵּאמֹר prep.-Qal inf. cstr. (55) *(saying)*

13:2

קַדֶּשׁ־לִי Pi. impv. 2 m.s. (872)-prep.-1 c.s. sf. *Consecrate to me*

כָל־בְּכוֹר n.m.s. cstr. (481)-n.m.s. (114) *all the first-born*

פֶּטֶר n.m.s. cstr. (809) *whatever is the first to open*

כָּל־רֶחֶם n.m.s. cstr. (481)-n.m.s. (933) *the womb*

בִּבְנֵי יִשְׂרָאֵל prep.-n.m.p. cstr. (119) - pr.n. (975) *among the people of Israel*

בָּאָדָם prep.-def. art.-n.m.s. (9) *both of man*

וּבַבְּהֵמָה conj.-prep.-def. art.-n.f.s. (96) *and of beast*

לִי הוּא prep.-1 c.s. sf.-pers. pr. 3 m.s. (214) *is mine (it)*

13:3

וַיֹּאמֶר מֹשֶׁה consec.-Qal impf. 3 m.s. (55)-pr.n. (602) *and Moses said*

אֶל־הָעָם prep.-def. art.-n.m.s. (I 766) *to the people*

זָכוֹר Qal inf. abs. (זָכַר 269) *Remember*

אֶת־הַיּוֹם הַזֶּה dir. obj.-def. art.-n.m.s. (398)-def. art.-demons. adj. m.s. (260) *this day*

אֲשֶׁר rel. *in which*

יְצָאתֶם Qal pf. 2 m.p. (יָצָא 422) *you came out*

מִמִּצְרַיִם prep.-pr.n. (595) *from Egypt*

מִבֵּית prep.-n.m.s. cstr. (108) *out of the house of*

עֲבָדִים n.m.p. (712) *bondage*

כִּי בְּחֹזֶק conj.-prep.-n.m.s. cstr. (305) *for by strength of*

יָד n.f.s. (388) *hand*

הוֹצִיא יהוה Hi. pf. 3 m.s. (יָצָא 422)-pr.n. (217) *Yahweh brought out*

אֶתְכֶם dir. obj.-2 m.p. sf. *you*

מִזֶּה prep.-demons. adj. m.s. (260) *from this place*

וְלֹא יֵאָכֵל conj.-neg.-Ni. impf. 3 m.s. (37) *no ... shall be eaten*

חָמֵץ n.m.s. (329) *leavened bread*

13:4

הַיּוֹם def. art.-n.m.s. (398) *this day*

אַתֶּם יֹצְאִים pers. pr. 2 m.p. (61)-Qal act. ptc. m.p. (422) *you are to go forth*

בְּחֹדֶשׁ prep.-n.m.s. cstr. (II 294) *in the month of*

הָאָבִיב def. art.-pr.n. (1) *Abib*

13:5

וְהָיָה conj.-Qal pf. 3 m.s. (224) *and (it shall be)*

כִּי־יְבִיאֲךָ conj.-Hi. impf. 3 m.s.-2 m.s. sf. (בּוֹא 97) *when ... brings you*

יהוה pr.n. (217) *Yahweh*

אֶל־אֶרֶץ prep.-n.f.s. cstr. (75) *into the land of*

הַכְּנַעֲנִי def.art.-pr.n. (489) cf. 3:17 *the Canaanites*

וְהַחִתִּי conj.-def.art.-pr.n. (366) *the Hittites*

וְהָאֱמֹרִי conj.-def.art.-pr.n. (57) *the Amorites*

וְהַחִוִּי conj.-def.art.-pr.n. (295) *the Hivites*

וְהַיְבוּסִי conj.-def.art.-pr.n. (101) *and the Jebusites*

אֲשֶׁר נִשְׁבַּע rel.-Ni. pf. 3 m.s. (989) *which he swore*

לַאֲבֹתֶיךָ prep.-n.m.p.-2 m.s. sf. (3) *to your fathers*

לָתֶת לָךְ prep.-Qal inf. cstr. (נָתַן 678)-prep.-2 m.s. sf. paus. *to give you*

אֶרֶץ n.f.s. (75) *a land*

זָבַת Qal act. ptc. f.s. cstr. (זוב 264) *flowing with*

חָלָב n.m.s. (316) *milk*

וּדְבָשׁ conj.-n.m.s. paus. (185) *and honey*

וְעָבַדְתָּ conj.-Qal pf. 2 m.s. (עָבַד 712) *you shall keep*

אֶת־הָעֲבֹדָה dir.obj.-def.art.-n.f.s. (715) *service*

הַזֹּאת def.art.-demons. adj. f.s. (260) *this*

בַּחֹדֶשׁ הַזֶּה prep.-def.art.-n.m.s. (II 294)-def.art.-demons. adj. m.s. (260) *in this month*

13:6

שִׁבְעַת num. f.s. cstr. (988) *seven (of)*

יָמִים n.m.p. (398) *days*

תֹּאכַל Qal impf. 2 m.s. (37) *you shall eat*

מַצֹּת n.f.p. (595) *unleavened bread*

וּבַיּוֹם conj.-prep.-def.art.-n.m.s. (398) *and on the ... day*

הַשְּׁבִיעִי def.art.-num. adj. (988) *seventh*

חַג לַיהוה n.m.s. (290)-prep.-pr.n. (217) *a feast to Yahweh*

13:7

מַצּוֹת n.f.p. (595) *unleavened bread*

יֵאָכֵל Ni. impf. 3 m.s. (37) *shall be eaten*

אֵת שִׁבְעַת dir.obj.-n.f.s. cstr. (988) *for seven (of)*

הַיָּמִים def.art.-n.m.p. (398) *days*

וְלֹא־יֵרָאֶה conj.-neg.-Ni. impf. 3 m.s. (906) *no ... shall be seen*

לְךָ prep.-2 m.s. sf. *with you*

חָמֵץ n.m.s. (329) *leavened bread*

וְלֹא־יֵרָאֶה v.supra-v.supra *and no ... shall be seen*

לְךָ v.supra *with you*

שְׂאֹר n.m.s. (959) *leaven*

בְּכָל־גְּבֻלֶךָ prep.-n.m.s. cstr. (481)-n.m.s.-2 m.s. sf. (147) *in all your territory*

13:8

וְהִגַּדְתָּ conj.-Hi. pf. 2 m.s. (נָגַד 616) *and you shall tell*

לְבִנְךָ prep.-n.m.s.-2 m.s. sf. (119) *your son*

בַּיּוֹם הַהוּא prep.-def.art.-n.m.s. (398)-def.art.-demons. adj. m.s. (214) *on that day*

לֵאמֹר prep.-Qal inf. cstr. (55) *(saying)*

בַּעֲבוּר זֶה prep.-n.m.s. cstr. (II 721)-demons. adj. m.s. (260) *because of what*

עָשָׂה יהוה Qal pf. 3 m.s. (I 793) - pr.n. (217) *Yahweh did*

לִי prep.-1 c. s. sf. *for me*

בְּצֵאתִי prep.-Qal inf. cstr.-1 c.s. sf. (יָצָא 422) *when I came out*

מִמִּצְרָיִם prep.-pr.n. paus. (595) *of Egypt*

13:9

וְהָיָה לְךָ conj.-Qal pf. 3 m.s. (224)-prep.-2 m.s. sf. *and it shall be to you*

לְאוֹת prep.-n.m.s. (16) *as a sign*

עַל־יָדְךָ prep.-n.f.s.-2 m.s. sf. (388) *on your hand*

וּלְזִכָּרוֹן conj.-prep.-n.m.s. (272) *and as a memorial*

בֵּין עֵינֶיךָ prep.-n.f.p.-2 m.s. sf. (744) *between your eyes*

לְמַעַן prep.-prep. (775) *that*

תִּהְיֶה Qal impf. 3 f.s. (הָיָה 224) *may be*

תּוֹרַת יהוה n.f.s. cstr. (435)-pr.n. (217) *the law of Yahweh*

בְּפִיךָ prep.-n.m.s.-2 m.s. sf. (804) *in your mouth*

כִּי בְּיָד conj.-prep.-n.f.s. (388) *for with a ... hand*

חֲזָקָה adj. f.s. (305) *strong*

הוֹצִאֲךָ Hi. pf. 3 m.s.-2 m.s. sf. (יָצָא 422) *has brought you*

יהוה pr.n. (217) *Yahweh*

מִמִּצְרָיִם prep.-pr.n. paus. (595) *out of Egypt*

13:10

וְשָׁמַרְתָּ conj.-Qal pf. 2 m.s. (1036) *you shall therefore keep*

אֶת־הַחֻקָּה dir. obj.-def. art.-n.f.s. (349) *... ordinance*

הַזֹּאת def. art.-demons. adj. f.s. (260) *this*

לְמוֹעֲדָהּ prep.-n.m.s.-3 f.s. sf. (417) *at its appointed time*

מִיָּמִים prep.-n.m.p. (398) *from year*
יָמִימָה n.m.p.-dir. he (398) *to year*

13:11

וְהָיָה conj.-Qal pf. 3 m.s. (224) *and (it shall be)*
כִּי־יְבִאֲךָ יהוה conj.-Hi. impf. 3 m.s.-2 m.s. sf. (בּוֹא 97)-pr.n. (217) *when Yahweh brings you*
אֶל־אֶרֶץ prep.-n.f.s. cstr. (75) *into the land of*
הַכְּנַעֲנִי def. art.-pr.n. (489) *the Canaanites*
כַּאֲשֶׁר prep.-rel. *as*
נִשְׁבַּע Ni. pf. 3 m.s. (989) *he swore*
לְךָ prep.-2 m.s. sf. *to you*
וְלַאֲבֹתֶיךָ conj.-prep.-n.m.p.-2 m.s. sf. (3) *and your fathers*
וּנְתָנָהּ conj.-Qal pf. 3 m.s.-3 f.s. sf. (678) *and shall give it*
לָךְ prep.-2 m.s. sf. paus. *to you*

13:12

וְהַעֲבַרְתָּ conj.-Hi. pf. 2 m.s. (716) *you shall set apart*
כָל־פֶּטֶר־ n.m.s. cstr. (481)-n.m.s. cstr. (809) *all that first opens*
רֶחֶם n.m.s. (933) *the womb*
ליהוה prep.-pr.n. (217) *to Yahweh*
וְכָל־פֶּטֶר conj.-v.supra-v.supra *all the firstlings of*
שֶׁגֶר n.f.s. cstr. (993) *(offspring of)*
בְּהֵמָה n.f.s. (96) *cattle*
אֲשֶׁר יִהְיֶה rel.-Qal impf. 3 m.s. (הָיָה 224) *that are*
לְךָ prep.-2 m.s. sf. *your*
הַזְּכָרִים def. art.-n.m.p. (271) *males*
ליהוה prep.-pr.n. (217) *Yahweh's*

13:13

וְכָל־פֶּטֶר conj.-n.m.s. cstr. (481)-n.m.s. cstr. (809) *every firstling of*
חֲמֹר n.m.s. (331) *an ass*
תִּפְדֶּה Qal impf. 2 m.s. (804) *you shall redeem*
בְשֶׂה prep.-n.m.s. (961) *with a lamb*
וְאִם־לֹא תִפְדֶּה conj.-hypoth. part. (49)-neg.-Qal impf. 2 m.s. (804) *or if you will not redeem*
וַעֲרַפְתּוֹ conj.-Qal pf. 2 m.s.-3 m.s. sf. (עָרַף 791) *you shall break its neck*
וְכֹל בְּכוֹר conj.-n.m.s. cstr. (481)-n.m.s. cstr. (114) *every first-born of*
אָדָם n.m.s. (9) *man*
בְּבָנֶיךָ prep.-n.m.p.-2 m.s. sf. (119) *among your sons*
תִּפְדֶּה v. supra *you shall redeem*

13:14

וְהָיָה conj.-Qal pf. 3 m.s. (224) *and (it shall be)*
כִּי־יִשְׁאָלְךָ conj.-Qal impf. 3 m.s.-2 m.s. sf. (981) *when ... asks you*
בִנְךָ n.m.s.-2 m.s. sf. (119) *your son*
מָחָר adv. (563) *in time to come*
לֵאמֹר prep.-Qal inf. cstr. (55) *(saying)*
מַה־זֹּאת interr. (552)-demons. adj. f.s. (260) *what does this mean*
וְאָמַרְתָּ conj.-Qal pf. 2 m.s. (55) *you shall say*
אֵלָיו prep.-3 m.s. sf. *to him*
בְּחֹזֶק יָד prep.-n.m.s. cstr. (305)-n.f.s. (388) *By strength of hand*
הוֹצִיאָנוּ Hi. pf. 3 m.s.-1 c.p. sf. (יָצָא 422) *brought us out*
יהוה pr.n. (217) *Yahweh*
מִמִּצְרַיִם prep.-pr.n. (595) *of Egypt*
מִבֵּית prep.-n.m.s. cstr. (108) *from the house of*
עֲבָדִים n.m.p. (713) *bondage*

13:15

וַיְהִי consec.-Qal impf. 3 m.s. (224) *for (it shall be)*
כִּי־הִקְשָׁה conj.-Hi. pf. 3 m.s. (קָשָׁה 904) *when ... stubbornly refused*
פַרְעֹה pr.n. (829) *Pharaoh*
לְשַׁלְּחֵנוּ prep.-Pi. inf. cstr.-1 c.p. sf. (1018) *to let us go*
וַיַּהֲרֹג יהוה consec.-Qal impf. 3 m.s. (246)-pr.n. (217) *Yahweh slew*
כָּל־בְּכוֹר n.m.s. cstr. (481)-n.m.s. (114) *all the first-born*
בְּאֶרֶץ prep.-n.f.s. cstr. (75) *in the land of*

מִצְרַיִם pr.n. (595) *Egypt*

מִבְּכֹר אָדָם prep.-n.m.s. cstr. (114)-n.m.s. (9) *both the first-born of man*

וְעַד־בְּכוֹר conj.-prep.-n.m.s. cstr. (114) *and the first-born of*

בְּהֵמָה n.f.s. (96) *cattle*

עַל־כֵּן prep. - adv. (485) *therefore*

אֲנִי זֹבֵחַ pers.pr. 1 c.s. (58)-Qal act. ptc. (256) *I sacrifice*

ליהוה prep.-pr.n. (217) *to Yahweh*

כָּל־פֶּטֶר n.m.s. cstr. (481)-n.m.s. cstr. (809) *all that first open*

רֶחֶם n.m.s. (933) *the womb*

הַזְּכָרִים def.art.-n.m.p. (271) *the males*

וְכָל־בְּכוֹר conj.-n.m.s. cstr. (481)-n.m.s. cstr. (114) *but all the first-born of*

בָּנַי n.m.p.-1 c.s. sf. (119) *my sons*

אֶפְדֶּה Qal impf. 1 c.s. (פָּדָה 804) *I redeem*

13:16

וְהָיָה לְאוֹת conj.-Qal pf. 3 m.s. (224)-prep.-n.m.s. (16) *it shall be as a mark*

עַל־יָדְכָה prep.-n.f.s.-2 m.s. sf. (388) *on your hand*

וּלְטוֹטָפֹת conj.-prep.-n.f.p. (377) *or frontlets*

בֵּין עֵינֶיךָ prep.-n.f.p.-2 m.s. sf. (744) *between your eyes*

כִּי בְּחֹזֶק יָד conj.-prep.-n.m.s. cstr. (305)-n.f.s. (388) *for by a strong hand*

הוֹצִיאָנוּ Hi. pf. 3 m.s.-1 c.p. sf. (יָצָא 422) *brought us out*

יהוה pr.n. (217) *Yahweh*

מִמִּצְרָיִם prep.-pr.n. paus. (595) *of Egypt*

13:17

וַיְהִי consec.-Qal impf. 3 m.s. (הָיָה 224) *(and it was)*

בְּשַׁלַּח פַּרְעֹה prep.-Pi. inf. cstr. (1018)-pr.n. (829) *when Pharaoh let go*

אֶת־הָעָם dir. obj.-def. art.-n.m.s. (I 766) *the people*

וְלֹא־נָחָם conj.-neg.-Qal pf. 3 m.s.-3 m.p. sf. (נָחָה 634) *did not lead them*

אֱלֹהִים n.m.p. (43) *God*

דֶּרֶךְ n.m.s. cstr. (202) *by way of*

אֶרֶץ n.f.s. cstr. (75) *the land of*

פְּלִשְׁתִּים pr.n. adj. p. (814) *the Philistines*

כִּי קָרוֹב הוּא conj.-adj. (898)-pers. pr. 3 m.s. (214) *although that was near*

כִּי אָמַר conj.-Qal pf. 3 m.s. (55) *for ... said*

אֱלֹהִים n.m.p. (43) *God*

פֶּן־יִנָּחֵם conj. (814)-Ni. impf. 3 m.s. (נָחַם 636) *lest ... repent*

הָעָם def. art.-n.m.s. (I 766) *the people*

בִּרְאֹתָם prep.-Qal inf. cstr. (906)-3 m.p. sf. *when they see*

מִלְחָמָה n.f.s. (536) *war*

וְשָׁבוּ conj.-Qal pf. 3 c.p. (שׁוּב 996) *and return*

מִצְרָיְמָה pr.n.-dir. he (595) *to Egypt*

13:18

וַיַּסֵּב אֱלֹהִים consec.-Hi. impf. 3 m.s. (סָבַב 685)-n.m.p. (43) *but God led round*

אֶת־הָעָם dir. obj.-def. art.-n.m.s. (I 766) *the people*

דֶּרֶךְ n.m.s. cstr. (202) *by the way of*

הַמִּדְבָּר def. art.-n.m.s. (184) *the wilderness*

יַם־סוּף n.m.s. cstr. (410)-n.m.s. (I 693) *toward the Red Sea (sea of rushes)*

וַחֲמֻשִׁים conj.-adj. p. (332) *and equipped for battle*

עָלוּ Qal pf. 3 c.p. (עָלָה 748) *went up*

בְנֵי־יִשְׂרָאֵל n.m.p. cstr. (119)-pr.n. (975) *the people of Israel*

מֵאֶרֶץ prep.-n.f.s. cstr. (75) *out of the land of*

מִצְרָיִם pr.n. paus. (595) *Egypt*

13:19

וַיִּקַּח מֹשֶׁה consec.-Qal impf. 3 m.s.

(לָקַח 542)-pr.n. (602) *and Moses took*
אֶת־עַצְמוֹת dir. obj.-n.f.p. cstr. (782) *the bones of*
יוֹסֵף pr.n. (415) *Joseph*
עִמּוֹ prep.-3 m.s. sf. *with him*
כִּי הַשְׁבֵּעַ conj.-Hi. inf. abs. (989) *for ... solemnly*
הִשְׁבִּיעַ Hi. pf. 3 m.s. (989) *he had sworn*
אֶת־בְּנֵי dir. obj.-n.m.p. cstr. (119) *the people of*
יִשְׂרָאֵל pr.n. (975) *Israel*
לֵאמֹר prep.-Qal inf. cstr. (55) *saying*
פָּקֹד יִפְקֹד Qal inf. abs. (823)-Qal impf. 3 m.s. (823) *will visit*
אֱלֹהִים n.m.p. (43) *God*
אֶתְכֶם dir. obj.-2 m.p. sf. *you*
וְהַעֲלִיתֶם conj.-Hi. pf. 2 m.p. (עָלָה 748) *then you must carry*
אֶת־עַצְמֹתַי dir. obj.-n.f.p.-1 c.s. sf. (782) *my bones*
מִזֶּה prep.-demons. adj. (260) *from here*
אִתְּכֶם prep.-2 m.p. sf. (II 85) *with you*

13:20

וַיִּסְעוּ consec.-Qal impf. 3 m.p. (נָסַע I 652) *and they moved on*
מִסֻּכֹּת prep.-pr.n. (697) *from Succoth*
וַיַּחֲנוּ consec.-Qal impf. 3 m.p. (חָנָה 333) *and encamped*
בְאֵתָם prep.-pr.n. (87) *at Etham*
בִּקְצֵה prep.-n.m.s. cstr. (892) *on the edge of*
הַמִּדְבָּר def. art.-n.m.s. (184) *the wilderness*

13:21

ויהוה conj.-pr.n. (217) *and Yahweh*
הֹלֵךְ Qal act. ptc. (229) *went*
לִפְנֵיהֶם prep.-n.m.p.-3 m.p. sf. (815) *before them*
יוֹמָם adv. (401) *by day*
בְּעַמּוּד prep.-n.m.s. cstr. (765) *in a pillar of*
עָנָן n.m.s. (777) *cloud*
לַנְחֹתָם prep.-Qal inf. cstr.-3 m.p. sf. (נָחָה 634) *to lead them*
הַדֶּרֶךְ def. art.-n.m.s. (202) *along the way*
וְלַיְלָה conj.-n.m.s. (538) *and by night*
בְּעַמּוּד v. supra *in a pillar of*
אֵשׁ n.f.s. (77) *fire*
לְהָאִיר prep.-Hi. inf. cstr. (אוֹר 21) *to give light*
לָהֶם prep.-3 m.p. sf. *to them*
לָלֶכֶת prep.-Qal inf. cstr. (הָלַךְ 229) *that they might travel*
יוֹמָם v. supra *by day*
וָלָיְלָה conj.-n.m.s. as adv. paus. (538) *and by night*

13:22

לֹא־יָמִישׁ neg.-Hi. impf. 3 m.s. (מוּשׁ I 559) *did not depart from*
עַמּוּד n.m.s. cstr. (765) *the pillar of*
הֶעָנָן יוֹמָם def. art.-n.m.s. (777)-v. supra 13:21 *cloud by day*
וְעַמּוּד conj.-v. supra *and the pillar of*
הָאֵשׁ def. art.-n.f.s. (77) *fire*
לָיְלָה n.m.s. as adv. paus. (538) *by night*
לִפְנֵי prep.-n.m.p. cstr. (815) *before*
הָעָם def. art.-n.m.s. (I 766) *the people*

14:1

וַיְדַבֵּר consec.-Pi. impf. 3 m.s. (180) *then ... said*
יהוה pr.n. (217) *Yahweh*
אֶל־מֹשֶׁה prep.-pr.n. (602) *to Moses*
לֵּאמֹר prep.-Qal inf. cstr. (55) *(saying)*

14:2

דַּבֵּר Pi. impv. 2 m.s. (180) *Tell*
אֶל־בְּנֵי prep.-n.m.p. cstr. (119) *the people of*
יִשְׂרָאֵל pr.n. (975) *Israel*
וְיָשֻׁבוּ conj.-Qal impf. 3 m.p. (שׁוּב 996) *to turn back*
וְיַחֲנוּ conj.-Qal impf. 3 m.p. (חָנָה 333) *and encamp*
לִפְנֵי prep.-n.m.p. cstr. (815) *in front*

of

פִּי הַחִירֹת pr.n. (809) *Pihahiroth*

בֵּין מִגְדֹּל prep.-pr.n. (154) *between Migdol*

וּבֵין הַיָּם conj.-prep.-def. art.-n.m.s. (410) *and the sea*

לִפְנֵי v. supra *in front of*

בַּעַל צְפֹן pr.n. (128) *Baalzephon*

נִכְחוֹ adv. acc.-3 m.s. sf. (647) *over against it*

תַּחֲנוּ Qal impf. 2 m.p. (חָנָה 333) *you shall encamp*

עַל־הַיָּם prep.-def. art.-n.m.s. (410) *by the sea*

14:3

וְאָמַר conj.-Qal pf. 3 m.s. (55) *for ... will say*

פַּרְעֹה pr.n. (829) *Pharaoh*

לִבְנֵי prep.-n.m.p. cstr. (119) *of the people of*

יִשְׂרָאֵל pr.n. (975) *Israel*

נְבֻכִים Ni. pass. ptc. m.p. (בּוּךְ 100) *are entangled*

הֵם pers. pr. 3 m.p. (241) *they*

בָּאָרֶץ prep.-def. art.-n.f.s. (75) *in the land*

סָגַר Qal pf. 3 m.s. (688) *has shut in*

עֲלֵיהֶם prep.-3 m.p. sf. *them*

הַמִּדְבָּר def. art.-n.m.s. (184) *the wilderness*

14:4

וְחִזַּקְתִּי conj.-Hi. pf. 1 c.s. (חָזַק 304) *and I will harden*

אֶת־לֵב־ dir. obj.-n.m.s. cstr. (523) *the heart of*

פַּרְעֹה pr.n. (829) *Pharaoh*

וְרָדַף conj.-Qal pf. 3 m.s. (922) *and he will pursue*

אַחֲרֵיהֶם prep.-3 m.p. sf. (29) *(after) them*

וְאִכָּבְדָה conj.-Ni. impf. 1 c.s.-coh. he (כָּבֵד 457) *and I will get glory*

בְּפַרְעֹה prep.-pr.n. (829) *over Pharaoh*

וּבְכָל־חֵילוֹ conj.-prep.-n.m.s. cstr. (481)-n.m.s.-3 m.s. sf. (298) *and all his host*

וְיָדְעוּ conj.-Qal pf. 3 c.p. (393) *and ... shall know*

מִצְרַיִם pr.n. (595) *the Egyptians*

כִּי־אֲנִי conj.-pers. pr. 1 c.s. (58) *that I*

יהוה pr.n. (217) *Yahweh*

וַיַּעֲשׂוּ־כֵן consec.-Qal impf. 3 m. p. (עָשָׂה I 793) - adv.(485) *and they did so*

14:5

וַיֻּגַּד consec.-Ho. impf. 3 m.s. (נָגַד 616) *when it was told*

לְמֶלֶךְ prep.-n.m.s. cstr. (I 572) *the king of*

מִצְרַיִם pr.n. (595) *Egypt*

כִּי בָרַח conj.-Qal pf. 3 m.s. (137) *that had fled*

הָעָם def. art.-n.m.s. (I 766) *the people*

וַיֵּהָפֵךְ consec.-Ni. impf. 3 m.s. (הָפַךְ 245) *and was changed*

לְבַב פַּרְעֹה n.m.s. cstr. (523)-pr.n. (829) *the mind of Pharaoh*

וַעֲבָדָיו conj.-n.m.p.-3 m.s. sf. (713) *and his servants*

אֶל־הָעָם prep.-def. art.-n.m.s. (I 766) *toward the people*

וַיֹּאמְרוּ consec.-Qal impf. 3 m.p. (55) *and they said*

מַה־זֹּאת interr.(552)-demons. adj. f.s. (260) *what is this*

עָשִׂינוּ Qal pf. 1 c.p. (עָשָׂה I 793) *we have done*

כִּי־שִׁלַּחְנוּ conj.-Pi. pf. 1 c.p. (שָׁלַח 1018) *that we have let go*

אֶת־יִשְׂרָאֵל dir.obj.-pr.n. (975) *Israel*

מֵעָבְדֵנוּ prep.-Qal inf. cstr.-1 c.p. sf. (712) *from serving us*

14:6

וַיֶּאְסֹר consec.-Qal impf. 3 m.s. (אָסַר 63) *so he made ready*

אֶת־רִכְבּוֹ dir. obj.-n.m.s.-3 m.s. sf. (939) *his chariot*

וְאֶת־עַמּוֹ conj.-dir. obj.-n.m.s.-3 m.s. sf. (I 766) *and his army*

(people)

לָקַח עִמּוֹ Qal pf. 3 m.s. (542)-prep.-3 m.s. sf. *took with him*

14:7

וַיִּקַּח consec.-Qal impf. 3 m.s. (לָקַח 542) *and took*

שֵׁשׁ־מֵאוֹת num. (995)-n.f.p. cstr. (547) *six hundred (of)*

רֶכֶב n.m.s. (939) *chariots*

בָּחוּר Qal pass. ptc. (בָּחַר 103) *picked*

וְכֹל רֶכֶב conj.-n.m.s. cstr. (481)-n.m.s. cstr. (939) *and all the other chariots of*

מִצְרָיִם pr.n. paus. (595) *Egypt*

וְשָׁלִשִׁם conj.-n.m.p. (III 1026) *with officers*

עַל־כֻּלּוֹ prep.-n.m.s.-3 m.s. sf. (481) *over all of them*

14:8

וַיְחַזֵּק consec.-Pi. impf. 3 m.s. (חָזַק 304) *and hardened*

יהוה pr.n. (217) *Yahweh*

אֶת־לֵב dir. obj.-n.m.s. cstr. (523) *the heart of*

פַּרְעֹה pr.n. (829) *Pharaoh*

מֶלֶךְ n.m.s. cstr. (I 572) *king of*

מִצְרַיִם pr.n. (595) *Egypt*

וַיִּרְדֹּף consec.-Qal impf. 3 m.s. (רָדַף 922) and

וַיִּרְדֹּף consec.-Qal impf. 3 m.s. (רָדַף 922) *and he pursued*

אַחֲרֵי בְּנֵי prep. (29)-n.m.p. cstr. (119) *the people of*

יִשְׂרָאֵל pr.n. (975) *Israel*

וּבְנֵי יִשְׂרָאֵל conj.-n.m.p. cstr. (119)-pr.n. (975) *as they (the children of Israel)*

יֹצְאִים Qal act. ptc. m.p. (יָצָא 422) *went forth*

בְּיָד רָמָה prep.-n.f.s. (388)-Qal act. ptc. f.s. as adj. (926) *defiantly (with uplifted hand)*

14:9

וַיִּרְדְּפוּ consec.-Qal impf. 3 m.p. (רָדַף 922) *pursued*

מִצְרַיִם pr. n. (595) *the Egyptians*

אַחֲרֵיהֶם prep.-3 m.p. sf. (29) *(after) them*

וַיַּשִּׂיגוּ consec.-Hi. impf. 3 m.p. (נָשַׂג 673) *and overtook*

אוֹתָם dir.obj.-3 m.p. sf. *them*

חֹנִים Qal act. ptc. m.p. (חָנָה 333) *encamped*

עַל־הַיָּם prep.-def.art.-n.m.s. (410) *at the sea*

כָּל־סוּס n.m.s. cstr. (481)-n.m.s. cstr. (692) *all horses*

רֶכֶב n.m.s. cstr. (939) *chariots of*

פַּרְעֹה pr.n. (829) *Pharaoh*

וּפָרָשָׁיו conj.-n.m.p.-3 m.s. sf. (832) *and his horsemen*

וְחֵילוֹ conj.-n.m.s.-3 m.s. sf. (298) *and his army*

עַל־פִּי הַחִירֹת prep.-pr.n. (809) *by Pihahiroth*

לִפְנֵי prep.-n.m.p. cstr. (815) *in front of*

בַּעַל צְפֹן pr.n. (128) *Baalzephon*

14:10

וּפַרְעֹה conj.-pr.n. (829) *when Pharaoh*

הִקְרִיב Hi. pf. 3 m.s. (897) *drew near*

וַיִּשְׂאוּ consec.-Qal impf. 3 m.p. (נָשָׂא 669) *lifted up*

בְנֵי־יִשְׂרָאֵל n.m.p. cstr. (119)-pr.n. (975) *the people of Israel*

אֶת־עֵינֵיהֶם dir. obj.-n.f.p.-3 m.p. sf. (744) *their eyes*

וְהִנֵּה conj.-demons. part. (243) *and behold*

מִצְרַיִם pr.n. (595) *the Egyptians*

נֹסֵעַ Qal act. ptc. (נָסַע 652) *were marching*

אַחֲרֵיהֶם prep.-3 m.p. sf. (29) *after them*

וַיִּירְאוּ consec.-Qal impf. 3 m.p. (יָרֵא 431) *and they were in fear*

מְאֹד adv. (547) *great*

וַיִּצְעֲקוּ consec.-Qal impf. 3 m.p. (צָעַק 858) *and cried out*

בְנֵי־יִשְׂרָאֵל n.m.p. cstr. (119)-pr.n. (975) *the people of Israel*

אֶל־יהוה prep.-pr.n. (217) *to Yahweh*

14:11

וַיֹּאמְרוּ consec.-Qal impf. 3 m.p. (55) *and they said*

אֶל־מֹשֶׁה prep.-pr.n. (602) *to Moses*

הַמִבְּלִי interr. part.-prep.-subst. (115) *is it because*

אֵין־קְבָרִים subst. (II 34)-n.m.p. (868) *there are no graves*

בְּמִצְרַיִם prep.-pr.n. (595) *in Egypt*

לְקַחְתָּנוּ Qal pf. 2 m.s.-1 c.p. sf. (542) *that you have taken us away*

לָמוּת prep.-Qal inf. cstr. (מוּת 559) *to die*

בַּמִּדְבָּר prep.-def. art.-n.m.s. (184) *in the wilderness*

מַה־זֹּאת interr. (552)-demons. adj. f.s. (260) *What (this)*

עָשִׂיתָ לָּנוּ Qal pf. 2 m.s. (עָשָׂה I 793)-prep.-1 c.p. sf. *have you done to us*

לְהוֹצִיאָנוּ prep.-Hi. inf. cstr.-1 c.p. sf. (יָצָא 422) *in bringing us out*

מִמִּצְרָיִם prep.-pr.n. paus. (595) *of Egypt*

14:12

הֲלֹא־זֶה interr.part.-neg.-demons. adj. m.s. (260) *is not this*

הַדָּבָר def.art.-n.m.s. (182) *what (the word)*

אֲשֶׁר דִּבַּרְנוּ rel.-Pi. pf. 1 c.p. (180) *we said*

אֵלֶיךָ prep.-2 m.s. sf. *to you*

בְמִצְרַיִם prep.-pr.n. (595) *in Egypt*

לֵאמֹר prep.-Qal inf. cstr. (55) *(saying)*

חֲדַל Qal impv. 2 m.s. (292) *let alone*

מִמֶּנּוּ prep.-1 c.p. sf. *us*

וְנַעַבְדָה conj.-Qal impf. 1 c.p.-coh. he (עָבַד 712) *and let us serve*

אֶת־מִצְרָיִם dir.obj.-pr.n. paus. (595) *the Egyptians*

כִּי טוֹב לָנוּ conj.-adj. (I 373)-prep.-1 c.p. sf. *for it would have been better for us*

עֲבֹד Qal inf. cstr. (712) *to serve*

אֶת־מִצְרַיִם dir.obj.-pr.n. (595) *the Egyptians*

מִמֻּתֵנוּ prep.-Qal inf. cstr.-1 c.p. sf. (מוּת 559) *than to die*

בַּמִּדְבָּר prep.-def.art.-n.m.s. (184) *in the wilderness*

14:13

וַיֹּאמֶר consec.-Qal impf. 3 m.s. (55) *and ... said*

מֹשֶׁה pr.n. (602) *Moses*

אֶל־הָעָם prep.-def.art.-n.m.s. (I 766) *to the people*

אַל־תִּירָאוּ neg.-Qal impf. 2 m.p. (יָרֵא 431) *Fear not*

הִתְיַצְּבוּ Hith. impv. 2 m.p. (יָצַב 426) *stand firm*

וּרְאוּ conj.-Qal impv. 2 m.p. (רָאָה 906) *and see*

אֶת־יְשׁוּעַת dir.obj.-n.f.s. cstr. (447) *the salvation of*

יהוה pr.n. (217) *Yahweh*

אֲשֶׁר־יַעֲשֶׂה rel.-Qal impf. 3 m.s. (I 793) *which he will work*

לָכֶם prep.-2 m.p. sf. *for you*

הַיּוֹם def.art.-n.m.s. (398) *today*

כִּי אֲשֶׁר conj.-rel. *for whom*

רְאִיתֶם Qal pf. 2 m.p. (רָאָה 906) *you see*

אֶת־מִצְרַיִם dir.obj.-pr.n. (595) *the Egyptians*

הַיּוֹם v.supra *today*

לֹא תֹסִפוּ neg.-Hi. impf. 2 m.p. (יָסַף 414) *you shall never*

לִרְאֹתָם prep.-Qal inf. cstr.-3 m.p. sf. (רָאָה 906) *see (them)*

עוֹד adv. (728) *again*

עַד־עוֹלָם prep.-n.m.s. (761) *(until forever)*

14:14

יהוה pr.n. (217) *Yahweh*

יִלָּחֵם Ni. impf. 3 m.s. (לָחַם 535) *will fight*

לָכֶם prep.-2 m.p. sf. *for you*

וְאַתֶּם conj.-pers.pr. 2 m.p. (61) *and you*

תַּחֲרִישׁוּן Hi. impf. 2 m.p. (חָרֵשׁ II 361) *have only to be still*

14:15

וַיֹּאמֶר consec.-Qal impf. 3 m.s. (55)

said

יהוה pr.n. (217) *Yahweh*

אֶל־מֹשֶׁה prep.-pr.n. (602) *to Moses*

מַה־תִּצְעַק interr. (552)-Qal impf. 2 m.s. (858) *Why do you cry*

אֵלָי prep.-1 c.s. sf. paus. *to me*

דַּבֵּר Pi. impv. 2 m.s. (180) *Tell*

אֶל־בְּנֵי־ prep.-n.m.p. cstr. (119) *the people of*

יִשְׂרָאֵל pr.n. (975) *Israel*

וְיִסָּעוּ conj.-Qal impf. 3 m.p. paus. (נָסַע I 652) *to go forward*

14:16

וְאַתָּה conj.-pers. pr. 2 m.s. (61) *(and you)*

הָרֵם Hi. impv. 2 m.s. (רום 926) *lift up*

אֶת־מַטְּךָ dir. obj.-n.m.s.-2 m.s. sf. (641) *your rod*

וּנְטֵה conj.-Qal impv. 2 m.s. (נָטָה 639) *and stretch out*

אֶת־יָדְךָ dir. obj.-n.f.s.-2 m.s. sf. (388) *your hand*

עַל־הַיָּם prep.-def. art.-n.m.s. (410) *over the sea*

וּבְקָעֵהוּ conj.-Qal impv. 2 m.s.-3 m.s. sf. (בָּקַע 131) *and divide it*

וְיָבֹאוּ conj.-Qal impf. 3 m.p. (בּוֹא 97) *that ... may go*

בְנֵי־יִשְׂרָאֵל n.m.p. cstr. (119)-pr.n. (975) *the people of Israel*

בְּתוֹךְ הַיָּם prep.-n.m.s. cstr. (1063)-def. art.-n.m.s. (410) *through the sea*

בַּיַּבָּשָׁה prep.-def. art.-n.f.s. (387) *on dry ground*

14:17

וַאֲנִי conj.-pers. pr. 1 c.s. (58) *and I*

הִנְנִי demons. part.-1 c.s. sf. (243) *(behold I)*

מְחַזֵּק Pi. ptc. (חָזַק 304) *will harden*

אֶת־לֵב dir. obj.-n.m.s. cstr. (523) *the hearts of*

מִצְרַיִם pr.n. (595) *the Egyptians*

וְיָבֹאוּ conj.-Qal impf. 3 m.p. (בּוֹא 97) *so that they shall go in*

אַחֲרֵיהֶם prep.-3 m.p. sf. (29) *after them*

וְאִכָּבְדָה conj.-Ni. impf. 1 c.s.-vol. he (כָּבַד 457) *and I will get glory*

בְּפַרְעֹה prep.-pr.n. (829) *over Pharaoh*

וּבְכָל־חֵילוֹ conj.-prep.-n.m.s. cstr. (481)-n.m.s.-3 m.s. sf. (298) *and all his host*

בְּרִכְבּוֹ prep.-n.m.s.-3 m.s. sf. (939) *his chariots*

וּבְפָרָשָׁיו conj.-prep.-n.m.p.-3 m.s. sf. (832) *and his horsemen*

14:18

וְיָדְעוּ conj.-Qal pf. 3 c.p. (393) *and ... shall know*

מִצְרַיִם pr.n. (595) *the Egyptians*

כִּי־אֲנִי conj.-pers. pr. 1 c.s. (58) *that I*

יהוה pr.n. (217) *Yahweh*

בְּהִכָּבְדִי prep.-Ni. inf. cstr.-1 c.s. sf. (כָּבַד 457) *when I have gotten glory*

בְּפַרְעֹה prep.-pr.n. (829) *over Pharaoh*

בְּרִכְבּוֹ prep.-n.m.s.-3 m.s. sf. (939) *his chariots*

וּבְפָרָשָׁיו conj.-prep.-n.m.p.-3 m.s. sf. (832) *and his horsemen*

14:19

וַיִּסַּע consec.-Qal impf. 3 m.s. (נָסַע 652) *then ... moved*

מַלְאַךְ n.m.s. cstr. (521) *the angel of*

הָאֱלֹהִים def. art.-n.m.p. (43) *God*

הַהֹלֵךְ def. art.-Qal act. ptc. (הָלַךְ 229) *who went*

לִפְנֵי prep.-n.m.p. cstr. (815) *before*

מַחֲנֵה n.m.s. cstr. (334) *the host of*

יִשְׂרָאֵל pr.n. (975) *Israel*

וַיֵּלֶךְ consec.-Qal impf. 3 m.s. (הָלַךְ 229) *and went*

מֵאַחֲרֵיהֶם prep.-prep.-3 m.p. sf. (29) *behind them*

וַיִּסַּע v. supra *and moved*

עַמּוּד n.m.s. cstr. (765) *the pillar of*

הֶעָנָן def. art.-n.m.s. (777) *cloud*

מִפְּנֵיהֶם prep.-n.m.p.-3 m.p. sf. (815) *from before them*

וַיַּעֲמֹד consec.-Qal impf. 3 m.s. (763) *and stood*

מֵאַחֲרֵיהֶם v. supra *behind them*

14:20

וַיָּבֹא consec.-Qal impf. 3 m.s. (בּוֹא 97) *coming*

בֵּין מַחֲנֵה prep.-n.m.s. cstr. (334) *between the host of*

מִצְרַיִם pr.n. (595) *Egypt*

וּבֵין מַחֲנֵה conj.-v. supra-v. supra *and the host of*

יִשְׂרָאֵל pr.n. (975) *Israel*

וַיְהִי consec.-Qal impf. 3 m.s. (הָיָה 224) *and there was*

הֶעָנָן def. art.-n.m.s. (777) *the cloud*

וְהַחֹשֶׁךְ conj.-def. art.-n.m.s. (365) *and the darkness*

וַיָּאֶר consec.-Hi. impf. 3 m.s. (אוֹר 21) *and ... passed (caused to light)*

אֶת־הַלָּיְלָה dir. obj.-def. art.-n.m.s. paus. (538) *the night*

וְלֹא־קָרַב conj.-neg.-Qal pf. 3 m.s. (897) *without ... coming near*

זֶה demons. adj. (260) *one*

אֶל־זֶה prep.-demons. adj. (260) *(unto) the other*

כָּל־הַלָּיְלָה n.m.s. cstr. (481)-def. art.-n.m.s. paus. (538) *all night*

14:21

וַיֵּט consec.-Qal impf. 3 m.s. (נָטָה 639) *then ... stretched out*

מֹשֶׁה pr.n. (602) *Moses*

אֶת־יָדוֹ dir. obj.-n.f.s.-3 m.s. sf. (388) *his hand*

עַל־הַיָּם prep.-def. art.-n.m.s. (410) *over the sea*

וַיּוֹלֶךְ consec.-Hi. impf. 3 m.s. (הָלַךְ 229) *and ... drove back*

יהוה pr.n. (217) *Yahweh*

אֶת־הַיָּם dir. obj.-def. art.-n.m.s. (410) *the sea*

בְּרוּחַ קָדִים prep.-n.f.s. cstr. (924)-n.m.s. (870) *by a ... east wind*

עַזָּה adj. f.s. (738) *strong*

כָּל־הַלַּיְלָה n.m.s. cstr. (481)-def. art.-n.m.s. (538) *all night*

וַיָּשֶׂם consec.-Qal impf. 3 m.s. (שִׂים 962) *and made*

אֶת־הַיָּם dir. obj.-def. art.-n.m.s. (410) *the sea*

לֶחָרָבָה prep.-def. art.-n.f.s. (352) *dry land*

וַיִּבָּקְעוּ consec.-Ni. impf. 3 m.p. (בָּקַע 131) *and were divided*

הַמָּיִם def. art.-n.m.p. paus. (565) *the waters*

14:22

וַיָּבֹאוּ consec.-Qal impf. 3 m.p. (בּוֹא 97) *and ... went*

בְנֵי־יִשְׂרָאֵל n.m.p. cstr. (119)-pr.n. (975) *the people of Israel*

בְּתוֹךְ prep.-n.m.s. cstr. (תָּוֶךְ 1063) *into the midst of*

הַיָּם def. art.-n.m.s. (410) *the sea*

בַּיַּבָּשָׁה prep.-def. art.-n.f.s. (387) *on dry ground*

וְהַמַּיִם conj.-def. art.-n.m.p. (565) *(and) the waters*

לָהֶם prep.-3 m.p. sf. *to them*

חֹמָה n.f.s. (327) *a wall*

מִימִינָם prep.-n.f.s.-3 m.p. sf. (411) *on their right hand*

וּמִשְּׂמֹאלָם conj.-prep.-n.m.s.-3 m.p. sf. (969) *and on their left*

14:23

וַיִּרְדְּפוּ consec.-Qal impf. 3 m.p. (רָדַף 922) *pursued*

מִצְרַיִם pr.n. (595) *the Egyptians*

וַיָּבֹאוּ consec.-Qal impf. 3 m.p. (בּוֹא 97) *and went in*

אַחֲרֵיהֶם prep.-3 m.p. sf. (29) *after them*

כֹּל סוּס n.m.s. cstr. (481)-n.m.s. cstr. (692) *all horses (of)*

פַּרְעֹה pr.n. (829) *Pharaoh*

רִכְבּוֹ n.m.s.-3 m.s. sf. (939) *his chariots*

וּפָרָשָׁיו conj.-n.m.p.-3 m.s. sf. (832) *and his horsemen*

אֶל־תּוֹךְ prep.-n.m.s. cstr. (1063) *into the midst of*

הַיָּם def. art.-n.m.s. (410) *the sea*

14:24

וַיְהִי consec.-Qal impf. 3 m.s. (224)

and (it was)
בְּאַשְׁמֹרֶת prep.-n.f.s. cstr. (1038) *in the watch of*
הַבֹּקֶר def.art.-n.m.s. (133) *the morning*
וַיַּשְׁקֵף consec.-Hi. impf. 3 m.s. (שָׁקַף 1054) *looked down*
יהוה pr.n. (217) *Yahweh*
אֶל־מַחֲנֵה prep.-n.m.s. cstr. (334) *upon the host of*
מִצְרַיִם pr.n. (595) *the Egyptians*
בְּעַמּוּד prep.-n.m.s. cstr. (765) *in the pillar of*
אֵשׁ n.f.s. (77) *fire*
וְעָנָן conj.-n.m.s. (777) *and cloud*
וַיָּהָם consec.-Qal impf. 3 m.s. (הָמַם 243) *and discomfited*
אֵת מַחֲנֵה dir.obj.-v.supra *the host of*
מִצְרָיִם pr.n. paus. (595) *the Egyptians*

14:25

וַיָּסַר consec.-Qal impf. 3 m.s. (סוּר 693) *clogging (and he turned)*
אֵת אֹפַן dir.obj.-n.m.s. cstr. (66) *wheels of*
מַרְכְּבֹתָיו n.f.p.-3 m.s. sf. (939) *their chariots*
וַיְנַהֲגֵהוּ consec.-Pi. impf. 3 m.s.-3 m.s. sf. (נָהַג 624) *so that they drove*
בִּכְבֵדֻת prep.-n.f.s. (459) *heavily*
וַיֹּאמֶר consec.-Qal impf. 3 m.s. (55) *and ... said*
מִצְרַיִם pr.n. (595) *the Egyptians*
אָנוּסָה Qal impf. 1 c.s. - coh. he (נוּס 630) *let us flee*
מִפְּנֵי prep.-n.m.p. cstr. (815) *from before*
יִשְׂרָאֵל pr.n. (975) *Israel*
כִּי יהוה conj.-pr.n. (217) *for Yahweh*
נִלְחָם Ni. pf. 3 m.s. (לָחַם 535) *fights*
לָהֶם prep.-3 m.p. sf. *for them*
בְּמִצְרָיִם prep.-pr.n. paus. (595) *against the Egyptians*

14:26

וַיֹּאמֶר consec.-Qal impf. 3 m.s. (55) *then ... said*
יהוה pr.n. (217) *Yahweh*
אֶל־מֹשֶׁה prep.-pr.n. (602) *to Moses*
נְטֵה Qal impv. 2 m.s. (נָטָה 639) *stretch out*
אֶת־יָדְךָ dir.obj.-n.f.s.-2 m.s. sf. (388) *your hand*
עַל־הַיָּם prep.-def.art.-n.m.s. (410) *over the sea*
וְיָשֻׁבוּ conj.-Qal impf. 3 m.p. apoc. (שׁוּב 996) *that ... may come back*
הַמַּיִם def.art.-n.m.p. (565) *the water*
עַל־מִצְרַיִם prep.-pr.n. (595) *upon the Egyptians*
עַל־רִכְבּוֹ prep.-n.m.s.-3 m.s. sf. (939) *upon their chariots*
וְעַל־פָּרָשָׁיו conj.-prep.-n.m.p.-3 m.s. sf. (832) *and upon their horsemen*

14:27

וַיֵּט consec.-Qal impf. 3 m.s. (נָטָה 639) *so ... stretched forth*
מֹשֶׁה pr.n. (602) *Moses*
אֶת־יָדוֹ dir.obj.-n.f.s.-3 m.s. sf. (388) *his hand*
עַל־הַיָּם prep.-def.art.-n.m.s. (410) *over the sea*
וַיָּשָׁב consec.-Qal impf. 3 m.s. (שׁוּב 996) *and ... returned*
הַיָּם v.supra *the sea*
לִפְנוֹת prep.-Qal inf. cstr. (פָּנָה 815) *when ... appeared*
בֹּקֶר n.m.s. (133) *the morning*
לְאֵיתָנוֹ prep.-n.m.s.-3 m.s. sf. (I 450) *to its wonted flow*
וּמִצְרַיִם conj.-pr.n. (595) *and the Egyptians*
נָסִים Qal act. ptc. m.p. (נוּס 630) *fled*
לִקְרָאתוֹ prep.-Qal inf. cstr.-3 m.s. sf. (קָרָא 894) *into it*
וַיְנַעֵר consec.-Pi. impf. 3 m.s. (נָעַר II 654) *and ... routed (shook off)*
יהוה pr.n. (217) *Yahweh*
אֶת־מִצְרַיִם dir.obj.-pr.n. (595) *the Egyptians*
בְּתוֹךְ prep.-n.m.s. cstr. (1063) *in the midst of*

הַיָּם def.art.-n.m.s. (410) *the sea*

14:28

וַיָּשֻׁבוּ consec.-Qal impf. 3 m.p. (שׁוּב 996) *returned*

הַמַּיִם def.art.-n.m.p. (565) *the waters*

וַיְכַסּוּ consec.-Pi. impf. 3 m.p. (כָּסָה 491) *and covered*

אֶת־הָרֶכֶב dir.obj.-def.art.-n.m.s. (939) *the chariots*

וְאֶת־הַפָּרָשִׁים conj.-dir.obj.-def.art.-n.m.p. (832) *and the horsemen*

לְכֹל חֵיל prep.-n.m.s. cstr. (481)-n.m.s. cstr. (298) *(to) all the host of*

פַּרְעֹה pr.n. (829) *Pharaoh*

הַבָּאִים def.art.-Qal act. ptc. m.p. (בּוֹא 97) *that had followed (come)*

אַחֲרֵיהֶם prep.-3 m.p. sf. (29) *(after) them*

בַּיָּם prep.-def.art.-n.m.s. (410) *into the sea*

לֹא־נִשְׁאַר neg.-Ni. pf. 3 m.s. (שָׁאַר 983) *not ... remained*

בָּהֶם prep.-3 m.p. sf. *of them*

עַד־אֶחָד adv. (III 723)-num. m.s. (25) *so much as one*

14:29

וּבְנֵי conj.-n.m.p. cstr. (119) *but the people of*

יִשְׂרָאֵל pr.n. (975) *Israel*

הָלְכוּ Qal pf. 3 c.p. (הָלַךְ 229) *walked*

בַיַּבָּשָׁה prep.-def.art.-n.f.s. (387) *on dry ground*

בְּתוֹךְ prep.-n.m.s. cstr. (1063) *through*

הַיָּם def.art.-n.m.s. (410) *the sea*

וְהַמַּיִם conj.-def.art.-n.m.p. (565) *the waters*

לָהֶם prep.-3 m.p. sf. *to them*

חֹמָה n.f.s. (327) *a wall*

מִימִינָם v.14:22 prep.-n.f.s.-3 m.p. sf. (411) *on their right hand*

וּמִשְּׂמֹאלָם conj.-prep.-n.m.s.-3 m.p. sf. (969) *and on their left*

14:30

וַיּוֹשַׁע consec.-Hi. impf. 3 m.s. (יָשַׁע 446) *thus ... saved*

יהוה pr.n. (217) *Yahweh*

בַּיּוֹם הַהוּא prep.-def.art.-n.m.s. (398)-def.art.-demons. adj. m.s. (214) *(on) that day*

אֶת־יִשְׂרָאֵל dir.obj.-pr.n. (975) *Israel*

מִיַּד prep.-n.f.s. cstr. (388) *from the hand of*

מִצְרָיִם pr.n. paus. (595) *the Egyptians*

וַיַּרְא consec.-Qal impf. 3 m.s. (רָאָה 906) *and ... saw*

יִשְׂרָאֵל pr.n. (975) *Israel*

אֶת־מִצְרַיִם dir.obj.-pr.n. (595) *the Egyptians*

מֵת Qal act. ptc. (מוּת 559) *dead*

עַל־שְׂפַת prep.-n.f.s. cstr. (973) *upon the shore (lip) of*

הַיָּם def.art.-n.m.s. (410) *the sea*

14:31

וַיַּרְא v.14:30 consec.-Qal impf. 3 m.s. (רָאָה 906) *and ... saw*

יִשְׂרָאֵל pr.n. (975) *Israel*

אֶת־הַיָּד dir.obj.-def.art.-n.f.s. (388) *the ... work*

הַגְּדֹלָה def.art.-adj. f.s. (152) *great*

אֲשֶׁר rel.

עָשָׂה Qal pf. 3 m.s. (I 793) *did*

יהוה pr.n. (217) *Yahweh*

בְּמִצְרַיִם prep.-pr.n. (595) *against the Egyptians*

וַיִּירְאוּ consec.-Qal impf. 3 m.p. (יָרֵא 431) *and ... feared*

הָעָם def.art.-n.m.s. (I 766) *the people*

אֶת־יהוה dir.obj.-pr.n. (217) *Yahweh*

וַיַּאֲמִינוּ consec.-Hi. impf. 3 m.p. (אָמַן 52) *and they believed*

בּיהוה prep.-pr.n. (217) *in Yahweh*

וּבְמֹשֶׁה conj.-prep.-pr.n. (602) *and in Moses*

עַבְדּוֹ n.m.s.-3 m.s. sf. (713) *his servant*

15:1

אָז adv. (23) *then*

יָשִׁיר־מֹשֶׁה Qal impf. 3 m.s. (שִׁיר 1010) - pr.n. (602) *Moses sang*

וּבְנֵי conj.-n.m.p. cstr. (119) *and the people of*

יִשְׂרָאֵל pr.n. (975) *Israel*

אֶת־הַשִּׁירָה dir.obj.-def.art.-n.f.s. (1010) *song*

הַזֹּאת def.art.-demons.adj. f.s. (260) *this*

הַזֹּאז def.art.-demons. adj. f.s. (260) *this*

לַיהוה prep.-pr.n. (217) *to Yahweh*

וַיֹּאמְרוּ consec.-Qal impf. 3 m.p. (55) *(and said)*

לֵאמֹר prep.-Qal inf. cstr. (55) *saying*

אָשִׁירָה Qal impf. 1 c.s.-coh. he (1010) *I will sing*

לַיהוה prep.-pr.n. (217) *to Yahweh*

כִּי־גָאֹה גָּאָה conj.-Qal inf. abs. (גָּאָה 144) - Qal pf. 3 m.s. (144) *for he has triumphed gloriously*

סוּס n.m.s. (692) *horse*

וְרֹכְבוֹ conj.-Qal act. ptc.-3 m.s. sf. (938) *and his rider*

רָמָה Qal pf. 3 m.s. (I 941) *he has thrown*

בַיָּם prep.-def.art.-n.m.s. (410) *into the sea*

15:2

עָזִּי n.m.s.-1 c.s. sf. (738) *my strength*

וְזִמְרָת conj.-n.f.s. (I 274) *and my song*

יָהּ pr.n. (219) *Yahweh*

וַיְהִי־לִי consec.-Qal impf. 3 m.s. (הָיָה 224) - prep.-1 c.s. sf. *and he has become my*

לִישׁוּעָה prep.-n.f.s. (447) *salvation*

זֶה אֵלִי demons. adj. m.s. (260) - n.m.s.-1 c.s. sf. (42) *this is my God*

וְאַנְוֵהוּ conj.-Hi. impf. 1 c.s.-3 m.s. sf. (נָוָה I 627) *and I will praise him*

אֱלֹהֵי n.m.p. cstr. (43) *God of*

אָבִי n.m.s.-1 c.s. sf. (3) *my father*

וַאֲרֹמְמֶנְהוּ conj.-Polel impf. 1 c.s.-3 m.s. sf. (רוּם 926) *and I will exalt him*

15:3

יהוה pr.n. (217) *Yahweh*

אִישׁ n.m.s. cstr. (35) *a man of*

מִלְחָמָה n.f.s (526) *war*

יהוה v.supra *Yahweh*

שְׁמוֹ n.m.s.-3 m.s. sf. (1027) *his name*

15:4

מַרְכְּבֹת n.f.p. cstr. (939) *chariots of*

פַּרְעֹה pr.n. (829) *Pharaoh*

וְחֵילוֹ conj.-n.m.s.-3 m.s. sf. (298) *and his host*

יָרָה Qal pf. 3 m.s. (434) *he cast*

בַיָּם prep.-def.art.-n.m.s. (410) *into the sea*

וּמִבְחַר conj.-n.m.s. cstr. (103) *picked*

שָׁלִשָׁיו n.m.p.-3 m.s. sf. (III 1026) *his officers*

טֻבְּעוּ Pu. pf. 3 c.p. (טָבַע 371) *are sunk*

בְיַם־סוּף prep.-n.m.s. cstr. (410)-n.m.s. (I 693) *in the Red (?) Sea*

15:5

תְּהֹמֹת n.f.p. (1062) *floods*

יְכַסְיֻמוּ Pi. impf. 3 m.p.-3 m.p. sf. (כָּסָה 491) *cover them*

יָרְדוּ Qal pf. 3 c.p. (יָרַד 432) *they went down*

בִמְצוֹלֹת prep.-n.f.p. (846) *into the depths*

כְּמוֹ־אָבֶן prep.-n.f.s. paus. (6) *like a stone*

15:6

יְמִינְךָ n.f.s.-2 m.s. sf. (411) *thy right hand*

יהוה pr.n. (217) *O Yahweh*

נֶאְדָּרִי Ni. ptc. cstr. (אָדַר 12) *glorious*

בַּכֹּחַ prep.-def.art.-n.m.s. (470) *in power*

יְמִינְךָ v.supra *thy right hand*

יהוה pr.n. (217) *O Yahweh*

תִּרְעַץ Qal impf. 3 f.s. (רָעַץ 950) *shatters*

אוֹיֵב Qal act. ptc. (אָיַב 33) *the enemy*

15:7

וּבְרֹב conj.-prep.-n.m.s. cstr. (913) *in the greatness of*

גְּאוֹנְךָ n.m.s.-2 m.s. sf. (144) *thy majesty*

תַּהֲרֹס Qal impf. 2 m.s. (הָרַס 248) *thou overthrowest*

קָמֶיךָ Qal act. ptc. m.p.-2 m.s. sf. (קוּם 877) *thy adversaries*

תְּשַׁלַּח Pi. impf. 2 m.s. (1018) *thou sendest forth*

חֲרֹנְךָ n.m.s.-2 m.s. sf. (354) *thy fury*

יֹאכְלֵמוֹ Qal impf. 3 m.s.-3 m.p. sf. (אָכַל 37) *it consumes them*

כַּקַּשׁ prep.-def.art.-n.m.s. (905) *like stubble*

15:8

וּבְרוּחַ conj.-prep.-n.f.s. cstr. (924) *at the blast of*

אַפֶּיךָ n.m.p.-2 m.s. sf. (I 60) *thy nostrils*

נֶעֶרְמוּ Ni. pf. 3 c.p. (עָרַם 790) *piled up*

מַיִם n.m.p. (565) *waters*

נִצְּבוּ Ni. pf. 3 c.p. (נָצַב 662) *stood up*

כְמוֹ־נֵד prep. (455) n.m.s. (622) *in a heap*

נֹזְלִים Qal act. ptc. m.p. (נָזַל 633) *floods*

קָפְאוּ Qal pf. 3 c.p. (קָפָא 891) *congealed*

תְהֹמֹת n.f.p. (1062) *deeps*

בְּלֶב־יָם prep.-n.m.s. cstr. (523)-n.m.s. (410) *in the heart of the sea*

15:9

אָמַר Qal pf. 3 m.s. (55) *said*

אוֹיֵב Qal act. ptc. (אָיַב 33) *the enemy*

אֶרְדֹּף Qal impf. 1 c.s. (רָדַף 922) *I will pursue*

אַשִּׂיג Hi. impf. 1 c.s. (נָשַׂג 673) *I will overtake*

אֲחַלֵּק Pi. impf. 1 c.s. (חָלַק 323) *I will divide*

שָׁלָל n.m.s. (1021) *the spoil*

תִּמְלָאֵמוֹ Qal impf. 3 f.s.-3 m.p. sf. (מָלֵא 569) *shall have its fill of them*

נַפְשִׁי n.f.s.-1 c.s. sf. (659) *my desire*

אָרִיק Hi. impf. 1 c.s. (רִיק 937) *I will draw*

חַרְבִּי n.f.s.-1 c.s. sf. (352) *my sword*

תּוֹרִישֵׁמוֹ Hi. impf. 3 f.s.-3 m.p. sf. (יָרַשׁ 439) *shall destroy them*

יָדִי n.f.s.-1 c.s. sf. (388) *my hand*

15:10

נָשַׁפְתָּ Qal pf. 2 m.s. (נָשַׁף 676) *thou didst blow*

בְרוּחֲךָ prep.-n.f.s.-2 m.s. sf. (924) *with thy wind*

כִּסָּמוֹ Pi. pf. 3 m.s.-3 m.p. sf. (כָּסָה 491) *covered them*

יָם n.ms. (410) *the sea*

צָלֲלוּ Qal pf. 3 c.p. (צָלַל II 853) *they sank*

כַּעוֹפֶרֶת prep.-def.art.-n.f.s. (780) *as lead*

בְּמַיִם prep.-n.m.p. (565) *in ... waters*

אַדִּירִים adj. m.p. (12) *mighty*

15:11

מִי־כָמֹכָה interr. (566)-prep.-2 m.s. sf. *Who is like thee?*

בָּאֵלִם prep.-def.art.-n.m.p. (42) *among the gods*

יהוה pr.n. (217) *O Yahweh*

מִי כָּמֹכָה v.supra *who is like thee*

נֶאְדָּר Ni. ptc. (אָדַר 12) *majestic*

בַּקֹּדֶשׁ prep.-def.art.-n.m.s. (871) *in holiness*

נוֹרָא Ni. ptc. (יָרֵא 431) *terrible*

תְהִלֹּת n.f.p. (239) *in glorious deeds*

עֹשֵׂה Qal act. ptc. m.s. cstr. (I 793) *doing*

פֶלֶא n.m.s. (810) *wonders*

15:12

נָטִיתָ Qal pf. 2 m.s. (נָטָה 639) *thou didst stretch out*

יְמִינְךָ n.f.s.-2 m.s. sf. (411) *thy right hand*

תִּבְלָעֵמוֹ Qal impf. 3 f.s.-3 m.p. sf.

(בָּלַע 118) *swallowed them*

אָרֶץ n.f.s. paus. (75) *earth*

15:13

נָחִיתָ Qal pf. 2 m.s. (נָחָה 634) *thou hast led*

בְחַסְדְּךָ prep.-n.m.s.-2 m.s. sf. (338) *in thy stedfast love*

עַם־זוּ n.m.s. (I 766)-rel. (262) *people whom*

גָּאָלְתָּ Qal pf. 2 m.s. paus. (גָּאַל I 145) *thou hast redeemed*

נֵהַלְתָּ Pi. pf. 2 m.s. (נָהַל 624) *thou hast guided*

בְעָזְּךָ prep.-n.m.s.-2 m.s. sf. (738) *by thy strength*

אֶל־נְוֵה prep.-n.m.s. cstr. (627) *to ... abode (of)*

קָדְשֶׁךָ adj. m.s. - 2 m.s. sf. (872) *thy holy*

15:14

שָׁמְעוּ Qal pf. 3 c.p. (1033) *have heard*

עַמִּים n.m.p. (I 766) *peoples*

יִרְגָּזוּן Qal impf. 3 m.p. paus. (רָגַז 919) *they tremble*

חִיל n.m.s. (297) *pangs*

אָחַז Qal pf. 3 m.s. (28) *have seized on*

יֹשְׁבֵי Qal act. ptc. m.p. cstr. (442) *the inhabitants of*

פְּלָשֶׁת pr.n. paus. (814) *Philistia*

15:15

אָז adv. (23) *now*

נִבְהֲלוּ Ni. pf. 3 c.p. (בָּהַל 96) *are dismayed*

אַלּוּפֵי n.m.p. cstr. (II 49) *the chiefs of*

אֱדוֹם pr.n. (10) *Edom*

אֵילֵי n.m.p. cstr. (III 18) *the leaders of*

מוֹאָב pr.n. (555) *Moab*

יֹאחֲזֵמוֹ Qal impf. 3 m.s.-3 m.p. sf. (אָחַז 28) *seizes them*

רָעַד n.m.s. (944) *trembling*

נָמֹגוּ Ni. pf. 3 c.p. (מוּג 556) *have melted away*

כֹּל יֹשְׁבֵי n.m.s. cstr. (481) - Qal act.ptc. m.p. cstr. (442) *all the inhabitants of*

כְנָעַן pr.n. paus. (488) *Canaan*

15:16

תִּפֹּל Qal impf. 3 f.s. (נָפַל 656) *fall*

עֲלֵיהֶם prep.-3 m.p. sf. *upon them*

אֵימָתָה n.f.s. (33) *terror*

וָפַחַד conj.-n.m.s. (808) *and dread*

בִּגְדֹל prep.-adj. m.s. cstr. (152) *because of the greatness of*

זְרוֹעֲךָ n.f.s.-2 m.s. sf. (283) *thy arm*

יִדְּמוּ Qal impf. 3 m.p. (דָּמַם I 198) *they are still*

כָּאָבֶן prep.-def.art.-n.f.s. paus. (6) *as a stone*

עַד־יַעֲבֹר conj.-Qal impf. 3 m.s. (716) *till ... pass by*

עַמְּךָ n.m.s.-2 m.s. sf. (I 766) *thy people*

יהוה pr.n. (217) *O Yahweh*

עַד־יַעֲבֹר v.supra *till ... pass by*

עַם־זוּ v.15:13 n.m.s. (I 766)-rel. (262) *the people by whom*

קָנִיתָ Qal pf. 2 m.s. (קָנָה 888) *thou hast purchased*

15:17

תְּבִאֵמוֹ Hi. impf. 2 m.s. - 3 m.p. sf. (בּוֹא 97) *thou wilt bring them in*

וְתִטָּעֵמוֹ conj.-Qal impf. 2 m.s.-3 m.p. sf. (נָטַע 642) *and plant them*

בְּהַר prep.-n.m.s. cstr. (249) *on mount (of)*

נַחֲלָתְךָ n.f.s.-2 m.s. sf. (635) *thy own inheritance*

מָכוֹן n.m.s. (467) *place*

לְשִׁבְתְּךָ prep.-Qal inf. cstr.-2 m.s. sf. (יָשַׁב 442) *for thy abode*

פָּעַלְתָּ Qal pf. 2 m.s. (821) *thou hast made*

יהוה pr.n. (217) *O Yahweh*

מִקְּדָשׁ n.m.s. (874) *the sanctuary*

אֲדֹנָי pr.n. (10) *O Lord*

כּוֹנְנוּ Po'el pf. 3 c.p. (465) *have established*

יָדֶיךָ n.f.p.-2 m.s. sf. (388) *thy hands*

15:18

יהוה pr.n. (217) *Yahweh*

יִמְלֹךְ Qal impf. 3 m.s. (573) *will reign*

לְעֹלָם prep.-n.m.s. (761) *for ever*

וָעֶד conj.-n.m.s. (I 723) *and ever*

15:19

כִּי conj. *for when*

בָא Qal pf. 3 m.s. (בּוֹא 97) *went*

סוּס פַּרְעֹה n.m.s. cstr. (692)-pr.n. (829) *the horses of Pharaoh*

בְּרִכְבּוֹ prep.-n.m.s.-3 m.s. sf. (939) *with his chariots*

וּבְפָרָשָׁיו conj.-prep.-n.m.p.-3 m.s. sf. (832) *and his horsemen*

בַּיָּם prep.-def.art.-n.m.s. (410) *into the sea*

וַיָּשֶׁב consec.-Hi. impf. 3 m.s. (שׁוּב 996) *brought back*

יהוה pr.n. (217) *Yahweh*

עֲלֵהֶם prep.-3 m.p. sf. *upon them*

אֶת־מֵי dir.obj.-n.m.p. cstr. (565) *the waters of*

הַיָּם def.art.-n.m.s. (410) *the sea*

וּבְנֵי conj.-n.m.p. cstr. (119) *but the people of*

יִשְׂרָאֵל pr.n. (975) *Israel*

הָלְכוּ Qal pf. 3 c.p. (229) *walked*

בַיַּבָּשָׁה prep.-def.art.-n.f.s. (387) *on dry ground*

בְּתוֹךְ prep.-n.m.s. cstr. (1063) *in the midst of*

הַיָּם def. art.-n.m.s. (410) *the sea*

15:20

וַתִּקַּח consec.-Qal impf. 3 f.s. (לָקַח 542) *then ... took*

מִרְיָם pr.n. (599) *Miriam*

הַנְּבִיאָה def. art.-n.f.s. (612) *the prophetess*

אֲחוֹת n.f.s. cstr. (27) *the sister of*

אַהֲרֹן pr.n. (14) *Aaron*

אֶת־הַתֹּף dir. obj.-def. art.-n.m.s. (1074) *a timbrel*

בְּיָדָהּ prep.-n.f.s.-3 f.s. sf. (388) *in her hand*

וַתֵּצֶאןָ consec.-Qal impf. 3 f.p. (יָצָא 422) *and ... went out*

כָל־הַנָּשִׁים n.m.s. cstr. (481)-def. art.-n.f.p. (61) *all the women*

אַחֲרֶיהָ prep.-3 f.s. sf. (29) *after her*

בְּתֻפִּים prep.-n.m.p. (1074) *with timbrels*

וּבִמְחֹלֹת conj.-prep.-n.f.p. (298) *and dancing*

15:21

וַתַּעַן consec.-Qal impf. 3 f.s. (עָנָה IV 777) *and ... sang*

לָהֶם prep.-3 m.p. sf. *to them*

מִרְיָם pr.n. (599) *Miriam*

שִׁירוּ Qal impv. 2 m.p. (שִׁיר 1010) *Sing*

ליהוה prep.-pr.n. (217) *to Yahweh*

כִּי־ conj. *for*

גָאֹה גָּאָה Qal inf. abs. (144)-Qal pf. 3 m.s. (144) *he has triumphed gloriously*

סוּס n.m.s. (692) *the horse*

וְרֹכְבוֹ conj.-Qal act. ptc.-3 m.s. sf. (938) *and his rider*

רָמָה Qal pf. 3 m.s. (I 941) *he has thrown*

בַיָּם prep.-def. art.-n.m.s. (410) *into the sea*

15:22

וַיַּסַּע consec.-Qal impf. 3 m.s. (נָסַע 652) *then ... led*

מֹשֶׁה pr.n. (602) *Moses*

אֶת־יִשְׂרָאֵל dir.obj.-pr.n. (975) *Israel*

מִיַּם־סוּף prep.-n.m.s. cstr. (410) - n.m.s. (693) *from the Red Sea (of reeds)*

וַיֵּצְאוּ consec.-Qal impf. 3 m.p. (יָצָא 422) *they went*

אֶל־מִדְבַּר־ prep.-n.m.s. cstr. (184) *into the wilderness of*

שׁוּר pr.n. (III 1004) *Shur*

וַיֵּלְכוּ consec.-Qal impf. 3 m.p. (הָלַךְ 229) *they went*

שְׁלֹשֶׁת־ num. f.s. cstr. (1025) *three (of)*

יָמִים n.m.p. (398) *days*

בַּמִּדְבָּר prep.-def. art.-n.m.s. (184) *in the wilderness*

וְלֹא־מָצְאוּ conj.-neg.-Qal pf. 3 c.p. (592) *and found no*

מָיִם n.m.p. paus. (565) *water*

15:23

וַיָּבֹאוּ consec.-Qal impf. 3 m.p. (בּוֹא 97) *when they came*

מָרָתָה pr.n.-dir. he (600) *to Marah*

וְלֹא יָכְלוּ conj.-neg.-Qal pf. 3 c.p. (יָכֹל 407) *they could not*

לִשְׁתֹּת prep.-Qal inf. cstr. (שָׁתָה 1059) *drink*

מַיִם n.m.p. (565) *the water*

מִמָּרָה prep.-v. supra pr.n. (600) *of Marah*

כִּי מָרִים conj.-adj. m.p. (600) *because ... bitter*

הֵם pers. pr. m.p. (241) *it was (they)*

עַל־כֵּן prep.-adv. (485) *therefore*

קָרָא־שְׁמָהּ Qal pf. 3 m.s. (894)-n.m.s.-3 f.s. sf. (1027) *it was named*

מָרָה pr.n. (600) *Marah*

15:24

וַיִּלֹּנוּ consec.-Qal impf. 3 m.p. (לוּן II 534) *and ... murmured*

הָעָם def. art.-n.m.s. (I 766) *the people*

עַל־מֹשֶׁה prep.-pr.n. (602) *against Moses*

לֵּאמֹר prep.-Qal inf. cstr. (55) *saying*

מַה־נִּשְׁתֶּה interr. (552)-Qal impf. 1 c.p. (שָׁתָה 1059) *what shall we drink?*

15:25

וַיִּצְעַק consec.-Qal impf. 3 m.s. (858) *and he cried*

אֶל־יהוה prep.-pr.n. (217) *to Yahweh*

וַיּוֹרֵהוּ consec.-Hi. impf. 3 m.s.-3 m.s. sf. (יָרָה 434) *and showed him*

יהוה pr.n. (217) *Yahweh*

עֵץ n.m.s. (781) *a tree*

וַיַּשְׁלֵךְ consec.-Hi. impf. 3 m.s. (יָלַךְ 1020) *and he threw*

אֶל־הַמַּיִם prep.-def. art.-n.m.p. (565) *into the water*

וַיִּמְתְּקוּ consec.-Qal impf. 3 m.p. (מָתֹק 608) *and ... became sweet*

הַמָּיִם def. art.-n.m.p. paus. (565) *the water*

שָׁם adv. (1027) *there*

שָׂם Qal pf. 3 m.s. (שׂוּם 962) *made*

לוֹ prep.-3 m.s. sf. *for them*

חֹק n.m.s. (349) *a statute*

וּמִשְׁפָּט conj.-n.m.s. (1048) *and an ordinance*

וְשָׁם conj.-v. supra *and there*

נִסָּהוּ Pi. pf. 3 m.s.-3 m.s. sf. (נָסָה 650) *he proved them*

15:26

וַיֹּאמֶר consec.-Qal impf. 3 m.s. (55) *saying*

אִם־ hypoth. part. (49) *if*

שָׁמוֹעַ תִּשְׁמַע Qal inf. abs. (1033)-Qal impf. 2 m.s. (1033) *you will diligently hearken*

לְקוֹל יהוה prep.-n.m.s. cstr. (876)-pr.n. (217) *to the voice of Yahweh*

אֱלֹהֶיךָ n.m.p.-2 m.s. sf. (43) *your God*

וְהַיָּשָׁר conj.-def. art.-n.m.s. (449) *and that which is right*

בְּעֵינָיו prep.-n.f.p.-3 m.s. sf. (744) *in his eyes*

תַּעֲשֶׂה Qal impf. 2 m.s. (עָשָׂה I 793) *do*

וְהַאֲזַנְתָּ conj.-Hi. pf. 3 m.s. (אָזַן 24) *and give heed*

לְמִצְוֺתָיו prep.-n.f.p.-3 m.s. sf. (846) *to his commandments*

וְשָׁמַרְתָּ conj.-Qal pf. 2 m.s. (1036) *and keep*

כָּל־חֻקָּיו n.m.s. cstr. (481)-n.m.p.-3 m.s. sf. (349) *all his statutes*

כָּל־הַמַּחֲלָה n.m.s. cstr. (481)-def. art.-n.f.s. (318) *all the diseases*

אֲשֶׁר־שַׂמְתִּי rel.-Qal pf. 1 c.s. (שִׂים 962) *which I put*

בְּמִצְרַיִם prep.-pr.n. (595) *upon the Egyptians*

לֹא־אָשִׂים neg.-Qal impf. 1 c.s. (962) *I will not put*

עָלֶיךָ prep.-2 m.s. sf. *upon you*

כִּי אֲנִי conj.-pers. pr. 1 c.s. (58) *for I am*

יהוה pr.n. (217) *Yahweh*

רֹפְאֶךָ Qal act. ptc.-2 m.s. sf. (רָפָא 950) *your healer*

15:27

וַיָּבֹאוּ consec.-Qal impf. 3 m.p. (בּוֹא 97) *then they came*

אֵילִמָה pr.n.-dir. he (18) *to Elim*

וְשָׁם conj.-adv. (1027) *where there*

שְׁתֵּים num. (1040) *two*

עֶשְׂרֵה num. (797) *ten*

עֵינֹת n.f.p. cstr. (744) *springs of*

מַיִם n.m.p. (565) *water*

וְשִׁבְעִים conj.-num. p. (988) *and seventy*

תְּמָרִים n.m.p. (I 1071) *palm trees*

וַיַּחֲנוּ־ consec.-Qal impf. 3 m. p. (חָנָה 333) *and they encamped*

שָׁם v. supra adv. (1027) *there*

עַל־הַמָּיִם prep.-def. art.-n.m.p. paus. (565) *by the water*

16:1

וַיִּסְעוּ consec.-Qal impf. 3 m.p. (נָסַע 652) *They set out*

מֵאֵילִם prep.-pr.n. (18) *from Elim*

וַיָּבֹאוּ consec.-Qal impf. 3 m.p. (בּוֹא 97) *and ... came*

כָּל־עֲדַת n.m.s. cstr. (481)-n.f.s. cstr. (II 417) *all the congregation of*

בְּנֵי־יִשְׂרָאֵל n.m.p. cstr. (119) - pr.n. (975) *the people of Israel*

אֶל־מִדְבַּר־ prep.-n.m.s. cstr. (184) *to the wilderness of*

סִין pr.n. (II 695) *Sin*

אֲשֶׁר rel. *which is*

בֵּין־אֵילִם prep.-pr.n. (18) *between Elim*

וּבֵין סִינָי conj.-prep.-pr.n. paus. (696) *and Sinai*

בַּחֲמִשָּׁה prep.-num. f.s. (331) *on the five*

עָשָׂר num. m.s. (797) *ten*

יוֹם n.m.s. (398) *day*

לַחֹדֶשׁ prep.-def. art.-n.m.s. (II 294) *of the ... month*

הַשֵּׁנִי def. art.-num. adj. (1040) *second*

לְצֵאתָם prep.-Qal inf. cstr.-3 m.p. sf. (יָצָא 422) *after they had departed*

מֵאֶרֶץ prep.-n.f.s. cstr. (75) *from the land of*

מִצְרָיִם pr.n. paus. (595) *Egypt*

16:2

וַיִּלִּינוּ v.15:24 consec.-Qal impf. 3 m.p. (לוּן II 534) *and ... murmured*

כָּל־עֲדַת v.16:11 n.m.s. cstr. (481)-n.f.s. cstr. (II 417) *the whole congregation of*

בְּנֵי־יִשְׂרָאֵל n.m.p. cstr. (119)-pr.n. (975) *the people of Israel*

עַל־מֹשֶׁה prep.-pr.n. (602) *against Moses*

וְעַל־אַהֲרֹן conj.-prep.-pr.n. (14) *and Aaron*

בַּמִּדְבָּר prep.-def. art.-n.m.s. (184) *in the wilderness*

16:3

וַיֹּאמְרוּ consec.-Qal impf. 3 m.p. (55) *and said*

אֲלֵהֶם prep.-3 m.p. sf. *to them*

בְּנֵי יִשְׂרָאֵל n.m.p. cstr. (119)-pr.n. (975) *(the people of Israel)*

מִי־יִתֵּן interr. (566)-Qal impf. 3 m.s. (נָתַן 678) *would that*

מוּתֵנוּ Qal inf. cstr.-1 c.p. sf. (מוּת 559) *we had died*

בְיַד־יהוה prep.-n.f.s. cstr. (388)-pr.n. (217) *by the hand of Yahweh*

בְּאֶרֶץ prep.-n.f.s. cstr. (75) *in the land of*

מִצְרַיִם pr.n. (595) *Egypt*

בְּשִׁבְתֵּנוּ prep.-Qal inf. cstr.-1 c.p. sf. (יָשַׁב 442) *when we sat*

עַל־סִיר prep.-n.m.s. cstr. (I 696) *by the ... pots*

הַבָּשָׂר def. art.-n.m.s. (142) *flesh*

בְּאָכְלֵנוּ prep.-Qal inf. cstr.-1 c.p. sf. (37) *and ate*

לֶחֶם n.m.s. (536) *bread*

לָשֹׂבַע prep.-n.m.s. (שֹׂבַע 959) *to the full*

כִּי־הוֹצֵאתֶם conj.-Hi. pf. 2 m.p. (יָצָא 422) *for you have brought out*

אֹתָנוּ dir. obj.-1 c.p. sf. *us*

אֶל־הַמִּדְבָּר prep.-def. art.-n.m.s. (184) *into ... wilderness*

הַזֶּה def. art.-demons. adj. m.s. (260) *this*

לְהָמִית prep.-Hi. inf. cstr. (מוּת 559) *to kill*

אֶת־כָּל־ dir. obj.-n.m.s. cstr. (481) *whole*

הַקָּהָל הַזֶּה def. art.-n.m.s. (874)-v. supra *this assembly*

בָּרָעָב prep.-def. art.-n.m.s. (944) *with hunger*

16:4

וַיֹּאמֶר יהוה consec.-Qal impf. 3 m.s. (55)-pr.n. (217) *then Yahweh said*

אֶל־מֹשֶׁה prep.-pr.n. (602) *to Moses*

הִנְנִי demons. part.-1 c.s. sf. (243) *Behold, I*

מַמְטִיר Hi. ptc. (מָטַר 565) *will rain*

לָכֶם prep.-2 m.p. sf. *for you*

לֶחֶם n.m.s. (536) *bread*

מִן־הַשָּׁמָיִם prep.-def. art.-n.m.p. paus. (1029) *from heaven*

וְיָצָא conj.-Qal pf. 3 m.s. (422) *and ... shall go out*

הָעָם def. art.-n.m.s. (I 766) *the people*

וְלָקְטוּ conj.-Qal pf. 3 c.p. (544) *and gather*

דְּבַר־יוֹם n.m.s. cstr. (182)-n.m.s. (398) *a day's portion*

בְּיוֹמוֹ prep.-n.m.s.-3 m.s. sf. (398) *every day*

לְמַעַן prep.-prep. (775) *that*

אֲנַסֶּנּוּ Pi. impf. 1 c.s.-3 m.s. sf. (נָסָה 650) *I may prove them*

הֲיֵלֵךְ interr. part.-Qal impf. 3 m.s. (הָלַךְ 229) *whether they will walk*

בְּתוֹרָתִי prep.-n.f.s.-3 m.s. sf. (435) *in my law*

אִם־לֹא hypoth. part. (49)-neg. *or not*

16:5

וְהָיָה conj.-Qal pf. 3 m.s. (224) *(and it shall be)*

בַּיּוֹם הַשִּׁשִּׁי prep.-def. art.-n.m.s. (398)-def. art.-num. adj. (995) *on the sixth day*

וְהֵכִינוּ conj.-Hi. pf. 3 c.p. (כּוּן 465) *when they prepare*

אֵת אֲשֶׁר־ dir. obj.-rel. *what*

יָבִיאוּ Hi. impf. 3 m.p. (בּוֹא 97) *they bring in*

וְהָיָה conj.-Qal pf. 3 m.s. (224) *it will be*

מִשְׁנֶה n.m.s. (1041) *twice*

עַל אֲשֶׁר־ prep.-rel. *as much as*

יִלְקְטוּ Qal impf. 3 m.p. (544) *they gather*

יוֹם יוֹם n.m.s. (398)-n.m.s. (398) *daily*

16:6

וַיֹּאמֶר consec.-Qal impf. 3 m.s. (55) *so ... said*

מֹשֶׁה pr.n. (602) *Moses*

וְאַהֲרֹן conj.-pr.n. (14) *and Aaron*

אֶל־כָּל־ prep.-n.m.s. cstr. (481) *to all*

בְּנֵי n.m.p. cstr. (119) *the people of*

יִשְׂרָאֵל pr.n. (975) *Israel*

עֶרֶב n.m.s. (787) *At evening*

וִידַעְתֶּם conj.-Qal pf. 2 m.p. (393) *you shall know*

כִּי יהוה conj.-pr.n. (217) *that it was Yahweh*

הוֹצִיא Hi.pf.3 m.s. (יָצָא 422) *who brought*

אֶתְכֶם dir. obj.-2 m.p. sf. *you*

מֵאֶרֶץ prep.-n.f.s. cstr. (75) *out of the land of*

מִצְרָיִם pr.n. paus. (595) *Egypt*

16:7

וּבֹקֶר conj.-n.m.s. (133) *and in the morning*

וּרְאִיתֶם conj.-Qal pf. 2 m.p. (רָאָה 906) *you shall see*

אֶת־כְּבוֹד dir. obj.-n.m.s. cstr. (458) *the glory of*

יהוה pr.n. (217) *Yahweh*

בְּשָׁמְעוֹ prep.-Qal inf. cstr.-3 m.s. sf. (1033) *because he has heard*

אֶת־תְּלֻנֹּתֵיכֶם dir. obj.-n.f.p.-2 m.p. sf. (534) *your murmurings*

עַל־יהוה prep.-pr.n. (217) *against Yahweh*

וְנַחְנוּ conj.-pers. pr. 1 c.p. (59) *for ... we*

מָה interr. (552) *what*

כִּי תַלִּינוּ conj.-Hi. impf. 2 m.p. (לון II 534) *that you murmur*

עָלֵינוּ prep.-1 c.p. sf. *against us*

16:8

וַיֹּאמֶר consec.-Qal impf. 3 m.s. (55) *and ... said*

מֹשֶׁה pr.n. (602) *Moses*

בְּתֵת prep.-Qal inf. cstr. (נָתַן 678) *when ... gives*

יהוה pr.n. (217) *Yahweh*

לָכֶם prep.-2 m.p. sf. *you*

בָּעֶרֶב prep.-def. art.-n.m.s. (787) *in the evening*

בָּשָׂר n.m.s. (142) *flesh*

לֶאֱכֹל prep.-Qal inf. cstr. (37) *to eat*

וְלֶחֶם conj.-n.m.s. (536) *and bread*

בַּבֹּקֶר prep.-def. art.-n.m.s. (133) *in the morning*

לִשְׂבֹּעַ prep.-Qal inf. cstr. (959) *to the full*

בִּשְׁמֹעַ prep.-Qal inf. cstr. (1033) *because ... has heard*

יהוה pr.n. (217) *Yahweh*

אֶת־תְּלֻנֹּתֵיכֶם dir. obj.-n.f.p.-2 m.p. sf. (534) *your murmurings*

אֲשֶׁר־אַתֶּם rel.-pers. pr. 2 m.p. (61) *which you*

מַלִּינִם Hi. ptc. m.p. (לון II 534) *murmur*

עָלָיו prep.-3 m.s. sf. *against him*

וְנַחְנוּ conj.-pers. pr. 1 c.p. (59) *we*

מָה interr. (552) *what*

לֹא־עָלֵינוּ neg.-prep.-1 c.p. sf. *not against us*

תְּלֻנֹּתֵיכֶם v. supra *your murmurings*

כִּי conj. *but*

עַל־יהוה prep.-pr.n. (217) *against Yahweh*

16:9

וַיֹּאמֶר consec.-Qal impf. 3 m.s. (55) *and ... said*

מֹשֶׁה pr.n. (602) *Moses*

אֶל־אַהֲרֹן prep.-pr.n. (14) *to Aaron*

אֱמֹר Qal impv. 2 m.s. (55) *Say*

אֶל־כָּל־עֲדַת prep.-n.m.s. cstr. (481)-n.f.s. cstr. (II 417) *to the whole congregation of*

בְּנֵי n.m.p. cstr. (119) *the people of*

יִשְׂרָאֵל pr.n. (975) *Israel*

קִרְבוּ Qal impv. 2 m.p. (897) *Come near*

לִפְנֵי prep.-n.m.p. cstr. (815) *before*

יהוה pr.n. (217) *Yahweh*

כִּי שָׁמַע conj.-Qal pf. 3 m.s. (1033) *for he has heard*

אֵת תְּלֻנֹּתֵיכֶם dir. obj.-n.f.p.-2 m.p. sf. (534) *your murmurings*

16:10

וַיְהִי consec.-Qal impf. 3 m.s. (224) *and*

כְּדַבֵּר prep.-Pi. inf. cstr. (180) *as ... spoke*

אַהֲרֹן pr.n. (14) *Aaron*

אֶל־כָּל־ prep.-n.m.s. cstr. (481) *to the whole*

עֲדַת n.f.s. cstr. (II 417) *congregation of*

בְּנֵי־יִשְׂרָאֵל n.m.p. cstr. (119)-pr.n. (975) *the people of Israel*

וַיִּפְנוּ consec.-Qal impf. 3 m.p. (פָּנָה 815) *they looked*

אֶל־הַמִּדְבָּר prep.-def.art.-n.m.s. (184) *toward the wilderness*

וְהִנֵּה conj.-demons.part. (243) *and behold*

כְּבוֹד n.m.s. cstr. (458) *the glory of*

יהוה pr.n. (217) *Yahweh*

נִרְאָה Ni. pf. 3 m.s. (906) *appeared*

בֶּעָנָן prep.-def.art.-n.m.s. (777) *in the cloud*

16:11

וַיְדַבֵּר consec.-Pi. impf. 3 m.s. (180) *and ... said*

יהוה pr.n. (217) *Yahweh*

אֶל־מֹשֶׁה prep.-pr.n. (602) *to Moses*

לֵאמֹר prep.-Qal inf. cstr. (55) *(saying)*

16:12

שָׁמַעְתִּי Qal pf. 1 c.s. (1033) *I have heard*

אֶת־תְּלוּנֹּת dir.obj.-n.f.p. cstr. (534) *the murmurings of*

בְּנֵי יִשְׂרָאֵל n.m.p. cstr. (119)-pr.n. (975) *of the people of Israel*

דַּבֵּר Pi. impv. 2 m.s. (180) *say*

אֲלֵהֶם prep.-3 m.p. sf. *to them*

לֵאמֹר prep.-Qal inf. cstr. (55) *(saying)*

בֵּין הָעַרְבַּיִם prep. (107)-def.art.-n.m.p. (787) *at twilight*

תֹּאכְלוּ Qal impf. 2 m.p. (37) *you shall eat*

בָשָׂר n.m.s. (142) *flesh*

וּבַבֹּקֶר conj.-prep.-def.art.-n.m.s. (133) *and in the morning*

תִּשְׂבְּעוּ־ Qal impf. 2 m.p. (959) *you shall be filled with*

לָחֶם n.m.s. paus. (536) *bread*

וִידַעְתֶּם conj.-Qal pf. 2 m.p. (393) *then you shall know*

כִּי אֲנִי conj.-pers.pr. 1 c.s. (58) *that I*

יהוה pr.n. (217) *Yahweh*

אֱלֹהֵיכֶם n.m.p.-2 m.p. sf. (43) *your God*

16:13

וַיְהִי consec.-Qal impf. 3 m.s. (224)

בָעֶרֶב prep.-def.art.-n.m.s. (787) *in the evening*

וַתַּעַל consec.-Qal impf. 3 f.s. (עָלָה 748) *came up*

הַשְּׂלָו def.art.-n.f.s. (969) *quails*

וַתְּכַס consec.-Pi. impf. 3 f.s. (כָּסָה 491) *and covered*

אֶת־הַמַּחֲנֶה dir.obj.-def.art.-n.f.s. (334) *the camp*

וּבַבֹּקֶר conj.-prep.-def.art.-n.m.s. (133) *and in the morning*

הָיְתָה Qal pf. 3 f.s. (224) *(was)*

שִׁכְבַת n.f.s. cstr. (1012) *(layer of)*

הַטָּל def.art.-n.m.s. (378) *dew*

סָבִיב adv. (686) *round about*

לַמַּחֲנֶה prep.-def.art.-n.f.s. (334) *the camp*

16:14

וַתַּעַל consec.-Qal impf. 3 f.s. (עָלָה 748) *and when ... had gone up*

שִׁכְבַת הַטָּל n.f.s. cstr. (1012) - def.art.-n.m.s. paus. (378) *the dew*

וְהִנֵּה conj.-demons.part. (243) *there was (and behold)*

עַל־פְּנֵי הַמִּדְבָּר prep.-n.m.p. cstr. (815)-def.art.-n.m.s. (184) *on the face of the wilderness*

דַּק adj. (201) *a fine*

מְחֻסְפָּס Pu. ptc. (חַסְפַּס 341) *flake-like thing*

דַּק v.supra *fine*

כַּכְּפֹר prep.-def.art.-n.m.s. (II 499) *as hoar-frost*

עַל־הָאָרֶץ prep.-def.art.-n.f.s. (75) *on the ground*

16:15

וַיִּרְאוּ consec.-Qal impf. 3 m.p. (רָאָה 906) *when ... saw*

בְנֵי־יִשְׂרָאֵל n.m.p. cstr. (119)-pr.n. (975) *the people of Israel*

וַיֹּאמְרוּ consec.-Qal impf. 3 m.p. (55) *they said*

אִישׁ n.m.s. (35) *(each) one*

אֶל־אָחִיו prep.-n.m.s.-3 m.s. sf. (26) *to another (to his brother)*

מָן הוּא interr. (577)-pers. pr. 3 m.s. (214) *what is it?*

כִּי conj. *for*

לֹא יָדְעוּ neg.-Qal pf. 3 c.p. (393) *they did not know*

מַה־הוּא interr. (552)-pers. pr. 3 m.s. (214) *what it was*

וַיֹּאמֶר consec.-Qal impf. 3 m.s. (55) *and ... said*

מֹשֶׁה pr.n. (602) *Moses*

אֲלֵהֶם prep.-3 m.p. sf. *to them*

הוּא v.supra *it*

הַלֶּחֶם def.art.-n.m.s. (536) *the bread*

אֲשֶׁר rel. *which*

נָתַן יהוה Qal pf. 3 m.s. (678)-pr.n. (217) *Yahweh has given*

לָכֶם prep.-2 m.p. *you*

לְאָכְלָה prep.-n.f.s. (3) *to eat*

16:16

זֶה הַדָּבָר demons. adj. (260)-def.art.-n.m.s. (182) *this is (the matter)*

אֲשֶׁר rel. *what*

צִוָּה Pi. pf. 3 m.s. (845) *has commanded*

יהוה pr.n. (217) *Yahweh*

לִקְטוּ Qal impv. 2 m.p. (544) *gather*

מִמֶּנּוּ prep.-3 m.s. sf. *of it*

אִישׁ n.m.s. (35) *every man*

לְפִי אָכְלוֹ prep.-n.m.s. cstr. (804)-Qal inf. cstr.-3 m.s. sf. (37) *as much as he can eat*

עֹמֶר n.m.s. (II 771) *an omer*

לַגֻּלְגֹּלֶת prep.-def.art.-n.f.s. (166) *apiece*

מִסְפַּר n.m.s. cstr. (708) *according to the number of*

נַפְשֹׁתֵיכֶם n.f.p.-2 m.p. sf. (659) *the persons ... of you*

אִישׁ n.m.s. (35) *each*

לַאֲשֶׁר prep.-rel. *whom*

בְּאָהֳלוֹ prep.-n.m.s.-3 m.s. sf. (13) *in his tent*

תִּקָּחוּ Qal impf. 2 m.p. paus. (לָקַח 542) *you shall take*

16:17

וַיַּעֲשׂוּ־כֵן consec.-Qal impf. 3 m.p. (עָשָׂה I 793)-adv. (485) *and ... did so*

בְּנֵי יִשְׂרָאֵל n.m.p. cstr. (119)-pr.n. (975) *the people of Israel*

וַיִּלְקְטוּ consec.-Qal impf. 3 m.p. (544) *they gathered*

הַמַּרְבֶּה def.art.-Hi. ptc. (רָבָה 915) *some more*

וְהַמַּמְעִיט conj.-def.art.-Hi. ptc. (מָעַט 589) *some less*

16:18

וַיָּמֹדּוּ consec.-Qal impf. 3 m.p. (מָדַד 551) *but when they measured*

בָעֹמֶר prep.-def.art.-n.m.s. (II 771) *with an omer*

וְלֹא הֶעְדִּיף conj.-neg.-Hi. pf. 3 m.s. (עָדַף 727) *had nothing over*

הַמַּרְבֶּה v.16:17 *the much*

וְהַמַּמְעִיט conj.-def.art.-Hi. ptc. (מָעַט 589) *little*

לֹא הֶחְסִיר neg.-Hi. pf. 3 m.s. (341) *had no lack*

אִישׁ n.m.s. (35) *each*

לְפִי־אָכְלוֹ prep.-n.m.s. cstr. (804)-Qal inf. cstr.-3 m.s. sf. (37) *according to what he could eat*

לָקָטוּ Qal pf. 3 c.p. paus. (544) *gathered*

16:19

וַיֹּאמֶר consec.-Qal impf. 3 m.s. (55) *and ... said*

מֹשֶׁה pr.n. (602) *Moses*

אֲלֵהֶם prep.-3 m.p. sf. *to them*

אִישׁ n.m.s. (35) *man*

אַל־יוֹתֵר neg.-Hi. impf. 3 m.s. apoc. (יָתַר 451) *let no ... leave*

מִמֶּנּוּ prep.-3 m.s. sf. *of it*

עַד־בֹּקֶר prep. (III 723)-n.m.s. (133) *till the morning*

16:20

וְלֹא־שָׁמְעוּ neg.-Qal pf. 3 c.p. (1033) *but they did not listen*

אֶל־מֹשֶׁה prep.-pr.n. (602) *to Moses*

וַיּוֹתִרוּ consec.-Hi. impf. 3 m.p. (יָתַר 451) *and ... left*

אֲנָשִׁים n.m.p. (35) *some*

מִמֶּנּוּ prep.-3 m.s. sf. *of it*

עַד־בֹּקֶר v.16:19 prep. (III 723) - n.m.s. (133) *till the morning*

וַיָּרֻם consec.-Qal impf. 3 m.s. (רוּם 926) *and it bred*

תּוֹלָעִים n.f.p. (1069) *worms*

וַיִּבְאַשׁ consec.-Qal impf. 3 m.s. (92) *and became foul*

וַיִּקְצֹף consec.-Qal impf. 3 m.s. (893) *and was angry*

עֲלֵהֶם prep.-3 m.p. sf. *with them*

מֹשֶׁה pr.n. (602) *Moses*

16:21

וַיִּלְקְטוּ consec.-Qal impf. 3 m.p. (544) *they gathered*

אֹתוֹ dir.obj.-3 m.s. sf. *it*

בַּבֹּקֶר prep.-def.art.-n.m.s. (133) *morning*

בַּבֹּקֶר v.supra *by morning*

אִישׁ n.m.s. (35) *each*

כְּפִי אָכְלוֹ prep.-n.m.s. cstr. (804)-Qal inf. cstr.-3 m.s. sf. (37) *as much as he could eat*

וְחַם conj.-Qal pf. 3 m.s. (חָמַם 328) *but when ... grew hot*

הַשֶּׁמֶשׁ def.art.-n.m.s. (1039) *the sun*

וְנָמָס conj.-Ni. pf. 3 m.s. paus. (מָסַס 587) *it melted*

16:22

וַיְהִי consec.-Qal impf. 3 m.s. (224)

בַּיּוֹם הַשִּׁשִּׁי prep.-def.art.-n.m.s. (398)-def.art.-num. (995) *on the sixth day*

לָקְטוּ Qal pf. 3 c.p. (544) *they gathered*

לֶחֶם n.m.s. (536) *bread*

מִשְׁנֶה n.m.s. (1041) *twice*

שְׁנֵי הָעֹמֶר num.cstr. (1040) - def.art.-n.m.s. (II 771) *two omers*

לָאֶחָד prep.-def.art.-n.m.s. (25) *apiece*

וַיָּבֹאוּ consec.-Qal impf. 3 m.p. (בּוֹא 97) *and when ... came*

כָּל־נְשִׂיאֵי n.m.s. cstr. (481)-n.m.p. cstr. (672) *all the leaders of*

הָעֵדָה def.art.-n.f.s. (II 417) *the congregation*

וַיַּגִּידוּ consec.-Hi. impf. 3 m.p. (נָגַד 616) *and told*

לְמֹשֶׁה prep.-pr.n. (602) *Moses*

16:23

וַיֹּאמֶר consec.-Qal impf. 3 m.s. (55) *he said*

אֲלֵהֶם prep.-3 m.p. sf. *to them*

הוּא אֲשֶׁר demons. adj. (214)-rel. *this is what*

דִּבֶּר יהוה Pi. pf. 3 m.s. (180)-pr.n. (217) *Yahweh has commanded*

שַׁבָּתוֹן n.m.s. (992) *a day of solemn rest*

שַׁבַּת־קֹדֶשׁ n.f.s. cstr. (992) - n.m.s. (871) *a holy sabbath*

ליהוה prep.-pr.n. (217) *to Yahweh*

מָחָר n.m.s. paus. (563) *tomorrow*

אֵת אֲשֶׁר־ dir.obj.-rel. *what*

תֹּאפוּ Qal impf. 2 m.p. (אָפָה 66) *you will bake*

אֵפוּ Qal impv. 2 m.p. (אָפָה 66) *bake*

וְאֵת אֲשֶׁר־ conj.-dir.obj.-rel. *and what*

תְּבַשְּׁלוּ Pi. impf. 2 m.p. (143) *you will boil*

בַּשֵּׁלוּ Pi. impv. 2 m.p. paus. (143) *boil*

וְאֵת כָּל־ conj.-dir.obj.-n.m.s. cstr. (481) *and all*

הָעֹדֵף def.art.-Qal act. ptc. (727) *that is left over*

הַנִּיחוּ Hi. impv. 2 m.p. (נוּחַ 628) *lay by*

לָכֶם prep.-2 m.p. sf. (*for yourselves*)

לְמִשְׁמֶרֶת prep.-n.f.s. (1038) *to be kept*

עַד־הַבֹּקֶר prep.-def.art.-n.m.s. (133) *till the morning*

16:24

וַיַּנִּיחוּ consec.-Hi. impf. 3 m.p. (נוּחַ 628) *so they laid by*

אֹתוֹ dir.obj.-3 m.s. sf. *it*

עַד־הַבֹּקֶר v.16:23 *till the morning*

כַּאֲשֶׁר prep.-rel. *as*

צִוָּה Pi. pf. 3 m.s. (845) *bade*

מֹשֶׁה pr.n. (602) *Moses*

וְלֹא הִבְאִישׁ conj.-neg.-Hi. pf. 3 m.s. (בָּאַשׁ 92) *and it did not become foul*

וְרִמָּה conj.-n.f.s. (942) *worms*

לֹא־הָיְתָה neg.-Qal pf. 3 f.s. (224) *there were no*

בּוֹ prep.-3 m.s. sf. *in it*

16:25

וַיֹּאמֶר consec.-Qal impf. 3 m.s. (55)

said
מֹשֶׁה pr.n. (602) *Moses*
אִכְלֻהוּ Qal impv. 2 m.p.-3 m.s. sf. (37) *eat it*
הַיּוֹם def.art.-n.m.s. (398) *today*
כִּי־שַׁבָּת conj.-n.f.s. (992) *for a sabbath*
הַיּוֹם v.supra def.art.-n.m.s. (398) *today*
ליהוה prep.-pr.n. (217) *to Yahweh*
הַיּוֹם v.supra *today*
לֹא תִמְצָאֻהוּ neg.-Qal impf. 2 m.p.-3 m.s. sf. (592) *you will not find it*
בַּשָּׂדֶה prep.-def.art.-n.m.s. (961) *in the field*

16:26

שֵׁשֶׁת יָמִים num. f.s. cstr. (995)-n.m.p. (398) *six days*
תִּלְקְטֻהוּ Qal impf. 2 m.p.-3 m.s. sf. (544) *you shall gather it*
וּבַיּוֹם הַשְּׁבִיעִי conj.-prep.-def.art.-n.m.s. (398) - def.art. - num. adj. (988) *but on the seventh day*
שַׁבָּת n.f.s. (992) *a sabbath*
לֹא יִהְיֶה־בּוֹ neg.-Qal impf. 3 m.s. (224) - prep.-3 m.s. sf. *there will be none*

16:27

וַיְהִי consec.-Qal impf. 3 m.s. (224)
בַּיּוֹם הַשְּׁבִיעִי v.16:26 *on the seventh day*
יָצְאוּ Qal pf. 3 c.p. (422) *went out*
מִן־הָעָם prep.-def.art.-n.m.s. (I 766) *some of the people*
לִלְקֹט prep.-Qal inf. cstr. (544) *to gather*
וְלֹא מָצָאוּ conj.-neg.-Qal pf. 3 c.p. paus. (592) *and they found none*

16:28

וַיֹּאמֶר consec.-Qal impf. 3 m.s. (55) *and ... said*
יהוה pr.n. (217) *Yahweh*
אֶל־מֹשֶׁה prep.-pr.n. (602) *to Moses*
עַד־אָנָה adv. (III 723)-adv.-loc. he (33) *how long*
מֵאַנְתֶּם Pi. pf. 2 m.p. (549) *do you refuse*
לִשְׁמֹר prep.-Qal inf. cstr. (1036) *to keep*
מִצְוֹתַי n.f.p.-1 c.s. sf. (846) *my commandments*
וְתוֹרֹתָי conj.-n.f.p.-1 c.s. sf. paus. (435) *and my laws*

16:29

רְאוּ Qal impv. 2 m.p. (רָאָה 906) *see*
כִּי־יהוה conj.-pr.n. (217) *Yahweh*
נָתַן לָכֶם Qal pf. 3 m.s. (678)-prep.-2 m.p. sf. *has given you*
הַשַּׁבָּת def.art.-n.f.s. (992) *the sabbath*
עַל־כֵּן prep.-adv. (485) *therefore*
הוּא נֹתֵן pers.pr. 3 m.s. (214)-Qal act. ptc. (678) *he gives*
לָכֶם prep.-2 m.p. sf. *you*
בַּיּוֹם הַשִּׁשִּׁי prep.-def.art.-n.m.s. (398) - def.art. - num. adj. (995) *on the sixth day*
לֶחֶם n.m.s. (536) *bread*
יוֹמָיִם n.m. du. paus. (398) *for two days*
שְׁבוּ Qal impv. 2 m.p. (יָשַׁב 442) *remain*
אִישׁ n.m.s. (35) *every man*
תַּחְתָּיו prep.-3 m.s. sf. (1065) *in his place*
אַל־יֵצֵא neg.-Qal impf. 3 m.s. (יָצָא 422) *let no ... go out*
אִישׁ n.m.s. (35) *man*
מִמְּקֹמוֹ prep.-n.m.s.-3 m.s. sf. (879) *of his place*
בַּיּוֹם הַשְּׁבִיעִי prep.-def.art.-n.m.s. (398)-def.art.-num. adj. (988) *on the seventh day*

16:30

וַיִּשְׁבְּתוּ consec. - Qal impf. 3 m. p. (שָׁבַת 991) *so ... rested*
הָעָם def.art.-n.m.s. (I 766) *the people*
בַּיּוֹם הַשְּׁבִעִי v.16:29 *on the seventh day*

16:31

וַיִּקְרְאוּ consec.-Qal impf. 3 m.p. (894) *now ... called*

בֵּית־יִשְׂרָאֵל n.m.s. cstr. (108)-pr.n. (975) *the house of Israel*

אֶת־שְׁמוֹ dir.obj.-n.m.s.-3 m.s. sf. (1027) *its name*

מָן interr. (I 577) *Manna*

וְהוּא conj.-pers.pr. 3 m.s. (214) *it was*

כְּזֶרַע גַּד prep.-n.m.s. cstr. (282)-n.m.s. (I 151) *coriander seed*

לָבָן n.m.s. (526) *white*

וְטַעְמוֹ conj.-n.m.s.-3 m.s. sf. (381) *and the taste of it*

כְּצַפִּיחִת prep.-n.f.s. (860) *like wafers*

בִּדְבָשׁ prep.-n.m.s. paus. (185) *with honey*

16:32

וַיֹּאמֶר consec.-Qal impf. 3 m.s. (55) *and ... said*

מֹשֶׁה pr.n. (602) *Moses*

זֶה הַדָּבָר demons. adj. (260)-def.art.-n.m.s. (182) *this is (the thing)*

אֲשֶׁר rel. *what*

צִוָּה יהוה Pi. pf. 3 m.s. (צָוָה 845)-pr.n. (217) *Yahweh has commanded*

מְלֹא הָעֹמֶר n.m.s. cstr. (571)-def.art.-n.m.s. (II 771) *an omer*

מִמֶּנּוּ prep.-3 m.s. sf. *of it*

לְמִשְׁמֶרֶת prep.-n.f.s. (1038) *let be kept*

לְדֹרֹתֵיכֶם prep.-n.f.p.-2 m.p. sf. (189) *throughout your generations*

לְמַעַן prep.-prep. (775) *that*

יִרְאוּ Qal impf. 3 m.p. (רָאָה 906) *they may see*

אֶת־הַלֶּחֶם dir.obj.-def.art.-n.m.s. (536) *the bread*

אֲשֶׁר rel. *with which*

הֶאֱכַלְתִּי Hi. pf. 1 c.s. (אָכַל 37) *I fed*

אֶתְכֶם dir.obj.-2 m.p. sf. *you*

בַּמִּדְבָּר prep.-def.art.-n.m.s. (184) *in the wilderness*

בְּהוֹצִיאִי prep.-Hi. inf. cstr.-1 c.s. sf. (יָצָא 422) *when I brought*

אֶתְכֶם v.supra *you*

מֵאֶרֶץ prep.-n.f.s. cstr. (75) *out of the land of*

מִצְרָיִם pr.n. paus. (595) *Egypt*

16:33

וַיֹּאמֶר consec.-Qal impf. 3 m.s. (55) *and ... said*

מֹשֶׁה pr.n. (602) *Moses*

אֶל־אַהֲרֹן prep.-pr.n. (14) *to Aaron*

קַח Qal impv. 2 m.s. (לָקַח 542) *take*

צִנְצֶנֶת n.f.s. (857) *jar*

אַחַת adj. f.s. (25) *a*

וְתֶן־ conj.-Qal impv. 2 m.s. (נָתַן 678) *and put*

שָׁמָּה adv.-loc. he (1027) *in it*

מְלֹא־הָעֹמֶר n.m.s. cstr. (571)-def.art.-n.m.s. (II 771) *an omer*

מָן pr.n. (577) *manna*

וְהַנַּח conj.-Hi. impv. 2 m.s. (נוּחַ 628) *and place*

אֹתוֹ dir.obj.-3 m.s. sf. *it*

לִפְנֵי prep.-n.m.p. cstr. (815) *before*

יהוה pr.n. (217) *Yahweh*

לְמִשְׁמֶרֶת prep.-n.f.s. (1038) *to be kept*

לְדֹרֹתֵיכֶם prep.-n.m.p.-2 m.p. sf. (189) *throughout your generations*

16:34

כַּאֲשֶׁר prep.-rel. *as*

צִוָּה יהוה Pi. pf. 3 m.s. (צָוָה 845)-pr.n. (217) *Yahweh commanded*

אֶל־מֹשֶׁה prep.-pr.n. (602) *Moses*

וַיַּנִּיחֵהוּ consec.-Hi. impf. 3 m.p.-3 m.s. sf. (נוּחַ 628)*so ... placed it*

אַהֲרֹן pr.n. (14) *Aaron*

לִפְנֵי v. 16:33 *before*

הָעֵדֻת def. art.-n.f.s. (730) *the testimony*

לְמִשְׁמָרֶת v. 16:33 paus. *to be kept*

16:35

וּבְנֵי יִשְׂרָאֵל conj.-n.m.p. cstr. (119)-pr.n. (975) *and the people of Israel*

אָכְלוּ Qal pf. 3 c.p. (37) *ate*

אֶת־הַמָּן dir.obj.-def.art.-n.m.s. (577) *the manna*

אַרְבָּעִים num. p. (916) *forty*
שָׁנָה n.f.s. (1040) *years*
עַד־בֹּאָם prep.-Qal inf. cstr.-3 m.p. sf. (בּוֹא 97) *till they came*
אֶל־אֶרֶץ prep.-n.f.s. cstr. (75) *to a land*
נוֹשָׁבֶת Ni. ptc. f.s. paus. (יָשַׁב 442) *habitable*
אֶת־הַמָּן v.supra *the manna*
אָכְלוּ Qal pf. 3 c.p. (37) *they ate*
עַד־בֹּאָם v. supra *till they came*
אֶל־קְצֵה prep.-n.m.s. cstr. (892) *to the border of*
אֶרֶץ n.f.s. cstr. (75) *the land of*
כְּנָעַן pr.n. paus. (488) *Canaan*

16:36

וְהָעֹמֶר conj.-def. art.-n.m.s. (II 771) *an omer*
עֲשִׂרִית num. adj. f.s. cstr. (798) *the tenth part of*
הָאֵיפָה def. art.-n.f.s. (35) *an ephah*
הוּא pers. pr. 3 m.s. (214) *(it)*

17:1

וַיִּסְעוּ consec.-Qal impf. 3 m.p. (נָסַע I 652) *and ... moved on*
כָּל־עֲדַת n.m.s. cstr. (481)-n.f.s. cstr. (II 417) *all the congregation of*
בְּנֵי־יִשְׂרָאֵל n.m.p. cstr. (119)-pr.n. (975) *the people of Israel*
מִמִּדְבַּר־סִין prep.-n.m.s. cstr. (184)-pr.n. (II 695) *from the wilderness of Sin*
לְמַסְעֵיהֶם prep.-n.m.p.-3 m.p. sf. (652) *by stages*
עַל־פִּי prep.-n.m.s. cstr. (804) *according to the commandment of*
יהוה pr.n. (217) *Yahweh*
וַיַּחֲנוּ consec.-Qal impf. 3 m.p. (חָנָה 333) *and camped*
בִּרְפִידִים prep.-pr.n. (951) *at Rephidim*
וְאֵין מַיִם conj.-subst. cstr. (II 34)-n.m.p. (565) *but there was no water*
לִשְׁתֹּת prep.-Qal inf. cstr. (1059) *to drink*
הָעָם def. art.-n.m.s. (I 766) *the people*

17:2

וַיָּרֶב consec.-Qal impf. 3 m.s. (רִיב 936) *therefore ... found fault*
הָעָם def. art.-n.m.s. (I 766) *the people*
עִם־מֹשֶׁה prep.-pr.n. (602) *with Moses*
וַיֹּאמְרוּ consec.-Qal impf. 3 m.p. (55) *and said*
תְּנוּ־לָנוּ Qal impv. 2 m.p. (נָתַן 678)-prep.-1 c.p. sf. *Give us*
מַיִם n.m.p. (565) *water*
וְנִשְׁתֶּה conj.-Qal impf. 3 1 c.p. (1059) *to drink*
וַיֹּאמֶר consec.-Qal impf. 3 m.s. (55) *and ... said*
לָהֶם prep.-3 m.p. sf. *to them*
מֹשֶׁה pr.n. (602) *Moses*
מַה־תְּרִיבוּן interr. (552)-Qal impf. 2 m.p. (רִיב 936) *Why do you find fault*
עִמָּדִי prep. (767)-1 c.s. sf. *with me*
מַה־תְּנַסּוּן interr. (552)-Pi. impf. 2 m.p. (נָסָה 650) *why do you put to the proof*
אֶת־יהוה dir. obj.-pr.n. (217) *Yahweh*

17:3

וַיִּצְמָא consec.-Qal impf. 3 m.s. (צָמֵא 854) *but ... thirsted*
שָׁם adv. (1027) *there*
הָעָם def. art.-n.m.s. (I 766) *the people*
לַמַּיִם prep.-def. art.-n.m.p. (565) *for water*
וַיָּלֶן consec.-Hi. impf. 3 m.s. (לוּן II 534) *and murmured*
הָעָם v. supra *the people*
עַל־מֹשֶׁה prep.-pr.n. (602) *against Moses*
וַיֹּאמֶר consec.-Qal impf. 3 m.s. (55) *and said*
לָמָּה זֶּה prep.-interr. (552)-demons. adj. (260) *why*

הֶעֱלִיתָנוּ Hi. pf. 2 m.s.-1 c.p. sf. (עָלָה 748) *did you bring us up*

מִמִּצְרַיִם prep.-pr.n. (595) *out of Egypt*

לְהָמִית prep.-Hi. inf. cstr. (מוּת 559) *to kill*

אֹתִי dir. obj.-1 c.s. sf. *us (me)*

וְאֶת־בָּנַי conj.-dir.obj.-n.m.p.-1 c.s. sf. (119) *and our (my) children*

וְאֶת־מִקְנַי conj.-dir. obj.-n.m.p.-1 c.s. sf. (889) *and our (my) cattle*

בַּצָּמָא prep.-def. art.-n.m.s. (854) *with thirst*

17:4

וַיִּצְעַק consec.-Qal impf. 3 m.s. (צָעַק 858) *so ... cried*

מֹשֶׁה pr.n. (602) *Moses*

אֶל־יהוה prep.-pr.n. (217) *to Yahweh*

לֵאמֹר prep.-Qal inf. cstr. (55) *(saying)*

מָה interr. (552) *what*

אֶעֱשֶׂה Qal impf. 1 c.s. (עָשָׂה I 793) *shall I do*

לָעָם הַזֶּה prep.-def. art.-n.m.s. (I 766)-def. art.-demons. adj. m.s. (260) *with this people*

עוֹד מְעַט adv. (728)-adv. (589) *almost*

וּסְקָלֻנִי conj.-Qal pf. 3 c.p.-1 c.s. sf. (סָקַל 709) *they stone me*

17:5

וַיֹּאמֶר consec.-Qal impf. 3 m.s. (55) *and ... said*

יהוה pr.n. (217) *Yahweh*

אֶל־מֹשֶׁה prep.-pr.n. (602) *to Moses*

עֲבֹר Qal impv. 2 m.s. (716) *Pass on*

לִפְנֵי prep.-n.m.p. cstr. (815) *before*

הָעָם def. art.-n.m.s. (I 766) *the people*

וְקַח conj.-Qal impv. 2 m.s. (לָקַח 542) *taking*

אִתְּךָ prep.-2 m.s. sf. (II 85) *with you*

מִזִּקְנֵי prep.-n.m.p. cstr. (278) *some of the elders of*

יִשְׂרָאֵל pr.n. (975) *Israel*

וּמַטְּךָ conj.-n.m.s.-2 m.s. sf. (641) *and (your) rod*

אֲשֶׁר rel. *which*

הִכִּיתָ בּוֹ Hi. pf. 2 m.s. (נָכָה 645)-prep.-3 m.s. sf. *you struck (with it)*

אֶת־הַיְאֹר dir. obj.-def. art.-n.m.s. (384) *the Nile*

קַח v. supra Qal impv. 2 m.s. (לָקַח 542) *take*

בְּיָדְךָ prep.-n.f.s.-2 m.s. sf. (388) *in your hand*

וְהָלָכְתָּ conj.-Qal pf. 2 m.s. paus. (הָלַךְ 229) *and go*

17:6

הִנְנִי demons.part.-1 c.s. sf. (243) *behold I*

עֹמֵד Qal act. ptc. (763) *will stand*

לְפָנֶיךָ prep.-n.m.p.-2 m.s. sf. (815) *before you*

שָּׁם adv. (1027) *there*

עַל־הַצּוּר prep.-def. art.-n.m.s. (849) *on the rock*

בְּחֹרֵב prep.-pr.n. (352) *at Horeb*

וְהִכִּיתָ conj.-Hi. pf. 2 m.s. (נָכָה 645) *and you shall strike*

בַצּוּר prep.-def. art.-n.m.s. (849) *the rock*

וְיָצְאוּ conj.-Qal pf. 3 c.p. (יָצָא 422) *and shall come out*

מִמֶּנּוּ prep.-3 m.s. sf. *of it*

מַיִם n.m.p. (565) *water*

וְשָׁתָה conj.-Qal pf. 3 m.s. (שָׁתָה 1059) *that may drink*

הָעָם def. art.-n.m.s. (I 766) *the people*

וַיַּעַשׂ consec.-Qal impf. 3 m.s. (עָשָׂה I 793) *and ... did*

כֵּן adv. (485) *so*

מֹשֶׁה pr.n. (602) *Moses*

לְעֵינֵי prep.-n.f.p. cstr. (744) *in the sight of*

זִקְנֵי n.m.p. cstr. (278) *the elders of*

יִשְׂרָאֵל pr.n. (975) *Israel*

17:7

וַיִּקְרָא consec.-Qal impf. 3 m.s. (קָרָא 894) *and he called*

שֵׁם n.m.s. cstr. (1027) *the name of*
הַמָּקוֹם def. art.-n.m.s. (879) *the place*
מַסָּה pr.n. (III 650) *Massah*
וּמְרִיבָה conj.-pr.n. (II 937) *and Meribah*
עַל־רִיב conj.-Qal inf. cstr. (רִיב 936) *because of the faultfinding of*
בְּנֵי יִשְׂרָאֵל n.m.p. cstr. (119)-pr.n. (975) *the children of Israel*
וְעַל נַסֹּתָם conj.-prep.-Pi. inf. cstr.-3 m.p. sf. (נָסָה 650) *and because they put to the proof*
אֶת־יהוה dir. obj.-pr.n. (217) *Yahweh*
לֵאמֹר prep.-Qal inf. cstr. (55) *by saying*
הֲיֵשׁ יהוה interr.part.-subst. (441)-pr.n. (217) *is Yahweh?*
בְּקִרְבֵּנוּ prep.-n.m.s.-1 c.p. sf. (899) *among us*
אִם־אָיִן hypoth. part. (49)-subst. paus. (II 34) *or not*

17:8

וַיָּבֹא consec.-Qal impf. 3 m.s. (בּוֹא 97) *then came*
עֲמָלֵק pr.n. (766) *Amalek*
וַיִּלָּחֶם consec.-Ni. impf. 3 m.s. (לָחַם 535) *and fought*
עִם־יִשְׂרָאֵל prep.-pr.n. (975) *with Israel*
בִּרְפִידִם prep.-pr.n. (951) *at Rephidim*

17:9

וַיֹּאמֶר consec.-Qal impf. 3 m.s. (55) *and ... said*
מֹשֶׁה pr.n. (602) *Moses*
אֶל־יְהוֹשֻׁעַ prep.-pr.n. (221) *to Joshua*
בְּחַר־לָנוּ Qal impv. 2 m.s. (103)-prep.-1 c.p. sf. *choose for us*
אֲנָשִׁים n.m.p. (35) *men*
וְצֵא Qal impv. 2 m.s. (יָצָא 422) *and go out*
הִלָּחֵם Ni. impv. 2 m.s. (לָחַם 535) *fight*
בַּעֲמָלֵק prep.-pr.n. (766) *with Amalek*
מָחָר adv. (563) *tomorrow*
אָנֹכִי pers.pr. 1 c.s. (59) *I*
נִצָּב Ni. ptc. (נָצַב 662) *will stand*
עַל־רֹאשׁ prep.-n.m.s. cstr. (910) *on the top of*
הַגִּבְעָה def.art.-n.f.s. (148) *the hill*
וּמַטֵּה conj.-n.m.s. cstr. (641) *with the rod of*
הָאֱלֹהִים def.art.-n.m.p. (43) *God*
בְּיָדִי prep.-n.f.s.-1 c.s. sf. (388) *in my hand*

17:10

וַיַּעַשׂ consec.-Qal impf. 3 m.s. (עָשָׂה I 793) *so ... did*
יְהוֹשֻׁעַ pr.n. (221) *Joshua*
כַּאֲשֶׁר prep.-rel. *as*
אָמַר־לוֹ Qal pf. 3 m.s. (55)-prep.-3 m.s. sf. *told him*
מֹשֶׁה pr.n. (602) *Moses*
לְהִלָּחֵם prep.-Ni. inf. cstr. (535) *and fought*
בַּעֲמָלֵק prep.-pr.n. (766) *with Amalek*
וּמֹשֶׁה conj.-pr.n. (602) *and Moses*
אַהֲרֹן pr.n. (14) *Aaron*
וְחוּר conj.-pr.n. (301) *and Hur*
עָלוּ Qal pf. 3 c.p. (עָלָה 748) *went up*
רֹאשׁ n.m.s. cstr. (910) *to the top of*
הַגִּבְעָה dcf.art.-n.f.s. (148) *the hill*

17:11

וְהָיָה conj.-Qal pf. 3 m.s. (224) *(and it was)*
כַּאֲשֶׁר prep.-rel. *whenever*
יָרִים Hi. impf. 3 m.s. (רוּם 926) *held up*
מֹשֶׁה pr.n. (602) *Moses*
יָדוֹ n.f.s.-3 m.s. sf. (388) *his hand*
וְגָבַר conj.-Qal pf. 3 m.s. (149) *(and) prevailed*
יִשְׂרָאֵל pr.n. (975) *Israel*
וְכַאֲשֶׁר conj.-v.supra *and whenever*
יָנִיחַ Hi. impf. 3 m.s. (נוּחַ 628) *he lowered (rested)*
יָדוֹ v.supra *his hand*
וְגָבַר v.supra *(and) prevailed*
עֲמָלֵק pr.n. (766) *Amalek*

17:12

וִידֵי conj.-n.f.p. cstr. (388) *but hands (of)*

מֹשֶׁה pr.n. (602) *Moses*

כְּבֵדִים n.m.p. (458) *grew weary*

וַיִּקְחוּ־ consec.-Qal impf. 3 m.p. (לָקַח 542) *so they took*

אֶבֶן n.f.s. (6) *a stone*

וַיָּשִׂימוּ consec.-Qal impf. 3 m.p. (שִׂים 962) *and put*

תַחְתָּיו prep.-3 m.s. sf. (1065) *under him*

וַיֵּשֶׁב consec.-Qal impf. 3 m.s. (יָשַׁב 442) *and he sat*

עָלֶיהָ prep.-3 f.s. sf. *upon it*

וְאַהֲרֹן conj.-pr.n. (14) *and Aaron*

וְחוּר conj.-pr.n. (301) *and Hur*

תָּמְכוּ Qal pf. 3 c.p. (תָּמַךְ 1069) *held up*

בְיָדָיו prep.-n.f.p.-3 m.s. sf. (388) *his hands*

מִזֶּה אֶחָד prep.-demons. adj. (260)-n.m.s. (25) *one on one side (from this, one)*

וּמִזֶּה אֶחָד conj.-v.supra *and the other on the other side*

וַיְהִי consec.-Qal impf. 3 m.s. (הָיָה 224) *and so*

יָדָיו v.supra *his hands*

אֱמוּנָה Qal pass. ptc. f.s. (אָמַן 52) *were steady (confirmed)*

עַד־בֹּא prep. (III 723)-Qal inf. cstr. (בּוֹא 97) *until the going down of*

הַשָּׁמֶשׁ def.art.-n.f.s. paus. (1039) *the sun*

17:13

וַיַּחֲלֹשׁ consec.-Qal impf. 3 m.s. (חָלַשׁ 325) *and ... mowed down*

יְהוֹשֻׁעַ pr.n. (221) *Joshua*

אֶת־עֲמָלֵק dir.obj.-pr.n. (766) *Amalek*

וְאֶת־עַמּוֹ conj.-dir.obj.-n.m.s.-3 m.s. sf. (I 766) *and his people*

לְפִי־חָרֶב prep.-n.m.s. cstr. (804)-n.f.s. paus. (352) *with the edge of the sword*

17:14

וַיֹּאמֶר consec.-Qal impf. 3 m.s. (55) *and ... said*

יהוה pr.n. (217) *Yahweh*

אֶל־מֹשֶׁה prep.-pr.n. (602) *to Moses*

כְּתֹב Qal impv. 2 m.s. (507) *write*

זֹאת demons. adj. f.s. (260) *this*

זִכָּרוֹן n.m.s. (271) *as a memorial*

בַּסֵּפֶר prep.-def.art.-n.m.s. (706) *in a book*

וְשִׂים conj.-Qal impv. 2 m.s. (962) *and recite*

בְּאָזְנֵי prep.-n.f.p. cstr. (23) *in the ears of*

יְהוֹשֻׁעַ pr.n. (221) *Joshua*

כִּי־מָחֹה conj.-Qal inf. abs. (562) *that ... utterly*

אֶמְחֶה Qal impf. 1 c.s. (מָחָה 562) *I will blot out*

אֶת־זֵכֶר dir.obj.-n.m.s. cstr. (271) *the remembrance of*

עֲמָלֵק pr.n. (766) *Amalek*

מִתַּחַת prep.-prep. (1065) *from under*

הַשָּׁמָיִם def.art.-n.m.p. paus. (1029) *heaven*

17:15

וַיִּבֶן consec.-Qal impf. 3 m.s. (בָּנָה 124) *and ... built*

מֹשֶׁה pr.n. (602) *Moses*

מִזְבֵּחַ n.m.s. (258) *an altar*

וַיִּקְרָא consec.-Qal impf. 3 m.s. (894) *and called*

שְׁמוֹ n.m.s.-3 m.s. sf. (1027) *the name of it*

יהוה pr.n. (217) *Yahweh*

נִסִּי n.m.s.-1 c.s. sf. (נֵס 651) *my banner*

17:16

וַיֹּאמֶר consec.-Qal impf. 3 m.s. (55) *saying*

כִּי־יָד conj.-n.f.s. (388) *a hand*

עַל־כֵּסְיָהּ prep.-n.m.s. (כִּסֵּא 490)-pr.n. (219) *upon the banner of Yahweh*

מִלְחָמָה n.f.s. (536) *war*

ליהוה prep.-pr.n. (217) *Yahweh will have*

בַּעֲמָלֵק prep.-pr.n. (766) *with Amalek*

מִדֹּר דֹּר prep.-n.m.s. (189)-n.m.s. (189) *from generation to generation*

18:1

וַיִּשְׁמַע consec.-Qal impf. 3 m.s. (שָׁמַע 1033) *heard*

יִתְרוֹ pr.n. (452) *Jethro*

כֹהֵן n.m.s. cstr. (463) *priest of*

מִדְיָן pr.n. (193) *Midian*

חֹתֵן n.m.s. cstr. (368) *father-in-law of*

מֹשֶׁה pr.n. (602) *Moses*

אֵת כָּל־ dir.obj.-n.m.s. (481) *of all*

אֲשֶׁר rel. *that*

עָשָׂה Qal pf. 3 m.s. (I 793) *had done*

אֱלֹהִים n.m.p. (43) *God*

לְמֹשֶׁה prep.-pr.n. (602) *for Moses*

וּלְיִשְׂרָאֵל conj.-prep.-pr.n. (975) *and for Israel*

עַמּוֹ n.m.s.-3 m.s. sf. (I 766) *his people*

כִּי־הוֹצִיא conj.-Hi. pf. 3 m.s. (יָצָא 422) *for ... had brought out*

יהוה pr.n. (217) *Yahweh*

אֶת־יִשְׂרָאֵל dir.obj.-pr.n. (975) *Israel*

מִמִּצְרָיִם prep.-pr.n. paus. (595) *of Egypt*

18:2

וַיִּקַּח consec.-Qal impf. 3 m.s. (לָקַח 542) *now ... had taken*

יִתְרוֹ pr.n. (452) *Jethro*

חֹתֵן v.18:1 n.m.s. cstr. (368) *father-in-law of*

מֹשֶׁה pr.n. (602) *Moses*

אֶת־צִפֹּרָה dir.obj.-pr.n. (862) *Zipporah*

אֵשֶׁת n.f.s. cstr. (61) *wife of*

מֹשֶׁה pr.n. (602) *Moses*

אַחַר adv. (29) *after*

שִׁלּוּחֶיהָ n.m.p.-3 f.s. sf. (1019) *he had sent her away*

18:3

וְאֵת שְׁנֵי conj.-dir.obj.-n.m.p. cstr. (1040) *and ... two*

בָנֶיהָ n.m.p.-3 f.s. sf. (119) *her ... sons*

אֲשֶׁר שֵׁם rel.-n.m.s. cstr. (1027) *of whom the name of*

הָאֶחָד def.art.-n.m.s. (25) *the one*

גֵּרְשֹׁם pr.n. (177) *Gershom*

כִּי אָמַר conj.-Qal pf. 3 m.s. (55) *for he said*

גֵּר הָיִיתִי n.m.s. (158)-Qal pf. 1 c.s. (הָיָה 224) *I have been a sojourner*

בְּאֶרֶץ prep.-n.f.s. (75) *in a land*

נָכְרִיָּה adj. f.s. (648) *foreign*

18:4

וְשֵׁם conj.-n.m.s. cstr. (1027) *and the name of*

הָאֶחָד def.art.-n.m.s. (25) *the other*

אֱלִיעֶזֶר pr.n. (45) *Eliezer*

כִּי־אֱלֹהֵי conj.-n.m.p. cstr. (43) *for the God of*

אָבִי n.m.s.-1 c.s. sf. (3) *my father*

בְּעֶזְרִי prep.-n.m.s.-1 c.s. sf. (740) *my help*

וַיַּצִּלֵנִי consec.-Hi. impf. 3 m.s.-1 c.s. sf. (נָצַל 664) *and delivered me*

מֵחֶרֶב prep.-n.f.s. cstr. (352) *from the sword of*

פַּרְעֹה pr.n. (829) *Pharaoh*

18:5

וַיָּבֹא consec.-Qal impf. 3 m.s. (בּוֹא 97) *and ... came*

יִתְרוֹ pr.n. (452) *Jethro*

חֹתֵן v.18:2 n.m.s. cstr. (368) *father-in-law of*

מֹשֶׁה pr.n. (602) *Moses*

וּבָנָיו conj.-n.m.p.-3 m.s. sf. (119) *with his sons*

וְאִשְׁתּוֹ conj.-n.f.s.-3 m.s. sf. (61) *and his wife*

אֶל־מֹשֶׁה prep.-pr.n. (602) *to Moses*

אֶל־הַמִּדְבָּר prep.-def.art.-n.m.s. (184) *in the wilderness*

אֲשֶׁר־הוּא rel.-pers.pr. 3 m.s. (214) *where he*

חֹנֶה Qal act. ptc. (חָנָה 333) *was encamped*

שָׁם adv. (1027) *(there)*

הַר n.m.s. cstr. (249) *at the mountain of*

הָאֱלֹהִים def.art.-n.m.p. (43) *God*

18:6

וַיֹּאמֶר consec.-Qal impf. 3 m.s. (55) *and when one told*

אֶל־מֹשֶׁה prep.-pr.n. (602) *Moses*

אֲנִי pers. pr. 1 c.s. (58) *Lo (I)*

חֹתֶנְךָ n.m.s.-2 m.s. sf. (368) *your father-in-law*

יִתְרוֹ pr.n. (452) *Jethro*

בָּא Qal act. ptc. (בּוֹא 97) *is coming*

אֵלֶיךָ prep.-2 m.s. sf. *to you*

וְאִשְׁתְּךָ conj.-n.f.s.-2 m.s. sf. (61) *with your wife*

וּשְׁנֵי conj.-num. m.p. cstr. (1040) *and ... two*

בָנֶיהָ n.m.p.-3 f.s. sf. (119) *her ... sons*

עִמָּהּ prep.-3 f.s. sf. *with her*

18:7

וַיֵּצֵא consec.-Qal impf. 3 m.s. (יָצָא 422) *went out*

מֹשֶׁה pr.n. (602) *Moses*

לִקְרַאת prep.-Qal inf. cstr. (קָרָא 894) *to meet*

חֹתְנוֹ n.m.s.-3 m.s. sf. (368) *his father-in-law*

וַיִּשְׁתַּחוּ consec.-Hith. impf. 3 m.s. (שָׁחָה 1005) *and did obeisance*

וַיִּשַּׁק־לוֹ consec.-Qal impf. 3 m.s. (נָשַׁק I 676)-prep.-3 m.s. sf. *and kissed him*

וַיִּשְׁאֲלוּ consec.-Qal impf. 3 m.p. (שָׁאַל 981) *and they asked*

אִישׁ־לְרֵעֵהוּ n.m.s. (35)-prep.-n.m.s.-3 m.s. sf. (945) *each other*

לְשָׁלוֹם prep.-n.m.s. (1022) *of their welfare*

וַיָּבֹאוּ consec.-Qal impf. 3 m.p. (בּוֹא 97) *and went*

הָאֹהֱלָה def.art.-n.m.s.-dir.he (אֹהֶל 13) *into the tent*

18:8

וַיְסַפֵּר consec.-Pi. impf. 3 m.s. (סָפַר 707) *then told*

מֹשֶׁה pr.n. (602) *Moses*

לְחֹתְנוֹ prep.-n.m.s.-3 m.s. sf. (368) *his father-in-law*

כָּל־אֲשֶׁר dir.obj.-n.m.s. (481) - rel. *all that*

עָשָׂה Qal pf. 3 m.s. (I 793) *had done*

יהוה pr.n. (217) *Yahweh*

לְפַרְעֹה prep.-pr.n. (829) *to Pharaoh*

וּלְמִצְרַיִם conj.-prep.-pr.n. (595) *and to the Egyptians*

עַל אוֹדֹת prep.-n.f.p. cstr. (15) *for sake (of)*

יִשְׂרָאֵל pr.n. (975) *Israel*

אֵת כָּל־ dir.obj.-n.m.s. cstr. (481) *all*

הַתְּלָאָה def.art.-n.f.s. (521) *the hardship*

אֲשֶׁר rel. *that*

מְצָאָתַם Qal pf. 3 f.s.-3 m.p. sf. (מָצָא 592) *had come upon them*

בַּדֶּרֶךְ prep.-def.art.-n.m.s. (202) *in the way*

וַיַּצִּלֵם consec.-Hi. impf. 3 m.s.-3 m.p. sf. (נָצַל 664) *and how ... had delivered them*

יהוה pr.n. (217) *Yahweh*

18:9

וַיִּחַדְּ consec.-Qal impf. 3 m.s. (חָדָה II 292) *and ... rejoiced*

יִתְרוֹ pr.n. (452) *Jethro*

עַל כָּל־ prep.-n.m.s. cstr. (481) *for all*

הַטּוֹבָה def.art.-n.f.s. (375) *the good*

אֲשֶׁר־ rel. *which*

עָשָׂה Qal pf. 3 m.s. (I 793) *had done*

יהוה pr.n. (217) *Yahweh*

לְיִשְׂרָאֵל prep.-pr.n. (975) *to Israel*

אֲשֶׁר rel. *in that*

הִצִּילוֹ Hi. pf. 3 m.s.-3 m.s. sf. (נָצַל 664) *he had delivered them*

מִיַּד prep.-n.f.s. cstr. (388) *out of the hand of*

מִצְרָיִם pr.n. paus. (595) *the Egyptians*

18:10

וַיֹּאמֶר consec.-Qal impf. 3 m.s. (55) *and ... said*

יִתְרוֹ pr.n. (452) *Jethro*

בָּרוּךְ Qal pass. ptc. (138) *blessed be*

יהוה pr.n. (217) *Yahweh*

אֲשֶׁר הִצִּיל rel.-Hi. pf. 3 m.s. (נָצַל 664) *who has delivered*

אֶתְכֶם dir.obj.-2 m.p. sf. *you*

מִיַּד prep.-n.f.s. cstr. (388) *out of the hand of*

מִצְרַיִם pr.n. (595) *the Egyptians*

וּמִיַּד conj.-prep.-n.f.s. cstr. (388) *and out of the hand of*

פַּרְעֹה pr.n. (829) *Pharaoh*

אֲשֶׁר הִצִּיל v.supra *(because he has delivered)*

אֶת־הָעָם dir.obj.-def.art.-n.m.s. (I 766) *(the people)*

מִתַּחַת prep.-prep. (1065) *from under*

יַד־ n.f.s. cstr. (388) *the hand of*

מִצְרָיִם pr.n. paus. (595) *the Egyptians*

18:11

עַתָּה conj.-adv. (773) *now*

יָדַעְתִּי Qal pf. 1 c.s. (יָדַע 393) *I know*

כִּי־גָדוֹל conj.-adj. m.s. (152) *that ... is greater*

יהוה pr.n. (217) *Yahweh*

מִכָּל־ prep.-n.m.s. cstr. (481) *than all*

הָאֱלֹהִים def.art.-n.m.p. (43) *gods*

כִּי בַדָּבָר conj.-prep.-def.art.-n.m.s. (182) *when (in the matter)*

אֲשֶׁר rel.

זָדוּ Qal pf. 3 c.p. (זוּד 267) *they dealt arrogantly*

עֲלֵיהֶם prep.-3 m.p. sf. *with them*

18:12

וַיִּקַּח consec.-Qal impf. 3 m.s. (לָקַח 542) *and ... offered (took)*

יִתְרוֹ pr.n. (452) *Jethro*

חֹתֵן n.m.s. cstr. (368) *father-in-law (of)*

מֹשֶׁה pr.n. (602) *Moses*

עֹלָה n.f.s. (750) *a burnt offering*

וּזְבָחִים conj.-n.m.p. (257) *and sacrifices*

לֵאלֹהִים prep.-n.m.p. (43) *to God*

וַיָּבֹא consec.-Qal impf. 3 m.s. (בּוֹא 97) *and ... came*

אַהֲרֹן pr.n. (14) *Aaron*

וְכֹל זִקְנֵי conj.-n.m.s. cstr. (481)-n.m.p. cstr. (278) *with all the elders of*

יִשְׂרָאֵל pr.n. (975) *Israel*

לֶאֱכָל־ prep.-Qal inf. cstr. (37) *to eat*

לֶחֶם n.m.s. (536) *bread*

עִם־חֹתֵן prep.-n.m.s. cstr. (368) *with father-in-law (of)*

מֹשֶׁה pr.n. (602) *Moses*

לִפְנֵי prep.-n.m.p. cstr. (815) *before*

הָאֱלֹהִים def.art.-n.m.p. (43) *God*

18:13

וַיְהִי consec.-Qal impf. 3 m.s. (הָיָה 224) *and*

מִמָּחֳרָת prep.-n.f.s. (564) *on the morrow*

וַיֵּשֶׁב consec.-Qal impf. 3 m.s. (יָשַׁב 442) *sat*

מֹשֶׁה pr.n. (602) *Moses*

לִשְׁפֹּט prep.-Qal inf. cstr. (1047) *to judge*

אֶת־הָעָם dir.obj.-def.art.-n.m.s. (I 766) *the people*

וַיַּעֲמֹד consec.-Qal impf. 3 m.s. (763) *and ... stood*

הָעָם v.supra *the people*

עַל־מֹשֶׁה prep.-pr.n. (602) *about Moses*

מִן־הַבֹּקֶר prep.-def.art.-n.m.s. (133) *from morning*

עַד־הָעָרֶב prep.-def.art.-n.m.s. paus. (787) *till evening*

18:14

וַיַּרְא consec.-Qal impf. 3 m.s. (רָאָה 906) *when ... saw*

חֹתֵן n.m.s. cstr. (368) *father-in-law (of)*

מֹשֶׁה pr.n. (602) *Moses*

אֵת כָּל־ dir.obj.-n.m.s. (481) *all*

אֲשֶׁר־הוּא rel.-pers.pr. 3 m.s. (214) *that he*

עֹשֶׂה Qal act. ptc. (I 793) *was doing*

לָעָם prep.-def.art.-n.m.s. (I 766) *for the people*

וַיֹּאמֶר consec.-Qal impf. 3 m.s. (55) *he said*

מָה־הַדָּבָר interr. (552)-def.art.-n.m.s. (182) *what is ... (thing)*

הַזֶּה def.art.-demons. adj. (260) *this*

אֲשֶׁר אַתָּה rel.-pers. pr. 2 m.s. (61) *that you*

עֹשֶׂה v.supra *are doing*

לָעָם v.supra *for the people*

מַדּוּעַ interr. (396) *why*

אַתָּה v.supra *you*

יוֹשֵׁב Qal act. ptc. (יָשַׁב 442) *do sit*

לְבַדֶּךָ prep.-n.m.s.-2 m.s. sf. (94) *alone*

וְכָל־הָעָם conj.-n.m.s. cstr. (481)-def.art.-n.m.s. (I 766) *and all the people*

נִצָּב Ni. ptc. (נָצַב 662) *stand*

עָלֶיךָ prep.-2 m.s. sf. *about you*

מִן־בֹּקֶר v.18:13 prep.-n.m.s. (133) *from morning*

עַד־עָרֶב prep. (III 723)-n.m.s. paus. (787) *till evening*

18:15

וַיֹּאמֶר consec.-Qal impf. 3 m.s. (55) *and ... said*

מֹשֶׁה pr.n. (602) *Moses*

לְחֹתְנוֹ prep.-n.m.s.-3 m.s. sf. (368) *to his father-in-law*

כִּי־יָבֹא conj.-Qal impf. 3 m.s. (בּוֹא 97) *because ... come*

אֵלַי prep.-1 c.s. sf. *to me*

הָעָן def.art.-n.m.s. (I 766) *the people*

לִדְרשׁ prep.-Qal inf. cstr. (205) *to inquire of*

אֱלֹהִים n.m.p. (43) *God*

18:16

כִּי־יִהְיֶה conj.-Qal impf. 3 m.s. (הָיָה 224) *when*

לָהֶם prep.-3 m.p. sf. *they have (for them)*

דָּבָר n.m.s. (182) *a dispute*

בָּא Qal pf. 3 m.s. (בּוֹא 97) *they come*

אֵלַי prep.-1 c.s. sf. *to me*

וְשָׁפַטְתִּי conj.-Qal pf. 1 c.s. (1047) *and I decide*

בֵּין אִישׁ prep.-n.m.s. (35) *between a man*

וּבֵין רֵעֵהוּ conj.-prep.-n.m.s.-3 m.s. sf. (945) *and his neighbor*

וְהוֹדַעְתִּי conj.-Hi. pf. 1 c.s. (יָדַע 393) *and I make them know*

אֶת־חֻקֵּי dir.obj.-n.m.p. cstr. (349) *the statutes of*

הָאֱלֹהִים def.art.-n.m.p. (43) *God*

וְאֶת־תּוֹרֹתָיו conj.-dir.obj.-n.f.p.-3 m.s. sf. (435) *and his decisions*

18:17

וַיֹּאמֶר consec.-Qal impf. 3 m.s. (55) *said*

חֹתֵן n.m.s. cstr. (368) *father-in-law (of)*

מֹשֶׁה pr.n. (602) *Moses*

אֵלָיו prep.-3 m.s. sf. *to him*

לֹא־טוֹב neg.-adj. m.s. (373) *is not good*

הַדָּבָר def.art.-n.m.s. (182) *(the thing)*

אֲשֶׁר rel. *what*

אַתָּה עֹשֶׂה pers.pr. 2 m.s. (61)-Qal act. ptc. (I 793) *you are doing*

18:18

נָבֹל תִּבֹּל Qal inf. abs. (615)-Qal impf. 2 m.s. (נָבֵל 615) *will wear out*

גַּם־אַתָּה adv. (168)-pers. pr. 2 m.s. (61) *you*

גַּם־הָעָם adv. (168)-def.art.-n.m.s. (I 766) *and the people*

הַזֶּה def.art.-demons. adj. (260) *(this)*

אֲשֶׁר עִמָּךְ rel.-prep.-2 m.s. sf. paus. *with you*

כִּי־כָבֵד conj.-n.m.s. (458) *for too heavy*

מִמְּךָ prep.-2 m.s. sf. *for you*

הַדָּבָר def.art.-n.m.s. (182) *the thing*

לֹא־תוּכַל neg.-Qal impf. 2 m.s. (יָכֹל 407) *you are not able*

עֲשֹׂהוּ Qal inf. cstr.-3 m.s. sf. (עָשָׂה I 793) *to perform it*

לְבַדֶּךָ prep.-n.m.s.-2 m.s. sf. (94) *alone*

18:19

עַתָּה adv. (773) *now*

שְׁמַע Qal impv. 2 m.s. (1033) *listen*

בְּקֹלִי prep.-n.m.s.-1 c.s. sf. (876) *to my voice*

אִיעָצְךָ Qal impf. 1 c.s.-2 m.s. sf. (יָעַץ 419) *I will give you counsel*

וִיהִי conj.-Qal impf. 3 m.s. apoc. (הָיָה 224) *and be*

אֱלֹהִים n.m.p. (43) *God*

עִמָּךְ prep.-2 m.s. sf. *with you*

הֱיֵה Qal impv. 2 m.s. (224) *(be)*

אַתָּה pers.pr. 2 m.s. (61) *you*

לָעָם prep.-def.art.-n.m.s. (I 766) *(for) the people*

מוּל prep. (I 557) *before*

הָאֱלֹהִים def.art.-n.m.p. (43) *God*

וְהֵבֵאתָ conj.-Hi. pf. 2 m.s. (בּוֹא 97) *and bring*

אַתָּה v.supra *(you)*

אֶת־הַדְּבָרִים dir.obj.-def.art.-n.m.p. (182) *their cases*

אֶל־הָאֱלֹהִים prep.-def.art.-n.m.p. (43) *to God*

18:20

וְהִזְהַרְתָּה conj.-Hi. pf. 2 m.s. (זָהַר II 264) *and you shall teach*

אֶתְהֶם dir.obj.-3 m.p. sf. *them*

אֶת־הַחֻקִּים dir.obj.-def.art.-n.m.p. (חֹק 349) *the statutes*

וְאֶת־הַתּוֹרֹת conj.-dir.obj.-def.art.-n.f.p. (תּוֹרָה 435) *and the decisions*

וְהוֹדַעְתָּ conj.-Hi. pf. 2 m.s. (יָדַע 393) *and make ... know*

לָהֶם prep.-3 m.p. sf. *them*

אֶת־הַדֶּרֶךְ dir.obj.-def.art.-n.m.s. (202) *the way*

יֵלְכוּ Qal impf. 3 m.p. (הָלַךְ 229) *they must walk*

בָהּ prep.-3 f.s. sf. *in which*

וְאֶת־הַמַּעֲשֶׂה conj.-dir.obj.-def.art.-n.m.s. (795) *and (the deed)*

אֲשֶׁר rel. *what*

יַעֲשׂוּן Qal impf. 3 m.p. (עָשָׂה I 793) *they must do*

18:21

וְאַתָּה conj.-pers. pr. 2 m.s. (61) *moreover*

תֶחֱזֶה Qal impf. 2 m.s. (חָזָה 302) *choose (see)*

מִכָּל־הָעָם prep.-n.m.s. cstr. (481)-def.art.-n.m.s. (I 766) *from all the people*

אַנְשֵׁי־חַיִל n.m.p. cstr. (35)-n.m.s. (298) *able men*

יִרְאֵי אֱלֹהִים Qal act. ptc. m.p. cstr. (431) - n.m.p. (43) *such as fear God*

אַנְשֵׁי אֱמֶת v.supra-n.f.s. (54) *men who are trustworthy*

שֹׂנְאֵי בָצַע Qal act.ptc. m.p. cstr. (שָׂנֵא 971) - n.m.s. paus. (130) *and who hate a bribe*

וְשַׂמְתָּ עֲלֵהֶם conj.-Qal pf. 2 m.s. (שִׂים 962)-prep.-3 m.p. sf. *and place over the people (them)*

שָׂרֵי אֲלָפִים n.m.p. cstr. (978)-n.m.p. (48) *rulers of thousands*

שָׂרֵי מֵאוֹת v.supra-num. f.p. (547) *of hundreds*

שָׂרֵי חֲמִשִּׁים v.supra-num. m.p. (331) *of fifties*

וְשָׂרֵי עֲשָׂרֹת conj.-v.supra-num. f.p. (797) *and (rulers) of tens*

18:22

וְשָׁפְטוּ conj.-Qal pf. 3 c.p. (1047) *and let them judge*

אֶת־הָעָם dir.obj.-def.art.-n.m.s. (I 766) *the people*

בְּכָל־עֵת prep.-n.m.s. cstr. (481)-n.f.s. (773) *at all times*

וְהָיָה conj.-Qal pf. 3 m.s. (224)

כָּל־הַדָּבָר n.m.s. cstr. (481)-def.art.-n.m.s. (182) *every ... matter*

הַגָּדֹל def.art.-adj. m.s. (152) *great*

יְבִיאוּ אֵלֶיךָ Hi. impf. 3 m.p. (97)-prep.-2 m.s. sf. *they shall bring to you*

וְכָל־הַדָּבָר conj.-v.supra *and every ... matter*

הַקָּטֹן def.art.-adj. m.s. (882) *small*

יִשְׁפְּטוּ־הֵם Qal impf. 3 m.p. (1047) - pers.pr. 3 m.p. (241) *they shall decide*

וְהָקֵל conj.-Hi. inf. cstr. (קָלַל 886) *so it will be easier*

מֵעָלֶיךָ prep.-prep.-2 m.s. sf. *for you*

וְנָשְׂאוּ conj.-Qal pf. 3 c.p. (669) *and they will bear the burden*

אִתָּךְ prep. (II 85)-2 m.s. sf. paus. *with you*

18:23

אִם hypoth.part. (49) *if*

אֶת־הַדָּבָר dir.obj.-def.art.-n.m.s. (182) *(thing)*

הַזֶּה def.art.-demons. adj. m.s. (260) *this*

תַּעֲשֶׂה Qal impf. 2 m.s. (I 793) *you do*

וְצִוְּךָ conj.-Pi. pf. 3 m.s.-2 m.s. sf. (צָוָה 845) *and commands you*

אֱלֹהִים n.m.p. (43) *God*

וְיָכָלְתָּ conj.-Qal pf. 2 m.s. (407) *then you will be able*

עֲמֹד Qal inf. cstr. (763) *to stand*

וְגַם conj.-adv. (168) *and also*

כָּל־הָעָם n.m.s. cstr. (481)-def.art.-n.m.s. (I 766) *all ... people*

הַזֶּה def.art.-demons. adj. (260) *this*

עַל־מְקֹמוֹ prep.-n.m.s.-3 m.s. sf. (879) *to their place*

יָבֹא Qal impf. 3 m.s. (97) *will go*

בְשָׁלוֹם prep.-n.m.s. (1022) *in peace*

18:24

וַיִּשְׁמַע consec.-Qal impf. 3 m.s. (1033) *so ... gave heed*

מֹשֶׁה pr.n. (602) *Moses*

לְקוֹל prep.-n.m.s. cstr. (876) *to the voice of*

חֹתְנוֹ n.m.s.-3 m.s. sf. (368) *his father-in-law*

וַיַּעַשׂ consec.-Qal impf. 3 m.s. (עָשָׂה I 793) *and did*

כֹּל אֲשֶׁר n.m.s. (481)-rel. *all that*

אָמָר Qal pf. 3 m.s. paus. (55) *he had said*

18:25

וַיִּבְחַר consec.-Qal impf. 3 m.s. (103) *chose*

מֹשֶׁה pr.n. (602) *Moses*

אַנְשֵׁי־ n.m.p. cstr. (35) *men (of)*

חַיִל n.m.s. (298) *able*

מִכָּל־יִשְׂרָאֵל prep.-n.m.s. cstr. (481)-pr.n. (975) *out of all Israel*

וַיִּתֵּן consec.-Qal impf. 3 m.s. (נָתַן 678) *and made*

אֹתָם dir.obj.-3 m.p. sf. *them*

רָאשִׁים n.m.p. (910) *heads*

עַל־הָעָם prep.-def.art.-n.m.s. (I 766) *over the people*

שָׂרֵי v.18:21 n.m.p. cstr. (978) *rulers of*

אֲלָפִים num. m.p. (48) *thousands*

שָׂרֵי v.supra *(rulers) of*

מֵאוֹת num. f.p. (547) *hundreds*

שָׂרֵי v.supra *(rulers) of*

חֲמִשִּׁים num. m.p. (331) *fifties*

וְשָׂרֵי conj.-v.supra *and (rulers) of*

עֲשָׂרֹת num. f.p. (796) *tens*

18:26

וְשָׁפְטוּ conj.-Qal pf. 3 c.p. (1047) *and they judged*

אֶת־הָעָם dir.obj.-def.art.-n.m.s. (I 766) *the people*

בְּכָל־עֵת prep.-n.m.s. cstr. (481) - n.f.s. (773) *at all times*

אֶת־הַדָּבָר dir.obj.-def.art.-n.m.s. (182) *cases*

הַקָּשֶׁה def.art.-adj. m.s. (904) *hard*

יְבִיאוּן Hi. impf. 3 m.p. (בּוֹא 97)-*they brought*

אֶל־מֹשֶׁה prep.-pr.n. (602) *to Moses*

וְכָל־הַדָּבָר conj.-n.m.s. cstr. (481)-def. art.-n.m.s. (182) *but any ... matter*

הַקָּטֹן def.art.-adj. m.s. (882) *small*

יִשְׁפּוּטוּ Qal impf. 3 m.p. (1047) *they decided*

הֵם pers. pr. 3 m.p. (241) *themselves*

18:27

וַיְשַׁלַּח consec.-Pi. impf. 3 m.s. (1018) *then ... let depart*

מֹשֶׁה pr.n. (602) *Moses*

אֶת־חֹתְנוֹ dir.obj.-n.m.s.-3 m.s. sf. (368) *his father-in-law*

וַיֵּלֶךְ consec.-Qal impf. 3 m.s. (הָלַךְ 229) *and he went*

לוֹ prep.-3 m.s. sf. *his way*

אֶל־אַרְצוֹ prep.-n.f.s.-3 m.s. sf. (75) *to his own country*

19:1

בַּחֹדֶשׁ prep.-def. art.-n.m.s. (II 294) *on the ... new moon*

הַשְּׁלִישִׁי def. art.-num. adj. s. (1026) *third*

לְצֵאת prep.-Qal inf. cstr. (יָצָא 422) *after had gone forth*

בְּנֵי־יִשְׂרָאֵל n.m.p. cstr. (119)-pr.n. (975) *the people of Israel*

מֵאֶרֶץ prep.-n.f.s. cstr. (75) *out of the land of*

מִצְרָיִם pr.n. paus. (595) *Egypt*

בַּיּוֹם הַזֶּה prep.-def. art.-n.m.s. (398)-def. art.-demons. adj. m.s. (260) *on that day*

בָּאוּ Qal pf. 3 c.p. (בּוֹא 97) *they came*

מִדְבַּר n.m.s. cstr. (184) *into the wilderness of*

סִינָי pr.n. paus. (696) *Sinai*

19:2

וַיִּסְעוּ consec.-Qal impf. 3 m.p. (נָסַע I 652) *and when they set out*

מֵרְפִידִים prep.-pr.n. (951) *from Rephidim*

וַיָּבֹאוּ consec.-Qal impf. 3 m.p. (97) *and came into*

מִדְבַּר n.m.s. cstr. (184) *the wilderness of*

סִינַי pr.n. (696) *Sinai*

וַיַּחֲנוּ consec.-Qal impf. 3 m.p. (חָנָה 333) *they encamped*

בַּמִּדְבָּר prep.-def. art.-n.m.s. (184) *in the wilderness*

וַיִּחַן־שָׁם consec.-Qal impf. 3 m.s. (333)-adv. (1027) *and there ... encamped*

יִשְׂרָאֵל pr.n. (975) *Israel*

נֶגֶד הָהָר prep. (617)-def. art.-n.m.s. (249) *before the mountain*

19:3

וּמֹשֶׁה conj.-pr.n. (602) *and Moses*

עָלָה Qal pf. 3 m.s. (748) *went up*

אֶל־הָאֱלֹהִים prep.-def. art.-n.m.p. (43) *to God*

וַיִּקְרָא consec.-Qal impf. 3 m.s. (894) *and ... called*

אֵלָיו prep.-3 m.s. sf. *him*

יהוה pr.n. (217) *Yahweh*

מִן־הָהָר prep.-def. art.-n.m.s. (249) *out of the mountain*

לֵאמֹר prep.-Qal inf. cstr. (55) *saying*

כֹּה תֹאמַר adv. (462)-Qal impf. 2 m.s. (55) *Thus you shall say*

לְבֵית prep.-n.m.s. cstr. (108) *to the house of*

יַעֲקֹב pr.n. (784) *Jacob*

וְתַגֵּיד conj.-Hi. impf. 2 m.s. (נָגַד 616) *and tell*

לִבְנֵי prep.-n.m.p. cstr. (119) *the people of*

יִשְׂרָאֵל pr.n. (975) *Israel*

19:4

אַתֶּם pers. pr. 2 m.p. (61) *you*

רְאִיתֶם Qal pf. 2 m.p. (רָאָה 906) *have seen*

אֲשֶׁר rel. *what*

עָשִׂיתִי Qal pf. 1 c.s. (I 793) *I did*

לְמִצְרָיִם prep.-pr.n. paus. (595) *to the Egyptians*

וָאֶשָּׂא consec.-Qal impf. 1 c.s. (נָשָׂא 669) *and how I bore*

אֶתְכֶם dir. obj.-2 m.p. sf. *you*

עַל־כַּנְפֵי prep.-n.f.p. cstr. (489) *on wings (of)*

נְשָׁרִים n.m.p. (676) *eagles*

וָאָבִא consec.-Hi. impf. 1 c.s. (97) *and brought*

אֶתְכֶם v. supra *you*

אֵלָי prep.-1 c.s. sf. paus. *to myself*

19:5

וְעַתָּה conj.-adv. (773) *now therefore*

אִם־שָׁמוֹעַ hypoth. part.-Qal inf. abs. (1033) *if (utterly)*

תִּשְׁמְעוּ Qal impf. 2 m.p. (1033) *you will obey*

בְּקֹלִי prep.-n.m.s.-1 c.s. sf. (876) *my voice*

וּשְׁמַרְתֶּם conj.-Qal pf. 2 m.p. (1036) *and keep*

אֶת־בְּרִיתִי dir. obj.-n.f.s.-1 c.s. sf. (136) *my covenant*

וִהְיִיתֶם conj.-Qal pf. 2 m.p. (224) *you shall be*

לִי prep.-1 c.s. sf. *my*

סְגֻלָּה n.f.s. (688) *own possession*

מִכָּל־הָעַמִּים prep.-n.m.s. cstr. (481)-def. art.-n.m.p. (I 766) *among all peoples*

כִּי־לִי conj.-prep.-1 c.s. sf. *for ... is mine*

כָּל־הָאָרֶץ n.m.s. cstr. (481)-def. art.-n.f.s. (75) *all the earth*

19:6

וְאַתֶּם conj.-pers. pr. 2 m.p. (61) *and you*

תִּהְיוּ־לִי Qal impf. 2 m.p. (224)-prep.-1 c.s. sf. *shall be to me*

מַמְלֶכֶת n.f.s. cstr. (575) *a kingdom of*

כֹּהֲנִים n.m.p. (463) *priests*

וְגוֹי conj.-n.m.s. (156) *and a ... nation*

קָדוֹשׁ adj. m.s. (872) *holy*

אֵלֶּה demons. adj. m.p. (41) *these (are)*

הַדְּבָרִים def. art.-n.m.p. (182) *the words*

אֲשֶׁר rel. *which*

תְּדַבֵּר Pi. impf. 2 m.s. (180) *you shall speak*

אֶל־בְּנֵי prep.-n.m.p. cstr. (119) *to the children of*

יִשְׂרָאֵל pr.n. (975) *Israel*

19:7

וַיָּבֹא consec.-Qal impf. 3 m.s. (97) *so ... came*

מֹשֶׁה pr.n. (602) *Moses*

וַיִּקְרָא consec.-Qal impf. 3 m.s. (894) *and called*

לְזִקְנֵי prep.-n.m.p. cstr. (278) *the elders of*

הָעָם def. art.-n.m.s. (I 766) *the people*

וַיָּשֶׂם consec.-Qal impf. 3 m.s. (שִׂים 962) *and set*

לִפְנֵיהֶם prep.-n.m.p.-3 m.p. sf. (815) *before them*

אֵת כָּל־ dir. obj.-n.m.s. cstr. (481) *all*

הַדְּבָרִים def. art.-n.m.p. (182) *words*

הָאֵלֶּה def. art.-demons. adj. m.p. (41) *these*

אֲשֶׁר rel. *which*

צִוָּהוּ Pi. pf. 3 m.s.-3 m.s. sf. (צָוָה 845) *had commanded him*

יהוה pr.n. (217) *Yahweh*

19:8

וַיַּעֲנוּ consec.-Qal impf. 3 m.p. (עָנָה I 772) *and answered*

כָל־הָעָם n.m.s. cstr. (481)-def. art.-n.m.s. (I 766) *all the people*

יַחְדָּו adv. (403) *together*

וַיֹּאמְרוּ consec.-Qal impf. 3 m.p. (55) *and said*

כֹּל אֲשֶׁר־ n.m.s. (481)-rel. *All that*

דִּבֶּר Pi. pf. 3 m.s. (180) *has spoken*

יהוה pr.n. (217) *Yahweh*

נַעֲשֶׂה Qal impf. 1 c.p. (I 793) *we will do*

וַיָּשֶׁב consec.-Hi. impf. 3 m.s. (שׁוּב 996) *and reported*

מֹשֶׁה pr.n. (602) *Moses*

אֶת־דִּבְרֵי dir. obj.-n.m.p. cstr. (182) *the words of*

הָעָם def. art.-n.m.s. (I 766) *the people*

אֶל־יהוה prep.-pr.n. (217) *to Yahweh*

19:9

וַיֹּאמֶר consec.-Qal impf. 3 m.s. (55) *and ... said*

יהוה pr.n. (217) *Yahweh*

אֶל־מֹשֶׁה prep.-pr.n. (602) *to Moses*

הִנֵּה interj. (243) *Lo*

אָנֹכִי בָּא pers. pr. 1 c.s. (59)-Qal act. ptc. (97) *I am coming*

אֵלֶיךָ prep.-2 m.s. sf. *to you*

בְּעַב prep.-n.m.s. cstr. (II 728) *in a thick*

הֶעָנָן def. art.-n.m.s. (777) *cloud*

בַּעֲבוּר prep.-prep. (II 721) *that*

יִשְׁמַע Qal impf. 3 m.s. (1033) *may hear*

הָעָם def. art.-n.m.s. (I 766) *the people*

בְּדַבְּרִי prep.-Pi. inf. cstr.-1 c.s. sf. (180) *when I speak*

עִמָּךְ prep.-2 m.s. sf. paus. *with you*

וְגַם־ conj.-adv. (168) *and also*

בְּךָ prep.-2 m.s. sf. *you*

יַאֲמִינוּ Hi. impf. 3 m.p. (52) *may believe*

לְעוֹלָם prep.-n.m.s. (761) *for ever*

וַיַּגֵּד consec.-Hi. impf. 3 m.s. (נָגַד 616) *then told*

מֹשֶׁה pr.n. (602) *Moses*

אֶת־דִּבְרֵי dir. obj.-n.m.p. cstr. (182) *the words of*

הָעָם def. art.-n.m.s. (I 766) *the people*

אֶל־יהוה prep.-pr.n. (217) *to Yahweh*

19:10

וַיֹּאמֶר consec.-Qal impf. 3 m.s. (55) *and ... said*

יהוה pr.n. (217) *Yahweh*

אֶל־מֹשֶׁה prep.-pr.n. (602) *to Moses*

לֵךְ Qal impv. 2 m.s. (הָלַךְ 229) *go*

אֶל־הָעָם prep.-def.art.-n.m.s. (I 766) *to the people*

וְקִדַּשְׁתָּם conj.-Pi. pf. 2 m.s.-3 m.p. sf. (872) *and consecrate them*

הַיּוֹם def.art.-n.m.s. (398) *today*

וּמָחָר conj.-adv. (563) *and tomorrow*

וְכִבְּסוּ conj.-Pi. pf. 3 c.p. (460) *and let them wash*

שִׂמְלֹתָם n.f.p.-3 m.p. sf. (971) *their garments*

19:11

וְהָיוּ conj.-Qal pf. 3 c.p. (224) *and be*

נְכֹנִים Ni. ptc. m.p. (כּוּן I 465) *ready*

לַיּוֹם prep.-def.art.-n.m.s. (398) *by the ... day*

הַשְּׁלִישִׁי def.art.-num. (1026) *third*

כִּי conj. *for*

בַּיּוֹם prep.-v.supra *on the ... day*

הַשְּׁלִשִׁי v.supra *third*

יֵרֵד Qal impf. 3 m.s. (יָרַד 432) *will come down*

יהוה pr.n. (217) *Yahweh*

לְעֵינֵי prep.-n.f.p. cstr. (744) *in the sight of*

כָל־הָעָם n.m.s. cstr. (481)-def.art.-n.m.s. (I 766) *all the people*

עַל־הַר סִינָי prep.-n.m.s. cstr. (249) - pr.n. paus. (696) *upon Mount Sinai*

19:12

וְהִגְבַּלְתָּ conj.-Hi. pf. 2 m.s. (148) *and you shall set bounds for*

אֶת־הָעָם dir.obj.-def.art.-n.m.s. (I 766) *the people*

סָבִיב adv. (686) *round about*

לֵאמֹר prep.-Qal inf. cstr. (55) *saying*

הִשָּׁמְרוּ Ni. impv. 2 m.p. (1036) *take heed*

לָכֶם prep.-2 m.p. sf. *that you*

עֲלוֹת Qal inf. cstr. (עָלָה 748) *go up*

בָּהָר prep.-def.art.-n.m.s. (249) *into the mountain*

וּנְגֹעַ conj.-Qal inf. cstr. (619) *or touch*

בְּקָצֵהוּ prep.-n.m.s.-3 m.s. sf. (892) *the border of it*

כָּל־הַנֹּגֵעַ n.m.s. cstr. (481)-def.art.-Qal act. ptc. (619) *whoever touches*

בָּהָר prep.-def.art.-n.m.s. (249) *the mountain*

מוֹת יוּמָת Qal inf. abs. (מוּת 559) - Ho. impf. 3 m.s. paus. (559) *shall be put to death*

19:13

לֹא־תִגַּע neg.-Qal impf. 3 f.s. (נָגַע 619) *no ... shall touch*

בוֹ prep.-3 m.s. sf. *him*

יָד n.f.s. (388) *hand*

כִּי־סָקוֹל conj.-Qal inf. abs. (709) *but*
יִסָּקֵל Ni. impf. 3 m.s. (709) *he shall be stoned*
אוֹ־יָרֹה יִיָּרֶה conj. (14)-Qal inf. abs. (יָרָה 434) - Ni. impf. 3 m.s. (434) *or shot*
אִם־בְּהֵמָה conj. (49)-n.f.s. (96) *whether beast*
אִם־אִישׁ conj. (49)-n.m.s. (35) *or man*
לֹא יִחְיֶה neg.-Qal impf. 3 m.s. (חָיָה 310) *he shall not live*
בִּמְשֹׁךְ prep.-Qal inf. cstr. (מָשַׁךְ 604) *when ... sounds a long blast*
הַיֹּבֵל def.art.-n.m.s. (385) *the trumpet*
הֵמָּה pers. pr. 3 m.p. (241) *they*
יַעֲלוּ Qal impf. 3 m.p. (748) *shall come up*
בָהָר prep.-def.art.-n.m.s. (249) *to the mountain*

19:14

וַיֵּרֶד consec.-Qal impf. 3 m.s. (יָרַד 432) *so ... went down*
מֹשֶׁה pr.n. (602) *Moses*
מִן־הָהָר prep.-def.art.-n.m.s. (249) *from the mountain*
אֶל־הָעָם prep.-def.art.-n.m.s. (I 766) *to the people*
וַיְקַדֵּשׁ consec.-Pi. impf. 3 m.s. (872) *and consecrated*
אֶת־הָעָם dir.obj.-def.art.-n.m.s. (I 766) *the people*
וַיְכַבְּסוּ consec.-Pi. impf. 3 m.p. (כָּבַס 460) *and they washed*
שִׂמְלֹתָם n.f.p.-3 m.p. sf. (971) *their garments*

19:15

וַיֹּאמֶר consec.-Qal impf. 3 m.s. (55) *and he said*
אֶל־הָעָם prep.-def.art.-n.m.s. (I 766) *to the people*
הֱיוּ Qal impv. 2 m.p. (הָיָה 224) *be*
נְכֹנִים Ni. ptc. m.p. (כּוּן 465) *ready*
לִשְׁלֹשֶׁת prep.-num. f. cstr. (1025) *by the third (of)*
יָמִים n.m.p. (398) *day*

אַל־תִּגְּשׁוּ neg.-Qal impf. 2 m.p. (נָגַשׁ 620) *do not go near*
אֶל־אִשָּׁה prep.-n.f.s. (61) *a woman*

19:16

וַיְהִי consec.-Qal impf. 3 m.s. (224)
בַיּוֹם prep.-def.art.-n.m.s. (398) *on the ... day*
הַשְּׁלִישִׁי def.art.-adj. num. (1026) *third*
בִּהְיֹת prep.-Qal inf. cstr. (224) *on*
הַבֹּקֶר def.art.-n.m.s. (133) *the morning*
וַיְהִי consec.-Qal impf. 3 m.s. (224) *there were*
קֹלֹת n.m.p. (876) *thunders*
וּבְרָקִים conj.-n.m.p. (140) *and lightnings*
וְעָנָן conj.-n.m.s. (777) *and a ... cloud*
כָּבֵד adj. m.s. (458) *thick*
עַל־הָהָר prep.-def.art.-n.m.s. (249) *upon the mountain*
וְקֹל שֹׁפָר conj.-n.m.s. cstr. (876) - n.m.s. (1051) *and a trumpet blast*
חָזָק מְאֹד adj. m.s. (305)-adv. (547) *very loud*
וַיֶּחֱרַד consec.-Qal impf. 3 m.s. (353) *so that ... trembled*
כָּל־הָעָם n.m.s. cstr. (481)-def.art.-n.m.s. (I 766) *all the people*
אֲשֶׁר בַּמַּחֲנֶה rel.-prep.-def.art.-n.m.s. (334) *who were in the camp*

19:17

וַיּוֹצֵא consec.-Hi. impf. 3 m.s. (יָצָא 422) *then ... brought out*
מֹשֶׁה pr.n. (602) *Moses*
אֶת־הָעָם dir.obj.-def.art.-n.m.s. (I 766) *the people*
לִקְרַאת prep.-Qal inf. cstr. (II 896) *to meet*
הָאֱלֹהִים def.art.-n.m.p. (43) *God*
מִן־הַמַּחֲנֶה prep.-def.art.-n.m.s. (334) *out of the camp*
וַיִּתְיַצְּבוּ consec.-Hith. impf. 3 m.p. (יָצַב 426) *and they took their stand*
בְּתַחְתִּית prep.-adj. f.s. cstr. (1066) *at the foot of*

הָהָר def.art.-n.m.s. paus. (249) *the mountain*

19:18

וְהַר conj.-n.m.s. cstr. (249) *and Mount*

סִינַי pr.n. (696) *Sinai*

עָשַׁן Qal pf. 3 m.s. (798) *in smoke*

כֻּלּוֹ n.m.s.-3 m.s. sf. (481) *was wrapped in (all of it)*

מִפְּנֵי אֲשֶׁר prep.-n.m.p. cstr. (815)-rel. *because*

יָרַד Qal pf. 3 m.s. (432) *descended*

עָלָיו prep.-3 m.s. sf. *upon it*

יהוה pr.n. (217) *Yahweh*

בָּאֵשׁ prep.-def.art.-n.f.s. (77) *in fire*

וַיַּעַל consec.-Qal impf. 3 m.s. (עָלָה 748) *and went up*

עֲשָׁנוֹ n.m.s.-3 m.s. sf. (798) *the smoke of it*

כְּעֶשֶׁן prep.-n.m.s. cstr. (798) *like the smoke of*

הַכִּבְשָׁן def.art.-n.m.s. (461) *a kiln*

וַיֶּחֱרַד v.18:16 consec.-Qal impf. 3 m.s. (353) *and ... quaked*

כָּל־הָהָר n.m.s. cstr. (481)-def.art.-n.m.s. (249) *the whole mountain*

מְאֹד adv. (547) *greatly*

19:19

וַיְהִי consec.-Qal impf. 3 m.s. (224) *and (as)*

קוֹל n.m.s. cstr. (876) *the sound of*

הַשֹּׁפָר def.art.-n.m.s. (1051) *the trumpet*

הוֹלֵךְ Qal act. ptc. (229) *grew (walking)*

וְחָזֵק מְאֹד conj.-Qal act. ptc. (304) - adv. (547) *louder and louder*

מֹשֶׁה pr.n. (602) *Moses*

יְדַבֵּר Pi. impf. 3 m.s. (180) *spoke*

וְהָאֱלֹהִים conj.-def.art.-n.m.p. (43) *and God*

יַעֲנֶנּוּ Qal impf. 3 m.s.-3 m.s. sf. (I 772) *answered him*

בְקוֹל prep.-n.m.s. (876) *in thunder*

19:20

וַיֵּרֶד consec.-Qal impf. 3 m.s. (יָרַד 432) *and ... came down*

יהוה pr.n. (217) *Yahweh*

עַל־הַר סִינַי prep.-n.m.s. cstr. (249) - pr.n. (696) *upon Mount Sinai*

אֶל־רֹאשׁ הָהָר prep.-n.m.s. cstr. (910)-def. art.-n.m.s. (249) *to the top of the mountain*

וַיִּקְרָא consec.-Qal impf. 3 m.s. (894) *and ... called*

יהוה pr.n. (217) *Yahweh*

לְמֹשֶׁה prep.-pr.n. (602) *Moses*

אֶל־רֹאשׁ v.supra prep.-n.m.s. cstr. (910) *to the top of*

הָהָר def.art.-n.m.s. (249) *the mountain*

וַיַּעַל consec.-Qal impf. 3 m.s. (עָלָה 748) *and ... went up*

מֹשֶׁה pr.n. (602) *Moses*

19:21

וַיֹּאמֶר consec.-Qal impf. 3 m.s. (55) *and ... said*

יהוה pr.n. (217) *Yahweh*

אֶל־מֹשֶׁה prep.-pr.n. (602) *to Moses*

רֵד Qal impv.2 m.s. (יָרַד 432) *Go down*

הָעֵד Hi.impv.2 m.s. (עוּד 729) *warn*

בָּעָם prep.-def.art.-n.m.s. (I 766) *the people*

פֶּן־יֶהֶרְסוּ conj. (814)-Qal impf.3 m.p. (הָרַס 248) *lest they break through*

אֶל־יהוה prep.-pr.n. (217) *to Yahweh*

לִרְאוֹת prep.-Qal inf.cstr. (רָאָה 906) *to gaze*

וְנָפַל conj.-Qal pf.3 m.s. (656) *and perish*

מִמֶּנּוּ prep.-3 m.s. sf. *of them*

רָב adj.m.s. paus. (I 912) *many*

19:22

וְגַם conj.-adv. (168) *and also*

הַכֹּהֲנִים def.art.-n.m.p. (463) *the priests*

הַנִּגָּשִׁים def.art.-Ni.ptc.m.p. (620) *who come near*

אֶל־יהוה prep.-pr.n. (217) *to Yahweh*

יִתְקַדָּשׁוּ Hith.impf.3 m.p. paus. (קָדַשׁ 872) *let consecrate themselves*

פֶּן־ conj. (814) *lest*

יִפְרֹץ Qal impf.3 m.s. (I 829) *break out*

בָּהֶם prep.-3 m.p. *upon them*

יהוה pr.n. (217) *Yahweh*

19:23

וַיֹּאמֶר consec.-Qal impf.3 m.s. (55) *and said*

מֹשֶׁה pr.n. (602) *Moses*

אֶל־יהוה prep.-pr.n. (217) *to Yahweh*

לֹא־יוּכַל neg.-Qal impf.3 m.s. (יָכֹל 407) *cannot*

הָעָם def.art.-n.m.s. (I 766) *the people*

לַעֲלֹת prep.-Qal inf.cstr. (עָלָה 748) *come up*

אֶל־הַר סִינָי prep.-n.m.s. cstr. (249)-pr.n. paus. (696) *to Mount Sinai*

כִּי־אַתָּה conj.-pers.pr.2 m.s. (61) *for thou thyself*

הַעֵדֹתָה Hi.pf.2 m.s. (עוּד 729) *didst charge*

בָּנוּ prep.-1 c.p. sf. *us*

לֵאמֹר prep.-Qal inf.cstr. (55) *saying*

הַגְבֵּל Hi.impv.2 m.s. (148) *Set bounds*

אֶת־הָהָר dir.obj.-def.art.-n.m.s. (249) *about the mountain*

וְקִדַּשְׁתּוֹ conj.-Pi.pf.2 m.s.-3 m.s. sf. (872) *and consecrate it*

19:24

וַיֹּאמֶר consec.-Qal impf.3 m.s. (55) *and ... said*

אֵלָיו prep.-3 m.s.sf. *to him*

יהוה pr.n. (217) *Yahweh*

לֶךְ־ Qal impv. 2 m.s. (הָלַךְ 229) *Go*

רֵד Qal impv.2 m.s. (יָרַד 432) *down*

וְעָלִיתָ conj.-Qal pf.2 m.s. (עָלָה 748) *and come up*

אַתָּה pers.pr.2 m.s. (61) *(you)*

וְאַהֲרֹן conj.-pr.n. (217) *and Aaron*

עִמָּךְ prep.-2 m.s. sf. paus. *with you*

וְהַכֹּהֲנִים conj.-def.art.-n.m.p. (463) *but the priests*

וְהָעָם conj.-def.art.-n.m.s. (I 766) *and the people*

אַל־יֶהֶרְסוּ neg.-Qal impf.3 m.p. (הָרַס 248) *do not let break through*

לַעֲלֹת prep.-Qal inf.cstr. (עָלָה 748) *to come up*

אֶל־יהוה prep.-pr.n. (217) *to Yahweh*

פֶּן־יִפְרָץ־ conj. (814)-Qal impf.3 m.s. (I 829) *lest he break out*

בָּם prep.-3 m.p. sf. *against them*

19:25

וַיֵּרֶד consec.-Qal impf.3 m.s. (יָרַד 432) *so went down*

מֹשֶׁה pr.n. (602) *Moses*

אֶל־הָעָם prep.-def.art.-n.m.s. (I 766) *to the people*

וַיֹּאמֶר consec.-Qal impf.3 m.s. (55) *and told*

אֲלֵהֶם prep.-3 m.p. sf. *them*

20:1

וַיְדַבֵּר consec.-Pi.impf.3 m.s. (180) *and spoke*

אֱלֹהִים n.m.p. (43) *God*

אֵת כָּל־ dir.obj.-n.m.s. cstr. (481) *all*

הַדְּבָרִים הָאֵלֶּה def.art.-n.m.p. (182)-def.art.-demons. adj. m.p. (41) *these words*

לֵאמֹר prep.-Qal inf. cstr. (55) *saying*

20:2

אָנֹכִי pers.pr. 1 c.s. (59) *I am*

יהוה pr.n. (217) *Yahweh*

אֱלֹהֶיךָ n.m.p.-2 m.s. sf. (43) *your God*

אֲשֶׁר rel. *who*

הוֹצֵאתִיךָ Hi. pf. 1 c.s.-2 m.s. sf. (יָצָא 422) *brought you out*

מֵאֶרֶץ prep.-n.f.s. cstr. (75) *out of the land of*

מִצְרַיִם pr.n. (595) *Egypt*

מִבֵּית prep.-n.m.s. cstr. (108) *out of the house of*

עֲבָדִים n.m.p. (I 713) *bondage*

20:3

לֹא יִהְיֶה־ neg.-Qal impf. 3 m.s. (224) *shall have no*

לְךָ prep.-2 m.s. sf. *You (to you)*

אֱלֹהִים n.m.p. (43) *gods*

אֲחֵרִים adj.m.p. (29) *other*

עַל־פָּנָי prep.-n.m.p.-1 c.s. sf. (815) *before me*

20:4

לֹא תַעֲשֶׂה־ neg.-Qal impf. 2 m.s. (I 793) *you shall not make*

לְךָ prep.-2 m.s. sf. *yourself*

פֶסֶל n.m.s. (820) *a graven image*

וְכָל־ conj.-n.m.s. cstr. (481) *or any*

תְּמוּנָה n.f.s. (568) *likeness*

אֲשֶׁר rel. *that is*

בַּשָּׁמַיִם prep.-def.art.-n.m.p. (1029) *in heaven*

מִמַּעַל prep.-subst. (751) *above*

וַאֲשֶׁר conj.-rel. *or that is*

בָּאָרֶץ prep.-def.art.-n.f.s. (75) *in the earth*

מִתָּחַת prep.-adv. accus. paus. (1065) *beneath*

וַאֲשֶׁר conj.-rel. *or that is*

בַּמַּיִם prep.-def.art.-n.m.p. (565) *in the water*

מִתַּחַת v. supra *under*

לָאָרֶץ prep.-def.art.-n.f.s. (75) *the earth*

20:5

לֹא־תִשְׁתַּחְוֶה neg.-Hith.impf.2 m.s. (שָׁחָה 1005) *you shall not bow down*

לָהֶם prep.-3 m.p. sf. *to them*

וְלֹא תָעָבְדֵם conj.-neg.-Ho. impf. 2 m.s.-3 m.p. sf. (712) *or serve them (be caused to serve them)*

כִּי אָנֹכִי conj.-prs. pr. 1 c.s. (59) *for I*

יהוה pr.n. (217) *Yahweh*

אֱלֹהֶיךָ n.m.p.-2 m.s. sf. (43) *your God*

אֵל קַנָּא n.m.s. (42)-adj.m.s. (888) *a jealous God*

פֹּקֵד Qal act.ptc. (823) *visiting*

עֲוֹן n.m.s. cstr. (730) *the iniquity of*

אָבֹת n.m.p. (3) *the fathers*

עַל־בָּנִים prep.-n.m.p. (119) *upon the children*

עַל־שִׁלֵּשִׁים prep.-num. m.p. (II 1026) *to the third generation*

וְעַל־רִבֵּעִים conj.-prep.-num.adj.m.p. (918) *and the fourth generation*

לְשֹׂנְאָי prep.-Qal act. ptc. m.p.-1 c.p. sf. paus. (שָׂנֵא 971) *of those who hate me*

20:6

וְעֹשֶׂה conj.-Qal act.ptc. (I 793) *but showing*

חֶסֶד n.m.s. (338) *steadfast love*

לַאֲלָפִים prep.-num.m.p. (48) *to thousands*

לְאֹהֲבַי prep.-Qal act.ptc.m.p.-1 c.s. sf. (12) *of those who love me*

וּלְשֹׁמְרֵי conj.-prep.-Qal act. ptc. m.p. cstr. (1036) *and keep*

מִצְוֹתָי n.f.p.-1 c.s. sf. paus. (846) *my commandments*

20:7

לֹא תִשָּׂא neg.-Qal impf.2 m.s. (נָשָׂא 669) *you shall not take*

אֶת־שֵׁם־יהוה dir.obj.-n.m.s. cstr. (1027)-pr.n. (217) *the name of Yahweh*

אֱלֹהֶיךָ n.m.p.-2 m.s. sf. (43) *your God*

לַשָּׁוְא prep.-def.art.-n.m.s. (996) *in vain*

כִּי לֹא יְנַקֶּה conj.-neg.-Pi. impf. 3 m.s. (נָקָה 667) *for ... will not hold guiltless*

יהוה pr.n. (217) *Yahweh*

אֵת אֲשֶׁר־יִשָּׂא dir.obj.-rel.-Qal impf.3 m.s. (נָשָׂא 669) *who takes*

אֶת־שְׁמוֹ dir.obj.-n.m.s.-3 m.s. sf. (1027) *his name*

לַשָּׁוְא v. supra *in vain*

20:8

זָכוֹר Qal inf.abs. (269) *remembering*

אֶת־יוֹם dir.obj.-n.m.s. cstr. (398) *the day (of)*

הַשַּׁבָּת def.art.-n.f.s. (992) *the Sabbath*

לְקַדְּשׁוֹ prep.-Pi.inf.cstr.-3 m.s. sf. (872) *to keep it holy*

20:9

שֵׁשֶׁת n.f.s. cstr. (995) *Six (of)*

יָמִים n.m.p. (398) *days*

תַּעֲבֹד Qal impf.2 m.s. (712) *you shall labor*

וְעָשִׂיתָ conj.-Qal pf.2 m.s. (I 793) *and do*

כָּל־מְלַאכְתֶּךָ n.m.s. cstr. (481)-n.f.s.-2 m.s. sf. (521) *all your work*

20:10

וְיוֹם conj.-n.m.s. cstr. (398) *but the ... day (of)*

הַשְּׁבִיעִי def.art.-num. (988) *seventh*

שַׁבָּת n.f.s. (992) *a sabbath*

ליהוה prep.-pr.n. (217) *to Yahweh*

אֱלֹהֶיךָ n.m.p.-2 m.s. sf. (43) *your God*

לֹא־תַעֲשֶׂה neg.-Qal impf. 2 m.s. (I 793) *you shall not do*

כָל־מְלָאכָה n.m.s. cstr. (481)-n.f.s. (521) *any work*

אַתָּה pers.pr. 2 m.s. (61) *you*

וּבִנְךָ־ conj.-n.m.s.-2 m.s. sf. (119) *or your son*

וּבִתֶּךָ conj.-n.f.s.-2 m.s. sf. (I 123) *or your daughter*

עַבְדְּךָ n.m.s.-2 m.s. sf. (713) *your manservant*

וַאֲמָתְךָ conj.-n.f.s.-2 m.s. sf. (51) *or your maid servant*

וּבְהֶמְתֶּךָ conj.-n.f.s.-2 m.s. sf. (96) *or your cattle*

וְגֵרְךָ conj.-n.m.s.-2 m.s. sf. (158) *or the sojourner (of you)*

אֲשֶׁר rel. *who is*

בִּשְׁעָרֶיךָ prep.-n.m.p.-2 m.s. sf. (1044) *within your gates*

20:11

כִּי שֵׁשֶׁת־ conj.-v.20:9 n.f.s. cstr. (995) *for in six (of)*

יָמִים n.m.p. (398) *days*

עָשָׂה Qal pf. 3 m.s. (I 793) *made*

יהוה pr.n. (217) *Yahweh*

אֶת־הַשָּׁמַיִם dir.obj.-def.art.-n.m.p. (1029) *heaven*

וְאֶת־הָאָרֶץ conj.-dir.obj.-def.art.-n.f.s. (75) *and earth*

אֶת־הַיָּם dir.obj.-def.art.-n.m.s. (410) *the sea*

וְאֶת־כָּל־ conj.-dir.obj.-n.m.s. cstr. (481) *and all*

אֲשֶׁר־בָּם rel.-prep.-3 m.p. sf. *that is in them*

וַיָּנַח consec.-Qal impf. 3 m.s. (נוּחַ 628) *and rested*

בַּיּוֹם prep.-def.art.-n.m.s. (398) *(on) the ... day*

הַשְּׁבִיעִי def.art.-num. adj. (988) *seventh*

עַל־כֵּן prep.-adv. (485) *therefore*

בֵּרַךְ Pi. pf. 3 m.s. (138) *blessed*

יהוה pr.n. (217) *Yahweh*

אֶת־יוֹם dir.obj.-n.m.s. cstr. (398) *the day (of)*

הַשַּׁבָּת def.art.-n.f.s. (992) *the sabbath*

וַיְקַדְּשֵׁהוּ consec.-Pi. impf. 3 m.s.-3 m.s. sf. (872) *and hallowed it*

20:12

כַּבֵּד Pi. inf. abs. (or? Pi. impv. 2 m.s.) (457) *honor*

אֶת־אָבִיךָ dir.obj.-n.m.s.-2 m.s. sf. (3) *your father*

וְאֶת־אִמֶּךָ conj.-dir.obj.-n.f.s.-2 m.s. sf. (51) *and your mother*

לְמַעַן prep.-prep. (775) *that*

יַאֲרִכוּן Hi. impf. 3 m.p. (אָרַךְ 73) *may be long*

יָמֶיךָ n.m.p.-2 m.s. sf. (398) *your days*

עַל הָאֲדָמָה prep.-def.art.-n.f.s. (9) *in the land*

אֲשֶׁר־יהוה rel.-pr.n. (217) *which Yahweh*

אֱלֹהֶיךָ n.m.p.-2 m.s. sf. (43) *your God*

נֹתֵן Qal act. ptc. (678) *gives*

לָךְ prep.-2 m.s. sf. paus. *you*

20:13

לֹא תִּרְצָח neg.-Qal impf. 2 m.s. (רָצַח 953) *you shall not kill*

20:14

לֹא תִּנְאָף neg.-Qal impf. 2 m.s. (נָאַף 610) *you shall not commit adultery*

20:15

לֹא תִּגְנֹב neg.-Qal impf. 2 m.s. (גָּנַב 170) *you shall not steal*

20:16

לֹא־תַעֲנֶה neg.-Qal impf. 2 m.s. (עָנָה I 772) *you shall not bear*

בְרֵעֲךָ prep.-n.m.s.-2 m.s. sf. (רֵעַ 945) *against your neighbor*

עֵד שָׁקֶר n.m.s. cstr. (729)-n.m.s. paus. (1055) *false witness*

20:17

לֹא תַחְמֹד neg.-Qal impf. 2 m.s. (326) *you shall not covet*

בֵּית רֵעֶךָ n.m.s. cstr. (108)-n.m.s.-2 m.s. sf. (945) *your neighbor's house*

לֹא־תַחְמֹד v.supra neg.-Qal impf. 2 m.s. (326) *you shall not covet*

אֵשֶׁת רֵעֶךָ n.f.s. cstr. (61)-v.supra n.m.s.-2 m.s. sf. (945) *your neighbor's wife*

וְעַבְדּוֹ conj.-n.m.s.-3 m.s. sf. (713) *or his manservant*

וַאֲמָתוֹ conj.-n.f.s.-3 m.s. sf. (51) *or his maidservant*

וְשׁוֹרוֹ conj.-n.m.s.-3 m.s. sf. (1004) *or his ox*

וַחֲמֹרוֹ conj.-n.m.s.-3 m.s. sf. (331) *or his ass*

וְכֹל אֲשֶׁר conj.-n.m.s. (481)-rel. *or anything that*

לְרֵעֶךָ prep.-n.m.s.-2 m.s. sf. (945) *your neighbor's*

20:18

וְכָל־הָעָם conj.-n.m.s. cstr. (481)-def.art.-n.m.s. (I 766) *now when all the people*

רֹאִים Qal act. ptc. m.p. (רָאָה 906) *perceived*

אֶת־הַקּוֹלֹת dir.obj.-def.art.-n.m.p. (876) *the thunderings*

וְאֶת־הַלַּפִּידִם conj.-dir.obj.-def.art.-n.m.p. (542) *and the lightnings*

וְאֵת קוֹל conj.-dir.obj.-n.m.s. cstr. (876) *and the sound of*

הַשֹּׁפָר def.art.-n.m.s. (1051) *the trumpet*

וְאֶת־הָהָר conj.-dir.obj.-def.art.-n.m.s. (249) *and the mountain*

עָשֵׁן adj. m.s. (798) *smoking*

וַיַּרְא consec.-Qal impf. 3 m.s. (רָאָה 906; some rd. וַיִּרָא from יָרֵא 431) *were afraid*

הָעָם def.art.-n.m.s. (I 766) *the people*

וַיָּנֻעוּ consec.-Qal impf. 3 m.p. (נוּעַ 631) *and trembled*

וַיַּעַמְדוּ consec.-Qal impf. 3 m.p. (763) *and they stood*

מֵרָחֹק prep.-n.m.s. (935) *afar off*

20:19

וַיֹּאמְרוּ consec.-Qal impf. 3 m.p. (55) *and said*

אֶל־מֹשֶׁה prep.-pr.n. (602) *to Moses*

דַּבֵּר־אַתָּה Pi. impv. 2 m.s. (180)-pers. pr. 2 m.s. (61) *you speak*

עִמָּנוּ prep.-1 c.p. sf. *to us*

וְנִשְׁמָעָה conj.-Qal impf. 1 c.p.-vol. he (1033) *and we will hear*

וְאַל־יְדַבֵּר conj.-neg.-Pi. impf. 3 m.s. (180) *but let not speak*

עִמָּנוּ v.supra prep.-1 c.p. sf. *to us*

אֱלֹהִים n.m.p. (43) *God*

פֶּן־נָמוּת conj. (814)-Qal impf. 1 c.p. (מוּת 559) *lest we die*

20:20

וַיֹּאמֶר consec.-Qal impf. 3 m.s. (55) *and ... said*

מֹשֶׁה pr.n. (602) *Moses*

אֶל־הָעָם prep.-def.art.-n.m.s. (I 766) *to the people*

אַל־תִּירָאוּ neg.-Qal impf. 2 m.p. (יָרֵא 431) *do not fear*

כִּי לְבַעֲבוּר conj.-prep.-prep.-prep. (721) *for ... to*

נַסּוֹת Pi. inf. cstr. (נָסָה 650) *prove*

אֶתְכֶם dir.obj.-2 m.p. sf. *you*
בָּא Qal pf. 3 m.s. (בּוֹא 97) *has come*
הָאֱלֹהִים def.art.-n.m.p. (43) *God*
וּבַעֲבוּר conj.-v.supra prep.-prep. (721) *and that*
תִּהְיֶה Qal impf. 3 f.s. (224) *may be*
יִרְאָתוֹ n.f.s.-3 m.s. sf. (432) *the fear of him*
עַל־פְּנֵיכֶם prep.-n.m.p.-2 m.p. sf. (815) *before your eyes*
לְבִלְתִּי prep.-neg. (116) *that ... not*
תֶחֱטָאוּ Qal impf. 2 m.p. paus. (306) *you may sin*

20:21

וַיַּעֲמֹד consec.-Qal impf. 3 m.s. (763) *and ... stood*
הָעָם def.art.-n.m.s. (I 766) *the people*
מֵרָחֹק v.20:18 prep.-n.m.s. (935) *afar off*
וּמֹשֶׁה conj.-pr.n. (602) *while Moses*
נִגַּשׁ Ni. pf. 3 m.s. (נָגַשׁ 620) *drew near*
אֶל־הָעֲרָפֶל prep.-def.art.-n.m.s. (791) *to the thick cloud*
אֲשֶׁר־שָׁם rel.-adv. (1027) *where*
הָאֱלֹהִים def.art.-n.m.p. (43) *God was*

20:22

וַיֹּאמֶר consec.-Qal impf. 3 m.s. (55) *and ... said*
יהוה pr.n. (217) *Yahweh*
אֶל־מֹשֶׁה prep.-pr.n. (602) *to Moses*
כֹּה adv. (462) *thus*
תֹאמַר Qal impf. 2 m.s. (55) *you shall say*
אֶל־בְּנֵי prep.-n.m.p. cstr. (119) *to the people of*
יִשְׂרָאֵל pr.n. (975) *Israel*
אַתֶּם pers. pr. 2 m.p. (61) *you*
רְאִיתֶם Qal pf. 2 m.p. (רָאָה 906) *have seen*
כִּי מִן־ conj.-prep. *that ... from*
הַשָּׁמַיִם def.art.-n.m.p. (1029) *heaven*
דִּבַּרְתִּי Pi. pf. 1 c.s. (180) *I have talked*
עִמָּכֶם prep.-2 m.p. sf. *with you*

20:23

לֹא תַעֲשׂוּן neg.-Qal impf. 2 m.p. (I 793) *you shall not make*
אִתִּי prep.-1 c.s. sf. (II 85) *with me*
אֱלֹהֵי n.m.p. cstr. (43) *gods of*
כֶסֶף n.m.s. (494) *silver*
וֵאלֹהֵי conj.-n.m.p. cstr. (43) *nor gods of*
זָהָב n.m.s. (262) *gold*
לֹא תַעֲשׂוּ neg.-Qal impf. 2 m.p. (I 793) *shall you make*
לָכֶם prep.-2 m.p. sf. *for yourselves*

20:24

מִזְבַּח n.m.s. cstr. (258) *an altar of*
אֲדָמָה n.f.s. (9) *earth*
תַּעֲשֶׂה־לִּי Qal impf. 2 m.s. (I 793)-prep.-1 c.s. sf. *you shall make for me*
וְזָבַחְתָּ conj.-Qal pf. 2 m.s. (256) *and sacrifice*
עָלָיו prep.-3 m.s. sf. *on it*
אֶת־עֹלֹתֶיךָ dir.obj.-n.f.p.-2 m.s. sf. (750) *your burnt offerings*
וְאֶת־שְׁלָמֶיךָ conj.-dir.obj.-n.m.p.-2 m.s. sf. (1023) *and your peace offerings*
אֶת־צֹאנְךָ dir.obj.-n.f.s.-2 m.s. sf. (838) *your sheep*
וְאֶת־בְּקָרֶךָ conj.-dir.obj.-n.m.s.-2 m.s. sf. paus. (133) *and your oxen*
בְּכָל־ prep.-n.m.s. cstr. (481) *in every*
הַמָּקוֹם def.art.-n.m.s. (879) *place*
אֲשֶׁר אַזְכִּיר rel.-Hi. impf. 1 c.s. (269) *where I cause to be remembered*
אֶת־שְׁמִי dir.obj.-n.m.s.-1 c.s. sf. (1027) *my name*
אָבוֹא Qal impf. 1 c.s. (97) *I will come*
אֵלֶיךָ prep.-2 m.s. sf. *to you*
וּבֵרַכְתִּיךָ conj.-Pi. pf. 1 c.s.-2 m.s. sf. (138) *and bless you*

20:25

וְאִם־מִזְבַּח conj.-hypoth.part. (49) - n.m.s. cstr. (258) *and if ... an altar of*

אֲבָנִים n.f.p. (6) *stone*
תַּעֲשֶׂה־לִּי Qal impf. 2 m.s. (I 793)-prep.-1 c.s. sf. *you make me*
לֹא־תִבְנֶה neg.-Qal impf. 2 m.s. (124) *you shall not build*
אֶתְהֶן dir.obj.-3 f.p. sf. *it*
גָּזִית n.f.s. (159) *of hewn stones*
כִּי חַרְבְּךָ conj.-n.f.s.-2 m.s. sf. (352) *your tool*
הֵנַפְתָּ Hi. pf. 2 m.s. (נוּף I 631) *you wield*
עָלֶיהָ prep.-3 f.s. sf. *upon it*
וַתְּחַלְלֶהָ consec.-Pi. impf. 2 m.s.-3 f.s. sf. (חָלַל III 320) *you profane it*

20:26

וְלֹא־תַעֲלֶה conj.-neg.-Qal impf. 2 m.s. (748) *and you shall not go up*
בְמַעֲלֹת prep.-n.f.p. (752) *by steps*
עַל־מִזְבְּחִי prep.-n.m.s.-1 c.s. sf. (258) *to my altar*
אֲשֶׁר rel. *that*
לֹא־תִגָּלֶה neg.-Ni. impf. 3 f.s. (גָּלָה 162) *be not exposed*
עֶרְוָתְךָ n.f.s.-2 m.s. sf. (788) *your nakedness*
עָלָיו prep.-3 m.s. sf. *on it*

21:1

וְאֵלֶּה conj.-demons. adj. c.p. (41) *now these are*
הַמִּשְׁפָּטִים def.art.-n.m.p. (1048) *the ordinances*
אֲשֶׁר rel. *which*
תָּשִׂים Qal impf. 2 m.s. (שִׂים 962) *you shall set*
לִפְנֵיהֶם prep.-n.m.p.-3 m.p. sf. (815) *before them*

21:2

כִּי תִקְנֶה conj.-Qal impf. 2 m.s. (קָנָה 888) *when you buy*
עֶבֶד n.m.s. (713) *a slave*
עִבְרִי adj. gent. (I 720) *Hebrew*
שֵׁשׁ num. (995) *six*
שָׁנִים n.f.p. (1040) *years*
יַעֲבֹד Qal impf. 3 m.s. (712) *he shall serve*
וּבַשְּׁבִעִת conj.-prep.-def.art.-adj. f. num. (988) *and in the seventh*
יֵצֵא Qal impf. 3 m.s. (יָצָא 422) *he shall go out*
לַחָפְשִׁי prep.-def.art.- adj. (344) *free*
חִנָּם adv. (336) *for nothing*

21:3

אִם־בְּגַפּוֹ hypoth.part. (49)-prep.-n.m.s. - 3 m.s. sf. (172) *if ... in single*
יָבֹא Qal impf. 3 m.s. (97) *he comes in*
בְּגַפּוֹ v.supra *single*
יֵצֵא Qal impf. 3 m.s. (יָצָא 422) *he shall go out*
אִם־בַּעַל אִשָּׁה hypoth.part. (49) - n.m.s. cstr. (127) - n.f.s. (61) *if ... married (husband of a wife)*
הוּא pers. pr. 3 m.s. (214) *he*
וְיָצְאָה conj.-Qal pf. 3 f.s. (422) *then shall go out*
אִשְׁתּוֹ n.f.s.-3 m.s. sf. (61) *his wife*
עִמּוֹ prep.-3 m.s. sf. *with him*

21:4

אִם־אֲדֹנָיו hypoth.part. (49) - n.m.p.-3 m.s. sf. (10) *if his master*
יִתֶּן־ Qal impf. 3 m.s. (נָתַן 678) *gives*
לוֹ prep.-3 m.s. sf. *him*
אִשָּׁה n.f.s. (61) *a wife*
וְיָלְדָה־לוֹ conj.-Qal pf. 3 f.s. (408) - prep.-3 m.s. sf. *and she bears him*
בָנִים n.m.p. (119) *sons*
אוֹ בָנוֹת conj. (14)-n.f.p. (I 123) *or daughters*
הָאִשָּׁה def.art.-n.f.s. (61) *the wife*
וִילָדֶיהָ conj.-n.m.p.-3 f.s. sf. (409) *and her children*
תִּהְיֶה Qal impf. 3 f.s. (224) *shall be*
לַאדֹנֶיהָ prep.-n.m.p.-3 f.s. sf. (10) *her master's*
וְהוּא conj.-pers. pr. 3 m.s. (214) *and he*
יֵצֵא Qal impf. 3 m.s. (יָצָא 422) *shall go out*
בְגַפּוֹ v.21:3 prep.-n.m.s.-3 m.s. sf. (172) *alone*

21:5

וְאִם־אָמֹר conj.-hypoth.part. (49) - Qal inf. abs. (55) *but if ... plainly*

יֹאמַר Qal impf. 3 m.s. (55) *says*

הָעֶבֶד def.art.-n.m.s. (713) *the slave*

אָהַבְתִּי Qal pf. 1 c.s. (אָהַב 12) *I love*

אֶת־אֲדֹנִי dir.obj.-n.m.s.-1 c.s. sf. (10) *my master*

אֶת־אִשְׁתִּי dir.obj.-n.f.s.-1 c.s. sf. (61) *my wife*

וְאֶת־בָּנָי conj.-dir.obj.n.m.p.-1 c.s. sf. paus. (119) *and my children*

לֹא אֵצֵא neg.-Qal impf. 1 c.s. (יָצָא 422) *I will not go out*

חָפְשִׁי v.21:2 adj. (344) *free*

21:6

וְהִגִּישׁוֹ conj.-Hi. pf. 3 m.s.-3 m.s. sf. (נָגַשׁ 620) *then shall bring him*

אֲדֹנָיו n.m.p.-3 m.s. sf. (10) *his master*

אֶל־הָאֱלֹהִים prep.-def.art.-n.m.p. (43) *to God*

וְהִגִּישׁוֹ v.supra *and he shall bring him*

אֶל־הַדֶּלֶת prep.-def.art.-n.f.s. (195) *to the door*

אוֹ אֶל־הַמְּזוּזָה conj. (14)-prep.-def.art.-n.f.s. (265) *or the door-post*

וְרָצַע conj.-Qal pf. 3 m.s. (954) *and shall bore through*

אֲדֹנָיו n.m.p.-3 m.s. sf. (10) *his master*

אֶת־אָזְנוֹ dir.obj.-n.f.s.-3 m.s. sf. (23) *his ear*

בַּמַּרְצֵעַ prep.-def.art.-n.m.s. (954) *with an awl*

וַעֲבָדוֹ conj.-Qal pf. 3 m.s.-3 m.s. sf. *and he shall serve him*

לְעֹלָם prep.-n.m.s. (761) *for life*

21:7

וְכִי־יִמְכֹּר conj.-conj.-Qal impf. 3 m.s. (569) *when ... sells*

אִישׁ n.m.s. (35) *a man*

אֶת־בִּתּוֹ dir.obj.-n.f.s.-3 m.s. sf. (I 123) *his daughter*

לְאָמָה prep.-n.f.s. (51) *as a slave*

לֹא תֵצֵא neg.-Qal impf. 3 f.s. (422) *she shall not go out*

כְּצֵאת prep.-Qal inf. cstr. (יָצָא 422) *as ... do*

הָעֲבָדִים def.art.-n.m.p. (713) *the male slaves*

21:8

אִם־רָעָה hypoth.part. (49) - Qal pf. 3 f.s. (רָעַע 949) *if she does not please*

בְּעֵינֵי prep.-n.f.p. cstr. (744) *(in the sight of)*

אֲדֹנֶיהָ n.m.p.-3 f.s. sf. (10) *her master*

אֲשֶׁר־לֹא יְעָדָהּ rel.-neg.-Qal pf. 3 m.s.-3 f.s. sf. (יָעַד 416) *who has (not) designated her*

וְהֶפְדָּהּ conj.-Hi. pf. 3 m.s.-3 f.s. sf. (פָּדָה 804) *then he shall let her be redeemed*

לְעַם prep.-n.m.s. (I 766) *to a ... people*

נָכְרִי adj. (648) *foreign*

לֹא־יִמְשֹׁל neg.-Qal impf. 3 m.s. (III 605) *he shall have no right*

לְמָכְרָהּ prep.-Qal inf. cstr.-3 f.s. sf. (569) *to sell her*

בְּבִגְדוֹ־ prep.-Qal inf. cstr.-3 m.s. sf. (בָּגַד 93) *since he has dealt faithlessly*

בָהּ prep.-3 f.s. sf. *with her*

21:9

וְאִם־לִבְנוֹ conj.-hypoth.part. (49)-prep.-n.m.s.-3 m.s. sf. (119) *if ... for his son*

יִיעָדֶנָּה Qal impf. 3 m.s.-3 f.s. sf. (יָעַד 416) *he designates her*

כְּמִשְׁפַּט הַבָּנוֹת prep.-n.m.s. cstr. (1048)-def.art.-n.f.p. (I 123) *as with a daughter*

יַעֲשֶׂה־לָּהּ Qal impf. 3 m.s. (I 793)-prep.-3 f.s. sf. *he shall deal with her*

21:10

אִם־אַחֶרֶת hypoth.part. (49)-adj. f.s. (29) *if ... another wife*

יִקַּח־לוֹ Qal impf. 3 m.s. (לָקַח 542)-prep.-3 m.s. sf. *he takes to himself*

שְׁאֵרָהּ n.m.s.-3 f.s. sf. (984) *her food*

כְּסוּתָהּ n.f.s.-3 f.s. sf. (492) *her clothing*

וְעֹנָתָהּ conj.-n.f.s.-3 f.s. sf. (773) *or her marital rights*

לֹא יִגְרָע neg.-Qal impf. 3 m.s. paus. (גָּרַע 175) *he shall not diminish*

21:11

וְאִם־ conj.-hypoth. part. (49) *and if*

שְׁלָשׁ־אֵלֶּה num. (1025) - demons. adj. (41) *these three things*

לֹא יַעֲשֶׂה neg.-Qal impf. 3 m.s. (I 793) *he does not do*

לָהּ prep.-3 f.s. sf. *for her*

וְיָצְאָה conj.-Qal pf. 3 f.s. (422) *she shall go out*

חִנָּם v.21:2 adv. (336) *for nothing*

אֵין כָּסֶף subst. cstr. (II 34)-n.m.s. paus. (494) *without payment of money*

21:12

מַכֵּה Hi. ptc. m.s. cstr. (נָכָה 645) *whoever strikes*

אִישׁ n.m.s. (35) *a man*

וָמֵת conj.-Qal pf. 3 m.s. (מוּת 559) *so that he dies*

מוֹת יוּמָת Qal inf. abs. (559)-Ho. impf. 3 m.s. (559) *shall be put to death*

21:13

וַאֲשֶׁר conj.-rel. *but if*

לֹא צָדָה neg.-Qal pf. 3 m.s. (I 841) *he did not lie in wait*

הָאֱלֹהִים conj.-def.art.-n.m.p. (43) *but God*

אִנָּה Pi. pf. 3 m.s. (אָנָה III 58) *let him fall*

לְיָדוֹ prep.-n.f.s.-3 m.s. sf. (388) *in his hand*

וְשַׂמְתִּי conj.-Qal pf. 1 c.s. (שִׂים 962) *then I will appoint*

לְךָ prep.-2 m.s. sf. *for you*

מָקוֹם n.m.s. (879) *a place*

אֲשֶׁר rel. *which*

יָנוּס Qal impf. 3 m.s. (נוּס 630) *he may flee*

שָׁמָּה adv.-dir. he (1027) *(there)*

21:14

וְכִי־יָזִד conj.-conj.-Hi. impf. 3 m.s. (זִיד 267) *but if ... willfully attacks*

אִישׁ n.m.s. (35) *a man*

עַל־רֵעֵהוּ prep.-n.m.s.-3 m.s. sf. (945) *another*

לְהָרְגוֹ prep.-Qal inf. cstr. - 3 m.s. sf. (הָרַג 246) *to kill him*

בְעָרְמָה prep.-n.f.s. (791) *treacherously*

מֵעִם מִזְבְּחִי prep.-prep.-n.m.s.-1 c.s. sf. (258) *from my altar*

תִּקָּחֶנּוּ Qal impf. 2 m.s. - 3 m. s. sf. (לָקַח 542) *you shall take him*

לָמוּת prep.-Qal inf. cstr. (מוּת 559) *that he may die*

21:15

וּמַכֵּה conj.-Hi. ptc. m.s. cstr. (נָכָה 645) *whoever strikes*

אָבִיו n.m.s.-3 m.s. sf. (3) *his father*

וְאִמּוֹ conj.-n.f.s.-3 m.s. sf. (51) *or his mother*

מוֹת יוּמָת Qal inf. abs. (מוּת 559) - Ho. impf. 3 m.s. (559) *shall be put to death*

21:16

וְגֹנֵב conj.-Qal act. ptc. cstr. (170) *whoever steals*

אִישׁ n.m.s. (35) *a man*

וּמְכָרוֹ conj.-Qal pf. 3 m.s.-3 m.s. sf. (569) *whether he sells him*

וְנִמְצָא conj.-Ni. pf. 3 m.s. (מָצָא 592) *or is found*

בְיָדוֹ prep.-n.f.s.-3 m.s. sf. (388) *in possession of him*

מוֹת יוּמָת Qal inf. abs. (מוּת 559) - Ho. impf. 3 m.s. (559) *shall be put to death*

21:17

וּמְקַלֵּל conj.-Pi. ptc. cstr. (886) *whoever curses*

אָבִיו n.m.s.-3 m.s. sf. (3) *his father*

וְאִמּוֹ conj.-n.f.s.-3 m.s. sf. (51) *or his mother*

מוֹת יוּמָת v.21:16 *shall be put to death*

21:18

וְכִי־יְרִיבֻן conj.-conj.-Qal impf. 3 m.p. (רִיב 936) *when ... quarrel*

אֲנָשִׁין n.m.p. (35) *men*

וְהִכָּה־אִישׁ conj.-Hi. pf. 3 m.s. (נָכָה 645) *and one strikes*

אֶת־רֵעֵהוּ dir.obj.-n.m.s.-3 m.s. sf. (945) *the other*

בְּאֶבֶן prep.-n.f.s. (6) *with a stone*

אוֹ בְאֶגְרֹף conj. (14)-prep.-n.m.s. (175) *or with his fist*

וְלֹא יָמוּת conj.-neg.-Qal impf. 3 m.s. (559) *and does not die*

וְנָפַל conj.-Qal pf. 3 m.s. (656) *but keeps (falls)*

לְמִשְׁכָּב prep.-n.m.s. (1012) *to his bed*

21:19

אִם־יָקוּם hypoth. part. (49)-Qal impf. 3 m.s. (877) *then if ... rises again*

וְהִתְהַלֵּךְ conj.-Hith. pf. 3 m.s. (229) *and walks*

בַּחוּץ prep.-def.art.-n.m.s. (299) *abroad*

עַל־מִשְׁעַנְתּוֹ prep.-n.f.s.-3 m.s. sf. (1044) *with his staff*

וְנִקָּה conj.-Ni. pf. 3 m.s. (נָקָה 667) *shall be clear*

הַמַּכֶּה def.art.-Hi. ptc. (נָכָה 645) *he that struck him*

רַק adv. (956) *only*

שִׁבְתּוֹ n.f.s.-3 m.s. sf. (II 992) *the loss of his time (cessation)*

יִתֵּן Qal impf. 3 m.s. (נָתַן 678) *he shall pay*

וְרַפֹּא יְרַפֵּא conj.-Pi. inf. abs. (רָפָא 950) - Pi. mpf. 3 m.s. (950) *and shall have him thoroughly healed*

21:20

וְכִי־יַכֶּה conj.-conj.-Hi. impf. 3 m.s. (נָכָה 645) *when ... strikes*

אִישׁ n.m.s. (35) *a man*

אֶת־עַבְדּוֹ dir.obj.-n.m.s.-3 m.s. sf. (713) *his slave*

אוֹ אֶת־אֲמָתוֹ conj. (14)-dir.obj.-n.f.s. - 3 m.s. sf. (51) *or female (slave)*

בַּשֵּׁבֶט prep.-def.art.-n.m.s. (986) *with a rod*

וּמֵת conj.-Qal pf. 3 m.s. (559) *and (the slave) dies*

תַּחַת יָדוֹ prep. (1065)-n.f.s.-3 m.s. sf. (388) *under his hand*

נָקֹם יִנָּקֵם Qal inf.abs. (נָקַם 667)-Ni. impf. 3 m.s. (667) *he shall be punished*

21:21

אַךְ אִם־ adv. (36)-hypoth. part. (49) *but if*

יוֹם n.m.s. (398) *a day*

אוֹ יוֹמַיִם conj. (14)-n.m. du. (398) *or two (days)*

יַעֲמֹד Qal impf. 3 m.s. (712) *(the slave) survives*

לֹא יֻקַּם neg.-Ho. impf. 3 m.s. (נָקַם 667) *he is not to be punished*

כִּי כַסְפּוֹ conj.-n.m.s.-3 m.s. sf. (494) *for ... his money*

הוּא pers. pr. 3 m.s. (214) *the slave (he)*

21:22

וְכִי־יִנָּצוּ conj.-conj.-Ni. impf. 3 m.p. (נָצָה II 663) *when ... strive together*

אֲנָשִׁים n.m.p. (35) *men*

וְנָגְפוּ conj.-Qal pf. 3 c.p. (619) *and hurt*

אִשָּׁה הָרָה n.f.s. (61)- adj. f.s. (II 248) *a woman with child*

וְיָצְאוּ יְלָדֶיהָ conj.-Qal pf. 3 c.p. (422) - n.m.p.-3 f.s. sf. (409) *so that there is a miscarriage*

וְלֹא יִהְיֶה conj.-neg.-Qal impf. 3 m.s. (224) *and yet no ... follows*

אָסוֹן n.m.s. (62) *harm*

עָנוֹשׁ יֵעָנֵשׁ Qal inf. abs. (עָנַשׁ 778) - Ni. impf. 3 m.s. (778) *shall be fined*

כַּאֲשֶׁר prep.-rel. *according as*

יָשִׁית Qal impf. 3 m.s. (שִׁית 1011) *shall lay*

עָלָיו prep.-3 m.s. sf. *upon him*

בַּעַל n.m.s. cstr. (127) *the husband of*

הָאִשָּׁה def.art.-n.f.s. (61) *the woman*

וְנָתַן conj.-Qal pf. 3 m.s. (678) *and he shall pay*

בִּפְלִלִים prep.-n.m.p. (813) *as the judges determine*

21:23

וְאִם־ conj.-hypoth. part (49) *if*

אָסוֹן n.m.s. (62) *any harm*

יִהְיֶה Qal impf. 3 m.s. (224) *follows*

וְנָתַתָּה conj.-Qal pf. 2 m.s. (נָתַן 678) *then you shall give*

נֶפֶשׁ n.f.s. (659) *life*

תַּחַת נָפֶשׁ prep. (1065)-n.f.s. paus. (659) *for life*

21:24

עַיִן תַּחַת עַיִן n.f.s. (744)-prep. (1065)-n.f.s. (744) *eye for eye*

שֵׁן תַּחַת שֵׁן n.f.s. (1042)-v.supra - v.supra *tooth for tooth*

יָד תַּחַת יָד n.f.s. (388) - v.supra - v.supra *hand for hand*

רֶגֶל תַּחַת רָגֶל n.f.s. (919) - v.supra - v.supra paus. *foot for foot*

21:25

כְּוִיָּה תַּחַת כְּוִיָּה n.f.s. (465)-v.supra - v.supra *burn for burn*

פֶּצַע תחת פָּצַע n.m.s. (822)-v.supra - v.supra paus. *wound for wound*

חַבּוּרָה תַּחַת חַבּוּרָה n.f.s. (289) - v.supra - v.supra *stripe for stripe*

21:26

וְכִי־יַכֶּה conj.-conj.-Hi. impf. 3 m.s. (נָכָה 645) *when ... strikes*

אִישׁ n.m.s. (35) *a man*

אֶת־עֵין dir.obj.-n.f.s. cstr. (744) *the eye of*

עַבְדּוֹ n.m.s.-3 m.s. sf. (713) *his slave*

אוֹ־אֶת־עֵין conj. (14)-dir.obj. - v.supra *or (the eye of)*

אֲמָתוֹ n.f.s.-3 m.s. sf. (51) *female (slave)*

וְשִׁחֲתָהּ conj. - Pi. pf. 3 m.s. - 3 f.s. (שָׁחַת 1007) *and destroys it*

לַחָפְשִׁי prep.-def.art.-adj. (344) *free*

יְשַׁלְּחֶנּוּ Pi. impf. 3 m.s. - 3 m.s. sf. (שָׁלַח 1018) *he shall let (the slave) go*

תַּחַת עֵינוֹ prep. (1065)-n.f.s.-3 m.s. sf. (744) *for the eye's sake*

21:27

וְאִם־שֵׁן conj.-hypoth.part. (49) - n.f.s. cstr. (1042) *if the tooth of*

עַבְדּוֹ n.m.s.-3 m.s. sf. (713) *his slave*

אוֹ־שֵׁן conj. (14) - n.f.s. cstr. (1042) *or (the tooth of)*

אֲמָתוֹ n.f.s.-3 m.s. sf. (51) *female (slave)*

יַפִּיל Hi. impf. 3 m.s. (נָפַל 656) *he knocks out*

לַחָפְשִׁי v.21:26 prep.-def.art.-adj. (344) *free*

יְשַׁלְּחֶנּוּ Pi. impf. 3 m.s.-3 m.s. sf. (1018) *he shall let go the slave (him)*

תַּחַת שִׁנּוֹ v.21:26 prep. (1065) - n.f.s.-3 m.s. sf. (1042) *for the tooth's sake*

21:28

וְכִי־יִגַּח conj.-conj.-Qal impf. 3 m.s. (נָגַח 618) *when ... gores*

שׁוֹר n.m.s. (1004) *an ox*

אֶת־אִישׁ dir.obj.-n.m.s. (35) *a man*

אוֹ אֶת־אִשָּׁה conj. (14)-dir.obj.-n.f.s. (61) *or a woman*

וָמֵת conj.-Qal pf. 3 m.s. (מוּת 559) *to death*

סָקוֹל יִסָּקֵל Qal inf. abs. (709) - Ni. impf. 3 m.s. (709) *shall be stoned*

הַשּׁוֹר def.art.-n.m.s. (1004) *the ox*

וְלֹא יֵאָכֵל conj.-neg.-Ni. impf. 3 m.s. (37) *and shall not be eaten*

אֶת־בְּשָׂרוֹ dir.obj.-n.m.s.-3 m.s. sf. (142) *its flesh*

וּבַעַל conj.-n.m.s. cstr. (127) *but the owner of*

הַשּׁוֹר def.art.-n.m.s. (1004) *the ox*

נָקִי adj. (667) *shall be clear*

21:29

וְאִם שׁוֹר conj.-hypoth. part. (49) - n.m.s. (1004) *but if the ox*

נַגָּח adj. (618) *has been accustomed to gore*

הוּא pers. pr. 3 m.s. (214)

מִתְּמֹל שִׁלְשֹׁם prep.-adv. acc. (1069) - adv. (1026) *in the past*

וְהוּעַד conj.-Ho. pf. 3 m.s. (עוּד 729) *and has been warned*

בִּבְעָלָיו prep.-n.m.p.-3 m.s. sf. (127) *its owner*

וְלֹא יִשְׁמְרֶנּוּ conj.-neg.-Qal impf. 3 m.s.-3 m.s. sf. (שָׁמַר 1036) *but has not kept it in*

וְהֵמִית conj. - Hi. pf. 3 m.s. (מוּת 559) *and it kills*

אִישׁ n.m.s. (35) *a man*

אוֹ אִשָּׁה conj. (14)-n.f.s. (61) *or a woman*

הַשּׁוֹר def.art.-n.m.s. (1004) *the ox*

יִסָּקֵל Ni. impf. 3 m.s. (709) *shall be stoned*

וְגַם־בְּעָלָיו conj.-adv. (168) - n.m.p.-3 m.s. sf. (127) *and its owner also*

יוּמָת Ho. impf. 3 m.s. (מוּת 559) *shall be put to death*

21:30

אִם־כֹּפֶר hypoth. part. (49)-n.m.s. (I 497) *if a ransom*

יוּשַׁת Ho. impf. 3 m.s. (שִׁית 1011) *is laid*

עָלָיו prep.-3 m.s. sf. *on him*

וְנָתַן conj.-Qal pf. 3 m.s. (678) *then he shall give*

פִּדְיֹן n.m.s. cstr. (804) *for the redemption of*

נַפְשׁוֹ n.f.s.-3 m.s. sf. (659) *his life*

כְּכֹל אֲשֶׁר־ prep.-n.m.s. (481) - rel. *whatever*

יוּשַׁת v.supra Ho. impf. 3 m.s. (1011) *is laid*

עָלָיו prep.-3 m.s. sf. *upon him*

21:31

אוֹ־בֵן conj. (14)-n.m.s. (119) *if a son*

יִגָּח Qal impf. 3 m.s. (נָגַח 618) *it gores*

אוֹ־בַת יִגָּח conj. (14)-n.f.s. (I 123)-v. supra paus. *or daughter*

כַּמִּשְׁפָּט הַזֶּה prep.-def.art.-n.m.s. (1048) - def.art.-demons. adj. m.s. (260) *according to this same rule*

יֵעָשֶׂה Ni. impf. 3 m.s. (I 793) *shall be dealt with*

לוֹ prep.-3 m.s. sf. *(to him) he*

21:32

אִם־עֶבֶד hypoth.part. (49) - n.m.s. (713) *if a slave*

יִגַּח הַשּׁוֹר Qal impf. 3 m.s. (נָגַח 618) - def.art.-n.m.s. (1004) *the ox gores*

אוֹ אָמָה conj. (14)-n.f.s. (51) *or female*

כֶּסֶף n.m.s. cstr. (494) *silver of*

שְׁלֹשִׁים שְׁקָלִים num. m.p. (1026) - n.m.p. (1053) *thirty shekels*

יִתֵּן Qal impf. 3 m.s. (נָתַן 678) *shall give*

לַאדֹנָיו prep.-n.m.p.-3 m.s. sf. (10) *to their master*

וְהַשּׁוֹר conj.-def.art.-n.m.s. (1004) *and the ox*

יִסָּקֵל Ni. impf. 3 m.s. (709) *shall be stoned*

21:33

וְכִי־יִפְתַּח conj.-conj.-Qal impf. 3 m.s. (פָּתַח I 834) *when leaves open*

אִישׁ n.m.s. (35) *a man*

בּוֹר n.m.s. (92) *a pit*

אוֹ כִּי־יִכְרֶה conj. (14) - conj.-Qal impf. 3 m.s. (כָּרָה I 500) *or when ... digs*

אִישׁ n.m.s. (35) *a man*

בֹּר n.m.s. (92) *a pit*

וְלֹא יְכַסֶּנּוּ conj.-neg.-Pi. impf. 3 m.s.-3 m.s. sf. (כָּסָה 491) *and does not cover it*

וְנָפַל־ conj.-Qal pf. 3 m.s. (656) *and ... falls*

שָׁמָּה adv.-dir. he (1027) *into it (there)*

שׁוֹר n.m.s. (1004) *an ox*

אוֹ חֲמוֹר conj. (14) - n.m.s. (331) *or an ass*

21:34

בַּעַל n.m.s. cstr. (127) *the owner of*

הַבּוֹר def.art.-n.m.s. (92) *the pit*

יְשַׁלֵּם Pi. impf. 3 m.s. (1022) *shall make it good*

כֶּסֶף n.m.s. (494) *money*

יָשִׁיב Hi. impf. 3 m.s. (שׁוּב 996) *he shall give*

לִבְעָלָיו prep.-n.m.p.-3 m.s. sf. (127) *to its owner*

וְהַמֵּת conj. - def. art. - Qal act. ptc. (מוּת 559) *the dead beast*

יִהְיֶה־לּוֹ Qal impf. 3 m.s. (224)-prep.-3 m.s. sf. *shall be his*

21:35

וְכִי־יִגֹּף conj. - conj. - qal impf. 3 m.s. (נָגַף 619) *when ... hurts*

שׁוֹר־אִישׁ n.m.s. cstr. (1004) - n.m.s. (35) *one man's ox*

אֶת־שׁוֹר רֵעֵהוּ dir.obj.-n.m.s. cstr. (1004) - n.m.s.-3 m.s. sf. (945) *another's*

וָמֵת conj.-Qal pf. 3 m.s. (559) *so that it dies*

וּמָכְרוּ conj.-Qal pf. 3 c.p. (569) *then they shall sell*

אֶת־הַשּׁוֹר הַחַי dir.obj.-def.art.-n.m.s. (1004) - def.art.-adj. m.s. (311) *the live ox*

וְחָצוּ conj.-Qal pf. 3 c.p. (חָצָה 345) *and divide*

אֶת־כַּסְפּוֹ dir.obj.-n.m.s.-3 m.s. sf. (494) *the price of it*

וְגַם אֶת־הַמֵּת conj.-adv. (168)-dir.obj.-def.art.-Qal act. ptc. (559) *and also the dead beast*

יֶחֱצוּן Qal impf. 3 m.p. (345) *they shall divide*

21:36

אוֹ נוֹדַע conj. (14)-Ni. pf. 3 m.s. (יָדַע 393) *or if it is known*

כִּי שׁוֹר conj.-n.m.s. (1004) *that the ox*

נַגָּח הוּא v.21:29 adj. (618)-pers. pr. 3 m.s. (214) *has been accustomed to gore*

מִתְּמוֹל שִׁלְשֹׁם prep.-adv. acc. (1069)-adv. (1026) *in the past*

וְלֹא יִשְׁמְרֶנּוּ conj.-neg.-Qal impf. 3 m.s.-3 m.s. sf. (1036) *and has not kept it in*

בְּעָלָיו n.m.p.-3 m.s. sf. (127) *his owner*

שַׁלֵּם יְשַׁלֵּם Pi. inf. abs. (1022) - Pi. impf. 3 m.s. (1022) *he shall pay*

שׁוֹר n.m.s. (1004) *ox*

תַּחַת הַשּׁוֹר prep. (1065) - def.art.-n.m.s. (1004) *for ox*

וְהַמֵּת conj.-def.art.-Qal act. ptc. (559) *and the dead beast*

יִהְיֶה־לּוֹ Qal impf. 3 m.s. (224)-prep.-3 m.s. sf. *shall be his*

21:37 (Eng.22:1)

כִּי יִגְנֹב־ conj.-Qal impf. 3 m.s.(גָּנַב 170) *if ... steals*

אִישׁ n.m.s. (35) *a man*

שׁוֹר אוֹ־שֶׂה n.m.s. (1004) - conj. (14)-n.m.s. (961) *an ox or a sheep*

וּטְבָחוֹ conj.-Qal pf. 3 m.s.-3 m.s. sf. (370) *and kills it*

אוֹ מְכָרוֹ conj. (14)-Qal pf. 3 m.s.-3 m.s. sf. (569) *or sells it*

חֲמִשָּׁה num. f.s. (331) *five*

בָקָר n.m.s. (133) *oxen*

יְשַׁלֵּם Pi. impf. 3 m.s. (1022) *he shall pay*

תַּחַת הַשּׁוֹר prep. (1065)-def.art.-n.m.s. (1004) *for an ox*

וְאַרְבַּע־ conj.-num. (916) *and four*

צֹאן n.f.s. (838) *sheep*

תַּחַת הַשֶּׂה prep. (1065) - def.art.-n.m.s. (961) *for a sheep*

22:1

אִם־בַּמַּחְתֶּרֶת hypoth.part. (49) - prep.-def.art.-n.m.s. (369) *if ... in the breaking in*

יִמָּצֵא Ni. impf. 3 m.s. (592) *is found*

הַגַּנָּב def. art.-n.m.s. (170) *the thief*

וְהֻכָּה conj.-Ho. pf. 3 m.s. (נָכָה 645) *and is struck*

וָמֵת conj.-Qal pf. 3 m.s. (מוּת 559) *so that he dies*

אֵין לוֹ subst. cstr. (II 34)-prep.-3 m.s. sf. *there shall be no ... for him*

דָּמִים n.m.p. (196) *bloodguilt*

22:2

אִם־זָרְחָה hypoth. part. (49)-Qal pf. 3 f.s. (280) *but if ... has risen*

הַשֶּׁמֶשׁ def. art.-n.f.s. (1039) *the sun*

עָלָיו prep.-3 m.s. sf. *upon him*

דָּמִים לוֹ n.m.p. (196)-prep.-3 m.s. sf. *there shall be bloodguilt for him*

שַׁלֵּם יְשַׁלֵּם Pi. inf. abs. (1022)-Pi. impf. 3 m.s. (1022) v.22:1b Eng. *He shall make restitution*

אִם־אֵין לוֹ hypoth. part. (49)-subst. cstr. (II 34)-prep.-3 m.s. sf. *if he has nothing*

וְנִמְכַּר conj.-Ni. pf. 3 m.s. (מָכַר 569) *then he shall be sold*

בִּגְנֵבָתוֹ prep.-n.f.s.-3 m.s. sf. (170) *for his theft*

22:3

אִם־הִמָּצֵא תִמָּצֵא hypoth. part. (49)-Ni. inf. abs. (592)-Ni. impf. 3 f.s. (592) *if ... is found*

בְיָדוֹ prep.-n.f.s.-3 m.s. sf. (388) *in his possession*

הַגְּנֵבָה def. art.-n.f.s. (170) *the stolen beast*

מִשּׁוֹר prep.-n.m.s. (1004) *whether it is an ox*

עַד־חֲמוֹר conj. (723)-n.m.s. (331) *or an ass*

עַד־שֶׂה v. supra-n.m.s. (961) *or a sheep*

חַיִּים n.m.p. (313) *alive*

שְׁנַיִם num. m. (1040) *double*

יְשַׁלֵּם Pi. impf. 3 m.s. (1022) *he shall pay*

22:4

כִּי יַבְעֶר־אִישׁ conj.-Hi. impf. 3 m.s. (בָּעַר II 129)-n.m.s. (35) *when a man causes ... to be grazed over*

שָׂדֶה n.m.s. (961) *a field*

אוֹ־כֶרֶם conj. (14)-n.m.s. (501) *or a vineyard*

וְשִׁלַּח conj.-Pi. pf. 3 m.s. (1018) *or lets loose*

אֶת־בְּעִירֹה dir.obj.-n.m.s.-3 m.s. sf. (129) *his beast*

וּבִעֵר conj.-Pi. pf. 3 m.s. (II 129) *and it feeds*

בִּשְׂדֵה אַחֵר prep.-n.m.s. cstr. (961)-adj. m.s. (29) *in another man's field*

מֵיטַב שָׂדֵהוּ n.m.s. cstr. (406)-n.m.s.-3 m.s. sf. (961) *the best in his own field*

וּמֵיטַב כַּרְמוֹ conj.-v. supra-n.m.s.-3 m.s. sf. (501) *and in his own vineyard*

יְשַׁלֵּם Pi. impf. 3 m.s. (1022) *he shall make restitution*

22:5

כִּי־תֵצֵא אֵשׁ conj.-Qal impf. 3 f.s. (יָצָא 422)-n.f.s. (77) *when fire breaks out*

וּמָצְאָה conj.-Qal pf. 3 f.s. (592) *and catches*

קֹצִים n.m.p. (I 881) *in thorns*

וְנֶאֱכַל conj.-Ni. pf. 3 m.s. (אָכַל 37) *so that ... is consumed*

גָּדִישׁ n.m.s. (I 155) *the stacked grain*

אוֹ הַקָּמָה conj. (14)-def. art.-n.f.s. (879) *or the standing grain*

אוֹ הַשָּׂדֶה conj. (14)-def. art.-n.m.s. (961) *or the field*

שַׁלֵּם יְשַׁלֵּם Pi. inf. abs. (1022)-Pi. impf. 3 m.s. (1022) *shall make full restitution*

הַמַּבְעִר def.art.-Hi. ptc. m.s. (בָּעַר I 128) *he that kindled*

אֶת־הַבְּעֵרָה dir. obj.-def. art.-n.f.s. (129) *the fire*

22:6

כִּי־יִתֵּן אִישׁ conj.-Qal impf. 3 m.s. (נָתַן 678)-n.m.s. (35) *if a man delivers*

אֶל־רֵעֵהוּ prep.-n.m.s.-3 m.s. sf. (945) *to his neighbor*

כֶּסֶף n.m.s. (494) *money*

אוֹ־כֵלִים conj. (14)-n.m.p. (479) *or goods*

לִשְׁמֹר prep.-Qal inf. cstr. (1036) *to keep*

וְגֻנַּב conj.-Pi. pf. 3 m.s. (170) *and it is stolen*

מִבֵּית הָאִישׁ prep.-n.m.s. cstr. (108)-def. art.-n.m.s. (35) *out of the man's house*

אִם־יִמָּצֵא hypoth. part. (49)-Ni. impf. 3 m.s. (592) *then if ... is found*

הַגַּנָּב def. art.-n.m.s. (170) *the thief*

יְשַׁלֵּם שְׁנָיִם Pi. impf. 3 m.s. (1022)-num. m. paus. (104) *he shall pay double*

22:7

אִם־לֹא יִמָּצֵא hypoth. part. (49)-neg.-Ni. impf. 3 m.s. (592) *if ... is not found*

הַגַּנָּב def. art.-n.m.s. (170) *the thief*

וְנִקְרַב conj.-Ni. pf. 3 m.s. (קָרַב 897) *and ... shall come near*

בַּעַל־הַבַּיִת n.m.s. cstr. (127)-def. art.-n.m.s. (108) *the owner of the house*

אֶל־הָאֱלֹהִים prep.-def. art.-n.m.p. (43) *to God*

אִם־לֹא שָׁלַח hypoth. part. (49)-neg.-Qal pf. 3 m.s. (1018) *whether or not he has put*

יָדוֹ n.f.s.-3 m.s. sf. (388) *his hand*

בִּמְלֶאכֶת רֵעֵהוּ prep.-n.f.s. cstr. (521)-n.m.s.-3 m.s. sf. (945) *to his neighbor's goods*

22:8

עַל־כָּל־דְּבַר־ prep.-n.m.s. cstr. (481) - n.m.s. cstr. (182) *for every matter of*

פֶּשַׁע n.m.s. (833) *transgression*

עַל־שׁוֹר prep.-n.m.s. (1004) *whether it is for ox*

עַל־חֲמוֹר prep.-n.m.s. (331) *for ass*

עַל־שֶׂה prep.-n.m.s. (961) *for sheep*

עַל־שַׂלְמָה prep.-n.f.s. (971) *for clothing*

עַל־כָּל אֲבֵדָה prep.-n.m.s. cstr. (481) - n.f.s. (2) *or for any kind of lost thing*

אֲשֶׁר יֹאמַר rel.-Qal impf. 3 m.s. (55) *of which one says*

כִּי־הוּא זֶה conj.-pers. pr. 3 m.s. (214)-demons. adj. m.s. (260) *this is it*

עַד הָאֱלֹהִים prep.-def. art.-n.m.p. (43) *before God*

יָבֹא Qal impf. 3 m.s. (בּוֹא 97) *shall come*

דְּבַר־שְׁנֵיהֶם n.m.s. cstr. (182)-num. m.p.-3 m.p. sf. (1040) *the case of both parties*

אֲשֶׁר יַרְשִׁיעֻן rel.-Hi. impf. 3 m.p. (רָשַׁע 957) *he whom ... shall condemn*

אֱלֹהִים n.m.p. (43) *God*

יְשַׁלֵּם שְׁנַיִם Pi. impf. 3 m.s. (1022)-num. m. (1040) *shall pay double*

לְרֵעֵהוּ prep.-n.m.s.-3 m.s. sf. (945) *to his neighbor*

22:9

כִּי־יִתֵּן אִישׁ conj.-Qal impf. 3 m.s. (נָתַן 678)-n.m.s. (35) *if a man delivers*

אֶל־רֵעֵהוּ prep.-n.m.s.-3 m.s. sf. (945) *to his neighbor*

חֲמוֹר n.m.s. (331) *an ass*

אוֹ־שׁוֹר conj. (14)-n.m.s. (1004) *or an ox*

אוֹ־שֶׂה conj. (14)-n.m.s. (961) *or a sheep*

וְכָל־בְּהֵמָה conj.-n.m.s. cstr. (481)-n.f.s. (96) *or any beast*

לִשְׁמֹר prep.-Qal inf. cstr. (1036) *to keep*

וּמֵת conj.-Qal pf. 3 m.s. (מוּת 559) *and it dies*

אוֹ־נִשְׁבַּר conj. (14)-Ni. pf. 3 m.s. (990) *or is hurt*

אוֹ־נִשְׁבָּה conj. (14)-Ni. pf. 3 m.s. (שָׁבָה 985) *or is driven away (taken captive)*

אֵין רֹאֶה subst. cstr. (II 34)-Qal act. ptc. (רָאָה 906) *without any one seeing it*

22:10

שְׁבֻעַת יהוה n.f.s. cstr. (989)-pr.n. (217) *an oath by Yahweh*

תִּהְיֶה Qal impf. 3 f.s. (הָיָה 224) *shall be*

בֵּין שְׁנֵיהֶם prep.-num. m.p.-3 m.p. sf. (1040) *between them both*

אִם־לֹא שָׁלַח hypoth. part. (49)-neg.-Qal pf. 3 m.s. (1018) *whether he has not put*

יָדוֹ n.f.s.-3 m.s. sf. (388) *his hand*

בִּמְלֶאכֶת prep.-n.f.s. cstr. (521) *to the property of*

רֵעֵהוּ n.m.s.-3 m.s. sf. (945) *his neighbor*

וְלָקַח conj.-Qal pf. 3 m.s. (542) *and ... shall accept the oath*

בְּעָלָיו n.m.p.-3 m.s. sf. (127) *the owner*

וְלֹא יְשַׁלֵּם conj.-neg.-Pi. impf. 3 m.s. (1022) *and he shall not make restitution*

22:11

וְאִם־גָּנֹב יִגָּנֵב conj.-hypoth.part. (49) - Qal inf. abs. (170) - Ni. impf. 3 m.s. (170) *but if it is stolen*

מֵעִמּוֹ prep.-prep.-3 m.s. sf. *from him*

יְשַׁלֵּם לִבְעָלָיו Pi. impf. 3 m.s. (1022) - prep.-n.m.p.-3 m.s. sf. (127) *he shall make restitution to its owner*

22:12

אִם־טָרֹף יִטָּרֵף hypoth.part. (49) - Qal inf. abs. (382) - Ni. impf. 3 m.s. (382) *if it is torn by beasts*

יְבִאֵהוּ עֵד Hi. impf. 3 m.s.-3 m.s. sf. (aWbB 97) - n.m.s. (729) *let him bring it as evidence*

הַטְּרֵפָה def.art.-n.f.s. (383) *for what has been torn*

לֹא יְשַׁלֵּם neg.-Pi.impf.3 m.s. (1022) *he shall not make restitution*

22:13

וְכִי־יִשְׁאַל conj.-conj.-Qal impf.3 m.s. (981) *if ... borrows*

אִישׁ n.m.s. (35) *a man*

מֵעִם רֵעֵהוּ prep.-prep.-n.m.s.-3 m.s. sf. (945) *of his neighbor*

וְנִשְׁבַּר conj.-Ni. pf. 3 m.s. (990) *and it is hurt*

אוֹ־מֵת conj. (14) - Qal pf. 3 m.s. (מוּת 559) *or dies*

בְּעָלָיו n.m.p.-3 m.s. sf. (127) *his owner*

אֵין־עִמּוֹ subst. cstr. (II 34)-prep.-3 m.s. sf. *not being with it*

שַׁלֵּם יְשַׁלֵּם Pi.inf.abs. (1022)-Pi.impf.3 m.s. (1022) *he shall make full restitution*

22:14

אִם־בְּעָלָיו hypoth.part. (49)-n.m.p.-3 m.s. sf. (127) *if the owner*

עִמּוֹ prep.-3 m.s. sf. *with it*

לֹא יְשַׁלֵּם neg.-Pi.impf.3 m.s. (1022) *he shall not make restitution*

אִם־שָׂכִיר הוּא hypoth.part. (49)-adj.m.s. (969)-pers.pr.3 m.s. (214) *if it was hired*

בָּא בִּשְׂכָרוֹ Qal pf. 3 m.s. (בּוֹא 97) - prep.-n.m.s.-3 m.s. sf. (969) *it came for its hire*

22:15

וְכִי־יְפַתֶּה conj.-conj.-Pi.impf.3 m.s. (פָּתָה 834) *if ... seduces*

אִישׁ n.m.s. (35) *a man*

בְּתוּלָה n.f.s. (143) *a virgin*

אֲשֶׁר לֹא־אֹרָשָׂה rel.-neg.-Pu.pf.3 f.s. (אָרַשׂ 76) *who is not betrothed*

וְשָׁכַב עִמָּהּ conj.-Qal pf.3 m.s. (1011)-prep.-3 f.s. sf. *and lies with her*

מָהֹר יִמְהָרֶנָּה Qal inf.abs. (מָהַר III 555)-Qal impf.3 m.s.-3 f.s. sf. (III 555) *he shall give the marriage present for her*

לוֹ לְאִשָּׁה prep.-3 m.s. sf.-prep.-n.f.s. (61) *and make her his wife*

22:16

אִם־מָאֵן יְמָאֵן hypoth.part. (49)-Pi.inf.abs. (549)-Pi.impf.3 m.s. (549) *if ... utterly refuses*

אָבִיהָ n.m.s.-3 f.s. sf. (3) *her father*

לְתִתָּהּ לוֹ prep.-Qal inf. cstr.-3 f.s. sf. (נָתַן 678) - prep.-3 m.s. sf. *to give her to him*

כֶּסֶף n.m.s. (494) *money*

יִשְׁקֹל Qal impf.3 m.s. (1053) *he shall pay*

כְּמֹהַר הַבְּתוּלֹת prep.-n.m.s. cstr. (555)-def.art.-n.f.p. (143) *equivalent to the marriage present for virgins*

22:17

מְכַשֵּׁפָה Pi.ptc.f.s. (כָּשַׁף 506) *a sorceress*

לֹא תְחַיֶּה neg.-Pi.impf.2 m.s. (חָיָה 310) *you shall not permit to live*

22:18

כָּל־שֹׁכֵב n.m.s. cstr. (481)-Qal act.ptc. (1011) *whoever lies*

עִם־בְּהֵמָה prep.-n.f.s. (96) *with a beast*

מוֹת יוּמָת Qal inf. abs. (מוּת 559) - Ho. impf. 3 m.s. paus. (מוּת 559) *shall be put to death*

22:19

זֹבֵחַ Qal act.ptc. (256) *whoever sacrifices*

לָאֱלֹהִים prep.-def.art.-n.m.p. (43) *to any god*

יָחֳרָם Ho.impf.3 m.s. (חָרַם I 355) *shall be utterly destroyed*

בִּלְתִּי ליהוה לְבַדּוֹ neg. (116)-prep.-pr.n. (217)-prep.-n.m.s.-3 m.s. sf. (94) *save to Yahweh only*

22:20

וְגֵר conj.-n.m.s. (158) *a stranger*

לֹא־תוֹנֶה neg.-Hi.impf.2 m.s. (יָנָה 413) *you shall not wrong*

וְלֹא תִלְחָצֶנּוּ conj.-neg.-Qal impf. 2 m.s.-3 m.s. sf. (לָחַץ 537) *or oppress him*

כִּי־גֵרִים הֱיִיתֶם conj.-n.m.p. (158)-Qal pf.2 m.p. (הָיָה 224) *for you were strangers*

בְּאֶרֶץ מִצְרָיִם prep.-n.f.s. cstr. (75)-pr.n. paus. (595) *in the land of Egypt*

22:21

כָּל־אַלְמָנָה n.m.s. cstr. (481)-n.f.s. (48) *any widow*

וְיָתוֹם conj.-n.m.s. (450) *or orphan*

לֹא תְעַנּוּן neg.-Pi.impf.2 m.p. (עָנָה III 776) *you shall not afflict*

22:22

אִם־עַנֵּה תְעַנֶּה hypoth.part. (49) - Pi. inf. abs. (III 776) - Pi. impf. 2 m.s. (III 776) *if you do afflict*

אֹתוֹ dir.obj.-3 m.s. sf. *them*

כִּי אִם־צָעֹק יִצְעַק conj.-hypoth.part. (49) - Qal inf. abs. (858) - Qal impf. 3 m.s. (858) *and they cry out*

אֵלַי prep.-1 c.s. sf. *to me*

שָׁמֹעַ אֶשְׁמַע Qal inf.abs. (1033)-Qal impf.1 c.s. (1033) *I will surely hear*

צַעֲקָתוֹ n.f.s.-3 m.s. sf. (858) *their cry*

22:23

וְחָרָה אַפִּי conj.-Qal pf. 3 m.s. (354) - n.m.s.-1 c.s. sf. (I 60) *and my wrath will burn*

וְהָרַגְתִּי conj.-Qal pf. 1 c.s. (הָרַג 246) *and I will kill*

אֶתְכֶם dir.obj.-2 m.p. sf. *you*

בֶּחָרֶב prep.-def.art.-n.f.s. paus. (352) *with the sword*

וְהָיוּ conj.-Qal pf.3 c.p. (הָיָה 224) *and shall become*

נְשֵׁיכֶם n.f.p.-2 m.p. sf. (61) *your wives*

אַלְמָנוֹת n.f.p. (48) *widows*

וּבְנֵיכֶם conj.-n.m.p.-2 m.p. sf. (119) *and your children*

יְתֹמִים n.m.p. (450) *fatherless*

22:24

אִם־כֶּסֶף hypoth.part. (49)-n.m.s. (494) *if ... money*

תַּלְוֶה Hi.impf.2 m.s. (לָוָה II 531) *you lend*

אֶת־עַמִּי dir.obj.-n.m.s.-1 c.s. sf. (I 766) *to any of my people*

אֶת־הֶעָנִי עִמָּךְ dir.obj.-def.art.-adj. m.s. (776) - prep.-2 m.s. sf. paus. *with you who is poor*

לֹא־תִהְיֶה לוֹ neg.-Qal impf.2 m.s. (224)-prep.-3 m.s. sf. *you shall not be to him*

כְּנֹשֶׁה prep.-Qal act.ptc. (נָשָׁה I 674) *as a creditor*

לֹא־תְשִׂימוּן עָלָיו neg.-Qal impf. 2 m.p. (שִׂים 962) - prep.-3 m.s. sf. *and you shall not exact from him*

נֶשֶׁךְ n.m.s. (675) *interest*

22:25

אִם־חָבֹל תַּחְבֹּל hypoth.part. (49)-Qal inf.abs. (286)-Qal impf.2 m.s. (286) *if ever you take in pledge*

שַׂלְמַת רֵעֶךָ n.f.s. cstr. (971) - n.m.s.-2 m.s. sf. (945) *your neighbor's garment*

עַד־בֹּא הַשֶּׁמֶשׁ prep.(III 723)-Qal inf. cstr. (בּוֹא 97)-def.art.-n.f.s. (1039) *before the sun goes down*

תְּשִׁיבֶנּוּ Hi.impf.2 m.s.-3 m.s. sf. (שׁוּב 996) *you shall restore it*

לוֹ prep.-3 m.s. sf. *to him*

22:26

כִּי הִוא כְסוּתֹה conj.-pers.pr.3 f.s. (214)-n.f.s.-3 m.s. sf. (492) *for that is his ... covering*

לְבַדָּהּ prep.-n.m.s.-3 f.s. sf. (94) *only*

הִוא שִׂמְלָתוֹ v.supra-n.f.s.-3 m.s. sf. (971) *it is his mantle*

לְעֹרוֹ prep.-n.m.s.-3 m.s. sf. (736) *for his body*

בַּמֶּה prep.-def.art.-interr. (552) *in what else*

יִשְׁכָּב Qal impf.3 m.s. (1011) *shall he sleep*

וְהָיָה כִּי־יִצְעַק conj.-Qal pf.3 m.s. (224)-conj.-Qal impf.3 m.s. (858) *and if he cries*

אֵלַי prep.-1 c.s. sf. *to me*

וְשָׁמַעְתִּי conj.-Qal pf.1 c.s. (1033) *I will hear*

כִּי־חַנּוּן אָנִי conj.-adj. m.s. (337)-pers.pr. 1 c.s. (58) *for I am compassionate*

22:27

אֱלֹהִים n.m.p. (43) *God*

לֹא תְקַלֵּל neg.-Pi.impf.2 m.s. (886) *you shall not revile*

וְנָשִׂיא conj.-n.m.s. (I 672) *nor a ruler*

בְעַמְּךָ prep.-n.m.s.-2 m.s. sf. (I 766) *of your people*

לֹא תָאֹר neg.-Qal impf.2 m.s. (אָרַר 76) *curse*

22:28

מְלֵאָתְךָ n.f.s.-2 m.s. sf. (571) *from the fulness of your harvest*

וְדִמְעֲךָ conj.-n.m.s.-2 m.s. sf. (199) *and from the outflow of your presses*

לֹא תְאַחֵר neg.-Pi. impf. 2 m.s. (אָחַר 29) *you shall not delay*

בְּכוֹר בָּנֶיךָ n.m.s. cstr. (114) - n.m.p.-2 m.s. sf. (119) *the first-born of your sons*

תִּתֶּן־לִי Qal impf.2 m.s. (נָתַן 678)-prep.-1 c.s. sf. *you shall give to me*

22:29

כֵּן־תַּעֲשֶׂה adv. (485)-Qal impf.2 m.s. (עָשָׂה I 793) *you shall do likewise*

לְשֹׁרְךָ prep.-n.m.s.-2 m.s. sf. (1004) *with your oxen*

לְצֹאנֶךָ prep.-n.f.s.-2 m.s. sf. (838) *and with your sheep*

שִׁבְעַת יָמִים num.f.s. cstr. (988)-n.m.p. (398) *seven days*

יִהְיֶה Qal impf.3 m.s. (הָיָה 224) *it shall be*

עִם־אִמּוֹ prep.-n.f.s.-3 m.s. sf. (51) *with its dam*

בַּיּוֹם הַשְּׁמִינִי prep.-def.art.-n.m.s. (398) - def.art.-adj. num. (1033) *on the eighth day*

תִּתְּנוֹ־לִי Qal impf.2 m.s.-3 m.s. sf. (נָתַן 678)-prep.-1 c.s. sf. *you shall give it to me*

22:30

וְאַנְשֵׁי־קֹדֶשׁ conj.-n.m.p. cstr. (35) - n.m.s. (871) *men consecrated*

תִּהְיוּן לִי Qal impf. 2 m.p. (הָיָה 224) - prep.-1 c.s. sf. *you shall be to me*

וּבָשָׂר conj.-n.m.s. (142) *therefore any flesh*

בַּשָּׂדֶה prep.-def.art.-n.m.s. (961) *in the field*

טְרֵפָה n.f.s. (383) *that is torn by beasts*

לֹא תֹאכֵלוּ neg.-Qal impf.2 m.p. paus. (37) *you shall not eat*

לַכֶּלֶב prep.-def.art.-n.m.s. (476) *to the dogs*

תַּשְׁלִכוּן אֹתוֹ Hi. impf. 2 m.p. (שָׁלַךְ 1020) - dir.obj.3 m.s. sf. *you shall cast it*

23:1

לֹא תִשָּׂא neg.-Qal impf. 2 m.s. (נָשָׂא 669) *you shall not utter*

שֵׁמַע שָׁוְא n.m.s. cstr. (1034)-n.m.s. (996) *a false report*

אַל־תָּשֶׁת יָדְךָ neg.-Qal impf. 2 m.s. (שִׁית 1011)-n.f.s.-2 m.s. sf. (388) *you shall not join hands*

עִם־רָשָׁע prep.-adj. m.s. (957) *with a wicked man*

לִהְיֹת prep.-Qal inf. cstr. (הָיָה 224) *to be*

עֵד חָמָס n.m.s. cstr. (729)-n.m.s. (329) *a malicious witness*

23:2

לֹא־תִהְיֶה אַחֲרֵי־רַבִּים neg.-Qal impf. 2 m.s. (הָיָה 224)-prep. cstr. (29)-adj. m.p. (I 912) *you shall not follow a multitude*

לְרָעֹת prep.-adj. f.p. (I 948) *to do evil*

וְלֹא־תַעֲנֶה conj.-neg.-Qal impf. 2 m.s. (I 772) *nor shall you bear witness*

עַל־רִב prep.-n.m.s. (936) *in a suit*

לִנְטֹת prep.-Qal inf. cstr. (נָטָה 639) *turning aside*

אַחֲרֵי רַבִּים prep. cstr. (29)-adj. m.p. (I 912) *after a multitude*

לְהַטֹּת prep.-Hi. inf. cstr. (נָטָה 639) *so as to pervert justice*

23:3

וְדָל conj.-adj. m.s. paus. (195) *nor to a poor man*

לֹא תֶהְדַּר neg.-Qal impf. 2 m.s. (הָדַר 213) *(nor) shall you be partial*

בְּרִיבוֹ prep.-n.m.s.-3 m.s. sf. (936) *in his suit*

23:4

כִּי תִפְגַּע conj.-Qal impf. 2 m.s. (803) *if you meet*

שׁוֹר אֹיִבְךָ n.m.s. cstr. (1004)-Qal act. ptc.-2 m.s. sf. (33) *your enemy's ox*

אוֹ חֲמֹרוֹ conj. (14)-n.m.s.-3 m.s. sf. (331) *or his ass*

תֹּעֶה Qal act. ptc. (תָּעָה 1073) *going astray*

הָשֵׁב תְּשִׁיבֶנּוּ לוֹ Hi. inf. abs. (שׁוּב 996)-Hi. impf. 2 m.s.-3 m.s. sf. (שׁוּב 996)-prep.-3 m.s. sf. *you shall bring it back to him*

23:5

כִּי־תִרְאֶה conj.-Qal impf. 2 m.s. (רָאָה 906) *if you see*

חֲמוֹר שֹׂנַאֲךָ n.m.s. cstr. (331)-Qal act. ptc.-2 m.s. sf. (שָׂנֵא 971) *the ass of one who hates you*

רֹבֵץ Qal act. ptc. (918) *lying*

תַּחַת מַשָּׂאוֹ prep. (1065)-n.m.s.-3 m.s. sf. (II 672) *under its burden*

וְחָדַלְתָּ conj.-Qal pf. 2 m.s. (292) *you shall refrain*

מֵעֲזֹב לוֹ prep.-Qal inf. cstr. (I 736)-prep.-3 m.s. sf. *from leaving him with it*

עָזֹב תַּעֲזֹב Qal inf. abs. (I 736)-Qal impf. 2 m.s. (עָזַב I 736) *you shall by all means free*

עִמּוֹ prep.-3 m.s. sf. *it (with him)*

23:6

לֹא תַטֶּה neg.-Hi. impf. 2 m.s. (נָטָה 639) *you shall not pervert*

מִשְׁפַּט n.m.s. cstr. (1048) *the justice due to*

אֶבְיֹנְךָ n.m.s.-2 m.s. sf. (2) *your poor*

בְּרִיבוֹ prep.-n.m.s.-3 m.s. sf. (936) *in his suit*

23:7

מִדְּבַר־שֶׁקֶר prep.-n.m.s. cstr. (182)-n.m.s. (1055) *from a false charge*

תִּרְחָק Qal impf. 2 m.s. paus. (934) *keep far*

וְנָקִי וְצַדִּיק conj.-adj. m.s. (67)-conj.-adj. m.s. (843) *and the innocent and righteous*

אַל־תַּהֲרֹג neg.-Qal impf. 2 m.s. (הָרַג 246) *do not slay*

כִּי לֹא־אַצְדִּיק conj.-neg.-Hi. impf. 1 c.s. (842) *for I will not acquit*

רָשָׁע adj. m.s. (957) *the wicked*

23:8

וְשֹׁחַד conj.-n.m.s. (1005) *and a bribe*

לֹא תִקָּח neg.-Qal impf. 2 m.s. paus. (לָקַח 542) *you shall not take*

כִּי הַשֹּׁחַד conj.-def. art.-n.m.s. (1005) *for a bribe*

יְעַוֵּר Pi. impf. 3 m.s. (עָוַר 734) *blinds*

פִּקְחִים adj. m.p. (824) *the officials*

וְיסַלֵּף conj.-Pi. impf. 3 m.s. (סָלַף 701) *and subverts*

דִּבְרֵי צַדִּיקִים n.m.p. cstr. (182)-adj. m.p. (843) *the cause of those who are in the right*

23:9

וְגֵר conj.-n.m.s. (158) *and a stranger*

לֹא תִלְחָץ neg.-Qal impf. 2 m.s. paus. (537) *you shall not oppress*

וְאַתֶּם יְדַעְתֶּם conj.-pers. pr. 2 m.p. (61)-Qal pf. 2 m.p. (393) *you know*

אֶת־נֶפֶשׁ הַגֵּר dir. obj.-n.f.s. cstr. (659)-def. art.-n.m.s. (158) *the heart of a stranger*

כִּי־גֵרִים conj.-n.m.p. (158) *for strangers*

הֱיִיתֶם Qal pf. 2 m.p. (הָיָה 224) *you were*

בְּאֶרֶץ מִצְרָיִם prep.-n.f.s. cstr. (75)-pr.n. paus. (595) *in the land of Egypt*

23:10

וְשֵׁשׁ שָׁנִים conj.-num. (995)-n.f.p. (1040) *for six years*

תִּזְרַע Qal impf. 2 m.s. (281) *you shall sow*

אֶת־אַרְצֶךָ dir. obj.-n.f.s.-2 m.s. sf. (75) *your land*

וְאָסַפְתָּ conj.-Qal pf. 2 m.s. (62) *and gather in*

אֶת־תְּבוּאָתָהּ dir. obj.-n.f.s.-3 f.s. sf. (100) *its yield*

23:11

וְהַשְּׁבִיעִת conj.-def. art.-adj. f.s. (988) *but the seventh year*

תִּשְׁמְטֶנָּה Qal impf. 2 m.s.-3 f.s. sf. (שָׁמַט 1030) *you shall let it rest*

וּנְטַשְׁתָּהּ conj.-Qal pf. 2 m.s.-3 f.s. sf. (נָטַשׁ 643) *and lie fallow*

וְאָכְלוּ conj.-Qal pf. 3 c.p. (37) *that may eat*

אֶבְיֹנֵי עַמֶּךָ n.m.p. cstr. (2)-n.m.s.-2 m.s. sf. (I 766) *the poor of your people*

וְיִתְרָם conj.-n.m.s.-3 m.p. sf. (451) *and what they leave*

תֹּאכַל Qal impf. 3 f.s. (37) *may eat*

חַיַּת הַשָּׂדֶה n.f.s. cstr. (I 312)-def. art.-n.m.s. (961) *the wild beasts*

כֵּן־תַּעֲשֶׂה adv. (485)-Qal impf. 2 m.s. (I 793) *you shall do likewise*

לְכַרְמְךָ prep.-n.m.s.-2 m.s. sf. (501) *with your vineyard*

לְזֵיתֶךָ prep.-n.m.s.-2 m.s. sf. (268) *and with your olive orchard*

23:12

שֵׁשֶׁת יָמִים n.f.s. cstr. (995)-n.m.p. (398) *six days*

תַּעֲשֶׂה Qal impf. 2 m.s. (I 793) *you shall do*

מַעֲשֶׂיךָ n.m.p.-2 m.s. sf. (795) *your work*

וּבַיּוֹם הַשְּׁבִיעִי conj.-prep.-def. art.-n.m.s. (398)-def. art.-num. adj. (988) *but on the seventh day*

תִּשְׁבֹּת Qal impf. 2 m.s. (שָׁבַת 991) *you shall rest*

לְמַעַן יָנוּחַ prep.-prep. (775)-Qal impf. 3 m.s. (נוּחַ 628) *that may have rest*

שׁוֹרְךָ וַחֲמֹרֶךָ n.m.s.-2 m.s. sf. (1004)-conj.-n.m.s.-2 m.s. sf. (331) *your ox and your ass*

וְיִנָּפֵשׁ conj.-Ni. impf. 3 m.s. (נָפַשׁ 661) *and may be refreshed*

בֶּן־אֲמָתְךָ n.m.s. cstr. (119)-n.f.s.-2 m.s. sf. (51) *the son of your bondmaid*

וְהַגֵּר conj.-def. art.-n.m.s. (158) *and the alien*

23:13

וּבְכֹל אֲשֶׁר־ conj.-prep.-n.m.s. (481) - rel. *to all that*

אָמַרְתִּי Qal pf. 1 c.s. (55) *I have said*

אֲלֵיכֶם prep.-2 m.p. sf. *to you*

תִּשָּׁמֵרוּ Ni. impf. 2 m.p. paus. (1036) *take heed*

וְשֵׁם conj.-n.m.s. cstr. (1027) *and the names of*

אֱלֹהִים אֲחֵרִים n.m.p. (43) - adj. m.p. (29) *other gods*

לֹא תַזְכִּירוּ neg.-Hi. impf. 2 m.p. (269) *make no mention*

לֹא יִשָּׁמַע neg.-Ni. impf. 3 m.s. (1033) *nor let such be heard*

עַל־פִּיךָ prep.-n.m.s.-2 m.s. sf. (804) *out of your mouth*

23:14

שָׁלֹשׁ רְגָלִים num. (1025)-n.f.p. (919) *three times*

תָּחֹג לִי Qal impf. 2 m.s. (חָגַג 290) - prep.-1 c.s. sf. *you shall keep a feast to me*

בַּשָּׁנָה prep.-def.art.-n.f.s. (1040) *in the year*

23:15

אֶת־חַג הַמַּצּוֹת dir.obj.-n.m.s. cstr. (290) - def.art.-n.f.p. (I 595) *the feast of unleavened bread*

תִּשְׁמֹר Qal impf. 2 m.s. (1036) *you shall keep*

שִׁבְעַת יָמִים num. f.s. cstr. (988) - n.m.p. (398) *for seven days*

תֹּאכַל Qal impf. 2 m.s. (37) *you shall eat*

מַצּוֹת n.f.p. (I 595) *unleavened bread*

כַּאֲשֶׁר צִוִּיתִךָ prep.-rel.-Pi. pf. 1 c.s. - 2 m.s. sf. (צָוָה 845) *as I commanded you*

לְמוֹעֵד prep.-n.m.s. (417) *at the appointed time*

חֹדֶשׁ הָאָבִיב n.m.s. cstr. (294)-def.art.-pr.n. (1) *in the month of Abib*

כִּי־בוֹ יָצָאתָ conj.-prep.-3 m.s. sf.-Qal pf. 2 m.s. (422) *for in it you came out*

מִמִּצְרָיִם prep.-pr.n. paus. (595) *of Egypt*

וְלֹא־יֵרָאוּ conj.-neg.-Ni. impf. 3 m.p. (רָאָה 906) *and none shall appear*

פָנַי n.m.p.-1 c.s. sf. (815) *before me*

רֵיקָם adv. (938) *empty-handed*

23:16

וְחַג הַקָּצִיר conj.-n.m.s. cstr. (290)-def.art.-n.m.s. (I 894) *and the feast of harvest*

בִּכּוּרֵי n.m.p. cstr. (114) *the first fruits of*

מַעֲשֶׂיךָ n.m.p.-2 m.s. sf. (795) *your labor*

אֲשֶׁר תִּזְרַע rel.-Qal impf. 2 m.s. (281) *of what you sow*

בַּשָּׂדֶה prep.-def.art.-n.m.s. (961) *in the field*

וְחַג הָאָסִף conj.-n.m.s. cstr. (290) - def.art.-n.m.s. (63) *and the feast of ingathering*

בְּצֵאת הַשָּׁנָה prep.-Qal inf. cstr. (יָצָא 422)-def.art.-n.f.s. (1040) *at the end of the year*

בְּאָסְפְּךָ prep.-Qal inf. cstr.-2 m.s. sf. (אָסַף 62) *when you gather in*

אֶת־מַעֲשֶׂיךָ dir.obj.-n.m.p.-2 m.s. sf. (795) *the fruit of your labor*

מִן־הַשָּׂדֶה prep.-def.art.-n.m.s. (961) *from the field*

23:17

שָׁלֹשׁ פְּעָמִים num. (1025)-n.f.p. (821) *three times*

בַּשָּׁנָה prep.-def.art.-n.f.s. (1040) *in the year*

יֵרָאֶה Ni. impf. 3 m.s. (רָאָה 906) *shall appear*

כָּל־זְכוּרְךָ n.m.s. cstr. (481)-n.m.s.-2 m.s. sf. (271) *all your males*

אֶל־פְּנֵי prep.-n.m.p. cstr. (815) *before*

הָאָדֹן def.art.-n.m.s. (10) *the Lord*

יהוה pr.n. (217) *Yahweh*

23:18

לֹא תִזְבַּח neg.-Qal impf. 2 m.s. (256) *you shall not offer*

עַל־חָמֵץ prep.-n.m.s. (329) *with leavened bread*

דַּם־זִבְחִי n.m.s. cstr. (196)-n.m.s.-1 c.s. sf. (257) *the blood of my sacrifice*

וְלֹא־יָלִין conj.-neg.-Qal impf. 3 m.s. (I 533) *or let remain*

חֵלֶב־חַגִּי n.m.s. cstr. (316) - n.m.s.-1 c.s. sf. (290) *the fat of my feast*

עַד־בֹּקֶר prep.-n.m.s. (133) *until morning*

23:19

רֵאשִׁית n.f.s. cstr. (912) *the first of*

בִּכּוּרֵי n.m.p. cstr. (114) *the first fruits of*

אַדְמָתְךָ n.f.s.-2 m.s. sf. (9) *your ground*

תָּבִיא Hi. impf. 2 m.s. (בּוֹא 97) *you shall bring*

בֵּית יהוה n.m.s. cstr. (108)-pr.n. (217) *into the house of Yahweh*

אֱלֹהֶיךָ n.m.p.-2 m.s. sf. (43) *your God*

לֹא־תְבַשֵּׁל neg.-Pi. impf. 2 m.s. (בָּשַׁל 143) *you shall not boil*

גְּדִי n.m.s. (152) *a kid*

בַּחֲלֵב אִמּוֹ prep.-n.m.s. cstr. (316)-n.m.s.-3 m.s. sf. (51) *in its mother's milk*

23:20

הִנֵּה demons. part. (243) *behold*

אָנֹכִי שֹׁלֵחַ pers.pr.1 c.s. (59)-Qal act. ptc. (1018) *I send*

מַלְאָךְ n.m.s. (521) *an angel*

לְפָנֶיךָ prep.-n.m.p.-2 m.s. sf. (815) *before you*

לִשְׁמָרְךָ prep.-Qal inf. cstr.-2 m.s. sf. (1036) *to guard you*

בַּדָּרֶךְ prep.-def.art.-n.m.s. paus. (202) *on the way*

וְלַהֲבִיאֲךָ conj.-prep.-Hi. inf. cstr.-2 m.s. sf. (בּוֹא 97) *and to bring you*

אֶל־הַמָּקוֹם prep.-def.art.-n.m.s. (879) *to the place*

אֲשֶׁר הֲכִנֹתִי rel.-Hi. pf. 1 c.s. (כּוּן 465) *which I have prepared*

23:21

הִשָּׁמֶר Ni. impv. 2 m.s. (1036) *give heed*

מִפָּנָיו prep.-n.m.p.-3 m.s. sf. (815) *to him*

וּשְׁמַע conj.-Qal impv. 2 m.s. (1033) *and hearken*

בְּקֹלוֹ prep.-n.m.s.-3 m.s. sf. (876) *to his voice*

אַל־תַּמֵּר בּוֹ neg.-Hi. impf. 2 m.s. (מָרַר 600) - prep.-3 m.s. sf. *do not rebel against him*

כִּי לֹא יִשָּׂא conj.-neg.-Qal impf. 3 m.s. (נָשָׂא 669) *for he will not pardon*

לְפִשְׁעֲכֶם prep.-n.m.s.-2 m.p. sf. (833) *your transgression*

כִּי שְׁמִי conj.-n.m.s.-1 c.s. sf. (1027) *for my name*

בְּקִרְבּוֹ prep.-n.m.s.-3 m.s. sf. (899) *in him*

23:22

כִּי אִם־שָׁמֹעַ תִּשְׁמַע conj.-hypoth. part. (49) - Qal inf. abs. (1033) - Qal impf. 2 m.s. (1033) *but if you hearken attentively*

בְּקֹלוֹ prep.-n.m.s.-3 m.s. sf. (876) *to his voice*

וְעָשִׂיתָ conj.-Qal pf. 2 m.s. (עָשָׂה I 793) *and do*

כֹּל אֲשֶׁר n.m.s. (481)-rel. *all that*

אֲדַבֵּר Pi. impf. 1 c.s. (180) *I say*

וְאָיַבְתִּי conj.-Qal pf. 1 c.s. (אָיַב 33) *then I will be an enemy*

אֶת־אֹיְבֶיךָ dir.obj.-Qal act. ptc. m.p.-2 m.s. sf. (אָיַב 33) *to your enemies*

וְצַרְתִּי conj.-Qal pf. 1 c.s. (צוּר III 849) *and will be an adversary*

אֶת־צֹרְרֶיךָ dir.obj.-Qal act. ptc. m.p.-2 m.s. sf. (צָרַר II 865) *to your adversaries*

23:23

כִּי־יֵלֵךְ conj.-Qal impf. 3 m.s. (הָלַךְ 229) *when ... goes*

מַלְאָכִי n.m.s.-1 c.s. sf. (521) *my angel*

לְפָנֶיךָ prep.-n.m.p.-2 m.s. sf. (815) *before you*

וֶהֱבִיאֲךָ conj.-Hi. pf. 3 m.s.-2 m.s. sf. (בּוֹא 97) *and brings you in*

אֶל־הָאֱמֹרִי prep.-def.art.-pr.n. (57) *to the Amorites*

וְהַחִתִּי conj.-def.art.-pr.n. (366) *and the Hittites*

וְהַפְּרִזִּי conj.-def.art.-pr.n. (827) *and the Perizzites*

וְהַכְּנַעֲנִי conj.-def.art.-pr.n. (489) *and the Canaanites*

הַחִוִּי def.art.-pr.n. (295) *the Hivites*

וְהַיְבוּסִי conj.-def.art.-pr.n. (101) *and the Jebusites*

וְהִכְחַדְתִּיו conj.-Hi. pf. 1 c.s.-3 m.s. sf. (כָּחַד 470) *and I blot them out*

23:24

לֹא־תִשְׁתַּחֲוֶה neg.-Hithpalel impf. 2 m.s. (שָׁחָה 1005) *you shall not bow down*

לֵאלֹהֵיהֶם prep.-n.m.p.-3 m.p. sf. (43) *to their gods*

וְלֹא תָעָבְדֵם conj.-neg.-Ho. impf. 2 m.s.-3 m.p. sf. (עָבַד 712) *nor serve them*

וְלֹא תַעֲשֶׂה conj.-neg.-Qal impf. 2 m.s. (עָשָׂה I 793) *nor do*

כְּמַעֲשֵׂיהֶם prep.-n.m.p.-3 m.p. sf. (795) *according to their works*

כִּי הָרֵס תְּהָרְסֵם conj.-Pi. inf. abs. (הָרַס 248) - Pi. impf. 2 m.s.-3 m.p. sf. (הָרַס 248) *but you shall utterly overthrow them*

וְשַׁבֵּר תְּשַׁבֵּר conj.-Pi. inf. abs. (990) - Pi. impf. 2 m.s. (990) *and break in pieces*

מַצֵּבֹתֵיהֶם n.f.p.-3 m.p. sf. (663) *their pillars*

23:25

וַעֲבַדְתֶּם conj.-Qal pf. 2 m.p. (712) *you shall serve*

אֵת יהוה dir.obj.-pr.n. (217) *Yahweh*

אֱלֹהֵיכֶם n.m.p.-2 m.p. sf. (43) *your God*

וּבֵרַךְ conj.-Pi. pf. 3 m.s. (138) (LXX, V rd וּבֵרַכְתִּי) *and I will bless*

אֶת־לַחְמְךָ dir.obj.-n.m.s.-2 m.s. sf. (536) *your bread*

וְאֶת־מֵימֶיךָ conj.-dir.obj.-n.m.p.-2 m.s. sf. (565) *and your water*

וַהֲסִרֹתִי conj.-Hi. pf. 1 c.s. (סוּר 693) *and I will take away*

מַחֲלָה n.f.s. (318) *sickness*

מִקִּרְבֶּךָ prep.-n.m.s.-2 m.s. sf. (899) *from the midst of you*

23:26

לֹא תִהְיֶה neg.-Qal impf. 3 f.s. (הָיָה 224) *none shall be*

מְשַׁכֵּלָה Pi. ptc. f.s. (שָׁכֹל 1013) *casting her young*

וַעֲקָרָה conj.-adj. f.s. (785) *or be barren*

בְּאַרְצֶךָ prep.-n.f.s.-2 m.s. sf. (75) *in your land*

אֶת־מִסְפַּר dir.obj.-n.m.s. cstr. (708) *the number of*

יָמֶיךָ n.m.p.-2 m.s. sf. (398) *your days*

אֲמַלֵּא Pi. impf. 1 c.s. (569) *I will fulfil*

23:27

אֶת־אֵימָתִי dir.obj.-n.f.s.-1 c.s. sf. (33) *my terror*

אֲשַׁלַּח Pi. impf. 1 c.s. (1018) *I will send*

לְפָנֶיךָ prep.-n.m.p.-2 m.s. sf. (815) *before you*

וְהַמֹּתִי conj.-Qal pf. 1 c.s. (הָמַם 243) *and will throw into confusion*

אֶת־כָּל־הָעָם dir.obj.-n.m.s. cstr. (481)-def. art.-n.m.s. (I 766) *all the people*

אֲשֶׁר תָּבֹא בָּהֶם rel.-Qal impf. 2 m.s. (בּוֹא 97) - prep.-3 m.p. sf. *against whom you shall come*

וְנָתַתִּי conj.-Qal pf. 1 c.s. (נָתַן 678) *and I will make*

אֶת־כָּל־אֹיְבֶיךָ dir.obj.-n.m.s. cstr. (481)-Qal act. ptc. m.p.-2 m.s. sf. (33) *all your enemies*

אֵלֶיךָ עֹרֶף prep.-2 m.s. sf.-n.m.s. (791) *turn their backs to you*

23:28

וְשָׁלַחְתִּי conj.-Qal pf. 1 c.s. (1018) *and I will send*

אֶת־הַצִּרְעָה dir.obj.-def.art.-n.f. coll. (864) *hornets*

לְפָנֶיךָ prep.-n.m.p.-2 m.s. sf. (815) *before you*

וְגֵרְשָׁה conj.-Pi. pf. 3 f.s. (גָּרַשׁ 176) *which shall drive out*

אֶת־הַחִוִּי dir.obj.-def.art.-pr.n. (295) *Hivite*

אֶת־הַכְּנַעֲנִי dir.obj.-def.art.-pr.n. (489) *Canaanite*

וְאֶת־הַחִתִּי conj.-dir.obj.-def.art.-pr.n. (366) *and Hittite*

מִלְּפָנֶיךָ prep.-prep.-n.m.p.-2 m.s. sf. (815) *from before you*

23:29

לֹא אֲגָרְשֶׁנּוּ neg.-Pi. impf. 1 c.s.-3 m.s. sf. (גָּרַשׁ 176) *I will not drive them out*

מִפָּנֶיךָ prep.-n.m.p.-2 m.s. sf. (815) *from before you*

בְּשָׁנָה אֶחָת prep.-n.f.s. (1040)-adj. num. f.s. paus. (25) *in one year*

פֶּן־תִּהְיֶה conj. (814)-Qal impf. 3 f.s. (הָיָה 224) *lest ... become*

הָאָרֶץ def.art.-n.f.s. (75) *the land*

שְׁמָמָה n.f.s. (1031) *desolate*

וְרַבָּה עָלֶיךָ conj.-adj. f.s. (912)-prep.-2 m.s. sf. *and multiply against you*

חַיַּת הַשָּׂדֶה n.f.s. cstr. (I 312)-def.art.-n.m.s. (961) *the wild beasts*

23:30

מְעַט מְעַט subst (589)-subst. (589) *little by little*

אֲגָרְשֶׁנּוּ Pi. impf. 1 c.s.-3 m.s. sf. (גָּרַשׁ 176) *I will drive them out*

מִפָּנֶיךָ prep.-n.m.p.-2 m.s. sf. (815) *from before you*

עַד אֲשֶׁר תִּפְרֶה prep. (III 723)-rel.-Qal impf. 2 m.s. (פָּרָה 826) *until you are increased*

וְנָחַלְתָּ conj.-Qal pf. 2 m.s. (635) *and possess*

אֶת־הָאָרֶץ dir.obj.-def.art.-n.f.s. (75) *the land*

23:31

וְשַׁתִּי conj.-Qal pf. 1 c.s. (שִׁית 1011) *and I will set*

אֶת־גְּבֻלְךָ dir.obj.-n.m.s.-2 m.s. sf. (147) *your bounds*

מִיַּם־סוּף prep.-n.m.s. cstr. (410)-n.m.s. (693) *from the Red Sea (*lit. *sea of rushes)*

וְעַד־יָם conj.-prep. (III 723) - n.m.s. cstr. (410) *to the sea of*

פְּלִשְׁתִּים pr.n. (814) *the Philistines*

וּמִמִּדְבָּר conj.-prep.-n.m.s. (184) *and from the wilderness*

עַד־הַנָּהָר prep. (III 723)-def.art.-n.m.s. (625) *to the Euphrates*

כִּי אֶתֵּן conj.-Qal impf. 1 c.s. (נָתַן 678) *for I will deliver*

בְּיֶדְכֶם prep.-n.f.s.-2 m.p. sf. (388) *into your hand*

אֵת יֹשְׁבֵי הָאָרֶץ dir.obj.-Qal act. ptc. m.p. cstr. (442) - def.art.-n.f.s. (75) *the inhabitants of the land*

וְגֵרַשְׁתָּמוֹ conj.-Pi. pf. 2 m.s.-3 m.p. sf. (176) *and you shall drive them out*

מִפָּנֶיךָ prep.-n.m.p.-2 m.s. sf. (815) *before you*

23:32

לֹא־תִכְרֹת neg.-Qal impf. 2 m.s. (503) *you shall make no*

לָהֶם prep.-3 m.p. sf. *with them*

וְלֵאלֹהֵיהֶם conj.-prep.-n.m.p.-3 m.p. sf. (43) *or with their gods*

בְּרִית n.f.s. (136) *covenant*

23:33

לֹא יֵשְׁבוּ neg.-Qal impf. 3 m.p. (יָשַׁב 442) *they shall not dwell*

בְּאַרְצְךָ prep.-n.f.s.-2 m.s. sf. (75) *in your land*

פֶּן־יַחֲטִיאוּ conj. (814)-Hi. impf. 3 m.p. (306) *lest they make sin*

אֹתְךָ לִי dir.obj.-2 m.s. sf.-prep.-1 c.s. sf. *you ... against me*

כִּי תַעֲבֹד conj.-Qal impf. 2 m.s. (712) *for if you serve*

אֶת־אֱלֹהֵיהֶם dir.obj.-n.m.p.-3 m.p. sf. (43) *their gods*

כִּי־יִהְיֶה conj.-Qal impf. 3 m.s. (הָיָה 224) *it will surely be*

לְךָ prep.-2 m.s. sf. *to you*

לְמוֹקֵשׁ prep.-n.m.s. (430) *a snare*

24:1

וְאֶל־מֹשֶׁה conj.-prep.-pr.n. (602) *and to Moses*

אָמַר Qal pf. 3 m.s. (55) *he said*

עֲלֵה Qal impv. 2 m.s. (עָלָה 748) *come up*

אֶל־יהוה prep.-pr.n. (217) *to Yahweh*

אַתָּה וְאַהֲרֹן pers. pr. 2 m.s. (61)-conj.-pr.n. (14) *you and Aaron*

נָדָב וַאֲבִיהוּא pr.n. (621)-conj.-pr.n. (4) *Nadab, and Abihu*

וְשִׁבְעִים conj.-num. p. (988) *and seventy*

מִזִּקְנֵי יִשְׂרָאֵל prep.-n.m.p. cstr. (278)-pr.n. (975) *of the elders of Israel*

וְהִשְׁתַּחֲוִיתֶם conj.-Hithpalel pf. 2 m.p. (שָׁחָה 1005) *and worship*

מֵרָחֹק prep.-n.m.s. (935) *afar off*

24:2

וְנִגַּשׁ conj.-Ni. pf. 3 m.s. (נָגַשׁ 620) *shall come near*

מֹשֶׁה pr.n. (602) *Moses*

לְבַדּוֹ prep.-n.m.s.-3 m.s. sf. (94) *alone*

אֶל־יהוה prep.-pr.n. (217) *to Yahweh*

וְהֵם conj.-pers. pr. 3 m.p. (241) *but the others*

לֹא יִגָּשׁוּ neg.-Qal impf. 3 m.p. paus. (נָגַשׁ 620) *shall not come near*

וְהָעָם conj.-def.art.-n.m.s. (I 766) *and the people*

לֹא יַעֲלוּ neg.-Qal impf. 3 m.p. (עָלָה 748) *shall not come up*

עִמּוֹ prep.-3 m.s. sf. *with him*

24:3

וַיָּבֹא מֹשֶׁה consec.-Qal impf. 3 m.s. (בּוֹא 97) - pr.n. (602) *and Moses came*

וַיְסַפֵּר consec.-Pi. impf. 3 m.s. (707) *and told*

לָעָם prep.-def.art.-n.m.s. (I 766) *the people*

אֵת כָּל־דִּבְרֵי dir.obj.-n.m.s. cstr. (481)-n.m.p. cstr. (182) *all the words of*

יהוה pr.n. (217) *Yahweh*

וְאֵת כָּל־הַמִּשְׁפָּטִים conj.-dir.obj.-n.m.s. cstr. (481) - def.art.-n.m.p. (1048) *and all the ordinances*

וַיַּעַן consec.-Qal impf. 3 m.s. (עָנָה I 772) *and answered*

כָּל־הָעָם n.m.s. cstr. (481) - def.art.-n.m.s. (I 766) *all the people*

קוֹל אֶחָד n.m.s. (876)-num. adj. (25) *with one voice*

וַיֹּאמְרוּ consec.-Qal impf. 3 m.p. (55) *and said*

כָּל־הַדְּבָרִים n.m.s. cstr. (481) - def.art.-n.m.p. (182) *all the words*

אֲשֶׁר־דִּבֶּר יהוה rel.-Pi. pf. 3 m.s. (180)-pr.n. (217) *which Yahweh has spoken*

נַעֲשֶׂה Qal impf. 1 c.p. (עָשָׂה I 793) *we will do*

24:4

וַיִּכְתֹּב מֹשֶׁה consec.-Qal impf. 3 m.s. (507)-pr.n. (602) *and Moses wrote*

אֵת כָּל־דִּבְרֵי dir.obj.-n.m.s. cstr. (481)-n.m.p. cstr. (182) *all the words of*

יהוה pr.n. (217) *Yahweh*

וַיַּשְׁכֵּם consec.-Hi. impf. 3 m.p. (שָׁכַם 1014) *and he rose*

בַּבֹּקֶר prep.-def.art.-n.m.s. (133) *in the morning*

וַיִּבֶן consec.-Qal impf. 3 m.s. (בָּנָה 124) *and built*

מִזְבֵּחַ n.m.s. (258) *an altar*

תַּחַת הָהָר prep. (1065) - def.art.-n.m.s. (249) *at the foot of the mountain*

וּשְׁתֵּים עֶשְׂרֵה conj.-num. f. (1040) - num. (797) *and twelve*

מַצֵּבָה n.f.s. (663) *pillars*

לִשְׁנֵים עָשָׂר prep.-num. m. (1040) - num. m. (797) *according to the twelve*

שִׁבְטֵי יִשְׂרָאֵל n.m.p. cstr. (986) - pr.n. (975) *tribes of Israel*

24:5

וַיִּשְׁלַח consec.-Qal impf. 3 m.s. (1018) *and he sent*

אֶת־נַעֲרֵי dir.obj.-n.m.p. cstr. (654) *young men of*

בְּנֵי יִשְׂרָאֵל n.m.p. cstr. (119) - pr.n. (975) *the people of Israel*

וַיַּעֲלוּ consec.-Qal impf. 3 m.p. (עָלָה 748) *who offered*

עֹלֹת n.f.p. (750) *burnt-offerings*

וַיִּזְבְּחוּ זְבָחִים consec.-Qal impf. 3 m.p. (256) - n.m.p. (257) *and sacrificed sacrifices*

שְׁלָמִים n.m.p. (1023) *peace offerings*

ליהוה prep.-pr.n. (217) *to Yahweh*

פָּרִים n.m.p. (830) *of oxen*

24:6

וַיִּקַּח מֹשֶׁה consec.-Qal impf. 3 m.s. (לָקַח 542) - pr.n. (602) *and Moses took*

חֲצִי הַדָּם n.m.s. cstr. (345)-def.art.-n.m.s. (196) *half of the blood*

וַיָּשֶׂם consec.-Qal impf. 3 m.s. (שִׂים 962) *and put it*

בָּאַגָּנֹת prep.-def.art.-n.m.p. (8) *in basins*

וַחֲצִי הַדָּם conj.-v.supra-v.supra *and half of the blood*

זָרַק Qal pf. 3 m.s. (284) *he threw*

עַל־הַמִּזְבֵּחַ prep.-def.art.-n.m.s. (258) *against the altar*

24:7

וַיִּקַּח consec.-Qal impf. 3 m.s. (לָקַח 542) *then he took*

סֵפֶר הַבְּרִית n.m.s. cstr. (706) - def.art.-n.f.s. (136) *the book of the covenant*

וַיִּקְרָא consec.-Qal impf. 3 m.s. (894) *and read it*

בְּאָזְנֵי הָעָם prep.-n.f. du. cstr. (23) - def.art.-n.m.s. (I 766) *in the hearing of the people*

וַיֹּאמְרוּ consec.-Qal impf. 3 m.p. (55) *and they said*

כֹּל אֲשֶׁר־ n.m.s. (481) - rel. *all that*

דִּבֶּר יהוה Pi. pf. 3 m.s. (180) - pr.n. (217) *Yahweh has spoken*

נַעֲשֶׂה Qal impf. 1 c.p. (עָשָׂה I 793) *we will do*

וְנִשְׁמָע conj.-Qal impf. 1 c.p. paus. (1033) *and we will be obedient*

24:8

וַיִּקַּח מֹשֶׁה consec.-Qal impf. 3 m.s. (לָקַח 542) - pr.n. (602) *and Moses took*

אֶת־הַדָּם dir.obj.-def.art.-n.m.s. (196) *the blood*

וַיִּזְרֹק consec.-Qal impf. 3 m.s. (284) *and threw it*

עַל־הָעָם prep.-def.art.-n.m.s. (I 766) *upon the people*

וַיֹּאמֶר consec.-Qal impf. 3 m.s. (55) *and said*

הִנֵּה demons. part. (243) *behold*

דַם־הַבְּרִית n.m.s. cstr. (196) - def.art.-n.f.s. (136) *the blood of the covenant*

אֲשֶׁר כָּרַת יהוה rel.-Qal pf. 3 m.s. (503) - pr.n. (217) *which Yahweh has made*

עִמָּכֶם prep.-2 m.p. sf. *with you*

עַל כָּל־הַדְּבָרִים prep.-n.m.s. cstr. (481) - def.art.-n.m.p. (182) *in accordance with all ... words*

הָאֵלֶּה def.art.-demons. adj. c.p. (41) *these*

24:9

וַיַּעַל consec.-Qal impf. 3 m.s. (עָלָה 748) *then went up*

מֹשֶׁה וְאַהֲרֹן pr.n. (602) - conj.-pr.n. (14) *Moses and Aaron*

נָדָב וַאֲבִיהוּא pr.n. (621) - conj.-pr.n. (4) *Nadab, and Abihu*

וְשִׁבְעִים conj.-num. p. (988) *and seventy*

מִזִּקְנֵי יִשְׂרָאֵל prep.-adj. m.p. cstr. (278) - pr.n. (975) *of the elders of Israel*

24:10

וַיִּרְאוּ consec.-Qal impf. 3 m.p. (רָאָה 906) *and they saw*

אֵת אֱלֹהֵי יִשְׂרָאֵל dir.obj.-n.m.p. cstr. (43) - pr.n. (975) *the God of Israel*

וְתַחַת רַגְלָיו conj.-prep. (1065) - n.f.p.-3 m.s. sf. (919) *and under his feet*

כְּמַעֲשֵׂה לִבְנַת prep.-n.m.s. cstr. (795) - n.f.s. cstr. (527) *as it were a pavement of*

הַסַּפִּיר def.art.-n.m.s. (705) *sapphire stone*

וּכְעֶצֶם הַשָּׁמַיִם conj.-prep.-n.f.s. cstr. (782)-def.art.-n.m. du. (1029) *like the very heaven*

לָטֹהַר prep.-n.m.s. (372) *for clearness (*lit. *as the body of the heavens for purity)*

24:11

וְאֶל־אֲצִילֵי conj.-prep.-n.m.p. cstr. (69) *and on the chief men of*

בְּנֵי יִשְׂרָאֵל n.m.p. cstr. (119) - pr.n. (975) *the people of Israel*

לֹא שָׁלַח יָדוֹ neg.-Qal pf. 3 m.s. (1018) - n.f.s.-3 m.s. sf. (388) *he did not lay his hand*

וַיֶּחֱזוּ consec.-Qal impf. 3 m.p. (חָזָה 302) *they beheld*

אֶת־הָאֱלֹהִים dir.obj.-def.art.-n.m.p. (43) *God*

וַיֹּאכְלוּ consec.-Qal impf. 3 m.p. (37) *and ate*

וַיִּשְׁתּוּ consec.-Qal impf. 3 m.p. (שָׁתָה 1059) *and drank*

24:12

וַיֹּאמֶר יהוה consec.-Qal impf. 3 m.s. (55) - pr.n. (217) *and Yahweh said*

אֶל־מֹשֶׁה prep.-pr.n. (602) *to Moses*

עֲלֵה אֵלַי Qal impv. 2 m.s. (עָלָה 748) - prep.-1 c.s. sf. *come up to me*

הָהָרָה def.art.-n.m.s.-dir. he (249) *on the mountain*

וֶהְיֵה־שָׁם conj.-Qal impv. 2 m.s. (הָיָה 224) - adv. (1027) *and wait there*

וְאֶתְּנָה לְךָ conj.-Qal impf. 1 c.s. - coh. he (נָתַן 678) - prep.-2 m.s. sf. *and I will give you*

אֶת־לֻחֹת הָאֶבֶן dir.obj.-n.m.p. cstr. (531) - def.art.-n.f.s. (6) *the tables of stone*

וְהַתּוֹרָה conj.-def.art.-n.f.s. (435) *with the law*

וְהַמִּצְוָה conj.-def.art.-n.f.s. (846) *and the commandment*

אֲשֶׁר כָּתַבְתִּי rel.-Qal pf. 1 c.s. (507) *which I have written*

לְהוֹרֹתָם prep.-Hi. inf. cstr.-3 m.p. sf. (יָרָה 434) *for their instruction*

24:13

וַיָּקָם מֹשֶׁה consec.-Qal impf. 3 m.s. (קוּם 877) - pr.n. (602- *so Moses rose*

וִיהוֹשֻׁעַ מְשָׁרְתוֹ conj.-pr.n. (221) - Pi. ptc. - 3 m.s. sf. (שָׁרַת 1058) *with his servant Joshua*

וַיַּעַל מֹשֶׁה consec.-Qal impf. 3 m.s. (עָלָה 748) - pr.n. (602) *and Moses went up*

אֶל־הַר הָאֱלֹהִים prep.-n.m.s. cstr. (249) - def.art.-n.m.p. (43) *into the mountain of God*

24:14

וְאֶל־הַזְּקֵנִים conj.-prep.-def.art.-adj. m.p. (278) *and to the elders*

אָמַר Qal pf. 3 m.s. (55) *he said*

שְׁבוּ־לָנוּ Qal impv. 2 m.p. (יָשַׁב 442) - prep.-1 c.p. sf. *tarry for us*

בָזֶה prep.-demons. adj. (260) *here*

עַד אֲשֶׁר־נָשׁוּב prep. (III 723) - Qal impf. 1 c.p. (שׁוּב 996) *until we come again*

אֲלֵיכֶם prep.-2 m.p. sf. *to you*

וְהִנֵּה conj.-demons. part. (243) *and behold*

אַהֲרֹן וְחוּר pr.n. (14) - conj.-pr.n. (II 301) *Aaron and Hur*

עִמָּכֶם prep.-2 m.p. sf. *with you*

מִי־בַעַל דְּבָרִים interr. (566) - n.m.s. cstr. (127) - n.m.p. (182) *whoever has a cause*

יִגַּשׁ אֲלֵהֶם Qal impf. 3 m.s. (נָגַשׁ 620) - prep.-3 m.p. sf. *let him go to them*

24:15

וַיַּעַל מֹשֶׁה consec.-Qal impf. 3 m.s. (עָלָה 748) - pr.n. (602) *then Moses went up*

אֶל־הָהָר prep.-def.art.-n.m.s. (249) *on the mountain*

וַיְכַס הֶעָנָן consec.-Pi. impf. 3 m.s. (כָּסָה 491) - def.art.-n.m.s. (777) *and the cloud covered*

אֶת־הָהָר dir.obj.-v. supra *the mountain*

24:16

וַיִּשְׁכֹּן consec.-Qal impf. 3 m.s. (1014) *and settled*

כְּבוֹד־יהוה n.m.s. cstr. (458)-pr.n. (217) *the glory of Yahweh*

עַל־הַר סִינַי prep.-n.m.s. cstr. (249) - pr.n. (696) *on Mount Sinai*

וַיְכַסֵּהוּ consec.-Pi. impf. 3 m.s.-3 m.s. sf. (כָּסָה 491) *and covered it*

הֶעָנָן def.art.-n.m.s. (777) *the cloud*

שֵׁשֶׁת יָמִים num. f.s. cstr. (995) - n.m.p. (398) *six days*

וַיִּקְרָא consec.-Qal impf. 3 m.s. (894) *and he called*

אֶל־מֹשֶׁה prep.-pr.n. (602) *to Moses*

בַּיּוֹם הַשְּׁבִיעִי prep.-def.art.-n.m.s. (398) - def.art.-num. adj. (988) *on the seventh day*

מִתּוֹךְ הֶעָנָן prep.-n.m.s. cstr. (1063) - def.art.-n.m.s. (777) *out of the midst of the cloud*

24:17

וּמַרְאֵה conj.-n.m.s. cstr. (909) *now the appearance of*

כְּבוֹד יהוה n.m.s. cstr. (458)-pr.n. (217) *the glory of Yahweh*

כְּאֵשׁ אֹכֶלֶת prep.-n.f.s. (77)-Qal act. ptc. f.s. (37) *like a devouring fire*

בְּרֹאשׁ הָהָר prep.-n.m.s. cstr. (910)-def. art.-n.m.s. (249) *on the top of the mountain*

לְעֵינֵי prep.-n.f. du. cstr. (744) *in the sight of*

בְּנֵי יִשְׂרָאֵל n.m.p. cstr. (119)-pr.n. (975) *the people of Israel*

24:18

וַיָּבֹא מֹשֶׁה consec.-Qal impf. 3 m.s. (בּוֹא 97)-pr.n. (602) *and Moses entered*

בְּתוֹךְ הֶעָנָן prep.-n.m.s. cstr. (1063)-def. art.-n.m.s. (777) *the cloud*

וַיַּעַל consec.-Qal impf. 3 m.s. (עָלָה 748) *and went up*

אֶל־הָהָר prep.-def. art.-n.m.s. (249) *on the mountain*

וַיְהִי מֹשֶׁה consec.-Qal impf. 3 m.s. (הָיָה 224)-pr.n. (602) *and Moses was*

בָּהָר prep.-def. art.-n.m.s. (249) *on the mountain*

אַרְבָּעִים יוֹם num. p. (917)-n.m.s. (398) *forty days*

וְאַרְבָּעִים לָיְלָה conj.-num. p. (917)-n.m.s. paus. (538) *and forty nights*

25:1

וַיְדַבֵּר יהוה consec.-Pi. impf. 3 m.s. (180)-pr.n. (217) *and Yahweh said*

אֶל־מֹשֶׁה prep.-pr.n. (602) *to Moses*

לֵּאמֹר prep.-Qal inf. cstr. (55) *saying*

25:2

דַּבֵּר Pi. impv. 2 m.s. (180) *Speak*

אֶל־בְּנֵי יִשְׂרָאֵל prep.-n.m.p. cstr. (119)-pr.n. (975) *to the people of Israel*

וְיִקְחוּ־ conj.-Qal impf. 3 m.p. (לָקַח 542) *that they take*

לִי prep.-1 c.s. sf. *for me*

תְּרוּמָה n.f.s. (929) *an offering*

מֵאֵת כָּל־אִישׁ prep.-prep. (II 85)-n.m.s. cstr. (481)-n.m.s. (35) *from every man*

אֲשֶׁר יִדְּבֶנּוּ לִבּוֹ rel.-Qal impf. 3 m.s.-3 m.s. sf. (נָדַב 621)-n.m.s.-3 m.s. sf. (524) *whose heart makes him willing*

תִּקְחוּ Qal impf. 2 m.p. (לָקַח 542) *you shall receive*

אֶת־תְּרוּמָתִי dir. obj.-n.f.s.-1 c.s. sf. (929) *the offering for me*

25:3

וְזֹאת הַתְּרוּמָה conj.-demons. adj. f.s. (260)-def. art.-n.f.s. (929) *and this is the offering*

אֲשֶׁר תִּקְחוּ rel. - Qal impf. 2 m. p. (לָקַח 542) *which you shall receive*

מֵאִתָּם prep.-prep. (II 85)-3 m.p. sf. *from them*

זָהָב n.m.s. (262) *gold*

וָכֶסֶף conj.-n.m.s. (494) *and silver*

וּנְחֹשֶׁת conj.-n.f.s. (638) *and bronze*

25:4

וּתְכֵלֶת conj.-n.f.s. (1067) *blue*

וְאַרְגָּמָן conj.-n.m.s. (71) *and purple*

וְתוֹלַעַת שָׁנִי conj.-n.f.s. cstr. (1069)-n.m.s. (1040) *and scarlet stuff*

וְשֵׁשׁ conj.-n.m.s. (III 1058) *and fine twined linen*

וְעִזִּים conj.-n.f.p. (777) *and goat's hair*

25:5

וְעֹרֹת אֵילִם conj.-n.m.p. cstr. (736)-n.m.p. (17) *and rams' skins*

מְאָדָּמִים Pu. ptc. m.p. (אָדֹם 10) *tanned*

וְערֹת תְּחָשִׁים conj.-v. supra (736)-n.m.p. (I 1065) *goatskins*

וַעֲצֵי שִׁטִּים conj.-n.m.p. cstr. (781)-n.f.p. (1008) *acacia wood*

25:6

שֶׁמֶן n.m.s. (1032) *oil*

לַמָּאֹר prep.-def. art.-n.m.s. (22) *for the lamps*

בְּשָׂמִים n.m.p. (141) *spices*

לְשֶׁמֶן הַמִּשְׁחָה prep.-n.m.s. cstr. (1032)-def. art.-n.f.s. (603) *for the anointing oil*

וְלִקְטֹרֶת הַסַּמִּים conj.-prep.-n.f.s. cstr. (882)-def. art.-n.m.p. (702) *and for the fragrant incense*

25:7

אַבְנֵי־שֹׁהַם n.f.p. cstr. (6)-n.m.s. (I 995) *onyx stones*

וְאַבְנֵי מִלֻּאִים conj.-v. supra-n.m.p. (571) *and stones for setting*

לָאֵפֹד prep.-def. art.-n.m.s. (65) *for the ephod*

וְלַחֹשֶׁן conj.-prep.-def. art.-n.m.s. (365) *and for the breastpiece*

וְלַחֹשֶׁן conj.-prep.-def. art.-n.m.s. (365) *and for the breastpiece*

25:8

וְעָשׂוּ לִי conj.-Qal pf. 3 c.p. (עָשָׂה I 793)-prep.-1 c.s. sf. *and let them make me*

מִקְדָּשׁ n.m.s. (874) *a sanctuary*

וְשָׁכַנְתִּי conj.-Qal pf. 1 c.s. (שָׁכַן 1014) *that I may dwell*

בְּתוֹכָם prep.-n.m.s.-3 m.p. sf. (1063) *in their midst*

25:9

כְּכֹל אֲשֶׁר אֲנִי prep.-n.m.s. (481)-rel.-pers. pr. 1 c.s. (58) *according to all that I*

מַרְאֶה אוֹתְךָ Hi. ptc. (רָאָה 906)-dir. obj.-2 m.s. sf. *show you*

אֵת תַּבְנִית הַמִּשְׁכָּן dir. obj.-n.f.s. cstr. (125)-def. art.-n.m.s. (1015) *concerning the pattern of the tabernacle*

וְאֵת תַּבְנִית conj.-dir. obj.-v. supra *and (the pattern) of*

כָּל־כֵּלָיו n.m.s. cstr. (481)-n.m.p.-3 m.s. sf. (479) *all its furniture*

וְכֵן תַּעֲשׂוּ conj.-adv. (485)-Qal impf. 2 m.p. (עָשָׂה I 793) *so you shall make it*

25:10

וְעָשׂוּ conj.-Qal pf. 3 c.p. (עָשָׂה I 793) *they shall make*

אֲרוֹן n.m.s. cstr. (75) *an ark of*

עֲצֵי שִׁטִּים n.m.p. cstr. (781)-n.f.p. (1008) *acacia wood*

אַמָּתַיִם n.f. du. (II 52) *two cubits*

וָחֵצִי conj.-n.m.s. (345) *and a half*

אָרְכּוֹ n.m.s.-3 m.s. sf. (73) *its length*

וְאַמָּה וָחֵצִי conj.n.f.s. (II 52)-conj.-v. supra *and a cubit and a half*

רָחְבּוֹ n.m.s.-3 m.s. sf. (931) *its breadth*

וְאַמָּה וָחֵצִי v. supra-v. supra *and a cubit and a half*

קֹמָתוֹ n.f.s.-3 m.s. sf. (879) *its height*

25:11

וְצִפִּיתָ אֹתוֹ conj.-Pi. pf. 2 m.s. (צָפָה II 860)-dir. obj.-3 m.s. sf. *and you shall overlay it*

זָהָב טָהוֹר n.m.s. (262)-adj. (373) *with pure gold*

מִבַּיִת prep.-n.m.s. (108) *within*

וּמִחוּץ conj.-prep.-n.m.s. (299) *and without*

תְּצַפֶּנּוּ Pi. impf. 2 m.s.-3 m.s. sf. (צָפָה II 860) *shall you overlay it*

וְעָשִׂיתָ עָלָיו conj.-Qal pf. 2 m.s. (עָשָׂה I 793)-prep.-3 m.s. sf. *and you shall make upon it*

זֵר זָהָב n.m.s. (267)-n.m.s. (262) *a molding of gold*

סָבִיב adv. (686) *round about*

25:12

וְיָצַקְתָּ conj.-Qal pf. 2 m.s. (427) *and you shall cast*

לּוֹ prep.-3 m.s. sf. *for it*

אַרְבַּע טַבְּעֹת num. (I 916)-n.f.p. (371) *four rings*

זָהָב n.m.s. (262) *gold*

וְנָתַתָּה conj.-Qal pf. 2 m.s. (נָתַן 678) *and put them*

עַל אַרְבַּע פַּעֲמֹתָיו prep.-num. (I 916)-n.f.p.-3 m.s. sf. (821) *on its four feet*

וּשְׁתֵּי טַבָּעֹת conj.-num. cstr. (1040)-n.f.p. (371) *two rings*

עַל־צַלְעוֹ הָאֶחָת prep.-n.f.s.-3 m.s. sf. (854)-def. art.-num. f. (25) *on the one side of it*

וּשְׁתֵּי טַבָּעֹת conj.-v. supra-v. supra *and two rings*

עַל־צַלְעוֹ הַשֵּׁנִית v. supra-def. art.-num. adj. (1041) *on the other side of it*

25:13

וְעָשִׂיתָ conj.-Qal pf.2 m.s. (עָשָׂה I 793) *you shall make*

בַדֵּי n.m.p. cstr. (II 94) *poles of*

עֲצֵי שִׁטִּים n.m.p. cstr. (781)-n.f.p. (1008) *acacia wood*

וְצִפִּיתָ conj.-Qal pf.2 m.s. (צָפָה II 860) *and overlay*

אֹתָם dir.obj.-3 m.p. sf. *them*

זָהָב n.m.s. (262) *with gold*

25:14

וְהֵבֵאתָ conj.-Hi.pf. 2 m.s. (בּוֹא 97) *And you shall put*

אֶת־הַבַּדִּים dir.obj.-def.art.-n.m.p. (II 94) *the poles*

בַּטַּבָּעֹת prep.-def.art.-n.f.p. (371) *into the rings*

עַל צַלְעֹת הָאָרֹן prep.-n.f.p. cstr. (854)-def.art.-n.m.s. (75) *on the sides of the ark*

לָשֵׂאת prep.-Qal inf. cstr. (נָשָׂא 669) *to carry*

אֶת־הָאָרֹן dir.obj.-def.art.-n.m.s. (75) *the ark*

בָּהֶם prep.-3 m.p. sf. *by them*

25:15

בְּטַבְּעֹת הָאָרֹן prep.-n.f.p. cstr. (371)-def.art.-n.m.s. (75) *in the rings of the ark*

יִהְיוּ הַבַּדִּים Qal impf. 3 m.p. (הָיָה 224) - def.art.-n.m.p. (II 94) *the poles shall remain*

לֹא יָסֻרוּ מִמֶּנּוּ neg.-Qal impf. 3 m.p. (סוּר 693) - prep.-3 m.s. sf. *they shall not be taken from it*

25:16

וְנָתַתָּ conj.-Qal pf.2 m.s. (נָתַן 678) *and you shall put*

אֶל־הָאָרֹן prep.-def.art.-n.m.s. (75) *into the ark*

אֵת הָעֵדֻת dir.obj.-def.art.-n.f.s. (730) *the testimony*

אֲשֶׁר אֶתֵּן אֵלֶיךָ rel.-Qal impf. 1 c.s. (נָתַן 678) - prep.-2 m.s. sf. *which I shall give you*

25:17

וְעָשִׂיתָ conj.-Qal pf. 2 m.s. (עָשָׂה I 793) *then you shall make*

כַפֹּרֶת n.f.s. cstr. (498) *a mercy seat of (*lit. *propitiatory* or *cover)*

זָהָב טָהוֹר n.m.s. (262) - adj. m.s. (373) *pure gold*

אַמָּתַיִם וָחֵצִי n.f. du. (52)-conj.-n.m.s. (345) *two cubits and a half*

אָרְכָּהּ n.m.s.-3 f.s. sf. (73) *its length*

וְאַמָּה וָחֵצִי conj.-n.f.s. (52) - v.supra *and a cubit and a half*

רָחְבָּהּ n.m.s.-3 f.s. sf. (931) *its breadth*

25:18

וְעָשִׂיתָ conj.-Qal pf. 2 m.s. (עָשָׂה I 793) *and you shall make*

שְׁנַיִם כְּרֻבִים num. m. (1040) - n.m.p. (500) *two cherubim*

זָהָב n.m.s. (262) *of gold*

מִקְשָׁה n.f.s. (I 904) *of hammered work*

תַּעֲשֶׂה Qal impf.2 m.s. (עָשָׂה I 793) *shall you make*

אֹתָם dir.obj-3 m.p. sf. *them*

מִשְּׁנֵי prep.-num.m. cstr. (1040) *on the two*

קְצוֹת n.f.p. cstr. (892) *ends of*

הַכַּפֹּרֶת def.art.-n.f.s. (498) *the mercy seat*

25:19

וַעֲשֵׂה conj.-Qal impv.2 m.s. (עָשָׂה I 793) *make*

כְּרוּב אֶחָד n.m.s. (500)-adj.num. (25) *one cherub*

מִקָּצָה מִזֶּה prep.-n.f.s. 9892)-prep.-demons.adj. (260) *on the one end*

וּכְרוּב־אֶחָד conj.-n.m.s. (500)-adj.num.m. (25) *and one cherub*

מִקָּצָה מִזֶּה v.supra - v.supra *on the other end*

מִן־הַכַּפֹּרֶת prep.-def.art.-n.f.s. (498) *with the mercy seat*

תַּעֲשׂוּ Qal impf.2 m.p. (עָשָׂה I 793) *shall you make*

אֶת־הַכְּרֻבִים dir.obj.-def.art.-n.m.p. (500) *the cherubim*

עַל־שְׁנֵי קְצוֹתָיו prep.-num.m. cstr. (1040)-n.f.p.-3 m.s. sf. (892) *on its two ends*

25:20

וְהָיוּ הַכְּרֻבִים conj.-Qal pf. 3 c.p. (הָיָה 224) - def.art.-n.m.p. (500) *the cherubim shall*

פֹּרְשֵׂי Qal act.ptc.m.p. cstr. (831) *spread out*

כְנָפַיִם n.f. du. (489) *their wings*

לְמַעְלָה prep.-adv.-loc.he (751) *above*

סֹכְכִים Qal act. ptc. m.p. (סָכַךְ I 696) *overshadowing*

בְּכַנְפֵיהֶם prep.-n.f. du.-3 m.p. sf. (489) *with their wings*

עַל־הַכַּפֹּרֶת prep.-def.art.-n.f.s. (498) *the mercy seat*

וּפְנֵיהֶם conj.-n.m.p.-3 m.p. sf. (815) *their faces*

אִישׁ אֶל־אָחִיו n.m.s. (35)-prep.-n.m.s.-3 m.s. sf. (26) *one to another*

אֶל־הַכַּפֹּרֶת prep.-def.art.-n.f.s. (498) *toward the mercy seat*

יִהְיוּ Qal impf. 3 m.p. (הָיָה 224) *shall be*

פְּנֵי הַכְּרֻבִים n.m.p. cstr. (815)-def.art.-n.m.p. (500) *the faces of the cherubim*

25:21

וְנָתַתָּ conj.-Qal pf.2 m.s. (נָתַן 678) *and you shall put*

אֶת־הַכַּפֹּרֶת dir.obj.-def.art.-n.f.s. (498) *the mercy seat*

עַל־הָאָרֹן prep.-def.art.-n.m.s. (75) *on the ark*

מִלְמָעְלָה prep.-prep.-adv.-loc.he (751) *on the top*

וְאֶל־הָאָרֹן conj.-prep.-def.art.-n.m.s. (75) *and in the ark*

תִּתֵּן Qal impf.2 m.s. (נָתַן 678) *you shall put*

אֶת־הָעֵדֻת dir.obj.-def.art.-n.f.s. (730) *the testimony*

אֲשֶׁר אֶתֵּן אֵלֶיךָ rel.-Qal impf. 1 c.s. (נָתַן 678) - prep.-2 m.s. sf. *that I shall give you*

25:22

וְנוֹעַדְתִּי לְךָ conj.-Ni. pf. 1 c.s. (יָעַד 416) - prep.-2 m.s. sf. *I will meet you*

שָׁם adv. (1027) *there*

וְדִבַּרְתִּי אִתְּךָ conj.-Pi. pf. 1 c.s. (180) - prep.-2 m.s. sf. (II 85) *I will speak with you*

מֵעַל הַכַּפֹּרֶת prep.-prep.-def.art.-n.f.s. (498) *from above the mercy seat*

מִבֵּין שְׁנֵי הַכְּרֻבִים prep.-prep. (107) - num. m. cstr. (1040) - def.art.-n.m.p. (500) *from between the two cherubim*

אֲשֶׁר עַל־אֲרֹן הָעֵדֻת rel.-prep.-n.m.s. cstr. (75) - def.art.-n.f.s. (730) *that are upon the ark of the testimony*

אֵת כָּל־אֲשֶׁר dir.obj.-n.m.s. (481) - rel. *of all that*

אֲצַוֶּה אוֹתְךָ Pi. impf. 1 c.s. (צָוָה 845) - dir.obj.-2 m.s. sf. *I will give you in commandment*

אֶל־בְּנֵי יִשְׂרָאֵל prep.-n.m.p. cstr. (119)-pr.n. (975) *for the people of Israel*

25:23

וְעָשִׂיתָ conj.-Qal pf.2 m.s. (**עָשָׂה** I 793) *and you shall make*

שֻׁלְחָן עֲצֵי שִׁטִּים n.m.s. cstr. (1020) - n.m.p. cstr. (781) - n.f.p. (1008) *a table of acacia wood*

אַמָּתַיִם n.f. du. (52) *two cubits*

אָרְכּוֹ n.m.s.-3 m.s. sf. (73) *its length*

וְאַמָּה conj.-n.f.s. (52) *a cubit*

רָחְבּוֹ n.m.s.-3 m.s. sf. (931) *its breadth*

וְאַמָּה v.supra *and a cubit*

וָחֵצִי conj.-n.m.s. (345) *and a half*

קֹמָתוֹ n.f.s.-3 m.s. sf. (879) *its height*

25:24

וְצִפִּיתָ אֹתוֹ conj.-Pi. pf. 2 m.s. (**צָפָה** 860)-dir. obj.-3 m.s. sf. *you shall overlay it*

זָהָב טָהוֹר n.m.s. (262)-adj. m.s. (373) *with pure gold*

וְעָשִׂיתָ conj.-Qal pf. 2 m.s. (**עָשָׂה** I 793) *and make*

לוֹ prep.-3 m.s. sf. *it*

זֵר זָהָב n.m.s. cstr. (267)-n.m.s. (262) *a molding of gold*

סָבִיב adv. (686) *around*

25:25

וְעָשִׂיתָ לוֹ conj.-Qal pf. 2 m.s. (**עָשָׂה** I 793)-prep.-3 m.s. sf. *and you shall make it*

מִסְגֶּרֶת טֹפַח n.f.s. cstr. (689)-n.m.s. (381) *a frame a handbreadth wide*

סָבִיב adv. (686) *around*

וְעָשִׂיתָ conj.-Qal pf. 2 m.s. (**עָשָׂה** I 793) *(and you shall make)*

זֵר־זָהָב n.m.s. cstr. (267) - n.m.s. (262) *a molding of gold*

לְמִסְגַּרְתּוֹ סָבִיב prep.-n.f.s.-3 m.s. sf. (689) - adv. (686) *around the frame*

25:26

וְעָשִׂיתָ לוֹ conj.-Qal pf. 2 m.s. (**עָשָׂה** I 793)-prep.-3 m.s. sf. *and you shall make for it*

אַרְבַּע num. (916) *four*

טַבְּעֹת n.f.p. cstr. (371) *rings of*

זָהָב n.m.s. (262) *gold*

וְנָתַתָּ conj.-Qal pf. 2 m.s. (**נָתַן** 678) *and fasten*

אֶת־הַטַּבָּעֹת dir. obj.-def. art.-n.f.p. (71) *the rings*

עַל אַרְבַּע הַפֵּאֹת prep.-num. m.s. cstr. (916)-def. art.-n.f.p. (802) *to the four corners*

אֲשֶׁר לְאַרְבַּע רַגְלָיו rel.-prep.-num. m.s. cstr. (916)-n.f.p.-3 m.s. sf. (919) *at its four legs*

25:27

לְעֻמַּת הַמִּסְגֶּרֶת prep.-n.f.s. cstr. as prep. (769)-def. art.-n.f.s. (689) *close to the frame*

תִּהְיֶיןָ Qal impf. 3 f.p. (**הָיָה** 224) *shall lie*

הַטַּבָּעֹת def. art.-n.f.p. (371) *the rings*

לְבָתִּים prep.-n.m.p. (108) *as holders*

לְבַדִּים prep.-n.m.p. (II 94) *for poles*

לָשֵׂאת prep.-Qal inf. cstr. (**נָשָׂא** 669) *to carry*

אֶת־הַשֻּׁלְחָן dir. obj.-def. art.-n.m.s. paus. (1020) *the table*

25:28

וְעָשִׂיתָ conj.-Qal pf. 2 m.s. (**עָשָׂה** I 793) *you shall make*

אֶת־הַבַּדִּים dir. obj.-def. art.-n.m.p. (II 94) *the poles*

עֲצֵי שִׁטִּים n.m.p. cstr. (781)-n.f.p. (1008) *of acacia wood*

וְצִפִּיתָ אֹתָם conj.-Pi. pf. 2 m.s. (**צָפָה** II 860) - dir.obj.-3 m.p. sf. *and overlay them*

זָהָב n.m.s. (262) *with gold*

וְנִשָּׂא־בָם conj.-Ni. pf. 3 m.s. (**נָשָׂא** 669)-prep.-3 m.p. sf. *and shall be carried with these*

אֶת־הַשֻּׁלְחָן dir. obj.-def. art.-n.m.s. (1020) *the table*

25:29

וְעָשִׂיתָ conj.-Qal pf. 2 m.s. (**עָשָׂה** I 793) *and you shall make*

קְעָרֹתָיו n.f.p.-3 m.s. sf. (891) *its plates*

וְכַפֹּתָיו conj.-n.f.p.-3 m.s. sf. (496) *and dishes*

וּקְשׂוֹתָיו conj.-n.f.p.-3 m.s. sf. (903) *and its flagons*

וּמְנַקִּיֹּתָיו conj.-n.f.p.-3 m.s. sf. (667) *and bowls*

אֲשֶׁר יֻסַּךְ בָּהֵן rel.-Ho. impf. 3 m.s. (נָסַךְ 650)-prep.-3 f.p. sf. *with which to pour libations*

זָהָב טָהוֹר n.m.s. (262)-adj. m.s. (373) *of pure gold*

תַּעֲשֶׂה אֹתָם Qal impf. 2 m.s. (עָשָׂה I 793)-dir. obj.-3 m.p. sf. *you shall make them*

25:30

וְנָתַתָּ conj.-Qal pf. 2 m.s. (נָתַן 678) *and you shall set*

עַל־הַשֻּׁלְחָן prep.-def. art.-n.m.s. (1020) *on the table*

לֶחֶם פָּנִים n.m.s. cstr. (536)-n.m.p. (815) *the bread of the Presence*

לְפָנַי prep.-n.m.p.-1 c.s. sf. (815) *before me*

תָּמִיד adv. (556) *always*

25:31

וְעָשִׂיתָ conj.-Qal pf. 2 m.s. (עָשָׂה I 793) *and you shall make*

מְנֹרַת זָהָב טָהוֹר n.f.s cstr. (633)-n.m.s. (262)-adj. m.s. (373) *a lampstand of pure gold*

מִקְשָׁה n.f.s. (904) *of hammered work*

תֵּעָשֶׂה Ni. impf. 3 f.s. (עָשָׂה I 793) *shall be made*

הַמְּנוֹרָה def. art.-n.f.s. (633) *the lampstand*

יְרֵכָהּ n.f.s.-3 f.s. sf. (437) *its base*

וְקָנָהּ conj.-n.m.s.-3 f.s. sf. (889) *and its shaft*

גְּבִיעֶיהָ n.m.p.-3 f.s. sf. (149) *its cups*

כַּפְתֹּרֶיהָ n.m.p.-3 f.s. sf. (499) *its capitals*

וּפְרָחֶיהָ conj.-n.m.p.-3 f.s. sf. (827) *and its flowers*

מִמֶּנָּה prep.-3 f.s. sf. (577) *of one piece with it*

יִהְיוּ Qal impf. 3 m.p. (הָיָה 224) *shall be*

25:32

וְשִׁשָּׁה קָנִים conj.-num. f.s. (995)-n.m.p. (889) *and six branches*

יֹצְאִים Qal act. ptc. m.p. (יָצָא 422) *going out*

מִצִּדֶּיהָ prep.-n.m.p.-3 f.s. sf. (841) *of its sides*

שְׁלֹשָׁה קְנֵי num. f.s. (1025)-n.m.p. cstr. (889) *three branches of*

מְנֹרָה n.f.s. (633) *lampstand*

מִצִּדָּהּ הָאֶחָד prep.-n.m.s.-3 f.s. sf. (841)-def. art.-num. m.s. (25) *out of one side of it*

וּשְׁלֹשָׁה קְנֵי conj.-num. f.s. (1025)-n.m.p. cstr. (889) *and three branches of*

מְנֹרָה n.f.s. (633) *lampstand*

מִצִּדָּהּ הַשֵּׁנִי v. supra-def. art.-num. adj. m.s. (1041) *out of the other side of it*

25:33

שְׁלֹשָׁה גְבִעִים num. f.s. (1025)-n.m.p. (149) *three cups*

מְשֻׁקָּדִים Pu. ptc. m.p. (שָׁקַד 1052) *made like almonds*

בַּקָּנֶה הָאֶחָד prep.-def. art.-n.m.s. (889)-def. art.-num. adj. m.s. (25) *on one branch*

כַּפְתֹּר וָפֶרַח n.m.s. (499)-conj.-n.m.s. (827) *capital and flower*

וּשְׁלֹשָׁה גְבִעִים conj.-v. supra-v. supra *and three cups*

מְשֻׁקָּדִים v. supra *made like almonds*

בַּקָּנֶה הָאֶחָד v.supra - v.supra *on the other branch*

כַּפְתֹּר וָפָרַח v. supra-v. supra paus. *capital and flower*

כֵּן adv. (485) *so*

לְשֵׁשֶׁת הַקָּנִים prep.-num. f.s. cstr. (995) - def.art.-n.m.p. (889) *for the six branches*

הַיֹּצְאִים def. art.-Qal act. ptc. m.p. (יָצָא 422) *going out*

מִן־הַמְּנֹרָה prep.-def. art.-n.f.s. (633) *of the lampstand*

25:34

וּבַמְּנֹרָה conj.-prep.-def. art.-n.f.s. (633) *and on the lampstand*

אַרְבָּעָה גְבִעִים num. f.s. (916)-n.m.p. (149) *four cups*

מְשֻׁקָּדִים Pu. ptc. m.p. (שָׁקַד 1052) *made like almonds*

כַּפְתֹּרֶיהָ n.m.p.-3 f.s. sf. (499) *with their capitals*

וּפְרָחֶיהָ conj.-n.m.p.-3 f.s. sf. (827) *and flowers*

25:35

וְכַפְתֹּר conj.-n.m.s. (499) *and a capital*

תַּחַת שְׁנֵי prep. (1065)-num. m.p. cstr. (1040) *under each pair of*

הַקָּנִים def.art.-n.m.p. (889) *the branches*

מִמֶּנָּה prep.-3 f.s. sf. (577) *of one piece with it*

וְכַפְתֹּר v.supra *and a capital*

תַּחַת שְׁנֵי v.supra - v.supra *under each pair of*

הַקָּנִים מִמֶּנָּה v.supra - v.supra *the branches of one piece with it*

וְכַפְתֹּר v.supra *and a capital*

תַּחַת־שְׁנֵי v.supra - v.supra *under each pair of*

הַקָּנִים מִמֶּנָּה v.supra - v.supra *the branches of one piece with it*

לְשֵׁשֶׁת הַקָּנִים prep.-num. f.s. cstr. (995) - def.art.-n.m.p. (889) *of the six branches*

הַיֹּצְאִים def.art.-Qal act. ptc. m.p. (יָצָא 422) *going out*

מִן־הַמְּנֹרָה prep.-def.art.-n.f.s. (633) *from the lampstand*

25:36

כַּפְתֹּרֵיהֶם n.m.p.-3 m.p. sf. (I 499) *their capitals*

וּקְנֹתָם conj.-n.m.p.-3 m.p. sf. (889) *and their branches*

מִמֶּנָּה יִהְיוּ prep.-3 f.s. sf. - Qal impf. 3 m.p. (הָיָה 224) *shall be of one piece*

כֻּלָּהּ n.m.s.-3 f.s. sf. (481) *the whole of it*

מִקְשָׁה אַחַת n.f.s. (904) - adj. f.s. (25) *one piece of hammered work*

זָהָב טָהוֹר n.m.s. (262) - adj. m.s. (373) *pure gold*

25:37

וְעָשִׂיתָ conj.-Qal pf. 2 m.s. (עָשָׂה I 793) *and you shall make*

אֶת־נֵרֹתֶיהָ dir.obj.-n.m.p.-3 f.s. sf. (632) *the ... lamps for it*

שִׁבְעָה num. f.s. (987) *seven*

וְהֶעֱלָה conj.-Hi. pf. 3 m.s. (עָלָה 748) *and shall be set up*

אֶת־נֵרֹתֶיהָ v.supra *the lamps*

וְהֵאִיר conj.-Hi. pf. 3 m.s. (אוֹר 21) *so as to give light*

עַל־עֵבֶר פָּנֶיהָ prep.-n.m.s. cstr. (719) - n.m.p.-3 f.s. sf. (815) *upon the space in front of it*

25:38

וּמַלְקָחֶיהָ conj.-n.m. du.-3 f.s. sf. (544) (*(and) its snuffers*

וּמַחְתֹּתֶיהָ conj.-n.f.p.-3 f.s. sf. (367) *and their trays*

זָהָב טָהוֹר n.m.s. (262) - adj. m.s. (373) *pure gold*

25:39

כִּכָּר n.f.s. (503) *a talent*

זָהָב טָהוֹר n.m.s. (262) - adj. m.s. (373) *pure gold*

יַעֲשֶׂה אֹתָהּ Qal impf. 3 m.s. (עָשָׂה I 793) - dir.obj.-3 f.s. sf. *shall it be made*

אֵת כָּל־הַכֵּלִים הָאֵלֶּה prep. (II 85) - n.m.s. cstr. (481) - def.art.-n.m.p. (479) - def.art.-demons. adj. (41) *with all these utensils*

25:40

וּרְאֵה conj.-Qal impv. 2 m.s. (רָאָה 906) *and see*

וַעֲשֵׂה conj.-Qal impv. 2 m.s. (עָשָׂה I 793) *that you make*

בְּתַבְנִיתָם prep.-n.f.s.-3 m.p. sf. (125) *after the pattern for them*

אֲשֶׁר־אַתָּה מָרְאֶה rel.-pers. pr. 2 m.s. (61) - Ho. ptc. (רָאָה 906) *which is being shown you*

בָּהָר prep.-def.art.-n.m.s. (249) *on the mountain*

26:1

וְאֶת־הַמִּשְׁכָּן conj.-dir.obj.-def.art.-n.m.s. (1015) *moreover, the tabernacle*

תַּעֲשֶׂה Qal impf. 2 m.s. (עָשָׂה I 793) *you shall make*

עֶשֶׂר יְרִיעֹת n.m.s. cstr. (796) - n.f.p. (438) *ten curtains*

שֵׁשׁ מָשְׁזָר n.m.s. (III 1058) - Ho. ptc. (שָׁזַר 1004) *fine twined linen (byssus)*

וּתְכֵלֶת conj.-n.f.s. (1067) *and violet*

וְאַרְגָּמָן conj.-n.m.s. (71) *and purple*

וְתֹלַעַת שָׁנִי conj.-n.f.s. cstr. (1069) - n.m.s. (1040) *and scarlet stuff*

כְּרֻבִים n.m.p. (500) *cherubim*

מַעֲשֵׂה חֹשֵׁב n.m.s. cstr. (795) - Qal act. ptc. (362) *skilfully worked*

תַּעֲשֶׂה אֹתָם Qal impf. 2 m.s. (עָשָׂה I 793) - dir.obj.-3 m.p. sf. *shall you make them*

26:2

אֹרֶךְ n.m.s. cstr. (73) *the length of*

הַיְרִיעָה הָאַחַת def.art.-n.f.s. (438) - def.art.-adj. f.s. (25) *each curtain*

שְׁמֹנֶה וְעֶשְׂרִים num. (1032) - conj.-num. p. (797) *twenty-eight*

בָּאַמָּה prep.-def.art.-n.f.s. (52) *cubits*

וְרֹחַב conj.-n.m.s. (931) *and breadth*

אַרְבַּע בָּאַמָּה num. (916) - prep.-def.art.-n.f.s. (52) *four cubits*

הַיְרִיעָה הָאֶחָת v.supra-def.art.-adj. f.s. paus. (25) *each curtain*

מִדָּה אַחַת n.f.s. (551) - adj. f.s. (25) *one measure*

לְכָל־הַיְרִיעֹת prep.-n.m.s. cstr. (481) - def.art.-n.f.p. (438) *all the curtains*

26:3

חֲמֵשׁ הַיְרִיעֹת num. m. cstr. (331) - def.art.-n.f.p. (438) *five curtains*

תִּהְיֶיןָ Qal impf. 3 f.p. (הָיָה 224) *shall be*

חֹבְרֹת Qal act. ptc. f.p. (חָבַר 287) *coupled*

אִשָּׁה אֶל־אֲחֹתָהּ n.f.s. (61) - prep.-n.f.s.-3 f.s. sf. (27) *to one another*

וְחָמֵשׁ יְרִיעֹת conj.-num. (331) - n.f.p. (438) *and five curtains*

חֹבְרֹת v.supra *shall be coupled*

אִשָּׁה אֶל־אֲחֹתָהּ v.supra - v.supra - v.supra *to one another*

26:4

וְעָשִׂיתָ conj.-Qal pf. 2 m.s. (עָשָׂה I 793) *and you shall make*

לֻלְאֹת n.f.p. cstr. (533) *loops of*

תְּכֵלֶת n.f.s. (1067) *blue*

עַל שְׂפַת prep.-n.f.s. cstr. (973) *on the edge of*

הַיְרִיעָה הָאֶחָת def.art.-n.f.s. (438) - def.art.-adj. f.s. (25) *the one curtain*

מִקָּצָה prep.-n.f.s. (892) *at the end*

בַּחֹבָרֶת prep.-def.art.-n.f.s. paus. (289) *as joined together*

וְכֵן conj.-adv. (485) *and likewise*

תַּעֲשֶׂה Qal impf. 2 m.s. (עָשָׂה I 793) *you shall make*

בִּשְׂפַת prep.-n.f.s. cstr. (973) *on the edge of*

הַיְרִיעָה הַקִּיצוֹנָה def.art.-n.f.s. (438) - def.art.-adj. f.s. (894) *the outmost curtain*

בַּמַּחְבֶּרֶת הַשֵּׁנִית prep.-def.art.-n.f.s. (289) - def.art.-adj. num. f.s. (1041) *in the second set*

26:5

חֲמִשִּׁים לֻלָאֹת num. p. (332) - n.f.p. (533) *fifty loops*

תַּעֲשֶׂה Qal impf. 2 m.s. (עָשָׂה I 793) *you shall make*

בַּיְרִיעָה הָאֶחָת prep.-def.art.-n.f.s. (438) - def.art.-adj. f.s. (25) *on the one curtain*

וַחֲמִשִּׁים לֻלָאֹת conj.-v.supra - v.supra *and fifty loops*

תַּעֲשֶׂה v.supra *you shall make*

בִּקְצֵה הַיְרִיעָה prep.-n.m.s. cstr. (892) - def.art.-n.f.s. (438) *on the edge of the curtain*

אֲשֶׁר rel. *that is*

בַּמַּחְבֶּרֶת הַשֵּׁנִית prep.-def.art.-n.f.s. (289) - def.art.-adj. num. f. (1041) *in the second set*

מַקְבִּילֹת Hi. ptc. f.p. cstr. (קָבַל 867) *showing oppositeness of*

הַלֻּלָאֹת def.art.-n.f.p. (533) *the loops*

אִשָּׁה אֶל־אֲחֹתָהּ n.f.s. (61) - prep.-n.f.s.-3 f.s. sf. (27) *one to another*

26:6

וְעָשִׂיתָ conj.-Qal pf. 2 m.s. (עָשָׂה I 793) *and you shall make*

חֲמִשִּׁים num. p. (332) *fifty*

קַרְסֵי זָהָב n.m.p. cstr. (902) - n.m.s. (262) *clasps of gold*

וְחִבַּרְתָּ conj.-Pi. pf. 2 m.s. (חָבַר 287) *and couple*

אֶת־הַיְרִיעֹת dir.obj.-def.art.-n.f.p. (438) *the curtains*

אִשָּׁה אֶל־אֲחֹתָהּ n.f.s. (61) - prep.-n.f.s.-3 f.s. sf. (27) *one to the other*

בַּקְּרָסִים prep.-def.art.-n.m.p. (902) *with the clasps*

וְהָיָה conj.-Qal pf. 3 m.s. (224) *that may be*

הַמִּשְׁכָּן def.art.-n.m.s. (1015) *the tabernacle*

אֶחָד adj. num. (25) *one*

26:7

וְעָשִׂיתָ conj.-Qal pf. 2 m.s. (עָשָׂה I 793) *you shall also make*

יְרִיעֹת עִזִּים n.f.p. cstr. (438) - n.f.p. (777) *curtains of goats' hair*

לְאֹהֶל prep.-n.m.s. (13) *for a tent*

עַל־הַמִּשְׁכָּן prep.-def.art.-n.m.s. (1015) *over the tabernacle*

עַשְׁתֵּי־עֶשְׂרֵה num. (799) - num. (797) *eleven*

יְרִיעֹת n.f.p. (438) *curtains*

תַּעֲשֶׂה אֹתָם Qal impf. 2 m.s. (עָשָׂה I 793) - dir.obj.-3 m.p. sf. *shall you make (them)*

26:8

אֹרֶךְ הַיְרִיעָה n.m.s. cstr. (73) - def.art.-n.f.s. (438) *the length of ... curtain*

הָאַחַת def.art.-adj. f.s. (25) *each*

שְׁלֹשִׁים num. p. (1026) *thirty*

בָּאַמָּה prep.-def.art.-n.f.s. (52) *cubits*

וְרֹחַב conj.-n.m.s. (931) *and breadth*

אַרְבַּע בָּאַמָּה num. (916) - prep.-def.art.-n.f.s. (52) *four cubits*

הַיְרִיעָה הָאֶחָת def.art.-n.f.s. (438) - def.art.-adj. f.s. (25) *each curtain*

מִדָּה אַחַת n.f.s. (551) - adj. f.s. (25) *same measure*

לְעַשְׁתֵּי עֶשְׂרֵה prep.-num. (799) - num. (797) *the eleven*

יְרִיעֹת n.f.p. (438) *curtains*

26:9

וְחִבַּרְתָּ conj.-Pi. pf. 2 m.s. (287) *and shall couple*

אֶת־חֲמֵשׁ הַיְרִיעֹת dir.obj.-num. cstr. (331) - def.art.-n.f.p. (438) *five curtains*

לְבָד prep.-n.m.s. paus. (94) *by themselves*

וְאֶת־שֵׁשׁ הַיְרִיעֹת conj.-dir.obj.-num. cstr. (995) - v.supra *and six curtains*

לְבָד v.supra *by themselves*

וְכָפַלְתָּ conj.-Qal pf. 2 m.s. (495) *and you shall double over*

אֶת־הַיְרִיעָה הַשִּׁשִּׁית dir.obj.-def.art.-n.f.s. (438) - def.art.-adj. f.s. (995) *the sixth curtain*

אֶל־מוּל prep.-subst. as prep. (557) *at the front of*

פְּנֵי הָאֹהֶל n.m.p. cstr. (815) - def.art.-n.m.s. (13) *(face of) the tent*

26:10

וְעָשִׂיתָ conj.-Qal pf. 2 m.s. (עָשָׂה I 793) *and you shall make*

חֲמִשִּׁים לֻלָאֹת num. p. (332) - n.f.p. (533) *fifty loops*

עַל שְׂפַת prep.-n.f.s. cstr. (973) *on the edge of*

הַיְרִיעָה def.art.-n.f.s. (438) *the curtain*

הָאֶחָת def.art.-num. adj. f. paus. (25) *(one)*

הַקִּיצֹנָה def.art.-adj. f.s. (894) *outmost*

בַּחֹבָרֶת prep.-def.art.-n.f.s. paus. (289) *in one set*

וַחֲמִשִּׁים לֻלָאֹת conj.-num. p. (332) - v.supra (533) *and fifty loops*

עַל שְׂפַת הַיְרִיעָה v.supra.-v.supra-v.supra *on the edge of the curtain*

הַחֹבֶרֶת הַשֵּׁנִית def.art.-n.f.s. (289) - def.art.-num. adj. f. (1041) *in the second set*

26:11

וְעָשִׂיתָ conj.-Qal pf. 2 m.s. (עָשָׂה I 793) *and you shall make*

קַרְסֵי נְחֹשֶׁת n.m.p. cstr. (902) - n.m.s. (I 638) *clasps of bronze*

חֲמִשִּׁים num. p. (332) *fifty*

וְהֵבֵאתָ conj.-Hi. pf. 2 m.s. (בּוֹא 97) *and put*

אֶת־הַקְּרָסִים dir.obj.-def.art.-n.m.p. (902) *the clasps*

בַּלֻּלָאֹת prep.-def.art.-n.f.p. (533) *into the loops*

וְחִבַּרְתָּ conj.-Pi. pf. 2 m.s. (חָבַר 287) *and couple*

אֶת־הָאֹהֶל dir.obj.-def.art.-n.m.s. (13) *the tent*

וְהָיָה אֶחָד conj.-Qal pf. 3 m.s. (224) - num. adj. (25) *that it may be one whole*

26:12

וְסֶרַח הָעֹדֵף conj.-n.m.s. cstr. (710) - def.art.-Qal act. ptc. (עָדַף 727) *and the part that remains*

בִּירִיעֹת הָאֹהֶל prep.-n.f.p. cstr. (438) - def.art.-n.m.s. (13) *of the curtains of the tent*

חֲצִי הַיְרִיעָה n.m.s. cstr. (345) - def.art.-n.f.s. (438) *the half curtain*

הָעֹדֶפֶת def.art. - Qal act. ptc. f. s. (עָדַף 727) *that remains*

תִּסְרַח Qal impf. 3 f.s. (סָרַח 710) *shall hang*

עַל אֲחֹרֵי הַמִּשְׁכָּן prep.-subst. p. cstr. (30) - def.art.-n.m.s. (1015) *over the back of the tabernacle*

26:13

וְהָאַמָּה מִזֶּה conj.-def.art.-n.f.s. (52) - prep.-demons. adj. (260) *and the cubit on the one side*

וְהָאַמָּה מִזֶּה v.supra - v.supra *and the cubit on the other side*

בָּעֹדֵף prep. def.art. - Qal act. ptc. (עָדַף 727) *of what remains*

בְּאֹרֶךְ יְרִיעֹת prep.-n.m.s. cstr. (73) - n.f.p. cstr. (438) *in the length of the curtains of*

הָאֹהֶל def.art.-n.m.s. (13) *the tent*

יִהְיֶה סָרוּחַ Qal impf. 3 m.s. (הָיָה 224) - Qal pass. ptc. (סָרַח 710) *shall hang*

עַל־צִדֵּי הַמִּשְׁכָּן prep.-n.m.p. cstr. (841) - def.art.-n.m.s. (1015) *over the sides of the tabernacle*

מִזֶּה וּמִזֶּה prep.-demons. adj. m.s. (260) - conj. - v.supra *on this side and that side*

לְכַסֹּתוֹ prep.-Pi. inf. cstr.-3 m.s. sf. (כָּסָה 491) *to cover it*

26:14

וְעָשִׂיתָ conj.-Qal pf. 2 m.s. (עָשָׂה I 793) *and you shall make*

מִכְסֶה n.m.s. (492) *a covering*

לָאֹהֶל prep.-def.art.-n.m.s. (13) *for the tent*

עֹרֹת אֵילִם n.f.p. cstr. (736) - n.m.p. (I 17) *rams' skins*

מְאָדָּמִים Pu. ptc. m.p. (אָדֹם 10) *tanned*

וּמִכְסֵה עֹרֹת conj.-n.m.s. cstr. (492) - v.supra *and (a covering of) skins of*

תְּחָשִׁים n.m.p. (I 1065) *goats*

מִלְמָעְלָה prep.-prep.-subst.-loc. he as adv. (751, 2d) *(above)*

26:15

וְעָשִׂיתָ conj.-Qal pf. 2 m.s. (עָשָׂה I 793) *and you shall make*

אֶת־הַקְּרָשִׁים dir.obj.-def.art.-n.m.p. (903) *the frames (boards)*

לַמִּשְׁכָּן prep.-def.art.-n.m.s. (1015) *for the tabernacle*

עֲצֵי שִׁטִּים n.m.p. cstr. (781) - n.f.p. (1008) *of acacia wood*

עֹמְדִים Qal act. ptc. m.p. (עָמַד 763) *upright (standing)*

26:16

עֶשֶׂר אַמּוֹת num. (796) - n.f.p. (52) *ten cubits*

אֹרֶךְ הַקָּרֶשׁ n.m.s. cstr. (73) - def.art.-n.m.s. paus. (903) *the length of the frame (board)*

וְאַמָּה conj.-n.f.s. (52) *and a cubit*

וַחֲצִי הָאַמָּה conj.-n.m.s. cstr. (345) - def.art.-n.f.s. (52) *and a half (cubit)*

רֹחַב הַקֶּרֶשׁ n.m.s. cstr. (931) - def.art.-n.m.s. (903) *the breadth of ... frame*

הָאֶחָד def.art.adj. m.s. (25) *each*

26:17

שְׁתֵּי יָדוֹת num. f.s. cstr. (1040) - n.f.p. (388: 4f) *two tenons*

לַקֶּרֶשׁ הָאֶחָד prep.-def.art.-n.m.s. (903) - def.art.-adj. m.s. (25) *in each frame*

מְשֻׁלָּבֹת Pu. ptc. f.p. (שָׁלַב 1016) *joined*

אִשָּׁה אֶל־אֲחֹתָהּ n.f.s. (61) - prep.-n.f.s.-3 f.s. sf. (27) *together*

כֵּן תַּעֲשֶׂה adv. (485) - Qal impf. 2 m.s. (עָשָׂה I 793) *so shall you do*

לְכֹל קַרְשֵׁי prep.-n.m.s. cstr. (481) - n.m.p. cstr. (903) *for all the frames of*

הַמִּשְׁכָּן def.art.-n.m.s. (1015) *the tabernacle*

26:18

וְעָשִׂיתָ conj.-Qal pf. 2 m.s. (עָשָׂה I 793) *you shall make*

אֶת־הַקְּרָשִׁים dir.obj.-def.art.-n.m.p. (903) *the frames*

לַמִּשְׁכָּן prep.-def.art.-n.m.s. (1015) *for the tabernacle*

עֶשְׂרִים קֶרֶשׁ num. p. (797) - n.m.s. (903) *twenty frames*

לִפְאַת prep.-n.f.s. cstr. (802) *for the side (of)*

נֶגְבָּה תֵימָנָה n.m.s.-loc. he (616) - n.f.s.-loc. he (412) *south (toward the south)*

26:19

וְאַרְבָּעִים conj.-num. p. (917) *and forty*

אַדְנֵי־כֶסֶף n.m.p. cstr. (10)-n.m.s. (494) *bases of silver*

תַּעֲשֶׂה Qal impf. 2 m.s. (עָשָׂה I 793) *you shall make*

תַּחַת עֶשְׂרִים prep. (1065) - num. p. (797) *under the twenty*

הַקָּרֶשׁ def.art.-n.m.s. paus. (903) *frames*

שְׁנֵי אֲדָנִים num. m.s. cstr. (1040) - n.m.p. (10) *two bases*

תַּחַת־הַקֶּרֶשׁ prep. (1065) - def.art.-n.m.s. (903) *under ... frame*

הָאֶחָד def.art.-num. adj. m.s. (25) *one*

לִשְׁתֵּי יְדֹתָיו prep.-num. f.s. cstr. (1040) - n.f.p. - 3 m.s. sf. (388) *for its two tenons*

וּשְׁנֵי אֲדָנִים conj. - v.supra - v.supra *and two bases*

תַּחַת־הַקֶּרֶשׁ v.supra-v.supra *under ... frame*

הָאֶחָד v.supra *one*

לִשְׁתֵּי יְדֹתָיו v.supra - v.supra *for its two tenons*

26:20

וּלְצֶלַע conj.-prep.-n.f.s. cstr. (854) *and for the side of*

הַמִּשְׁכָּן def.art.-n.m.s. (1015) *the tabernacle*

הַשֵּׁנִית def.art.-num. adj. f. (1041) *second*

לִפְאַת צָפוֹן prep.-n.f.s. cstr. (802) - n.f.s. (860) *on the north side*

עֶשְׂרִים קָרֶשׁ num. p. (797) - n.m.s. paus. (903) *twenty frames*

26:21

וְאַרְבָּעִים אַדְנֵיהֶם conj.-num. p. (917) - n.m.p.-3 m.p. sf. (10) *and their forty bases*

כָּסֶף n.m.s. paus. (494) *of silver*

שְׁנֵי אֲדָנִים num. m. cstr. (1040) - n.m.p. (10) *two bases*

תַּחַת הַקֶּרֶשׁ prep. (1065) - def.art.-n.m.s. (903) *under ... frame*

הָאֶחָד def.art.-num. adj. m.s. (25) *one*

וּשְׁנֵי אֲדָנִים conj.-num. m.s. cstr. (1040) - n.m.p. (10) *and two bases*

תַּחַת הַקֶּרֶשׁ prep. (1065) - def.art.-n.m.s. (903) *under ... frame*

הָאֶחָד v.supra *one*

26:22

וּלְיַרְכְּתֵי conj.-prep.-n.f. du. cstr. (438) *and for the rear of*

הַמִּשְׁכָּן def.art.-n.m.s. (1015) *the tabernacle*

יָמָּה n.m.s.-loc. he (410; 9) *westward*

תַּעֲשֶׂה Qal impf. 2 m.s. (עָשָׂה I 793) *you shall make*

שִׁשָּׁה קְרָשִׁים num. f.s. (995) - n.m.p. (903) *six frames*

26:23

וּשְׁנֵי קְרָשִׁים conj.-num. m.s. cstr. (1040) - n.m.p. (903) *and two frames*

תַּעֲשֶׂה Qal impf. 2 m.s. (עָשָׂה I 793) *you shall make*

לִמְקֻצְעֹת prep.-n.m.p. cstr. (893) *for the corners of*

הַמִּשְׁכָּן def.art.-n.m.s. (1015) *the tabernacle*

בַּיַּרְכָתָיִם prep.-def.art.-n.f. du. paus. (438) *in the rear*

26:24

וְיִהְיוּ conj.-Qal impf. 3 m.p. (הָיָה 224) *and they shall be*

תֹאֲמִים Qal act. ptc. m.p. (תָּאַם 1060) *separate (double)*

מִלְּמַטָּה prep.-prep.-adv. (641; 3) *beneath*

וְיַחְדָּו conj.-adv. (403) *but together*

יִהְיוּ Qal impf. 3 m.p. (הָיָה 224) *shall be*

תַּמִּים Qal act. ptc.m.p. (תָּאַם 1060) *joined (double)*

עַל־רֹאשׁוֹ prep.-n.m.s.-3 m.s. sf. (910) *at the top*

אֶל־הַטַּבַּעַת prep.-def.art.-n.f.s. (371) *at the ... ring*

הָאֶחָת def.art.-adj. f.s. paus. (25) *first*

כֵּן יִהְיֶה adv. (485) - Qal impf. 3 m.p. (הָיָה 224) *thus shall it be*

לִשְׁנֵיהֶם prep.-num. m.s.-3 m.p. sf. (1040) *with both of them*

לִשְׁנֵי הַמִּקְצֹעֹת prep.-num. m.s. cstr. (1040) - def.art.-n.m.p. (893) *the two corners*

יִהְיוּ Qal impf. 3 m.p. (הָיָה 224) *they shall form*

26:25

וְהָיוּ conj.-Qal pf. 3 c.p. (הָיָה 224) *and there shall be*

שְׁמֹנָה קְרָשִׁים num. f.s. (1032) - n.m.p. (903) *eight frames*

וְאַדְנֵיהֶם conj.-n.m.p.-3 m.p. sf. (10) *with their bases*

כֶּסֶף n.m.s. (494) *silver*

שִׁשָּׁה עָשָׂר num. f.s. (995) - num. m.s. (797) *sixteen*

אֲדָנִים n.m.p. (10) *bases*

שְׁנֵי אֲדָנִים num. m.s. cstr. (1040) - n.m.p. (10) *two bases*

תַּחַת הַקֶּרֶשׁ prep. (1065) - def.art.-n.m.s. (903) *under ... frame*

הָאֶחָד def.art.-adj. m.s. (25) *one*

וּשְׁנֵי אֲדָנִים conj.-num. m.s. cstr. (1040) - n.m.p. (10) *and two bases*

תַּחַת הַקֶּרֶשׁ v.supra-v.supra *under ... frame*

הָאֶחָד v.supra *another*

26:26

וְעָשִׂיתָ conj.-Qal pf. 2 m.s. (עָשָׂה I 793) *and you shall make*

בְרִיחִם n.m.p. (138) *bars*

עֲצֵי שִׁטִּים n.m.p. cstr. (781) - n.f.p. (1008) *acacia wood*

חֲמִשָּׁה לְקַרְשֵׁי num. f.s. (331) - prep.-n.m.p. cstr. (903) *five for the frames of*

צֶלַע־ n.f.s. cstr. (854) *the side of*

הַמִּשְׁכָּן def.art.-n.m.s. (1015) *the tabernacle*

הָאֶחָד def.art.-adj. m.s. (25) *one*

26:27

וַחֲמִשָּׁה בְרִיחִם conj.-num. f.s. (331) - n.f.p. (138) *and five bars*

לְקַרְשֵׁי prep.-n.m.p. cstr. (903) *for the frames of*

צֶלַע־הַמִּשְׁכָּן n.f.s. cstr. (854) - def.art.-n.m.s. (1015) *the ... side of the tabernacle*

הַשֵּׁנִית def.art.-adj. f.s. (1041) *other (second)*

וַחֲמִשָּׁה בְרִיחִם v.supra - v.supra *and five bars*

לְקַרְשֵׁי v.supra *for the frames of*

צֶלַע הַמִּשְׁכָּן v.supra *the tabernacle*

לַיַּרְכָתַיִם prep.-def.art.-n.f. du. (438) *at the rear*

יָמָּה n.m.s.-loc. he (410; 9) *westward*

26:28

וְהַבְּרִיחַ הַתִּיכֹן conj.-def.art.-n.m.s. (138) - def.art.-adj. m.s. (1064) *and the middle bar*

בְּתוֹךְ הַקְּרָשִׁים prep.-n.m.s. cstr. (1063) - def.art.-n.m.p. (903) *halfway up the frames*

מַבְרִחַ Hi. ptc. (בָּרַח 137) *shall pass through*

מִן־הַקָּצֶה אֶל־הַקָּצֶה prep.-def.art.-n.m.s. (892) - prep.-v.supra *from end to end*

26:29

וְאֶת־הַקְּרָשִׁים conj.-dir.obj.-def.art.-n.m.p. (903) *and the frames*

תְּצַפֶּה Pi. impf. 2 m.s. (צָפָה II 860) *you shall overlay*

זָהָב n.m.s. (262) *with gold*

וְאֶת־טַבְּעֹתֵיהֶם conj.-dir.obj.-n.f.p.-3 m.p. sf. (371) *and their rings*

תַּעֲשֶׂה Qal impf. 2 m.s. (עָשָׂה I 793) *you shall make*

זָהָב v.supra *of gold*

בָּתִּים n.m.p. (108; 3) *holders*

לַבְּרִיחִם prep.-def.art.-n.m.p. (138) *for the bars*

וְצִפִּיתָ conj.-Pi. pf. 2 m.s. (צָפָה II 860) *and you shall overlay*

אֶת־הַבְּרִיחִם dir.obj.-def.art.-n.m.p. (138) *the bars*

זָהָב v.supra *with gold*

26:30

וַהֲקֵמֹתָ conj.-Hi. pf. 2 m.s. (קוּם 877) *and you shall erect*

אֶת־הַמִּשְׁכָּן dir.obj.-def.art.-n.m.s. paus. (1015) *the tabernacle*

כְּמִשְׁפָּטוֹ prep.-n.m.s.-3 m.s. sf. (1048; 6d) *according to the plan for it*

אֲשֶׁר הָרְאֵיתָ rel.-Ho. pf. 2 m.s. (רָאָה 906) *which has been shown you*

בָּהָר prep.-def.art.-n.m.s. (249) *on the mountain*

26:31

וְעָשִׂיתָ conj.-Qal pf. 2 m.s. (עָשָׂה I 793) *and you shall make*

פָרֹכֶת n.f.s. (827) *a veil*

תְּכֵלֶת n.f.s. (1067) *blue (violet)*

וְאַרְגָּמָן conj.-n.m.s. (71) *and purple*

וְתוֹלַעַת שָׁנִי conj.-n.f.s. cstr. (1069) - n.m.s. (1040) *and scarlet stuff*

וְשֵׁשׁ מָשְׁזָר conj.-n.m.s. (III 1058) - Ho. ptc. (שָׁזַר 1004) *and fine twined linen*

מַעֲשֵׂה חֹשֵׁב n.m.s. cstr. (795) -Qal act. ptc. (חָשַׁב 362; 5) *in skilled work*

יַעֲשֶׂה Qal impf. 3 m.s. (I 793) *one shall make*

אֹתָהּ dir.obj.-3 f.s. sf. *it*

כְּרֻבִים n.m.p. (500) *with cherubim*

26:32

וְנָתַתָּה אֹתָהּ conj.-Qal pf. 2 m.s. (נָתַן 678) - dir.obj.-3 f.s. sf. *and you shall hang it*

עַל־אַרְבָּעָה prep.-num. f.s. (916) *upon four*

עַמּוּדֵי שִׁטִּים n.m.p. cstr. (765) - n.f.p. (1008) *pillars of acacia*

מְצֻפִּים זָהָב Pu. ptc. m.p. (צָפָה II 860) - n.m.s. (262) *overlaid with gold*

וָוֵיהֶם conj.-n.m.p.-3 m.p. sf. (255) *and their hooks*

זָהָב v.supra *gold*

עַל־אַרְבָּעָה prep.-num. f.s. (916) *upon four*

אַדְנֵי־כָסֶף n.m.p. cstr. (10) - n.m.s. paus. (494) *bases of silver*

26:33

וְנָתַתָּה conj.-Qal pf. 2 m.s. (נָתַן 678) *and you shall hang*

אֶת־הַפָּרֹכֶת dir.obj.-def.art.-n.f.s. (827) *the veil*

תַּחַת הַקְּרָסִים prep. (1065) - def.art.-n.m.p. (902) *from the clasps*

וְהֵבֵאתָ conj.-Hi. pf. 2 m.s. (בּוֹא 97) *and bring*

שָׁמָּה adv.-dir. he (1027) *in thither*

מִבֵּית לַפָּרֹכֶת prep.-n.m.s. cstr. (108; 8b; cf. GK 130) - prep.-def.art.-n.f.s. (827) *within the veil*

אֵת אֲרוֹן הָעֵדוּת dir.obj.-n.m.s. cstr. (75) - def.art.-n.f.s. (730) *the ark of the testimony*

וְהִבְדִּילָה conj.-Hi. pf. 3 f.s. (בָּדַל 95) *and shall separate*

הַפָּרֹכֶת def.art.-n.f.s. (827) *the veil*

לָכֶם prep.-2 m.p. *for you*

בֵּין הַקֹּדֶשׁ prep. (107) - def.art.-n.m.s. (871) *the holy place*

וּבֵין קֹדֶשׁ הַקֳּדָשִׁים conj.-prep. (107) - n.m.s. cstr. (871) - def.art.-n.m.p. (871)*from the most holy*

26:34

וְנָתַתָּ conj.-Qal pf. 2 m.s. (נָתַן 678) *and you shall put*

אֶת־הַכַּפֹּרֶת dir. obj.-def. art.-n.f.s. (498) *the mercy seat (propitiatory)*

עַל אֲרוֹן הָעֵדֻת prep.-n.m.s. cstr. (75)-def. art.-n.f.s. (730) *upon the ark of the testimony*

בְּקֹדֶשׁ הַקֳּדָשִׁים prep.-n.m.s. cstr. (871)-def. art.-n.m.p. (871) *in the most holy place*

26:35

וְשַׂמְתָּ conj.-Qal pf. 2 m.s. (שִׂים I 962) *and you shall set*

אֶת־הַשֻּׁלְחָן dir. obj.-def. art.-n.m.s. (1020) *the table*

מִחוּץ לַפָּרֹכֶת prep.-n.m.s. (299)-prep.-def. art.-n.f.s. (827) *outside the veil*

וְאֶת־הַמְּנֹרָה conj.-dir. obj.-n.f.s. (633) *and the lampstand*

נֹכַח הַשֻּׁלְחָן prep. (647)-v. supra *opposite the table*

עַל צֶלַע הַמִּשְׁכָּן prep.-n.f.s. cstr. (854)-def. art.-n.m.s. (1015) *on the ... side of the tabernacle*

תֵּימָנָה n.f.s.-loc. he (412) *south*

וְהַשֻּׁלְחָן conj.-def. art.-n.m.s. (1020) *and the table*

תִּתֵּן Qal impf. 2 m.s. (נָתַן 678) *you shall put*

עַל־צֶלַע v. supra-v. supra *on the side*

צָפוֹן n.f.s. (860) *north*

26:36

וְעָשִׂיתָ conj.-Qal pf. 2 m.s. (עָשָׂה I 793) *and you shall make*

מָסָךְ n.m.s. (697) *a screen*

לְפֶתַח הָאֹהֶל prep.-n.m.s. cstr. (835)-def. art.-n.m.s. (13) *for the door of the tent*

תְּכֵלֶת n.f.s. (1067) *blue*

וְאַרְגָּמָן conj.-n.m.s. (71) *and purple*

וְתוֹלַעַת שָׁנִי conj.-n.f.s. cstr. (1069)-n.m.s. (1040) *and scarlet stuff*

וְשֵׁשׁ מָשְׁזָר conj.-n.m.s. (III 1058)-Ho. ptc. (שָׁזַר 1004) *and fine twined linen*

מַעֲשֵׂה רֹקֵם n.m.s. cstr. (795)-Qal act. ptc. (955) *embroidered with needlework*

26:37

וְעָשִׂיתָ conj.-Qal pf. 2 m.s. (עָשָׂה I 793) *and you shall make*

לַמָּסָךְ prep.-def. art.-n.m.s. (697) *for the screen*

חֲמִשָּׁה num. f. (331) *five*

עַמּוּדֵי שִׁטִּים n.m.p. cstr. (765)-n.f.p. (1008) *pillars of acacia*

וְצִפִּיתָ conj.-Pi. pf. 2 m.s. (צָפָה II 860) *and overlay*

אֹתָם dir. obj.-3 m.p. sf. *them*

זָהָב n.m.s. (262) *with gold*

וָוֵיהֶם conj.-n.m.p.-3 m.p. sf. (255) *and their hooks*

זָהָב v. supra *gold*

וְיָצַקְתָּ conj.-Qal pf. 2 m.s. (יָצַק 427) *and you shall cast*

לָהֶם prep.-3 m.p. sf. *for them*
חֲמִשָּׁה num. f.s. (331) *five*
אַדְנֵי נְחֹשֶׁת n.m.p. cstr. (10)-n.f.s. (638) *bases of bronze*

27:1

וְעָשִׂיתָ conj.-Qal pf. 2 m.s. (עָשָׂה I 793) *and you shall make*
אֶת־הַמִּזְבֵּחַ dir. obj.-def. art.-n.m.s. (258) *the altar*
עֲצֵי שִׁטִּים n.m.p. cstr. (781)-n.f.p. (1008) *acacia wood*
חָמֵשׁ אַמּוֹת num. (331)-n.f.p. cstr. (52) *five cubits (of)*
אֹרֶךְ n.m.s. (73) *long (length)*
וְחָמֵשׁ אַמּוֹת conj.-v. supra-v. supra *and five cubits (of)*
רֹחַב n.m.s. (931) *broad (breadth)*
רָבוּעַ יִהְיֶה Qal pass. ptc. (רָבַע 917)-Qal impf. 3 m.s. (224) *shall be square*
הַמִּזְבֵּחַ v. supra *the altar*
וְשָׁלֹשׁ אַמּוֹת conj.-num. (1025)-n.f.p. cstr. (52) *and three cubits (of)*
קֹמָתוֹ n.f.s.-3 m.s. sf. (879) *its height*

27:2

וְעָשִׂיתָ conj.-Qal pf. 2 m.s. (עָשָׂה I 793) *and you shall make*
קַרְנֹתָיו n.f.p.-3 m.s. sf. (901) *horns*
עַל אַרְבַּע פִּנֹּתָיו prep.-num. m.s. cstr. (916)-n.f.p.-3 m.s. sf. (819) *on its four corners*
מִמֶּנּוּ prep.-3 m.s. sf. *of one piece with it (from it)*
תִּהְיֶיןָ Qal impf. 3 f.p. (הָיָה 224) *shall be*
קַרְנֹתָיו v. supra *its horns*
וְצִפִּיתָ conj.-Pi. pf. 2 m.s. (צָפָה II 860) *and you shall overlay*
אֹתוֹ dir. obj.-3 m.s. sf. *it*
נְחֹשֶׁת n.f.s. (638) *with bronze*

27:3

וְעָשִׂיתָ conj.-Qal pf. 2 m.s. (עָשָׂה I 793) *and you shall make*
סִּירֹתָיו n.m.p.-3 m.s. sf. (I 696) *pots for it*
לְדַשְּׁנוֹ prep.-Pi. inf. cstr.-3 m.s. sf. (דָּשֵׁן 206) *to receive its ashes*
וְיָעָיו conj.-n.m.p.-3 m.s. sf. (418) *and (its) shovels*
וּמִזְרְקֹתָיו conj.-n.m.p.-3 m.s. sf. (284) *and basins*
וּמִזְלְגֹתָיו conj.-n.f.p.-3 m.s. sf. (272) *and forks*
וּמַחְתֹּתָיו conj.-n.f.p.-3 m.s. sf. (367) *and fire pans*
לְכָל־כֵּלָיו prep.-n.m.s. cstr. (481)-n.m.p.-3 m.s. sf. (479) *all its utensils*
תַּעֲשֶׂה Qal impf. 2 m.s. (עָשָׂה I 793) *you shall make*
נְחֹשֶׁת n.m.s. (638) *of bronze*

27:4

וְעָשִׂיתָ conj.-Qal pf. 2 m.s. (עָשָׂה I 793) *you shall also make*
לּוֹ prep.-3 m.s. sf. *for it*
מִכְבָּר n.m.s. (460) *a grating*
מַעֲשֵׂה רֶשֶׁת n.m.s. cstr. (795)-n.f.s. cstr. (440) *a network of*
נְחֹשֶׁת n.m.s. (638) *bronze*
וְעָשִׂיתָ v. supra *and you shall make*
עַל־הָרֶשֶׁת prep.-def. art.-n.f.s. (440) *upon the net*
אַרְבַּע num. (916) *four*
טַבְּעֹת נְחֹשֶׁת n.f.p. cstr. (371)-n.m.s. (638) *bronze rings*
עַל אַרְבַּע prep.-num. (916) *at ... four*
קְצוֹתָיו n.f.p.-3 m.s. sf. (892) *its ... corners*

27:5

וְנָתַתָּה אֹתָהּ conj.-Qal pf. 2 m.s. (נָתַן 678)-dir. obj.-3 f.s. sf. *and you shall set it*
תַּחַת כַּרְכֹּב prep. (1065)-n.m.s. cstr. (501) *under the ledge of*
הַמִּזְבֵּחַ def. art.-n.m.s. (258) *the altar*
מִלְּמָטָּה prep.-prep.-adv. paus. (641: 3) *(beneath)*
וְהָיְתָה conj.-Qal pf. 3 f.s. (הָיָה 224) *so that ... shall extend*
הָרֶשֶׁת def. art.-n.f.s. (440) *the net*

עַד חֲצִי prep. (III 723)-n.m.s. cstr. (345) *half way down*

הַמִּזְבֵּחַ v. supra *the altar*

27:6

וְעָשִׂיתָ conj.-Qal pf. 2 m.s. (עָשָׂה I 793) *and you shall make*

בַדִּים n.m.p. (94: 3) *poles*

לַמִּזְבֵּחַ prep.-def.art.-n.m.s. (258) *for the altar*

בַּדֵּי n.m.p. cstr. (II 94: 3) *poles of*

עֲצֵי שִׁטִּים n.m.p. cstr. (781)-n.f.p. (1008) *acacia wood*

וְצִפִּיתָ אֹתָם conj.-Pi. pf. 2 m.s. (צָפָה II 860)-dir. obj.-3 m.p. sf. *and overlay them*

נְחֹשֶׁת n.m.s. (638) *with bronze*

27:7

וְהוּבָא conj.-Ho. pf. 3 m.s. (בּוֹא 97; Ho. c) *and shall be put*

אֶת־בַּדָּיו dir. obj.-n.m.p.-3 m.s. sf. (94) *its poles*

בַּטַּבָּעֹת prep.-def. art.-n.f.p. (371) *through the rings*

וְהָיוּ הַבַּדִּים conj.-Qal pf. 3 c.p. (הָיָה 224)-def. art.-n.m.p. (94) *so that the poles shall be*

עַל־שְׁתֵּי צַלְעֹת prep.-num. f. cstr. (1040)-n.f.p. cstr. (854) *upon the two sides of*

הַמִּזְבֵּחַ def. art.-n.m.s. (258) *the altar*

בִּשְׂאֵת אֹתוֹ prep.-Qal inf. cstr. (נָשָׂא 669)-dir. obj.-3 m.s. sf. *when it is carried*

27:8

נְבוּב לֻחֹת Qal pass.ptc. cstr. (נָבַב 612)-n.m.p. (531) *hollow with boards*

תַּעֲשֶׂה אֹתוֹ Qal impf.2 m.s. (עָשָׂה I 793) - dir.obj.-3 m.s. sf. *and you shall make it*

כַּאֲשֶׁר הֶרְאָה prep.-rel.-Hi. pf. 3 m.s. (רָאָה 906) *as it has been shown*

אֹתְךָ dir.obj.-2 m.s. sf. *you*

בָּהָר prep.-def.art.-n.m.s. (249) *on the mountain*

כֵּן יַעֲשׂוּ adv. (485) - Qal impf. 3 m.p. (עָשָׂה I 793) *so shall it be made*

27:9

וְעָשִׂיתָ conj.-Qal pf.2 m.s. (עָשָׂה I 793) *and you shall make*

אֵת חֲצַר dir.obj.-n.m.s. cstr. (I 346) *the court of*

הַמִּשְׁכָּן def.art.-n.m.s. (1015) *the tabernacle*

לִפְאַת נֶגֶב־ prep.-n.f.s. cstr. (802)-n.m.s. cstr. (616) *on the south side*

תֵּימָנָה n.f.s.-loc.he (412) *(southward)*

קְלָעִים n.m.p. (II 887) *hangings*

לֶחָצֵר prep.-def.art.-n.m.s. (I 346) *of the court*

שֵׁשׁ מָשְׁזָר n.m.s. (III 1058)-Ho.ptc. (שָׁזַר 1004) *fine twined linen*

מֵאָה בָאַמָּה n.f.s. (547)-prep.-def.art.-n.f.s. (52) *a hundred cubits*

אֹרֶךְ n.m.s. (73) *long*

לַפֵּאָה הָאֶחָת prep.-def.art.-n.f.s. (802)-def.art.-adj.f.s. (25) *for one side*

27:10

וְעַמֻּדָיו conj.-n.m.p.-3 m.s. sf. (765) *and their pillars*

עֶשְׂרִים num.p. (797) *twenty*

וְאַדְנֵיהֶם conj.-n.m.p.-3 m.p. sf. (10) *and their bases*

עֶשְׂרִים v.supra *twenty*

נְחֹשֶׁת n.m.s. (638) *of bronze*

וָוֵי הָעַמֻּדִים n.m.p. cstr. (255)-def.art.-n.m.p. (765) *the hooks of the pillars*

וַחֲשֻׁקֵיהֶם conj.-n.m.p.-3 m.p. sf. (366) *and their fillets*

כָּסֶף n.m.s. paus. (494) *of silver*

27:11

וְכֵן conj.-adv. (485) *and likewise*

לִפְאַת צָפוֹן prep.-n.f.s. cstr. (802)-n.f.s. (860) *on the north side*

בָּאֹרֶךְ prep.-def.art.-n.m.s. (73) *for its length*

קְלָעִים n.m.p. (II 887) *hangings*

מֵאָה אֹרֶךְ n.f.s. (547) - n.m.s. (73) *a hundred long*

וְעַמֻּדָו conj.-n.m.p.-3 m.s. sf. (765) *and their pillars*

עֶשְׂרִים num.p. (797) *twenty*

וְאַדְנֵיהֶם conj.-n.m.p.-3 m.p. sf. (10) *and their bases*

עֶשְׂרִים v.supra *twenty*

נְחֹשֶׁת n.m.s. (638) *of bronze*

וָוֵי הָעַמֻּדִים n.m.p. cstr. (255)-def.art.-n.m.p. (765) *the hooks of the pillars*

וַחֲשֻׁקֵיהֶם conj.-n.m.p.-3 m.p. sf. (366) *and their fillets*

כָּסֶף n.m.s. paus. (494) *of silver*

27:12

וְרֹחַב הֶחָצֵר conj.-n.m.s. cstr. (931) - def.art.-n.m.s. (I 346) *and for the breadth of the court*

לִפְאַת־יָם prep.-n.f.s. cstr. (802)-n.m.s. (410) *on the west side*

קְלָעִים n.m.p. (II 887) *hangings*

חֲמִשִּׁים אַמָּה num.p. (332)-n.f.s. (52) *for fifty cubits*

עַמֻּדֵיהֶם n.m.p.-3 m.p. sf. (765) *their pillars*

עֲשָׂרָה n.f.s. (796) *ten*

וְאַדְנֵיהֶם conj.-n.m.p.-3 m.p. sf. (10) *and their bases*

עֲשָׂרָה v. supra *ten*

27:13

וְרֹחַב הֶחָצֵר conj.-n.m.s. cstr. (931) - def.art.-n.m.s. (I 346) *the breadth of the court*

לִפְאַת קֵדְמָה prep.-n.f.s. cstr. (802) - adv.-loc. he (870) *on the front to the east*

מִזְרָחָה n.m.s.-loc. he (280) *(eastward)*

חֲמִשִּׁים אַמָּה num.p. (332)-n.f.s. (52) *fifty cubits*

27:14

וַחֲמֵשׁ עֶשְׂרֵה conj.-num. (331)-num. (797) *and fifteen*

אַמָּה n.f.s. (52) *cubits*

קְלָעִים n.m.p. (II 887) *hangings*

לַכָּתֵף prep.-def.art.-n.f.s. (509 θ2b) *for the one side (of the gate)*

עַמֻּדֵיהֶם n.m.p.-3 m.p. sf. (765) *their pillars*

שְׁלֹשָׁה num.f.s. (1025) *three*

וְאַדְנֵיהֶם conj.-n.m.p.-3 m.p. sf. (10) *and their bases*

שְׁלֹשָׁה v.supra *three*

27:15

וְלַכָּתֵף conj.-prep.-def.art.-n.f.s. (509; 2b) *on the ... side*

הַשֵּׁנִית def.art.-num.adj. (1041) *other*

חֲמֵשׁ עֶשְׂרֵה num.m. cstr. (331)-num. (797) *fifteen*

קְלָעִים n.m.p. (II 887) *hangings*

עַמֻּדֵיהֶם n.m.p.-3 m.p. sf. (765) *their pillars*

שְׁלֹשָׁה num.f.s. (1025) *three*

וְאַדְנֵיהֶם conj.-n.m.p.-3 m.p. sf. (10) *and their bases*

שְׁלֹשָׁה v.supra *three*

27:16

וּלְשַׁעַר הֶחָצֵר conj.-prep.-n.m.s. cstr. (1044) - def.art.-n.m.s. (I 346) *for the gate of the court*

מָסָךְ n.m.s. (697) *a screen*

עֶשְׂרִים אַמָּה num. p. (797) - n.f.s. (52) *twenty cubits*

תְּכֵלֶת n.f.s. (1067) *blue*

וְאַרְגָּמָן conj.-n.m.s. (71) *and purple*

וְתוֹלַעַת שָׁנִי conj.-n.f.s. cstr. (1069)-n.m.s. (1040) *and scarlet stuff*

וְשֵׁשׁ מָשְׁזָר conj.-n.m.s. (III 1058)-Ho.ptc. (שָׁזַר 1004) *and fine twisted linen*

מַעֲשֵׂה רֹקֵם n.m.s. cstr. (795) - Qal act. ptc. as subst. (955) *embroidered with needlework*

עַמֻּדֵיהֶם n.m.p.-3 m.p. sf. (765) *their pillars*

אַרְבָּעָה num.f. (916) *four*

וְאַדְנֵיהֶם conj.-n.m.p.-3 m.p. sf. (10) *and their bases*

אַרְבָּעָה v.supra *four*

27:17

כָּל־עַמּוּדֵי n.m.s. cstr. (481)-n.m.p. cstr. (765) *all the pillars of*

הֶחָצֵר def.art.-n.m.s. (I 346) *the court*

סָבִיב adv. (686) *around*

מְחֻשָּׁקִים Pu.ptc.m.p. (חָשַׁק II 366) *shall be filleted*

כֶּסֶף n.m.s. (494) *with silver*

וָוֵיהֶם n.m.p.-3 m.p. sf. (255) *their hooks*

כָּסֶף n.m.s. paus. (494) *with silver*

וְאַדְנֵיהֶם conj.-n.m.p.-3 m.p. sf. (10) *and their bases*

נְחֹשֶׁת n.m.s. (638) *of bronze*

27:18

אֹרֶךְ הֶחָצֵר n.m.s. cstr. (73) - def.art.-n.m.s. (I 346) *the length of the court*

מֵאָה בָאַמָּה n.f.s. (547)-prep.-def.art.-n.f.s. (52) *a hundred cubits*

וְרֹחַב conj.-n.m.s. (931) *and breadth*

חֲמִשִּׁים num.p. (332) *fifty*

בַּחֲמִשִּׁים prep.-def.art.-num.p. (332) *(with the fifty)*

וְקֹמָה conj.-n.f.s. (879) *and height*

חָמֵשׁ אַמּוֹת num. (331)-n.f.p. (52) *five cubits*

שֵׁשׁ מָשְׁזָר n.m.s. (III 1058)-Ho.ptc. (שָׁזַר 1004) *fine twined linen*

וְאַדְנֵיהֶם conj.-n.m.p.-3 m.p. sf. (10) *and their bases*

נְחֹשֶׁת n.m.s. (638) *of bronze*

27:19

לְכֹל כְּלֵי prep.-n.m.s. cstr. (481)-n.m.p. cstr. (479) *all the utensils of*

הַמִּשְׁכָּן def.art.n.m.s. (1015) *the tabernacle*

בְּכֹל עֲבֹדָתוֹ prep.-n.m.s. cstr. (481)-n.f.s.-3 m.s. sf. (715) *for every use*

וְכָל־יְתֵדֹתָיו conj.-n.m.s. cstr. (481)-n.f.p.-3 m.s. sf. (450) *and all its pegs*

וְכָל־יִתְדֹת conj.-n.m.s. cstr. (481)-n.f.p. cstr. (450) *and all the pegs of*

הֶחָצֵר def.art.-n.m.s. (I 346) *the court*

נְחֹשֶׁת n.m.s. (638) *of bronze*

27:20

וְאַתָּה תְּצַוֶּה conj.-pers.pr. 2 m.s. (61) - Pi. impf. 2 m.s. (צָוָה 845) *and you shall command*

אֶת־בְּנֵי יִשְׂרָאֵל dir.obj.-n.m.p. cstr. (119)-pr.n. (975) *the people of Israel*

וְיִקְחוּ conj.-Qal impf.3 m.p. (לָקַח 542) *that they bring*

אֵלֶיךָ prep.-2 m.s. sf. *to you*

שֶׁמֶן זַיִת n.m.s. cstr. (1032) - n.m.s. (268) *olive oil*

זָךְ adj. m.s. paus. (269) *pure*

כָּתִית adj.m.s. (510) *beaten*

לַמָּאוֹר prep.-def.art.-n.m.s. (22) *for the light*

לְהַעֲלֹת prep.-Hi.inf.cstr. (עָלָה 748.θ4) *that ... may set up (to burn)*

נֵר n.m.s. (632) *a lamp*

תָּמִיד n.m.s. as. adv. (556) *continually*

27:21

בְּאֹהֶל מוֹעֵד prep.-n.m.s. cstr. (13)-n.m.s. (417) *in tent of meeting*

מִחוּץ prep.-n.m.s. (299; 1 b, d) *outside*

לַפָּרֹכֶת prep.-def.art.-n.f.s. (827) *of the veil*

אֲשֶׁר עַל־הָעֵדֻת rel.-prep.-def.art.-n.f.s. (730) *which is before the testimony*

יַעֲרֹךְ אֹתוֹ Qal impf. 3 m.s. (עָרַךְ 789) - dir.obj.-3 m.s. sf. *shall tend it*

אַהֲרֹן וּבָנָיו pr.n. (14)-conj.-n.m.p.-3 m.s. sf. (119) *Aaron and his sons*

מֵעֶרֶב prep.-n.m.s. (787) *from evening*

עַד־בֹּקֶר prep.-n.m.s. (133) *to morning*

לִפְנֵי יהוה prep.-n.m.p. cstr. (815)-pr.n. (217) *before Yahweh*

חֻקַּת עוֹלָם n.f.s. cstr. (349) - n.m.s. (761) *a statute for ever*

לְדֹרֹתָם prep.-n.m.p.-3 m.p. sf. (189) *throughout their generations*

מֵאֵת בְּנֵי יִשְׂרָאֵל prep.-prep. (II 85) - n.m.p. cstr. (119) - pr.n. (975) *by the people of Israel*

28:1

וְאַתָּה הַקְרֵב conj.-pers.pr. 2 m.s. (61) - Hi. impv. 2 m.s. (קָרַב 897) *then bring (thou) near*

אֵלֶיךָ prep.-2 m.s. sf. *to you*

אֶת־אַהֲרֹן אָחִיךָ dir.obj.-pr.n. (14) - n.m.s.-2 m.s. sf. (26) *Aaron your brother*

וְאֶת־בָּנָיו conj.-dir.obj.-n.m.p.-3 m.s. sf. (119) *and his sons*

אִתּוֹ prep.-3 m.s. sf. (II 85) *with him*

מִתּוֹךְ prep.-n.m.s. cstr. (1063) *from among*

בְּנֵי יִשְׂרָאֵל n.m.p. cstr. (119) - pr.n. (975) *the people of Israel*

לְכַהֲנוֹ־לִי prep.-Pi. inf. cstr.-3 m.s. sf. (כָּהַן II 464) - prep.-1 c.s. sf. *to serve me as priests*

אַהֲרֹן pr.n. (14) *Aaron*

נָדָב pr.n. (621) *Nadab*

וַאֲבִיהוּא conj.-pr.n. (4) *and Abihu*

אֶלְעָזָר pr.n. (46) *Eleazar*

וְאִיתָמָר conj.-pr.n. (16) *and Ithamar*

בְּנֵי אַהֲרֹן n.m.p. cstr. (119) - pr.n. (14) *Aaron's sons*

28:2

וְעָשִׂיתָ conj.-Qal pf. 2 m.s. (עָשָׂה I 793) *and you shall make*

בִגְדֵי־קֹדֶשׁ n.m.p. cstr. (93) - n.m.s. (871) *holy garments*

לְאַהֲרֹן אָחִיךָ prep.-pr.n. (14) - n.m.s.-2 m.s. sf. (26) *for Aaron your brother*

לְכָבוֹד prep.-n.m.s. (458) *for glory*

וּלְתִפְאָרֶת conj.-prep.-n.f.s. paus. (802) *and for beauty*

28:3

וְאַתָּה תְּדַבֵּר conj.-pers. pr. 2 m.s. (61) - Pi. impf. 2 m.s. (דָּבַר 180) *and you shall speak*

אֶל־כָּל־חַכְמֵי לֵב prep.-n.m.s. cstr. (481) - adj. m.p. cstr. (314) - n.m.s. (523) *to all who have ability (wise of heart)*

אֲשֶׁר מִלֵּאתִיו rel.-Pi.pf.1 c.s. - 3 m.s. sf. (מָלֵא 569) *whom I have endowed with*

רוּחַ חָכְמָה n.f.s. (924)-n.f.s. (315) *an able mind (wise spirit)*

וְעָשׂוּ conj.-Qal pf.3 c.p. (עָשָׂה I 793) *that they make*

אֶת־בִּגְדֵי אַהֲרֹן dir.obj.-n.m.p. cstr. (93)-pr.n. (14) *Aaron's garments*

לְקַדְּשׁוֹ prep.-Pi.inf.cstr.-3 m.s. sf. (872) *to consecrate him*

לְכַהֲנוֹ־לִי prep.-Pi. inf. cstr. - 3 m.s. sf. (כָּהַן II 464) - prep.-1 c.s. sf. *for my priesthood*

28:4

וְאֵלֶּה הַבְּגָדִים conj.-demons. adj. c.p. (41) - def.art.-n.m.p. (93) *these are the garments*

אֲשֶׁר יַעֲשׂוּ rel.-Qal impf. 3 m.p. (עָשָׂה I 793) *which they shall make*

חֹשֶׁן n.m.s. (365) *a breastpiece*

וְאֵפוֹד conj.-n.m.s. (65) *and an ephod*

וּמְעִיל conj.-n.m.s. (591) *and a robe*

וּכְתֹנֶת conj.-n.f.s. cstr. (509) *and a coat of*

תַּשְׁבֵּץ n.m.s. (990) *checker work*

מִצְנֶפֶת n.f.s. (857) *a turban*

וְאַבְנֵט conj.-n.m.s. (126) *and a girdle*

וְעָשׂוּ conj.-Qal pf. 3 c.p. (עָשָׂה I 793) *and they shall make*

בִגְדֵי־קֹדֶשׁ n.m.p. cstr. (93) - n.m.s. (871) *holy garments*

לְאַהֲרֹן אָחִיךָ prep.-pr.n. (14) - n.m.s.-2 m.s. sf. (26) *for Aaron your brother*

וּלְבָנָיו conj.-prep.-n.m.p.-3 m.s. sf. (119) *and his sons*

לְכַהֲנוֹ־לִי prep.-Pi. inf. cstr.-3 m.s. sf. (464) - prep.-1 c.s. sf. *to serve me as priests*

28:5

וְהֵם יִקְחוּ conj.-pers. pr. 3 m.p. (241) - Qal impf. 3 m.p. (לָקַח 542) *and they shall receive*

אֶת־הַזָּהָב dir.obj.-def.art.-n.m.s. (262) *gold*

וְאֶת־הַתְּכֵלֶת conj.-dir.obj.-def.art.-n.f.s. (1067) *and blue*

וְאֶת־הָאַרְגָּמָן conj.-dir.obj.-def.art.-n.m.s. (71) *and purple*

וְאֶת־תּוֹלַעַת הַשָּׁנִי conj.-dir.obj.-n.f.s. cstr. (1069) - def.art.-n.m.s. (1040) *and scarlet stuff*

וְאֶת־הַשֵּׁשׁ conj.-dir.obj.-def.art.-n.m.s. (III 1058) *and fine twined linen*

28:6

וְעָשׂוּ conj.-Qal pf. 3 c.p. (עָשָׂה I 793) *and they shall make*

אֶת־הָאֵפֹד dir.obj.-def.art.-n.m.s. (65) *the ephod*

זָהָב n.m.s. (262) *of gold*

תְּכֵלֶת n.f.s. (1067) *of blue*

וְאַרְגָּמָן conj.-n.m.s. (71) *and purple*

תּוֹלַעַת שָׁנִי n.f.s. cstr. (1069) - n.m.s. (1040) *scarlet stuff*

וְשֵׁשׁ מָשְׁזָר conj.-n.m.s. (III 1058) - Ho. ptc. (שָׁזַר 1004) *and of fine twined linen*

מַעֲשֵׂה חֹשֵׁב n.m.s. cstr. (795) - Qal act. ptc. (362) *skilfully worked*

28:7

שְׁתֵּי כְתֵפֹת n.f. du. cstr. (1040) - n.f.p. (509) *two shoulder-pieces*

חֹבְרֹת Qal act. ptc. f.p. (חָבַר 287) *attached*

יִהְיֶה־לּוֹ Qal impf. 3 m.s. (הָיָה 224) - prep.-3 m.s. sf. *it shall have*

אֶל־שְׁנֵי קְצוֹתָיו prep.-n.m. du. cstr. (1040) - n.f.p.-3 m.s. sf. (892) *to its two edges*

וְחֻבָּר conj.-Pu. pf. 3 m.s. paus. (חָבַר 287) *that it may be joined together*

28:8

וְחֵשֶׁב אֲפֻדָּתוֹ conj.-n.m.s. cstr. (363) - n.f.s.-3 m.s. sf. (65) *and the skilfully woven band (of his ephod)*

אֲשֶׁר עָלָיו rel.-prep.-3 m.s. sf. *upon it*

כְּמַעֲשֵׂהוּ prep.-n.m.s.-3 m.s. sf. (795) *of the same workmanship*

מִמֶּנּוּ prep.-3 m.s. sf. *(from it)*

יִהְיֶה Qal impf. 3 m.s. (הָיָה 224) *shall be*

זָהָב n.m.s. (262) *of gold*

תְּכֵלֶת n.f.s. (1067) *blue*

וְאַרְגָּמָן conj.-n.m.s. (71) *and purple*

וְתוֹלַעַת שָׁנִי conj.-n.f.s. (1069) - n.m.s. (1040) *and scarlet stuff*

וְשֵׁשׁ מָשְׁזָר conj.-n.m.s. (III 1058) - Ho. ptc. (שָׁזַר 1004) *and fine twined linen*

28:9

וְלָקַחְתָּ conj.-Qal pf. 2 m.s. (לָקַח 542) *and you shall take*

אֶת־שְׁתֵּי dir.obj.-n.f. du. cstr. (1040) *two*

אַבְנֵי־שֹׁהַם n.f.p. cstr. (6) - n.m.s. (I 995) *onyx stones*

וּפִתַּחְתָּ conj.-Pi. pf. 2 m.s. (פָּתַח II 836) *and engrave*

עֲלֵיהֶם prep.-3 m.p. sf. *on them*

שְׁמוֹת בְּנֵי יִשְׂרָאֵל n.m.p. cstr. (1027) - n.m.p. cstr. (119) - pr.n. (975) *the names of the sons of Israel*

28:10

שִׁשָּׁה num. f.s. (995) *six*

מִשְּׁמֹתָם prep.-n.m.p.-3 m.p. sf. (1027) *of their names*

עַל הָאֶבֶן הָאֶחָת prep.-def.art.-n.f.s. (6) - def.art.adj. f.s. (25) *on the one stone*

וְאֶת־שְׁמוֹת conj.-dir.obj.-n.m.p. cstr. (1027) *and the names of*

הַשִּׁשָּׁה הַנּוֹתָרִים def.art.-num. f.s. (995) - def.art.-Ni. ptc. m.p. (יָתַר 451) *the remaining six*

עַל־הָאֶבֶן הַשֵּׁנִית prep.-def.art.-n.f.s. (6) - def.art. - num. adj. f.s. (1041) *on the other stone*

כְּתוֹלְדֹתָם prep.-n.f.p.-3 m.p. sf. (410) *in the order of their birth*

28:11

מַעֲשֵׂה חָרַשׁ אֶבֶן n.m.s. cstr. (795) - n.m.s. cstr. (360) - n.f.s. (6) *as a jeweler (*lit. *work of an artificer of a stone)*

פִּתּוּחֵי חֹתָם n.m.p. cstr. (836) - n.m.s. (368) *engraves signets*

תְּפַתַּח Pi. impf. 2 m.s. (פָּתַח II 836) *so shall you engrave*

אֶת־שְׁתֵּי הָאֲבָנִים dir.obj.-n.f. du. cstr. (1040) - def.art.-n.f.p. (6) *the two stones*

עַל־שְׁמֹת prep.-n.f.p. cstr. (1027) *with the names of*

בְּנֵי יִשְׂרָאֵל n.m.p. cstr. (119) - pr.n. (975) *the sons of Israel*

מֻסַבֹּת מִשְׁבְּצוֹת Ho. ptc. f. p. cstr. (סָבַב 686) - n.f.p. (990) *in settings of filigree*

זָהָב n.m.s. (262) *of gold*

תַּעֲשֶׂה אֹתָם Qal impf. 2 m.s. (עָשָׂה I 793) - dir.obj.-3 m.p. sf. *you shall enclose them*

28:12

וְשַׂמְתָּ conj.-Qal pf. 2 m.s. (שִׂים I 962) *and you shall set*

אֶת־שְׁתֵּי הָאֲבָנִים dir.obj.-num. f. du. cstr. (1040) - def.art.-n.f.p. (6) *the two stones*

עַל כִּתְפֹת הָאֵפֹד prep.-n.f.p. cstr. (509) - def.art.-n.m.s. (65) *upon the shoulder-pieces of the ephod*

אַבְנֵי זִכָּרֹן n.f.p. cstr. (6) - n.m.s. (272) *as stones of remembrance*

לִבְנֵי יִשְׂרָאֵל prep.-n.m.p. cstr. (119) - pr.n. (975) *for the sons of Israel*

וְנָשָׂא אַהֲרֹן conj.-Qal pf. 3 m.s. (669) - pr.n. (14) *and Aaron shall bear*

אֶת־שְׁמוֹתָם dir.obj.-n.m.p.-3 m.p. sf. (1027) *their names*

לִפְנֵי יהוה prep.-n.m.p. cstr. (815) - pr.n. (217) *before Yahweh*

עַל־שְׁתֵּי כְתֵפָיו prep.-num. f. du. cstr. (1040) - n.f.p.-3 m.s. sf. (509) *upon his two shoulders*

לְזִכָּרֹן prep.-n.m.s. (272) *for remembrance*

28:13

וְעָשִׂיתָ conj.-Qal pf. 2 m.s. (עָשָׂה I 793) *and you shall make*

מִשְׁבְּצֹת זָהָב n.f.p. cstr. (990) - n.m.s. (262) *settings of gold*

28:14

וּשְׁתֵּי שַׁרְשְׁרֹת conj.-num. f. du. cstr. (1040) - n.f.p. cstr. (1057) *and two chains of*

זָהָב טָהוֹר n.m.s. (252) - adj. m.s. (373) *pure gold*

מִגְבָּלֹת n.f.p. (148) *twisted*

תַּעֲשֶׂה אֹתָם Qal impf. 2 m.s. (עָשָׂה I 793) - dir.obj.-3 m.p. sf. *(you shall make them)*

מַעֲשֵׂה עֲבֹת n.m.s. cstr. (795) - n.m.s. (721) *like cords (cordage-work)*

וְנָתַתָּה conj.-Qal pf. 2 m.s. (נָתַן 678) *and you shall attach*

אֶת־שַׁרְשְׁרֹת הָעֲבֹתֹת dir.obj.-n.f.p. cstr. (1057) - def.art.-n.m.p. (721) *the corded chains*

עַל־הַמִּשְׁבְּצֹת prep.-def.art.-n.f.p. (990) *to the settings*

28:15

וְעָשִׂיתָ conj.-Qal pf. 2 m.s. (עָשָׂה I 793) *and you shall make*

חֹשֶׁן מִשְׁפָּט n.m.s. cstr. (365) - n.m.s. (1048) *a breastpiece of judgment*

מַעֲשֵׂה חֹשֵׁב n.m.s. cstr. (795) - Qal act. ptc. (362) *in skilled work*

כְּמַעֲשֵׂה אֵפֹד prep.-n.m.s. cstr. (795) - n.m.s. (65) *like the work of the ephod*

תַּעֲשֶׂנּוּ Qal impf. 2 m.s. - 3 m.s. sf. (עָשָׂה I 793) *you shall make it*

זָהָב n.m.s. (262) *of gold*

תְּכֵלֶת n.f.s. (1067) *blue*

וְאַרְגָּמָן conj.-n.m.s. (71) *and purple*

וְתוֹלַעַת שָׁנִי conj.-n.f.s. cstr. (1069) - n.m.s. (1040) *and scarlet stuff*

וְשֵׁשׁ מָשְׁזָר conj.-n.m.s. (III 1058) - Ho. ptc. (שָׁזַר 1004) *and fine twined linen*

תַּעֲשֶׂה אֹתוֹ Qal impf. 2 m.s. (עָשָׂה I 793) - dir.obj.-3 m.s. sf. *shall you make it*

28:16

רָבוּעַ יִהְיֶה Qal pass. ptc. (רָבַע 917) - Qal impf. 3 m.s. (הָיָה 224) *it shall be square*

כָּפוּל Qal pass. ptc. (495) *double*

זֶרֶת n.f.s. (284) *a span*

אָרְכּוֹ n.m.s.-3 m.s. sf. (73) *its length*

וְזֶרֶת conj.-n.f.s. (284) *and a span*

רָחְבּוֹ n.m.s.-3 m.s. sf. (931) *its breadth*

28:17

וּמִלֵּאתָ בוֹ conj.-Pi. pf. 2 m.s. (מָלֵא 569) - prep.-3 m.s. sf. *and you shall set in it*

מִלֻּאַת אֶבֶן n.f.s. cstr. (571) - n.f.s. (6) *a setting of stone*

אַרְבָּעָה טוּרִים num. f.s. (916) - n.m.p. (377) *four rows*

אָבֶן n.f.s. paus. (6) *stones*

טוּר אֹדֶם n.m.s. cstr. (377) - n.f.s. (10) *a row of sardius (carnelian)*

פִּטְדָה n.f.s. (809) *topaz*

וּבָרֶקֶת conj.-n.f.s. (140) *and carbuncle*

הַטּוּר הָאֶחָד def.art.-n.m.s. (377) - def.art.-adj. m.s. (25) *the first row*

28:18

וְהַטּוּר הַשֵּׁנִי conj.-def.art.-n.m.s. (377) - def.art.-num. adj. m.s. (1041) *and the second row*

נֹפֶךְ n.m.s. (656) *an emerald*

סַפִּיר n.m.s. (705) *a sapphire*

וְיָהֲלֹם conj.-n.m.s. (240) *and a diamond*

28:19

וְהַטּוּר הַשְּׁלִישִׁי conj.-def.art.-n.m.s. (377) - def.art.-num. adj. m.s. (1026) *and the third row*

לֶשֶׁם n.m.s. (I 545) *a jacinth*

שְׁבוֹ n.f.s. (986) *an agate*

וְאַחְלָמָה conj.-n.f.s. paus. (29) *and an amethyst*

28:20

וְהַטּוּר הָרְבִיעִי conj.-def.art.-n.m.s. (377) - def.art.-num. adj. m.s. (917) *and the fourth row*

תַּרְשִׁישׁ n.m.s. (I 1076) *a beryl*

וְשֹׁהַם conj.-n.m.s. (I 995) *and an onyx*

וְיָשְׁפֵה conj.-n.m.s. paus. (448) *and a jasper*

מְשֻׁבָּצִים Pu. ptc. m.p. (שָׁבַץ 990) *be set (inwoven)*

זָהָב n.m.s. (262) *gold*

יִהְיוּ Qal impf. 3 mp. (הָיָה 224) *they shall be*

בְּמִלּוּאֹתָם prep.-n.f.p.-3 m.p. sf. (571) *(in their setting)*

28:21

וְהָאֲבָנִים conj.-def.art.-n.f.p. (6) *and the stones*

תִּהְיֶיןָ Qal impf. 3 f.p. (הָיָה 224) *shall be*

עַל־שְׁמֹת prep.-n.m.p. cstr. (1027) *with the names of*

בְּנֵי־יִשְׂרָאֵל n.m.p. cstr. (119) - pr.n. (975) *the sons of Israel*

שְׁתֵּים עֶשְׂרֵה num. (1040) - num. (797) *twelve*

עַל־שְׁמֹתָם prep.-n.m.p.-3 m.p. sf. (1027) *according to their names*

פִּתּוּחֵי חוֹתָם n.m.p. cstr. (836) - n.m.s. (I 369) *engravings of a signet-ring*

אִישׁ עַל־שְׁמוֹ n.m.s. (35) - prep.-n.m.s.-3 m.s. sf. (1027) *each with its name*

תִּהְיֶיןָ Qal impf. 3 f.p. (הָיָה 224) *they shall be*

לִשְׁנֵי עָשָׂר prep.-num. m. du. cstr. (1040) - num. (797) *for the twelve*

שָׁבֶט n.m.s. paus. (986) *tribes*

28:22

וְעָשִׂיתָ conj.-Qal pf. 2 m.s. (עָשָׂה I 793) *and you shall make*

עַל־הַחֹשֶׁן prep.-def.art.-n.m.s. (365) *for the breastpiece*

שַׁרְשֹׁת גַּבְלֻת n.f.p. cstr. (1057) - n.f.s. (148) *twisted chains*

מַעֲשֵׂה עֲבֹת n.m.s. cstr. (795) - n.m.s. (721) *like cords*

זָהָב טָהוֹר n.m.s. (262) - adj. m.s. (373) *of pure gold*

28:23

וְעָשִׂיתָ conj.-Qal pf. 2 m.s. (עָשָׂה I 793) *and you shall make*

עַל־הַחֹשֶׁן prep.-def.art.-n.m.s. (365) *for the breastpiece*

שְׁתֵּי טַבְּעוֹת num. f. du. cstr. (1040) - n.f.p. cstr. (371) *two rings of*

זָהָב n.m.s. (262) *gold*

וְנָתַתָּ conj.-Qal pf. 2 m.s. (נָתַן 678) *and put*

אֶת־שְׁתֵּי הַטַּבָּעוֹת dir.obj.-num. f. du. cstr. (1040) - def.art.-n.f.p. (371) *the two rings*

עַל־שְׁנֵי קְצוֹת prep.-num. m.du. cstr. (1040) - n.f.p. cstr. (892) *on the two edges of*

הַחֹשֶׁן def.art.-n.m.s. (365) *the breastpiece*

28:24

וְנָתַתָּה conj.-Qal pf. 2 m.s. (נָתַן 678) *and you shall put*

אֶת־שְׁתֵּי עֲבֹתֹת dir.obj.-num. f.du. cstr. (1040) - n.m.p. cstr. (721) *the two cords of*

הַזָּהָב def.art.-n.m.s. (262) *gold*

עַל־שְׁתֵּי הַטַּבָּעֹת prep.-num. f.du. cstr. (1040) - def.art.-n.f.p. (371) *in the two rings*

אֶל־קְצוֹת prep.-n.f.p. cstr. (892) *at the edges of*

הַחֹשֶׁן def.art.-n.m.s. (365) *the breastpiece*

28:25

וְאֵת שְׁתֵּי conj.-dir.obj.-num. f.du. cstr. (1040) *and the two*

קְצוֹת שְׁתֵּי n.f.p. cstr. (892) - v.supra *edges of the two*

הָעֲבֹתֹת def.art.-n.m.p. (721) *cords*

תִּתֵּן Qal impf. 2 m.s. (נָתַן 678) *you shall attach*

עַל־שְׁתֵּי הַמִּשְׁבְּצוֹת prep.-num. f.du. cstr. (1040) - def.art.-n.f.p. (990) *to the two settings of filigree*

וְנָתַתָּה conj.-Qal pf. 2 m.s. (נָתַן 678) *and so attach*

עַל־כִּתְפוֹת prep.-n.f.p. cstr. (509) *to the shoulder-pieces of*

הָאֵפֹד def.art.-n.m.s. (65) *the ephod*

אֶל־מוּל פָּנָיו prep.-subst. (I 557) - n.m.p.-3 m.s. sf. (815) *in front*

28:26

וְעָשִׂיתָ conj.-Qal pf. 2 m.s. (עָשָׂה I 793) *and you shall make*

שְׁתֵּי טַבְּעוֹת num. f. du. cstr. (1040)- n.f.p. cstr. (371) *two rings of*

זָהָב n.m.s. (262) *gold*

וְשַׂמְתָּ אֹתָם conj.-Qal pf. 2 m.s. (שִׂים I 962) - dir.obj.-3 m.p. sf. *and put them*

עַל־שְׁנֵי קְצוֹת prep.-num. m.du. cstr. (1040) - n.f.p. cstr. (892) *at the ends of*

הַחֹשֶׁן def.art.-n.m.s. (365) *the breastpiece*

עַל־שְׂפָתוֹ prep.-n.f.s.-3 m.s. sf. (973) *on its edge*

אֲשֶׁר אֶל־עֵבֶר rel.-prep.-n.m.s. cstr. (719) *which on the side of*

הָאֵפֹד def.art.-n.m.s. (65) *the ephod*

בָּיְתָה n.m.s.-loc. he (108; 7) *inside*

28:27

וְעָשִׂיתָ conj.-Qal pf. 2 m.s. (עָשָׂה I 793) *and you shall make*

שְׁתֵּי טַבְּעוֹת num. f.du. cstr. (1040) -n.f.p. cstr. (371) *two rings of*

זָהָב n.m.s. (262) *gold*

וְנָתַתָּה conj.-Qal pf. 2 m.s. (נָתַן 678) *and attach*

אֹתָם dir.obj.-3 m.p. sf. *them*

עַל־שְׁתֵּי כִתְפוֹת prep.-num. f.du. cstr. (1040) - n.f.p. cstr. (509) *on the two shoulder-pieces of*

הָאֵפוֹד def.art.-n.m.s. (65) *the ephod*

מִלְּמַטָּה prep.-prep.-adv. (641; 3) *to the lower part (beneath)*

מִמּוּל פָּנָיו prep.-subst. (557) - n.m.p.-3 m.s. sf. (815) *in front*

לְעֻמַּת prep.-n.f.s. cstr. as prep. (769) *close by*

מֶחְבַּרְתּוֹ n.f.s.-3 m.s. sf. (289) *at its joining*

מִמַּעַל לְחֵשֶׁב prep.-prep. (751; 1b) - prep.-n.m.s. cstr. (363) *above the band of*

הָאֵפוֹד def.art.-n.m.s. (65) *the ephod*

28:28

וְיִרְכְּסוּ conj.-Qal impf. 3 m.p. (רָכַס 940) *and they shall bind*

אֶת־הַחֹשֶׁן dir.obj.-def.art.-n.m.s. (365) *the breastpiece*

מִטַּבְּעֹתָו prep.-n.f.p.-3 m.s. sf. (371) *by its rings*

אֶל־טַבְּעֹת הָאֵפֹד prep.-n.f.p. cstr. (371) - def.art.-n.m.s. (65) *to the rings of the ephod*

בִּפְתִיל תְּכֵלֶת prep.-n.m.s. cstr. - n.f.s. (1067) *with a lace of blue*

לִהְיוֹת prep.-Qal inf. cstr. (הָיָה 224) *that it may lie*

עַל־חֵשֶׁב הָאֵפוֹד prep.-n.m.s. cstr. (363) - def.art.-n.m.s. (65) *upon the skilfully woven band of the ephod*

וְלֹא־יִזַּח הַחֹשֶׁן conj.-neg.-Ni. impf. 3 m.s. (זָחַח 267) - def.art.-n.m.s. (365) *and that the breastpiece shall not come loose*

מֵעַל הָאֵפוֹד prep.-prep.-def.art.-n.m.s. (65) *from the ephod*

28:29

וְנָשָׂא אַהֲרֹן conj.-Qal pf. 3 m.s. (669)-pr.n. (14) *so Aaron shall bear*

אֶת־שְׁמוֹת dir.obj.-n.m.p. cstr. (1027) *the names of*

בְּנֵי־יִשְׂרָאֵל n.m.p. cstr. (119) - pr.n. (975) *the sons of Israel*

בְּחֹשֶׁן הַמִּשְׁפָּט prep.-n.m.s. cstr. (365) - def.art.-n.m.s. (1048) *in the breastpiece of judgment*

עַל־לִבּוֹ prep.-n.m.s.-3 m.s. sf. (523) *upon his heart*

בְּבֹאוֹ prep.-Qal inf. cstr.-3 m.s. sf. (בּוֹא 97) *when he goes*

אֶל־הַקֹּדֶשׁ prep.-def.art.-n.m.s. (871) *into the holy place*

לְזִכָּרֹן prep.-n.m.s. (272) *to remembrance*

לִפְנֵי־יהוה prep.-n.m.p. cstr. (815) - pr.n. (217) *before Yahweh*

תָּמִיד n.m.s. as adv. (556) *continual*

28:30

וְנָתַתָּ conj.-Qal pf. 2 m.s. (נָתַן 678) *and you shall put*

אֶל־חֹשֶׁן הַמִּשְׁפָּט prep.-n.m.s. cstr. (365) - def.art.-n.m.s. (1048) *in the breastpiece of judgment*

אֶת־הָאוּרִים dir.obj.-def.art.-n.m.p. (22) *the Urim*

וְאֶת־הַתֻּמִּים conj.-dir.obj.-def.art.-n.m.p. (1070; 4) *and the Thummim*

וְהָיוּ conj.-Qal pf. 3 c.p. (הָיָה 224) *and they shall be*

עַל־לֵב אַהֲרֹן prep.-n.m.s. cstr. (523) - pr.n. (14) *upon Aaron's heart*

בְּבֹאוֹ prep.-Qal inf. cstr.-3 m.s. sf. (בּוֹא 97) *when he goes in*

לִפְנֵי יהוה prep.-n.m.p. cstr. (815) - pr.n. (217) *before Yahweh*

וְנָשָׂא אַהֲרֹן conj.-Qal pf. 3 m.s. (669) - pr.n. (14) *and Aaron shall bear*

אֶת־מִשְׁפַּט dir.obj.-n.m.s. cstr. (1048) *the judgment of*

בְּנֵי־יִשְׂרָאֵל n.m.p. cstr. (119) - pr.n. (975) *the people of Israel*

עַל־לִבּוֹ prep.-n.m.s.-3 m.s. sf. (523) *upon his heart*

לִפְנֵי יהוה v.supra - v.supra *before Yahweh*

תָּמִיד n.m.s. as adv. (556) *continually*

28:31

וְעָשִׂיתָ conj.-Qal pf. 2 m.s. (עָשָׂה I 793) *and you shall make*

אֶת־מְעִיל הָאֵפוֹד dir.obj.-n.m.s. cstr. (591)-def.art.-n.m.s. (65) *the robe of the ephod*

כְּלִיל תְּכֵלֶת adj. cstr. (483)-n.f.s. (1067) *all of blue*

28:32

וְהָיָה conj.-Qal pf. 3 m.s. (224) *and it shall have*

פִּי־רֹאשׁוֹ n.m.s. cstr. (804)-n.m.s.-3 m.s. sf. (910) *an opening for the head*

בְּתוֹכוֹ prep.-n.m.s.-3 m.s. sf. (1063) *in it*

שָׂפָה יִהְיֶה n.f.s. (973)-Qal impf. 3 m.s. (הָיָה 224) *an edge shall be*

לְפִיו prep.-n.m.s.-3 m.s. sf. (804) *to its opening*

סָבִיב adv. (686) *around*

מַעֲשֵׂה אֹרֵג n.m.s. cstr. (795)-Qal act. ptc. (אָרַג 70) *a work of a weaver*

כְּפִי prep.-n.m.s. cstr. (804) *like the opening of*

תַחְרָא n.m.s. (1065) *a garment*

יִהְיֶה־לּוֹ Qal impf. 3 m.s. (הָיָה 224)-prep.-3 m.s. sf. *(it shall be)*

לֹא יִקָּרֵעַ neg.-Ni. impf. 3 m.s. (902) *that it may not be torn*

28:33

וְעָשִׂיתָ conj.-Qal pf. 2 m.s. (עָשָׂה I 793) *and you shall make*

עַל־שׁוּלָיו prep.-n.m.p.-3 m.s. sf. (1002) *on its skirts*

רִמֹּנֵי תְּכֵלֶת n.m.p. cstr. (I 941)-n.f.s. (1067) *pomegranates of blue*

וְאַרְגָּמָן conj.-n.m.s. (71) *and purple*

וְתוֹלַעַת שָׁנִי conj.-n.f.s. cstr. (1069)-n.m.s. (1040) *and scarlet stuff*

עַל־שׁוּלָיו v. supra-v. supra *its skirts*

סָבִיב adv. (686) *around*

וּפַעֲמֹנֵי זָהָב conj.-n.m.p. cstr. (822)-n.m.s. (262) *with bells of gold*

בְּתוֹכָם סָבִיב prep.-n.m.s.-3 m.p. sf. (1063)-v. supra *between them (around)*

28:34

פַּעֲמֹן זָהָב n.m.s. cstr. (822)-n.m.s. (262) *a golden bell*

וְרִמּוֹן conj.-n.m.s. (I 941) *and a pomegranate*

פַּעֲמֹן זָהָב v. supra-v. supra *a golden bell*

וְרִמּוֹן v. supra *and a pomegranate*

עַל־שׁוּלֵי prep.-n.m.p. cstr. (1002) *on the skirts of*

הַמְּעִיל def.art.-n.m.s. (591) *the robe*

סָבִיב adv. (686) *round about*

28:35

וְהָיָה conj.-Qal pf. 3 m.s. (224) *and it shall be*

עַל־אַהֲרֹן prep.-pr.n. (14) *upon Aaron*

לְשָׁרֵת prep.-Pi. inf. cstr. (שָׁרַת 1058) *when he ministers*

וְנִשְׁמַע קוֹלוֹ conj.-Ni. pf. 3 m.s. (שָׁמַע 1033)-n.m.s.-3 m.s. sf. (876) *and its sound shall be heard*

בְּבֹאוֹ prep.-Qal inf. cstr.-3 m.s. sf. (בּוֹא 97) *when he goes*

אֶל־הַקֹּדֶשׁ prep.-def.art.-n.m.s. (871) *into the holy place*

לִפְנֵי יהוה prep.-n.m.p. cstr. (815)-pr.n. (217) *before Yahweh*

וּבְצֵאתוֹ conj.-prep.-Qal inf. cstr.-3 m.s. sf. (יָצָא 422) *and when he comes out*

וְלֹא יָמוּת conj.-neg.-Qal impf. 3 m.s. (מוּת 559) *lest he die*

28:36

וְעָשִׂיתָ conj.-Qal pf. 2 m.s. (עָשָׂה I 793) *and you shall make*

צִּיץ זָהָב טָהוֹר n.m.s. cstr. (847; 2)-n.m.s. (262)-adj. m.s. (373) *a plate of pure gold*

וּפִתַּחְתָּ conj.-Pi. pf. 2 m.s. (פָּתַח II 836) *and engrave*

עָלָיו prep.-3 m.s. sf. *on it*

פִּתּוּחֵי חֹתָם n.m.p. cstr. (836)-n.m.s. (I 368) *like an engraving of a signet*

קֹדֶשׁ לַיהוה n.m.s. (871)-prep.-pr.n. (217) *Holy to Yahweh*

28:37

וְשַׂמְתָּ conj.-Qal pf. 2 m.s. (שִׂים I 962) *and you shall fasten*

אֹתוֹ dir.obj.-3 m.s. sf. *it*

עַל־פְּתִיל תְּכֵלֶת prep.-n.m.s. cstr. (836)-n.f.s. (1067) *by a lace of blue*

וְהָיָה conj.-Qal pf. 3 m.s. (224) *it shall be*

עַל־הַמִּצְנָפֶת prep.-def.art.-n.f.s. paus. (857) *on the turban*

אֶל־מוּל prep.-subst. (I 557) *on the front of*

פְּנֵי־הַמִּצְנֶפֶת n.m.p. cstr. (815)-def.art.-n.f.s. (857) *the turban*

יִהְיֶה Qal impf. 3 m.s. (הָיָה 224) *it shall xe*

28:38

יִהְיֶה Qal impf. 3 m.s. (הָיָה 224) *it shall be*

עַל־מֵצַח אַהֲרֹן prep.-n.m.s. cstr. (594)-pr.n. (14) *upon Aaron's forehead*

וְנָשָׂא אַהֲרֹן conj.-Qal pf. 3 m.s. (669)-pr.n. (14) *and Aaron shall take*

אֶת־עֲוֹן dir.obj.-n.m.s. cstr. (730) *guilt incurred in*

הַקֳּדָשִׁים def.art.-n.m.p. (871) *the holy offering*

אֲשֶׁר יַקְדִּישׁוּ rel.-Hi. impf. 3 m.p. (קָדַשׁ 872) *which ... hallow*

בְּנֵי יִשְׂרָאֵל n.m.p. cstr. (119)-pr.n. (975) *the people of Israel*

לְכָל־מַתְּנֹת prep.-n.m.s. cstr. (481)-n.f.p. cstr. (682) *as all the gifts of*

קָדְשֵׁיהֶם n.m.p.-3 m.p. sf. (871) *their holiness (their holy gifts)*

וְהָיָה conj.-Qal pf. 3 m.s. (224) *and it shall be*

עַל־מִצְחוֹ prep.-n.m.s.-3 m.s. sf. (594) *upon his forehead*

תָּמִיד adv. (556) *always*

לְרָצוֹן לָהֶם prep.-n.m.s. (953)-prep.-3 m.p. sf. *that they may be accepted*

לִפְנֵי יהוה prep.-n.m.p. cstr. (815)-pr.n. (217) *before Yahweh*

28:39

וְשִׁבַּצְתָּ conj.-Pi. pf. 2 m.s. (שָׁבַץ 990) *and you shall weave*

הַכְּתֹנֶת def.art.-n.f.s. (509) *the coat*

שֵׁשׁ n.m.s. (III 1058) *in checker work of fine linen*

וְעָשִׂיתָ conj.-Qal pf. 2 m.s. (עָשָׂה I 793) *and you shall make*

מִצְנֶפֶת שֵׁשׁ n.f.s. cstr. (857)-n.m.s. (III 1058) *a turban of fine linen*

וְאַבְנֵט conj.-n.m.s. (126) *and a girdle*

תַּעֲשֶׂה Qal impf. 2 m.s. (עָשָׂה I 793) *you shall make*

מַעֲשֵׂה רֹקֵם n.m.s. cstr. (795)-Qal act. ptc. (955) *embroidered with needlework*

28:40

וְלִבְנֵי אַהֲרֹן conj.-prep.-n.m.p. cstr. (119)-pr.n. (14) *and for Aaron's sons*

תַּעֲשֶׂה Qal impf. 2 m.s. (עָשָׂה I 793) *you shall make*

כֻּתֳּנֹת n.f.p. (509) *coats*

וְעָשִׂיתָ conj.-Qal pf. 2 m.s. (עָשָׂה I 793) *and you shall make*

לָהֶם prep.-3 m.p. sf. *them*

אַבְנֵטִים n.m.p. (126) *girdles*

וּמִגְבָּעוֹת conj.-n.f.p. (149) *and caps*

תַּעֲשֶׂה v. supra *you shall make*

לָהֶם v. supra *them*

לְכָבוֹד prep.-n.m.s. (458) *for glory*

וּלְתִפְאָרֶת conj.-prep.-n.f.s. paus. (802) *and (for) beauty*

28:41

וְהִלְבַּשְׁתָּ אֹתָם conj.-Hi. pf. 2 m.s. (לָבַשׁ 527)-dir.obj.-3 m.p. sf. *and you shall put them upon*

אֶת־אַהֲרֹן אָחִיךָ dir.obj.-pr.n. (14)-n.m.s.-2 m.s. sf. (26) *Aaron your brother*

וְאֶת־בָּנָיו אִתּוֹ conj.-dir.obj.-n.m.p.-3 m.s. sf. (119)-prep.-3 m.s. sf. (II 85) *and upon his sons with him*

וּמָשַׁחְתָּ conj.-Qal pf. 2 m.s. (602) *and shall anoint*

אֹתָם dir.obj.-3 m.p. sf. *them*

וּמִלֵּאתָ אֶת־יָדָם conj.-Pi. pf. 2 m.s. (569)-dir.obj.-n.f.s.-3 m.p. sf. (388) *and ordain them*

וְקִדַּשְׁתָּ אֹתָם conj.-Pi. pf. 2 m.s. (872)-dir.obj.-3 m.p. sf. *and consecrate them*

וְכִהֲנוּ לִי conj.-Pi. pf. 3 c.p. (II 464)-prep.-1 c.s. sf. *that they may serve me as priests*

28:42

וַעֲשֵׂה לָהֶם conj.-Qal impv. 2 m.s. (עָשָׂה I 793)-prep.-3 m.p. sf. *and you shall make for them*

מִכְנְסֵי־בָד n.m.p. cstr. (488)-n.m.s. paus. (I 94) *linen breeches*

לְכַסּוֹת prep.-Pi.inf. cstr. (כָּסָה 491) *to cover*

בְּשַׂר עֶרְוָה n.m.s. cstr. (142)-n.f.s. (788) *naked flesh*

מִמָּתְנַיִם prep.-n.m. du. (608) *from loins*

וְעַד־יְרֵכַיִם conj.-prep.-n.f. du. (437) *to thighs*

יִהְיוּ Qal impf. 3 m.p. (הָיָה 224) *they shall reach*

28:43

וְהָיוּ conj.-Qal pf. 3 c.p. (הָיָה 224) *and they shall be*

עַל־אַהֲרֹן prep.-pr.n. (14) *upon Aaron*

וְעַל־בָּנָיו conj.-prep.-n.m.p.-3 m.s. sf. (119) *and upon his sons*

בְּבֹאָם prep.-Qal inf. cstr.-3 m.p. sf. (בּוֹא 97) *when they go*

אֶל־אֹהֶל מוֹעֵד prep.-n.m.s. cstr. (13)-n.m.s. (417) *into the tent of meeting*

אוֹ בְגִשְׁתָּם conj. (14)-prep.-Qal inf. cstr.-3 m.p. sf. (נָגַשׁ 620) *or when they come near*

אֶל־הַמִּזְבֵּחַ prep.-def.art.-n.m.s. (258) *the altar*

לְשָׁרֵת prep.-Pi.inf. cstr. (שָׁרַת 1058) *to minister*

בַּקֹּדֶשׁ prep.-def.art.-n.m.s. (871) *in the holy place*

וְלֹא־יִשְׂאוּ עָוֹן conj.-neg.-Qal impf. 3 m.p. (נָשָׂא 669)-n.m.s. (730) *lest they bring guilt*

וָמֵתוּ conj.-Qal pf. 3 c.p. (מוּת 559) *and die*

חֻקַּת עוֹלָם n.f.s. cstr. (349)-n.m.s. (761) *a perpetual statute*

לוֹ prep.-3 m.s. sf. *for him*

וּלְזַרְעוֹ conj.-prep.-n.m.s.-3 m.s. sf. (282) *and for his descendants*

אַחֲרָיו prep.-3 m.s. sf. (29) *after him*

29:1

וְזֶה הַדָּבָר conj.-demons. adj. m.s. (260)-def.art.-n.m.s. (182) *now this is what (the thing)*

אֲשֶׁר־תַּעֲשֶׂה rel.-Qal impf. 2 m.s. (עָשָׂה I 793) *(which) you shall do*

לָהֶם prep.-3 m.p. sf. *to them*

לְקַדֵּשׁ אֹתָם prep.-Pi. inf. cstr. (872)-dir.obj.-3 m.p. sf. *to consecrate them*

לְכַהֵן לִי prep.-Pi. inf. cstr. (II 464) - prep.-1 c.s. sf. *that they may serve me as priests*

לְקַח Qal impv. 2 m.s. (לָקַח 542) *take*

פַּר אֶחָד n.m.s. (830)-num. adj. m.s. (25) *one ... bull*

בֶּן־בָּקָר n.m.s. cstr. (119)-n.m.s. (133) *young*

וְאֵילִם שְׁנַיִם conj.-n.m.p. (I 17)-num. m. du. (1040) *and two rams*

תְּמִימִם adj. m.p. (1071) *without blemish*

29:2

וְלֶחֶם מַצּוֹת conj.-n.m.s. cstr. (536) - n.f.p. (595) *and unleavened bread*

וְחַלֹּת מַצֹּת conj.-n.f.p. cstr. (319)-n.f.p. (595) *and unleavened cakes*

בְּלוּלֹת Qal pass. ptc. f.p. (בָּלַל I 117) *mixed*

בַּשֶּׁמֶן prep.-def.art.-n.m.s. (1032) *with oil*

וּרְקִיקֵי מַצּוֹת conj.-n.m.p. cstr. (956)-n.f.p. (595) *and unleavened wafers*

מְשֻׁחִים Qal pass. ptc. m.p. (מָשַׁח 602) *spread*

בַּשָּׁמֶן prep.-def.art.-n.m.s. paus. (1032) *with oil*

סֹלֶת חִטִּים n.f.s. cstr. (701)-n.f.p. (334) *of fine wheat flour*

תַּעֲשֶׂה אֹתָם Qal impf. 2 m. s. (עָשָׂה I 793) - dir.obj.-3 m.p. sf. *you shall make them*

29:3

וְנָתַתָּ conj.-Qal pf. 2 m.s. (נָתַן 678) *and you shall put*

אוֹתָם dir.obj.-3 m.p. sf. *them*

עַל־סַל אֶחָד prep.-n.m.s. (700)-num. adj. m.s. (25) *in one basket*

וְהִקְרַבְתָּ conj.-Hi. pf. 2 m.s. (קָרַב 897) *and bring*

אֹתָם dir.obj.-3 m.p. sf. *them*

בַּסָּל prep.-def.art.-n.m.s. paus. (700) *in the basket*

וְאֶת־הַפָּר conj.-dir.obj.-def.art.-n.m.s. (830) *and the bull*

וְאֵת שְׁנֵי הָאֵילִם conj.-dir.obj.-num. m.du. cstr. (1040) - def.art.-n.m.p. (I 17) *and the two rams*

29:4

וְאֶת־אַהֲרֹן conj.-dir.obj.-pr.n. (14) *and Aaron*

וְאֶת־בָּנָיו conj.-dir.obj.-n.m.p.-3 m.s. sf. (119) *and his sons*

תַּקְרִיב Hi. impf. 2 m.s. (קָרַב 897) *you shall bring*

אֶל־פֶּתַח אֹהֶל מוֹעֵד prep.-n.m.s. cstr. (835)-n.m.s. cstr. (13)-n.m.s. (417) *to the door of the tent of meeting*

וְרָחַצְתָּ conj.-Qal pf. 2 m.s. (934) *and wash*

אֹתָם dir.obj.-3 m.p. sf. *them*

בַּמָּיִם prep.-def.art.-n.m.p. paus. (565) *with water*

29:5

וְלָקַחְתָּ conj.-Qal pf. 2 m.s. (לָקַח 542) *and you shall take*

אֶת־הַבְּגָדִים dir.obj.-def.art.-n.m.p. (93) *the garments*

וְהִלְבַּשְׁתָּ conj.-Hi. pf. 2 m.s. (לָבַשׁ 527) *and put on*

אֶת־אַהֲרֹן dir.obj.-pr.n. (14) *Aaron*

אֶת־הַכֻּתֹּנֶת dir.obj.-def.art.-n.f.s. (509) *the coat*

וְאֵת מְעִיל הָאֵפֹד conj.-dir.obj.-n.m.s. cstr. (591)-def.art.-n.m.s. (65) *and the robe of the ephod*

וְאֶת־הָאֵפֹד conj.-dir.obj.-def.art.-n.m.s. (65) *and the ephod*

וְאֶת־הַחֹשֶׁן conj.-dir.obj.-def.art.-n.m.s. (365) *and the breastpiece*

וְאָפַדְתָּ לוֹ conj.-Qal pf. 2 m.s. (אָפַד 65)-prep.-3 m.s. sf. *and gird him*

בְּחֵשֶׁב הָאֵפֹד prep.-n.m.s. cstr. (363) - def.art.-n.m.s. (65) *with the skilfully woven band of the ephod*

29:6

וְשַׂמְתָּ conj.-Qal pf. 2 m.s. (שִׂים I 962) *and you shall set*

הַמִּצְנֶפֶת def.art.-n.f.s. (857) *the turban*

עַל־רֹאשׁוֹ prep.-n.m.s.-3 m.s. sf. (910) *on his head*

וְנָתַתָּ conj.-Qal pf. 2 m.s. (נָתַן 678) *and put*

אֶת־נֵזֶר הַקֹּדֶשׁ dir.obj.-n.m.s. cstr. (634) - def.art.-n.m.s. (871) *the holy crown*

עַל־הַמִּצְנָפֶת prep.-def.art.-n.f.s. paus. (857) *upon the turban*

29:7

וְלָקַחְתָּ conj.-Qal pf. 2 m.s. (לָקַח 542) *and you shall take*

אֶת־שֶׁמֶן הַמִּשְׁחָה dir.obj.-n.m.s. cstr. (1032)-def.art.-n.f.s. (603) *the anointing oil*

וְיָצַקְתָּ conj.-Qal pf. 2 m.s. (יָצַק 427) *and pour*

עַל־רֹאשׁוֹ prep.-n.m.s.-3 m.s. sf. (910) *on his head*

וּמָשַׁחְתָּ אֹתוֹ conj.-Qal pf. 2 m.s. (מָשַׁח 602)-dir.obj.-3 m.s. sf. *and anoint him*

29:8

וְאֶת־בָּנָיו conj.-dir.obj.-n.m.p.-3 m.s. sf. (119) *then his sons*

תַּקְרִיב Hi. impf. 2 m.s. (קָרַב 897) *you shall bring*

וְהִלְבַּשְׁתָּם conj.-Hi. pf. 2 m.s.-3 m.p. sf. (לָבַשׁ 527) *and put on them*

כֻּתֳּנֹת n.f.p. (509) *coats*

29:9

וְחָגַרְתָּ אֹתָם conj.-Qal pf. 2 m.s. (חָגַר 291)-dir.obj.-3 m.p. sf. *and you shall gird them*

אַבְנֵט n.m.s. (126) *with girdles*

אַהֲרֹן וּבָנָיו pr.n. (14)-conj.-n.m.p.-3 m.s. sf. (119) *Aaron and his sons*

וְחָבַשְׁתָּ לָהֶם conj.-Qal pf. 2 m.s. (חָבַשׁ 289)-prep.-3 m.p. sf. *and bind on them*

מִגְבָּעֹת n.f.p. (149) *caps*

וְהָיְתָה לָהֶם conj.-Qal pf. 3 f.s. (הָיָה 224)-prep.-3 m.p. sf. *shall be theirs*

כְּהֻנָּה n.f.s. (464) *priesthood*

לְחֻקַּת עוֹלָם prep.-n.f.s. cstr. (349)-n.m.s. (761) *by a perpetual statute*

וּמִלֵּאתָ יַד־ conj.-Pi. pf. 2 m.s. (569)-n.f.s. cstr. (388) *thus you shall ordain*

אַהֲרֹן וְיַד־בָּנָיו pr.n. (14) - conj.-n.f.s. cstr. (388) - n.m.p.-3 m.s. sf. (119) *Aaron and his sons*

29:10

וְהִקְרַבְתָּ conj.-Hi. pf. 2 m.s. (קָרַב 897) *then you shall bring*

אֶת־הַפָּר dir.obj.-def.art.-n.m.s. paus. (830) *the bull*

לִפְנֵי prep.-n.m.p. cstr. (815) *before*

אֹהֶל מוֹעֵד n.m.s. cstr. (13) - n.m.s. (417) *tent of meeting*

וְסָמַךְ conj.-Qal pf. 3 m.s. (701) *and shall lay*

אַהֲרֹן וּבָנָיו pr.n. (14) - conj.-n.m.p.-3 m.s. sf. (119) *Aaron and his sons*

אֶת־יְדֵיהֶם dir.obj.-n.f.p.-3 m.p. sf. (388) *their hands*

עַל־רֹאשׁ הַפָּר prep.-n.m.s. cstr. (910) - def.art.-n.m.s. paus. (830) *upon the head of the bull*

29:11

וְשָׁחַטְתָּ conj.-Qal pf. 2 m.s. (שָׁחַט 1006) *and you shall kill*

אֶת־הַפָּר dir.obj.-def.art.-n.m.s. (830) *the bull*

לִפְנֵי יהוה prep.-n.m.p. cstr. (815) - pr.n. (217) *before Yahweh*

פֶּתַח n.m.s. cstr. (835) *at door of*

אֹהֶל מוֹעֵד n.m.s. cstr. (13) - n.m.s. (417) *tent of meeting*

29:12

וְלָקַחְתָּ conj.-Qal pf. 2 m.s. (לָקַח 542) *and shall take*

מִדַּם הַפָּר prep.-n.m.s. cstr. (196) - def.art.-n.m.s. (830) *part of the blood of the bull*

וְנָתַתָּה conj.-Qal pf. 2 m.s. (נָתַן 678) *and put*

עַל־קַרְנֹת prep.-n.f.p. cstr. (901) *upon the horns of*

הַמִּזְבֵּחַ def.art.-n.m.s. (258) *the altar*

בְּאֶצְבָּעֶךָ prep.-n.f.s.-2 m.s. sf. (840) *with your finger*

וְאֶת־כָּל־הַדָּם conj.-dir.obj.-n.m.s. cstr. (481) - def.art.-n.m.s. (196) *and the rest of the blood*

תִּשְׁפֹּךְ Qal impf. 2 m.s. (שָׁפַךְ 1049) *you shall pour out*

אֶל־יְסוֹד הַמִּזְבֵּחַ prep.-n.f.s. cstr. (414) - def.art.-n.m.s. (258) *at the base of the altar*

29:13

וְלָקַחְתָּ conj.-Qal pf. 2 m.s. (לָקַח 542) *and you shall take*

אֶת־כָּל־הַחֵלֶב dir.obj.-n.m.s. cstr. (481) - def.art.-n.m.s. (316) *all the fat*

הַמְכַסֶּה def.art.-Pi. ptc. (כָּסָה 491) *that covers*

אֶת־הַקֶּרֶב dir.obj.-def.art.-n.m.s. (899) *the entrails*

וְאֵת הַיֹּתֶרֶת conj.-dir.obj.-def.art.-n.f.s. (452) *and the appendage*

עַל הַכָּבֵד prep.-def.art.-n.m.s. (458) *of the liver*

וְאֵת שְׁתֵּי הַכְּלָיֹת conj.-dir.obj.-num. f.du. cstr. (1040)-def.art.-n.f.p. (480) *and the two kidneys*

וְאֶת־הַחֵלֶב conj.-dir.obj.-v.supra *and the fat*

אֲשֶׁר עֲלֵיהֶן rel.-prep.-3 f.p. sf. *that is on them*

וְהִקְטַרְתָּ conj.-Hi. pf. 2 m.s. (קָטַר 882) *and burn*

הַמִּזְבֵּחָה def.art.-n.m.s.-loc. he (258) *upon the altar*

29:14

וְאֶת־בְּשַׂר הַפָּר conj.-dir.obj.-n.m.s. cstr. (142) - def.art.-n.m.s. (830) *but the flesh of the bull*

וְאֶת־עֹרוֹ conj.-dir.obj.-n.m.s.-3 m.s. sf. (736) *and its skin*

וְאֶת־פִּרְשׁוֹ conj.-dir.obj.-n.m.s.-3 m.s. sf. (I 831) *and its dung*

תִּשְׂרֹף Qal impf. 2 m.s. (שָׂרַף 976) *you shall burn*

בָּאֵשׁ prep.-def.art.-n.f.s. (77) *with fire*

מִחוּץ לַמַּחֲנֶה prep.-n.m.s. cstr. (299) - prep.-def.art.-n.m.s. (334) *outside the camp*

חַטָּאת הוּא n.f.s. (308) - pers.pr. 3 m.s. (214) *it is a sin offering*

29:15

וְאֶת־הָאַיִל הָאֶחָד conj.-dir.obj.-def.art.-n.m.s. (I 17) -def.art.-num. adj. (25) *then one of the rams*

תִּקָּח Qal impf. 2 m.s. paus. (לָקַח 542) *you shall take*

וְסָמְכוּ conj.-Qal pf. 3 c.p. (סָמַךְ 701) *and shall lay*

אַהֲרֹן וּבָנָיו pr.n. (14) - conj.-n.m.p.-3 m.s. sf. (119) *Aaron and his sons*

אֶת־יְדֵיהֶם dir.obj. nf.p.-3 m.p. sf. (388) *their hands*

עַל־רֹאשׁ הָאָיִל prep.-n.m.s. cstr. (910) - def.art.-n.m.s. paus. (I 17) *upon the head of the ram*

29:16

וְשָׁחַטְתָּ conj.-Qal pf. 2 m.s. (שָׁחַט 1006) *and you shall slaughter*

אֶת־הָאָיִל dir.obj.-def.art.-n.m.s. paus. (I 17) *the ram*

וְלָקַחְתָּ conj.-Qal pf. 2 m.s. (לָקַח 542) *and shall take*

אֶת־דָּמוֹ dir.obj.-n.m.s.-3 m.s. sf. (196) *its blood*

וְזָרַקְתָּ conj.-Qal pf. 2 m.s. (זָרַק 284) *and throw*

עַל־הַמִּזְבֵּחַ prep.-def.art.-n.m.s. (258) *against the altar*

סָבִיב adv. (686) *round about*

29:17

וְאֶת־הָאַיִל conj.-dir.obj.-def.art.-n.m.s. (I 17) *then the ram*

תְּנַתֵּחַ Pi. mpf. 2 m.s. (נָתַח 677) *you shall cut*

לִנְתָחָיו prep.-n.m.p.-3 m.s. sf. (677) *into pieces*

וְרָחַצְתָּ conj.-Qal pf. 2 m.s. (רָחַץ 934) *and wash*

קִרְבּוֹ n.m.s.-3 m.s. sf. (899) *its entrails*

וּכְרָעָיו conj.-n.f.p.-3 m.s. sf. (502) *and its legs*

וְנָתַתָּ conj.-Qal pf. 2 m.s. (נָתַן 678) *and put*

עַל־נְתָחָיו prep.-n.m.p.-3 m.s. sf. (677) *with its pieces*

וְעַל־רֹאשׁוֹ conj.-prep.-n.m.s.-3 m.s. sf. (910) *and its head*

29:18

וְהִקְטַרְתָּ conj.-Hi. pf. 2 m.s. (קָטַר 882) *and burn*

אֶת־כָּל־הָאַיִל dir.obj.-n.m.s. cstr. (481) - def.art.-n.m.s. (I 17) *the whole ram*

הַמִּזְבֵּחָה def.art.-n.m.s.-loc. he (258) *upon the altar*

עֹלָה הוּא n.f.s. (750) - pers.pr. 3 m.s. (214) *it is a burnt offering*

ליהוה prep.-pr.n. (217) *to Yahweh*

רֵיחַ נִיחוֹחַ n.m.s. cstr. (926) - n.m.s. (629) *a pleasing odor*

אִשֶּׁה n.m.s. (77) *an offering by fire*

ליהוה v.supra *to Yahweh*

הוּא pers.pr. 3 m.s. (214) *it is*

29:19

וְלָקַחְתָּ conj.-Qal pf. 2 m.s. (לָקַח 542) *and you shall take*

אֵת הָאַיִל הַשֵּׁנִי dir.obj.-def.art.-n.m.s. (I 17) - def.art.-num. adj. m. (1041) *the other ram*

וְסָמַךְ conj.-Qal pf. 3 m.s. (סָמַךְ 701) *and shall lay*

אַהֲרֹן וּבָנָיו pr.n. (14) - conj.-n.m.p.-3 m.s. sf. (119) *Aaron and his sons*

אֶת־יְדֵיהֶם dir.obj.-n.f.p.-3 m.p. sf. (388) *their hands*

עַל־רֹאשׁ הָאָיִל prep.-n.m.s. cstr. (910) - def.art.-n.m.s. paus. (I 17) *upon the head of the ram*

29:20

וְשָׁחַטְתָּ conj.-Qal pf. 2 m.s. (שָׁחַט 1006) *and you shall kill*

אֶת־הָאַיִל dir.obj.-def.art.-n.m.s. (I 17) *the ram*

וְלָקַחְתָּ conj.-Qal pf. 2 m.s. (לָקַח 542) *and take*

מִדָּמוֹ prep.-n.m.s.-3 m.s. sf. (196) *part of its blood*

וְנָתַתָּה conj.-Qal pf. 2 m.s. (נָתַן 678) *and put*

עַל־תְּנוּךְ prep.-n.m.s. cstr. (1072) *upon the tip of*

אֹזֶן n.f.s. cstr. (23) *the ear of*

אַהֲרֹן pr.n. (14) *Aaron*

וְעַל־תְּנוּךְ conj.-v.supra - v.supra *and upon the tips of*

אֹזֶן בָּנָיו v.supra-n.m.p.-3 m.s. sf. (119) *the ... ears of his sons*

הַיְמָנִית def.art.-adj. f.s. (412) *right*

וְעַל־בֹּהֶן יָדָם conj.-prep.-n.f.s. cstr. (97) - n.f.s.-3 m.p. sf. (388) *and upon the thumbs of their ... hands*

הַיְמָנִית def.art.-adj. f.s. (412) *right*

וְעַל־בֹּהֶן v.supra - v.supra *and upon the great toes of*

רַגְלָם n.f.s.-3 m.p. sf. (919) *their ... feet*

הַיְמָנִית v.supra *right*

וְזָרַקְתָּ conj.-Qal pf. 2 m.s. (זָרַק 284) *and throw*

אֶת־הַדָּם dir.obj.-def.art.-n.m.s. (196) *the rest of the blood*

עַל־הַמִּזְבֵּחַ prep.-def.art.-n.m.s. (258) *against the altar*

סָבִיב adv. (686) *round about*

29:21

וְלָקַחְתָּ conj.-Qal pf. 2 m.s. (לָקַח 542) *then you shall take*

מִן־הַדָּם prep.-def.art.-n.m.s. (196) *part of the blood*

אֲשֶׁר עַל־הַמִּזְבֵּחַ rel.-prep.-def.art.-n.m.s. (258) *that is on the altar*

וּמִשֶּׁמֶן conj.-prep.-n.m.s. cstr. (1032) *and of the oil of*

הַמִּשְׁחָה def.art.-n.f.s. (603) *the anointing*

וְהִזֵּיתָ conj.-Hi. pf. 2 m.s. (נָזָה I 633) *and sprinkle*

עַל־אַהֲרֹן prep.-pr.n. (14) *upon Aaron*

וְעַל־בְּגָדָיו conj.-prep.-n.m.p.-3 m.s. sf. (93) *and his garments*

וְעַל־בָּנָיו conj.-prep.-n.m.p.-3 m.s. sf. (119) *and upon his sons*

וְעַל־בִּגְדֵי בָנָיו conj.-prep.-n.m.p. cstr. (93) - n.m.p.-3 m.s. sf. (119) *and his sons' garments*

אִתּוֹ prep.-3 m.s. sf. (II 85) *with him*
וְקָדַשׁ conj.-Qal pf. 3 m.s. (872) *and shall be holy*
הוּא וּבְגָדָיו pers.pr. 3 m.s. (214) - conj.-n.m.p.-3 m.s. sf. (93) *he and his garments*
וּבָנָיו conj.-n.m.p.-3 m.s. sf. (119) *and his sons*
וּבִגְדֵי בָנָיו conj.-n.m.p. cstr. (93) - v.supra *and his sons' garments*
אִתּוֹ v.supra *with him*

29:22

וְלָקַחְתָּ conj.-Qal pf. 2 m.s. (לָקַח 542) *you shall also take*
מִן־הָאַיִל prep.-def.art.-n.m.s. (I 17) *of the ram*
הַחֵלֶב def.art.-n.m.s. (316) *the fat*
וְהָאַלְיָה conj.-def.art.-n.f.s. (46) *and the fat tail*
וְאֶת־הַחֵלֶב conj.-dir.obj.-def.art.-n.m.s. (316) *and the fat*
הַמְכַסֶּה def.art.-Pi. ptc. (כָּסָה 491) *that covers*
אֶת־הַקֶּרֶב dir.obj.-def.art.-n.m.s. (899) *the entrails*
וְאֵת יֹתֶרֶת conj.-dir.obj.-n.f.s. cstr. (452) *and the appendage of*
הַכָּבֵד def.art.-n.m.s. (458) *the liver*
וְאֵת שְׁתֵּי conj.-dir.obj.-num. f.du. cstr. (1040) *and the two*
הַכְּלָיֹת def.art.-n.f.p. (480) *kidneys*
וְאֶת־הַחֵלֶב conj.-dir.obj.-def.art.-n.m.s. (316) *with the fat*
אֲשֶׁר עֲלֵהֶן rel.-prep.-3 f.p. sf. *that is on them*
וְאֵת שׁוֹק הַיָּמִין conj.-dir.obj.-n.f.s. cstr. (1003) - def.art.-n.f.s. (411) *and the right thigh*
כִּי אֵיל conj.-n.m.s. cstr. (I 17) *for a ram of*
מִלֻּאִים n.m.p. (571) *ordination*
הוּא pers.pr. 3 m.s. (214) *it is*

29:23

וְכִכַּר לֶחֶם conj.-n.f.s. cstr. (503) - n.m.s. (536) *and ... loaf of bread*
אַחַת adj. num. f.s. (25) *one*
וַחַלַּת לֶחֶם conj.-n.f.s. cstr. - v.supra *and ... cake of bread*
שֶׁמֶן n.m.s. (1032) *with oil*
אַחַת v.supra *one*
וְרָקִיק אֶחָד conj.-n.m.s. (956) - num. adj. m.s. (25) *and one wafer*
מִסַּל־הַמַּצּוֹת prep.-n.m.s. cstr. (700) - def.art.-n.f.p. (595) *out of the basket of unleavened bread*
אֲשֶׁר לִפְנֵי יהוה rel.-prep.-n.m.p. cstr. (815) - pr.n. (217) *that is before Yahweh*

29:24

וְשַׂמְתָּ conj.-Qal pf. 2 m.s. (שִׂים I 962) *and you shall put*
הַכֹּל def.art.-n.m.s. (481) *all these*
עַל כַּפֵּי prep.-n.f.p. cstr. (496) *in the hands of*
אַהֲרֹן pr.n. (14) *Aaron*
וְעַל כַּפֵּי conj.-prep.-v.supra *and in the hands of*
בָנָיו n.m.p.-3 m.s. sf. (119) *his sons*
וְהֵנַפְתָּ אֹתָם conj.-Hi. pf. 2 m.s. (נוּף 631) - dir.obj.-3 m.p. sf. *and wave them*
תְּנוּפָה n.f.s. (632) *for a wave offering*
לִפְנֵי יהוה prep.-n.m.p. cstr. (815) - pr.n. (217) *before Yahweh*

29:25

וְלָקַחְתָּ conj.-Qal pf. 2 m.s. (לָקַח 542) *then you shall take*
אֹתָם dir.obj.-3 m.p. sf. *them*
מִיָּדָם prep.-n.f.s.-3 m.p. sf. (388) *from their hands*
וְהִקְטַרְתָּ conj.-Hi. pf. 2 m.s. (קָטַר 882) *and burn*
הַמִּזְבֵּחָה def.art.-n.m.s.-loc. he (258) *on the altar*
עַל־הָעֹלָה prep.-def.art.-n.f.s. (750) *in addition to the burnt offering*
לְרֵיחַ נִיחוֹחַ prep.-n.m.s. cstr. (926) - n.m.s. (629) *as a pleasing odor*
לִפְנֵי יהוה prep.-n.m.p. cstr. (815) - pr.n. (217) *before Yahweh*
אִשֶּׁה n.m.s. (77) *an offering by fire*
הוּא ליהוה pers.pr. 3 m.s. (214) - prep.-pr.n. (217) *it is to Yahweh*

29:26

וְלָקַחְתָּ conj.-Qal pf. 2 m.s. (לָקַח 542) *and you shall take*

אֶת־הֶחָזֶה dir.obj.-def.art.-n.m.s. (303) *the breast*

מֵאֵיל prep.-n.m.s. cstr. (I 17) *of the ram of*

הַמִּלֻּאִים def.art.-n.m.p. (571) *the ordination*

אֲשֶׁר לְאַהֲרֹן prep.-pr.n. (14) *of Aaron*

וְהֵנַפְתָּ conj.-Hi. pf. 2 m.s. (631) *and wave*

אֹתוֹ dir.obj.-3 m.s. sf. *it*

תְּנוּפָה n.f.s. (632) *for a wave offering*

לִפְנֵי יהוה prep.-n.m.p. cstr. (815) - pr.n. (217) *before Yahweh*

וְהָיָה לְךָ conj.-Qal pf. 3 m.s. (224)- prep.-2 m.s. sf. *and it shall be for you*

לְמָנָה prep.-n.f.s. (584) *for a portion*

29:27

וְקִדַּשְׁתָּ conj.-Pi. pf. 2 m.s. (872) *and you shall consecrate*

אֵת חֲזֵה dir.obj.-n.m.s. cstr. (303) *the breast of*

הַתְּנוּפָה def.art.-n.f.s. (632) *the wave offering*

וְאֵת שׁוֹק conj.-dir.obj.-n.f.s. cstr. (1003) *and the thigh of*

הַתְּרוּמָה def.art.-n.f.s. (929) *the priests' portion (offering)*

אֲשֶׁר הוּנַף rel.-Ho. pf. 3 m.s. (נוּף 631) *which is waved*

וַאֲשֶׁר הוּרָם conj.-rel.-Ho. pf. 3 m.s. (רוּם 926) *and which is offered*

מֵאֵיל הַמִּלֻּאִים prep.-n.m.s. cstr. (I 17) - def.art.-n.m.p. (571) *from the ram of ordination*

מֵאֲשֶׁר לְאַהֲרֹן prep.-rel.-prep.-pr.n. (14) *since it is for Aaron*

וּמֵאֲשֶׁר לְבָנָיו conj.-prep.-rel.-prep.- n.m.p.-3 m.s. sf. (119) *and for his sons*

29:28

וְהָיָה conj.-Qal pf. 3 m.s. (224) *and it shall be*

לְאַהֲרֹן וּלְבָנָיו prep.-pr.n. (14) - conj.- prep.-n.m.p.- 3 m.s. sf. (119) *for Aaron and his sons*

לְחָק־עוֹלָם prep.-n.m.s. cstr. (349) - n.m.s. (761) *as a perpetual due*

מֵאֵת בְּנֵי יִשְׂרָאֵל prep.-prep. (II 85) - n.m.p. cstr. (119) - pr.n. (975) *from the people of Israel*

כִּי תְרוּמָה הוּא conj.-n.f.s. (929) - pers.pr. 3 m.s. (214) *for it is the priests' portion*

וּתְרוּמָה יִהְיֶה conj.-n.f.s. (929) - Qal impf. 3 m.s. (הָיָה 224) *to be offered*

מֵאֵת בְּנֵי־ v.supra - v.supra *by the people of*

יִשְׂרָאֵל v.supra *Israel*

מִזִּבְחֵי שַׁלְמֵיהֶם prep.-n.m.p. cstr. (257) - n.m.p.-3 m.p. sf. (1023) *from their peace offerings*

תְּרוּמָתָם לַיהוה n.f.s.-3 m.p. sf. (929) - prep.-pr.n. (217) *it is their offering to Yahweh*

29:29

וּבִגְדֵי הַקֹּדֶשׁ conj.-n.m.p. cstr. (93) - def.art.-n.m.s. (871) *the holy garments*

אֲשֶׁר לְאַהֲרֹן rel.-prep.-pr.n. (14) *of Aaron*

יִהְיוּ לְבָנָיו Qal impf. 3 m.p. (הָיָה 224) - prep.-n.m.p.-3 m.s. sf. (119) *shall be for his sons*

אַחֲרָיו prep.-3 m.s. sf. (29) *after him*

לְמָשְׁחָה בָהֶם prep. - Qal inf. cstr. (מָשַׁח 602) - prep.-3 m.p. sf. *to be anointed in them*

וּלְמַלֵּא־בָם conj.-prep.-Pi. inf. cstr. (מָלֵא 569) - prep.-3 m.p. sf. *and ordained in them (*lit. *to fill in them)*

אֶת־יָדָם dir.obj.-n.f.s.-3 m.p. sf. (388) *(their hand)*

29:30

שִׁבְעַת יָמִים num. f.s. cstr. (987) - n.m.p. (398) *seven days*

יִלְבָּשָׁם Qal impf. 3 m.s.-3 m.p. sf. (לָבַשׁ 527) *shall wear them*

הַכֹּהֵן def.art.-n.m.s. (463) *the priest*

תַּחְתָּיו prep.-3 m.s. sf. (1065) *in his place*

מִבָּנָיו prep.-n.m.p.-3 m.s. sf. (119) *from his sons*

אֲשֶׁר יָבֹא rel.-Qal impf. 3 m.s. (בּוֹא 97) *when he comes*

אֶל־אֹהֶל מוֹעֵד prep.-n.m.s. cstr. (13) - n.m.s. (417) *into the tent of meeting*

לְשָׁרֵת prep.-Pi. inf. cstr. (שָׁרַת 1058) *to minister*

בַּקֹּדֶשׁ prep.-def.art.-n.m.s. (871) *in the holy place*

29:31

וְאֵת אֵיל conj.-dir.obj.-n.m.s. cstr. (I 17) *and the ram of*

הַמִּלֻּאִים def.art.-n.m.p. (571) *ordination*

תִּקָּח Qal impf. 2 m.s. paus. (לָקַח 542) *you shall take*

וּבִשַּׁלְתָּ conj.-Pi. pf. 2 m.s. (בָּשַׁל 143) *and boil*

אֶת־בְּשָׂרוֹ dir.obj.-n.m.s.-3 m.s. sf. (142) *its flesh*

בְּמָקֹם קָדֹשׁ prep.-n.m.s. (879) - adj. m.s. (872) *in a holy place*

29:32

וְאָכַל conj.-Qal pf. 3 m.s. (37) *and shall eat*

אַהֲרֹן וּבָנָיו pr.n. (14) - conj.-n.m.p.-3 m.s. sf. (119) *Aaron and his sons*

אֶת־בְּשַׂר הָאַיִל dir.obj.-n.m.s. cstr. (142) - def.art.-n.m.s. (I 17) *the flesh of the ram*

וְאֶת־הַלֶּחֶם conj.-dir.obj.-def.art.-n.m.s. (536) *and the bread*

אֲשֶׁר בַּסָּל rel.-prep.-def.art.-n.m.s. paus. (700) *that is in the basket*

פֶּתַח אֹהֶל n.m.s. cstr. (835) - n.m.s. cstr. (13) *at the door of the tent of*

מוֹעֵד n.m.s. (417) *meeting*

29:33

וְאָכְלוּ conj.-Qal pf. 3 c.p. (אָכַל 37) *and they shall eat*

אֹתָם אֲשֶׁר dir.obj.-3 m.p. sf.-rel. *those things with which*

כֻּפַּר בָּהֶם Pu. pf. 3 m.s. (497) - prep.-3 m.p. sf. *atonement was made (by them)*

לְמַלֵּא אֶת־יָדָם prep.-Pi. inf. cstr. (569) - dir.obj.-n.m.s.-3 m.p. sf. (388) *to ordain (*lit. *fill their hand)*

לְקַדֵּשׁ אֹתָם prep.-Pi. inf. cstr. (872) - dir.obj.-3 m.p. sf. *and consecrate them*

וְזָר conj.-Qal act. ptc. as n. (זוּר 266) *but an outsider*

לֹא־יֹאכַל neg.-Qal impf. 3 m.s. (אָכַל 37) *shall not eat*

כִּי־קֹדֶשׁ הֵם conj.-n.m.s. (871) - pers.pr. 3 m.p. (241) *because they are holy*

29:34

וְאִם־יִוָּתֵר conj.-hypoth. part. (49) - Ni. impf. 3 m.s. (יָתַר 451) *and if ... remain*

מִבְּשַׂר הַמִּלֻּאִים prep.-n.m.s. cstr. (142) - def.art.-n.m.p. (571) *any of the flesh for the ordination*

וּמִן־הַלֶּחֶם conj.-prep.-def.art.-n.m.s. (536) *or of the bread*

עַד־הַבֹּקֶר prep.-def.art.-n.m.s. (133) *until the morning*

וְשָׂרַפְתָּ conj.-Qal pf. 2 m.s. (שָׂרַף 976) *then you shall burn*

אֶת־הַנּוֹתָר dir.obj.-def.art.-Ni. ptc. (יָתַר 451) *the remainder*

בָּאֵשׁ prep.-def.art.-n.f.s. (77) *with fire*

לֹא יֵאָכֵל neg.-Ni. impf. 3 m.s. (אָכַל 37) *it shall not be eaten*

כִּי־קֹדֶשׁ הוּא conj.-n.m.s. (871) - pers.pr. 3 m.s. (214) *because it is holy*

29:35

וְעָשִׂיתָ conj.-Qal pf. 2 m.s. (עָשָׂה I 793) *thus you shall do*

לְאַהֲרֹן prep.pr.n. (14) *to Aaron*

וּלְבָנָיו conj.-prep.-n.m.p.-3 m.s. sf. (119) *and to his sons*

כָּכָה כְּכֹל adv. (462) - prep.-n.m.s. (481) *according to all*

אֲשֶׁר־צִוִּיתִי rel.-Pi. pf. 1 c.s. (צָוָה 845) *that I have commanded*

אֹתָכָה dir.obj.-2 m.s. sf. paus. *you*

שִׁבְעַת יָמִים num. f.s. cstr. (987) - n.m.p. (398) *through seven days*

תְּמַלֵּא יָדָם Pi. impf. 2 m.s. (מָלֵא 569) - n.f.s.-3 m.p. sf. (388) *shall you ordain them*

29:36

וּפַר חַטָּאת conj.-n.m.s. cstr. (830) - n.f.s. (308) *and a bull as a sin offering*

תַּעֲשֶׂה Qal impf. 2 m.s. (עָשָׂה I 793) *you shall offer*

לַיּוֹם prep.-def.art.-n.m.s. (398) *every day*

עַל־הַכִּפֻּרִים prep.-def.art.-n.m.p. (498) *for atonement*

וְחִטֵּאתָ conj.-Pi. pf. 2 m.s. (חָטָא 306) *also you shall offer a sin offering*

עַל־הַמִּזְבֵּחַ prep.-def.art.-n.m.s. (258) *for the altar*

בְּכַפֶּרְךָ prep.-Pi. inf. cstr.-2 m.s. sf. (כָּפַר 497) *when you make atonement*

עָלָיו prep.-3 m.s. sf. *for it*

וּמָשַׁחְתָּ conj.-Qal pf. 2 m.s. (מָשַׁח 602) *and you shall anoint*

אֹתוֹ dir.obj.-3 m.s. sf. *it*

לְקַדְּשׁוֹ prep.-Pi. inf. cstr.-3 m.s. sf. (קָדַשׁ 872) *to consecrate it*

29:37

שִׁבְעַת יָמִים num. f.s. cstr. (987) - n.m.p. (398) *seven days*

תְּכַפֵּר Pi. impf. 2 m.s. (כָּפַר 497) *you shall make atonement*

עַל־הַמִּזְבֵּחַ prep.-def.art.-n.m.s. (258) *for the altar*

וְקִדַּשְׁתָּ conj.-Pi. pf. 2 m.s. (קָדַשׁ 872) *and consecrate*

אֹתוֹ dir.obj.-3 m.s. sf. *it*

וְהָיָה הַמִּזְבֵּחַ conj.-Qal pf. 3 m.s. (224) - def.art.-n.m.s. (258) *and the altar shall be*

קֹדֶשׁ קָדָשִׁים n.m.s. cstr. (871) - n.m.p. (871) *most holy (*lit. *holy of holies)*

כָּל־הַנֹּגֵעַ n.m.s. cstr. (481) - def.art.-Qal act. ptc. (נָגַע 619) *whatever touches*

בַּמִּזְבֵּחַ prep.-def.art.-n.m.s. (258) *the altar*

יִקְדָּשׁ Qal impf. 3 m.s. (קָדַשׁ 872) *shall become holy*

29:38

וְזֶה conj.-demons. adj. (260) *now this is*

אֲשֶׁר תַּעֲשֶׂה rel.-Qal impf. 2 m.s. (עָשָׂה I 793) *what you shall offer*

עַל־הַמִּזְבֵּחַ prep.-def.art.-n.m.s. (258) *upon the altar*

כְּבָשִׂים n.m.p. (461) *lambs*

בְּנֵי־שָׁנָה n.m.p. cstr. (119) - n.f.s. (1040) *a year old*

שְׁנַיִם num. m.du. (1040) *two*

לַיּוֹם prep.-def.art.-n.m.s. (398) *day by day*

תָּמִיד adv. (556) *continually*

29:39

אֶת־הַכֶּבֶשׂ הָאֶחָד dir.obj.-def.art.-n.m.s. (461) - def.art.-num. adj. (25) *one lamb*

תַּעֲשֶׂה Qal impf. 2 m.s. (עָשָׂה I 793) *you shall offer*

בַבֹּקֶר prep.-def.art.-n.m.s. (133) *in the morning*

וְאֵת הַכֶּבֶשׂ הַשֵּׁנִי conj.-dir.obj.-def.art.-n.m.s. (461) - def.art.-num. adj. m. (1041) *and the other lamb*

תַּעֲשֶׂה v.supra *you shall offer*

בֵּין הָעַרְבָּיִם prep. (107) - def.art.-n.m.p. (787) *in the evening*

29:40

וְעִשָּׂרֹן conj.-n.m.s. (798) *and a tenth measure*

סֹלֶת n.f.s. (701) *fine flour*

בָּלוּל Qal pass. ptc. (בָּלַל I 117) *mingled*

בְּשֶׁמֶן כָּתִית prep.-n.m.s. (1032) -adj. m.s. (510) *with beaten oil*

רֶבַע הַהִין n.m.s. cstr. (I 917) - def.art.-n.m.s. (228) *a fourth of a hin*

וְנֶסֶךְ conj.-n.m.s. (651) *and a drink-offering*

רְבִעִית הַהִין adj. f.s. cstr. (917) - def.art.-n.m.s. (228) *a fourth of a hin*

יָיִן n.m.s. paus. (406) *wine*

לַכֶּבֶשׂ prep.-def.art.-n.m.s. (461) *with the ... lamb*

הָאֶחָד def.art.-num. adj. m. (25) *first*

29:41

וְאֵת הַכֶּבֶשׂ conj.-dir.obj.-def.art.-n.m.s. (461) *and the ... lamb*

הַשֵּׁנִי def.art.-num. adj. m. (1041) *other*

תַּעֲשֶׂה Qal impf. 2 m.s. (עָשָׂה I 793) *you shall offer*

בֵּין הָעַרְבַּיִם prep. (107) - def.art.-n.m.p. paus. (787) *in the evening*

כְּמִנְחַת הַבֹּקֶר prep.-n.f.s. cstr. (585) - def.art.-n.m.s. (133) *as an offering in the morning*

וּכְנִסְכָּהּ conj.-prep.-n.m.s.-3 f.s. sf. (651) *and its libation*

תַּעֲשֶׂה־לָּהּ v.supra - prep.-3 f.s. sf. *and shall offer with it*

לְרֵיחַ נִיחֹחַ prep.-n.m.s. cstr. (926) - n.m.s. (629) *for a pleasing odor*

אִשֶּׁה n.m.s. (77) *an offering by fire*

ליהוה prep.-pr.n. (217) *to Yahweh*

29:42

עֹלַת תָּמִיד n.f.s. cstr. (750) - n.m.s. (556) *a continual burnt offering*

לְדֹרֹתֵיכֶם prep.-n.m.p.-2 m.p. sf. (189) *throughout your generations*

פֶּתַח אֹהֶל־ n.m.s. cstr. (835) - n.m.s. cstr. (13) *at the door of the tent of*

מוֹעֵד n.m.s. (417) *meeting*

לִפְנֵי יהוה prep.-n.m.p. cstr. (815) - pr.n. (217) *before Yahweh*

אֲשֶׁר אִוָּעֵד rel.-Ni. impf. 1 c.s. (יָעַד 416) *where I will meet*

לָכֶם prep.-2 m.p. sf. *with you*

שָׁמָּה adv.-loc. he (1027) *(there)*

לְדַבֵּר אֵלֶיךָ prep.-Pi. inf. cstr. (180) - prep.-2 m.s. sf. *to speak to you*

שָׁם adv. (1027) *there*

29:43

וְנֹעַדְתִּי conj.-Ni. pf. 1 c.s. (יָעַד 416) *and I will meet*

שָׁמָּה adv.-loc. he (1027) *there*

לִבְנֵי יִשְׂרָאֵל prep.-n.m.p. cstr. (119) - pr.n. (975) *with the people of Israel*

וְנִקְדַּשׁ conj.-Ni. pf. 3 m.s. (קָדַשׁ 872) *and it shall be sanctified*

בִּכְבֹדִי prep.-n.m.s.-1 c.s. sf. (II 458) *by my glory*

29:44

וְקִדַּשְׁתִּי conj.-Pi. pf. 1 c.s. (קָדַשׁ 872) *and I will consecrate*

אֶת־אֹהֶל מוֹעֵד dir.obj.-n.m.s. cstr. (13) - n.m.s. (417) *the tent of meeting*

וְאֶת־הַמִּזְבֵּחַ conj.-dir.obj.-def.art.-n.m.s. (258) *and the altar*

וְאֶת־אַהֲרֹן conj.-dir.bj.-pr.n. (14) *Aaron also*

וְאֶת־בָּנָיו conj.-dir.obj.-n.m.p.-3 m.s. sf. (119) *and his sons*

אֲקַדֵּשׁ Pi. impf. 1 c.s. (קָדַשׁ 872) *I will consecrate*

לְכַהֵן לִי prep.-Pi. inf. cstr. (II 464) - prep.-1 c.s. sf. *to serve me as priests*

29:45

וְשָׁכַנְתִּי conj.-Qal pf. 1 c.s. (שָׁכַן 1014) *and I will dwell*

בְּתוֹךְ prep.-n.m.s. cstr. (1063) *among*

בְּנֵי יִשְׂרָאֵל n.m.p. cstr. (119) - pr.n. (975) *the people of Israel*

וְהָיִיתִי conj.-Qal pf. 1 c.s. (הָיָה 224) *and will be*

לָהֶם לֵאלֹהִים prep.-3 m.p. sf. - prep.-n.m.p. (43) *their God*

29:46

וְיָדְעוּ conj.-Qal pf. 3 c.p. (יָדַע 393) *and they shall know*

כִּי אֲנִי conj.-pers.pr. 1 c.s. (58) *that I am*

יהוה אֱלֹהֵיהֶם pr.n. (217) - n.m.p.-3 m.p. sf. (43) *Yahweh their God*

אֲשֶׁר הוֹצֵאתִי rel.-Hi. pf. 1 c.s. (יָצָא 422) *who brought forth*

אֹתָם dir.obj.-3 m.p. sf. *them*

מֵאֶרֶץ מִצְרַיִם prep.-n.f.s. cstr. (75) - pr.n. (595) *out of the land of Egypt*

לְשָׁכְנִי prep.-Qal inf. cstr.-1 cs. sf. (שָׁכַן 1014) *that I might dwell*

בְתוֹכָם prep.-n.m.s.-3 m.p. sf. (1063) *among them*

אֲנִי יהוה pers.pr. 1 c.s. (58) - pr.n. (217) *I am Yahweh*

אֱלֹהֵיהֶם v.supra *their God*

30:1

וְעָשִׂיתָ conj.-Qal pf. 2 m.s. (עָשָׂה I 793) *and you shall make*

מִזְבֵּחַ n.m.s. (258) *an altar*

מִקְטַר קְטֹרֶת n.m.s. cstr. (883)-n.f.s. (882) *to burn incense upon*

עֲצֵי שִׁטִּים n.m.p. cstr. (781)-n.f.p. (1008) *of acacia wood*

תַּעֲשֶׂה אֹתוֹ Qal impf. 2 m.s. (עָשָׂה I 793)-dir.obj.-3 m.s. sf. *shall you make it*

30:2

אַמָּה אָרְכּוֹ n.f.s. (52)-n.m.s.-3 m.s. sf. (73) *a cubit shall be its length*

וְאַמָּה רָחְבּוֹ conj.-n.f.s. (52)-n.m.s.-3 m.s. sf. (931) *and a cubit its breadth*

רָבוּעַ יִהְיֶה Qal pass. ptc. (רָבַע 917)-Qal impf. 3 m.s. (הָיָה 224) *it shall be square*

וְאַמָּתַיִם conj.-n.f. du. (52) *and two cubits*

קֹמָתוֹ n.f.s.-3 m.s. sf. (879) *its height*

מִמֶּנּוּ קַרְנֹתָיו prep.-3 m.s. sf.-n.f. du.-3 m.s. sf. (901) *its horns shall be of one piece with it*

30:3

וְצִפִּיתָ אֹתוֹ conj.-Pi. pf. 2 m.s. (צָפָה II 860) - dir.obj.-3 m.s. sf. *and you shall overlay it*

זָהָב טָהוֹר n.m.s. (262)-adj.m.s. (373) *with pure gold*

אֶת־גַּגּוֹ dir.obj.-n.m.s.-3 m.s. sf. (150) *its top*

וְאֶת־קִירֹתָיו conj.-dir.obj.-n.m.p.-3 m.s. sf. (885;θ4) *and its sides*

סָבִיב adv. (686) *round about*

וְאֶת־קַרְנֹתָיו conj.-dir.obj.-n.f.p.-3 m.s. sf. (901) *and its horns*

וְעָשִׂיתָ לּוֹ conj.-Qal pf. 2 m.s. (עָשָׂה I 793)-prep.-3 m.s. sf. *and you shall make for it*

זֵר זָהָב n.m.s. cstr. (267)-n.m.s. (262) *a molding of gold*

סָבִיב v.supra *round about*

30:4

וּשְׁתֵּי conj.-num. f.du. cstr. (1040) *and two*

טַבְּעֹת זָהָב n.f.p. cstr. (371)-n.m.s. (262) *golden rings*

תַּעֲשֶׂה־לּוֹ Qal impf. 2 m.s. (עָשָׂה I 793)-prep.-3 m.s. sf. *shall you make for it*

מִתַּחַת לְזֵרוֹ prep.-prep. (1065)-prep.-n.m.s.-3 m.s. sf. (267) *from beneath its molding*

עַל שְׁתֵּי prep.-v.supra *on two of*

צַלְעֹתָיו n.f.p.-3 m.s. sf. (854) *its sides*

תַּעֲשֶׂה v.supra *shall you make*

עַל־שְׁנֵי צִדָּיו prep.-num. m.du. cstr. (1040)-n.m.p.-3 m.s. sf. (841) *on its two sides*

וְהָיָה conj.-Qal pf. 3 m.s. (224) *and they shall be*

לְבָתִּים לְבַדִּים prep.-n.m.p. (108; 3) - prep.-n.m.p. (94; 3) *holders for poles*

לָשֵׂאת אֹתוֹ בָּהֵמָּה prep.-Qal inf. cstr. (נָשָׂא 669)-dir.obj.-3 m.s. sf.-prep.-pers.pr. 3 m.s. (241) *with which to carry it*

30:5

וְעָשִׂיתָ conj.-Qal pf. 2 m.s. (עָשָׂה I 793) *and you shall make*

אֶת־הַבַּדִּים dir.obj.-def.art.-n.m.p. (II 94) *the poles*

עֲצֵי שִׁטִּים n.m.p. cstr. (781)-n.f.p. (1008) *of acacia wood*

וְצִפִּיתָ אֹתָם conj.-Pi. pf. 2 m.s. (צָפָה II 860) - dir.obj.-3 m.p. sf. *and overlay them*

זָהָב n.m.s. (262) *with gold*

30:6

וְנָתַתָּה אֹתוֹ conj.-Qal pf. 2 m.s. (נָתַן 678)-dir.obj.-3 m.s. sf. *and you shall put it*

לִפְנֵי הַפָּרֹכֶת prep.-n.m.p. cstr. (815) - def.art.-n.f.s. (827) *before the veil*

אֲשֶׁר עַל־אֲרֹן rel.-prep.-n.m.s. cstr. (75) *that is by the ark of*

הָעֵדֻת def.art.-n.f.s. (730) *the testimony*

לִפְנֵי הַכַּפֹּרֶת v.supra-def.art.-n.f.s. (498) *before the mercy seat*

אֲשֶׁר עַל־הָעֵדֻת rel.-prep.-v.supra *that is over the testimony*

אֲשֶׁר אִוָּעֵד rel.-Ni. impf. 1 c.s. (יָעַד 416) *where I will meet*

לְךָ prep.-2 m.s. sf. *with you*

שָׁמָּה adv.-loc. he (1027) *(there)*

30:7

וְהִקְטִיר עָלָיו conj. - Hi. pf. 3 m.s. (קָטַר 882) - prep.-3 m.s. sf. *and shall burn on it*

אַהֲרֹן pr.n. (14) *Aaron*

קְטֹרֶת סַמִּים n.f.s. cstr. (882)-n.m.p. (702) *fragrant incense*

בַּבֹּקֶר בַּבֹּקֶר prep.-def.art.-n.m.s. (133)-v.supra *every morning*

בְּהֵיטִיבוֹ prep.-Hi. inf. cstr.-3 m.s. sf. (יָטַב 405) *when he dresses*

אֶת־הַנֵּרֹת dir.obj.-n.m.p. (632) *the lamps*

יַקְטִירֶנָּה Hi. impf. 3 m.s. - 3 f.s. sf. (קָטַר 882) *he shall burn it*

30:8

וּבְהַעֲלֹת אַהֲרֹן conj.-prep.-Hi. inf. cstr. (עָלָה 748)-pr.n. (14) *and when Aaron sets up*

אֶת־הַנֵּרֹת dir.obj.-def.art.-n.m.p. (632) *the lamps*

בֵּין הָעַרְבַּיִם prep. (107)-def.art.-n.m.p. (787) *in the evening*

יַקְטִירֶנָּה Hi. impf. 3 m.s.-3 f.s. sf. (קָטַר 882) *he shall burn it*

קְטֹרֶת תָּמִיד n.f.s. cstr. (882)-n.m.s. (556) *a perpetual incense*

לִפְנֵי יהוה prep.-n.m.p. cstr. (815)-pr.n. (217) *before Yahweh*

לְדֹרֹתֵיכֶם prep.-n.m.p.-2 m.p. sf. (189) *throughout your generations*

30:9

לֹא־תַעֲלוּ neg.-Qal impf. 2 m.p. (עָלָה 748) *you shall offer no*

עָלָיו prep.-3 m.s. sf. *thereon*

קְטֹרֶת זָרָה n.f.s. cstr. (882)-Qal act. ptc. f.s. (זור I 266) *unholy incense*

וְעֹלָה conj.-n.f.s. (750) *nor burnt offering*

וּמִנְחָה conj.-n.f.s. (585) *nor cereal offering*

וְנֶסֶךְ conj.-n.m.s. (651) *and libation*

לֹא תִסְּכוּ neg.-Qal impf. 2 m.p. (נָסַךְ 650) *you shall not pour out*

עָלָיו prep.-3 m.s. sf. *thereon*

30:10

וְכִפֶּר אַהֲרֹן conj.-Pi. pf. 3 m.s. (כָּפַר 497)-pr.n. (14) *and Aaron shall make atonement*

עַל־קַרְנֹתָיו prep.-n.f.p.-3 m.s. sf. (901) *upon its horns*

אַחַת בַּשָּׁנָה num. adj. f.s. (25)-prep.-def.art.-n.f.s. (1040) *once a year*

מִדַּם חַטַּאת prep.-n.m.s. cstr. (196)-n.f.s. cstr. (308) *with the blood of the sin offering of*

הַכִּפֻּרִים def.art.-n.m.p. (498) *atonement*

אַחַת בַּשָּׁנָה v.supra-v.supra *once in the year*

יְכַפֵּר עָלָיו Pi. impf. 3 m.s. (כָּפַר 497)-prep.-3 m.s. sf. *he shall make atonement for it*

לְדֹרֹתֵיכֶם prep.-n.m.p.-2 m.p. sf. (189) *throughout your generations*

קֹדֶשׁ־קָדָשִׁים n.m.s. cstr. (871)-n.m.p. (871) *most holy*

הוּא pers.pr. 3 m.s. (214) *it is*

לַיהוה prep.-pr.n. (217) *to Yahweh*

30:11

וַיְדַבֵּר יהוה consec.-Pi. impf. 3 m.s. (דָּבַר 180)-pr.n. (217) *then Yahweh said*

אֶל־מֹשֶׁה prep.-pr.n. (602) *to Moses*

לֵּאמֹר prep.-Qal inf. cstr. (55) *(saying)*

30:12

כִּי תִשָּׂא conj.-Qal impf. 2 m.s. (נָשָׂא 669) *when you take*

אֶת־רֹאשׁ dir.obj.-n.m.s. cstr. (910; 7) *the census of*

בְּנֵי־יִשְׂרָאֵל n.m.p. cstr. (119)-pr.n. (975) *the people of Israel*

לִפְקֻדֵיהֶם prep.-Qal pass. ptc. m.p.-3 m.p. sf. (פָּקַד 823; A4) *in their being numbered*

וְנָתְנוּ conj.-Qal pf. 3 c.p. (נָתַן 678) *then shall give*

אִישׁ n.m.s. (35) *each*

כֹּפֶר n.m.s. (497) *a ransom*

נַפְשׁוֹ n.f.s.-3 m.s. sf. (659) *for himself*

לַיהוה prep.-pr.n. (217) *to Yahweh*

בִּפְקֹד אֹתָם prep.-Qal inf. cstr. (פָּקַד 823)-dir.obj.-3 m.p. sf. *when you number them*

וְלֹא־יִהְיֶה בָהֶם conj.-neg.-Qal impf. 3 m.s. (הָיָה 224)-prep.-3 m.p. sf. *that there be no ... among them*

נֶגֶף n.m.s. (620) *plague*

בִּפְקֹד אֹתָם v.supra-v.supra *when you number them*

30:13

זֶה יִתְּנוּ demons. adj. (260)-Qal impf. 3 m.p. (נָתַן 678) *shall give this*

כָּל־הָעֹבֵר n.m.s. cstr. (481)-def.art.-Qal act. ptc. (עָבַר 716) *each who is numbered (passes over)*

עַל־הַפְּקֻדִים prep.-def.art.-Qal pass. ptc. m.p. (פָּקַד 823) *in the census*

מַחֲצִית הַשֶּׁקֶל n.f.s. cstr. (345)-def.art.-n.m.s. (1053) *half a shekel*

בְּשֶׁקֶל הַקֹּדֶשׁ prep.-n.m.s. cstr. (1053) - def.art.-n.m.s. (871) *according to the shekel of the sanctuary*

עֶשְׂרִים גֵּרָה num. p. (797)-n.f.s. (II 176) *twenty gerahs*

הַשֶּׁקֶל v.supra *the shekel*

מַחֲצִית הַשֶּׁקֶל v.supra-v.supra *half a shekel*

תְּרוּמָה n.f.s. (929) *as an offering*

לַיהוה prep.-pr.n. (217) *to Yahweh*

30:14

כֹּל הָעֹבֵר n.m.s. cstr. (481)-def.art.-Qal act. ptc. (עָבַר 716) *every one who is numbered*

עַל־הַפְּקֻדִים prep.-def.art.-Qal pass. ptc. m.p. (פָּקַד 823) *in the census*

מִבֶּן prep.-n.m.s. cstr. (119) *from ... old*

עֶשְׂרִים שָׁנָה num. p. (797)-n.f.s. (1040) *twenty years*

וָמָעְלָה conj.-adv.-loc. he paus. (751; 2) *and upward*

יִתֵּן Qal impf. 3 m.s. (נָתַן 678) *shall give*

תְּרוּמַת יהוה n.f.s. cstr. (929)-pr.n. (217) *Yahweh's offering*

30:15

הֶעָשִׁיר def.art.-n.m.s. (799) *the rich*

לֹא־יַרְבֶּה neg.-Hi. impf. 3 m.s. (רָבָה I 915) *shall not give more*

וְהַדַּל conj.-def.art.-n.m.s. (195) *and the poor*

לֹא יַמְעִיט neg.-Hi. impf. 3 m.s. (מָעַט 589) *shall not give less*

מִמַּחֲצִית הַשָּׁקֶל prep.-n.f.s. cstr. (345) - def.art.-n.m.s. paus. (1053) *than the half shekel*

לָתֵת prep.-Qal inf. cstr. (נָתַן 678) *when you give*

אֶת־תְּרוּמַת יהוה dir.obj.-n.f.s. cstr. (929)-pr.n. (217) *Yahweh's offering*

לְכַפֵּר prep.-Pi. inf. cstr. (כָּפַר 497) *to make atonement*

עַל־נַפְשֹׁתֵיכֶם prep.-n.f.p.-2 m.p. sf. (659) *for yourselves*

30:16

וְלָקַחְתָּ conj.-Qal pf. 2 m.s. (לָקַח 542) *and you shall take*

אֶת־כֶּסֶף dir.obj.-n.m.s. cstr. (494) *the money of*

הַכִּפֻּרִים def.art.-n.m.p. (498) *the atonement*

מֵאֵת בְּנֵי יִשְׂרָאֵל prep.-prep. (II 85)-n.m.p. cstr. (119)-pr.n. (975) *from the people of Israel*

וְנָתַתָּ אֹתוֹ conj.-Qal pf. 2 m.s. (נָתַן 678)-dir.obj.-3 m.s. sf. *and shall appoint it*

עַל־עֲבֹדַת prep.-n.f.s. cstr. (715) *for the service of*

אֹהֶל מוֹעֵד n.m.s. cstr. (13)-n.m.s. (417) *the tent of meeting*

וְהָיָה conj.-Qal pf. 3 m.s. (224) *that it may bring*

לִבְנֵי יִשְׂרָאֵל prep.-n.m.p. cstr. (119)-pr.n. (975) *the people of Israel*

לְזִכָּרוֹן prep.-n.m.s. (272) *to remembrance*

לִפְנֵי יהוה prep.-n.m.p. cstr. (815)-pr.n. (217) *before Yahweh*

לְכַפֵּר prep.-Pi. inf. cstr. (497) *so as to make atonement*

עַל־נַפְשֹׁתֵיכֶם prep.-n.f.p.-2 m.p. sf. (659) *for yourselves*

30:17

וַיְדַבֵּר יהוה consec.-Pi. impf. 3 m.s. (180)-pr.n. (217) *then Yahweh said*

אֶל־מֹשֶׁה prep.-pr.n. (602) *to Moses*

לֵּאמֹר prep.-Qal inf. cstr. (55) *(saying)*

30:18

וְעָשִׂיתָ conj.-Qal pf. 2 m.s. (עָשָׂה I 793) *you shall also make*

כִּיּוֹר נְחֹשֶׁת n.m.s. cstr. (468)-n.m.s. (638) *a laver of bronze*

וְכַנּוֹ conj.-n.m.s.-3 m.s. sf. (III 487) *and its base*

נְחֹשֶׁת n.m.s. (638) *bronze*

לְרָחְצָה prep.-Qal inf. cstr. (רָחַץ 934) *for washing*

וְנָתַתָּ אֹתוֹ conj.-Qal pf. 2 m.s. (נָתַן 678)-dir.obj.-3 m.s. sf. *and you shall put it*

בֵּין־אֹהֶל מוֹעֵד prep. (107)-n.m.s. cstr. (13)-n.m.s. (417) *between the tent of meeting*

וּבֵין הַמִּזְבֵּחַ conj.-prep. (107) - def.art.-n.m.s. (258) *and (between) the altar*

וְנָתַתָּ conj.-Qal pf. 2 m.s. (נָתַן 678) *and you shall put*

שָׁמָּה adv.-loc. he (1027) *in it (there)*

מָיִם n.m.p. paus. (565) *water*

30:19

וְרָחֲצוּ conj.-Qal pf. 3 c.p. (934) *and shall wash*

אַהֲרֹן וּבָנָיו pr.n. (14) - conj. - n.m.p. - 3 m.s. sf. (119) *Aaron and his sons*

מִמֶּנּוּ prep.-3 m.s. sf. *with which*

אֶת־יְדֵיהֶם dir.obj.-n.f.p.-3 m.p. sf. (388) *their hands*

וְאֶת־רַגְלֵיהֶם conj.-dir.obj.-n.f.p.-3 m.p. sf. (919) *and their feet*

30:20

בְּבֹאָם prep.-Qal inf. cstr.-3 m.p. sf. (בּוֹא 97) *when they go*

אֶל־אֹהֶל מוֹעֵד prep.-n.m.s. cstr. (13) - n.m.s. (417) *into the tent of meeting*

יִרְחֲצוּ־מַיִם Qal impf. 3 m.p. (רָחַץ 934) - n.m.p. (565) *they shall wash with water*

וְלֹא יָמֻתוּ conj.-neg.-Qal impf. 3 m.p. (מוּת 559) *lest they die (and they shall not die)*

אוֹ בְגִשְׁתָּם conj.- (14) - prep.-Qal inf. cstr.-3 m.p. sf. (נָגַשׁ 620) *or when they come near*

אֶל־הַמִּזְבֵּחַ prep.-def.art.-n.m.s. (258) *the altar*

לְשָׁרֵת prep.-Pi. inf. cstr. (שָׁרַת 1058) *to minister*

לְהַקְטִיר prep.-Hi. inf. cstr. (קָטַר 882) *to burn*

אִשֶּׁה n.m.s. (77) *an offering by fire*

ליהוה prep.-pr.n. (217) *to Yahweh*

30:21

וְרָחֲצוּ conj.-Qal pf. 3 c.p. (רָחַץ 934) *and they shall wash*

יְדֵיהֶם n.f.p.-3 m.p. sf. (388) *their hands*

וְרַגְלֵיהֶם conj.-n.f.p.-3 m.p. sf. (919) *and their feet*

וְלֹא יָמֻתוּ conj.-neg.-Qal impf. 3 m.p. (מוּת 559) *lest they die*

וְהָיְתָה conj.-Qal pf. 3 f.s. (הָיָה 224) *and it shall be*

לָהֶם prep.-3 m.p. sf. *to them*

חָק־עוֹלָם n.m.s. cstr. (349) - n.m.s. (761) *a statute for ever*

לוֹ prep.-3 m.s. sf. *even to him*

וּלְזַרְעוֹ conj.-prep.-n.m.s.-3 m.s. sf. (282) *and to his descendants*

לְדֹרֹתָם prep.-n.m.p.-3 m.p. sf. (189) *throughout their generations*

30:22

וַיְדַבֵּר יהוה consec.-Pi. impf. 3 m.s. (180) - pr.n. (217) *moreover Yahweh said*

אֶל־מֹשֶׁה prep.- pr.n. (602) *to Moses*

לֵאמֹר prep.-Qal inf. cstr. (55) *(saying)*

30:23

וְאַתָּה conj.-pers.pr. 2 m.s. (61) *(and you)*

קַח־לְךָ Qal impv. 2 m.s. (לָקַח 542) - prep.-2 m.s. sf. *take*

בְּשָׂמִים n.m.p. (141) *spices*

רֹאשׁ n.m.s. (910; 5) *finest*

מָר־דְּרוֹר n.m.s. cstr. (600) - n.m.s. (I 204) *of liquid myrrh*

חֲמֵשׁ מֵאוֹת num. m. cstr. (331) - n.f.p. (547) *five hundred*

וְקִנְּמָן־בֶּשֶׂם conj.-n.m.s. cstr. (890) - n.m.s. (141) *of sweet-smelling cinnamon*

מַחֲצִיתוֹ n.f.s.-3 m.s. sf. (345) *half as much*

חֲמִשִּׁים וּמָאתָיִם num. p. (332) - conj.-n.f.du. paus. (547) *two hundred and fifty*

וּקְנֵה־בֹשֶׂם conj.-n.m.s. cstr. (889) - n.m.s. (141) *and of aromatic cane*

חֲמִשִּׁים וּמָאתָיִם num. p. (332) - conj.-n.f.du. paus. (547) *two hundred and fifty*

30:24

וְקִדָּה conj.-n.f.s. (869) *and of acacia*

חֲמֵשׁ מֵאוֹת num. m. cstr. (331) - n.f.p. (547) *five hundred*

בְּשֶׁקֶל הַקֹּדֶשׁ prep.-n.m.s. cstr. (1053) - def.art.-n.m.s. (871) *according to the shekel of the sanctuary*

וְשֶׁמֶן זַיִת conj.-n.m.s. cstr. (1032)-n.m.s. (268) *and of olive oil*

הִין n.m.s. (228) *a hin*

30:25

וְעָשִׂיתָ conj.-Qal pf. 2 m.s. (עָשָׂה I 793) *and you shall make*

אֹתוֹ dir.obj.-3 m.s. sf. *of these*

שֶׁמֶן מִשְׁחַת־קֹדֶשׁ n.m.s. cstr. (1032) - n.f.s. cstr. (603) - n.m.s. (871) *a sacred anointing oil*

רֹקַח מִרְקַחַת n.m.s. cstr. (955) - n.f.s. (955) *blended (perfume of an ointment-pot)*

מַעֲשֵׂה רֹקֵחַ n.m.s. cstr. (795) - Qal act. ptc. (רָקַח 955) *as by the perfumer*

שֶׁמֶן מִשְׁחַת־קֹדֶשׁ v.supra - v.supra v.supra *a holy anointing oil*

יִהְיֶה Qal impf. 3 m.s. (הָיָה 224) *it shall be*

30:26

וּמָשַׁחְתָּ conj.-Qal pf. 2 m.s. (מָשַׁח 602) *and you shall anoint*

בוֹ prep.-3 m.s. sf. *with it*

אֶת־אֹהֶל מוֹעֵד dir.obj.-n.m.s. cstr. (13) - n.m.s. (417) *the tent of meeting*

וְאֵת אֲרוֹן הָעֵדֻת conj.-dir.obj.-n.m.s. cstr. (75) - def.art.-n.f.s. (730) *and the ark of the testimony*

30:27

וְאֶת־הַשֻּׁלְחָן conj.-dir.obj.-def.art.-n.m.s. (1020) *and the table*

וְאֶת־כָּל־כֵּלָיו conj.-dir.obj.-n.m.s. cstr. (481) - n.m.p.-3 m.s. sf. (479) *and all its utensils*

וְאֶת־הַמְּנֹרָה conj.-dir.obj.-def.art.-n.f.s. (633) *and the lampstand*

וְאֶת־כֵּלֶיהָ conj.-dir.obj.-n.m.p.-3 f.s. sf. (479) *and its utensils*

וְאֵת מִזְבַּח הַקְּטֹרֶת conj.-dir.obj.-n.m.s. cstr. (258) - def.art.-n.f.s. (882) *and the altar of incense*

30:28

וְאֶת־מִזְבַּח הָעֹלָה conj.-dir.obj.-n.m.s. cstr. (258) - def.art.-n.f.s. (750) *and the altar of burnt offering*

וְאֶת־כָּל־כֵּלָיו conj.-dir.obj.-n.m.s. cstr. (481) - n.m.p.-3 m.s. sf. (479) *with all its utensils*

וְאֶת־הַכִּיֹּר conj.-dir.obj.-def.art.-n.m.s. (468) *and the laver*

וְאֶת־כַּנּוֹ conj.-dir.obj.-n.m.s.-3 m.s. sf. (III 487) *and its base*

30:29

וְקִדַּשְׁתָּ conj.-Pi. pf. 2 m.s. (קָדַשׁ 872) *and you shall consecrate*

אֹתָם dir.obj.-3 m.p. sf. *them*

וְהָיוּ conj.-Qal pf. 3 c.p. (הָיָה 224) *that they may be*

קֹדֶשׁ קָדָשִׁים n.m.s. cstr. (871) - n.m.p. (871) *most holy*

כָּל־הַנֹּגֵעַ n.m.s. cstr. (481) - def.art.-Qal act. ptc. (נָגַע 619) *whatever touches*

בָּהֶם prep.-3 m.p. sf. *them*

יִקְדָּשׁ Qal impf. 3 m.s. (קָדַשׁ 872) *will become holy*

30:30

וְאֶת־אַהֲרֹן conj.-dir.obj.-pr.n. (14) *and Aaron*

וְאֶת־בָּנָיו conj.-dir.obj.-n.m.p.-3 m.s. sf. (119) *and his sons*

תִּמְשָׁח Qal impf. 2 m.s. paus. (מָשַׁח 602) *you shall anoint*

וְקִדַּשְׁתָּ conj.-Pi. pf. 2 m.s. (קָדַשׁ 872) *and consecrate*

אֹתָם dir.obj.-3 m.p. sf. *them*

לְכַהֵן לִי prep.-Pi. inf. cstr. (כָּהַן II 464) - prep.-1 c.s. sf. *that they may serve me as priests*

30:31

וְאֶל־בְּנֵי יִשְׂרָאֵל conj.-prep.-n.m.p. cstr. (119) - pr.n. (975) *and to the people of Israel*

תְּדַבֵּר Pi. impf. 2 m.s. (180) *you shall say*

לֵאמֹר prep.-Qal inf. cstr. (55) *(saying)*

שֶׁמֶן n.m.s. cstr. (1032) *an oil of*

מִשְׁחַת־קֹדֶשׁ n.f.s. cstr. (603) - n.m.s. (871) *holy anointing*

יִהְיֶה זֶה לִי Qal impf. 3 m.s. (הָיָה 224) - demons. (260) - prep.-1 c.s. sf. *this shall be to me*

לְדֹרֹתֵיכֶם prep.-n.m.p.-2 m.p. sf. (189) *throughout your generations*

30:32

עַל־בְּשַׂר prep.-n.m.s. cstr. (142) *upon the bodies of*

אָדָם n.m.s. (9) *ordinary men*

לֹא יִיסָךְ neg.-Qal impf. 3 m.s. paus. (414; but rd. from סוּךְ I 691) *it shall not be poured*

וּבְמַתְכֻּנְתּוֹ conj.-prep.-n.f.s.-3 m.s. sf. (1067) *in composition*

לֹא תַעֲשׂוּ neg.-Qal impf. 2 m.p. (עָשָׂה I 793) *you shall not make*

כָּמֹהוּ prep.-3 m.s. sf. *like it*

קֹדֶשׁ הוּא n.m.s. (871) - pers. pr. 3 m.s. (214) *it is holy*

קֹדֶשׁ יִהְיֶה v.supra - Qal impf. 3 m.s. (הָיָה 224) *and it shall be holy*

לָכֶם prep.-2 m.p. sf. *to you*

30:33

אִישׁ אֲשֶׁר n.m.s. (35) - rel. *whoever*

יִרְקַח Qal impf. 3 m.s. (רָקַח 955) *compounds*

כָּמֹהוּ prep.-3 m.s. sf. *any like it*

וַאֲשֶׁר יִתֵּן conj.-rel.-Qal impf. 3 m.s. (נָתַן 678) *or whoever puts*

מִמֶּנּוּ prep.-3 m.s. sf. *any of it*

עַל־זָר prep.-Qal act. ptc. (זוּר I 266) *on an outsider*

וְנִכְרַת conj.-Ni. pf. 3 m.s. (כָּרַת 503) *shall be cut off*

מֵעַמָּיו prep.-n.m.p.-3 m.s. sf. (I 766) *from his people*

30:34

וַיֹּאמֶר יהוה consec.-Qal impf. 3 m.s. (55) - pr.n. (217) *and Yahweh said*

אֶל־מֹשֶׁה prep. - pr.n. (602) *to Moses*

קַח־לְךָ Qal impv. 2 m.s. (לָקַח 542) - prep.-2 m.s. sf. *take*

סַמִּים n.m.p. (702) *sweet spices*

נָטָף n.m.s. (II 643) *stacte*

וּשְׁחֵלֶת conj.-n.f.s. (1006) *and onycha*

וְחֶלְבְּנָה conj.-n.f.s. (317) *and galbanum*

סַמִּים v.supra *sweet spices*

וּלְבֹנָה זַכָּה conj.-n.f.s. (526) - adj. f.s. (269) *with pure frankincense*

בַּד בְּבַד n.m.s. (II 94; 2) - prep.-v.supra *part for part*

יִהְיֶה Qal impf. 3 m.s. (הָיָה 224) *shall there be*

30:35

וְעָשִׂיתָ אֹתָהּ conj.-Qal pf. 2 m.s. (עָשָׂה I 793) - dir.obj.-3 f.s. sf. *and make (it)*

קְטֹרֶת n.f.s. (882) *an incense*

רֹקַח מַעֲשֵׂה n.m.s. cstr. (955) - n.m.s. cstr. (795) *blended as by*

רוֹקֵחַ Qal act. ptc. (רָקַח 955) *a perfumer*

מְמֻלָּח Pu. ptc. (מָלַח III 572) *seasoned with salt*

טָהוֹר adj. (373) *pure*

קֹדֶשׁ n.m.s. (871) *holy*

30:36

וְשָׁחַקְתָּ conj.-Qal pf. 2 m.s. (שָׁחַק 1006) *and you shall beat*

מִמֶּנָּה prep.-3 f.s. sf. *some of it*

הָדֵק Hi. inf. abs. (דָּקַק 200) *very small*

וְנָתַתָּה conj.-Qal pf. 2 m.s. (נָתַן 678) *and put*

מִמֶּנָּה v.supra *part of it*

לִפְנֵי הָעֵדֻת prep.-n.m.p. cstr. (815) - def.art.-n.f.s. (730) *before the testimony*

בְּאֹהֶל מוֹעֵד prep.-n.m.s. cstr. (13) - n.m.s. (417) *in the tent of meeting*

אֲשֶׁר אִוָּעֵד rel.-Ni. impf. 1 c.s. (יָעַד 416) *where I shall meet*

לְךָ שָׁמָּה prep.-2 m.s. sf.-adv.-loc. he (1027) *with you (there)*

קֹדֶשׁ קָדָשִׁים n.m.s. cstr. (871) - n.m.p. (871) *most holy*

תִּהְיֶה לָכֶם Qal impf. 3 f.s. (הָיָה 224) - prep.-2 m.p. sf. *it shall be for you*

30:37

וְהַקְּטֹרֶת conj.-def.art.-n.f.s. (882) *and the incense*

אֲשֶׁר תַּעֲשֶׂה rel.-Qal impf. 2 m.s. (עָשָׂה I 793) *which you shall make*

בְּמַתְכֻּנְתָּהּ prep.-n.f.s.-3 f.s. sf. (1067) *according to its composition*

לֹא תַעֲשׂוּ neg.-Qal impf. 2 m.p. (עָשָׂה I 793) *you shall not make*

לָכֶם prep.-2 m.p. sf. *for yourselves*

קֹדֶשׁ תִּהְיֶה n.m.s. (871) - Qal impf. 3 f.s. (הָיָה 224) *it shall be holy*

לְךָ prep.-2 m.s. sf. *for you*

ליהוה prep.-pr.n. (217) *to Yahweh*

30:38

אִישׁ אֲשֶׁר־ n.m.s. (35) - rel. *whoever*

יַעֲשֶׂה Qal impf. 3 m.s. (עָשָׂה I 793) *makes*

כָמוֹהָ prep.-3 f.s. sf. *any like it*

לְהָרִיחַ prep.-Hi. inf. cstr. (רִיחַ 926) *to use as perfume*

בָהּ prep.-3 f.s. sf. *it*

וְנִכְרַת conj.-Ni. pf. 3 m.s. (כָּרַת 503) *shall be cut off*

מֵעַמָּיו prep.-n.m.p.-3 m.s. sf. (I 766) *from his people*

31:1

וַיְדַבֵּר יהוה consec.-Pi. impf. 3 m.s. (180)-pr.n. (217) *then Yahweh said*

אֶל־מֹשֶׁה prep.-pr.n. (602) *to Moses*

לֵּאמֹר prep.-Qal inf. cstr. (55) *(saying)*

31:2

רְאֵה Qal impv. 2 m.s. (רָאָה 906) *see*

קָרָאתִי Qal pf. 1 c.s. (קָרָא 894) *I have called*

בְשֵׁם prep.-n.m.s. (1027) *by name*

בְּצַלְאֵל pr.n. (130) *Bezalel*

בֶּן־אוּרִי n.m.s. cstr. (119)-pr.n. (22) *son of Uri*

בֶן־חוּר n.m.s. cstr. (119)-pr.n. (II 301) *son of Hur*

לְמַטֵּה יְהוּדָה prep.-n.m.s. cstr. (641)-pr.n. (397) *of the tribe of Judah*

31:3

וָאֲמַלֵּא אֹתוֹ consec.-Pi. impf. 1 c.s. (מָלֵא 569)-dir.obj.-3 m.s. sf. *and I have filled him*

רוּחַ אֱלֹהִים n.f.s. cstr. (924)-n.m.p. (43) *the Spirit of God*

בְּחָכְמָה prep.-n.f.s. (315) *with ability*

וּבִתְבוּנָה conj.-prep.-n.f.s. (108) *and (with) intelligence*

וּבְדַעַת conj.-prep.-n.f.s. (395) *and with knowledge*

וּבְכָל־מְלָאכָה conj.-prep.-n.m.s. cstr. (481)-n.f.s. (521) *and all craftmanship*

31:4

לַחְשֹׁב prep.-Qal inf. cstr. (חָשַׁב 362) *to devise*

מַחֲשָׁבֹת n.f.p. (364) *artistic designs*

לַעֲשׂוֹת prep.-Qal inf. cstr. (עָשָׂה I 793) *to work*

בַּזָּהָב prep.-def.art.-n.m.s. (262) *in gold*

וּבַכֶּסֶף conj.-prep.-def.art.-n.m.s. (494) *and in silver*

וּבַנְּחֹשֶׁת conj.-prep.-def.art.-n.m.s. (638) *and in bronze*

31:5

וּבַחֲרֹשֶׁת conj.-prep.-n.f.s. cstr. (I 360) *and in cutting*

אֶבֶן n.f.s. (6) *stones*

לְמַלֹּאת prep.-Pi. inf. cstr. (מָלֵא 569) *for setting*

וּבַחֲרֹשֶׁת v.supra-v.supra *and in carving*

עֵץ n.m.s. (781) *wood*

לַעֲשׂוֹת prep.-Qal inf. cstr. (עָשָׂה I 793) *for work*

בְּכָל־מְלָאכָה prep.-n.m.s. cstr. (481)-n.f.s. (521) *in every craft*

31:6

וַאֲנִי הִנֵּה conj.-pers.pr. 1 c.s. (58)-demons. part. (243) *and behold I*

נָתַתִּי אִתּוֹ Qal pf. 1 c.s. (נָתַן 678)-prep.-3 m.s. sf. (II 85) *I have appointed with him*

אֵת אָהֳלִיאָב dir.obj.-pr.n. (14) *Oholiab*

בֶּן־אֲחִיסָמָךְ n.m.s. cstr. (119)-pr.n. (27) *the son of Ahisamach*

לְמַטֵּה־דָן prep.-n.m.s. cstr. (641)-pr.n. (192) *of the tribe of Dan*

וּבְלֵב conj.-prep.-n.m.s. cstr. (524) *and in the heart*

כָּל־חֲכַם־לֵב n.m.s. cstr. (481)-adj. m.s. cstr. (314)-n.m.s. (524) *all able men*

נָתַתִּי Qal pf. 1 c.s. (נָתַן 678) *I have given*

חָכְמָה n.f.s. (315) *ability*

וְעָשׂוּ conj.-Qal pf. 3 c.p. (עָשָׂה I 793) *that they may make*

אֵת כָּל־אֲשֶׁר צִוִּיתִךָ dir.obj.-n.m.s.-rel.-Pi. pf. 1 c.s.-2 m.s. sf. (צָוָה 845) *all that I have commanded you*

31:7

אֵת אֹהֶל מוֹעֵד dir.obj.-n.m.s. cstr. (13)-n.m.s. (417) *the tent of meeting*

וְאֶת־הָאָרֹן conj.-dir.obj.-def.art.-n.m.s. (75) *and the ark*

לָעֵדֻת prep.-def.art.-n.f.s. (730) *of the testimony*

וְאֶת־הַכַּפֹּרֶת conj.-dir.obj.-def.art.-n.f.s. (498) *and the mercy seat*

אֲשֶׁר עָלָיו rel.-prep.-3 m.s. sf. *that is thereon*

וְאֵת כָּל־כְּלֵי conj.-dir.obj.-n.m.s. cstr. (481)-n.m.p. cstr. (479) *and all the furnishings of*

הָאֹהֶל def.art.-n.m.s. (13) *the tent*

31:8

וְאֶת־הַשֻּׁלְחָן conj.-dir.obj.-def.art.-n.m.s. (1020) *and the table*

וְאֶת־כֵּלָיו conj.-dir.obj.-n.m.p.-3 m.s. sf. (479) *and its utensils*

וְאֶת־הַמְּנֹרָה conj.-dir.obj.-def.art.-n.f.s. (633) *and the ... lampstand*

הַטְּהֹרָה def.art.-adj. f.s. (373) *pure*

וְאֶת־כָּל־כֵּלֶיהָ conj.-dir.obj.-n.m.s. cstr. (481)-n.m.p.-3 f.s. sf. (479) *with all its utensils*

וְאֵת מִזְבַּח conj.-dir.obj.-n.m.s. cstr. (258) *and the altar of*

הַקְּטֹרֶת def.art.-n.f.s. (882) *incense*

31:9

וְאֶת־מִזְבַּח conj.-dir. obj.-n.m.s. cstr. (258) *and the altar of*

הָעֹלָה def.art.-n.f.s. (750) *burnt offering*

וְאֶת־כָּל־כֵּלָיו conj.-dir.obj.-n.m.s. cstr. (481) - n.m.p.-3 m.s. sf. (479) *with all its utensils*

וְאֶת־הַכִּיּוֹר conj.-dir.obj.-def.art.-n.m.s. (468) *and the laver*

וְאֶת־כַּנּוֹ conj.-dir.obj.-n.m.s.-3 m.s. sf. (III 487) *and its base*

31:10

וְאֵת בִּגְדֵי conj.-dir.obj.-n.m.p. cstr. (93) *and the garments (of)*

הַשְּׂרָד def.art.-n.m.s. (975) *finely worked*

וְאֶת־בִּגְדֵי הַקֹּדֶשׁ conj.-dir.obj.-n.m.p. cstr. (93)-def.art.-n.m.s. (871) *and the holy garments*

לְאַהֲרֹן prep.-pr.n. (14) *for Aaron*

הַכֹּהֵן def.art.-n.m.s. (463) *the priest*

וְאֶת־בִּגְדֵי v. supra-v. supra *and the garments of*

בָנָיו n.m.p.-3 m.s. sf. (119) *his sons*

לְכַהֵן prep.-Pi. inf. cstr. (כָּהַן 464) *for their service as priests*

31:11

וְאֵת שֶׁמֶן הַמִּשְׁחָה conj.-dir.obj.-n.m.s. cstr. (1032)-def.art.-n.f.s. (603) *and the anointing oil*

וְאֶת־קְטֹרֶת הַסַּמִּים conj.-dir.obj.-n.f.s. cstr. (882)-def.art.-n.m.p. (702) *and the fragrant incense*

לַקֹּדֶשׁ prep.-def.art.-n.m.s. (871) *for the holy place*

כְּכֹל אֲשֶׁר־ prep.-n.m.s. (481)-rel. *according to all that*

צִוִּיתִךָ Pi. pf. 1 c.s.-2 m.s. sf. (צָוָה 845) *I have commanded you*

יַעֲשׂוּ Qal impf. 3 m.p. (עָשָׂה I 793) *(they) shall do*

31:12

וַיֹּאמֶר יהוה consec.-Qal impf. 3 m.s. (55)-pr.n. (217) *and Yahweh said*

אֶל־מֹשֶׁה prep.-pr.n. (602) *to Moses*

לֵּאמֹר prep.-Qal inf. cstr. (55) *(saying)*

31:13

וְאַתָּה conj.-pers.pr. 2 m.s. (61) *(and you)*

דַּבֵּר Pi. impv. 2 m.s. (180) *say*

אֶל־בְּנֵי יִשְׂרָאֵל prep.-n.m.p. cstr. (119)-pr.n. (975) *to the people of Israel*

לֵאמֹר prep.-Qal inf. cstr. (55) *(saying)*

אַךְ אֶת־שַׁבְּתֹתַי adv. (36)-dir.obj.-n.f.p.-1 c.s. sf. (992) *surely my sabbaths*

תִּשְׁמֹרוּ Qal impf. 2 m.p. (שָׁמַר 1036) *you shall keep*

כִּי אוֹת הִוא conj.-n.m.s. (16)-pers.pr. 3 f.s. (214) *for this is a sign*

בֵּינִי וּבֵינֵיכֶם prep.-1 c.s. sf. (107)-conj.-prep.-2 m.p. sf. (107) *between me and you*

לְדֹרֹתֵיכֶם prep.-n.m.p.-2 m.p. sf. (189) *throughout your generations*

לָדַעַת prep.-Qal inf. cstr. (יָדַע 393) *that you may know*

כִּי אֲנִי conj.-pers.pr. 1 c.s. (58) *that I*

יהוה pr.n. (217) *Yahweh*

מְקַדִּשְׁכֶם Pi. ptc.-2 m.p. sf. (קָדַשׁ 872) *sanctify you*

31:14

וּשְׁמַרְתֶּם conj.-Qal pf. 2 m.p. (שָׁמַר 1036) *you shall keep*

אֶת־הַשַּׁבָּת dir.obj.-def.art.-n.f.s. (992) *the sabbath*

כִּי קֹדֶשׁ הוּא conj.-n.m.s. (871)-pers.pr. 3 m.s. (214) *because it is holy*

לָכֶם prep.-2 m.p. sf. *for you*

מְחַלְלֶיהָ Pi. ptc. m.p.-3 f.s. sf. (חָלַל III 320) *every one who profanes it*

מוֹת יוּמָת Qal inf. abs. (559)-Ho. impf. 3 m.s. paus. (מוּת 559) *shall be put to death*

כִּי כָּל־הָעֹשֶׂה conj.-n.m.s. cstr. (481)-def.art.-Qal act. ptc. (עָשָׂה I 793) *whoever does*

בָהּ מְלָאכָה prep.-3 f.s. sf.-n.f.s. (521) *in it any work*

וְנִכְרְתָה conj.-Ni. pf. 3 f.s. (כָּרַת 503) *shall be cut off*

הַנֶּפֶשׁ הַהִוא def.art.-n.f.s. (659)-def.art.-demons. adj. f.s. (214) *that soul*

מִקֶּרֶב עַמֶּיהָ prep.-n.m.s. cstr. (899)-n.m.p.-3 f.s. sf. (I 766) *from its people*

31:15

שֵׁשֶׁת יָמִים num. f.s. cstr. (995)-n.m.p. (398) *six days*

יֵעָשֶׂה Ni. impf. 3 m.s. (עָשָׂה I 793) *shall be done*

מְלָאכָה n.f.s. (521) *work*

וּבַיּוֹם הַשְּׁבִיעִי conj.-prep.-def.art.-n.m.s. (398)-def.art.-num. adj. m.s. (988) *but the seventh day*

שַׁבַּת שַׁבָּתוֹן n.f.s. cstr. (992)-n.m.s. (992) *a sabbath of solemn rest*

קֹדֶשׁ ליהוה n.m.s. (871)-prep.-pr.n. (217) *holy to Yahweh*

כָּל־הָעֹשֶׂה n.m.s. cstr. (481)-def.art.-Qal act. ptc. (עָשָׂה I 793) *whoever does*

מְלָאכָה n.f.s. (521) *any work*

בְּיוֹם הַשַּׁבָּת prep.-n.m.s. cstr. (398)-def.art.-n.f.s. (992) *on the sabbath day*

מוֹת יוּמָת Qal inf. abs. (559)-Ho. impf. 3 m.s. (מוּת 559) *shall be put to death*

31:16

וְשָׁמְרוּ conj.-Qal pf. 3 c.p. (שָׁמַר 1036) *wherefore ... shall keep*

בְנֵי־יִשְׂרָאֵל n.m.p. cstr. (119)-pr.n. (975) *the people of Israel*

אֶת־הַשַּׁבָּת dir.obj.-def.art.-n.f.s. (992) *the sabbath*

לַעֲשׂוֹת prep.-Qal inf. cstr. (עָשָׂה I 793) *observing*

אֶת־הַשַּׁבָּת v. supra *the sabbath*

לְדֹרֹתָם prep.-n.m.p.-3 m.p. sf. (189) *throughout their generations*

בְּרִית עוֹלָם n.f.s. cstr. (136)-n.m.s. (761) *as a perpetual covenant*

31:17

בֵּינִי וּבֵין prep.-1 c.s. sf. (107) - conj.-prep. (107) *between me and (between)*

בְּנֵי יִשְׂרָאֵל n.m.p. cstr. (119) - pr.n. (975) *the people of Israel*

אוֹת הִוא n.m.s. (16) - pers.pr. 3 f.s. (214) *it is a sign*

לְעֹלָם prep.-n.m.s. (761) *for ever*

כִּי־שֵׁשֶׁת יָמִים conj.-num. f.s. cstr. (995) - n.m.p. (398) *that in six days*

עָשָׂה יהוה Qal pf. 3 m.s. (I 793) - pr.n. (217) *Yahweh made*

אֶת־הַשָּׁמַיִם dir.obj.-def.art.-n.m. du. (1029) *heaven*

וְאֶת־הָאָרֶץ conj.-dir.obj.-def.art.-n.f.s. (75) *and earth*

וּבַיּוֹם הַשְּׁבִיעִי conj.-prep.-def.art.-n.m.s. (398) - def.art.-num. adj. m. (988) *and on the seventh day*

שָׁבַת Qal pf. 3 m.s. (991) *he rested*

וַיִּנָּפַשׁ consec.-Ni. impf. 3 m.s. (נָפַשׁ 661) *and was refreshed*

31:18

וַיִּתֵּן consec.-Qal impf. 3 m.s. (נָתַן 678) *and he gave*

אֶל־מֹשֶׁה prep.-pr.n. (602) *to Moses*

כְּכַלֹּתוֹ prep.-Pi. inf. cstr.- 3 m.s. sf. (כָּלָה 477) *when he had made an end*

לְדַבֵּר אִתּוֹ prep.-Pi. inf. cstr. (180) - prep.-3 m.s. sf. (II 85) *of speaking with him*

בְּהַר סִינַי prep.-n.m.s. cstr. (249) - pr.n. (696) *upon Mount Sinai*

שְׁנֵי לֻחֹת num. m. du. cstr. (1040) - n.m.p. cstr. (531) *the two tables of*

הָעֵדֻת def.art.-n.f.s. (730) *the testimony*

לֻחֹת אֶבֶן n.m.p. cstr. (531) - n.f.s. (6) *tables of stone*

כְּתֻבִים Qal pass. ptc. m.p. (כָּתַב 507) *written*

בְּאֶצְבַּע אֱלֹהִים prep.-n.f.s. cstr. (840) - n.m.p. (43) *with the finger of God*

32:1

וַיַּרְא הָעָם consec. - Qal impf. 3 m.s. (רָאָה 906) - def.art.-n.m.s. (I 766) *when the people saw*

כִּי־בֹשֵׁשׁ conj. - Polel pf. 3 m.s. (בּוֹשׁ 101) *that ... delayed (in shame)*

מֹשֶׁה pr.n. (602) *Moses*

לָרֶדֶת prep.-Qal inf. cstr. (יָרַד 432) *to come down*

מִן־הָהָר prep.-def.art.-n.m.s. (249) *from the mountains*

וַיִּקָּהֵל consec.-Ni. impf. 3 m.s. (קָהַל 874) *and ... gathered themselves*

הָעָם def.art.-n.m.s. (I 766) *the people*

עַל־אַהֲרֹן prep.-pr.n. (14) *to Aaron*

וַיֹּאמְרוּ אֵלָיו consec.-Qal impf. 3 m.s. (55)-prep.-3 m.s. sf. *and said to him*

קוּם Qal impv. 2 m.s. (קוּם 877) *up*

עֲשֵׂה־לָנוּ Qal impv. 2 m.s. (עָשָׂה I 793)-prep.-1 c.p. sf. *make us*

אֱלֹהִים n.m.p. (43) *gods*

אֲשֶׁר יֵלְכוּ rel.-Qal impf. 3 m.p. (הָלַךְ 229) *who shall go*

לְפָנֵינוּ prep.-n.m.p.1 c.p. sf. (815) *before us*

כִּי־זֶה מֹשֶׁה conj.-demons. adj. (260)-pr.n. (602) *as for this Moses*

הָאִישׁ אֲשֶׁר הֶעֱלָנוּ def.art.-n.m.s. (35) - rel. - Hi. pf. 3 m.s.-1 c.p. sf. (עָלָה 748) *the man who brought us up*

מֵאֶרֶץ מִצְרַיִם prep.-n.f.s. cstr. (75)-pr.n. (595) *out of the land of Egypt*

לֹא יָדַעְנוּ neg.-Qal pf. 1 c.p. (יָדַע 393) *we do not know*

מֶה־הָיָה לוֹ interr. (552) - Qal pf. 3 m.s. (224) - prep.-3 m.s. sf. *what has become of him*

32:2

וַיֹּאמֶר אֲלֵהֶם consec.-Qal impf. 3 m.s. (55)prep.3 m.p. sf. *and ... said to them*

אַהֲרֹן pr.n. (14) *Aaron*

פָּרְקוּ Pi. impv. 2 m.p. (פָּרַק 830) *take off*

נִזְמֵי הַזָּהָב n.m.p. cstr. (633)-def.art.-n.m.s. (262) *the rings of gold*

אֲשֶׁר בְּאָזְנֵי rel.-prep.-n.f.p. cstr. (23) *which are in the ears of*

נְשֵׁיכֶם n.f.p.-2 m.p. sf. (אִשָּׁה 61) *your wives*

בְּנֵיכֶם n.m.p.-2 m.p. sf. (119) *your sons*

וּבְנֹתֵיכֶם conj.-n.f.p.-2 m.p. sf. (I 123) *and your daughters*

וְהָבִיאוּ אֵלָי conj.-Hi. impv. 2 m. p. (בּוֹא 97) - prep.-1 c.s. sf. paus. *and bring them to me*

32:3

וַיִּתְפָּרְקוּ consec.-Hith. impf. 3 m.p. (פָּרַק 830) *so ... took of*

כָּל־הָעָם n.m.s. cstr. (481) - def.art.-n.m.s. (I 766) *all the people*

אֶת־נִזְמֵי הַזָּהָב dir.obj.-n.m.p. cstr. (633)-def.art.-n.m.s. (262) *the rings of gold*

אֲשֶׁר בְּאָזְנֵיהֶם rel.-prep.-n.f.p.-3 m.p. sf. (23) *which were in their ears*

וַיָּבִיאוּ consec.-Hi. impf. 3 m.p. (בּוֹא 97) *and brought*

אֶל־אַהֲרֹן prep.-pr.n. (14) *to Aaron*

32:4

וַיִּקַּח consec.-Qal impf. 3 m.s. (לָקַח 542) *and he received*

מִיָּדָם prep.-n.f.s.-3 m.p. sf. (388) *at their hand*

וַיָּצַר אֹתוֹ consec.-Qal impf. 3 m. s. (צוּר IV 849) - dir.obj.-3 m.s. sf. *and fashioned it*

בַּחֶרֶט prep.-def.art.-n.m.s. (354) *with a graving tool*

וַיַּעֲשֵׂהוּ consec.-Qal impf. 3 m.s.-3 m.s. sf. (עָשָׂה I 793) *and made (it)*

עֵגֶל מַסֵּכָה n.m.s. cstr. (722)-n.f.s. (651) *a molten calf*

וַיֹּאמְרוּ consec.-Qal impf. 3 m.p. (55) *and they said*

אֵלֶּה אֱלֹהֶיךָ demons. adj. c.p. (41)-n.m.p.-2 m.s. sf. (43) *these are your gods*

יִשְׂרָאֵל pr.n. (975) *O Israel*

אֲשֶׁר הֶעֱלוּךָ rel.-Hi. pf. 3 c.p.-2 m.s. sf. (עָלָה 748) *who brought you up*

מֵאֶרֶץ מִצְרָיִם prep.-n.f.s. cstr. (75) - pr.n. paus. (595) *out of the land of Egypt*

32:5

וַיַּרְא אַהֲרֹן consec.-Qal impf. 3 m.s. (רָאָה 906) - pr.n. (14) *when Aaron saw*

וַיִּבֶן consec.-Qal impf. 3 m.s. (בָּנָה 124) *he built*

מִזְבֵּחַ n.m.s. (258) *an altar*

לְפָנָיו prep.-n.m.p.-3 m.s. sf. (815) *before it*

וַיִּקְרָא אַהֲרֹן consec.-Qal impf. 3 m.s. (קָרָא 894)-pr.n. (14) *and Aaron made proclamation*

וַיֹּאמַר consec.-Qal impf. 3 m.s. (55) *and said*

חַג לַיהוה n.m.s. (290)-prep.-pr.n. (217) *a feast to Yahweh*

מָחָר n.m.s. (563) *tomorrow*

32:6

וַיַּשְׁכִּימוּ consec.-Hi. impf. 3 m.p. (שָׁכַם 1014) *and they rose up early*

מִמָּחֳרָת prep.-n.f.s. (564) *on the morrow*

וַיַּעֲלוּ consec.-Qal impf. 3 m.p. (עָלָה 748) *and offered*

עֹלֹת n.f.p. (750) *burnt offerings*

וַיַּגִּשׁוּ consec.-Hi. impf. 3 m.p. (נָגַשׁ 620) *and brought*

שְׁלָמִים n.m.p. (1023) *peace offerings*

וַיֵּשֶׁב הָעָם consec.-Qal impf. 3 m.p. (יָשַׁב 442)-def.art.-n.m.s. (I 766) *and the people sat*

לֶאֱכֹל prep.-Qal inf. cstr. (אָכַל 37) *to eat*

וְשָׁתוֹ conj.-Qal pf. 3 c.p. (שָׁתָה 1059) *and they drank*

וַיָּקֻמוּ consec.-Qal impf. 3 m.p. (קוּם 877) *and rose up*

לְצַחֵק prep.-Pi. inf. cstr. (850) *to play*

32:7

וַיְדַבֵּר יהוה consec.-Pi. impf. 3 m.s. (180)-pr.n. (217) *and Yahweh said*

אֶל־מֹשֶׁה prep.-pr.n. (602) *to Moses*

לֶךְ־רֵד Qal impv. 2 m.s. (הָלַךְ 229)-Qal impv. 2 m.s. (יָרַד 432) *go down*

כִּי שִׁחֵת conj.-Pi. pf. 3 m.s. (שָׁחַת 1007) *for ... have corrupted themselves*

עַמְּךָ n.m.s.-2 m.s. sf. (I 766) *your people*

אֲשֶׁר הֶעֱלֵיתָ rel.-Hi. pf. 2 m.s. (עָלָה 748) *whom you brought up*

מֵאֶרֶץ מִצְרָיִם prep.-n.f.s. cstr. (75)-pr.n. paus. (595) *out of the land of Egypt*

32:8

סָרוּ Qal pf. 3 c.p. (סוּר 693) *they have turned aside*

מַהֵר adv. (II 555) *quickly*

מִן־הַדֶּרֶךְ prep.-def.art.-n.m.s. (202) *out of the way*

אֲשֶׁר צִוִּיתִם rel.-Pi. pf. 1 c.s.-3 m.p. sf. (צָוָה 845) *which I commanded them*

עָשׂוּ לָהֶם Qal pf. 3 c.p. (עָשָׂה I 793)-prep.-3 m.p. sf. *they have made for themselves*

עֵגֶל מַסֵּכָה n.m.s. cstr. (722)n.f.s. (651) *a molten calf*

וַיִּשְׁתַּחֲווּ־לוֹ consec.-Hithpalel impf. 3 m.p. (שָׁחָה 1005) - prep.-3 m.s. sf. *and have worshiped it*

וַיִּזְבְּחוּ־לוֹ consec.-Qal impf. 3 m.p. (זָבַח 256) - prep.-3 m.s. sf. *and sacrificed to it*

וַיֹּאמְרוּ consec.-Qal impf. 3 m.p. (55) *and said*

אֵלֶּה אֱלֹהֶיךָ demons. adj. c.p. (41)-n.m.p.-2 m.s. sf. (43) *these are your gods*

יִשְׂרָאֵל pr.n. (975) *O Israel*

אֲשֶׁר הֶעֱלוּךָ rel.-Hi. pf. 3 c.p.-2 m.s. sf. (עָלָה 748) *who brought you up*

מֵאֶרֶץ מִצְרָיִם prep.-n.f.s. cstr. (75)-pr.n. paus. (595) *out of the land of Egypt*

32:9

וַיֹּאמֶר יהוה consec.-Qal impf. 3 m.s. (55)-pr.n. (217) *and Yahweh said*

אֶל־מֹשֶׁה prep.-pr.n. (602) *to Moses*

רָאִיתִי Qal pf. 1 c.s. (רָאָה 906) *I have seen*

אֶת־הָעָם הַזֶּה dir.obj.-def.art.-n.m.s. (I 766) - def.art.-demons.adj. m.s. (260) *this people*

לֶפֶפְּ שיהת

וְהִנֵּה conj.-demons. part. (243) *and behold*

עַם־קְשֵׁה־עֹרֶף n.m.s. cstr. (I 766)-adj. m.s. cstr. (904)-n.m.s. (791) *a stiff-necked people*

הוּא pers. pr. 3 m.s. (214) *it is*

32:10

וְעַתָּה conj.-adv. (773) *now therefore*

הַנִּיחָה לִּי Hi. impv. 2 m.s.-vol. he (נוּחַ 628;Hi.B, 5)-prep.-1 c.s. sf. *let me alone*

וְיִחַר־אַפִּי conj.-Qal impf. 3 m.s. (חָרָה 354)-n.m.s.-1 c.s. sf. (I 60) *that my wrath may burn hot*

בָּהֶם prep.-3 m.p. sf. *against them*

וַאֲכַלֵּם conj.-Pi. impf. 1 c.s.-3 m.p. sf. (אָכַל 37) *and I may consume them*

וְאֶעֱשֶׂה אוֹתְךָ conj.-Qal impf. 1 c.s. (עָשָׂה I 793)-dir.obj.-2 m.s. sf. *but of you I will make*

לְגוֹי גָּדוֹל prep.-n.m.s. (156)-adj. m.s. (152) *a great nation*

32:11

וַיְחַל מֹשֶׁה consec.-Pi. impf. 3 m.s. (חָלָה II 318)-pr.n. (602) *but Moses besought*

אֶת־פְּנֵי יהוה dir.obj.-n.m.p. cstr. (815)-pr.n. (217) *Yahweh*

אֱלֹהָיו n.m.p.-3 m.s. sf. (43) *his God*

וַיֹּאמֶר consec.-Qal impf. 3 m.s. (55) *and said*

לָמָה יהוה prep.-interr. (552; 4d)-pr.n. (217) *why O Yahweh*

יֶחֱרֶה אַפְּךָ Qal impf. 3 m.s. (חָרָה 354)-n.m.s.-2 m.s. sf. (I 60) *does thy wrath burn hot*

בְּעַמֶּךָ prep.-n.m.s.-2 m.s. sf. (I 766) *against thy people*

אֲשֶׁר הוֹצֵאתָ rel.-Hi. pf. 2 m.s. (יָצָא 422) *whom thou hast brought forth*

מֵאֶרֶץ מִצְרַיִם prep.-n.f.s. cstr. (75)-pr.n. (595) *out of the land of Egypt*

בְּכֹחַ גָּדוֹל prep.-n.m.s. (470)-adj. m.s. (152) *with great power*

וּבְיָד חֲזָקָה conj.-prep.-n.f.s. (388)-adj. f.s. (305) *and with a mighty hand*

32:12

לָמָּה prep.-interr. (552) *why*

יֹאמְרוּ מִצְרַיִם Qal impf. 3 m.p. (55)-pr.n. (595) *should the Egyptians say*

לֵאמֹר prep.-Qal inf. cstr. (55) *(saying)*

בְּרָעָה prep.-n.f.s. (949) *with evil intent*

הוֹצִיאָם Hi. pf. 3 m.s.-3 m.p. sf. (יָצָא 422) *did he bring them forth*

לַהֲרֹג prep.-Qal inf. cstr. (הָרַג 246) *to slay*

אֹתָם dir.obj.-3 m.p. sf. *them*

בֶּהָרִים prep.-def.art.-n.m.p. (249) *in the mountains*

וּלְכַלֹּתָם conj.-prep.-Pi. inf. cstr.-3 m.p. sf. (כָּלָה 477) *and to consume them*

מֵעַל פְּנֵי prep.-prep.-n.m.p. cstr. (815) *from the face of*

הָאֲדָמָה def.art.-n.f.s. (9) *the earth*

שׁוּב Qal impv. 2 m.s. (שׁוּב 996) *turn*

מֵחֲרוֹן אַפֶּךָ prep.-n.m.s. cstr. (354)-n.m.s.-2 m.s. sf. (I 60) *from thy fierce wrath*

וְהִנָּחֵם conj.-Ni. impv. 2 m.s. (נָחַם 636) *and repent*

עַל־הָרָעָה prep.-def.art.-n.f.s. (949) *of this evil*

לְעַמֶּךָ prep.-n.m.s.-2 m.s. sf. (I 766) *against thy people*

32:13

זְכֹר Qal impv. 2 m.s. (269) *remember*

לְאַבְרָהָם prep.-pr.n. (4) *Abraham*

לְיִצְחָק prep.-pr.n. (850) *Isaac*

וּלְיִשְׂרָאֵל conj.-prep.-pr.n. (975) *and Israel*

עֲבָדֶיךָ n.m.p.-2 m.s. sf. (712) *thy servants*

אֲשֶׁר נִשְׁבַּעְתָּ לָהֶם rel.-Ni. pf. 2 m.s. (שָׁבַע 989)-prep.-3 m.p. sf. *to whom thou didst swear*

בָּךְ prep.-2 m.s. sf. paus. *by thine own self*

וַתְּדַבֵּר consec.-Pi. impf. 2 m.s. (180) *and didst say*

אֲלֵהֶם prep.-3 m.p. sf. *to them*

אַרְבֶּה Hi. impf. 1 c.s. (רָבָה I 915) *I will multiply*

אֶת־זַרְעֲכֶם dir.obj.-n.m.s.-2 m.p. sf. (282) *your descendants*

כְּכוֹכְבֵי prep.-n.m.p. cstr. (456) *as the stars of*

הַשָּׁמָיִם def.art.-n.m. du. paus. (1029) *heaven*

וְכָל־הָאָרֶץ הַזֹּאת conj.-n.m.s. cstr. (481)-def.art.-n.f.s. (75)-def.art.-demons. adj. f.s. (260) *and all this land*

אֲשֶׁר אָמַרְתִּי rel.-Qal pf. 1 c.s. (55) *that I have promised*

אֶתֵּן Qal impf. 1 c.s. (נָתַן 678) *I will give*

לְזַרְעֲכֶם prep.-n.m.s.-2 m.p. sf. (282) *to your descendants*

וְנָחֲלוּ conj.-Qal pf. 3 c.p. (נחל 635) *and they shall inherit*

לְעֹלָם prep.-n.m.s. (761) *for ever*

32:14

וַיִּנָּחֶם יהוה consec.-Ni. impf. 3 m.s. (נָחַם 636)-pr.n. (217) *and Yahweh repented*

עַל־הָרָעָה prep.-def.art.-n.f.s. (949) *of the evil*

אֲשֶׁר דִּבֶּר rel.-Pi. pf. 3 m.s. (180) *which he thought*

לַעֲשׂוֹת prep.-Qal inf. cstr. (עָשָׂה I 793) *to do*

לְעַמּוֹ prep.-n.m.s.-3 m.s. sf. (I 766) *to his people*

32:15

וַיִּפֶן consec.-Qal impf. 3 m.s. (פָּנָה 815) *and turned*

וַיֵּרֶד consec.-Qal impf. 3 m.s. (יָרַד 432) *and went down*

מֹשֶׁה pr.n. (602) *Moses*

מִן־הָהָר prep.-def.art.-n.m.s. (249) *from the mountain*

וּשְׁנֵי לֻחֹת conj.-num. m. du. cstr. (1040)-n.m.p. cstr. (531) *with the two tables of*

הָעֵדֻת def.art.-n.f.s. (730) *the testimony*

בְּיָדוֹ prep.-n.f.s.-3 m.s. sf. (388) *in his hands*

לֻחֹת n.m.p. (531) *tables*

כְּתֻבִים Qal pass. ptc. m.p. (כָּתַב 507) *that were written*

מִשְּׁנֵי עֶבְרֵיהֶם prep.-num. m. du. cstr. (1040)-n.m.p.-3 m.p. sf. (I 719) *on both sides*

מִזֶּה וּמִזֶּה prep.-demons. (260)-conj.-prep.-demons. (260) *on the one side and on the other*

הֵם כְּתֻבִים pers.pr. 3 m.p. (241)-Qal pass. ptc. m.p. (כָּתַב 507) *were they written*

32:16

וְהַלֻּחֹת conj.-def.art.-n.m.p. (531) *and the tables (were)*

מַעֲשֵׂה אֱלֹהִים n.m.s. cstr. (795)-n.m.p. (43) *the work of God*

הֵמָּה pers.pr. 3 m.p. (241) *(they)*

וְהַמִּכְתָּב conj.-def.art.-n.m.s. (508) *and the writing*

מִכְתַּב אֱלֹהִים n.m.s. cstr. (508)-n.m.p. (43) *the writing of God*

הוּא pers.pr. 3 m.s. (214) *(it)*

חָרוּת Qal pass. ptc. (חָרַת 362) *graven*

עַל־הַלֻּחֹת prep.-def.art.-n.m.p. (531) *upon the tables*

32:17

וַיִּשְׁמַע consec.-Qal impf. 3 m.s. (שָׁמַע 1033) *when ... heard*

יְהוֹשֻׁעַ pr.n. (221) *Joshua*

אֶת־קוֹל הָעָם dir.obj.-n.m.s. cstr. (876)-def.art.-n.m.s. (I 766) *the noise of the people*

בְּרֵעֹה verb. n. (I 929) *as they shouted*

וַיֹּאמֶר consec.-Qal impf. 3 m.s. (55) *then he said*

אֶל־מֹשֶׁה prep.-pr.n. (602) *to Moses*

קוֹל מִלְחָמָה n.m.s. cstr. (876)-n.f.s. (536) *a noise of war*

בַּמַּחֲנֶה prep.-def.art.-n.m.s. (334) *in the camp*

32:18

וַיֹּאמֶר consec.-Qal impf. 3 m.s. (55) *but he said*

אֵין קוֹל subst. cstr. (II 34)-n.m.s. cstr. (876) *it is not the sound of*

עֲנוֹת Qal inf. cstr. (עָנָה IV 777) *shouting for*

גְּבוּרָה n.f.s. (150) *victory*

וְאֵין קוֹל conj.-v. supra-v. supra *or the sound of*

עֲנוֹת v. supra *the cry of*

חֲלוּשָׁה n.f.s. (325) *defeat*

קוֹל עַנּוֹת v. supra-Pi. inf. cstr. (עָנָה IV 777) *sound of singing*

אָנֹכִי שֹׁמֵעַ pers.pr. 1 c.s. (59)-Qal act. ptc. (שָׁמַע 1033) *I hear*

32:19

וַיְהִי כַּאֲשֶׁר consec.-Qal impf. 3 m.s. (הָיָה 224)-prep.-rel. *and as soon as*

קָרַב Qal pf. 3 m.s. (897) *he came near*

אֶל־הַמַּחֲנֶה prep.-def.art.-n.m.s. (334) *the camp*

וַיַּרְא consec.-Qal impf. 3 m.s. (רָאָה 906) *and saw*

אֶת־הָעֵגֶל dir.obj.-def.art.-n.m.s. (722) *the calf*

וּמְחֹלֹת conj.-n.f.p. (298) *and dancing*

וַיִּחַר־ consec.-Qal impf. 3 m.s. (חָרָה 354) *then ... burned hot*

אַף מֹשֶׁה n.m.s. cstr. (I 60)-pr.n. (602) *Moses' anger*

וַיַּשְׁלֵךְ consec.-Hi. impf. 3 m.s. (שָׁלַךְ 1020) *and he threw*

מִיָּדָו prep.-n.f.s.-3 m.s. sf. (388) *out of his hands*

אֶת־הַלֻּחֹת dir.obj.-def.art.-n.m.p. (531) *the tables*

וַיְשַׁבֵּר אֹתָם consec.-Pi. impf. 3 m.s. (שָׁבַר 990)-dir.obj.-3 m.p. sf. *and broke them*

תַּחַת הָהָר prep. (1065)-def.art.-n.m.s. (249) *at the foot of the mountain*

32:20

וַיִּקַּח consec.-Qal impf. 3 m.s. (לָקַח 542) *and he took*

אֶת־הָעֵגֶל dir.obj.-def.art.-n.m.s. (722) *the calf*

אֲשֶׁר עָשׂוּ rel.-Qal pf. 3 c.p. (עָשָׂה I 793) *which they had made*

וַיִּשְׂרֹף consec.-Qal impf. 3 m.s. (שָׂרַף 976) *and burnt*

בָּאֵשׁ prep.-def.art.-n.f.s. (77) *with fire*

וַיִּטְחַן consec.-Qal impf. 3 m.s. (טָחַן 377) *and ground*

עַד אֲשֶׁר־דָּק prep.-rel.-Qal pf. 3 m.s. paus. (דָּקַק 200) *to powder (until it was pulverized)*

וַיִּזֶר consec.-Qal impf. 3 m.s. (זָרָה 279) *and scattered*

עַל־פְּנֵי הַמַּיִם prep.-n.m.p. cstr. (814)-def.art.-n.m.p. (565) *upon the water*

וַיַּשְׁקְ consec.-Hi. impf. 3 m.s. (שָׁקָה 1052) *and made ... drink*

אֶת־בְּנֵי dir.obj.-n.m.p. cstr. (119) *the people of*

יִשְׂרָאֵל pr.n. (975) *Israel*

32:21

וַיֹּאמֶר מֹשֶׁה consec.-Qal impf. 3 m.s. (55)-pr.n. (602) *and Moses said*

אֶל־אַהֲרֹן prep.-pr.n. (14) *Aaron*

מֶה־עָשָׂה interr. (552) - Qal pf. 3 m.s. (I 793) *what did ... do*

לְךָ הָעָם הַזֶּה prep.-2 m.s. sf.-def.art.-n.m.s. (I 766)-def.art.-demons. adj. (260) *to you this people*

כִּי־הֵבֵאתָ conj.-Hi. pf. 2 m.s. (בּוֹא 97) *that you have brought*

עָלָיו prep.-3 m.s. sf. *upon them*

חֲטָאָה גְדֹלָה n.f.s. (308) - adj. f.s. (152) *a great sin*

32:22

וַיֹּאמֶר consec.-Qal impf. 3 m.s. (55) *and said*

אַהֲרֹן pr.n. (14) *Aaron*

אַל־יִחַר neg. (39)-Qal impf. 3 m.s. (חָרָה 354) *let not ... burn hot*

אַף אֲדֹנִי n.m.s. cstr. (I 60)-n.m.s.-1 c.s. sf. (10) *the anger of my lord*

אַתָּה יָדַעְתָּ pers.pr. 2 m.s. (61)-Qal pf. 2 m.s. (יָדַע 393) *you know*

אֶת־הָעָם dir.obj.-def.art.-n.m.s. (I 766) *the people*

כִּי בְרָע הוּא conj.-prep.-n.m.s. (II 948) - pers. pr. 3 m.s. (214) *that they are set on evil*

32:23

וַיֹּאמְרוּ לִי consec.-Qal impf. 3 m.p. (55) - prep.-1 c.s. sf. *for they said to me*

עֲשֵׂה־לָנוּ Qal impv. 2 m.s. (עָשָׂה I 793)-prep.-1 c.p. sf. *make (for)us*

אֱלֹהִים n.m.p. (43) *gods*

אֲשֶׁר יֵלְכוּ rel.-Qal impf. 3 m.p. (הָלַךְ 229) *who shall go*

לְפָנֵינוּ prep.-n.m.p.-1 c.p. sf. (815) *before us*

כִּי־זֶה מֹשֶׁה conj.-demons. adj. m.s. (260)-pr.n. (602) *as for this Moses*

הָאִישׁ אֲשֶׁר def.art.-n.m.s. (35)-rel. *the man who*

הֶעֱלָנוּ Hi. pf. 3 m.s.-1 c.p. sf. (עָלָה 748) *brought us up*

מֵאֶרֶץ מִצְרַיִם prep.-n.f.s. cstr. (75)-pr.n. (595) *out of the land of Egypt*

לֹא יָדַעְנוּ neg.-Qal pf. 1 c.p. (יָדַע 393) *we do not know*

מֶה־הָיָה לוֹ interr. (522)-Qal pf. 3 m.s. (224)-prep.-3 m.s. sf. *what has become of him*

32:24

וָאֹמַר לָהֶם consec.-Qal impf. 1 c.s. (אָמַר 55)-prep.-3 m.p. sf. *and I said to them*

לְמִי זָהָב prep.-interr. (566)-n.m.s. (262) *let any who have gold*

הִתְפָּרָקוּ Hith. impv. 2 m.p. paus. (פָּרַק 830) *take it off*

וַיִּתְּנוּ־לִי consec.-Qal impf. 3 m.p. (נָתַן 678) - prep.-1 c.s. sf. *so they gave it to me*

וָאַשְׁלִכֵהוּ consec.-Hi. impf. 1 c.s.- 3 m.s. sf. (שָׁלַךְ 1020) *and I threw it*

בָאֵשׁ prep.-def.art.-n.f.s. (77) *into the fire*

וַיֵּצֵא consec.-Qal impf. 3 m.s. (יָצָא 422) *and there came out*

הָעֵגֶל הַזֶּה def.art.-n.m.s. (722)-def.art.-demons. adj. (260) *this calf*

32:25

וַיַּרְא מֹשֶׁה consec.-Qal impf. 3 m.s. (רָאָה 906)-pr.n. (602) *and when Moses saw*

אֶת־הָעָם dir.obj.-def.art.-n.m.s. (I 766) *the people*

כִּי פָרֻעַ הוּא conj.-Qal pass. ptc. (פָּרַע III 828)-pers.pr. 3 m.s. (214) *that they had broken loose*

כִּי פְרָעֹה conj.-Qal pf. 3 m.s.-3 m.s. sf. (פָּרַע III 828) *for ... had let them break loose*

אַהֲרֹן pr.n. (14) *Aaron*

לְשִׁמְצָה prep.-n.f.s. (1036) *to their shame*

בְּקָמֵיהֶם prep.-Qal act. ptc. m.p.-3 m.p. sf. (קוּם 877; Qal 2) *among their enemies*

32:26

וַיַּעֲמֹד consec.-Qal impf. 3 m.s. (עָמַד 763) *then stood*

מֹשֶׁה pr.n. (60) *Moses*

בְּשַׁעַר prep.-n.m.s. cstr. (1044) *in the gate of*

הַמַּחֲנֶה def.art.-n.m.s. (334) *the camp*

וַיֹּאמֶר consec.-Qal impf. 3 m.s. (55) *and said*

מִי לַיהוה interr. (566)-prep.-pr.n. (217) *whoever to Yahweh*

אֵלָי prep.-1 c.s. sf. paus. *to me*

וַיֵּאָסְפוּ consec. - Ni. impf. 3 m. p. (אָסַף 62) *then gathered themselves*

אֵלָיו prep.-3 m.s. sf. *to him*

כָּל־בְּנֵי n.m.s. cstr. (481)-n.m.p. cstr. (119) *all the sons of*

לֵוִי pr.n. (I 532) *Levi*

32:27

וַיֹּאמֶר לָהֶם consec.-Qal impf. 3 m.s. (55)-prep.-3 m.p. sf. *and he said to them*

כֹּה־אָמַר adv. (462)-Qal pf. 3 m.s. (55) *thus says*

יהוה pr.n. (217) *Yahweh*

אֱלֹהֵי יִשְׂרָאֵל n.m.p. cstr. (43)-pr.n. (975) *God of Israel*

שִׂימוּ Qal impv. 2 m.p. (שִׂים I 962) *put*

אִישׁ־חַרְבּוֹ n.m.s. (35)-n.f.s.-3 m.s. sf. (352) *every man his sword*

עַל־יְרֵכוֹ prep.-n.f.s.-3 m.s. sf. (437) *on his side*

עִבְרוּ וָשׁוּבוּ Qal impv. 2 m.p. (עָבַר 716)-conj.-Qal impv. 2 m.p. (שׁוּב 966) *go to and fro*

מִשַּׁעַר לָשַׁעַר prep.-n.m.s. (1044)-prep.-n.m.s. (1044) *from gate to gate*

בַּמַּחֲנֶה prep.-def.art.-n.m.s. (334) *throughout the camp*

וְהִרְגוּ conj.-Qal impv. 2 m.p. (הָרַג 246) *and slay*

אִישׁ־אֶת־אָחִיו n.m.s. (35)-dir.obj.-n.m.s.-3 m.s. sf. (26) *every man his brother*

וְאִישׁ אֶת־רֵעֵהוּ conj.-n.m.s. (35)-dir.obj.-n.m.s.-3 m.s. sf. (945) *and every man his companion*

וְאִישׁ אֶת־קְרֹבוֹ v.supra-dir.obj.-adj. m.s.-3 m.s. sf. (898) *and every man his neighbor*

32:28

וַיַּעֲשׂוּ consec.-Qal impf. 3 m.p. (עָשָׂה I 793) *and did*

בְנֵי־לֵוִי n.m.p. cstr. (119)-pr.n. (I 532) *the sons of Levi*

כִּדְבַר מֹשֶׁה prep.n.m.s. cstr. (182)-pr.n. (602) *according to the word of Moses*

וַיִּפֹּל consec.-Qal impf. 3 m.s. (נָפַל 656) *and there fell*

מִן־הָעָם prep.-def.art.-n.m.s. (I 766) *of the people*

בַּיּוֹם הַהוּא prep.-def.art.-n.m.s. (398)-def.art.-demons. adj. (214) *that day*

כִּשְׁלֹשֶׁת אַלְפֵי prep.-num.f.s. cstr. (1025)-n.m.p. cstr. (48) *about three thousand*

אִישׁ n.m.s. (35) *men*

32:29

וַיֹּאמֶר מֹשֶׁה consec.-Qal impf. 3 m.s. (55)-pr.n. (602) *and Moses said*

מִלְאוּ יֶדְכֶם Qal impv. 2 m.p. (מָלֵא 569)-n.f.s.-2 m.p. sf. (388) *ordain yourselves*

הַיּוֹם def.art.-n.m.s. (398) *today*

ליהוה prep.-pr.n. (217) *for Yahweh*

כִּי אִישׁ בִּבְנוֹ conj.-n.m.s. (35)-prep.-n.m.s.-3 m.s. sf. (119) *each one at the cost of his son*

וּבְאָחִיו conj.-prep.-n.m.s.-3 m.s. sf. (26) *and of his brother*

וְלָתֵת conj.-prep.-Qal inf. cstr. (נָתַן 678) *that he may bestow*

עֲלֵיכֶם prep.-2 m.p. sf. *upon you*

הַיּוֹם def.art.-n.m.s. (398) *this day*

בְּרָכָה n.f.s. (139) *a blessing*

32:30

וַיְהִי מִמָּחֳרָת consec.-Qal impf. 3 m.s. (הָיָה 224)-prep.-n.f.s. (564) *on the morrow*

וַיֹּאמֶר מֹשֶׁה consec.-Qal impf. 3 m.s. (55)-pr.n. (602) *and Moses said*

אֶל־הָעָם prep.-def.art.-n.m.s. (I 766) *to the people*

אַתֶּם חֲטָאתֶם pers.pr. 2 m.p. (61)-Qal pf. 2 m.p. (חָטָא 306) *you have sinned*

חֲטָאָה גְדֹלָה n.f.s. (308)-adj. f.s. (152) *a great sin*

וְעַתָּה conj.-adv. (773) *and now*

אֶעֱלֶה Qal impf. 1 c.s. (עָלָה 748) *I will go up*

אֶל־יהוה prep.-pr.n. (217) *to Yahweh*

אוּלַי אֲכַפְּרָה adv. (II 19)-Pi. impf. 1 c.s.-vol. he (כָּפַר 497) *perhaps I can make atonement*

בְּעַד חַטַּאתְכֶם prep. (126)-n.f.s.-2 m.p. sf. (308) *for your sin*

32:31

וַיָּשָׁב מֹשֶׁה consec.-Qal impf. 3 m.s. (שׁוּב 996)-pr.n. (602) *So Moses returned*

אֶל־יהוה prep.-pr.n. (217) *to Yahweh*

וַיֹּאמַר consec.-Qal impf. 3 m.s. (55) *and said*

אָנָּה interj. (58) *alas*

חָטָא Qal pf. 3 m.s. (306) *have sinned*

הָעָם הַזֶּה def.art.-n.m.s. (I 766)-def.art.-demons. adj. (260) *this people*

חֲטָאָה גְדֹלָה n.f.s. (308)-adj. f.s. (152) *a great sin*

וַיַּעֲשׂוּ consec.-Qal impf. 3 m.p. (עָשָׂה I 793) *and they have made*

לָהֶם prep.-3 m.p. sf. *for themselves*

אֱלֹהֵי זָהָב n.m.p. cstr. (43)-n.m.s. (262) *gods of gold*

32:32

וְעַתָּה conj.-adv. (773) *but now*

אִם־תִּשָּׂא hypoth. part. (49)-Qal impf. 2 m.s. (נָשָׂא 669) *if thou wilt forgive*

חַטָּאתָם n.f.s.-3 m.p. sf. (308) *their sin*

וְאִם־אַיִן conj.-hypoth. part. (49)-subst. (II 34) *and if not*

מְחֵנִי נָא Qal impv. 2 m.s.-1 c.s. sf. (מָחָה I 562)-part. of entreaty (609) *blot me, I pray thee*

מִסִּפְרְךָ prep.-n.m.s.-2 m.s. sf. (706) *out of thy book*

אֲשֶׁר כָּתָבְתָּ rel.-Qal pf. 2 m.s. (כָּתַב 507) *which you hast written*

32:33

וַיֹּאמֶר יהוה consec.-Qal impf. 3 m.s. (55)-pr.n. (217) *but Yahweh said*

אֶל־מֹשֶׁה prep.-pr.n. (602) *to Moses*

מִי אֲשֶׁר interr. (566)-rel. *whoever*

חָטָא־לִי Qal pf. 3 m.s. (306)-prep.-1 c.s. sf. *has sinned against me*

אֶמְחֶנּוּ Qal impf. 1 c.s. - 3 m. s. sf. (מָחָה I 562) *him will I blot out*

מִסִּפְרִי prep.-n.m.s.-1 c.s. sf. (706) *of my book*

32:34

וְעַתָּה conj.-adv. (773) *but now*

לֵךְ Qal impv. 2 m.s. (הָלַךְ 229) *go*

נְחֵה Qal impv. 2 m.s. (נָחָה 634) *lead*

אֶת־הָעָם dir.obj.-def.art.-n.m.s. (I 766) *the people*

אֶל אֲשֶׁר־דִּבַּרְתִּי לָךְ prep.-rel.-Pi. pf. 1 c.s. (דָּבַר 180)-prep.-2 m.s. sf. paus. *to the place of which I have spoken to you*

הִנֵּה demons. part. (243) *behold*

מַלְאָכִי n.m.s.-1 c.s. sf. (521) *my angel*

יֵלֵךְ Qal impf. 3 m.s. (הָלַךְ 229) *shall go*

לְפָנֶיךָ prep.-n.m.p.-2 m.s. sf. (815) *before you*

וּבְיוֹם conj.-prep.-n.m.s. cstr. (398) *nevertheless in the day when*

פָּקְדִי Qal inf. cstr.-1 c.s. sf. (פָּקַד 823) *I visit*

וּפָקַדְתִּי conj.-Qal pf. 1 c.s. (פָּקַד 823) *I will visit*

עֲלֵיהֶם prep.-3 m.p. sf. *upon them*

חַטָּאתָם n.f.s.-3 m.p. sf. (308) *their sin*

32:35

וַיִּגֹּף יהוה consec.-Qal impf. 3 m.s. (נָגַף 619)-pr.n. (217) *and Yahweh sent a plague*

אֶת־הָעָם dir.obj.-def.art.-n.m.s. (I 766) *upon the people*

עַל אֲשֶׁר עָשׂוּ prep.-rel.-Qal pf. 3 c.p. (עָשָׂה I 793) *because they made*

אֶת־הָעֵגֶל dir.obj.-def.art.-n.m.s. (722) *the calf*

אֲשֶׁר עָשָׂה אַהֲרֹן rel.-Qal pf. 3 m.s. (I 793)-pr.n. (14) *which Aaron made*

33:1

וַיְדַבֵּר יהוה consec.-Pi. impf. 3 m.s. (דָּבַר 180)-pr.n. (217) *then Yahweh said*

אֶל־מֹשֶׁה prep.-pr.n. (602) *to Moses*

לֵךְ עֲלֵה Qal impv. 2 m.s. (הָלַךְ 229)-Qal impv. 2 m.s. (עָלָה 748) *depart go up*

מִזֶּה prep.-demons. adj. (260) *hence*

אַתָּה וְהָעָם pers.pr. 2 m.s. (61)-conj.-def.art.-n.m.s. (I 766) *you and the people*

אֲשֶׁר הֶעֱלִיתָ rel.-Hi. pf. 2 m.s. (עָלָה 748) *whom you have brought up*

מֵאֶרֶץ מִצְרָיִם prep.-n.f.s. cstr. (75)-pr.n. paus. (595) *out of the land of Egypt*

אֶל־הָאָרֶץ prep.-def.art.-n.f.s. (75) *to the land*

אֲשֶׁר נִשְׁבַּעְתִּי rel.-Ni. pf. 1 c.s. (שָׁבַע 989) *of which I swore*

לְאַבְרָהָם prep.-pr.n. (4) *to Abraham*

לְיִצְחָק prep.-pr.n. (850) *to Isaac*

וּלְיַעֲקֹב conj.-prep.-pr.n. (784) *and to Jacob*

לֵאמֹר prep.-Qal inf. cstr. (55) *saying*

לְזַרְעֲךָ prep.-n.m.s.-2 m.s. sf. (282) *to your descendants*

אֶתְּנֶנָּה Qal impf. 1 c.s.-3 f.s. sf. (נָתַן 678) *I will give it*

33:2

וְשָׁלַחְתִּי conj.-Qal pf. 1 c.s. (שָׁלַח 1018) *and I will send*

לְפָנֶיךָ prep.-n.m.p.-2 m.s. sf. (815) *before you*

מַלְאָךְ n.m.s. paus. (521) *an angel*

וְגֵרַשְׁתִּי conj.-Pi. pf. 1 c.s. (גָּרַשׁ 176) *and I will drive out*

אֶת־הַכְּנַעֲנִי dir.obj.-def.art.-pr.n. (489) *the Canaanites*

הָאֱמֹרִי def.art.-pr.n. (57) *the Amorites*

וְהַחִתִּי conj.-def.art.-pr.n. (366) *the Hittites*

וְהַפְּרִזִּי conj.-def.art.-pr.n. (827) *the Perizzites*

הַחִוִּי def.art.-pr.n. (295) *the Hivites*

וְהַיְבוּסִי conj.-def.art.-pr.n. (101) *and the Jebusites*

33:3

אֶל־אֶרֶץ prep.-n.f.s. cstr. (75) *to a land*

זָבַת חָלָב Qal act. ptc. f.s. cstr. (זוּב 264)-n.m.s. (316) *flowing with milk*

וּדְבָשׁ conj.-n.m.s. paus. (185) *and honey*

כִּי לֹא אֶעֱלֶה conj.-neg.-Qal impf. 1 c.s. (עָלָה 748) *but I will not go up*

בְּקִרְבְּךָ prep.-n.m.s.-2 m.s. sf. (899) *among you*

כִּי עַם־ conj.-n.m.s. cstr. (I 766) *for a people*

קְשֵׁה־עֹרֶף adj. cstr. (904)-n.m.s. (791) *stiff-necked*

אַתָּה pers. pr. 2 m.s. (61) *you are*

פֶּן־אֲכֶלְךָ conj. (814) - Pi. impf. 1 c.s.-2 m.s. sf. (כָּלָה I 477) *lest I consume you*

בַּדָּֽרֶךְ prep.-def.art.-n.m.s. paus. (202) *in the way*

33:4

וַיִּשְׁמַע הָעָם consec.-Qal impf. 3 m.s. (שָׁמַע 1033)-def.art.-n.m.s. (I 766) *when the people heard*

אֶת־הַדָּבָר הָרָע הַזֶּה dir.obj.-def.art.-n.m.s. (182)-def.art.-adj. (948)-def.art.-demons. adj. (260) *these evil tidings*

וַיִּתְאַבָּלוּ consec.-Hith. impf. 3 m.p. paus. (אָבַל 5) *they mourned*

וְלֹא־שָׁתוּ אִישׁ conj.-neg.-Qal pf. 3 c.p. (שִׁיתוּ 1011)-n.m.s. (35) *and no man put*

עֶדְיוֹ n.m.s.-3 m.s. sf. (725) *his ornaments*

עָלָיו prep.-3 m.s. sf. *(on him)*

33:5

וַיֹּאמֶר יהוה consec.-Qal impf. 3 m.s. (55)-pr.n. (217) *for Yahweh had said*

אֶל־מֹשֶׁה prep.-pr.n. (602) *to Moses*

אֱמֹר Qal impv. 2 m.s. (55) *say*

אֶל־בְּנֵי־יִשְׂרָאֵל prep.-n.m.p. cstr. (119)-pr.n. (975) *to the people of Israel*

אתֶּם pers.pr. 2 m.s. (61) *you are*

עַם־קְשֵׁה־עֹרֶף n.m.s. cstr. (I 766)-adj. cstr. (904)-n.m.s. (791) *a stiff-necked people*

רֶגַע אֶחָד n.m.s. (921)-num. adj. (25) *for a single moment*

אֶעֱלֶה Qal impf. 1 c.s. (עָלָה 748) *I should go up*

בְקִרְבְּךָ prep.-n.m.s.-2 m.s. sf. (899) *among you*

וְכִלִּיתִיךָ conj.-Pi. pf. 1 c.s.-2 m.s. sf. (כָּלָה 477) *I would consume you*

וְעַתָּה conj.-adv. (773) *so now*

הוֹרֵד Hi. impv. 2 m.s. (יָרַד 432) *put off*

עֶדְיְךָ n.m.s.-2 m.s. sf. (725) *your ornaments*

מֵעָלֶיךָ prep.-prep.-2 m.s. sf. *from you*

וְאֵדְעָה conj.-Qal impf. 1 c.s.-vol. he (יָדַע 393) *that I may know*

מָה אֶעֱשֶׂה־לָּךְ interr. (552)-Qal impf. 1 c.s. (עָשָׂה I 793)-prep.-2 m.s. sf. paus. *what to do with you*

33:6

וַיִּתְנַצְּלוּ consec.-Hith. impf. 3 m.p. (נָצַל 664) *therefore ... stripped themselves*

בְנֵי־יִשְׂרָאֵל n.m.p. cstr. (119)-pr.n. (975) *the people of Israel*

אֶת־עֶדְיָם dir.obj.-n.m.s.-3 m.p. sf. (725) *of their ornaments*

מֵהַר חוֹרֵב prep.-n.m.s. cstr. (249) - pr.n. (352) *from Mount Horeb*

33:7

וּמֹשֶׁה יִקַּח conj.-pr.n. (602)-Qal impf. 3 m.s. (לָקַח 542) *now Moses used to take*

אֶת־הָאֹהֶל dir.obj.-def.art.-n.m.s. (13) *the tent*

וְנָטָה־לוֹ conj.-Qal pf. 3 m.s. (639)-prep.-3 m.s. sf. *and pitch it*

מִחוּץ לַמַּחֲנֶה prep.-n.m.s. (299)-prep.-def.art.-n.m.s. (334) *outside the camp*

הַרְחֵק Hi. inf. abs. as adv. (רָחַק 934) *far off*

מִן־הַמַּחֲנֶה prep.-def.art.-n.m.s. (334) *from the camp*

וְקָרָא לוֹ conj.-Qal pf. 3 m.s. (894)-prep.-3 m.s. sf. *and he called it*

אֹהֶל מוֹעֵד n.m.s. cstr. (13)-n.m.s. (417) *tent of meeting*

וְהָיָה conj.-Qal pf. 3 m.s. (224) *(and it was)*

כָּל־מְבַקֵּשׁ n.m.s. cstr. (481) - Pi. ptc. (בָּקַשׁ 134) *and every one who sought*

יהוה pr.n. (217) *Yahweh*

יֵצֵא Qal impf. 3 m.s. (יָצָא 422) *would go out*

אֶל־אֹהֶל מוֹעֵד prep.-n.m.s. cstr. (13) - n.m.s. (417) *to the tent of meeting*

אֲשֶׁר מִחוּץ rel.-prep.-n.m.s. (299) *which was outside*

לַמַּחֲנֶה prep.-def.art.-n.m.s. (334) *the camp*

33:8

וְהָיָה כְּצֵאת conj.-Qal pf. 3 m.s. (224)-prep.-Qal inf. cstr. (יָצָא 422) *(and it was) whenever ... went out*

מֹשֶׁה *pr.n. (602) Moses*

אֶל־הָאֹהֶל prep.-def.art.-n.m.s. (13) *to the tent*

יָקוּמוּ Qal impf. 3 m.s. (קוּם 877) *rose*

כָּל־הָעָם n.m.s. cstr. (481)-def.art.-n.m.s. (I 766) *all the people*

וְנִצְּבוּ conj.-Ni. pf. 3 c.p. (נָצַב 662) *and stood*

אִישׁ n.m.s. (35) *every man*

פֶּתַח אָהֳלוֹ n.m.s. cstr. (835)-n.m.s.-3 m.s. sf. (13) *at his tent door*

וְהִבִּיטוּ conj.-Hi. pf. 3 c.p. (נָבַט 613) *and looked*

אַחֲרֵי מֹשֶׁה prep. (29)-pr.n. (602) *after Moses*

עַד־בֹּאוֹ prep.-Qal inf. cstr.-3 m.s. sf. (בּוֹא 97) *until he had gone*

הָאֹהֱלָה def.art.-n.m.s.-dir. he (13) *into the tent*

33:9

וְהָיָה כְּבֹא conj.-Qal pf. 3 m.s. (224)-prep.-Qal inf. cstr. (בּוֹא 97) *when ... entered*

מֹשֶׁה pr.n. (602) *Moses*

הָאֹהֱלָה def.art.-n.m.s.-dir.he (13) *the tent*

יֵרֵד Qal impf. 3 m.s. (יָרַד 432) *would descend*

עַמּוּד הֶעָנָן n.m.s. cstr. (765)-def.art.-n.m.s. (777) *the pillar of cloud*

וְעָמַד conj.-Qal pf. 3 m.s. (763) *and stand*

פֶּתַח הָאֹהֶל n.m.s. cstr. (835)-def.art.-n.m.s. (13) *at the door of the tent*

וְדִבֶּר conj.-Pi. pf. 3 m.s. (180) *and spoke*

עִם־מֹשֶׁה prep.-pr.n. (602) *with Moses*

33:10

וְרָאָה conj.-Qal pf. 3 m.s. (906) *and when ... saw*

כָּל־הָעָם n.m.s. cstr. (481)-def.art.-n.m.s. (I 766) *all the people*

אֶת־עַמּוּד הֶעָנָן dir.obj.-n.m.s. cstr. (765)-def.art.-n.m.s. (777) *the pillar of cloud*

עֹמֵד Qal act. ptc. (763) *standing*

פֶּתַח הָאֹהֶל n.m.s. cstr. (835)-def.art.-n.m.s. (13) *at the door of the tent*

וְקָם conj.-Qal pf. 3 m.s. (קוּם 877) *and would rise up*

כָּל־הָעָם n.m.s. cstr. (481)-def.art.-n.m.s. (I 766) *all the people*

וְהִשְׁתַּחֲווּ conj.-Hithpalel pf. 3 c.p. (שָׁחָה 1005) *and worship*

אִישׁ n.m.s. (35) *every man*

פֶּתַח אָהֳלוֹ n.m.s. cstr. (835)-n.m.s.-3 m.s. sf. (13) *at his tent door*

33:11

וְדִבֶּר יהוה conj.-Pi. pf. 3 m.s. (180)-pr.n. (217) *thus Yahweh used to speak*

אֶל־מֹשֶׁה prep.-pr.n. (602) *to Moses*

פָּנִים אֶל־פָּנִים n.m.p. (815)-prep.-n.m.p. (815) *face to face*

כַּאֲשֶׁר יְדַבֵּר prep.-rel.-Pi. impf. 3 m.s. (180) *as ... speaks*

אִישׁ n.m.s. (35) *a man*

אֶל־רֵעֵהוּ prep.-n.m.s.-3 m.s. sf. (945) *to his friend*

וְשָׁב conj.-Qal pf. 3 m.s. (שׁוּב 996) *when he turned again*

אֶל־הַמַּחֲנֶה prep.-def.art.-n.m.s. (334) *into the camp*

וּמְשָׁרְתוֹ conj.-Pi. ptc.-3 m.s. sf. (שָׁרַת 1058) *and his servant*

יְהוֹשֻׁעַ pr.n. (221) *Joshua*

בִּן־נוּן n.m.s. cstr. (119)-pr.n. (630) *the son of Nun*

נַעַר n.m.s. (654) *a young man*

לֹא יָמִישׁ neg.-Hi. impf. 3 m.s. (swR

לֹא יָמִישׁ neg.-Hi. impf. 3 m.s. (מוּשׁ I 559) *did not depart*

מִתּוֹךְ הָאֹהֶל prep.-n.m.s. cstr. (1063)-def.art.-n.m.s. (13) *from the tent*

33:12

וַיֹּאמֶר מֹשֶׁה consec.-Qal impf. 3 m.s. (55)-pr.n. (602) *then Moses said*

אֶל־יהוה prep.-pr.n. (217) *to Yahweh*

רְאֵה Qal impv. 2 m.s. (906) *see*

אַתָּה אֹמֵר אֵלַי pers.pr. 2 m.s. (61)-Qal act. ptc. (55)-prep.-1 c.s. sf. *thou sayest to me*

הַעַל Hi. impv. 2 m. s. (עָלָה 748) *bring up*

אֶת־הָעָם הַזֶּה dir.obj.-def.art.-n.m.s. (I 766)-def.art.-demons. adj. (260) *this people*

וְאַתָּה conj.-pers.pr. 2 m.s. (61) *but thou*

לֹא הוֹדַעְתַּנִי neg.-Hi. pf. 2 m.s.-1 c.s. sf. (יָדַע 393) *hast not let me know*

אֵת אֲשֶׁר־תִּשְׁלַח dir.obj.-rel.-Qal impf. 2 m.s. (שָׁלַח 1018) *whom thou wilt send*

עִמִּי prep.-1 c.s. sf. *with me*

וְאַתָּה אָמַרְתָּ v.supra-Qal pf. 2 m.s. (55) *yet thou hast said*

יְדַעְתִּיךָ Qal pf. 1 c.s.-2 m.s. sf. (יָדַע 393) *I know you*

בְשֵׁם prep.-n.m.s. (1027) *by name*

וְגַם־מָצָאתָ conj.-adv. (168)-Qal pf. 2 m.s. (מָצָא 592) *and you have also found*

חֵן n.m.s. (336) *favor*

בְּעֵינָי prep.-n.f.p.-1 c.s. sf. paus. (744) *in my sight*

33:13

וְעַתָּה conj.-adv. (773) *now therefore*

אִם־נָא hypoth.part. (49) - part. of entreaty (609) *I pray thee, if*

מָצָאתִי Qal pf. 1 c.s. (מָצָא 592) *I have found*

חֵן n.m.s. (336) *favor*

בְּעֵינֶיךָ prep.-n.f.p.-2 m.s. sf. (744) *in thy sight*

הוֹדִעֵנִי נָא Hi. impv. 2 m.s.-1 c.s. sf. (יָדַע 393)-part. of entreaty (609) *show me now*

אֶת־דְּרָכֶךָ dir.obj.-n.m.s.-2 m.s. sf. paus. (202) *thy way*

וְאֵדָעֲךָ conj.-Qal impf. 1 c.s.-2 m.s. sf. (יָדַע 393) *that I may know thee*

לְמַעַן אֶמְצָא־ prep. (775) - Qal impf. 1 c.s. (מָצָא 592) *that I may find*

חֵן n.m.s. (336) *favor*

בְּעֵינֶיךָ v.supra *in thy sight*

וּרְאֵה conj.-Qal impv. 2 m.s. (906) *consider too*

כִּי עַמְּךָ conj.-n.m.s.-2 m.s. sf. (I 766) *that thy people*

הַגּוֹי הַזֶּה def.art.-n.m.s. (156)-def.art.-demons. adj. (260) *this nation*

33:14

וַיֹּאמַר consec.-Qal impf. 3 m.s. (55) *and he said*

פָּנַי יֵלֵכוּ n.m.p.-1 c.s. sf. (815)-Qal impf. 3 m.s. paus. (הָלַךְ 229) *my presence will go*

וַהֲנִחֹתִי לָךְ conj.-Hi. pf. 1 c.s. (נוּחַ 628)-prep.-2 m.s. sf. paus. *and I will give you rest*

33:15

וַיֹּאמֶר אֵלָיו consec.-Qal impf. 3 m.s. (55)-prep.-3 m.s. sf. *and he said to him*

אִם־אֵין פָּנֶיךָ hypoth. part. (49)-subst. cstr. (II 34)-n.m.p.-2 m.s. sf. (815) *if thy presence will not*

הֹלְכִים Qal act. ptc. m.p. (הָלַךְ 229) *go*

אַל־תַּעֲלֵנוּ neg.-Hi. impf. 2 m.s.-1 c.p. sf. (עָלָה 748) *do not carry us up*

מִזֶּה prep.-demons. adj. (260) *from here*

33:16

וּבַמֶּה conj.-prep.-def.art.-interr. (552) *for how*

יִוָּדַע אֵפוֹא Ni. impf. 3 m.s. (יָדַע 393)-enclitic part. (66) *shall it be known then*

כִּי־מָצָאתִי חֵן conj.-Qal pf. 1 c.s. (מָצָא 592)-n.m.s. (336) *that I have found favor*

בְּעֵינֶיךָ prep.-n.f.p.-2 m.s. sf. (744) *in thy sight*

אֲנִי וְעַמֶּךָ pers. pr. 1 c.s. (58)-conj.-n.m.s.-2 m.s. sf. (I 766) *I and thy people*

הֲלוֹא בְּלֶכְתְּךָ interr.-neg.-prep.-Qal inf. cstr.-2 m.s. sf. (הָלַךְ 229) *is it not in thy going*

עִמָּנוּ prep.-1 c.p. sf. *with us*

וְנִפְלֵינוּ conj.-Ni. pf. 1 c.p. (פָּלָה 811) *so that we are distinct*

אֲנִי וְעַמְּךָ v.supra-v.supra *I and thy people*

מִכָּל־הָעָם prep.-n.m.s. cstr. (481)-def.art.-n.m.s. (I 766) *from all other people*

אֲשֶׁר עַל־פְּנֵי rel.-prep.-n.m.p. cstr. (815) *that are upon the face of*

הָאֲדָמָה def.art.-n.f.s. (9) *the earth*

33:17

וַיֹּאמֶר יהוה consec.-Qal impf. 3 m.s. (55)-pr.n. (217) *and Yahweh said*

אֶל־מֹשֶׁה prep.-pr.n. (602) *to Moses*

גַּם אֶת־הַדָּבָר הַזֶּה adv. (168)-dir.obj.-def.art.-n.m.s. (182)-def.art.-demons. adj. (260) *this very thing*

אֲשֶׁר דִּבַּרְתָּ rel.-Pi. pf. 2 m.s. (180) *that you have spoken*

אֶעֱשֶׂה Qal impf. 1 c.s. (עָשָׂה I 793) *I will do*

כִּי־מָצָאתָ חֵן conj.-Qal pf. 2 m.s. (592)-n.m.s. (336) *for you have found favor*

בְּעֵינַי prep.-n.f.p.-1 c.s. sf. (744) *in my sight*

וָאֵדָעֲךָ consec.-Qal impf. 1 c.s.-2 m.s. sf. (יָדַע 393) *and I know you*

בְּשֵׁם prep.-n.m.s. (1027) *by name*

33:18

וַיֹּאמַר consec.-Qal impf. 3 m.s. (55) *and he said*

הַרְאֵנִי נָא Hi. impv. 2 m.s.-1 c.s. sf. (רָאָה 906)-part. of entreaty (609) *show me, I pray thee*

אֶת־כְּבֹדֶךָ dir.obj.-n.m.s.-2 m.s. sf. (458) *thy glory*

33:19

וַיֹּאמֶר consec.-Qal impf. 3 m.s. (55) *and he said*

אֲנִי אַעֲבִיר pers.pr. 1 c.s. (58)-Hi. impf. 1 c.s. (עָבַר 716) *I will make pass*

כָּל־טוּבִי n.m.s. cstr. (481)-n.m.s.-1 c.s. sf. (375) *all my goodness*

עַל־פָּנֶיךָ prep.-n.m.p.-2 m.s. sf. (815) *before you*

וְקָרָאתִי conj.-Qal pf. 1 c.s. (קָרָא 894) *and will proclaim*

בְשֵׁם prep.-n.m.s. (1027) *by name (LXX rds. my name)*

יהוה pr.n. (217) *Yahweh*

לְפָנֶיךָ prep.-n.m.p.-2 m.s. sf. (815) *before you*

וְחַנֹּתִי conj.-Qal pf. 1 c.s. (חָנַן I 335) *and I will be gracious*

אֶת־אֲשֶׁר אָחֹן dir.obj.-rel.-Qal impf. 1 c.s. (חָנַן I 335) *to whom I will be gracious*

וְרִחַמְתִּי conj.-Pi. pf. 1 c.s. (933) *and will show mercy*

אֶת־אֲשֶׁר אֲרַחֵם dir.obj.-rel.-Pi. impf. 1 c.s. (933) *on whom I will show mercy*

33:20

וַיֹּאמֶר consec.-Qal impf. 3 m.s. (55) *and he said*

לֹא תוּכַל neg.-Qal impf. 2 m.s. (יָכֹל 407) *you cannot*

לִרְאֹת prep.-Qal inf. cstr. (רָאָה 906) *see*

אֶת־פָּנָי dir.obj.-n.m.p.-1 c.s. sf. paus. (815) *my face*

כִּי לֹא־יִרְאַנִי conj.-neg.-Qal impf. 3 m.s.-1 c.s. sf. (רָאָה 906) *for ... shall not see me*

הָאָדָם def.art.-n.m.s. (9) *man*

וָחָי conj.-Qal pf. 3 m.s. paus. (חָיָה 310) *and live*

33:21

וַיֹּאמֶר יהוה consec.-Qal impf. 3 m.s. (55)-pr.n. (217) *and Yahweh said*

הִנֵּה demons. part. (243) *behold*

מָקוֹם אִתִּי n.m.s. (879)-prep.-1 c.s. sf. (II 85) *a place by me*

וְנִצַּבְתָּ conj.-Ni. pf. 2 m.s. (נָצַב 662) *where you shall stand*

עַל־הַצּוּר prep.-def.art.-n.m.s. (849) *upon the rock*

33:22

וְהָיָה בַּעֲבֹר conj.-Qal pf. 3 m.s. (224)-prep.-Qal inf. cstr. (עָבַר 716) *and while ... passes by*

כְּבֹדִי n.m.s.-1 c.s. sf. (458) *my glory*

וְשַׂמְתִּיךָ conj.-Qal pf. 1 c.s.-2 m.s. sf. (שִׂים I 962) *I will put you*

בְּנִקְרַת הַצּוּר prep.-n.f.s. cstr. (669)-def.art.-n.m.s. (849) *in a cleft of the rock*

וְשַׂכֹּתִי conj.-Qal pf. 1 c.s. (שָׂכַךְ I 967) *and I will cover*

כַפִּי n.f.s.-1 c.s. sf. (496) *with my hand*

עָלֶיךָ prep.-2 m.s. sf. *you*

עַד־עָבְרִי prep.-Qal inf. cstr.-1 c.s. sf. (עָבַר 716) *until I have passed by*

33:23

וַהֲסִרֹתִי conj.-Hi. pf. 1 c.s. (סוּר 696) *then I will take away*

אֶת־כַּפִּי dir.obj.-n.f.s.-1 c.s. sf. (496) *my hand*

וְרָאִיתָ conj.-Qal pf. 2 m.s. (רָאָה 906) *and you shall see*

אֶת־אֲחֹרָי dir.obj.-subst. p. cstr. paus. (30) *my back*

וּפָנַי conj.-n.m.p.-1 c.s. sf. (815) *but my face*

לֹא יֵרָאוּ neg.-Ni. impf. 3 m.p. (רָאָה 906) *shall not be seen*

34:1

וַיֹּאמֶר יהוה consec.-Qal impf. 3 m.s. (55)-pr.n. (217) *and Yahweh said*

אֶל־מֹשֶׁה prep.-pr.n. (602) *to Moses*

פְּסָל־לְךָ Qal impv. 2 m.s. (פָּסַל 820)-prep.-2 m.s. sf. *cut (for yourself)*

שְׁנֵי־לֻחֹת num.m.p. cstr. (1040)-n.m.p. cstr. (531) *two tables of*

אֲבָנִים n.f.p. (6) *stone*

כָּרִאשֹׁנִים prep.-def.art.-adj. m.p. (911) *like the first*

וְכָתַבְתִּי conj.-Qal pf. 1 c.s. (כָּתַב 507) *and I will write*

עַל־הַלֻּחֹת prep.-def.art.-n.m.p. (531) *upon the tables*

אֶת־הַדְּבָרִים dir.obj.-def.art.-n.m.p. (182) *the words*

אֲשֶׁר הָיוּ rel.-Qal pf. 3 c.p. (הָיָה 224) *that were*

עַל־הַלֻּחֹת v.supra *on the tables*

הָרִאשֹׁנִים def.art.-adj. m.p. (911) *first*

אֲשֶׁר שִׁבַּרְתָּ rel.-Pi. pf. 2 m.s. (שָׁבַר 990) *which you broke*

34:2

וֶהְיֵה נָכוֹן conj.-Qal impv. 2 m.s. (הָיָה 224)-Ni. ptc. (כּוּן 465) *and be ready*

לַבֹּקֶר prep.-def.art.-n.m.s. (133) *in the morning*

וְעָלִיתָ conj.-Qal pf. 2 m.s. (עָלָה 748) *and come up*

בַבֹּקֶר prep.-def.art.-n.m.s. (133) *in the morning*

אֶל־הַר סִינַי prep.-n.m.s. cstr. (249)-pr.n. (696) *to Mount Sinai*

וְנִצַּבְתָּ לִי conj.-Ni. pf. 2 m.s. (נָצַב 662)-prep.-1 c.s. sf. *and present yourself to me*

שָׁם adv. (1027) *there*

עַל־רֹאשׁ הָהָר prep.-n.m.s. cstr. (910)-def.art.-n.m.s. (249) *on the top of the mountain*

34:3

וְאִישׁ conj.-n.m.s. (35) *and a man*

לֹא־יַעֲלֶה neg.-Qal impf. 3 m.s. (עָלָה 748) *shall not come up*

עִמָּךְ prep.-2 m.s. sf. paus. *with you*

וְגַם־אִישׁ conj.-adv. (168)-n.m.s. (35) *and also a man*

אַל־יֵרָא neg.-Ni. impf. 3 m.s. (רָאָה 906) *let not be seen*

בְּכָל־הָהָר prep.-n.m.s. cstr. (481)-def.art.-n.m.s. (249) *throughout all the mountain*

גַּם־הַצֹּאן adv. (168)-def.art.-n.f.s. (838) *also flocks*

וְהַבָּקָר conj.-def.art.-n.m.s. (133) *or herds*

אַל־יִרְעוּ neg.-Qal impf. 3 m.p. (רָעָה I 944) *let not feed*

אֶל־מוּל prep.-prep. (I 557) *before*

הָהָר הַהוּא def.art.-n.m.s. (249)-def.art.-demons. adj. (214) *that mountain*

34:4

וַיִּפְסֹל consec.-Qal impf. 3 m.s. (פָּסַל 820) *so he cut*

שְׁנֵי־לֻחֹת num. m.p. cstr. (1040)-n.m.p. cstr. (531) *two tables of*

אֲבָנִים n.f.p. (6) *stone*

כָּרִאשֹׁנִים prep.-def.art.-adj. m.p. (911) *like the first*

וַיַּשְׁכֵּם מֹשֶׁה consec.-Hi. impf. 3 m.s. (שָׁכַם 1014)-pr.n. (602) *and Moses rose early*

בַבֹּקֶר prep.-def.art.-n.m.s. (133) *in the morning*

וַיַּעַל consec.-Qal impf. 3 m.s. (עָלָה 748) *and went up*

אֶל־הַר סִינַי prep.-n.m.s. cstr. (249)-pr.n. (696) *on Mount Sinai*

כַּאֲשֶׁר צִוָּה prep.-rel.-Pi. pf. 3 m.s. (צָוָה 845) *as ... had commanded*

יהוה pr.n. (217) *Yahweh*

אֹתוֹ dir.obj.-3 m.s. sf. *him*

וַיִּקַּח consec.-Qal impf. 3 m.s. (לָקַח 542) *and took*

בְּיָדוֹ prep.-n.f.s.-3 m.s. sf. (388) *in his hand*

שְׁנֵי לֻחֹת v.supra-v.supra *two tablets of*

אֲבָנִים v.supra *stone*

34:5

וַיֵּרֶד יהוה consec.-Qal impf. 3 m.s. (יָרַד 432)-pr.n. (217) *and Yahweh descended*

בֶּעָנָן prep.-def.art.-n.m.s. (777) *in the cloud*

וַיִּתְיַצֵּב consec.-Hith. impf. 3 m.s. (יָצַב 426) *and stood*

עִמּוֹ שָׁם prep.-3 m.s. sf.-adv. (1027) *with him there*

וַיִּקְרָא consec.-Qal impf. 3 m.s. (894) *and proclaimed*

בְשֵׁם יהוה prep.-n.m.s. cstr. (1027)-pr.n. (217) *the name of Yahweh*

34:6

וַיַּעֲבֹר יהוה consec.-Qal impf. 3 m.s. (עָבַר 716)-pr.n. (217) *and Yahweh passed*

עַל־פָּנָיו prep.-n.m.p.-1 c.s. sf. (815) *before him*

וַיִּקְרָא consec.-Qal impf. 3 m.s. (894) *and proclaimed*

יהוה יהוה pr.n. (217)-pr.n. (217) *Yahweh, Yahweh*

אֵל n.m.s. (42) *a God*

רַחוּם וְחַנּוּן adj. (933)-conj.-adj. (337) *merciful and gracious*

אֶרֶךְ אַפַּיִם adj. cstr. (74)-n.m. du. (60) *slow to anger*

וְרַב־חֶסֶד conj.-adj. cstr. (I 912)-n.m.s. (338) *and abounding in steadfast love*

וֶאֱמֶת conj.-n.f.s. (54) *and faithfulness*

34:7

נֹצֵר Qal act. ptc. (נָצַר 665) *keeping*

חֶסֶד n.m.s. (338) *steadfast love*

לָאֲלָפִים prep.-def.art.-n.m.p. (48) *for thousands*

נֹשֵׂא Qal act. ptc. (נָשָׂא 669) *forgiving*

עָוֹן n.m.s. (730) *iniquity*

וָפֶשַׁע conj.-n.m.s. (833) *and transgression*

וְחַטָּאָה conj.-n.f.s. (308) *and sin*

וְנַקֵּה לֹא יְנַקֶּה conj.-Pi. inf. abs. (נָקָה 667)-neg.-Pi. impf. 3 m.s. (נָקָה 667) *but who will by no means clear the guilty*

פֹּקֵד Qal act. ptc. (פָּקַד 823) *visiting*

עֲוֺן אָבוֹת n.m.s. cstr. (730)-n.m.p. (3) *the iniquity of the fathers*

עַל־בָּנִים prep.-n.m.p. (119) *upon the children*

וְעַל־בְּנֵי בָנִים conj.-prep.-n.m.p. cstr. (119)-n.m.p. (119) *and the children's children*

עַל־שִׁלֵּשִׁים prep.-adj. p. (II 1026) *to the third*

וְעַל־רִבֵּעִים conj.-prep.-adj. p. (918) *and the fourth (generation)*

34:8

וַיְמַהֵר מֹשֶׁה consec.-Pi. impf. 3 m.s. (מָהַר I 554)-pr.n. (602) *and Moses made haste*

וַיִּקֹּד consec.-Qal impf. 3 m.s. (קָדַד I 869) *and bowed his head*

אַרְצָה n.f.s.-dir. he (75) *toward the earth*

וַיִּשְׁתָּחוּ consec.-Hithpalel impf. 3 m.s. (שָׁחָה 1005) *and worshiped*

34:9

וַיֹּאמֶר consec.-Qal impf. 3 m.s. (55) *and he said*

אִם־נָא hypoth. part. (49)-part. of entreaty (609) *if now*

מָצָאתִי חֵן Qal pf. 1 c.s. (מָצָא 592)-n.m.s. (336) *I have found favor*

בְּעֵינֶיךָ prep.-n.f.p.-2 m.s. sf. (744) *in thy sight*

אֲדֹנָי n.m.p.-1 c.s. sf. (10) *O Lord*

יֵלֶךְ־נָא Qal impf. 3 m.s. (הָלַךְ 229)-part. of entreaty (609) *let ... go I pray thee*

אֲדֹנָי v. supra *the Lord*

בְּקִרְבֵּנוּ prep.-n.m.s.-1 c.p. sf. (899) *in the midst of us*

כִּי עַם־ conj.-n.m.s. cstr. (I 766) *although a people*

קְשֵׁה־עֹרֶף adj. cstr. (904)-n.m.s. (791) *stiff-necked*

הוּא pers.pr. 3 m.s. (214) *it is*

וְסָלַחְתָּ conj.-Qal pf. 2 m.s. (סָלַח 699) *and pardon*

לַעֲוֺנֵנוּ prep.-n.m.s.-1 c.p. sf. (730) *our iniquity*

וּלְחַטָּאתֵנוּ conj.-prep.-n.f.s.-1 c.p. sf. (308) *and our sin*

וּנְחַלְתָּנוּ conj.-Qal pf. 2 m.s.-1 c.p. sf. (נָחַל 635) *and take us for thy inheritance*

34:10

וַיֹּאמֶר consec.-Qal impf. 3 m.s. (55) *and he said*

הִנֵּה demons. part. (243) *behold*

אָנֹכִי כֹּרֵת pers.pr. 1 c.s. (59)-Qal act. ptc. (503) *I make*

בְּרִית n.f.s. (136) *a covenant*

נֶגֶד כָּל־עַמְּךָ prep. (617) - n.m.s. cstr. (481) - n.m.s.-2 m.s. sf. (I 766) *before all your people*

אֶעֱשֶׂה Qal impf. 1 c.s. (עָשָׂה I 793) *I will do*

נִפְלָאֹת Ni. ptc. f.p. (פָּלָא 810) *marvels*

אֲשֶׁר לֹא־נִבְרְאוּ rel.-neg.-Ni. pf. 3 c.p. (בָּרָא 135) *such as have not been wrought*

בְּכָל־הָאָרֶץ prep.-n.m.s. cstr. (481)-def.art.-n.f.s. (75) *in all the earth*

וּבְכָל־הַגּוֹיִם conj.-prep.-n.m.s. cstr. (481)-def.art.-n.m.p. (156) *or in any nation*

וְרָאָה conj.-Qal pf. 3 m.s. (906) *and shall see*

כָל־הָעָם n.m.s. cstr. (471)-def.art.-n.m.s. (I 766) *all the people*

אֲשֶׁר־אַתָּה בְקִרְבּוֹ rel.-pers.pr. 2 m.s. (61)-prep.-n.m.s.-3 m.s. sf. (899) *among whom you are*

אֶת־מַעֲשֵׂה יהוה dir.obj.-n.m.s. cstr. (795)-pr.n. (217) *the work of Yahweh*

כִּי־נוֹרָא הוּא conj.-Ni. ptc. (יָרֵא 431)-pers.pr. 3 m.s. (214) *for it is a terrible thing*

אֲשֶׁר אֲנִי עֹשֶׂה rel.-pers.pr. 1 c.s. (58)-Qal act. ptc. (עָשָׂה I 793) *that I will do*

עִמָּךְ prep.-2 m.s. sf. paus. *with you*

34:11

שְׁמָר־לְךָ Qal impv. 2 m.s. (שָׁמַר 1036)-prep.-2 m.s. sf. *observe*

אֵת אֲשֶׁר אָנֹכִי dir.obj.-rel.-pers.pr. 1 c.s. (59) *what I*

מְצַוְּךָ Pi. ptc.-2 m.s. sf. (צָוָה 845) *command you*

הַיּוֹם def.art.-n.m.s. (398) *this day*

הִנְנִי demons. part.-1 c.s. sf. (243) *behold I*

גֹרֵשׁ Qal act. ptc. (176) *will drive out*

מִפָּנֶיךָ prep.-n.m.p.-2 m.s. sf. (815) *before you*

אֶת־הָאֱמֹרִי dir.obj.-def.art.-pr.n. gent. (57) *the Amorites*

וְהַכְּנַעֲנִי conj.-def.art.-pr.n. gent. (489) *the Canaanites*

וְהַחִתִּי conj.-def.art.-pr.n. gent. (366) *the Hittites*

וְהַפְּרִזִּי conj.-def.art.-pr.n. gent. (827) *the Perizzites*

וְהַחִוִּי conj.-def.art.-pr.n. gent. (295) *the Hivites*

וְהַיְבוּסִי conj.-def.art.-pr.n. gent. (101) *and the Jebusites*

34:12

הִשָּׁמֶר לְךָ Ni. impv.2 m.s. (שָׁמַר 1036) - prep.-2 m.s. sf. *take heed to yourself*

פֶּן־תִּכְרֹת adv. (814) - Qal impf. 2 m.s. (כָּרַת 503) *lest you make*

בְּרִית n.f.s. (136) *a covenant*

לְיוֹשֵׁב הָאָרֶץ prep.-Qal act. ptc. cstr. (יָשַׁב 442)-def.art.-n.f.s. (75) *with the inhabitants of the land*

אֲשֶׁר אַתָּה rel.-pers.pr. 2 m.s. (61) *which you*

בָּא עָלֶיהָ Qal act. ptc. (בּוֹא 97)-prep.-3 f.s. sf. *go unto it*

פֶּן־יִהְיֶה adv. (814)-Qal impf. 3 m.s. (הָיָה 224) *lest it become*

לְמוֹקֵשׁ prep.-n.m.s. (430) *a snare*

בְּקִרְבֶּךָ prep.-n.m.s.2 m.s. sf. (899) *in the midst of you*

34:13

כִּי אֶת־מִזְבְּחֹתָם conj.-dir.obj.-n.m.p.-3 m.p. sf. (258) *for their altars*

תִּתֹּצוּן Qal impf. 2 m.p. (נָתַץ 683) *you shall tear down*

וְאֶת־מַצֵּבֹתָם conj.-dir.obj.-n.f.p.-3 m.p. sf. (663) *and their pillars*

תְּשַׁבֵּרוּן Pi. impf. 2 m.p. (שָׁבַר 990) *break*

וְאֶת־אֲשֵׁרָיו conj.-dir.obj.-n.f.p.-3 m.s. sf. (81) *and their Asherim*

תִּכְרֹתוּן Qal impf. 2 m.p. paus. (כָּרַת 503) *cut down*

34:14

כִּי לֹא תִשְׁתַּחֲוֶה conj.-neg.-Hithpalel impf. 2 m.s. (שָׁחָה 1005) *for you shall not worship*

לְאֵל אַחֵר prep.-n.m.s. (42)-adj. (29) *another god*

כִּי יהוה conj.-pr.n. (217) *for Yahweh*

קַנָּא adj. (888) *jealous*

שְׁמוֹ n.m.s.-3 m.s.sf. (1027) *is his name*

אֵל קַנָּא n.m.s. (42)-adj. (888) *a jealous God*

הוּא pers.pr. 3 m.s. (214) *he is*

34:15

פֶּן־תִּכְרֹת adv. (814) - Qal impf. 2 m.s. (כָּרַת 503) *lest you make*

בְּרִית n.f.s. (136) *a covenant*

לְיוֹשֵׁב הָאָרֶץ prep.-Qal act. ptc. cstr. (יָשַׁב 442)-def.art.-n.f.s. (75) *with the inhabitants of the land*

וְזָנוּ conj.-Qal pf. 3 c.p. (זָנָה 275) *when they play the harlot*

אַחֲרֵי אֱלֹהֵיהֶם prep. (29)-n.m.p.-3 m.p. sf. (43) *after their gods*

וְזָבְחוּ conj.-Qal pf. 3 c.p. (256) *and sacrifice*

לֵאלֹהֵיהֶם prep.-n.m.p.-3 m.p. sf. (43) *to their gods*

וְקָרָא לְךָ conj.-Qal pf. 3 m.s. (894)-prep.-2 m.s. sf. *and one invites you*

וְאָכַלְתָּ conj.-Qal pf. 2 m.s. (אָכַל 37) *and you eat*

מִזִּבְחוֹ prep.-n.m.s.-3 m.s. sf. (257) *of his sacrifice*

34:16

וְלָקַחְתָּ conj.-Qal pf. 2 m.s. (542) *and you take*

מִבְּנֹתָיו prep.-n.f.p.-3 m.s. sf. (I 123) *of their daughters*

לְבָנֶיךָ prep.-n.m.p.-2 m.s. sf. (119) *for your sons*

וְזָנוּ conj.-Qal pf. 3 c.p. (זָנָה 275) *and play the harlot*

בְנֹתָיו n.f.p.-3 m.s. sf. (I 123) *their daughters*

אַחֲרֵי אֱלֹהֵיהֶן prep. (29)-n.m.p.-3 f.p. sf. (43) *after their gods*

וְהִזְנוּ conj.-Hi. pf. 3 c.p. (זָנָה 275) *and make play the harlot*

אֶת־בָּנֶיךָ dir.obj.-n.m.p.-2 m.s. sf. (119) *your sons*

אַחֲרֵי אֱלֹהֵיהֶן v.supra-v.supra *after their gods*

34:17

אֱלֹהֵי מַסֵּכָה n.m.p. cstr. (43)-n.f.s. (651) *molten gods*

לֹא תַעֲשֶׂה־לָּךְ neg.-Qal impf. 2 m.s. (עָשָׂה I 793)-prep.-2 m.s. sf. paus. *you shall not make for yourself*

34:18

אֶת־חַג הַמַּצּוֹת dir.obj.-n.m.s. cstr. (290) - def.art.-n.f.p. (595) *the feast of unleavened bread*

תִּשְׁמֹר Qal impf. 2 m.s. (שָׁמַר 1036) *you shall keep*

שִׁבְעַת יָמִים num. f.s. cstr. (987)-n.m.p. (398) *seven days*

תֹּאכַל Qal impf. 2 m.s. (אָכַל 37) *you shall eat*

מַצּוֹת n.f.p. (595) *unleavened bread*

אֲשֶׁר צִוִּיתִךָ rel.-Pi. pf. 1 c.s.-2 m.s. sf. (צָוָה 845) *as I commanded you*

לְמוֹעֵד prep.-n.m.s. (417) *at the time appointed*

חֹדֶשׁ הָאָבִיב n.m.s. cstr. (II 294)-def.art.-n.m.s. (1) *in the month Abib*

כִּי בְּחֹדֶשׁ הָאָבִיב conj.-prep.-n.m.s. cstr. (II 294)-def.art.-n.m.s. (1) *for in the month Abib*

יָצָאתָ Qal pf. 2 m.s. (יָצָא 422) *you came out*

מִמִּצְרָיִם prep.-pr.n. paus. (595) *from Egypt*

34:19

כָּל־פֶּטֶר n.m.s. cstr. (481)-n.m.s. cstr. (809) *all that opens*

רֶחֶם n.m.s. (933) *a womb*

לִי prep.-1 c.s. sf. *is mine*

וְכָל־מִקְנְךָ conj.-n.m.s. cstr. (481)-n.m.s.-2 m.s. sf. (889) *all your cattle*

תִּזָּכָר Ni. impf. 3 f.s. (זָכַר 269; pb.rd. הַזָּכָר - *male*) (? *are remembered*)

פֶּטֶר n.m.s. cstr. (809) *the firstlings of*

שׁוֹר וָשֶׂה n.m.s. (1004) - conj.-n.m.s. (961) *cow and sheep*

34:20

וּפֶטֶר חֲמוֹר conj.-n.m.s. cstr. (809) - n.m.s. (331) *and the firstling of an ass*

תִּפְדֶּה Qal impf. 2 m.s. (פָּדָה 804) *you shall redeem*

בְשֶׂה prep.-n.m.s. (961) *with a lamb*

וְאִם־לֹא תִפְדֶּה conj.-hypoth.part. (49)-neg.-Qal impf. 2 m.s. (פָּדָה 804) *or if you will not redeem*

וַעֲרַפְתּוֹ conj.-Qal pf. 2 m.s.-3 m.s. sf. (עָרַף 791) *you shall break its neck*

כֹּל בְּכוֹר n.m.s. cstr. (481)-n.m.s. cstr. (114) *all the first-born*

בָּנֶיךָ n.m.p.-2 m.s. sf. (119) *your sons*

תִּפְדֶּה v.supra *you shall redeem*

וְלֹא־יֵרָאוּ conj.-neg.-Ni. impf. 3 m.p. (רָאָה 906) *and none shall appear*

פָנַי n.m.p.-1 c.s. sf. (815) *before me*

רֵיקָם adv. (938) *empty*

34:21

שֵׁשֶׁת יָמִים num. f. cstr. (995)-n.m.p. (398) *six days*

תַּעֲבֹד Qal impf. 2 m.s. (עָבַד 712) *you shall work*

וּבַיּוֹם הַשְּׁבִיעִי conj.-prep.-def.art.-n.m.s. (398)-def.art.-adj. num. (988) *but on the seventh day*

תִּשְׁבֹּת Qal impf. 2 m.s. (שָׁבַת 991) *you shall rest*

בֶּחָרִישׁ prep.-def.art.-n.m.s. (361) *in plowing time*

וּבַקָּצִיר conj.-prep.-def.art.-n.m.s. (894) *and in harvest*

תִּשְׁבֹּת v. supra *you shall rest*

34:22

וְחַג שָׁבֻעֹת conj.-n.m.s. cstr. (290)-n.m.p. (988) *and the feast of weeks*

תַּעֲשֶׂה לְךָ Qal impf. 2 m.s. (עָשָׂה I 793)-prep.-2 m.s. sf. *you shall observe*

בִּכּוּרֵי קְצִיר n.m.p. cstr. (114)-n.m.s. cstr. (894) *the first fruits of harvest of*

חִטִּים n.f.p. (334) *wheat*

וְחַג הָאָסִיף conj.-n.m.s. cstr. (290)-def.art.-n.m.s. (63) *and the feast of ingathering*

תְּקוּפַת הַשָּׁנָה n.f.s. cstr. (880)-def.art.-n.f.s. (1040) *at the year's end*

34:23

שָׁלֹשׁ פְּעָמִים num. (1025) - n.f.p. (821) *three times*

בַּשָּׁנָה prep.-def.art.-n.f.s. (1040) *in the year*

יֵרָאֶה Ni. impf. 3 m.s. (רָאָה 906) *shall appear*

כָּל־זְכוּרְךָ n.m.s. cstr. (481)-n.m.s.-2 m.s. sf. (271) *all your males*

אֶת־פְּנֵי הָאָדֹן dir.obj.-n.m.p. cstr. (815)-def.art.-n.m.s. (10) *before the Lord*

יהוה pr.n. (217) *Yahweh*

אֱלֹהֵי יִשְׂרָאֵל n.m.p. cstr. (43) - pr.n. (975) *the God of Israel*

34:24

כִּי־אוֹרִישׁ conj.-Hi. impf. 1 c.s. (יָרַשׁ 439) *for I will cast out*

גּוֹיִם n.m.p. (156) *nations*

מִפָּנֶיךָ prep.-n.m.p.-2 m.s. sf. (815) *before you*

וְהִרְחַבְתִּי conj.-Hi. pf. 1 c.s. (רָחַב 931) *and enlarge*

אֶת־גְּבוּלֶךָ dir.obj.-n.m.s.-2 m.s. sf. (147) *your borders*

וְלֹא־יַחְמֹד conj.-neg.-Qal impf. 3 m.s. (חָמַד 326) *neither shall desire*

אִישׁ n.m.s. (35) *any man*

אֶת־אַרְצְךָ dir.obj.-n.f.s.-2 m.s. sf. (75) *your land*

בַּעֲלֹתְךָ prep.-Qal inf. cstr.-2 m.s. sf. (עָלָה 748) *when you go up*

לֵרָאוֹת prep.-Ni. inf. cstr. (רָאָה 906) *to appear*

אֶת־פְּנֵי יהוה dir.obj.-n.m.p. cstr. (815)-pr.n. (217) *before Yahweh*

אֱלֹהֶיךָ n.m.p.-2 m.s. sf. (43) *your God*

שָׁלֹשׁ פְּעָמִים num. (1025)-n.f.p. (821) *three times*

בַּשָּׁנָה prep.-def.art.-n.f.s. (1040) *in the year*

34:25

לֹא־תִשְׁחַט neg.-Qal impf. 2 m.s. (שָׁחַט 1006) *you shall not offer (slaughter)*

עַל־חָמֵץ prep.-n.m.s. (329) *with leaven*

דַּם־זִבְחִי n.m.s. cstr. (196)-n.m.s.-1 c.s. sf. (257) *the blood of my sacrifice*

וְלֹא־יָלִין conj.-neg.-Qal impf. 3 m.s. (לִין I 533; 1c) *neither shall be left*

לַבֹּקֶר prep.-def.art.-n.m.s. (133) *until the morning*

זֶבַח חַג n.m.s. cstr. (257)-n.m.s. cstr. (290) *the sacrifice of the feast of*

הַפָּסַח def.art.-n.m.s. paus. (820) *the passover*

34:26

רֵאשִׁית n.f.s. cstr. (912) *the first of*

בִּכּוּרֵי n.m.p. cstr. (114) *the first fruits of*

אַדְמָתְךָ n.f.s.-2 m.s. sf. (9) *your ground*

תָּבִיא Hi. impf. 2 m.s. (בּוֹא 97) *you shall bring*

בֵּית יהוה n.m.s. cstr. (108)-pr.n. (217) *to the house of Yahweh*

אֱלֹהֶיךָ n.m.p.-2 m.s. sf. (43) *your God*

לֹא־תְבַשֵּׁל neg.-Pi. impf. 2 m.s. (143) *you shall not boil*

גְּדִי n.m.s. (152) *a kid*

בַּחֲלֵב אִמּוֹ prep.-n.m.s. cstr. (316)-n.f.s.-3 m.s. sf. (51) *in its mother's milk*

34:27

וַיֹּאמֶר יהוה consec.-Qal impf. 3 m.s. (55)-pr.n. (217) *and Yahweh said*

אֶל־מֹשֶׁה prep.-pr.n. (602) *to Moses*

כְּתָב־לְךָ Qal impv. 2 m.s. (כָּתַב 507)-prep.-2 m.s. sf. *write (for yourself)*

אֶת־הַדְּבָרִים הָאֵלֶּה dir.obj.-def.art.-n.m.p. (182)-def.art.-demons. adj. c.p. (41) *these words*

כִּי עַל־פִּי conj.-prep.-n.m.s. cstr. (804) *for in accordance with*

הַדְּבָרִים הָאֵלֶּה v.supra-v.supra *these words*

כָּרַתִּי אִתְּךָ Qal pf. 1 c.s. (כָּרַת 503)-prep.-2 m.s. (II 85) *I have made with you*

בְּרִית n.f.s. (136) *a covenant*

וְאֶת־יִשְׂרָאֵל conj.-prep. (II 85)-pr.n. (975) *and with Israel*

34:28

וַיְהִי־שָׁם consec.-Qal impf. 3 m.s. (הָיָה 224)-adv. (1027) *and he was there*

עִם־יהוה prep.-pr.n. (217) *with Yahweh*

אַרְבָּעִים יוֹם num. p. (917)-n.m.s. (398) *forty days*

וְאַרְבָּעִים לַיְלָה conj.-num. p. (917)-n.m.s. (538) *and forty nights*

לֶחֶם n.m.s. (536) *bread*

לֹא אָכַל neg.-Qal pf. 3 m.s. (37) *he did not eat*

וּמַיִם conj.-n.m. p. (565) *and water*

לֹא שָׁתָה neg.-Qal pf. 3 m.s. (1059) *he did not drink*

וַיִּכְתֹּב consec.-Qal impf. 3 m.s. (כָּתַב 507) *and he wrote*

עַל־הַלֻּחֹת prep.-def.art.-n.m.p. (531) *upon the tables*

אֵת דִּבְרֵי הַבְּרִית dir.obj.-n.m.p. cstr. (182)-def.art.-n.f.s. (136) *the words of the covenant*

עֲשֶׂרֶת הַדְּבָרִים num. f. cstr. (796)-def.art.-n.m.p. (182) *the ten commandments (words)*

34:29

וַיְהִי בְּרֶדֶת consec.-Qal impf. 3 m.s. (הָיָה 224)-prep.-Qal inf. cstr. (יָרַד 432) *when ... came down*

מֹשֶׁה pr.n. (602) *Moses*

מֵהַר סִינַי prep.-n.m.s. cstr. (249)-pr.n. (696) *from Mount Sinai*

וּשְׁנֵי לֻחֹת conj.-num. m. du. cstr. (1040)-n.m.p. cstr. (531) *with the two tables of*

הָעֵדֻת def.art.-n.f.s. (730) *the testimony*

בְּיַד־מֹשֶׁה prep.-n.f.s. cstr. (388)-pr.n. (602) *in the hand of Moses*

בְּרִדְתּוֹ prep.-Qal inf. cstr.-3 m.s. sf. (יָרַד 432) *as he came down*

מִן־הָהָר prep.-def.art.-n.m.s. (249) *from the mountain*

וּמֹשֶׁה conj.-pr.n. (602) *and Moses*

לֹא־יָדַע neg.-Qal pf. 3 m.s. (393) *did not know*

כִּי קָרַן עוֹר פָּנָיו conj.-Qal pf. 3 m.s. (קָרַן 902)-n.m.s. cstr. (736)-n.m.p.-3 m.s. sf. (815) *that the skin of his face shone*

בְּדַבְּרוֹ אִתּוֹ prep.-Pi. inf. cstr.-3 m.s. sf.-prep.-3 m.s. (II 85) *because he had been talking with him*

34:30

וַיַּרְא אַהֲרֹן consec.-Qal impf. 3 m.s. (רָאָה 906)-pr.n. (14) *and when Aaron saw*

וְכָל־בְּנֵי conj.-n.m.s. cstr. (481)-n.m.p. cstr. (119) *and all the people of*

יִשְׂרָאֵל pr.n. (975) *Israel*

אֶת־מֹשֶׁה dir.obj.-pr.n. (602) *Moses*

וְהִנֵּה conj.-demons. part. (243) *and behold*

קָרַן Qal pf. 3 m.s. (902) *shone*

עוֹר פָּנָיו n.m.s. cstr. (736)-n.m.p.-3 m.s. sf. (815) *the skin of his face*

וַיִּירְאוּ consec.-Qal impf. 3 m.p. (יָרֵא 431) *and they were afraid*

מִגֶּשֶׁת אֵלָיו prep.-Qal inf. cstr. (נָגַשׁ 620)-prep.-3 m.s. sf. *to come near him*

34:31

וַיִּקְרָא consec.-Qal impf. 3 m.s. (קָרָא 894) *and called*

אֲלֵהֶם מֹשֶׁה prep.-3 m.p. sf.-pr.n. (602) *to them Moses*

וַיָּשֻׁבוּ consec.-Qal impf. 3 m.p. (שׁוּב 996) *and returned*

אֵלָיו אַהֲרֹן prep.-3 m.s. sf.-pr.n. (14) *to him Aaron*

וְכָל־הַנְּשִׂאִים conj.-n.m.s. cstr. (481) - def.art.-n.m.p. (I 672) *and all the leaders*

בָּעֵדָה prep.-def.art.-n.f.s. (II 417) *of the congregation*

וַיְדַבֵּר consec.-Pi. impf. 3 m.s. (180) *and talked*

מֹשֶׁה אֲלֵהֶם pr.n. (602)-prep.-3 m.p. sf. *Moses ... with them*

34:32

וְאַחֲרֵי־כֵן conj.-prep. (29)-adv. (485) *and afterward*

נִגְּשׁוּ Ni. pf. 3 c.p. (נָגַשׁ 620) *came near*

כָּל־בְּנֵי n.m.s. cstr. (481)-n.m.p. cstr. (119) *all the people of*

יִשְׂרָאֵל pr.n. (975) *Israel*

וַיְצַוֵּם consec.-Pi. impf. 3 m.s.-3 m.p. sf. (צָוָה 845) *and he gave them in commandment*

אֵת כָּל־אֲשֶׁר dir.obj.-n.m.s. (481)-rel. *all that*

דִּבֶּר יהוה Pi. pf. 3 m.s. (180)-pr.n. (217) *Yahweh had spoken*

אִתּוֹ prep.-3 m.s. sf. (II 85) *with him*

בְּהַר סִינָי prep.-n.m.s. cstr. (249)-pr.n. (696) *in Mount Sinai*

34:33

וַיְכַל מֹשֶׁה consec.-Pi. impf. 3 m.s. (כָּלָה 477)-pr.n. (602) *and when Moses had finished*

מִדַּבֵּר prep.-Pi. inf. cstr. (180) *speaking*

אִתָּם prep.-3 m.p. sf. (II 85) *with them*

וַיִּתֵּן consec.-Qal impf. 3 m.s. (נָתַן 678) *he put*

עַל־פָּנָיו prep.-n.m.p.-3 m.s. sf. (815) *on his face*

מַסְוֶה n.m.s. (691) *a veil*

34:34

וּבְבֹא מֹשֶׁה conj.-prep.-Qal inf. cstr. (בּוֹא 97)-pr.n. (602) *but whenever Moses went in*

לִפְנֵי יהוה prep.-n.m.p. cstr. (815)-pr.n. (217) *before Yahweh*

לְדַבֵּר אִתּוֹ prep.-Pi. inf. cstr. (180)-prep.-3 m.s. sf. (II 85) *to speak with him*

יָסִיר Hi. impf. 3 m.s. (סוּר 693) *he took off*

אֶת־הַמַּסְוֶה dir.obj.-n.m.s. (691) *the veil*

עַד־צֵאתוֹ prep.-Qal inf. cstr.-3 m.s. sf. (יָצָא 422) *until he came out*

וְיָצָא conj.-Qal pf. 3 m.s. (422) *and when he came out*

וְדִבֶּר conj.-Pi. pf. 3 m.s. (180) *and told*

אֶל־בְּנֵי יִשְׂרָאֵל prep.-n.m.p. cstr. (119)-pr.n. (975) *the people of Israel*

אֵת אֲשֶׁר יְצֻוֶּה dir.obj.-rel.-Pu. impf. 3 m.s. (צָוָה 845) *what he was commanded*

34:35

וְרָאוּ conj.-Qal pf. 3 c.p. (רָאָה 906) *and saw*

בְנֵי־יִשְׂרָאֵל n.m.p. cstr. (119)-pr.n. (975) *the people of Israel*

אֶת־פְּנֵי מֹשֶׁה dir.obj.-n.m.p. cstr. (815)-pr.n. (602) *the face of Moses*

כִּי קָרַן conj.-Qal pf. 3 m.s. (902) *that shone*

עוֹר פְּנֵי מֹשֶׁה n.m.s. cstr. (736)-n.m.p. cstr. (815)-pr.n. (602) *the skin of Moses' face*

וְהֵשִׁיב מֹשֶׁה conj.-Hi. pf. 3 m.s. (שׁוּב 996)-pr.n. (602) *and Moses would put again*

אֶת־הַמַּסְוֶה dir.obj.-def.art.-n.m.s. (691) *the veil*

עַל־פָּנָיו prep.-n.m.p.-3 m.s. sf. (815) *upon his face*

עַד־בֹּאוֹ prep.-Qal inf. cstr.-3 m.s. sf. (בּוֹא 97) *until he went in*

לְדַבֵּר אִתּוֹ prep.-Pi. inf. cstr. (180)-prep.-3 m.s. sf. (II 85) *to speak with him*

35:1

וַיַּקְהֵל consec.-Hi. impf. 3 m.s. (קָהַל 874) *and assembled*

מֹשֶׁה pr.n. (602) *Moses*

אֶת־כָּל־עֲדַת dir.obj.-n.m.s. cstr. (481)-n.f.s. cstr. (II 417) *all the congregation of*

בְּנֵי־יִשְׂרָאֵל n.m.p. cstr. (119)-pr.n. (975) *the people of Israel*

וַיֹּאמֶר אֲלֵהֶם consec.-Qal impf. 3 m.s. (55)-prep.-3 m.p. sf. *and said to them*

אֵלֶּה demons. adj. c.p. (41) *these are*

הַדְּבָרִים def.art.-n.m.p. (182) *the things*

אֲשֶׁר־צִוָּה יהוה rel.-Pi. pf. 3 m.s. (צָוָה 845)-pr.n. (217) *which Yahweh has commanded*

לַעֲשֹׂת אֹתָם prep.-Qal inf. cstr. (עָשָׂה I 793)-dir.obj.-3 m.p. sf. *to do (them)*

35:2

שֵׁשֶׁת יָמִים num. f. cstr. (995)-n.m.p. (398) *six days*

תֵּעָשֶׂה Ni. impf. 3 f.s. (עָשָׂה I 793) *shall be done*

מְלָאכָה n.f.s. (521) *work*

וּבַיּוֹם הַשְּׁבִיעִי conj.-prep.-def.art.-n.m.s. (398)-def.art.-num. adj. (988) *but on the seventh day*

יִהְיֶה לָכֶם Qal impf. 3 m.s. (הָיָה 224)-prep.-2 m.p. sf. *you shall have*

קֹדֶשׁ n.m.s. cstr. (871) *a holy*

שַׁבַּת שַׁבָּתוֹן n.f.s. cstr. (992)-n.m.s. (992) *sabbath of solemn rest*

ליהוה prep.-pr.n. (217) *to Yahweh*

כָּל־הָעֹשֶׂה n.m.s. cstr. (481)-def.art.-Qal act. ptc. (עָשָׂה I 793) *whoever does*

בוֹ prep.-3 m.s. sf. *on it*

מְלָאכָה n.f.s. (521) *any work*

יוּמָת Ho. impf. 3 m.s. (מוּת 559) *shall be put to death*

35:3

לֹא־תְבַעֲרוּ neg.-Pi. impf. 2 m.p. (בָּעַר 128) *you shall not kindle*

אֵשׁ n.f.s. (77) *fire*

בְּכֹל מֹשְׁבֹתֵיכֶם prep.-n.m.s. cstr. (481)-n.m.p.2 m.p. sf. (444) *in all your habitations*

בְּיוֹם הַשַּׁבָּת prep.-n.m.s. cstr. (398)-def.art.-n.f.s. paus. (992) *on the sabbath day*

35:4

וַיֹּאמֶר מֹשֶׁה consec.-Qal impf. 3 m.s. (55)-pr.n. (602) *and Moses said*

אֶל־כָּל־עֲדַת prep.-n.m.s. cstr. (481)-n.f.s. cstr. (II 417) *to all the congregation of*

בְּנֵי־יִשְׂרָאֵל n.m.p. cstr. (119)-pr.n. (975) *the people of Israel*

לֵאמֹר prep.-Qal inf. cstr. (55) *(saying)*

זֶה demons. adj. (260) *this is*

הַדָּבָר def.art.-n.m.s. (182) *the thing*

אֲשֶׁר־צִוָּה rel.-Pi. pf. 3 m.s. (צָוָה 845) *which has commanded*

יהוה לֵאמֹר pr.n. (217)-prep.-Qal inf. cstr. (55) *Yahweh (saying)*

35:5

קְחוּ Qal impv. 2 m.p. (לָקַח 542) *take*

מֵאִתְּכֶם prep.-prep.-2 m.p. sf. (II 85) *from among you*

תְּרוּמָה n.f.s. (929) *an offering*

ליהוה prep.-pr.n. (217) *to Yahweh*

כֹּל נְדִיב n.m.s. cstr. (481)-adj. m.s. cst. (622) *whoever is generous of*

לִבּוֹ n.m.s.-3 m.s. sf. (524) *his heart*

יְבִיאֶהָ Hi. impf. 3 m.s.-3 f.s. sf. (בּוֹא 97) *let him bring (it)*

אֵת תְּרוּמַת dir.obj.-n.f.s. cstr. (929) *the offering of*

יהוה pr.n. (217) *Yahweh*

זָהָב n.m.s. (262) *gold*

וָכֶסֶף conj.-n.m.s. (494) *and silver*

וּנְחֹשֶׁת conj.-n.m.s. (638) *and bronze*

35:6

וּתְכֵלֶת conj.-n.f.s. (1067) *and blue*

וְאַרְגָּמָן conj.-n.m.s. (71) *and purple*

וְתוֹלַעַת שָׁנִי conj.-n.f.s. cstr. (1069)-n.m.s. (1040) *and scarlet stuff*

וְשֵׁשׁ conj.-n.m.s. (III 1058) *and fine twined linen*

וְעִזִּים conj.-n.f.p. (777) *and goats' hair*

35:7

וְעֹרֹת אֵילִם conj.-n.m.p. cstr. (736) - n.m.p. (I 17) *and rams' skins*

מְאָדָּמִים Pu. ptc. m.p. (אָדֹם 10) *tanned*

וְעֹרֹת תְּחָשִׁים v. supra-n.m.p. (I 1065) *and goatskins*

וַעֲצֵי שִׁטִּים conj.-n.m.p. cstr. (781)-n.f.p. (1008) *and acacia wood*

35:8

וְשֶׁמֶן conj.-n.m.s. (1032) *and oil*

לַמָּאוֹר prep.-def. art.-n.m.s. (22) *for the light*

וּבְשָׂמִים conj.-n.m.p. (141) *and spices*

לְשֶׁמֶן הַמִּשְׁחָה prep.-n.m.s. cstr. (1032)-def. art.-n.f.s. (603) *for the anointing oil*

וְלִקְטֹרֶת הַסַּמִּים conj.-prep.-n.f.s. cstr. (882)-def. art.-n.m.p. (702) *and for the fragrant incense*

35:9

וְאַבְנֵי־שֹׁהַם conj.-n.f.p. cstr. (6)-n.m.s. (I 995) *and onyx stones*

וְאַבְנֵי מִלֻּאִים v. supra-n.m.p. (571) *and stones for setting*

לָאֵפוֹד prep.-def. art.-n.m.s. (65) *for the ephod*

וְלַחֹשֶׁן conj.-prep.-def. art.-n.m.s. (365) *and for the breastpiece*

35:10

וְכָל־חֲכַם־לֵב conj.-n.m.s. cstr. (481)-adj. m.s. cstr. (314)-n.m.s. (524) *and every able man*

בָּכֶם prep.-2 m.p. sf. *among you*

יָבֹאוּ Qal impf. 3 m.p. (בּוֹא 97) *let come*

וְיַעֲשׂוּ conj.-Qal impf. 3 m.p. (עָשָׂה I 793) *and make*

אֵת כָּל־אֲשֶׁר dir. obj.-n.m.s. (481)-rel. *all that*

צִוָּה יהוה Pi. pf. 3 m.s. (צָוָה 845)-pr.n. (217) *Yahweh has commanded*

35:11

אֶת־הַמִּשְׁכָּן dir. obj.-def. art.-n.m.s. (1015) *the tabernacle*

אֶת־אָהֳלוֹ dir. obj.-n.m.s.-3 m.s. sf. (13) *its tent*

וְאֶת־מִכְסֵהוּ conj.-dir. obj.-n.m.s.-3 m.s. sf. (492) *and its covering*

אֶת־קְרָסָיו dir. obj.-n.m.p.-3 m.s. sf. (902) *its hooks*

וְאֶת־קְרָשָׁיו conj.-dir. obj.-n.m.p.-3 m.s. sf. (903) *and its frames*

אֶת־בְּרִיחָו dir. obj.-n.m.p.-3 m.s. sf. (138) *its bars*

אֶת־עַמֻּדָיו dir. obj.-n.m.p.-3 m.s. sf. (765) *its pillars*

וְאֶת־אֲדָנָיו conj.-dir. obj.-n.m.p.-3 m.s. sf. (10) *and its bases*

35:12

אֶת־הָאָרֹן dir. obj.-def. art.-n.m.s. (75) *the ark*

וְאֶת־בַּדָּיו conj.-dir. obj.-n.m.p.-3 m.s. sf. (II 94) *with its poles*

אֶת־הַכַּפֹּרֶת dir. obj.-def. art.-n.f.s. (498) *the mercy seat*

וְאֵת פָּרֹכֶת הַמָּסָךְ conj.-dir. obj.-n.f.s. cstr. (827)-def. art.-n.m.s. paus. (697) *and the veil of the screen*

35:13

אֶת־הַשֻּׁלְחָן dir. obj.-def. art.-n.m.s. (1020) *the table*

וְאֶת־בַּדָּיו conj.-dir. obj.-n.m.p.-3 m.s. sf. (II 94) *with its poles*

וְאֶת־כָּל־כֵּלָיו conj.-dir. obj.-n.m.s. cstr. (481)-n.m.p.-3 m.s. sf. (479) *and all its utensils*

וְאֵת לֶחֶם הַפָּנִים conj.-dir. obj.-n.m.s. cstr. (536)-def. art.-n.m.p. (815) *and the bread of the Presence*

35:14

וְאֶת־מְנֹרַת הַמָּאוֹר conj.-dir. obj.-n.f.s. cstr. (633)-def. art.-n.m.s. (22) *the lampstand also for the light*

וְאֶת־כֵּלֶיהָ conj.-dir. obj.-n.m.p.-3 f.s. sf. (479) *with its utensils*

וְאֶת־נֵרֹתֶיהָ conj.-dir. obj.-n.m.p.-3 f.s. sf. (632) *and its lamps*

וְאֵת שֶׁמֶן הַמָּאוֹר conj.-dir. obj.-n.m.s. cstr. (1032)-def. art.-n.m.s. (22) *and the oil for the light*

35:15

וְאֶת־מִזְבַּח הַקְּטֹרֶת conj.-dir. obj.-n.m.s. cstr. (258)-def. art.-n.f.s. (882) *and the altar of incense*

וְאֶת־בַּדָּיו conj.-dir. obj.-n.m.p.-3 m.s. sf. (II 94) *with its poles*

וְאֵת שֶׁמֶן הַמִּשְׁחָה conj.-dir. obj.-n.m.s. cstr. (1032)-def. art.-n.f.s. (603) *and the anointing oil*

וְאֵת קְטֹרֶת הַסַּמִּים conj.-dir. obj.-n.f.s. cstr. (882)-def. art.-n.m.p. (702) *and the fragrant incense*

וְאֶת־מָסַךְ הַפֶּתַח conj.-dir. obj.-n.m.s. cstr. (697)-def. art.-n.m.s. (835) *and the screen for the door*

לְפֶתַח הַמִּשְׁכָּן prep.-n.m.s. cstr. (835)-def. art.-n.m.s. (1015) *at the door of the tabernacle*

35:16

אֵת מִזְבַּח הָעֹלָה dir.obj.-n.m.s. cstr. (258)-def.art.-n.f.s. (750) *the altar of burnt offering*

וְאֶת־מִכְבַּר הַנְּחֹשֶׁת conj.-dir.obj.-n.m.s. cstr. (460)-def.art.-n.m.s. (638) *with grating of bronze*

אֲשֶׁר־לוֹ rel.-prep.-3 m.s. sf. *its*

אֶת־בַּדָּיו dir.obj.-n.m.p.-3 m.s. sf. (II 94) *its poles*

וְאֶת־כָּל־כֵּלָיו conj.-dir.obj.-n.m.s. cstr. (481)-n.m.p.-3 m.s. sf. (479) *and all its utensils*

אֶת־הַכִּיֹּר dir.obj.-def.art.-n.m.s. (468) *the laver*

וְאֶת־כַּנּוֹ conj.-dir.obj.-n.m.s.-3 m.s. sf. (III 487) *and its base*

35:17

אֵת קַלְעֵי הֶחָצֵר dir.obj.-n.m.p. cstr. (II 887)-def.art.-n.m.s. (I 346) *the hangings of the court*

אֶת־עַמֻּדָיו dir.obj.-n.m.p.-3 m.s. sf. (765) *its pillars*

וְאֶת־אֲדָנֶיהָ conj.-dir.obj.-n.m.p.-3 f.s. sf. (10) *and its bases*

וְאֵת מָסַךְ conj.-dir.obj.-n.m.s. cstr. (697) *and the screen for*

שַׁעַר הֶחָצֵר n.m.s. cstr. (1044)-def.art.-n.m.s. (I 346) *the gate of the court*

35:18

אֶת־יִתְדֹת הַמִּשְׁכָּן dir.obj.-n.f.p. cstr. (450)-def.art.-n.m.s. (1015) *the pegs of the tabernacle*

וְאֶת־יִתְדֹת הֶחָצֵר conj.-dir.obj.-n.f.p. cstr. (450)-def.art.-n.m.s. (I 346) *and the pegs of the court*

וְאֶת־מֵיתְרֵיהֶם conj.-dir.obj.-n.m.p.-3 m.p. sf. (452) *and their cords*

35:19

אֶת־בִּגְדֵי הַשְּׂרָד dir.obj.-n.m.p. cstr. (93)-def.art.-n.m.s. (975) *the finely wrought garments*

לְשָׁרֵת prep.-Pi. inf. cstr. (שָׁרַת 1058) *for ministering*

בַּקֹּדֶשׁ prep.-def.art.-n.m.s. (871) *in the holy place*

אֶת־בִּגְדֵי הַקֹּדֶשׁ dir.obj.-n.m.p. cstr. (93)-def.art.-n.m.s. (871) *the holy garments*

לְאַהֲרֹן prep.-pr.n. (14) *for Aaron*

הַכֹּהֵן def.art.-n.m.s. (463) *the priest*

וְאֶת־בִּגְדֵי conj.-dir.obj.-n.m.p. cstr. (93) *and the garments of*

בָנָיו n.m.p.-3 m.s. sf. (119) *his sons*

לְכַהֵן prep.-Pi. inf. cstr. (כָּהַן 464) *for their service as priests*

35:20

וַיֵּצְאוּ consec.-Qal impf. 3 m.p. (יָצָא 422) *then departed*

כָּל־עֲדַת n.m.s. cstr. (481)-n.f.s. cstr. (II 417) *all the congregation of*

בְּנֵי־יִשְׂרָאֵל n.m.p. cstr. (119)-pr.n. (975) *the people of Israel*

מִלִּפְנֵי מֹשֶׁה prep.-prep.-n.m.p. cstr. (815)-pr.n. (602) *from the presence of Moses*

35:21

וַיָּבֹאוּ consec.-Qal impf. 3 m.p. (בּוֹא 97) *and they came*

כָּל־אִישׁ n.m.s. cstr. (481)-n.m.s. (35) *every one*

אֲשֶׁר־נְשָׂאוֹ לִבּוֹ rel.-Qal pf. 3 m.s.-3 m.s. sf. (נָשָׂא 669)-n.m.s.-3 m.s. sf. (524) *whose heart stirred him*

וְכֹל conj.-n.m.s. (481) *and every one*

אֲשֶׁר נָדְבָה רוּחוֹ rel. - Qal pf. 3 f.s. (נָדַב 621) - n.f.s.-3 m.s. sf. (924) *whose spirit moved*

אֹתוֹ dir.obj.-3 m.s. sf. *him*

הֵבִיאוּ Hi. pf. 3 c.p. (בּוֹא 97) *they brought*

אֶת־תְּרוּמַת יהוה dir.obj.-n.f.s. cstr. (929)-pr.n. (217) *Yahweh's offering*

לִמְלֶאכֶת אֹהֶל prep.-n.f.s. cstr. (521)-n.m.s. cstr. (13) *to be used for the tent of*

מוֹעֵד n.m.s. (417) *meeting*

וּלְכָל־עֲבֹדָתוֹ conj.-prep.-n.m.s. cstr. (481)-n.f.p.-3 m.s. sf. (715) *and for all its service*

וּלְבִגְדֵי conj.-prep.-n.m.p. cstr. (93) *and for the garments of*

הַקֹּדֶשׁ def.art.-n.m.s. (871) *the holy place*

35:22

וַיָּבֹאוּ consec.-Qal impf. 3 m.p. (בּוֹא 97) *so they came*

הָאֲנָשִׁים def.art.-n.m.p. (35) *the men*

עַל־הַנָּשִׁים prep.-def.art.-n.f.p. (61) *and the women*

כֹּל נְדִיב לֵב n.m.s. cstr. (481)-adj. cstr. (622)-n.m.s. (524) *all who were of a willing heart*

הֵבִיאוּ Hi. pf. 3 c.p. (בּוֹא 97) *brought*

חָח n.m.s. (296) *brooches*

וָנֶזֶם conj.-n.m.s. (633) *and earrings*

וְטַבַּעַת conj.-n.f.s. (371) *and signet rings*

וְכוּמָז conj.-n.m.s. (484) *and armlets*

כָּל־כְּלִי n.m.s. cstr. (481)-n.m.s. cstr. (479) *all sorts of*

זָהָב n.m.s. (262) *gold objects*

וְכָל־אִישׁ אֲשֶׁר conj.-n.m.s. cstr. (481)-n.m.s. (35)-rel. *and every man who*

הֵנִיף Hi. pf. 3 m.s. (נוּף I 631; 4) *dedicated*

תְּנוּפַת n.f.s. cstr. (632) *an offering of*

זָהָב n.m.s. (262) *gold*

ליהוה prep.-pr.n. (217) *to Yahweh*

35:23

וְכָל־אִישׁ conj.-n.m.s. cstr. (481)-n.m.s. (35) *and every man*

אֲשֶׁר־נִמְצָא אִתּוֹ rel.-Ni. pf. 3 m.s. (מָצָא 592)-prep.-3 m.s. sf. (II 85) *with whom was found*

תְּכֵלֶת n.f.s. (1067) *blue*

וְאַרְגָּמָן conj.-n.m.s. (71) *or purple*

וְתוֹלַעַת שָׁנִי conj.-n.f.s. cstr. (1069)-n.m.s. (1040) *or scarlet stuff*

וְשֵׁשׁ conj.-n.m.s. (III 1058) *or fine linen*

וְעִזִּים conj.-n.f.p. (777) *or goats' hair*

וְעֹרֹת אֵילִם conj.-n.m.p. cstr. (736)-n.m.p. (I 17) *or rams' skins*

מְאָדָּמִים Pu. ptc. m.p. (אָדֹם 10) *tanned*

וְעֹרֹת תְּחָשִׁים conj.-n.m.p. cstr. (736)-n.m.p. (I 1065) *or goatskins*

הֵבִיאוּ Hi. pf. 3 c.p. (בּוֹא 97) *brought*

35:24

כָּל־מֵרִים n.m.s. cstr. (481)-Hi. ptc. (רוּם 926) *every one who could make*

תְּרוּמַת n.f.s. cstr. (929) *an offering of*

כֶּסֶף n.m.s. (494) *silver*

וּנְחֹשֶׁת conj.-n.m.s. (638) *or bronze*

הֵבִיאוּ Hi. pf. 3 c.p. (בּוֹא 97) *brought*

אֵת תְּרוּמַת dir.obj.-v. supra *as the offering of*

יהוה pr.n. (217) *Yahweh*

וְכֹל conj.-n.m.s. (481) *and every man*

אֲשֶׁר נִמְצָא אִתּוֹ rel.-Ni. pf. 3 m.s. (מָצָא 592)-prep.-3 m.s. sf. (II 85) *with whom was found*

עֲצֵי שִׁטִּים n.m.p. cstr. (781)-n.f.p. (1008) *acacia wood*

לְכָל־מְלֶאכֶת prep.-n.m.s. cstr. (481)-n.f.s. cstr. (521) *of any use in*

הָעֲבֹדָה def.art.-n.f.s. (715) *the work*

הֵבִיאוּ Hi. pf. 3 c.p. (בּוֹא 97) *brought*

35:25

וְכָל־אִשָּׁה conj.-n.m.s. cstr. (481)-n.f.s. (61) *and all women*

חַכְמַת־לֵב adj. f.s. cstr. (314) - n.m.s. (524) *who had ability*

בְּיָדֶיהָ prep.-n.f.p.-3 f.s. sf. (388) *with their hands*

טָווּ Qal pf. 3 c.p. (טָוָה 376) *spun*

וַיָּבִיאוּ consec.-Hi. impf. 3 m.p. (בּוֹא 97) *and brought*

מַטְוֶה n.m.s. (376) *what they had spun*

אֶת־הַתְּכֵלֶת dir.obj.-def.art.-n.f.s. (1067) *in blue*

וְאֶת־הָאַרְגָּמָן conj.-dir.obj.-def.art.-n.m.s. (71) *and purple*

אֶת־תּוֹלַעַת הַשָּׁנִי dir.obj.-n.f.s. cstr. (1069) - def.art.-n.m.s. (1040) *and scarlet stuff*

וְאֶת־הַשֵּׁשׁ conj.-dir.obj.-def.art.-n.m.s. (III 1058) *and fine twined linen*

35:26

וְכָל־הַנָּשִׁים conj.-n.m.s. cstr. (481)-def.art.-n.f.p. (61) *and all the women*

אֲשֶׁר נָשָׂא rel.-Qal pf. 3 m.s. (669) *which moved*

לִבָּן n.m.s.-3 f.p. sf. (524) *their hearts*

אֹתָנָה dir.obj.-3 f.p. sf. *them*

בְּחָכְמָה prep.-n.f.s. (315) *with ability*

טָווּ Qal pf. 3 c.p. (טָוָה 376) *spun*

אֶת־הָעִזִּים dir.obj.-def.art.-n.f.p. (777) *the goats' hair*

35:27

וְהַנְּשִׂאִם conj.-def.art.-n.m.p. (672) *and the leaders*

הֵבִיאוּ Hi. pf. 3 c.p. (בּוֹא 97) *brought*

אֵת אַבְנֵי הַשֹּׁהַם dir.obj.-n.f.p. cstr. (6)-def.art.-n.m.s. (I 995) *onyx stones*

וְאֵת אַבְנֵי הַמִּלֻּאִים conj.-dir.obj.-v. supra-def.art.-n.m.p. (571) *and stones to be set*

לָאֵפוֹד prep.-def.art.-n.m.s. (65) *for the ephod*

וְלַחֹשֶׁן conj.-prep.-def.art.-n.m.s. (365) *and for the breastpiece*

35:28

וְאֶת־הַבֹּשֶׂם conj.-dir.obj.-def.art.-n.m.s. (141) *and spices*

וְאֶת־הַשָּׁמֶן conj.-dir.obj.-def.art.-n.m.s. paus. (1032) *and oil*

לְמָאוֹר prep.-n.m.s. (22) *for the light*

וּלְשֶׁמֶן הַמִּשְׁחָה conj.-prep.-n.m.s. cstr. (1032)-def.art.-n.f.s. (603) *and for the anointing oil*

וְלִקְטֹרֶת הַסַּמִּים conj.-prep.-n.f.s. cstr. (882)-def.art.-n.m.p. (702) *and for the fragrant incense*

35:29

כָּל־אִישׁ n.m.s. cstr. (481)-n.m.s. (35) *all the men*

וְאִשָּׁה conj.-n.f.s. (61) *and women*

אֲשֶׁר נָדַב לִבָּם rel.-Qal pf. 3 m.s. (621)-n.m.s.-3 m.p. sf. (524) *whose heart moved*

אֹתָם dir.obj.-3 m.p. sf. *them*

לְהָבִיא prep.-Hi. inf. cstr. (בּוֹא 97) *to bring*

לְכָל־הַמְּלָאכָה prep.-n.m.s. cstr. (481)-def.art.-n.f.s. (521) *anything for the work*

אֲשֶׁר צִוָּה rel.-Pi. pf. 3 m.s. (צָוָה 845) *which ... had commanded*

יהוה pr.n. (217) *Yahweh*

לַעֲשׂוֹת prep.-Qal inf. cstr. (עָשָׂה I 793) *to be done*

בְּיַד־מֹשֶׁה prep.-n.f.s. cstr. (388)-pr.n. (602) *by (the hand of) Moses* .

הֵבִיאוּ Hi. pf. 3 c.p. (בּוֹא 97) *brought*

בְנֵי־יִשְׂרָאֵל n.m.p. cstr. (119)-pr.n. (975) *the people of Israel*

נְדָבָה n.f.s. (621) *a freewill offering*

ליהוה prep.-pr.n. (217) *to Yahweh*

35:30

וַיֹּאמֶר מֹשֶׁה consec.-Qal impf. 3 m.s. (55)-pr.n. (602) *and Moses said*

אֶל־בְּנֵי יִשְׂרָאֵל prep.-n.m.p. cstr. (119)-pr.n. (975) *to the people of Israel*

רְאוּ Qal impv. 2 m.s. (רָאָה 906) *see*

קָרָא יהוה Qal pf. 3 m.s. (894)-pr.n. (217) *Yahweh has called*

בְשֵׁם prep.-n.m.s. (1027) *by name*

בְּצַלְאֵל pr.n. (130) *Bezalel*

בֶּן־אוּרִי n.m.s. cstr. (119)-pr.n. (22) *the son of Uri*

בֶן־חוּר v. supra-pr.n. (II 301) *son of Hur*

לְמַטֵּה יְהוּדָה prep.-n.m.s. cstr. (641)-pr.n. (397) *of the tribe of Judah*

35:31

וַיְמַלֵּא consec.-Pi. impf. 3 m.s. (מָלֵא 569) *and he has filled*

אֹתוֹ dir.obj.-3 m.s. sf. *him*

רוּחַ אֱלֹהִים n.f.s. cstr. (924)-n.m.p. (43) *with the Spirit of God*

בְּחָכְמָה prep.-n.f.s. (315) *with ability*

בִּתְבוּנָה prep.-n.f.s. (108) *with intelligence*

וּבְדַעַת conj.-prep.-n.f.s. (395) *and with knowledge*

וּבְכָל־מְלָאכָה conj.-prep.-n.m.s. cstr. (481)-n.f.s. (521) *and with all craftmanship*

35:32

וְלַחְשֹׁב conj. - prep. - Qal inf. cstr. (חָשַׁב 362) *and to devise*

מַחֲשָׁבֹת n.f.p. (364) *artistic designs*

לַעֲשֹׂת prep.-Qal inf. cstr. (עָשָׂה I 793) *to work*

בַּזָּהָב prep.-def.art.-n.m.s. (262) *in gold*

וּבַכֶּסֶף conj.-prep.-def.art.-n.m.s. (494) *and silver*

וּבַנְּחֹשֶׁת conj.-prep.-def.art.-n.m.s. (638) *and bronze*

35:33

וּבַחֲרֹשֶׁת אֶבֶן conj.-prep.-n.f.s. cstr. (I 360)-n.f.s. (6) *and in cutting stones*

לְמַלֹּאת prep.-Pi. inf. cstr. (מָלֵא 569) *for setting*

וּבַחֲרֹשֶׁת עֵץ v. supra-n.m.s. (781) *and in carving wood*

לַעֲשׂוֹת prep.-Qal inf. cstr. (עָשָׂה I 793) *for work*

בְּכָל־מְלֶאכֶת מַחֲשָׁבֶת prep.-n.m.s. cstr. (481)-n.f.s. cstr. (521)-n.f.s. paus. (364) *in every skilled craft*

35:34

וּלְהוֹרֹת prep.-Hi. inf. cstr. (יָרָה 434) *to teach*

נָתַן בְּלִבּוֹ Qal pf. 3 m.s. (678)-prep.-n.m.s.-3 m.s. sf. (524) *he has inspired him*

הוּא וְאָהֳלִיאָב pers.pr. 3 m.s. (214)-conj.-pr.n. (14) *both him and Oholiab*

בֶּן־אֲחִיסָמָךְ n.m.s. cstr. (119)-pr.n. (27) *the son of Ahisamach*

לְמַטֵּה־דָן prep.-n.m.s. cstr. (641)-pr.n. (192) *of the tribe of Dan*

35:35

מִלֵּא Pi. pf. 3 m.s. (מָלֵא 569) *he has filled*

אֹתָם dir.obj.-3 m.p. sf. *them*

חָכְמַת־לֵב n.f.s. cstr. (315)-n.m.s. (524) *with ability*

לַעֲשׂוֹת prep.-Qal inf. cstr. (עָשָׂה I 793) *to do*

כָּל־מְלֶאכֶת n.m.s. cstr. (481)-n.f.s. (521) *every sort of work*

חָרָשׁ n.m.s. (360) *by a craftsman*

וְחֹשֵׁב conj.-Qal act. ptc. (חָשַׁב 362) *or by a designer*

וְרֹקֵם conj.-Qal act. ptc. (רָקַם 955) *or by an embroiderer*

בַּתְּכֵלֶת prep.-def.art.-n.f.s. (1067) *in blue*

וּבָאַרְגָּמָן conj.-prep.-def.art.-n.m.s. (71) *and purple*

בְּתוֹלַעַת הַשָּׁנִי prep.-n.f.s. cstr. (1069) - def.art.-n.m.s. (1040) *and scarlet stuff*

וּבַשֵּׁשׁ conj.-prep.-def.art.-n.m.s. (III 1058) *and fine twined linen*

וְאֹרֵג conj.-Qal act. ptc. (אָרַג 70) *or by a weaver*

עֹשֵׂי כָּל־מְלָאכָה Qal act. ptc. m.p. cstr. (עָשָׂה I 793)-n.m.s. cstr. (481)-n.f.s. (521) *by any sort of workman*

וְחֹשְׁבֵי מַחֲשָׁבֹת conj.-Qal act. ptc. m.p. cstr. (חָשַׁב 362)-n.f.p. (364) *or skilled designer*

36:1

וְעָשָׂה conj.-Qal pf. 3 m.s. (עָשָׂה I 793) *and shall work*

בְצַלְאֵל pr.n. (130) *Bezalel*

וְאָהֳלִיאָב conj.-pr.n. (14) *and Oholiab*

וְכֹל אִישׁ conj.-n.m.s. cstr. (481)-n.m.s. (35) *and every man*

חֲכַם־לֵב adj. cstr. (314)-n.m.s. (524) *able (wise of heart)*

אֲשֶׁר נָתַן יהוה rel.-Qal pf. 3 m.s. (678)-pr.n. (217) *in whom Yahweh has put*

חָכְמָה n.f.s. (315) *ability*

וּתְבוּנָה conj.-n.f.s. (108) *and intelligence*

בָּהֵמָּה prep.-pers.pr. 3 m.p. (241) *(in them)*

לָדַעַת prep.-Qal inf. cstr. (יָדַע 393) *to know how*

לַעֲשֹׂת prep.-Qal inf. cstr. (עָשָׂה I 793) *to do*

אֶת־כָּל־מְלֶאכֶת dir.obj.-n.m.s. cstr. (481)-n.f.s. cstr. (521) *any work in*

עֲבֹדַת הַקֹּדֶשׁ n.f.s. cstr. (715)-def.art.-n.m.s. (871) *the construction of the sanctuary*

לְכֹל אֲשֶׁר־ prep.-n.m.s. (481)-rel. *in accordance with all that*

צִוָּה יהוה Pi. pf. 3 m.s. (צָוָה 845)-pr.n. (217) *Yahweh has commanded*

36:2

וַיִּקְרָא מֹשֶׁה consec.-Qal impf. 3 m.s. (894)-pr.n. (602) *and Moses called*

אֶל־בְּצַלְאֵל prep.-pr.n. (130) *Bezalel*

וְאֶל־אָהֳלִיאָב conj.-prep.-pr.n. (14) *and Oholiab*

וְאֶל כָּל־אִישׁ conj.-prep.-n.m.s. cstr. (481)-n.m.s. (35) *and every man*

חֲכַם־לֵב adj. cstr. (314)-n.m.s. (524) *able*

אֲשֶׁר נָתַן יהוה rel.-Qal pf. 3 m.s. (678)-pr.n. (217) *which Yahweh had put*

חָכְמָה n.f.s. (315) *ability*

בְּלִבּוֹ prep.-n.m.s.-3 m.s. sf. (524) *in whose mind*

כֹּל אֲשֶׁר n.m.s. (481)-rel. *every one which*

נְשָׂאוֹ Qal pf. 3 m.s.-3 m.s. sf. (נָשָׂא 669) *stirred him up*

לִבּוֹ n.m.s.-3 m.s. sf. (524) *whose heart*

לְקָרְבָה prep.-Qal inf. cstr. (קָרַב 897) *to come*

אֶל־הַמְּלָאכָה prep.-def.art.-n.f.s. (521) *unto the work*

לַעֲשֹׂת אֹתָהּ prep.-Qal inf. cstr. (עָשָׂה I 793) - dir.obj.-3 f.s. sf. *to do it*

36:3

וַיִּקְחוּ consec.-Qal impf. 3 m.p. (לָקַח 542) *and they received*

מִלִּפְנֵי מֹשֶׁה prep.-prep.-n.m.p. cstr. (815)-pr.n. (602) *from Moses*

אֵת כָּל־הַתְּרוּמָה dir.obj.-n.m.s. cstr. (481)-def.art.-n.f.s. (929) *all the freewill offering*

אֲשֶׁר הֵבִיאוּ rel.-Hi. pf. 3 c.p. (בּוֹא 97) *which ... had brought*

בְּנֵי יִשְׂרָאֵל n.m.p. cstr. (119) - pr.n. (975) *the people of Israel*

לִמְלֶאכֶת עֲבֹדַת prep.-n.f.s. cstr. (521)-n.f.s. cstr. (715) *the work on*

הַקֹּדֶשׁ def.art.-n.m.s. (871) *the sanctuary*

לַעֲשֹׂת אֹתָהּ prep.-Qal inf. cstr. (עָשָׂה I 793) - dir.obj.-3 f.s. sf. *(to do it)*

וְהֵם הֵבִיאוּ conj.-pers.pr. 3 m.p. (241)-Hi. pf. 3 c.p. (בּוֹא 97) *and they kept bringing*

אֵלָיו prep.-3 m.s. sf. *him*

עוֹד adv. (728) *still*

נְדָבָה n.f.s. (621) *freewill offerings*

בַּבֹּקֶר בַּבֹּקֶר prep.-def.art.-n.m.s. (133)-v.supra *every morning*

36:4

וַיָּבֹאוּ consec.-Qal impf. 3 m.p. (בּוֹא 97) *so that came*

כָּל־הַחֲכָמִים n.m.s. cstr. (481)-def.art.-adj. m.p. (314) *all the able men*

הָעֹשִׂים def.art.-Qal act. ptc. m.p. (עָשָׂה I 793) *who were doing*

אֵת כָּל־מְלֶאכֶת dir.obj.-n.m.s. cstr. (481) - n.f.s. cstr. (521) *every sort of task on*

הַקֹּדֶשׁ def.art.-n.m.s. (871) *the sanctuary*

אִישׁ־אִישׁ n.m.s. (35)-v.supra *each*

מִמְּלַאכְתּוֹ prep.-n.f.s.-3 m.s. sf. (521) *from the task (of him)*

אֲשֶׁר־הֵמָּה עֹשִׂים rel.-pers.pr. 3 m.p. (241)-Qal act. ptc. m.p. (עָשָׂה I 793) *that he was doing*

36:5

וַיֹּאמְרוּ consec.-Qal impf. 3m.p. (55) *and said*

אֶל־מֹשֶׁה prep.-pr.n. (602) *to Moses*

לֵאמֹר prep.-Qal inf. cstr. (55) *(saying)*

מַרְבִּים Hi. ptc. m.p. (רָבָה I 915) *much more*

הָעָם def.art.-n.m.s. (I 766) *the people*

לְהָבִיא prep.-Hi. inf. cstr. (בּוֹא 97) *bring*

מִדֵּי prep.-subst. cstr. (191) *than enough of*

הָעֲבֹדָה def.art.-n.f.s. (715) *the labor*

לַמְּלָאכָה prep.-def.art.-n.f.s. (521) *for the work*

אֲשֶׁר־צִוָּה יהוה rel.-Pi. pf. 3 m.s. (צָוָה 845)-pr.n. (217) *which Yahweh has commanded*

לַעֲשֹׂת אֹתָהּ prep.-Qal inf. cstr. (עָשָׂה I 793) - dir.obj.-3 f.s. sf. *to do (it)*

36:6

וַיְצַו מֹשֶׁה consec.-Pi. impf. 3 m.s. (צָוָה 845)-pr.n. (602) *so Moses gave command*

וַיַּעֲבִירוּ קוֹל consec.-Hi. impf. 3 m.p. (עָבַר 716)-n.m.s. (876) *and word was proclaimed*

בַּמַּחֲנֶה prep.-def.art.-n.m.s. (334) *throughout the camp*

לֵאמֹר prep.-Qal inf. cstr. (55) *(saying)*

אִישׁ וְאִשָּׁה n.m.s. (35) - conj.-n.f.s. (61) *man nor woman*

אַל־יַעֲשׂוּ־עוֹד neg.-Qal impf. 3 m.p. (עָשָׂה I 793) - adv. (728) *let do nothing more*

מְלָאכָה n.f.s. (521) *(work)*

לִתְרוּמַת הַקֹּדֶשׁ prep.-n.f.s. cstr. (929)-def.art.-n.m.s. (871) *for the offering for the sanctuary*

וַיִּכָּלֵא הָעָם consec.-Ni. impf. 3 m.s. (כָּלָא 476)-def.art.-n.m.s, (I 766) *so the people were restrained*

מֵהָבִיא prep.-Hi. inf. cstr. (בּוֹא 97) *from bringing*

36:7

וְהַמְּלָאכָה conj.-def.art.-n.f.s. (521) *for the stuff*

הָיְתָה דַיָּם Qal pf. 3 f.s. (הָיָה 224)-subst. 3 m.p. sf. *was sufficient*

לְכָל־הַמְּלָאכָה prep.-n.m.s. cstr. (481)-def.art.-n.f.s. (521) *for all the work*

לַעֲשׂוֹת אֹתָהּ prep.-Qal inf. cstr. (עָשָׂה I 793) - dir.obj.-3 f.s. sf. *to do it*

וְהוֹתֵר conj.-Hi. inf. abs. (יָתַר 451) *and more*

36:8

וַיַּעֲשׂוּ consec.-Qal impf. 3 m.p. (עָשָׂה I 793) *and made*

כָל־חֲכַם־לֵב n.m.s. cstr. (481)-adj. cstr. (314)-n.m.s. (524) *all the able men*

בְּעֹשֵׂי הַמְּלָאכָה prep.-Qal act. ptc. m.p. cstr. (עָשָׂה I 793)-def.art.-n.f.s. (521) *among the workmen*

אֶת־הַמִּשְׁכָּן dir.obj.-def.art.-n.m.s. (1015) *the tabernacle*

עֶשֶׂר יְרִיעֹת num. (796) - n.f.p. (438) *with ten curtains*

שֵׁשׁ מָשְׁזָר n.m.s. (III 1058)-Ho. ptc. (1004) *fine twined linen*

וּתְכֵלֶת conj.-n.f.s. (1067) *and blue*

וְאַרְגָּמָן conj.-n.m.s. (71) *and purple*

וְתוֹלַעַת שָׁנִי conj.-n.f.s. cstr. (1069)-n.m.s. (1040) *and scarlet stuff*

כְּרֻבִים n.m.p. (500) *with cherubim*

מַעֲשֵׂה חֹשֵׁב עָשָׂה אֹתָם n.m.s. cstr. (795)-Qal act. ptc. (חָשַׁב 362)-Qal pf. 3 m.s. (עָשָׂה I 793)-dir.obj.-3 m.p. sf. *skilfully worked*

36:9

אֹרֶךְ הַיְרִיעָה n.m.s. cstr. (73)-def.art.-n.f.s. (438) *the length of ... curtain*

הָאַחַת def.art.-adj.f.s. (25) *each*

שְׁמֹנֶה וְעֶשְׂרִים num. (1032)-num. p. (797) *twenty-eight*

בָּאַמָּה prep.-def.art.-n.f.s. (52) *cubits*

וְרֹחַב conj.-n.m.s. (931) *and breadth*

אַרְבַּע בָּאַמָּה num. (916)-prep.-def.art.-n.f.s. (52) *four cubits*

הַיְרִיעָה הָאֶחָת def.art.-n.f.s. (438)-def.art.-adj. f.s. paus. (25) *each curtain*

מִדָּה אַחַת n.f.s. (551)-num. adj. f.s. (25) *same measure*

לְכָל־הַיְרִיעֹת prep.-n.m.s. cstr. (481)-def.art.-n.f.p. (438) *all the curtains*

36:10

וַיְחַבֵּר consec.-Pil impf. 3 m.s. (חָבַר 287) *and he coupled*

אֶת־חֲמֵשׁ הַיְרִיעֹת dir.obj.-num. cstr. (331)-def.art.-n.f.p. (438) *five curtains*

אַחַת אֶל־אֶחָת num. adj. f.s. (25)-prep.-num. adj. f.s. paus. (25) *to one another*

וְחָמֵשׁ יְרִיעֹת conj.-num. (331)-n.f.p. (438) *and the other five curtains*

חִבַּר Pi. pf. 3 m.s. (חָבַר 287) *he coupled*

אַחַת אֶל־אֶחָת v.supra-v.supra *to one another*

36:11

וַיַּעַשׂ consec.-Qal impf. 3 m.s. (עָשָׂה I 793) *and he made*

לֻלְאֹת תְּכֵלֶת n.f.p. cstr. (533)-n.f.s. (1067) *loops of blue*

עַל שְׂפַת prep.-n.f.s. cstr. (973) *on the edge of*

הַיְרִיעָה הָאֶחָת def.art.-n.f.s. (438)-def.art.-num. adj. f.s. (25) *the one curtain*

מִקָּצָה בַּמַּחְבָּרֶת prep.-n.m.s. (892)-prep.-def.art.-n.f.s. paus. (289) *at the end of the thing joined*

כֵּן עָשָׂה adv. (485)-Qal pf. 3 m.s. (I 793) *likewise he made*

בִּשְׂפַת prep.-n.f.s. cstr. (973) *on the edge of*

הַיְרִיעָה הַקִּיצוֹנָה def.art.-n.f.s. (438)-def.art.-adj. f.s. (894) *the outmost curtain*

בַּמַּחְבֶּרֶת הַשֵּׁנִית prep.-def.art.-n.f.s. (289)-def.art.-num. adj. f.s. (1041) *of the second set*

36:12

חֲמִשִּׁים לֻלָאֹת num. p. (332)-n.f.p. (533) *fifty loops*

עָשָׂה Qal pf. 3 m.s. (I 793) *he made*

בַּיְרִיעָה הָאֶחָת prep.-def.art.-n.f.s. (438)-def.art.-num. adj. f.s. (25) *on the one curtain*

וַחֲמִשִּׁים לֻלָאֹת conj.-num. p. (332)-v. supra *and fifty loops*

עָשָׂה v. supra *he made*

בִּקְצֵה הַיְרִיעָה prep.-n.m.s. cstr. (892)-def.art.-n.f.s. (438) *on the edge of the curtain*

אֲשֶׁר בַּמַּחְבֶּרֶת הַשֵּׁנִית rel.-prep.-def.art.-n.f.s. (289)-def.art.-num. adj. f.s. (1041) *that was in the second set*

מַקְבִּילֹת הַלֻּלָאֹת Hi. ptc. f.p. (קָבַל 867)-def.art.-n.f.p. (438) *the loops were opposite*

אַחַת אֶל־אֶחָת num. adj. f.s. (25)-prep.-num. adj. f.s. paus. (25) *one another*

36:13

וַיַּעַשׂ consec.-Qal impf. 3 m.s. (עָשָׂה I 793) *and he made*

חֲמִשִּׁים קַרְסֵי num. p. (332)-n.m.p. cstr. (902) *fifty clasps of*

זָהָב n.m.s. (262) *gold*

וַיְחַבֵּר consec.-Pi. impf. 3 m.s. (חָבַר 287) *and coupled*

אֶת־הַיְרִיעֹת dir.obj.-def.art.-n.f.p. (438) *the curtains*

אַחַת אֶל־אַחַת num. adj. f.s. (25)-prep.-v. supra *one to the other*

בַּקְּרָסִים prep.-def.art.-n.m.p. (902) *with clasps*

וַיְהִי הַמִּשְׁכָּן consec.-Qal impf. 3 m.s. (הָיָה 224)-def.art.-n.m.s. (1015) *so the tabernacle was*

אֶחָד num. adj. m.s. (25) *one whole*

36:14

וַיַּעַשׂ consec.-Qal impf. 3 m.s. (עָשָׂה I 793) *he also made*

יְרִיעֹת עִזִּים n.f.p. cstr. (438)-n.f.p. (777) *curtains of goats' hair*

לְאֹהֶל prep.-n.m.s. (13) *for a tent*

עַל־הַמִּשְׁכָּן prep.-def.art.-n.m.s. (1015) *over the tabernacle*

עַשְׁתֵּי־עֶשְׂרֵה num. (799)-num. (797) *eleven*

יְרִיעֹת n.f.p. (438) *curtains*

עָשָׂה אֹתָם Qal pf. 3 m.s. (I 793)-dir.obj.-3 m.p. sf. *he made (them)*

36:15

אֹרֶךְ n.m.s. cstr. (73) *the length of*

הַיְרִיעָה הָאַחַת def.art.-n.f.s. (438)-def.art.-num. adj. f.s. (25) *each curtain*

שְׁלֹשִׁים בָּאַמָּה num. p. (1026)-prep.-def.art.-n.f.s. (52) *thirty cubits*

וְאַרְבַּע אַמּוֹת conj.-num. (916)-n.f.p. (52) *and four cubits*

רֹחַב n.m.s. cstr. (931) *the breadth of*

הַיְרִיעָה הָאֶחָת def.art.-n.f.s. (438)-def.art.-num. adj. f.s. paus. (25) *each curtain*

מִדָּה אַחַת n.f.s. (551)-num. adj. f.s. (25) *the same measure*

לְעַשְׁתֵּי עֶשְׂרֵה prep.-num. (799)-num. (797) *for eleven*

יְרִיעֹת n.f.p. (438) *curtains*

36:16

וַיְחַבֵּר consec.-Pi. impf. 3 m.s. (חָבַר 287) *and he coupled*

אֶת־חֲמֵשׁ dir.obj.-num. cstr. (331) *five*

הַיְרִיעֹת def.art.-n.f.p. (438) *curtains*

לְבָד prep.-n.m.. paus. (94) *by themselves*

וְאֶת־שֵׁשׁ conj.-dir.obj.-num. cstr. (995) *and six*

הַיְרִיעֹת v. supra *curtains*

לְבָד v. supra *by themselves*

36:17

וַיַּעַשׂ consec.-Qal impf. 3 m.s. (עָשָׂה I 793) *and he made*

לֻלָאֹת חֲמִשִּׁים n.f.p. (533)-num. m.p. (332) *fifty loops*

עַל שְׂפַת prep.-n.f.s. cstr. (973) *on the edge of*

הַיְרִיעָה הַקִּיצֹנָה def.art.-n.f.s. (438)-def.art.-adj. f.s. (894) *the outmost curtain*

בַּמַּחְבָּרֶת prep.-def.art.-n.f.s. paus. (289) *of the one set*

וַחֲמִשִּׁים לֻלָאֹת conj.-num.p. (332)-n.f.p. (533) *and fifty loops*

עָשָׂה Qal pf. 3 m.s. (I 793) *he made*

עַל־שְׂפַת v. supra *on the edge of*

הַיְרִיעָה v. supra *the curtain*

הַחֹבֶרֶת הַשֵּׁנִית def.art.-n.f.s. (289)-

def.art.-num. adj. f.s. (1041) *the second set*

36:18

וַיַּעַשׂ consec.-Qal impf. 3 m.s. (עָשָׂה I 793) *and he made*

קַרְסֵי נְחֹשֶׁת n.m.p. cstr. (902)-n.m.s. (638) *clasps of bronze*

חֲמִשִּׁים num. p. (332) *fifty*

לְחַבֵּר prep.-Pi. inf. cstr. (חָבַר 287) *to couple*

אֶת־הָאֹהֶל dir.obj.-def.art.-n.m.s. (13) *the tent*

לִהְיֹת אֶחָד prep.-Qal inf. cstr. (הָיָה 224)-num. adj. m.s. (25) *that it might be one whole*

36:19

וַיַּעַשׂ consec.-Qal impf. 3 m.s. (עָשָׂה I 793) *and he made*

מִכְסֶה n.m.s. (492) *a covering*

לָאֹהֶל prep.-def.art.-n.m.s. (13) *for the tent*

עֹרֹת אֵילִם n.m.p. cstr. (736)-n.m.p. (I 17) *rams' skins*

מְאָדָּמִים Pu. ptc. m.p. (אָדֹם 10) *tanned*

וּמִכְסֵה conj.-n.m.s. cstr. (492) *(and a covering of)*

עֹרֹת תְּחָשִׁים v. supra-n.m.p. (I 1065) *goatskins*

מִלְמָעְלָה prep.-prep.-subst.-loc. he (751; 2) *(upwards)*

36:20

וַיַּעַשׂ consec.-Qal impf. 3 m.s. (עָשָׂה I 793) *then he made*

אֶת־הַקְּרָשִׁים dir.obj.-def.art.-n.m.p. (903) *the frames*

לַמִּשְׁכָּן prep.-def.art.-n.m.s. (1015) *for the tabernacle*

עֲצֵי שִׁטִּים n.m.p. cstr. (781) - n.f.p. (1008) *acacia wood*

עֹמְדִים Qal act. ptc. (עָמַד 763) *upright*

36:21

עֶשֶׂר אַמֹּת num. (796)-n.f.p. (52) *ten cubits*

אֹרֶךְ הַקָּרֶשׁ n.m.s. cstr. (73)-def.art.-n.m.s. (903) *the length of the frame*

וְאַמָּה וַחֲצִי הָאַמָּה conj.-n.f.s. (52)-conj.-n.m.s. cstr. (345)-def.art.-n.f.s. (52) *and a cubit and a half*

רֹחַב n.m.s. cstr. (931) *the breadth of*

הַקֶּרֶשׁ הָאֶחָד def.art.-n.m.s. (903)-def.art.-num. adj. m.s. (25) *each frame*

36:22

שְׁתֵּי יְדֹת num. f.s. cstr. (1040)-n.f.p. (388; 4f) *two tenons*

לַקֶּרֶשׁ הָאֶחָד prep.-def.art.-n.m.s. (903)-def.art.-num. adj. (25) *each frame*

מְשֻׁלָּבֹת Pu. ptc. f.p. (שָׁלַב 1016) *for fitting*

אַחַת אֶל־אֶחָת num. adj. f.s. (25)-prep.-num. adj. f.s. paus. (25) *together*

כֵּן עָשָׂה adv. (485)-Qal pf. 3 m.s. (I 793) *he did this*

לְכֹל קַרְשֵׁי prep.-n.m.s. cstr. (481)-n.m.p. cstr. (903) *for all the frames of*

הַמִּשְׁכָּן def. art.-n.m.s. (1015) *the tabernacle*

36.23

וַיַּעַשׂ consec. Qal impf. 3 m.s. (עָשָׂה I 793) *he made thus*

אֶת־הַקְּרָשִׁים dir.obj.-def.art.-n.m.p. (903) *the frames*

לַמִּשְׁכָּן prep.-def.art.-n.m.s. (1015) *for the tabernacle*

עֶשְׂרִים קְרָשִׁים num. (797)-n.m.p. (903) *twenty frames*

לִפְאַת prep.-n.f.s. cstr. (802) *for the side*

נֶגֶב תֵּימָנָה n.m.s. (616)-n.f.s.-loc. he (412) *south*

36:24

וְאַרְבָּעִים conj.-num. p. (917) *and forty*

אַדְנֵי־כֶסֶף n.m.p. cstr. (10)-n.m.s. (494) *bases of silver*

עָשָׂה Qal pf. 3 m.s. (I 793) *he made*

תַּחַת עֶשְׂרִים prep.(1065)-num. p. (797) *under the twenty*

הַקְּרָשִׁים def.art.-n.m.p. (903) *frames*

שְׁנֵי אֲדָנִים num. m. cstr. (1040)-n.m.p. (10) *two bases*

תַּחַת־הַקֶּרֶשׁ הָאֶחָד prep. (1065)-def.art.-n.m.s. (903)-def.art.-num. adj. (25) *under one frame*

לִשְׁתֵּי יְדֹתָיו prep.-num. f. cstr. (1040)-n.f.p.-3 m.s. sf. (388; 4f) *for its two tenons*

וּשְׁנֵי אֲדָנִים conj.-num. m. cstr. (1040)-n.m.p. (10) *and two bases*

תַּחַת־הַקֶּרֶשׁ הָאֶחָד v. supra-v. supra-v. supra *under another frame*

לִשְׁתֵּי יְדֹתָיו v. supra-v. supra *for its two tenons*

36:25

וּלְצֶלַע conj.-prep.-n.f.s. cstr. (854) *and for the side of*

הַמִּשְׁכָּן def.art.-n.m.s. (1015) *the tabernacle*

הַשֵּׁנִית def.art.-num. adj. f.s. (1041) *the second*

לִפְאַת צָפוֹן prep.-n.f.s. cstr. (802)-n.f.s. (I 860) *on the north side*

עָשָׂה Qal pf. 3 m.s. (I 793) *he made*

עֶשְׂרִים קְרָשִׁים num. p. (797)-n.m.p. (903) *twenty frames*

36:26

וְאַרְבָּעִים conj.-num. p. (917) *and forty*

אַדְנֵיהֶם n.m.p.-3 m.p. sf. (10) *their bases*

כָּסֶף n.m.s. paus. (494) *of silver*

שְׁנֵי אֲדָנִים num. m. cstr. (1040)-n.m.p. (10) *two bases*

תַּחַת הַקֶּרֶשׁ הָאֶחָד prep. (1065)-def.art.-n.m.s. (903)-def.art.-num. adj. (25) *under one frame*

וּשְׁנֵי אֲדָנִים conj.-v.supra-v.supra *and two bases*

תַּחַת הַקֶּרֶשׁ הָאֶחָד v.supra-v.supra-v.supra *under another frame*

36:27

וּלְיַרְכְּתֵי conj.-prep.-n.f.du. cstr. (438) *and for the rear of*

הַמִּשְׁכָּן def.art.-n.m.s. (1015) *the tabernacle*

יָמָּה n.m.s.-dir. he (410) *westward*

עָשָׂה Qal pf. 3 m.s. (I 793) *he made*

שִׁשָּׁה קְרָשִׁים num. f. (995)-n.m.p. (903) *six frames*

36:28

וּשְׁנֵי קְרָשִׁים conj.-num. m. cstr. (1040)-n.m.p. (903) *and two frames*

עָשָׂה Qal pf. 3 m.s. (I 793) *he made*

לִמְקֻצְעֹת prep.-n.m.p. cstr. (893) *for corners of*

הַמִּשְׁכָּן def.art.-n.m.s. (1015) *the tabernacle*

בַּיַּרְכָתָיִם prep.-def.art.-n.f. du. paus. (438) *in the rear*

36:29

וְהָיוּ conj.-Qal pf. 3 c.p. (הָיָה 224) *and they were*

תוֹאֲמִם Qal act. ptc. m.p. (תָּאַם 1060) *separate*

מִלְּמַטָּה prep.-prep.-adv. (641; 3) *beneath*

וְיַחְדָּו יִהְיוּ conj.-adv. (403)-Qal impf. 3 m.p. (הָיָה 224) *and together they shall be*

תַּמִּים Qal act. ptc. m.p. (תָּאַם 1060) *joined*

אֶל־רֹאשׁוֹ prep.-n.m.s.-3 m.s. sf. (910) *at the top*

אֶל־הַטַּבַּעַת הָאֶחָת prep.-def.art.-n.f.s. (371)-def.art.-num. adj. f.s. (25) *at the first ring*

כֵּן עָשָׂה adv. (485)-Qal pf. 3 m.s. (I 793) *he made thus*

לִשְׁנֵיהֶם prep.-num. m.-3 m.p. sf. (1040) *two of them*

לִשְׁנֵי הַמִּקְצֹעֹת prep.-num. m. cstr. (1040)-def.art.-n.m.p. (893) *for the two corners*

36:30

וְהָיוּ conj.-Qal pf. 3 c.p. (הָיָה 224) *and there were*

שְׁמֹנָה קְרָשִׁים num. (1032)-n.m.p. (903) *eight frames*

וְאַדְנֵיהֶם conj.-n.m.p.-3 m.p. sf. (10) *with their frames*

כֶּסֶף n.m.s. (494) *of silver*

שִׁשָּׁה עָשָׂר num. f. (995)-num. (797) *sixteen*

אֲדָנִים n.m.p. (10) *bases*

שְׁנֵי אֲדָנִים num. m. cstr. (1040)-n.m.p. (10) *two bases*

שְׁנֵי אֲדָנִים v.supra-v.supra *two bases*

תַּחַת הַקֶּרֶשׁ הָאֶחָד prep. (1065)-def.art.-n.m.s. (903)-def.art.-num. adj. (25) *under every frame*

36:31

וַיַּעַשׂ consec.-Qal impf. 3 m.s. (עָשָׂה I 793) *and he made*

בְּרִיחֵי n.m.p. cstr. (138) *bars of*

עֲצֵי שִׁטִּים n.m.p. cstr. (781)-n.f.p. (1008) *acacia wood*

חֲמִשָּׁה num. f. (331) *five*

לְקַרְשֵׁי prep.-n.m.p. cstr. (903) *for the frames of*

צֶלַע־ n.f.s. cstr. (854) *the side of*

הַמִּשְׁכָּן def.art.-n.m.s. (1015) *the tabernacle*

הָאֶחָת def.art.-adj. f.s. (25) *one*

36:32

וַחֲמִשָּׁה בְרִיחִם conj.-num. f. (331)-n.m.p. (138) *and five bars*

לְקַרְשֵׁי prep.-n.m.p. cstr. (903) *for the frames of*

צֶלַע־ n.f.s. cstr. (854) *the side of*

הַמִּשְׁכָּן def.art.-n.m.s. (1015) *the tabernacle*

הַשֵּׁנִית def.art.-num. adj. f. (1041) *other*

וַחֲמִשָּׁה בְרִיחִם v.supra-v.supra *and five bars*

לְקַרְשֵׁי v.supra *for the frames of*

הַמִּשְׁכָּן v.supra *the tabernacle*

לַיַּרְכָתַיִם prep.-def.art.-n.f. du. (438) *at the rear*

יָמָּה n.m.s.-dir. he (410) *westward*

36:33

וַיַּעַשׂ consec.-Qal impf. 3 m.s. (עָשָׂה I 793) *and he made*

אֶת־הַבְּרִיחַ הַתִּיכֹן dir.obj.-def.art.-n.m.s. (138)-def.art.-adj. m.s. (1064) *the middle bar*

לִבְרֹחַ prep.-Qal inf. cstr. (בָּרַח 137) *to pass through*

בְּתוֹךְ הַקְּרָשִׁים prep.-n.m.s. cstr. (1063)-def.art.-n.m.p. (903) *the midst of the frames*

מִן־הַקָּצֶה prep.-def.art.-n.m.s. (892) *from end*

אֶל־הַקָּצֶה prep.-v.supra *to end*

36:34

וְאֶת־הַקְּרָשִׁים conj.-dir.obj.-def.art.-n.m.p. (903) *and the frames*

צִפָּה Pi. pf. 3 m.s. (צָפָה II 860) *he overlaid*

זָהָב n.m.s. (262) *with gold*

וְאֶת־טַבְּעֹתָם conj.-dir.obj.-n.f.p.-3 m.p. sf. (371) *and their rings*

עָשָׂה Qal pf. 3 m.s. (I 793) *he made*

זָהָב v.supra *of gold*

בָּתִּים n.m.p. (108; 3) *holders*

לַבְּרִיחִם prep.-def.art.-n.m.p. (138) *for the bars*

וַיְצַף consec.-Pi. impf. 3 m.s. (צָפָה II 860) *and overlaid*

אֶת־הַבְּרִיחִם dir.obj.-def.art.-n.m.p. (138) *the bars*

זָהָב v.supra *with gold*

36:35

וַיַּעַשׂ consec.-Qal impf. 3 m.s. (עָשָׂה I 793) *and he made*

אֶת־הַפָּרֹכֶת dir.obj.-def.art.-n.f.s. (827) *the veil*

תְּכֵלֶת n.f.s. (1067) *of blue*

וְאַרְגָּמָן conj.-n.m.s. (71) *and purple*

וְתוֹלַעַת שָׁנִי conj.-n.f.s. cstr. (1069)-n.m.s. (1040) *and scarlet stuff*

וְשֵׁשׁ מָשְׁזָר conj.-n.m.s. (III 1058)-Ho. ptc. (שָׁזַר 1004) *and fine twined linen*

מַעֲשֵׂה חֹשֵׁב n.m.s. cstr. (795)-Qal act. ptc. (חָשַׁב 362) *skilfully worked*

עָשָׂה אֹתָהּ Qal pf. 3 m.s. (I 793)-dir.obj.-3 f.s. sf. *he made it*

כְּרֻבִים n.m.p. (500) *with cherubim*

36:36

וַיַּעַשׂ לָהּ consec.-Qal impf. 3 m.s. (עָשָׂה I 793) - prep.-3 f.s. sf. *and for it he made*

אַרְבָּעָה עַמּוּדֵי num. (916) - n.m.p. cstr. (765) *four pillars of*

שִׁטִּים n.f.p. (1008) *acacia*

וַיְצַפֵּם consec.-Pi. impf. 3 m.s. - 3 m.p. sf. (צָפָה I 860) *and overlaid them*

זָהָב n.m.s. (262) *with gold*

וָוֵיהֶם conj.-n.m.p.-3 m.p. sf. (255) *and their hooks*

זָהָב v.supra *of gold*

וַיִּצֹק consec.-Qal impf. 3 m.s. (יָצַק 427) *and he cast*

לָהֶם prep.-3 m.p. sf. *for them*

אַרְבָּעָה num. f. (916) *four*

אַדְנֵי־כָסֶף n.m.p. cstr. (10) - n.m.s. paus. (494) *bases of silver*

36:37

וַיַּעַשׂ consec.-Qal impf. 3 m.s. (עָשָׂה I 793) *he also made*

מָסָךְ n.m.s. (697) *a screen*

לְפֶתַח הָאֹהֶל prep.-n.m.s. cstr. (835) - def.art.-n.m.s. (13) *for the door of the tent*

תְּכֵלֶת n.f.s. (1067) *of blue*

וְאַרְגָּמָן conj.-n.m.s. (71) *and purple*

וְתוֹלַעַת שָׁנִי conj.-n.f.s. cstr. (1069) - n.m.s. (1040) *and scarlet stuff*

וְשֵׁשׁ מָשְׁזָר conj.-n.m.s. (III 1058) - Ho. ptc. (שָׁזַר 1004) *and fine twined linen*

מַעֲשֵׂה רֹקֵם n.m.s. cstr. (795) - Qal act. ptc. (רָקַם 955) *embroidered with needlework*

36:38

וְאֶת־עַמּוּדָיו conj.-dir.obj.-n.m.p.-3 m.s. sf. (765) *and its pillars*

חֲמִשָּׁה num. f. (331) *five*

וְאֶת־וָוֵיהֶם conj.-dir.obj.-n.m.p.-3 m.p. sf. (255) *with their hooks*

וְצִפָּה conj.-Pi. pf. 3 m.s. (צָפָה II 860) *and he overlaid*

רָאשֵׁיהֶם n.m.p.-3 m.p. sf. (I 910) *their capitals*

וַחֲשֻׁקֵיהֶם conj.-n.m.p.-3 m.p. sf. (366) *and their fillets*

זָהָב n.m.s. (262) *of gold*

וְאַדְנֵיהֶם conj.-n.m.p.-3 m.p. sf. (10) *but their bases*

חֲמִשָּׁה num. f. (331) *five*

נְחֹשֶׁת n.m.s. (638) *of bronze*

37:1

וַיַּעַשׂ consec.-Qal impf. 3 m.s. (עָשָׂה I 793) *and made*

בְּצַלְאֵל pr.n. (130) *Bezalel*

אֶת־הָאָרֹן dir.obj.-def.art.-n.m.s. (75) *the ark*

עֲצֵי שִׁטִּים n.m.p. cstr. (781) - n.f.p. (1008) *of acacia wood*

אַמָּתַיִם וָחֵצִי n.f. du. (52) - conj.-n.m.s. (345) *two cubits and a half*

אָרְכּוֹ n.m.s.-3 m.s. sf. (73) *its length*

וְאַמָּה וָחֵצִי conj.-n.f.s. (52) - v.supra *a cubit and a half*

רָחְבּוֹ n.m.s.-3 m.s. sf. (931) *its breadth*

וְאַמָּה וָחֵצִי conj.-n.f.s. (52) - v.supra *and a cubit and a half*

קֹמָתוֹ n.f.s.-3 m.s. sf. (879) *its height*

37:2

וַיְצַפֵּהוּ consec.-Pi. impf. 3 m.s. - 3 m.s. sf. (צָפָה II 860) *and he overlaid it*

זָהָב טָהוֹר n.m.s. (262) - adj. m.s. (373) *with pure gold*

מִבַּיִת prep.-n.m.s. (108; 8) *within*

וּמִחוּץ conj.-prep.-n.m.s. (299) *and without*

וַיַּעַשׂ לוֹ consec.-Qal impf. 3 m.s. (עָשָׂה I 793) - prep.-3 m.s. sf. *and made for it*

זֵר זָהָב n.m.s. cstr. (267) - n.m.s. (262) *a molding of gold*

סָבִיב adv. (686) *around*

37:3

וַיִּצֹק לוֹ consec.-Qal impf. 3 m.s. (יָצַק 427) - prep.-3 m.s. sf. *and he cast for it*

אַרְבַּע num. (916) *four*

טַבְּעֹת זָהָב n.f.p. cstr. (371) - n.m.s. (262) *rings of gold*

עַל אַרְבַּע prep.-num. (916) *for four*

פַּעֲמֹתָיו n.f.p.-3 m.s. sf. (821) *its corners*

וּשְׁתֵּי טַבָּעֹת conj.-num. f. cstr. (1040) - n.f.p. (371) *and two rings*

עַל־צַלְעוֹ prep.-n.f.s.-3 m.s. sf. (854) *on its side*

הָאֶחָת def.art.-adj. f.s. (25) *one*

וּשְׁתֵּי טַבָּעוֹת v.supra - v.supra *and two rings*

עַל־צַלְעוֹ v.supra - v.supra *on its side*

הַשֵּׁנִית def.art.-num. adj. f. (1041) *other*

37:4

וַיַּעַשׂ consec.-Qal impf. 3 m.s. (עָשָׂה I 793) *and he made*

בַּדֵּי n.m.p. cstr. (II 94) *poles of*

עֲצֵי שִׁטִּים n.m.p. cstr. (781) - n.f.p. (1008) *acacia wood*

וַיְצַף אֹתָם consec.-Pi. impf. 3 m.s. (צָפָה II 860) - dir.obj.-3 m.p. sf. *and overlaid them*

זָהָב n.m.s. (262) *with gold*

37:5

וַיָּבֵא consec.-Hi. impf. 3 m.s. (בּוֹא 97) *and put*

אֶת־הַבַּדִּים dir.obj.-def.art.-n.m.p. (II 94) *the poles*

בַּטַּבָּעֹת prep.-def.art.-n.f.p. (371) *into the rings*

עַל צַלְעֹת הָאָרֹן prep.-n.f.p. cstr. (854)-def.art.-n.m.s. (75) *on the sides of the ark*

לָשֵׂאת prep.-Qal inf. cstr. (נָשָׂא 669) *to carry*

אֶת־הָאָרֹן dir.obj.-def.art.-n.m.s. (75) *the ark*

37:6

וַיַּעַשׂ consec.-Qal impf. 3 m.s. (עָשָׂה I 793) *and he made*

כַּפֹּרֶת n.f.s. (498) *a mercy seat*

זָהָב טָהוֹר n.m.s. (262)-adj. m.s. (373) *of pure gold*

אַמָּתַיִם וָחֵצִי n.f. du. (52)-conj.-n.m.s. (345) *two cubits and a half*

אָרְכָּהּ n.m.s.-3 f.s. sf. (73) *its length*

וְאַמָּה וָחֵצִי conj.-n.f.s. (52)-v.supra *and a cubit and a half*

רָחְבָּהּ n.m.s.-3 f.s. sf. (931) *its breadth*

37:7

וַיַּעַשׂ consec.-Qal impf. 3 m.s. (עָשָׂה I 793) *and he made*

שְׁנֵי כְרֻבִים num. m. cstr. (1040)-n.m.p. (500) *two cherubim*

זָהָב n.m.s. (262) *of gold*

מִקְשָׁה n.f.s. (I 904) *hammered work*

עָשָׂה אֹתָם Qal pf. 3 m.s. (I 793)-dir.obj.-3 m.p. sf. *he made them*

מִשְּׁנֵי קְצוֹת prep.-num. m. cstr. (1040)-n.f.p. cstr. (892) *on the two ends of*

הַכַּפֹּרֶת def.art.-n.f.s. (498) *the mercy seat*

37:8

כְּרוּב־אֶחָד n.m.s. (500)-adj. m.s. (25) *one cherub*

מִקָּצָה מִזֶּה prep.-n.f.s. (892)-prep.-demons. adj. (260) *on the one end*

וּכְרוּב־אֶחָד conj.-v.supra - v.supra *and one cherub*

מִקָּצָה מִזֶּה v.supra - v. supra *on the other end*

מִן־הַכַּפֹּרֶת prep.-def.art.-n.f.s. (498) *from the mercy seat*

עָשָׂה Qal pf. 3 m.s. (I 793) *he made*

אֶת־הַכְּרֻבִים dir.obj.-def.art.-n.m.p. (500) *the cherubim*

מִשְּׁנֵי קְצוֹוֹתָו prep.-num. m. cstr. (1040)-n.f.p.-3 m.s. sf. (892) *on its two ends*

37:9

וַיִּהְיוּ consec.-Qal impf. 3 m.p. (הָיָה 224) *and were*

הַכְּרֻבִים def.art.-n.m.p. (500) *the cherubim*

פֹּרְשֵׂי Qal act. ptc. m.p. cstr. (פָּרַשׂ 831) *spreading out*

כְנָפַיִם n.f. du. (489) *wings*

לְמַעְלָה prep.-subst.-loc. he (751) *above*

סֹכְכִים Qal act. ptc. m.p. (סָכַךְ I 696) *overshadowing*

בְּכַנְפֵיהֶם prep.-n.f. du.-3 m.p. sf. (489) *with their wings*

עַל־הַכַּפֹּרֶת prep.-def.art.-n.f.s. (498) *the mercy seat*

וּפְנֵיהֶם conj.-n.m.p.-3 m.p. sf. (815) *with their faces*

אִישׁ אֶל־אָחִיו n.m.s. (35)-prep.-n.m.s.-3 m.s. sf. (26) *one to another*

אֶל־הַכַּפֹּרֶת prep.-def.art.-n.f.s. (498) *toward the mercy seat*

הָיוּ Qal pf. 3 c.p. (הָיָה 224) *were*

פְּנֵי הַכְּרֻבִים n.m.p. cstr. (815)-def.art.-n.m.p. (500) *the faces of the cherubim*

37:10

וַיַּעַשׂ consec.-Qal impf. 3 m.s. (עָשָׂה I 793) *and he made*

אֶת־הַשֻּׁלְחָן dir.obj.-def.art.-n.m.s. (1020) *the table*

עֲצֵי שִׁטִּים n.m.p. cstr. (781) - n.f.p. (1008) *of acacia wood*

אַמָּתַיִם n.f. du. (52) *two cubits*

אָרְכּוֹ n.m.s.-3 m.s. sf. (73) *its length*

וְאַמָּה conj.-n.f.s. (52) *and a cubit*

רָחְבּוֹ n.m.s.-3 m.s. sf. (931) *its breadth*

וְאַמָּה וָחֵצִי conj.-n.f.s. (52) - conj.-n.m.s. (345) *and a cubit and a half*

קֹמָתוֹ n.f.s.-3 m.s. sf. (879) *its height*

37:11

וַיְצַף אֹתוֹ consec.-Pi. impf. 3 m.s. (צָפָה II 860) - dir.obj.-3 m.s. sf. *and he overlaid it*

זָהָב טָהוֹר n.m.s. (262) - adj. m.s. (373) *with pure gold*

וַיַּעַשׂ לוֹ consec.-Qal impf. 3 m.s. (עָשָׂה I 793) - prep.-3 m.s. sf. *and made for it*

זֵר זָהָב n.m.s. cstr. (267) - n.m.s. (262) *a molding of gold*

סָבִיב adv. (686) *around*

37:12

וַיַּעַשׂ לוֹ consec.-Qal impf. 3 m.s. (עָשָׂה I 793) - prep.-3 m.s. sf. *and he made for it*

מִסְגֶּרֶת טֹפַח n.f.s. cstr. (689) - n.m.s. (381) *a frame a handbreadth wide*

סָבִיב adv. (686) *around*

וַיַּעַשׂ consec.-Qal impf. 3 m.s. (עָשָׂה I 793) *and made*

זֵר־זָהָב n.m.s. cstr. (267) - n.m.s. (262) *a molding of gold*

לְמִסְגַּרְתּוֹ prep.-n.f.s.-3 m.s. sf. (689) *for its frame*

סָבִיב adv. (686) *around*

37:13

וַיִּצֹק לוֹ consec.-Qal impf. 3 m.s. (יָצַק 427) - prep.-3 m.s. sf. *and he cast for it*

אַרְבַּע טַבְּעֹת num. (916) - n.f.p. cstr. (371) *four rings of*

זָהָב n.m.s. (262) *gold*

וַיִּתֵּן consec.-Qal impf. 3 m.s. (נָתַן 678) *and fastened*

אֶת־הַטַּבָּעֹת dir.obj.-def.art.-n.f.p. (371) *the rings*

עַל אַרְבַּע prep.-num. cstr. (916) *to the four*

הַפֵּאֹת def.art.-n.f.p. (802) *corners*

אֲשֶׁר לְאַרְבַּע rel.-prep.-num. cstr. (916) *at four*

רַגְלָיו n.f.p.-3 m.s. sf. (919) *its legs*

37:14

לְעֻמַּת הַמִּסְגֶּרֶת prep.-n.f.s. cstr. (I 769) - def.art.-n.f.s. (689) *close to the frame*

הָיוּ Qal pf. 3 c.p. (הָיָה 224) *were*

הַטַּבָּעֹת def.art.-n.f.p. (371) *the rings*

בָּתִּים לַבַּדִּים n.m.p. (108) - prep.-def.art.-n.m.p. (II 94) *as holders for the poles*

לָשֵׂאת prep.-Qal inf. cstr. (נָשָׂא 669) *to carry*

אֶת־הַשֻּׁלְחָן dir.obj.-def.art.-n.m.s. (1020) *the table*

37:15

וַיַּעַשׂ consec.-Qal impf. 3 m.s. (עָשָׂה I 793) *and he made*

אֶת־הַבַּדִּים dir.obj.-def.art.-n.m.p. (II 94) *the poles*

עֲצֵי שִׁטִּים n.m.p. cstr. (781) - n.f.p. (1008) *of acacia wood*

וַיְצַף אֹתָם consec.-Pi. impf. 3 m.s. (צָפָה II 860) - dir.obj.-3 m.p. sf. *and overlaid them*

זָהָב n.m.s. (262) *gold*

לָשֵׂאת prep.-Qal inf. cstr. (נָשָׂא 669) *to carry*

אֶת־הַשֻּׁלְחָן dir.obj.-def.art.-n.m.s. (1020) *the table*

37:16

וַיַּעַשׂ consec.-Qal impf. 3 m.s. (עָשָׂה I 793) *and he made*

אֶת־הַכֵּלִים dir.obj.-def.art.-n.m.p. (479) *the vessels*

אֲשֶׁר עַל־הַשֻּׁלְחָן rel.-prep.-def.art.-n.m.s. (1020) *which were to be upon the table*

אֶת־קְעָרֹתָיו dir.obj.-n.f.p.-3 m.s. sf. (891) *its plates*

וְאֶת־כַּפֹּתָיו conj.-dir.obj.-n.f.p.-3 m.s. sf. (496; 4b) *and its dishes for incense*

וְאֵת מְנַקִּיֹּתָיו conj.-dir.obj.-n.f.p.-3 m.s. sf. (667) *and its bowls*

וְאֶת־הַקְּשָׂוֹת conj.-dir.obj.-def.art.-n.f.p. (903) *and flagons*

אֲשֶׁר יֻסַּךְ בָּהֵן rel.-Ho. impf. 3 m.s. (נָסַךְ I 650)-prep.-3 f.p. sf. *with which to pour libations*

זָהָב טָהוֹר n.m.s. (262)-adj. m.s. (373) *of pure gold*

37:17

וַיַּעַשׂ consec.-Qal impf. 3 m.s. (עָשָׂה I 793) *he also made*

אֶת־הַמְּנֹרָה dir.obj.-def.art.-n.f.s. (633) *the lampstand*

זָהָב טָהוֹר n.m.s. (262)-adj. m.s. (373) *of pure gold*

מִקְשָׁה n.f.s. (I 904) *of hammered work*

עָשָׂה Qal pf. 3 m.s. (I 793) *he made*

אֶת־הַמְּנֹרָה dir.obj.-def.art.-n.f.s. (633) *the lampstand*

יְרֵכָהּ n.f.s.-3 f.s. sf. (437) *its base*

וְקָנָהּ conj.-n.m.s.-3 f.s. sf. (889) *and its shaft*

גְּבִיעֶיהָ n.m.p.-3 f.s. sf. (149) *its cups*

כַּפְתֹּרֶיהָ n.m.p.-3 f.s. sf. (I 499) *its capitals*

וּפְרָחֶיהָ conj.-n.m.p.-3 f.s. sf. (827) *and its flowers*

מִמֶּנָּה הָיוּ prep.-3 f.s. sf.-Qal pf. 3 c.p. (fhioho 224) *were of one piece with it*

37:18

וְשִׁשָּׁה קָנִים conj.-num. f. (995)-n.m.p. (889) *and six branches*

יֹצְאִים Qal act. ptc. m.p. (יָצָא 422) *were going out*

מִצִּדֶּיהָ prep.-n.m.p.-3 f.s. sf. (841) *of its sides*

שְׁלֹשָׁה קְנֵי num. f. (1025)-n.m.p. cstr. (889) *three branches of*

מְנֹרָה n.f.s. (633) *lampstand*

מִצִּדָּהּ prep.-n.m.s.-3 f.s. sf. (841) *out of ... side of it*

הָאֶחָד def.art.-num. adj. (25) *one*

וּשְׁלֹשָׁה קְנֵי conj.-v.supra - v.supra *and three branches of*

מְנֹרָה v.supra *lampstand*

מִצִּדָּהּ v.supra *out of ... side of it*

הַשֵּׁנִי def.art.-num. adj. (1041) *other*

37:19

שְׁלֹשָׁה גְבִעִים num. f. (1025)-n.m.p. (149) *three cups*

מְשֻׁקָּדִים Pu. ptc. m.p. (שָׁקַד 1052) *made like almonds*

בַּקָּנֶה הָאֶחָד prep.-def.art.-n.m.s. (889) - def.art.-num. adj. (25) *on one branch*

כַּפְתֹּר n.m.s. (I 499) *capital*

וָפֶרַח conj.-n.m.s. (827) *and flower*

וּשְׁלֹשָׁה conj.-v.supra *and three*

גְבִעִים v.supra *cups*

מְשֻׁקָּדִים v.supra *made like almonds*

בְּקָנֶה אֶחָד prep.-n.m.s. (889)-num. adj. (25) *on the other branch*

כַּפְתֹּר v.supra *capital*

וָפָרַח conj.-n.m.s. paus. (827) *and flower*

כֵּן לְשֵׁשֶׁת adv. (485)-prep.-num. f. cstr. (995) *so for the six*

הַקָּנִים def.art.-n.m.p. (889) *branches*

הַיֹּצְאִים def.art.-Qal act. ptc. m.p. (422) *going out*

מִן־הַמְּנֹרָה prep.-def.art.-n.f.s. (633) *of the lampstand*

37:20

וּבַמְּנֹרָה conj.-prep.-def.art.-n.f.s. (633) *and on the lampstand*

אַרְבָּעָה גְבִעִים num. f. (916)-n.m.p. (149) *four cups*

מְשֻׁקָּדִים Pu. ptc. m.p. (שָׁקַד 1052) *made like almonds*

כַּפְתֹּרֶיהָ n.m.p.-3 f.s. sf. (I 499) *with their capitals*

וּפְרָחֶיהָ conj.-n.m.p.-3 f.s. sf. (827) *and flowers*

37:21

וְכַפְתֹּר conj.-n.m.s. (I 499) *and a capital*

תַּחַת שְׁנֵי prep. (1065)-num. m. cstr. (1040) *under each pair of*

הַקָּנִים def.art.-n.m.p. (889) *the branches*

מִמֶּנָּה prep.-3 f.s. sf. *of one piece with it*

וְכַפְתֹּר v.supra *and a capital*

תַּחַת שְׁנֵי v.supra - v.supra *under each pair of*

הַקָּנִים v.supra *the branches*

מִמֶּנָּה v.supra *of one piece with it*

וְכַפְתֹּר v.supra *and a capital*

תַּחַת־שְׁנֵי v.supra - v.supra *under each pair of*

הַקָּנִים v.supra *the branches*

מִמֶּנָּה v.supra *of one piece with it*

לְשֵׁשֶׁת הַקָּנִים prep.-num. cstr. (995)-def.art.-n.m.p. (889) *of the six branches*

הַיֹּצְאִים def.art.-Qal act. ptc. m.p. (יָצָא 422) *going out*

מִמֶּנָּה v.supra *of it*

37:22

כַּפְתֹּרֵיהֶם n.m.p.-3 m.p. sf. (I 499) *their capitals*

וּקְנֹתָם conj.-n.m.p.-3 m.p. sf. (889) *and their branches*

מִמֶּנָּה prep.-3 f.s. sf. *of one piece with it*

הָיוּ Qal pf. 3 c.p. (הָיָה 224) *were*

כֻּלָּהּ n.m.s.-3 f.s. sf. (481) *the whole of it*

מִקְשָׁה n.f.s. (I 904) *of hammered work*

אַחַת num. adj. f. (25) *one piece*

זָהָב טָהוֹר n.m.s. (262)-adj. m.s. (373) *pure gold*

37:23

וַיַּעַשׂ consec.-Qal impf. 3 m.s. (עָשָׂה I 793) *and he made*

אֶת־נֵרֹתֶיהָ dir.obj.-n.m.p.-3 f.s. sf. (I 632) *its lamps*

שִׁבְעָה num. f. (987) *seven*

וּמַלְקָחֶיהָ conj.-n.m. du.-3 f.s. sf. (544) *and its snuffers*

וּמַחְתֹּתֶיהָ conj.-n.f.p.-3 f.s. sf. (367) *and its trays (fire-pans)*

זָהָב טָהוֹר n.m.s. (262)-adj. m.s. (373) *of pure gold*

37:24

כִּכָּר n.f.s. (503) *a talent*

זָהָב טָהוֹר n.m.s. (262)-adj. m.s. (373) *of pure gold*

עָשָׂה אֹתָהּ Qal pf. 3 m.s. (I 793)-dir.obj.-3 f.s. sf. *he made it*

וְאֵת כָּל־כֵּלֶיהָ conj.-dir.obj.-n.m.s. cstr. (481)-n.m.p.-3 f.s. sf. (479) *and all its utensils*

37:25

וַיַּעַשׂ consec.-Qal impf. 3 m.s. (עָשָׂה I 793) *and he made*

אֶת־מִזְבַּח dir.obj.-n.m.s. cstr. (258) *the altar of*

הַקְּטֹרֶת drf.art.-n.f.s. (882) *incense*

עֲצֵי שִׁטִּים n.m.p. cstr. (781) - n.f.p. (1008) *of acacia wood*

אַמָּה n.f.s. (52) *a cubit*

אָרְכּוֹ n.m.s.-3 m.s. sf. (73) *its length*

וְאַמָּה conj.-n.f.s. (52) *and a cubit*

רָחְבּוֹ n.m.s.-3 m.s. sf. (931) *its breadth*

רָבוּעַ Qal pass. ptc. (רָבַע 917) *it was square*

וְאַמָּתַיִם conj.-n.f. du. (52) *and two cubits*

קֹמָתוֹ n.f.s.-3 m.s. sf. (879) *its height*

מִמֶּנּוּ הָיוּ prep.-3 m.s. sf.-Qal pf. 3 c.p. (הָיָה 224) *were of one piece with it*

קַרְנֹתָיו n.f.p.-3 m.s. sf. (901) *its horns*

37:26

וַיְצַף אֹתוֹ consec.-Pi. impf. 3 m.s. (צָפָה II 860)-dir.obj.-3 m.s. sf. *and he overlaid it*

זָהָב טָהוֹר n.m.s. (262)-adj. m.s. (373) *with pure gold*

אֶת־גַּגּוֹ dir.obj.-n.m.s.-3 m.s. sf. (150) *its top*

וְאֶת־קִירֹתָיו conj.-dir.obj.-n.m.p.-3 m.s. sf. (I 885; 4) *and its sides*

סָבִיב adv. (686) *around*

וְאֶת־קַרְנֹתָיו conj.-dir.obj.-n.f.p.-3 m.s. sf. (901) *and its horns*

וַיַּעַשׂ לוֹ consec.-Qal impf. 3 m.s. (עָשָׂה I 793)-prep.-3 m.s. sf. *and he made about it*

זֵר זָהָב n.m.s. cstr. (267)-n.m.s. (262) *a molding of gold*

סָבִיב adv. (686) *round*

37:27

וּשְׁתֵּי טַבְּעֹת conj.-num. f. cstr. (1040)-n.f.p. cstr. (371) *and two rings of*

זָהָב n.m.s. (262) *gold*

עָשָׂה־לוֹ Qal pf. 3 m.s. (I 793)-prep.-3 m.s. sf. *he made on it*

מִתַּחַת לְזֵרוֹ prep.-prep. (1065)-prep.-n.m.s.-3 m.s. sf. (267) *under its molding*

עַל שְׁתֵּי צַלְעֹתָיו prep.-num. f. cstr. (104)-n.f.p.-3 m.s. sf. (854) *on its two sides*

עַל שְׁנֵי צִדָּיו prep.-num. m. cstr. (1040)-n.m.p.-3 m.s. sf. (841) *on its two sides*

לְבָתִּים prep.-n.m.p. (108) *as holders*

לְבַדִּים prep.-n.m.p. (II 94) *for poles*

לָשֵׂאת prep.-Qal inf. cstr. (נָשָׂא 669) *to carry*

אֹתוֹ בָּהֶם dir.obj.-3 m.s. sf.-prep.-3 m.p. sf. *with which ... on them*

37:28

וַיַּעַשׂ consec.-Qal impf. 3 m.s. (עָשָׂה I 793) *and he made*

אֶת־הַבַּדִּים dir.obj.-def.art.-n.m.p. (II 94) *the poles*

עֲצֵי שִׁטִּים n.m.p. cstr. (781)-n.f.p. (1008) *of acacia wood*

וַיְצַף consec.-Pi. impf. 3 m.s. (צָפָה II 860) *and overlaid*

אֹתָם dir.obj.-3 m.p. sf. *them*

זָהָב n.m.s. (262) *with gold*

37:29

וַיַּעַשׂ consec.-Qal impf. 3 m.s. (עָשָׂה I 793) *and he made*

אֶת־שֶׁמֶן dir.obj.-n.m.s. cstr. (1032) *the oil of*

הַמִּשְׁחָה def.art.-n.f.s. (603) *anointing*

קֹדֶשׁ n.m.s. (871) *holy*

וְאֶת־קְטֹרֶת הַסַּמִּים conj.-dir.obj.-n.f.s. cstr. (882)-def.art.-n.m.p. (702) *and the fragrant incense*

טָהוֹר adj. m.s. (373) *pure*

מַעֲשֵׂה רֹקֵחַ n.m.s. cstr. (795)-Qal act. ptc. (רָקַח 955) *blended as by the perfumer*

38:1

וַיַּעַשׂ consec.-Qal impf. 3 m.s. (עָשָׂה I 793) *and he made*

אֶת־מִזְבַּח dir.obj.-n.m.s. cstr. (258) *the altar of*

הָעֹלָה n.f.s. (750) *burnt offering*

עֲצֵי שִׁטִּים n.m.p. cstr. (781)-n.f.p. (1008) *of acacia wood*

חָמֵשׁ אַמּוֹת num. (331)-n.f.p. (52) *five cubits*

אָרְכּוֹ n.m.s.-3 m.s. sf. (73) *its length*

וְחָמֵשׁ־אַמּוֹת conj.-num. (331)-n.f.p. (52) *and five cubits*

רָחְבּוֹ n.m.s.-3 m.s. sf. (931) *its breadth*

רָבוּעַ Qal pass. ptc. (רָבַע 917) *it was square*

וְשָׁלֹשׁ אַמּוֹת conj.-num. (1025)-n.f.p. (52) *and three cubits*

קֹמָתוֹ n.f.s.-3 m.s. sf. (879) *its height*

38:2

וַיַּעַשׂ consec.-Qal impf. 3 m.s. (**עָשָׂה** I 793) *and he made*

קַרְנֹתָיו n.f.p.-3 m.s. sf. (901) *horns for it*

עַל אַרְבַּע פִּנֹּתָיו prep.-num. (916)-n.f.p.-3 m.s. sf. (819) *on its four corners*

מִמֶּנּוּ prep.-3 m.s. sf. *of one piece with it*

הָיוּ קַרְנֹתָיו Qal pf. 3 c.p. (**הָיָה** 224)-n.f.p.-3 m.s. sf. (901) *its horns were*

וַיְצַף אֹתוֹ consec.-Pi. impf. 3 m.s. (**צָפָה** II 860)-dir.obj.-3 m.s. sf. *and he overlaid it*

נְחֹשֶׁת n.m.s. (638) *with bronze*

38:3

וַיַּעַשׂ consec.-Qal impf. 3 m.s. (**עָשָׂה** I 793) *and he made*

אֶת־כָּל־כְּלֵי dir.obj.-n.m.s. cstr. (481)-n.m.p. cstr. *all the utensils of*

הַמִּזְבֵּחַ def.art.-n.m.s. (258) *the altar*

אֶת־הַסִּירֹת dir.obj.-def.art.-n.m.p. (I 696) *the pots*

וְאֶת־הַיָּעִים conj.-dir.obj.-def.art.-n.m.p. (418) *the shovels*

וְאֶת־הַמִּזְרָקֹת conj.-dir.obj.-def.art.-n.m.p. (284) *the basins*

אֶת־הַמִּזְלָגֹת dir.obj.-def.art.-n.f.p. (272) *the forks*

וְאֶת־הַמַּחְתֹּת conj.-dir.obj.-def.art.-n.f.p. (367) *and the fire pans*

כָּל־כֵּלָיו n.m.s. cstr. (481)-n.m.p.-3 m.s. sf. (479) *all its utensils*

עָשָׂה Qal pf. 3 m.s. (I 793) *he made*

נְחֹשֶׁת n.m.s. (638) *of bronze*

38:4

וַיַּעַשׂ consec.-Qal impf. 3 m.s. (**עָשָׂה** I 793) *and he made*

לַמִּזְבֵּחַ prep.-def.art.-n.m.s. (258) *for the altar*

מִכְבָּר n.m.s. (460) *a grating*

מַעֲשֵׂה רֶשֶׁת n.m.s. cstr. (795)-n.f.s. cstr. (440) *a network of*

נְחֹשֶׁת n.m.s. (638) *bronze*

תַּחַת כַּרְכֻּבּוֹ prep. (1065)-n.m.s.-3 m.s. sf. (501) *under its ledge*

מִלְמַטָּה prep.-prep.-adv.-loc. he (641) *down*

עַד־חֶצְיוֹ prep.-n.m.s.-3 m.s. sf. (345) *extending halfway*

38:5

וַיִּצֹק consec.-Qal impf. 3 m.s. (**יָצַק** 427) *and he cast*

אַרְבַּע טַבָּעֹת num. (916)-n.f.p. (371) *four rings*

בְּאַרְבַּע הַקְּצָוֹת prep.-num. cstr. (916)-def.art.-n.f.p. (892) *on the four corners*

לְמִכְבַּר prep.-n.m.s. cstr. (460) *of the ... grating*

הַנְּחֹשֶׁת def.art.-n.m.s. (638) *bronze*

בָּתִּים n.m.p. (108) *as holders*

לַבַּדִּים prep.-def.art.-n.m.p. (II 94) *for the poles*

38:6

וַיַּעַשׂ consec.-Qal impf. 3 m.s. (**עָשָׂה** I 793) *and he made*

אֶת־הַבַּדִּים dir.obj.-def.art.-n.m.p. (II 94) *the poles*

עֲצֵי שִׁטִּים n.m.p. cstr. (781)-n.f.p. (1008) *of acacia wood*

וַיְצַף אֹתָם consec.-Pi. impf. 3 m.s. (**צָפָה** II 860)-dir.obj.-3 m.p. sf. *and overlaid them*

נְחֹשֶׁת n.m.s. (638) *with bronze*

38:7

וַיָּבֵא consec.-Hi. impf. 3 m.s. (**בּוֹא** 97) *and he put*

אֶת־הַבַּדִּים dir.obj.-def.art.-n.m.p. (II 94) *the poles*

בַּטַּבָּעֹת prep.-def.art.-n.f.p. (371) *through the rings*

עַל צַלְעֹת prep.-n.f.p. cstr. (854) *on the sides of*

הַמִּזְבֵּחַ def.art.-n.m.s. (258) *the altar*

לָשֵׂאת אֹתוֹ prep.-Qal inf. cstr. (**נָשָׂא** 669)-dir.obj.-3 m.s. sf. *to carry it*

בָּהֶם prep.-3 m.p. sf. *with them*

נְבוּב Qal pass. ptc. cstr. (נָבַב 612) *hollow with*

לֻחֹת n.f.p. (531) *boards*

עָשָׂה אֹתוֹ Qal pf. 3 m.s. (I 793)-dir.obj.-3 m.s. sf. *he made it*

38:8

וַיַּעַשׂ consec.-Qal impf. 3 m.s. (עָשָׂה I 793) *and he made*

אֵת הַכִּיּוֹר dir.obj.-def.art.-n.m.s. (468) *the laver*

נְחֹשֶׁת n.m.s. (638) *of bronze*

וְאֵת כַּנּוֹ conj.-dir.obj.-n.m.s.-3 m.s. sf. (III 487) *and its base*

נְחֹשֶׁת v.supra *of bronze*

בְּמַרְאֹת prep.-n.f.p. cstr. (II 909) *from the mirrors of*

הַצֹּבְאֹת def.art.-Qal act. ptc. f.p. (צָבָא 838) *the ministering women*

אֲשֶׁר צָבְאוּ rel.-Qal pf. 3 c.p. (838) *who ministered*

פֶּתַח n.m.s. cstr. (835) *at the door of*

אֹהֶל מוֹעֵד n.m.s. cstr. (13)-n.m.s. (417) *tent of meeting*

38:9

וַיַּעַשׂ consec.-Qal impf. 3 m.s. (עָשָׂה I 793) *and he made*

אֶת־הֶחָצֵר dir.obj.-def.art.-n.m.s. (I 346) *the court*

לִפְאַת prep.-n.f.s. cstr. (802) *for the side*

נֶגֶב תֵּימָנָה n.m.s. (616)-n.f.s.loc. he (I 412) *south*

קַלְעֵי הֶחָצֵר n.m.p. cstr. (II 887)-v.supra *the hangings of the court*

שֵׁשׁ מָשְׁזָר n.m.s. (III 1058)-Ho. ptc. (שָׁזַר 1004) *of fine twisted linen*

מֵאָה בָּאַמָּה n.f.s. (547)-prep.-def.art.-n.f.s. (52) *a hundred cubits*

38:10

עַמּוּדֵיהֶם n.m.p.-3 m.p. sf. (765) *their pillars*

עֶשְׂרִים num. p. (797) *twenty*

וְאַדְנֵיהֶם conj.-n.m.p.-3 m.p. sf. (10) *and their bases*

עֶשְׂרִים v.supra *twenty*

נְחֹשֶׁת n.m.s. (638) *of bronze*

וָוֵי הָעַמֻּדִים n.m.p. cstr. (255)-def.art.-n.m.p. (765) *the hooks of the pillars*

וַחֲשֻׁקֵיהֶם conj.-n.m.p.-3 m.p. sf. (366) *and their fillets*

כָּסֶף n.m.s. paus. (494) *of silver*

38:11

וְלִפְאַת conj.-prep.-n.f.s. cstr. (802) *and for the side*

צָפוֹן n.f.s. (860) *north*

מֵאָה בָאַמָּה n.f.s. (547)-prep.-def.art.-n.f.s. (52) *a hundred cubits*

עַמּוּדֵיהֶם n.m.p.-3 m.p. sf. (765) *their pillars*

עֶשְׂרִים num. p. (797) *twenty*

וְאַדְנֵיהֶם conj.-n.m.p.-3 m.p. sf. (10) *and their bases*

עֶשְׂרִים v.supra *twenty*

נְחֹשֶׁת n.m.s. (638) *of bronze*

וָוֵי הָעַמּוּדִים n.m.p. cstr. (255)-def.art.-n.m.p. (765) *the hooks of the pillars*

וַחֲשֻׁקֵיהֶם conj.-n.m.p.-3 m.p. sf. (366) *and their fillets*

כָּסֶף n.m.s. paus. (494) *of silver*

38:12

וְלִפְאַת־ conj.-prep.-n.f.s. cstr. (802) *and for the side*

יָם n.m.s. (410) *west*

קְלָעִים n.m.p. (II 887) *hangings*

חֲמִשִּׁים בָּאַמָּה num. p. (332)-prep.-def.art.-n.f.s. (52) *fifty cubits*

עַמּוּדֵיהֶם n.m.p.-3 m.p. sf. (765) *their pillars*

עֲשָׂרָה num. (796) *ten*

וְאַדְנֵיהֶם conj.-n.m.p.-3 m.p. sf. (10) *and their sockets (bases)*

עֲשָׂרָה וָוֵי הָעַמֻּדִים num. (796) - n.m.p. cstr. (255) - def.art.-n.m.p. (765) *the hooks of the pillars*

וַחֲשׁוּקֵיהֶם conj.-n.m.p.-3 m.p. sf. (366) *and their fillets*

כָּסֶף n.m.s. paus. (494) *of silver*

38:13

וְלִפְאַת conj.-prep.-n.f.s. cstr. (802) *and for the side*

קֵדְמָה adv.-loc. he (870) *east*

מִזְרָחָה n.m.s. cstr.-loc. he (280) *east*

חֲמִשִּׁים אַמָּה num. p. (332)-n.f.s. (52) *fifty cubits*

38:14

קְלָעִים n.m.p. (II 887) *hangings*

חֲמֵשׁ־עֶשְׂרֵה num. cstr. (331)-num. (797) *fifteen*

אַמָּה n.f.s. (52) *cubits*

אֶל־הַכָּתֵף prep.-def.art.-n.f.s. (509) *for one side of the gate*

עַמּוּדֵיהֶם n.m.p.-3 m.p. sf. (765) *their pillars*

שְׁלֹשָׁה num. (1025) *three*

וְאַדְנֵיהֶם conj.-n.m.p.-3 m.p. sf. (10) *and their bases*

שְׁלֹשָׁה v. supra *three*

38:15

וְלַכָּתֵף הַשֵּׁנִית conj.-prep.-def.art.-n.f.s. (509)-def.art.-num. adj. f. (1041) *and so for the other side*

מִזֶּה prep.-demons. adj. (260) *on this hand*

וּמִזֶּה conj.-v. supra *and that hand*

לְשַׁעַר הֶחָצֵר prep.-n.m.s. cstr. (1004)-def.art.-n.m.s. (I 346) *by the gate of the court*

קְלָעִים n.m.p. (II 887) *hangings*

חֲמֵשׁ עֶשְׂרֵה num. cstr. (331)-num. (797) *fifteen*

אַמָּה n.f.s. (52) *cubits*

עַמֻּדֵיהֶם n.m.p.-3 m.p. sf. (765) *their pillars*

שְׁלֹשָׁה num. (1025) *three*

וְאַדְנֵיהֶם conj.-n.m.p.-3 m.p. sf. (10) *and their bases*

שְׁלֹשָׁה v. supra *three*

38:16

כָּל־קַלְעֵי n.m.s. cstr. (481)-n.m.p. cstr. (II 887) *all the hangings of*

הֶחָצֵר def.art.-n.m.s. (I 346) *the court*

סָבִיב adv. (686) *round about*

שֵׁשׁ מָשְׁזָר n.m.s. (III 1058)-Ho. ptc. (שָׁזַר 1004) *of fine twined linen*

38:17

וְהָאֲדָנִים conj.-def.art.-n.m.p. (10) *and the bases*

לָעַמֻּדִים prep.-def.art.-n.m.p. (765) *for the pillars*

נְחֹשֶׁת n.m.s. (638) *of bronze*

וָוֵי הָעַמּוּדִים n.m.p. cstr. (255)-def.art.-n.m.p. (765) *the hooks of the pillars*

וַחֲשׁוּקֵיהֶם conj.-n.m.p.-3 m.p. sf. (366) *and their fillets*

כָּסֶף n.m.s. (494) *of silver*

וְצִפּוּי רָאשֵׁיהֶם conj.-n.m.s. cstr. (860)-n.m.p.-3 m.p. sf. (910) *the overlaying of their capitals*

כָּסֶף n.m.s. paus. (494) *of silver*

וְהֵם מְחֻשָּׁקִים conj.-pers. pr. 3 m.p. (241)-Pu. ptc. m.p. (חָשַׁק II 366) *and they were filleted*

כֶּסֶף n.m.s. (494) *with silver*

כֹּל עַמֻּדֵי n.m.s. cstr. (481)-n.m.p. cstr. (765) *all the pillars of*

הֶחָצֵר def.art.-n.m.s. (I 346) *the court*

38:18

וּמָסַךְ conj.-n.m.s. cstr. (697) *and the screen of*

שַׁעַר הֶחָצֵר n.m.s. cstr. (1044)-def.art.-n.m.s. (I 346) *the gate of the court*

מַעֲשֵׂה רֹקֵם n.m.s. cstr. (795)-Qal act. ptc. (רָקַם 955) *embroidered with needlework*

תְּכֵלֶת n.f.s. (1067) *in blue*

וְאַרְגָּמָן conj.-n.m.s. (71) *and purple*

וְתוֹלַעַת שָׁנִי conj.-n.f.s. cstr. (1069)-n.m.s. (1040) *and scarlet stuff*

וְשֵׁשׁ מָשְׁזָר conj.-n.m.s. (III 1058)-Ho. ptc. (שָׁזַר 1004) *and fine twined linen*

וְעֶשְׂרִים conj.-num. p. (797) *twenty*

אַמָּה n.f.s. (52) *cubits*

אֹרֶךְ n.m.s. (73) *long*

וְקוֹמָה conj.-n.f.s. (879) *and high*

בְּרֹחַב prep.-n.m.s. (931) *in breadth*

חָמֵשׁ אַמּוֹת num. (331)-n.f.p. (52) *five cubits*

לְעֻמַּת prep.-n.f.s. cstr. (769) *corresponding to*

קַלְעֵי הֶחָצֵר n.m.p. cstr. (II 887)-def.art.-n.m.s. (I 346) *the hangings of the court*

38:19

וְעַמֻּדֵיהֶם conj.-n.m.p.-3 m.p. sf. (765) *and their pillars*

אַרְבָּעָה num. (916) *four*

וְאַדְנֵיהֶם conj.-n.m.p.-3 m.p. sf. (10) *and their bases*

אַרְבָּעָה num. f. (916) *four*

נְחֹשֶׁת n.m.s. (638) *of bronze*

וָוֵיהֶם n.m.p.-3 m.p. sf. (255) *their hooks*

כֶּסֶף n.m.s. (494) *of silver*

וְצִפּוּי רָאשֵׁיהֶם conj.-n.m.s. cstr. (860)-n.m.p.-3 m.p. sf. (910) *and the overlayings of their capitals*

וַחֲשֻׁקֵיהֶם conj.-n.m.p.-3 m.p. sf. (366) *and their fillets*

כָּסֶף n.m.s. paus. (494) *of silver*

38:20

וְכָל־הַיְתֵדֹת conj.-n.m.s. cstr. (481)-def.art.-n.f.p. (450) *and all the pegs*

לַמִּשְׁכָּן prep.-def.art.-n.m.s. (1015) *for the tabernacle*

וְלֶחָצֵר conj.-prep.-def.art.-n.m.s. (I 346) *and for the court*

סָבִיב adv. (686) *round about*

נְחֹשֶׁת n.m.s. (638) *of bronze*

38:21

אֵלֶּה demons. adj. c.p. (41) *this is*

פְקוּדֵי הַמִּשְׁכָּן n.m.p. cstr. (824)-def.art.-n.m.s. (1015) *the sum of the things for the tabernacle*

מִשְׁכַּן הָעֵדֻת n.m.s. cstr. (1015)-def.art.-n.f.s. (730) *the tabernacle of the testimony*

אֲשֶׁר פֻּקַּד rel.-Pu. pf. 3 m.s. (פָּקַד 823) *as they were counted*

עַל־פִּי מֹשֶׁה prep.-n.m.s. cstr. (804)-pr.n. (602) *at the commandment of Moses*

עֲבֹדַת הַלְוִיִּם n.f.s. cstr. (715)-def.art.-pr.n. p. (I 532) *for the work of the Levites*

בְּיַד אִיתָמָר prep.-n.f.s. cstr. (388)-pr.n. (16) *under the direction of Ithamar*

בֶּן־אַהֲרֹן n.m.s. cstr. (119)-pr.n. (14) *the son of Aaron*

הַכֹּהֵן def.art.-n.m.s. (463) *the priest*

38:22

וּבְצַלְאֵל conj.-pr.n. (130) *and Bezalel*

בֶּן־אוּרִי n.m.s. cstr. (119)-pr.n. (22) *the son of Uri*

בֶן־חוּר n.m.s. cstr. (119)-pr.n. (II 301) *son of Hur*

לְמַטֵּה יְהוּדָה prep.-n.m.s. cstr. (641)-pr.n. (397) *of the tribe of Judah*

עָשָׂה Qal pf. 3 m.s. (I 793) *made*

אֵת כָּל־אֲשֶׁר־ dir.obj.-n.m.s. (481)-rel. *all that*

צִוָּה יהוה Pi. pf. 3 m.s. (צָוָה 845)-pr.n. (217) *Yahweh commanded*

אֶת־מֹשֶׁה dir.obj.-pr.n. (602) *Moses*

38:23

וְאִתּוֹ conj.-prep.-3 m.s. sf. (II 85) *and with him*

אָהֳלִיאָב pr.n. (14) *Oholiab*

בֶּן־אֲחִיסָמָךְ n.m.s. cstr. (119) - pr.n. (27) *the son of Ahisamach*

לְמַטֵּה־דָן prep.-n.m.s. cstr. (641)-pr.n. (192) *of the tribe of Dan*

חָרָשׁ n.m.s. (360) *a craftsman*

וְחֹשֵׁב conj.-Qal act. ptc. (חָשַׁב 362) *and designer*

וְרֹקֵם conj.-Qal act. ptc. (רָקַם 955) *and embroiderer*

בַּתְּכֵלֶת prep.-def.art.-n.f.s. (1067) *in blue*

וּבָאַרְגָּמָן conj.-prep.-def.art.-n.m.s. (71) *and purple*

וּבְתוֹלַעַת הַשָּׁנִי conj.-prep.-n.f.s. cstr. (1069)-def.art.-n.m.s. (1040) *and scarlet stuff*

וּבַשֵּׁשׁ conj.-prep.-def.art.-n.m.s. (III 1058) *and fine twined linen*

38:24

כָּל־הַזָּהָב n.m.s. cstr. (481)-def.art.-n.m.s. (262) *all the gold*

הֶעָשׂוּי def.art.-Qal pass. ptc. (עָשָׂה I 793) *that was used*

לַמְּלָאכָה prep.-def.art.-n.f.s. (521) *for the work*

בְּכֹל מְלֶאכֶת prep.-n.m.s. cstr. (481)-n.f.s. cstr. (521) *in all the construction of*

הַקֹּדֶשׁ def.art.-n.m.s. (871) *the sanctuary*

וַיְהִי consec.-Qal impf. 3 m.s. (הָיָה 224) *and ... was*

זְהַב הַתְּנוּפָה n.m.s. cstr. (262)-def.art.-n.f.s. (632) *the gold from the offering*

תֵּשַׁע וְעֶשְׂרִים num. (1077)-conj.-num. p. (797) *twenty-nine*

כִּכָּר n.f.s. (503) *talents*

וּשְׁבַע מֵאוֹת conj.-num. cstr. (987)-n.f.p. (547) *and seven hundred*

וּשְׁלֹשִׁים conj.-num. p. (1026) *and thirty*

שֶׁקֶל n.m.s. (1053) *shekels*

בְּשֶׁקֶל prep.-n.m.s. cstr. (1053) *by the shekel of*

הַקֹּדֶשׁ def.art.-n.m.s. (871) *the sanctuary*

38:25

וְכֶסֶף conj.-n.m.s. cstr. (494) *and the silver from*

פְּקוּדֵי הָעֵדָה n.m.p. cstr. (824)-def.art.-n.f.s. *those of the congregation who were numbered*

מְאַת כִּכָּר n.f.s. cstr. (547)-n.f.s. (503) *a hundred talents*

וְאֶלֶף conj.-n.m.s. (48) *and a thousand*

וּשְׁבַע מֵאוֹת conj.-num. cstr. (987) - n.f.p. (547) *and seven hundred*

וַחֲמִשָּׁה וְשִׁבְעִים conj.-num. f. (331)-conj.-num. p. (988) *and seventy-five*

שֶׁקֶל n.m.s. (1053) *shekels*

בְּשֶׁקֶל prep.-n.m.s. cstr. (1053) *by the shekel of*

הַקֹּדֶשׁ def.art-n.m.s. (871) *the sanctuary*

38:26

בֶּקַע n.m.s. (132) *a beka*

לַגֻּלְגֹּלֶת prep.-def.art.-n.f.s. (166) *a head*

מַחֲצִית הַשֶּׁקֶל n.f.s. cstr. (345)-def.art.-n.m.s. (1053) *half a shekel*

בְּשֶׁקֶל הַקֹּדֶשׁ prep.-n.m.s. cstr. (1053)-def.art.-n.m.s. (871) *by the shekel of the sanctuary*

לְכֹל הָעֹבֵר prep.-n.m.s. cstr. (481)-def.art.-Qal act. ptc. (עָבַר 716) *for every one who passed over*

עַל־הַפְּקֻדִים prep.-def.art.-n.m.p. (824) *to be numbered in the census*

מִבֶּן עֶשְׂרִים prep.-n.m.s. cstr. (119) - num. p. (797) *from twenty*

שָׁנָה n.f.s. (1040) *years*

וָמַעְלָה conj.-adv.-loc. he (751) *and upward*

לְשֵׁשׁ־מֵאוֹת prep.-num. (995)-n.f.p. cstr. (547) *for six hundred*

אֶלֶף n.m.s. (48) *thousand*

וּשְׁלֹשֶׁת אֲלָפִים conj.-num. (1026)-n.m.p. (48) *and three thousand*

וַחֲמֵשׁ מֵאוֹת conj.-num. cstr. (331)-n.f.p. (547) *and five hundred*

וַחֲמִשִּׁים conj.-num. p. (332) *and fifty*

38:27

וַיְהִי consec.-Qal impf. 3 m.s. (הָיָה 224) *and were*

מְאַת כִּכַּר n.f.s. cstr. (547)-n.f.s. cstr. (503) *hundred talents of*

הַכֶּסֶף def.art.-n.m.s. (494) *silver*

לָצֶקֶת prep.-Qal inf. cstr. (יָצַק 427) *for casting*

אֵת אַדְנֵי dir.obj.-n.m.p. cstr. (10) *the bases of*

הַקֹּדֶשׁ def.art.-n.m.s. (871) *the sanctuary*

וְאֵת אַדְנֵי conj.-dir.obj.-n.m.p. cstr. (10) *and the bases of*

הַפָּרֹכֶת def.art.-n.f.s. (827) *the veil*

מְאַת אֲדָנִים n.f.s. cstr. (547)-n.m.p.

(10) *a hundred bases*

לְמְאַת הַכִּכָּר prep.-n.f.s. cstr. (547)-def.art.-n.f.s. (503) *for the hundred talents*

כִּכָּר לָאָדֶן n.f.s. (503)-prep.-def.art.-n.m.s. (10) *a talent for a base*

38:28

וְאֶת־הָאֶלֶף conj.-dir.obj.-def.art.-n.m.s. (48) *and of the thousand*

וּשְׁבַע הַמֵּאוֹת conj.-num. cstr. (987)-def.art.-n.f.p. (547) *and seven hundred*

וַחֲמִשָּׁה conj.-num. f. (331) *and five*

וְשִׁבְעִים conj.-num. p. (988) *and seventy*

עָשָׂה Qal pf. 3 m.s. (I 793) *he made*

וָוִים n.m.p. (255) *hooks*

לָעַמּוּדִים prep.-def.art.-n.m.p. (765) *for the pillars*

וְצִפָּה conj.-Pi. pf. 3 m.s. (עָפָה II 860) *and overlaid*

רָאשֵׁיהֶם n.m.p.-3 m.p. sf. (910) *their capitals*

וְחִשַּׁק conj.-Pi. pf. 3 m.s. (חשק II 366) *and made fillets*

אֹתָם dir.obj.-3 m.p. sf. *for them*

38:29

וּנְחֹשֶׁת conj.-n.m.s. cstr. (638) *and the bronze that*

הַתְּנוּפָה def.art.-n.f.s. (632) *that was contributed*

שִׁבְעִים כִּכָּר num. p. (988)-n.f.s. (503) *seventy talents*

וְאַלְפַּיִם conj.-n.m. du. (48) *and two thousand*

וְאַרְבַּע־מֵאוֹת conj.-num. (916)-n.f.p. (547) *and four hundred*

שָׁקֶל n.m.s. paus. (1053) *shekels*

38:30

וַיַּעַשׂ בָּהּ consec.-Qal impf. 3 m.s. (עָשָׂה I 793)-prep.-3 f.s. sf. *with it he made*

אֶת־אַדְנֵי dir.obj.-n.m.p. cstr. (10) *the bases for*

פֶּתַח n.m.s. cstr. (835) *the door of*

אֹהֶל מוֹעֵד n.m.s. cstr. (13)-n.m.s. (417) *the tent of meeting*

וְאֵת מִזְבַּח conj.-dir.obj.-n.m.s. cstr. (258) *and the altar of*

הַנְּחֹשֶׁת def.art.-n.m.s. (638) *bronze*

וְאֶת־מִכְבַּר conj.-dir.obj.-n.m.s. cstr. (460) *and the grating of*

הַנְּחֹשֶׁת v.supra *bronze*

אֲשֶׁר־לוֹ rel.-prep.-3 m.s. sf. *for it*

וְאֵת כָּל־ conj.-dir.obj.-n.m.s. cstr. (481) *and all*

כְּלֵי הַמִּזְבֵּחַ n.m.p. cstr. (479)-def.art.-n.m.s. (258) *the utensils of the altar*

38:31

וְאֶת־אַדְנֵי conj.-dir.obj.-n.m.p. cstr. (10) *and the bases of*

הֶחָצֵר def.art.-n.m.s. (I 346) *the court*

סָבִיב adv. (686) *round about*

וְאֶת־אַדְנֵי v.supra *and the bases of*

שַׁעַר הֶחָצֵר n.m.s. cstr. (1044)-def.art.-n.m.s. (I 346) *the gate of the court*

וְאֵת כָּל־ conj.-dir.obj.-n.m.s. cstr. (491) *and all*

יִתְדֹת n.f.p. cstr. (450) *the pegs of*

הַמִּשְׁכָּן def.art.-n.m.s. (1015) *the tabernacle*

וְאֶת־כָּל־ conj.-dir.obj.-n.m.s. cstr. (481) *and all*

יִתְדֹת v.supra *the pegs of*

הֶחָצֵר v.supra *the court*

סָבִיב v.supra *round about*

39:1

וּמִן־הַתְּכֵלֶת conj.-prep.-def.art.-n.f.s. (1067) *and of the blue*

וְהָאַרְגָּמָן conj.-def.art.-n.m.s. (71) *and purple*

וְתוֹלַעַת הַשָּׁנִי conj.-n.f.s. cstr. (1069)-def.art.-n.m.s. (104) *and scarlet stuff*

עָשׂוּ Qal pf. 3 c.p. (עָשָׂה I 793) *they made*

בִּגְדֵי־שְׂרָד n.m.p. cstr. (93)-n.m.s. (975) *finely wrought garments*

לְשָׁרֵת prep.-Pi. inf. cstr. (1058) *for ministering*

בַּקֹּדֶשׁ prep.def.art.-n.m.s. (871) *in the holy place*

וַיַּעֲשׂוּ consec.-Qal impf. 3 m.p. (עָשָׂה I 793) *they made*

אֶת־בִּגְדֵי dir.obj.-n.m.p. cstr. (93) *the ... garments*

הַקֹּדֶשׁ def.art.-n.m.s. (871) *holy*

אֲשֶׁר לְאַהֲרֹן rel.-prep.-pr.n. (14) *for Aaron*

כַּאֲשֶׁר צִוָּה prep.-rel.-Pi. pf. 3 m.s. (צָוָה 845) *as ... had commanded*

יהוה pr.n. (217) *Yahweh*

אֶת־מֹשֶׁה dir.obj.-pr.n. (602) *Moses*

39:2

וַיַּעַשׂ consec.-Qal impf. 3 m.s. (עָשָׂה I 793) *and he made*

אֶת־הָאֵפֹד dir.obj.-def.art.-n.m.s. (65) *the ephod*

זָהָב n.m.s. (262) *of gold*

תְּכֵלֶת n.f.s. (1067) *blue*

וְאַרְגָּמָן conj.-n.m.s. (71) *and purple*

וְתוֹלַעַת שָׁנִי conj.-n.f.s. cstr. (1069)-n.m.s. (1040) *and scarlet stuff*

וְשֵׁשׁ מָשְׁזָר conj.-n.m.s. (III 1058) - Ho. ptc. (שָׁזַר 1004) *and fine twined linen*

39:3

וַיְרַקְּעוּ consec.-Pi. impf. 3 m.p. (רָקַע 955) *and was hammered out*

אֶת־פַּחֵי הַזָּהָב dir.obj.-n.m.p. cstr. (II 809) - def.art.-n.m.s. (262) *gold leaf*

וְקִצֵּץ conj.-Pi. pf. 3 m.s. (קָצַץ 893) *and cut*

פְּתִילִם n.m.p. (836) *into threads*

לַעֲשׂוֹת prep.-Qal inf. cstr. (עָשָׂה I 793) *to work*

בְּתוֹךְ prep.-n.m.s. cstr. (1063) *into*

הַתְּכֵלֶת def.art.-n.f.s. (1067) *the blue*

וּבְתוֹךְ הָאַרְגָּמָן conj.-v.supra-def.art.-n.m.s. (71) *and purple*

וּבְתוֹךְ תּוֹלַעַת הַשָּׁנִי v.supra-n.f.s. cstr. (1069)-def.art.-n.m.s. (1040) *and the scarlet stuff*

וּבְתוֹךְ הַשֵּׁשׁ v.supra-def.art.-n.m.s. (III 1058) *and into the fine twined linen*

מַעֲשֵׂה חֹשֵׁב n.m.s. cstr. (795) - Qal act. ptc. (362) *in skilled design*

39:4

כְּתֵפֹת n.f.p. (509) *shoulder-pieces*

עָשׂוּ־לוֹ Qal pf. 3 c.p. (עָשָׂה I 793)-prep.-3 m.s. sf. *they made for it*

חֹבְרֹת Qal act. ptc. f.p. (חָבַר 287) *(joining)*

עַל־שְׁנֵי קְצוֹותָו prep.-num. cstr. (1040) - n.f.p.-3 m.s. sf. (892) *at its two edges*

חֻבָּר Pu. pf. 3 m.s. paus. (חָבַר 287) *joined*

39:5

וְחֵשֶׁב אֲפֻדָּתוֹ n.m.s. cstr. (363)-n.f.s.-3 m.s. sf. (65) *the skilfully woven band of his ephod*

אֲשֶׁר עָלָיו rel.-prep.-3 m.s. sf. *upon it*

מִמֶּנּוּ הוּא prep.-3 m.s. sf.-pers. pr. 3 m.s. (214) *of the same materials*

כְּמַעֲשֵׂהוּ prep.-n.m.s.-3 m.s. sf. (795) *and workmanship*

זָהָב n.m.s. (262) *of gold*

תְּכֵלֶת n.f.s. (1067) *blue*

וְאַרְגָּמָן conj.-n.m.s. (71) *and purple*

וְתוֹלַעַת שָׁנִי conj.-n.f.s. cstr. (1069)-n.m.s. (1040) *and scarlet stuff*

וְשֵׁשׁ מָשְׁזָר conj.-n.m.s. (III 1058)-Ho. ptc. (שָׁזַר 1004) *and fine twined linen*

כַּאֲשֶׁר צִוָּה prep.-rel.-Pi. pf. 3 m.s. (צָוָה 845) *as ... had commanded*

יהוה pr.n. (217) *Yahweh*

אֶת־מֹשֶׁה dir.obj.-pr.n. (602) *Moses*

39:6

וַיַּעֲשׂוּ consec.-Qal impf. 3 m.p. (עָשָׂה I 793) *and they prepared*

אֶת־אַבְנֵי הַשֹּׁהַם dir.obj.-n.f.p. cstr. (6)-def.art.-n.m.s. (I 995) *the onyx stones*

מֻסַבֹּת Ho. ptc. f.p. cstr. (סָבַב 685) *enclosed in*

מִשְׁבְּצוֹת זָהָב n.f.p. cstr. (990)-n.m.s. (262) *settings of gold filigree*

מְפֻתָּחֹת Pu. ptc. f.p. (פָּתַח II 836) *engraved*

פִּתּוּחֵי חוֹתָם n.m.p. cstr. (836)-n.m.s. (I 368) *like the engravings of a signet*

עַל־שְׁמוֹת prep.-n.m.p. cstr. (1027) *according to the names of*

בְּנֵי יִשְׂרָאֵל n.m.p. cstr. (119)-pr.n. (975) *the sons of Israel*

39:7

וַיָּשֶׂם consec.-Qal impf. 3 m.s. (שִׂים I 962) *and he set*

אֹתָם dir.obj.-3 m.p. sf. *them*

עַל כִּתְפֹת prep.-n.f.p. cstr. (509) *on the shoulder-pieces of*

הָאֵפֹד def.art.-n.m.s. (65) *the ephod*

אַבְנֵי זִכָּרוֹן n.f.p. cstr. (6)-n.m.s. (272) *stones of remembrance*

לִבְנֵי יִשְׂרָאֵל prep.-n.m.p. cstr. (119)-pr.n. (975) *for the sons of Israel*

כַּאֲשֶׁר צִוָּה prep.-rel.-Pi. pf. 3 m.s. (צָוָה 845) *as ... had commanded*

יהוה pr.n. (217) *Yahweh*

אֶת־מֹשֶׁה dir.obj.-pr.n. (602) *Moses*

39:8

וַיַּעַשׂ consec.-Qal impf. 3 m.s. (עָשָׂה I 793) *he made*

אֶת־הַחֹשֶׁן dir.obj.-def.art.-n.m.s. (365) *the breastpiece*

מַעֲשֵׂה חֹשֵׁב n.m.s. cstr. (795)-Qal act. ptc. (362) *in skilled work*

כְּמַעֲשֵׂה אֵפֹד prep.-n.m.s. cstr. (795)-n.m.s. (65) *like the work of the ephod*

זָהָב n.m.s. (262) *of gold*

תְּכֵלֶת n.f.s. (1067) *blue*

וְאַרְגָּמָן conj.-n.m.s. (71) *and purple*

וְתוֹלַעַת שָׁנִי conj.-n.f.s. cstr. (1069)-n.m.s. (1040) *and scarlet stuff*

וְשֵׁשׁ מָשְׁזָר conj.-n.m.s. (III 1058)-Ho. ptc. (שָׁזַר 1004) *and fine twined linen*

39:9

רָבוּעַ הָיָה Qall pass. ptc. (רָבַע 917)-Qal pf. 3 m.s. (224) *it was square*

כָּפוּל Qal pass. ptc. (כָּפַל 495) *double*

עָשׂוּ Qal pf. 3 c.p. (עָשָׂה I 793) *they made*

אֶת־הַחֹשֶׁן dir.obj.-def.art.-n.m.s. (365) *the breastpiece*

זֶרֶת אָרְכּוֹ n.f.s. (284)-n.m.s.-3 m.s. sf. (73) *a span its length*

וְזֶרֶת רָחְבּוֹ conj.-n.f.s. (284)-n.m.s.-3 m.s. sf. (931) *and a span its breadth*

כָּפוּל Qal pass. ptc. (כָּפַל 495) *when doubled*

39:10

וַיְמַלְאוּ־בוֹ consec.-Pi. impf. 3 m.p. (מָלֵא 569)-prep.-3 m.s. sf. *and they set in it*

אַרְבָּעָה טוּרֵי num. f. (916)-n.m.p. cstr. (377) *four rows of*

אָבֶן n.f.s. paus. (6) *stones*

טוּר אֹדֶם n.m.s. cstr. (377) - n.f.s. (10) *a row of sardius*

פִּטְדָה n.f.s. (809) *topaz*

וּבָרֶקֶת conj.-n.f.s. (140) *and carbuncle*

הַטּוּר הָאֶחָד def.art.-n.m.s. (377)-def.art.-num. adj. (25) *the first row*

39:11

וְהַטּוּר הַשֵּׁנִי conj.-def.art.-n.m.s. (377) - def.art.-num. adj. (1041) *and the second row*

נֹפֶךְ n.m.s. (656) *an emerald*

סַפִּיר n.m.s. (705) *a sapphire*

וְיָהֲלֹם conj.-n.m.s. (240) *and a diamond*

39:12

וְהַטּוּר הַשְּׁלִישִׁי conj.-def.art.-n.m.s. (377)-def.art.-num. adj. (1026) *and the third row*

לֶשֶׁם n.m.s. (I 545) *a jacinth*

שְׁבוֹ n.f.s. (986) *an agate*

וְאַחְלָמָה conj.-n.f.s. (29) *and an amethyst*

39:13

וְהַטּוּר הָרְבִיעִי conj.-def.arg.-n.m.s. (377)-def.art.-num. adj. (917) *and the fourth row*

תַּרְשִׁישׁ n.m.s. (I 1076) *a beryl (yellow jasper)*

שֹׁהַם n.m.s. (I 995) *an onyx*

וְיָשְׁפֵה conj.-n.m.s. (448) *and a jasper*

מוּסַבֹּת Ho. ptc. f.p. cstr. (סָבַב 685) *enclosed in*

מִשְׁבְּצוֹת n.f.p. cstr. (990) *settings of*

זָהָב n.m.s. (262) *n.m.s.*

זָהָב n.m.s. (262) *gold*

בְּמִלֻּאֹתָם prep.-n.f.p.-3 m.p. sf. (571) *in their settings*

39:14

וְהָאֲבָנִים conj.-def.art.-n.f.p. (6) *and the stones*

עַל־שְׁמֹת prep.-n.m.p. cstr. (1027) *with the names of*

בְּנֵי־יִשְׂרָאֵל n.m.p. cstr. (119)-pr.n. (975) *the sons of Israel*

הֵנָּה pers.pr. 3 f.p. (241) *they*

שְׁתֵּים עֶשְׂרֵה num. (1040) - num. (797) *twelve*

עַל־שְׁמֹתָם prep.-n.m.p.-3 m.p. sf. (1027) *according to their names*

פִּתּוּחֵי חֹתָם n.m.p. cstr. (836)-n.m.s. (I 368) *engravings of a signet*

אִישׁ עַל־שְׁמוֹ n.m.s. (35)-prep.-n.m.s.-3 m.s. sf. (1027) *each with its name*

לִשְׁנֵים עָשָׂר prep.-num. (1040)-num. (797) *for the twelve*

שָׁבֶט n.m.s. paus. (986) *tribes*

39:15

וַיַּעֲשׂוּ consec.-Qal impf. 3 m.p. (עָשָׂה I 793) *and they made*

עַל־הַחֹשֶׁן prep.-def.art.-n.m.s. (365) *on the breastpiece*

שַׁרְשְׁרֹת n.f.p. cstr. (1057) *chains of*

גַּבְלֻת n.f.s. (148) *twisted*

מַעֲשֵׂה עֲבֹת n.m.s. cstr. (795)-n.m.s. (721) *like cords*

זָהָב טָהוֹר n.m.s. (262)-adj. m.s. (373) *of pure gold*

39:16

וַיַּעֲשׂוּ consec.-Qal impf. 3 m.p. (עָשָׂה I 793) *and they made*

שְׁתֵּי מִשְׁבְּצֹת num. f. cstr. (1040)-n.f.p. cstr. (990) *two settings of*

זָהָב n.m.s. (262) *gold*

וּשְׁתֵּי טַבְּעֹת conj.-v. supra-n.f.p. cstr. (371) *and two rings of*

זָהָב n.m.s. (262) *gold*

וַיִּתְּנוּ consec.-Qal impf. 3 m.p. (נָתַן 678) *and put*

אֶת־שְׁתֵּי הַטַּבָּעֹת dir.obj.-v. supra-def.art.-n.f.p. (371) *the two rings*

עַל־שְׁנֵי קְצוֹת prep.-num. cstr. (1040)-n.f.p. cstr. (892) *on the two edges of*

הַחֹשֶׁן def.art.-n.m.s. (365) *the breastpiece*

39:17

וַיִּתְּנוּ consec.-Qal impf. 3 m.p. (נָתַן 678) *and they put*

שְׁתֵּי הָעֲבֹתֹת num. f. cstr. (1040)-def.art.-n.m.p. (721) *the two cords*

הַזָּהָב def.art.-n.m.s. (262) *of gold*

עַל־שְׁתֵּי הַטַּבָּעֹת prep.-num. cstr. (1040)-def.art.-n.f.p. (371) *in the two rings*

עַל־קְצוֹת prep.-n.f.p. cstr. (892) *at the edges of*

הַחֹשֶׁן def.art.-n.m.s. (365) *the breastpiece*

39:18

וְאֵת שְׁתֵּי קְצוֹת conj.-dir.obj.-num. cstr. (1040)-n.f.p. cstr. (892) *and two ends of*

שְׁתֵּי הָעֲבֹתֹת num. cstr. (1040)-def.art.-n.m.p. (721) *the two cords*

נָתְנוּ Qal pf. 3 c.p. (נָתַן 678) *they had attached*

עַל־שְׁתֵּי הַמִּשְׁבְּצֹת prep.-num. cstr. (1040)-def.art.-n.f.p. (990) *to the two settings*

וַיִּתְּנֻם consec.-Qal impf. 3 m.p.-3 m.p. sf. (נָתַן 678) *thus they attached*

עַל־כִּתְפֹת prep.-n.f.p. cstr. (509) *to the shoulder-pieces of*

הָאֵפֹד def.art.-n.m.s. (65) *the ephod*

אֶל־מוּל פָּנָיו prep.-subst. cstr. (557)-n.m.p.-3 m.s. sf. (815) *in front*

39:19

וַיַּעֲשׂוּ consec.-Qal impf. 3 m.p. (עָשָׂה I 793) *then they made*

שְׁתֵּי טַבְּעֹת num. cstr. (1040)-n.f.p. cstr. (371) *two rings of*

זָהָב n.m.s. (262) *gold*

וַיָּשִׂימוּ consec.-Qal impf. 3 m.p. (שִׂים I 962) *and put*

עַל־שְׁנֵי קְצוֹת prep.-num. cstr. (1040)-n.f.p. cstr. (892) *at the two ends of*

הַחֹשֶׁן def.art.-n.m.s. (365) *the breastpiece*

עַל־שְׂפָתוֹ prep.-n.f.s.-3 m.s. sf. (973) *on its side*

אֲשֶׁר אֶל־עֵבֶר rel.-prep.-n.m.s. cstr. (719) *which on the side of*

הָאֵפֹד def.art.-n.m.s. (65) *the ephod*

בָּיְתָה n.m.s.-loc. he (108, 7) *inwards*

39:20

וַיַּעֲשׂוּ consec.-Qal impf. 3 m.s. (עָשָׂה I 793) *and they made*

שְׁתֵּי טַבְּעֹת num. cstr. (1040)-n.f.p. cstr. (371) *two rings of*

זָהָב n.m.s. (262) *gold*

וַיִּתְּנֻם consec.-Qal impf. 3 m.p.-3 m.p. sf. (נָתַן 678) *and attached them*

עַל־שְׁתֵּי כִתְפֹת prep.-num. cstr. (1040)-n.f.p. cstr. (509) *on the two shoulder-pieces of*

הָאֵפֹד def.art.-n.m.s. (65) *the ephod*

מִלְמַטָּה prep.-prep.-adv. (641) *beneath*

מִמּוּל פָּנָיו prep.-subst. cstr. (557)-n.m.p.-3 m.s. sf. (815) *in front*

לְעֻמַּת מֶחְבַּרְתּוֹ prep.-n.f.s. cstr. (769)-n.f.s.-3 m.s. sf. (289) *at its joining*

מִמַּעַל prep.-subst. (751) *above*

לְחֵשֶׁב הָאֵפֹד prep.-n.m.s. cstr. (363) - def.art.-n.m.s. (65) *the skilfully woven band of the ephod*

39:21

וַיִּרְכְּסוּ consec.-Qal impf. 3 m.p. (רָכַס 940) *and they bound*

אֶת־הַחֹשֶׁן dir.obj.-def.art.-n.m.s. (365) *the breastpiece*

מִטַּבְּעֹתָיו prep.-n.f.p.-3 m.s. sf. (371) *by its rings*

אֶל־טַבְּעֹת הָאֵפֹד prep.-n.f.p. cstr. (371)-def.art.-n.m.s. (65) *to the rings of the ephod*

בִּפְתִיל תְּכֵלֶת prep.-n.m.s. cstr. (836)-n.f.s. (1067) *with a cord of blue*

לִהְיֹת prep.-Qal inf. cstr. (הָיָה 224) *so that it should lie*

עַל־חֵשֶׁב הָאֵפֹד prep.-n.m.s. cstr. (363)-def.art.-n.m.s. (65) *upon the skilfully woven band of the ephod*

וְלֹא־יִזַּח conj.-neg.-Ni. impf. 3 m.s. (זָחַח 267) *that should not come loose*

הַחֹשֶׁן def.art.-n.m.s. (365) *the breastpiece*

מֵעַל הָאֵפֹד prep.-prep.-def.art.-n.m.s. (65) *from the ephod*

כַּאֲשֶׁר צִוָּה prep.-rel.-Pi. pf. 3 m.s. (צָוָה 845) *as ... had commanded*

יהוה pr.n. (217) *Yahweh*

אֶת־מֹשֶׁה dir.obj.-pr.n. (602) *Moses*

39:22

וַיַּעַשׂ consec.-Qal impf. 3 m.s. (עָשָׂה I 793) *he also made*

אֶת־מְעִיל הָאֵפֹד dir.obj.-n.m.s. cstr. (591) - def.art.-n.m.s. (65) *the robe of the ephod*

מַעֲשֵׂה אֹרֵג n.m.s. cstr. (795)-Qal act. ptc. (אָרַג 70) *woven*

כְּלִיל תְּכֵלֶת adj. cstr. (483)-n.f.s. (1067) *all of blue*

39:23

וּפִי־הַמְּעִיל conj.-n.m.s. cstr. (804)-def.art.-n.m.s. (591) *and the opening of the robe*

בְּתוֹכוֹ prep.-n.m.s.-3 m.s. sf. (1063) *in it*

כְּפִי תַחְרָא prep.-n.m.s. cstr. (804)-n.m.s. (1065) *like the opening in a garment*

שָׂפָה לְפִיו n.f.s. (973)-prep.-n.m.s.-3 m.s. sf. (804) *with a binding for its opening*

סָבִיב adv. (686) *round about*

לֹא יִקָּרֵעַ neg.-Ni. impf. 3 m.s. (קָרַע 902) *that it might not be torn*

39:24

וַיַּעֲשׂוּ consec.-Qal impf 3 m.p. (עָשָׂה I 793) *and they made*

עַל־שׁוּלֵי הַמְּעִיל prep.-n.m.p. cstr. (1002)-def.art.-n.m.s. (591) *on the skirts of the robe*

רִמּוֹנֵי n.m.p. cstr. (I 941) *pomegranates of*

תְּכֵלֶת n.f.s. (1067) *blue*

וְאַרְגָּמָן conj.-n.m.s. (71) *and purple*

וְתוֹלַעַת שָׁנִי conj.-n.f.s. cstr. (1069)-n.m.s. (1040) *and scarlet stuff*

מָשְׁזָר Ho. ptc. (שָׁזַר 1004) *and fine twined linen*

39:25

וַיַּעֲשׂוּ consec.-Qal impf. 3 m.p. (עָשָׂה I 793) *they also made*

פַעֲמֹנֵי n.m.p. cstr. (822) *bells of*

זָהָב טָהוֹר n.m.s. (262)-adj. m.s. (373) *pure gold*

וַיִּתְּנוּ consec.-Qal impf. 3 m.p. (נָתַן 678) *and put*

אֶת־הַפַּעֲמֹנִים dir.obj.-def.art.-n.m.p. (822) *the bells*

בְּתוֹךְ prep.-n.m.s. cstr. (1063) *between*

הָרִמֹּנִים def.art.-n.m.p. (I 941) *the pomegranates*

עַל־שׁוּלֵי הַמְּעִיל prep.-n.m.p. cstr. (1002)-def.art.-n.m.s. (591) *upon the skirts of the robe*

סָבִיב adv. (686) *round about*

בְּתוֹךְ v.supra *between*

הָרִמֹּנִים v.supra *the pomegranates*

39:26

פַּעֲמֹן וְרִמֹּן n.m.s. (822)-conj.-n.m.s. (I 941) *a bell and a pomegranate*

פַּעֲמֹן v.supra *a bell*

וְרִמֹּן v.supra *and a pomegranate*

עַל־שׁוּלֵי prep.-n.m.p. cstr. (1002) *upon the skirts of*

הַמְּעִיל def.art.-n.m.s. (591) *the robe*

סָבִיב adv. (686) *round about*

לְשָׁרֵת prep.-Pi. inf. cstr. (שָׁרַת 1058) *for ministering*

כַּאֲשֶׁר צִוָּה prep.-rel.-Pi. pf. 3 m.s. (צָוָה 845) *as ... had commanded*

יהוה pr. n. (217) *Yahweh*

אֶת־מֹשֶׁה dir.obj.-pr.n. (602) *Moses*

39:27

וַיַּעֲשׂוּ consec.-Qal impf. 3 m.p. (עָשָׂה I 793) *they also made*

אֶת־הַכָּתְנֹת dir.obj.-def.art.-n.f.p. (509) *the coats*

שֵׁשׁ n.m.s. (III 1058) *fine linen*

מַעֲשֵׂה אֹרֵג n.m.s. cstr. (795)-Qal act. ptc. (אָרַג 70) *woven*

לְאַהֲרֹן prep.-pr.n. (14) *for Aaron*

וּלְבָנָיו conj.-prep.-n.m.p.-3 m.s. sf. (119) *and his sons*

39:28

וְאֵת הַמִּצְנֶפֶת conj.-dir.obj.-def.art.-n.f.s. (857) *and the turban*

שֵׁשׁ n.m.s. (III 1058) *of fine linen*

וְאֶת־פַּאֲרֵי הַמִּגְבָּעֹת conj.-dir.obj.-n.m.p. cstr. (802)-def.art.-n.f.p. (149) *and the caps*

שֵׁשׁ v.supra *of fine linen*

וְאֶת־מִכְנְסֵי הַבָּד conj.-dir.obj.-n.m. du. cstr. (488)-def.art.-n.m.s. paus. (I 94) *and the linen breeches*

שֵׁשׁ מָשְׁזָר v.supra-Ho. ptc. (שָׁזַר 1004) *of fine twined linen*

39:29

וְאֶת־הָאַבְנֵט conj.-dir.obj.-def.art.-n.m.s. (126) *and the girdle*

שֵׁשׁ מָשְׁזָר n.m.s. (III 1058)-Ho. ptc. (שָׁזַר 1004) *of fine twined linen*

וּתְכֵלֶת conj.-n.f.s. (1067) *and of blue*

וְאַרְגָּמָן conj.-n.m.s. (71) *and purple*

וְתוֹלַעַת שָׁנִי conj.-n.f.s. cstr. (1069)-n.m.s. (1040) *and scarlet stuff*

מַעֲשֵׂה רֹקֵם n.m.s. cstr. (795)-Qal act. ptc. (רָקַם 955) *embroidered with needlework*

כַּאֲשֶׁר צִוָּה prep.-rel.-Pi. pf. 3 m.s. (צָוָה 845) *as ... had commanded*

יהוה pr.n. (217) *Yahweh*

אֶת־מֹשֶׁה dir.obj.-pr.n. (602) *Moses*

39:30

וַיַּעֲשׂוּ consec.-Qal impf. 3 m.p. (עָשָׂה I 793) *and they made*

אֶת־צִיץ dir.obj.-n.m.s. cstr. (I 847) *the plate of*

נֵזֶר־ n.m.s. cstr. (634) *the crown*

הַקֹּדֶשׁ def.art.-n.m.s. (871) *holy*

זָהָב טָהוֹר n.m.s. (262)-adj. m.s. (373) *of pure gold*

וַיִּכְתְּבוּ consec.-Qal impf. 3 m. p. (כָּתַב 507) *and wrote*

עָלָיו prep.-3 m.s. sf. *upon it*

מִכְתַּב n.m.s. cstr. (508) *an inscription like*

פִּתּוּחֵי חוֹתָם n.m.p. cstr. (836) - n.m.s. (I 368) *engraving of a signet*

קֹדֶשׁ ליהוה n.m.s. (871) - prep.-pr.n. (217) *Holy to Yahweh*

39:31

וַיִּתְּנוּ עָלָיו consec.-Qal impf. 3 m.p. (נָתַן 678)-prep.-3 m.s. sf. *and they tied to it*

פְּתִיל n.m.s. cstr. (836) *a cord of*

תְּכֵלֶת n.f.s. (1067) *blue*

לָתֵת prep.-Qal inf. cstr. (נָתַן 678) *to fasten it*

עַל־הַמִּצְנֶפֶת prep.-def.art.-n.f.s. (857) *on the turban*

מִלְמָעְלָה prep.-prep.-subst.-loc. he (751) *above*

כַּאֲשֶׁר צִוָּה prep.-rel.-Pi. pf. 3 m.s. (צָוָה 845) *as ... had commanded*

יהוה pr.n. (217) *Yahweh*

אֶת־מֹשֶׁה dir.obj.-pr.n. (602) *Moses*

39:32

וַתֵּכֶל consec.-Qal impf. 3 f.s. (כָּלָה I 477) *thus was finished*

כָּל־עֲבֹדַת n.m.s. cstr. (481)-n.f.s. cstr. (715) *all the work of*

מִשְׁכַּן n.m.s. cstr. (1015) *the tabernacle of*

אֹהֶל מוֹעֵד n.m.s. cstr. (13)-n.m.s. (417) *the tent of meeting*

וַיַּעֲשׂוּ consec.-Qal impf. 3 m.p. (עָשָׂה I 793) *and ... made*

בְּנֵי יִשְׂרָאֵל n.m.p. cstr. (119)-pr.n. (975) *the people of Israel*

כְּכֹל אֲשֶׁר prep.-n.m.s. (481)-rel. *according to all that*

צִוָּה יהוה Pi. pf. 3 m.s. (צָוָה 845)-pr.n. (217) *Yahweh had commanded*

אֶת־מֹשֶׁה dir.obj.-pr.n. (602) *Moses*

כֵּן עָשׂוּ adv. (485)-Qal pf. 3 c.p. (עָשָׂה I 793) *so had they done*

39:33

וַיָּבִיאוּ consec.-Hi. impf. 3 m.p. (בּוֹא 97) *and they brought*

אֶת־הַמִּשְׁכָּן dir.obj.-def.art.-n.m.s. (1015) *the tabernacle*

אֶל־מֹשֶׁה prep.-pr.n. (602) *to Moses*

אֶת־הָאֹהֶל dir.obj.-def.art.-n.m.s. (13) *the tent*

וְאֶת־כָּל־כֵּלָיו conj.-dir.obj.-n.m.s. cstr. (481)-n.m.p.-3 m.s. sf. (479) *and all its utensils*

קְרָסָיו n.m.p.-3 m.s. sf. (902) *its hooks*

קְרָשָׁיו n.m.p.-3 m.s. sf. (903) *its frames*

בְּרִיחָו n.m.p.-3 m.s. sf. (138) *its bars*

וְעַמֻּדָיו conj.-n.m.p.-3 m.s. sf. (765) *and its pillars*

וַאֲדָנָיו conj.-n.m.p.-3 m.s. sf. (10) *and its bases*

39:34

וְאֶת־מִכְסֵה conj.-dir.obj.-n.m.s. cstr. (492) *and the covering of*

עוֹרֹת הָאֵילִם n.m.p. cstr. (736) - def.art.-n.m.p. (I 17) *rams' skins*

הַמְאָדָּמִים def.art. - Pu. ptc. m.p. (אָדֹם 10) *tanned*

וְאֶת־מִכְסֵה v.supra *and (the covering of)*

עֹרֹת הַתְּחָשִׁים v.supra-def.art.-n.m.p. (I 1065) *goatskins*

וְאֵת פָּרֹכֶת conj.-dir.obj.-n.f.s. cstr. (827) *and the veil of*

הַמָּסָךְ def.art.-n.m.s. (697) *the screen*

39:35

אֶת־אֲרֹן dir.obj.-n.m.s. cstr. (75) *the ark of*

הָעֵדֻת def.art.-n.f.s. (730) *the testimony*

וְאֶת־בַּדָּיו conj.-dir.obj.-n.m.p.-3 m.s. sf. (II 94) *with its poles*

וְאֵת הַכַּפֹּרֶת conj.-dir.obj.-def.art.-n.f.s. (498) *and the mercy seat*

39:36

אֶת־הַשֻּׁלְחָן dir.obj.-def.art.-n.m.s. (1020) *the table*

אֶת־כָּל־כֵּלָיו dir.obj.-n.m.s. cstr. (481)-n.m.p.-3 m.s. sf. (479) *with all its utensils*

וְאֵת לֶחֶם conj.-dir.obj.-n.m.s. cstr. (536) *and the bread of*

הַפָּנִים def.art.-n.m.p. (815) *the Presence*

39:37

אֶת־הַמְּנֹרָה dir.obj.-def.at.-n.f.s. (633) *the lampstand*

הַטְּהֹרָה def.art.-adj. f.s. (373) *pure*

אֶת־נֵרֹתֶיהָ dir.obj.-n.m.p.-3 f.s. sf. (632) *and its lamps*

נֵרֹת n.m.p. cstr. (632) *with the lamps*

הַמַּעֲרָכָה def.art.-n.f.s. (790) *set (in a row)*

וְאֶת־כָּל־כֵּלֶיהָ conj.-dir.obj.-n.m.s. cstr. (481)-n.m.p.-3 f.s. sf. (479) *and all its utensils*

וְאֵת שֶׁמֶן conj.-dir.obj.-n.m.s. cstr. (1032) *and the oil for*

הַמָּאוֹר def.art.-n.m.s. (22) *the light*

39:38

וְאֵת מִזְבַּח conj.-dir.obj.-n.m.s. cstr. (258) *and the altar (of)*

הַזָּהָב def.art.-n.m.s. (262) *gold*

וְאֵת שֶׁמֶן conj.-dir.obj.-n.m.s. cstr. (1032) *and the oil of*

הַמִּשְׁחָה def.art.-n.f.s. (603) *anointing*

וְאֵת קְטֹרֶת הַסַּמִּים conj.-dir.obj.-n.f.s. cstr. (882)-def.art.-n.m.p. (702) *and the fragrant incense*

וְאֵת מָסַךְ conj.-dir.obj.-n.m.s. cstr. (697) *and the screen for*

פֶּתַח n.m.s. cstr. (835) *the door of*

הָאֹהֶל def.art.-n.m.s. (13) *the tent*

39:39

אֵת מִזְבַּח dir.obj.-n.m.s. cstr. (258) *the altar of*

הַנְּחֹשֶׁת def.art.-n.m.s. (638) *bronze*

וְאֶת־מִכְבַּר conj.-dir.obj.-n.m.s. cstr. (460) *and the grating of*

הַנְּחֹשֶׁת v. supra *bronze*

אֲשֶׁר־לוֹ rel.-prep.-3 m.s. sf. *its*

אֶת־בַּדָּיו dir.obj.-n.m.p.-3 m.s. sf. (II 94) *its poles*

וְאֶת־כָּל־כֵּלָיו conj.-dir.obj.-n.m.s. cstr. (481)-n.m.p.-3 m.s. sf. (479) *and all its utensils*

אֶת־הַכִּיֹּר dir.obj.-def.art.-n.m.s. (468) *the laver*

וְאֶת־כַּנּוֹ conj.-dir.obj.-n.m.s.-3 m.s. sf. (II 487) *and its base*

39:40

אֵת קַלְעֵי dir.obj.-n.m.p. cstr. (II 887) *the hangings of*

הֶחָצֵר def.art.-n.m.s. (I 346) *the court*

אֶת־עַמֻּדֶיהָ dir.obj.-n.m.p.-3 f.s. sf. (765) *its pillars*

וְאֶת־אֲדָנֶיהָ conj.-dir.obj.-n.m.p.-3 f.s. sf. (10) *and its bases*

וְאֶת־הַמָּסָךְ conj.-dir.obj.-def.art.-n.m.s. (697) *and the screen*

לְשַׁעַר prep.-n.m.s. cstr. (1044) *for the gate of*

הֶחָצֵר v. supra *the court*

אֶת־מֵיתָרָיו dir.obj.-n.m.p.-3 m.s. sf. (452) *its cords*

וִיתֵדֹתֶיהָ conj.-n.f.p.-3 f.s. sf. (450) *and its pegs*

וְאֵת כָּל־כְּלֵי conj.-dir.obj.-n.m.s. cstr. (481)-n.m.p. cstr. (479) *and all the utensils for*

עֲבֹדַת n.f.s. cstr. (715) *the service of*

הַמִּשְׁכָּן def.art.-n.m.s. (1015) *the tabernacle*

לְאֹהֶל prep.-n.m.s. cstr. (13) *for the tent of*

מוֹעֵד n.m.s. (417) *meeting*

39:41

אֶת־בִּגְדֵי הַשְּׂרָד dir.obj.-n.m.p. cstr. (93)-def.art.-n.m.s. (975) *the finely worked garments*

לְשָׁרֵת prep.-Pi. inf. cstr. (1058) *for ministering*

בַּקֹּדֶשׁ prep.-def.art.-n.m.s. (871) *in the holy place*

אֶת־בִּגְדֵי הַקֹּדֶשׁ dir.obj.-n.m.p. cstr. (93) - def.art.-n.m.s. (871) *the holy garments*

לְאַהֲרֹן prep.-pr.n. (14) *for Aaron*

הַכֹּהֵן def.art.-n.m.s. (463) *the priest*

וְאֶת־בִּגְדֵי conj.-dir.obj.-n.m.p. cstr. (93) *and the garments of*

בָנָיו n.m.p.-3 m.s. sf. (119) *his sons*

לְכַהֵן prep.-Pi. inf. cstr. (II 464) *to serve as priests*

39:42

כְּכֹל אֲשֶׁר־ prep.-n.m.s. (481)-rel. *according to all that*

צִוָּה יהוה Pi. pf. 3 m.s. (צָוָה 845)-pr.n. (217) *Yahweh had commanded*

אֶת־מֹשֶׁה dir.obj.-pr.n. (602) *Moses*

כֵּן עָשׂוּ adv. (485)-Qal pf. 3 c.p. (עָשָׂה I 793) *so ... had done*

בְּנֵי יִשְׂרָאֵל n.m.p. cstr. (119)-pr.n. (975) *the people of Israel*

אֵת כָּל־הָעֲבֹדָה dir.obj.-n.m.s. cstr. (481)-def.art.-n.f.s. (715) *all the work*

39:43

וַיַּרְא מֹשֶׁה consec.-Qal impf. 3 m.s. (רָאָה 906)-pr.n. (602) *and Moses saw*

אֶת־כָּל־ dir.obj.-n.m.s. cstr. (481) *all*

הַמְּלָאכָה def.art.-n.f.s. (521) *the work*

וְהִנֵּה conj.-demons. part. (243) *and behold*

עָשׂוּ אֹתָהּ Qal pf. 3 c.p. (עָשָׂה I 793)-dir.obj.-3 f.s. sf. *they had done it*

כַּאֲשֶׁר צִוָּה prep.-rel.-Pi. pf. 3 m.s. (צָוָה 845) *as ... had commanded*

יהוה pr.n. (217) *Yahweh*

כֵּן עָשׂוּ adv. (485)-Qal pf. 3 c.p. (עָשָׂה I 793) *so had they done*

וַיְבָרֶךְ אֹתָם consec.-Pi. impf. 3 m.s. (בָּרַךְ 138)-dir.obj.-3 m.p. sf. *and ... blessed them*

מֹשֶׁה pr.n. (602) *Moses*

40:1

וַיְדַבֵּר יהוה consec.-Pi. impf. 3 m.s. (180)-pr.n. (217) *and Yahweh said*

אֶל־מֹשֶׁה prep.-pr.n. (602) *to Moses*

לֵּאמֹר prep.-Qal inf. cstr. (55) *(saying)*

40:2

בְּיוֹם prep.-n.m.s. cstr. (398) *on the day of*

הַחֹדֶשׁ הָרִאשׁוֹן def.art.-n.m.s. (I 294)-def.art.-adj. (911) *the first month*

בְּאֶחָד לַחֹדֶשׁ prep.-num. (25)-prep.-def.art.-n.m.s. (I 294) *on the first of the month*

תָּקִים Hi. impf. 2 m.s. (קוּם 877) *you shall erect*

אֶת־מִשְׁכַּן dir.obj.-n.m.s. cstr. (1015) *the tabernacle of*

אֹהֶל מוֹעֵד n.m.s. cstr. (13)-n.m.s. (417) *the tent of meeting*

40:3

וְשַׂמְתָּ שָׁם conj.-Qal pf. 2 m.s. (שִׂים I 962)-adv. (1027) *and you shall put in it*

אֵת אֲרוֹן הָעֵדוּת dir.obj.-n.m.s. cstr. (75)-def.art.-n.f.s. (730) *the ark of the testimony*

וְסַכֹּתָ conj.-Qal pf. 2 m.s. (סָכַךְ I 696) *and you shall screen*

עַל־הָאָרֹן prep.-def.art.-n.m.s. (75) *the ark*

אֶת־הַפָּרֹכֶת prep. (II 85)-def.art.-n.f.s. (827) *with the veil*

40:4

וְהֵבֵאתָ conj.-Hi. pf. 2 m.s. (בּוֹא 97) *and you shall bring in*

אֶת־הַשֻּׁלְחָן dir.obj.-def.art.-n.m.s. (1020) *the table*

וְעָרַכְתָּ conj.-Qal pf. 2 m.s. (עָרַךְ 789) *and set*

אֶת־עֶרְכּוֹ dir.obj.-n.m.s.-3 m.s. sf. (789) *its arrangements*

וְהֵבֵאתָ v. supra *and you shall bring in*

אֶת־הַמְּנֹרָה dir.obj.-def.art.-n.f.s. (633) *the lampstand*

וְהַעֲלֵיתָ conj.-Hi. pf. 2 m.s. (עָלָה 748) *and set up*

אֶת־נֵרֹתֶיהָ dir.obj.-n.m.p.-3 f.s. sf. (632) *its lamps*

40:5

וְנָתַתָּה conj.-Qal pf. 2 m.s. (נָתַן 678) *and you shall put*

אֶת־מִזְבַּח dir.obj.-n.m.s. cstr. (258) *the altar of*

הַזָּהָב def.art.-n.m.s. (262) *gold*

לִקְטֹרֶת prep.-n.f.s. (882) *for incense*

לִפְנֵי prep.-n.m.p. cstr. (815) *before*

אֲרוֹן הָעֵדֻת n.m.s. cstr. (75)-def.art.-n.f.s. (730) *the ark of the testimony*

וְשַׂמְתָּ conj.-Qal pf. 2 m.s. (שִׂים I 962) *and set up*

אֶת־מָסַךְ dir.obj.-n.m.s. cstr. (697) *the screen for*

הַפֶּתַח def.art.-n.m.s. (835) *the door*

לַמִּשְׁכָּן prep.-def.art.-n.m.s. (1015) *of the tabernacle*

40:6

וְנָתַתָּה conj.-Qal pf. 2 m.s. (נָתַן 678) *and you shall set*

אֵת מִזְבַּח dir.obj.-n.m.s. cstr. (258) *the altar of*

הָעֹלָה def.art.-n.f.s. (750) *burnt offering*

לִפְנֵי prep.-n.m.p. cstr. (815) *before*

פֶּתַח n.m.s. cstr. (835) *the door of*

מִשְׁכַּן n.m.s. cstr. (1015) *the tabernacle of*

אֹהֶל־מוֹעֵד n.m.s. cstr. (13)-n.m.s. (417) *the tent of meeting*

40:7

וְנָתַתָּ conj.-Qal pf. 2 m.s. (נָתַן 678) *and place*

אֶת־הַכִּיֹּר dir.obj.-def.art.-n.m.s. (468) *the laver*

בֵּין־אֹהֶל מוֹעֵד prep. (107)-n.m.s. cstr. (13)-n.m.s. (417) *between the tent of meeting*

וּבֵין הַמִּזְבֵּחַ conj.-prep. (107)-def.art.-n.m.s. (258) *and the altar*

וְנָתַתָּ conj.-Qal pf. 2 m.s. (נָתַן 678) *and put*

שָׁם מָיִם adv. (1027)-n.m.p. paus. (565) *water in it*

40:8

וְשַׂמְתָּ conj.-Qal pf. 2 m.s. (שִׂים I 962) *and you shall set up*

אֶת־הֶחָצֵר dir.obj.-def.art.-n.m.s. (I 346) *the court*

סָבִיב adv. (686) *round about*

וְנָתַתָּ conj.-Qal pf. 2 m.s. (נָתַן 678) *and hang up*

אֶת־מָסַךְ dir.obj.-n.m.s. cstr. (697) *the screen for*

שַׁעַר n.m.s. cstr. (1044) *the gate of*

הֶחָצֵר def.art.-n.m.s. (I 346) *the court*

40:9

וְלָקַחְתָּ conj.-Qal pf. 2 m.s. (לָקַח 542) *then you shall take*

אֶת־שֶׁמֶן dir.obj.-n.m.s. cstr. (1032) *the oil of*

הַמִּשְׁחָה def.art.-n.f.s. (603) *anointing*

וּמָשַׁחְתָּ conj.-Qal pf. 2 m.s. (מָשַׁח 602) *and anoint*

אֶת־הַמִּשְׁכָּן dir.obj.-def.art.-n.m.s. (1014) *the tabernacle*

וְאֶת־כָּל־אֲשֶׁר־בּוֹ conj.-dir.obj.-n.m.s. (481)-rel.-prep.-3 m.s. sf. *and all that is in it*

וְקִדַּשְׁתָּ conj.-Pi. pf. 2 m.s. (קָדַשׁ 872) *and consecrate*

אֹתוֹ dir.obj.-3 m.s. sf. *it*

וְאֶת־כָּל־כֵּלָיו conj.-dir.obj.-n.m.s. cstr. (481)-n.m.p.-3 m.s. sf. (479) *and all its furniture*

וְהָיָה קֹדֶשׁ conj.-Qal pf. 3 m.s. (224)-n.m.s. (871) *and it shall become holy*

40:10

וּמָשַׁחְתָּ conj.-Qal pf. 2 m.s. (מָשַׁח 602) *you shall also anoint*

אֶת־מִזְבַּח dir.obj.-n.m.s. cstr. (258) *the altar of*

הָעֹלָה def.art.-n.f.s. (750) *burnt offering*

וְאֶת־כָּל־כֵּלָיו conj.-dir.obj.-n.m.s. cstr. (481)-n.m.p.-3 m.s. sf. (479) *and all its utensils*

וְקִדַּשְׁתָּ conj.-Pi. pf. 2 m.s. (קָדַשׁ 872) *and consecrate*

אֶת־הַמִּזְבֵּחַ dir.obj.-def.art.-n.m.s. (258) *the altar*

וְהָיָה הַמִּזְבֵּחַ conj.-Qal pf. 3 m.s. (224) - def.art.-n.m.s. (258) *and the altar shall be*

קֹדֶשׁ קָדָשִׁים n.m.s. cstr. (871)-n.m.p. (871) *most holy*

40:11

וּמָשַׁחְתָּ conj.-Qal pf. 2 m.s. (מָשַׁח 602) *you shall also anoint*

אֶת־הַכִּיֹּר dir.obj.-def.art.-n.m.s. (468) *the laver*

וְאֶת־כַּנּוֹ conj.-dir.obj.-n.m.s.-3 m.s. sf. (III 487) *and its base*

וְקִדַּשְׁתָּ אֹתוֹ conj.-Pi. pf. 2 m.s. (קָדַשׁ 872) - dir.obj.-3 m.s. sf. *and consecrate it*

40:12

וְהִקְרַבְתָּ conj.-Hi. pf. 2 m.s. (קָרַב 897) *then you shall bring near*

אֶת־אַהֲרֹן dir.obj.-pr.n. (14) *Aaron*

וְאֶת־בָּנָיו conj.-dir.obj.-n.m.p.-3 m.s. sf. (119) *and his sons*

אֶל־פֶּתַח prep.-n.m.s. cstr. (835) *to the door of*

אֹהֶל מוֹעֵד n.m.s. cstr. (13)-n.m.s. (417) *the tent of meeting*

וְרָחַצְתָּ conj.-Qal pf. 2 m.s. (רָחַץ 934) *and shall wash*

אֹתָם dir.obj.-3 m.p. sf. *them*

בַּמָּיִם prep.-def.art.-n.m.p. paus. (565) *with water*

40:13

וְהִלְבַּשְׁתָּ conj.-Hi. pf. 2 m.s. (לָבַשׁ 527) *and put upon*

אֶת־אַהֲרֹן dir.obj.-pr.n. (14) *Aaron*

אֵת בִּגְדֵי dir.obj.-n.m.p. cstr. (93) *the garments*

הַקֹּדֶשׁ def.art.-n.m.s. (871) *holy*

וּמָשַׁחְתָּ אֹתוֹ conj. - Qal pf. 2 m.s. (מָשַׁח 602) - dir.obj.-3 m.s. sf. *and you shall anoint him*

וְקִדַּשְׁתָּ אֹתוֹ conj.-Pi. pf. 2 m.s. (קָדַשׁ 872)-dir.obj.-3 m.s. sf. *and consecrate him*

וְכִהֵן לִי conj.-Pi. pf. 3 m.s. (464)-prep.-1 c.s. sf. *that he may serve me as priest*

40:14

וְאֶת־בָּנָיו conj.-dir.obj.-n.m.p.-3 m.s. sf. (119) *and his sons*

תַּקְרִיב Hi. impf. 2 m.s. (קָרַב 897) *you shall bring*

וְהִלְבַּשְׁתָּ אֹתָם conj.-Hi. pf. 2 m.s. (לָבַשׁ 527)-dir.obj.-3 m.p. sf. *and put on them*

כֻּתֳּנֹת n.f.p. (509) *coats*

40:15

וּמָשַׁחְתָּ אֹתָם conj. - Qal pf. 2 m. s. (מָשַׁח 602) - dir.obj.-3 m.p. sf. *and anoint them*

כַּאֲשֶׁר מָשַׁחְתָּ prep.-rel.-Qal pf. 2 m.s. (מָשַׁח 602) *as you anointed*

אֶת־אֲבִיהֶם dir.obj.-n.m.s.-3 m.p. sf. (3) *their father*

וְכִהֲנוּ לִי conj.-Pi. pf. 3 c.p. (464)-prep.-1 c.s. sf. *that they may serve me as priests*

וְהָיְתָה לִהְיֹת לָהֶם conj.-Qal pf. 3 f.s. (הָיָה 224)-prep.-Qal inf. cstr. (הָיָה 224)-prep.-3 m.p. sf. *shall admit them*

מָשְׁחָתָם Qal inf. cstr. - 3 m.p. sf. (מָשַׁח 602) *their anointing*

לִכְהֻנַּת עוֹלָם prep.-n.f.s. cstr. (464)-n.m.s. (761) *to a perpetual priesthood*

לְדֹרֹתָם prep.-n.m.p.-3 m.p. sf. (189) *throughout their generations*

40:16

וַיַּעַשׂ מֹשֶׁה consec.-Qal impf. 3 m.s. (עָשָׂה I 793)-pr.n. (602) *thus did Moses*

כְּכֹל אֲשֶׁר prep.-n.m.s. (481)-rel. *according to all that*

צִוָּה יהוה Pi. pf. 3 m.s. (צָוָה 845)-pr.n. (217) *Yahweh commanded*

אֹתוֹ dir.obj.-3 m.s. sf. *him*

כֵּן עָשָׂה adv. (485)-Qal pf. 3 m.s. (793) *so he did*

40:17

וַיְהִי consec.-Qal impf. 3 m.s. (הָיָה 224) *and (it proceeded to be)*

בַּחֹדֶשׁ הָרִאשׁוֹן prep.-def.art.-n.m.s. (I 294)-def.art.-adj. (911) *in the first month*

בַּשָּׁנָה הַשֵּׁנִית prep.-def.art.-n.f.s. (1040)-def.art.-num. adj. (1041) *in the second year*

בְּאֶחָד לַחֹדֶשׁ prep.-num. (25)-prep.-def.art.-n.m.s. (I 294) *on the first day of the month*

הוּקַם Ho. pf. 3 m.s. (קוּם 877) *was erected*

הַמִּשְׁכָּן def.art.-n.m.s. (1015) *the tabernacle*

40:18

וַיָּקֶם מֹשֶׁה consec. - Hi. impf. 3 m.s. (קוּם 877) - pr.n. (602) *and Moses erected*

אֶת־הַמִּשְׁכָּן dir.obj.-def.art.-n.m.s. (1015) *the tabernacle*

וַיִּתֵּן consec.-Qal impf. 3 m.s. (נָתַן 678) *and he laid*

אֶת־אֲדָנָיו dir.obj.-n.m.p.-3 m.s. sf. (10) *its bases*

וַיָּשֶׂם consec.-Qal impf. 3 m.s. (שִׂים I 962) *and set up*

אֶת־קְרָשָׁיו dir.obj.-n.m.p.-3 m.s. sf. (903) *its frames*

וַיִּתֵּן consec.-Qal impf. 3 m.s. (נָתַן 678) *and put*

אֶת־בְּרִיחָיו dir.obj.-n.m.p.-3 m.s. sf. (138) *its bars*

וַיָּקֶם consec.-Hi. impf. 3 m.s. (קוּם 877) *and raised up*

אֶת־עַמּוּדָיו dir.obj.-n.m.p.-3 m.s. sf. (765) *its pillars*

40:19

וַיִּפְרֹשׂ consec.-Qal impf. 3 m.s. (פָּרַשׂ 831) *and he spread*

אֶת־הָאֹהֶל dir.obj.-def.art.-n.m.s. (13) *the tent*

עַל־הַמִּשְׁכָּן prep.-def.art.-n.m.s. (1015) *over the tabernacle*

וַיָּשֶׂם consec.-Qal impf. 3 m.s. (שִׂים I 962) *and put*

אֶת־מִכְסֵה dir.obj.-n.m.s. cstr. (492) *the covering of*

הָאֹהֶל def.art.-n.m.s. (13) *the tent*

עָלָיו prep.-3 m.s. sf. over it

מִלְמָעְלָה prep.-prep.-subst.-loc. he (751) *(above)*

כַּאֲשֶׁר צִוָּה prep.-rel.-Pi. pf. 3 m.s. (צָוָה 845) *as ... had commanded*

יהוה pr.n. (217) *Yahweh*

אֶת־מֹשֶׁה dir.obj.-pr.n. (602) *Moses*

40:20

וַיִּקַּח consec.-Qal impf. 3 m.s. (לָקַח 542) *and he took*

וַיִּתֵּן consec.-Qal impf. 3 m.s. (נָתַן 678) *and put*

אֶת־הָעֵדֻת dir.obj.-def.art.-n.f.s. (730) *the testimony*

אֶל־הָאָרֹן prep.-def.art.-n.m.s. (75) *into the ark*

וַיָּשֶׂם consec.-Qal impf. 3 m.s. (שִׂים I 962) *and put*

אֶת־הַבַּדִּים dir.obj.-def.art.-n.m.p. (II 94) *the poles*

עַל־הָאָרֹן prep.-def.art.-n.m.s. (75) *on the ark*

וַיִּתֵּן consec.-Qal impf. 3 m.s. (נָתַן 678) *and set*

אֶת־הַכַּפֹּרֶת dir.obj.-def.art.-n.f.s. (498) *the mercy seat*

עַל־הָאָרֹן prep.-def.art.-n.m.s. (75) *on the ark*

מִלְמָעְלָה prep.-prep.subst.-loc. he (751) *above*

40:21

וַיָּבֵא consec.-Hi. impf. 3 m.s. (בּוֹא 97) *and he brought*

אֶת־הָאָרֹן dir.obj.-def.art.-n.m.s. (75) *the ark*

אֶל־הַמִּשְׁכָּן prep.-def.art.-n.m.s. (1015) *into the tabernacle*

וַיָּשֶׂם consec.-Qal impf. 3 m.s. (שִׂים I

962) *and set up*
אֶת פָּרֹכֶת dir.obj.-n.f.s. cstr. (827) *the veil of*
הַמָּסָךְ def.art.-n.m.s. (697) *the screen*
וַיָּסֶךְ consec.-Hi. impf. 3 m.s. (סָכַךְ I 696) *and screened*
עַל אֲרוֹן prep.-n.m.s. cstr. (75) *the ark of*
הָעֵדוּת def.art.-n.f.s. (730) *the testimony*
כַּאֲשֶׁר צִוָּה prep.-rel.-Pi. pf. 3 m.s. (צָוָה 845) *as ... had commanded*
יהוה pr.n. (217) *Yahweh*
אֶת־מֹשֶׁה dir.obj.-pr.n. (602) *Moses*

40:22

וַיִּתֵּן consec.-Qal impf. 3 m.s. (נָתַן 678) *and he put*
אֶת־הַשֻּׁלְחָן dir.obj.-def.art.-n.m.s. (1020) *the table*
בְּאֹהֶל מוֹעֵד prep.-n.m.s. cstr. (13)-n.m.s. (417) *in the tent of meeting*
עַל יֶרֶךְ prep.-n.f.s. cstr. (437) *on the side of*
הַמִּשְׁכָּן def.art.-n.m.s. (1015) *the tabernacle*
צָפֹנָה n.f.s.-loc. he (860) *north*
מִחוּץ prep.-n.m.s. (299) *outside*
לַפָּרֹכֶת prep.-def.art.-n.f.s. (827) *the veil*

40:23

וַיַּעֲרֹךְ עָלָיו עֵרֶךְ consec.-Qal impf. 3 m.s. (עָרַךְ 789)-prep.-3 m.s. sf.-n.m.s. (789) *and set in order on it*
לֶחֶם n.m.s. (536) *the bread*
לִפְנֵי יהוה prep.-n.m.p. cstr. (815)-pr.n. (217) *before Yahweh*
כַּאֲשֶׁר צִוָּה prep.-rel.-Pi. pf. 3 m.s. (צָוָה 845) *as ... had commanded*
יהוה pr.n. (217) *Yahweh*
אֶת־מֹשֶׁה dir.obj.-pr.n. (602) *Moses*

40:24

וַיָּשֶׂם consec.-Qal impf. 3 m.s. (שִׂים I 962) *and he put*
אֶת־הַמְּנֹרָה dir.obj.-def.art.-n.f.s. (633) *the lampstand*
בְּאֹהֶל מוֹעֵד prep.-n.m.s. cstr. (13)-n.m.s. (417) *in the tent of meeting*
נֹכַח הַשֻּׁלְחָן subst. (647)-def.art.-n.m.s. (1020) *opposite the table*
עַל יֶרֶךְ prep.-n.f.s. cstr. (437) *on the side of*
הַמִּשְׁכָּן def.art.-n.m.s. (1015) *the tabernacle*
נֶגְבָּה n.m.s.-loc. he (616) *south*

40:25

וַיַּעַל consec.-Qal impf. 3 m.s. (עָלָה 748) *and set up*
הַנֵּרֹת def.art.-n.m.p. (632) *the lamps*
לִפְנֵי יהוה prep.-n.m.p. cstr. (815)-pr.n. (217) *before Yahweh*
כַּאֲשֶׁר צִוָּה יהוה prep.-rel.-Pi. pf. 3 m.s. (צָוָה 845)-pr.n. (217) *as Yahweh had commanded*
אֶת־מֹשֶׁה dir.obj.-pr.n. (602) *Moses*

40:26

וַיָּשֶׂם consec.-Qal impf. 3 m.s. (שִׂים I 962) *and he put*
אֶת־מִזְבַּח dir.obj.-n.m.s. cstr. (258) *the altar of*
הַזָּהָב def.art.-n.m.s. (262) *the gold*
בְּאֹהֶל מוֹעֵד prep.-n.m.s. cstr. (13)-n.m.s. (417) *in the tent of meeting*
לִפְנֵי הַפָּרֹכֶת prep.-n.m.p. cstr. (815)-def.art.-n.f.s. (827) *before the veil*

40:27

וַיַּקְטֵר עָלָיו consec.-Hi. impf. 3 m.s. (קָטַר 882)-prep.-3 m.s. sf. *and burnt upon it*
קְטֹרֶת סַמִּים n.f.s. cstr. (882)-n.m.p. (702) *fragrant incense*
כַּאֲשֶׁר צִוָּה prep.-rel.-Pi. pf. 3 m.s. (צָוָה 845) *as ... had commanded*
יהוה pr.n. (217) *Yahweh*
אֶת־מֹשֶׁה dir.obj.-pr.n. (602) *Moses*

40:28

וַיָּשֶׂם consec.-Qal impf. 3 m.s. (שִׂים I 962) *and he put*
אֶת־מָסַךְ dir.obj.-n.m.s. cstr. (697) *the screen for*
הַפֶּתַח def.art.-n.m.s. (835) *the door*
לַמִּשְׁכָּן prep.-def.art.-n.m.s. (1015) *of the tabernacle*

40:29

וְאֵת מִזְבַּח conj.-dir.obj.-n.m.s. cstr. (258) *and the altar of*

הָעֹלָה def.art.-n.f.s. (750) *burnt offering*

שָׂם Qal pf. 3 m.s. (שִׂים I 962) *he set*

פֶּתַח מִשְׁכַּן n.m.s. cstr. (835)-n.m.s. cstr. (1015) *at the door of the tabernacle of*

אהֶלמוֹעֵד n.m.s. cstr. (13) - n.m.s. (417) *the tent of meeting*

וַיַּעַל עָלָיו consec.-Hi. impf. 3 m.s. (עָלָה 748)-prep.-3 m.s. sf. *and offered upon it*

אֶת־הָעֹלָה dir.obj.-def.art.-n.f.s. (750) *the burnt offering*

וְאֶת־הַמִּנְחָה conj.-dir.obj.-def.art.-n.f.s. (585) *and the cereal offering*

כַּאֲשֶׁר צִוָּה prep.-rel.-Pi. pf. 3 m.s. (צָוָה 845) *as ... had commanded*

יהוה pr.n. (217) *Yahweh*

אֶת־מֹשֶׁה dir.obj.-pr.n. (602) *Moses*

40:30

וַיָּשֶׂם consec.-Qal impf. 3 m.s. (שִׂים I 962) *and he set*

אֶת־הַכִּיֹּר dir.obj.-def.art.-n.m.s. (468) *the laver*

בֵּין־אֹהֶל מוֹעֵד prep. (107)-n.m.s. cstr. (13)-n.m.s. (417) *between the tent of meeting*

וּבֵין הַמִּזְבֵּחַ conj.-prep. (107)-def.art.-n.m.s. (258) *and the altar*

וַיִּתֵּן שָׁמָּה consec.-Qal impf. 3 m.s. (נָתַן 678)-adv.-loc. he (1027) *and put in it*

מַיִם n.m.p. (565) *water*

לְרָחְצָה prep.-Qal inf. cstr. (רָחַץ 934) *for washing*

40:31

וְרָחֲצוּ conj.-Qal pf. 3 c.p. (רָחַץ 934) *and washed*

מִמֶּנּוּ prep.-3 m.s. sf. *from it (with which)*

מֹשֶׁה pr.n. (602) *Moses*

וְאַהֲרֹן conj.-pr.n. (14) *and Aaron*

וּבָנָיו conj.-n.m.p.-3 m.s. sf. (119) *and his sons*

אֶת־יְדֵיהֶם dir.obj.-n.f.p.-3 m.p. sf. (388) *their hands*

וְאֶת־רַגְלֵיהֶם conj.-dir.obj.-n.f.p.-3 m.p. sf. (919) *and their feet*

40.32

בְּבֹאָם prep.-Qal inf. cstr.-3 m.p. sf. (בּוֹא 97) *when they went*

אֶל־אֹהֶל מוֹעֵד prep.n.m.s. cstr. (13)-n.m.s. (417) *into the tent of meeting*

וּבְקָרְבָתָם conj.-prep.-Qal inf. cstr.-3 m.p. sf. (קָרַב I 897) *and when they approached*

אֶל־הַמִּזְבֵּחַ prep.-def.art.-n.m.s. (258) *the altar*

יִרְחָצוּ Qal impf. 3 m.p. paus. (רָחַץ 934) *they washed*

כַּאֲשֶׁר צִוָּה prep.-rel.-Pi. pf. 3 m.s. (צָוָה 845) *as ... commanded*

יהוה pr.n. (217) *Yahweh*

אֶת־מֹשֶׁה dir.obj.-pr.n. (602) *Moses*

40:33

וַיָּקֶם consec.-Hi. impf. 3 m.s. (קוּם 877) *and he erected*

אֶת־הֶחָצֵר dir.obj.-def.art.-n.m.s. (I 346) *the court*

סָבִיב adv. (686) *round*

לַמִּשְׁכָּן prep.-def.art.-n.m.s. (1015) *the tabernacle*

וְלַמִּזְבֵּחַ conj.-prep.-def.art.-n.m.s. (258) *and the altar*

וַיִּתֵּן consec.-Qal impf. 3 m.s. (נָתַן 678) *and set up*

אֶת־מָסַךְ dir.obj.-n.m.s. cstr. (697) *the screen of*

שַׁעַר n.m.s. cstr. (1044) *the gate of*

הֶחָצֵר v.supra *the court*

וַיְכַל מֹשֶׁה consec.-Pi. impf. 3 m.s. (כָּלָה 477)-pr.n. (602) *so Moses finished*

אֶת־הַמְּלָאכָה dir.obj.-def.art.-n.f.s. (521) *the work*

40:34

וַיְכַס consec.-Pi. impf. 3 m.s. (כָּסָה 491) *then covered*

הֶעָנָן def.art.-n.m.s. (777) *the cloud*

אֶת־אֹהֶל מוֹעֵד dir.obj.-n.m.s. cstr.

(13)-n.m.s. (417) *the tent of meeting*

וּכְבוֹד יהוה conj.-n.m.s. cstr. (458)-pr.n. (217) *and the glory of Yahweh*

מָלֵא Qal pf. 3 m.s. (569) *filled*

אֶת־הַמִּשְׁכָּן dir.obj.-def.art.-n.m.s. (1015) *the tabernacle*

40:35

וְלֹא יָכֹל conj.-neg.-Qal pf. 3 m.s. (יָכֹל 407) *and was not able*

מֹשֶׁה pr.n. (602) *Moses*

לָבוֹא prep.-Qal inf. cstr. (בּוֹא 97) *to enter*

אֶל־אֹהֶל מוֹעֵד prep.-n.m.s. cstr. (13)-n.m.s. (417) *the tent of meeting*

כִּי־שָׁכַן conj.-Qal pf. 3 m.s. (1014) *because abode*

עָלָיו prep.-3 m.s. sf. *upon it*

הֶעָנָן def.art.-n.m.s. (777) *the cloud*

וּכְבוֹד יהוה conj.-n.m.s. cstr. (458)-pr.n. (217) *and the glory of Yahweh*

מָלֵא Qal pf. 3 m.s. (569) *filled*

אֶת־הַמִּשְׁכָּן dir.obj.-def.art.-n.m.s. (1015) *the tabernacle*

40:36

וּבְהֵעָלוֹת conj.-prep.-Ni. inf cstr. (עָלָה 748) *whenever ... was taken up*

הֶעָנָן def.art.-n.m.s. (777) *the cloud*

מֵעַל הַמִּשְׁכָּן prep.-prep.-def.art.-n.m.s. (1015) *from over the tabernacle*

יִסְעוּ Qal impf. 3 m.p. (נָסַע I 652) *would go onward*

בְּנֵי יִשְׂרָאֵל n.m.p. cstr. (119) - pr.n. (975) *the people of Israel*

בְּכֹל מַסְעֵיהֶם prep.-n.m.s. cstr. (481) - n.m.p. - 3 m.p. sf. (652) *throughout all their journeys*

40:37

וְאִם־ conj.-hypoth.part. (49) *but if*

לֹא יֵעָלֶה neg.-Ni. impf. 3 m.s. (עָלָה 748) *was not taken up*

הֶעָנָן def.art.-n.m.s. (777) *the cloud*

וְלֹא יִסְעוּ conj.-neg.-Qal impf. 3 m.p. (נָסַע I 652) *then they did not go onward*

עַד־יוֹם prep.-n.m.s. cstr. (398) *till the day that*

הֵעָלֹתוֹ Ni. inf. cstr.-3 m.s. sf. (עָלָה 748) *it was taken up*

40:38

כִּי עֲנַן יהוה conj.-n.m.s. cstr. (777)-pr.n. (217) *for the cloud of Yahweh*

עַל־הַמִּשְׁכָּן prep.-def.art.-n.m.s. (1015) *upon the tabernacle*

יוֹמָם adv. (401) *by day*

וְאֵשׁ conj.-n.f.s. (77) *and fire*

תִּהְיֶה Qal impf. 3 f.s. (הָיָה 224) *was*

לַיְלָה בּוֹ n.m.s. (538)-prep.-3 m.s. sf. *by night in it*

לְעֵינֵי prep.-n.f.p. cstr. (744) *in the sight of*

כָל־בֵּית־ n.m.s. cstr. (481)-n.m.s. cstr. (108) *all the house of*

יִשְׂרָאֵל pr.n. (975) *Israel*

בְּכָל־מַסְעֵיהֶם prep.-n.m.s. cstr. (481)-n.m.p.-3 m.p. sf. (652) *throughout all their journeys*

Key to Abbreviations

abs.–absolute
acc.–accusative
act.–active
adj.–adjective
adv.–adverb
advers.–adversative
apoc.–apocopated
art.–article

BDB–Brown, Driver, and Briggs*

c.–common
–with
cf.–compare
coh.–cohortative
coll.–collective
cond.–condition
conj.–conjunction
–conjunctive
consec.–consecutive
crpt.–corrupt
cstr.–construct

def.–definite
defect.–defective
demons.–demonstrative
diff.–difficult
dir.–direct
–directive
dl.–delete
du.–dual
dub.–dubious

ep.–epenthetic
exclam.–exclamation

f.–feminine

gent.–gentilic
GK–Gesenius-Kautzsch†

Heb.–Hebrew
Hi.–Hiph'il
Hith.–Hithpa'el
Ho.–Hoph'al
hypoth.–hypothetical

impf.–imperfect
impv.–imperative
inf.–infinitive
intens.–intensive
interj.–interjection
interr.–interrogative

juss.–jussive

KB–Koehler-Baumgartner††

lit.–literal
loc.–locative
–place
LXX–Septuagint

m.–masculine
mlt.–many
mng.–meaning
Ms.–manuscript

n.–noun
neg.–negative
Ni.–Niph'al
num.–number
–numeral

obj.–object

p.–plural
part.–particle
pass.–passive
paus.–pausal form
pers.–personal
pf.–perfect
Pi.–Pi'el
poss.–possible
–possibly
pr.–proper
–pronoun
prb.–probable
pred.–predicative
prep.–preposition
prp.–proposed
ptc.–participle
Pu.–Pu'al

rd.–read
rel.–relative

s.–singular
S–Syriac
segh.–segholate
sf.–suffix
subst.–substantive
supra–above
synon.–synonymous

T–Targum
txt.–text

v.–see
V–Vulgate
vb.–verb
–verbal
vol.–voluntative

---

* Francis Brown, S. R. Driver, and Charles A. Briggs, *A Hebrew and English Lexicon of the Old Testament* (Oxford: Clarendon Press, 1975).

† E. Kautzsch, ed., *Gesenius' Hebrew Grammar*, 2nd English ed., revised by A. E. Cowley (Oxford: Clarendon Press, 1910).

†† Ludwig Koehler and Walter Baumgartner, eds., *Lexicon in Veteris Testamenti Libros* (Leiden: E. J. Brill, 1958).